CE — **200** — **250** — **313** — **320** — **410** — **632** —

Goths invade Europe from Asia. Over the next 1100 years, Franks, Huns, Vandals, and Mongols migrate westward into Europe	Classical period of Mayan civilization (250–900) in present-day Mexico	Constantine legalizes Christianity in Roman Empire	Seat of Roman Empire transferred from Rome to Constantinople (Istanbul)

Gupta Empire (320–550) unites much of present-day India, Bangladesh, and Pakistan | Ostrogoths sacking of Rome marks decline of Western Roman Empire | Death of Mohammed: Islam begins to expand |

— **1520** — **1556** — **1625** — **1644** — **1648** — **1651** —

Sulieman the Magnificent (1520–1566) extends the Ottoman Empire into the Balkans, the Persian Gulf, and Northern Africa	Mughal Empire in South Asia begins period of growth and cultural development, lasting until 19th century	Hugo Grotius publishes *The Law of War and Peace*, modernizing the study of international law	Qing (Manchu) Dynasty begins in China, lasting until 1912	The Treaty of Westphalia establishes the rights of sovereign states	Thomas Hobbes' *Leviathan* promotes the ideas of a social contract and absolute rule

— **1789** — **1799** — **1815** — **1817** — **1825** — **1839–1842** —

The French Revolution overthrows the monarchy to establish the French Republic	Napolean comes to power in France and conquers much of Europe	Napolean exiled to St. Helena	David Ricardo publishes *On the Principles of Political Economy and Taxation*, laying out the theory of comparative advantage	Revolutions in Latin America (1816–1825) replace the Spanish Empire with independent countries	Opium War between England and China leads to the first of the "unequal treaties" between the West and China

— **1871** — **1880s** — **1898** — **1904–1905** — **1914–1918** — **1917** —

Germany is formed from Prussia, Bavaria, and many smaller states	The race among European powers to colonize Africa begins	Spanish-American War: United States annexes Cuba and Philippines	Russo-Japanese War results in defeat of Russia	World War I	The Russian Revolution establishes a communist state

continued on inside back cover

INTERNATIONAL POLITICS

SECOND EDITION

INTERNATIONAL POLITICS

Power and Purpose in Global Affairs

Paul D'Anieri
University of Florida

WADSWORTH
CENGAGE Learning™

Australia • Brazil • Japan • Korea • Mexico • Singapore • Spain • United Kingdom • United States

WADSWORTH
CENGAGE Learning™

International Politics: Power and Purpose in Global Affairs, 2e, International Edition

Paul D'Anieri

Publisher: Suzanne Jeans

Executive Editor: Carolyn Merrill

Development Editor: Rebecca Green

Associate Development Editor:
  Katherine Hayes

Editorial Assistant: Angela Hodge

Media Editor: Laura Hildebrand

Marketing Manager: Lydia LeStar

Marketing Coordinator: Josh Hendrick

Marketing Communications Manager:
  Heather Baxley

Content Project Manager: Jill Clark

Art Director: Linda Helcher

Print Buyer: Fola Orekoya

Rights Acquisition Specialist, Image:
  Mandy Groszko

Rights Acquisition Specialist, Text:
  Shalice Shah-Caldwell

Production Service: Cadmus
  Communications, Inc.

Text Designer: Red Hanger Design

Cover Designer: Rokusek Design

Cover Image: fpm/© istockphoto

Compositor: Cadmus Communications

International Edition:
ISBN-13: 978-1-1113-4603-4
ISBN-10: 1-1113-4603-8

Cengage Learning International Offices

Asia
www.cengageasia.com
tel: (65) 6410 1200

Australia/New Zealand
www.cengage.com.au
tel: (61) 3 9685 4111

Brazil
www.cengage.com.br
tel: (55) 11 3665 9900

India
www.cengage.co.in
tel: (91) 11 4364 1111

Latin America
www.cengage.com.mx
tel: (52) 55 1500 6000

UK/Europe/Middle East/Africa
www.cengage.co.uk
tel: (44) 0 1264 332 424

Represented in Canada by Nelson Education, Ltd.
tel: (416) 752 9100 / (800) 668 0671
www.nelson.com

Cengage Learning is a leading provider of customized learning solutions with office locations around the globe, including Singapore, the United Kingdom, Australia, Mexico, Brazil, and Japan. Locate your local office at:
www.cengage.com/global

For product information: **www.cengage.com/international**
Visit your local office: **www.cengage.com/global**
Visit our corporate website: **www.cengage.com**

AVAILABILITY OF RESOURCES MAY DIFFER BY REGION. Check with your local Cengage Learning representative for details.

Printed in Canada
1 2 3 4 5 6 7 14 13 12 11 10

To My Children
Jacey, Courtney, Zachary, Joe, and Lily

Brief Contents

Contents

PART II   Theoretical Approaches: Explaining System and State Behavior

CHAPTER 6: Bureaucracies, Groups, and Individuals in the Foreign Policy Process   148

PART III   International Conflict and Security

CHAPTER 7: International Insecurity and the Causes of War and Peace   178

CHAPTER 8: The Use of Force   206

PART IV   International Political Economy

CHAPTER 11: The Problem of Global Inequality   300

PART V   The Evolving Agenda

CHAPTER 12: International Organizations and Transnational Actors   332

CHAPTER 13: International Law, Norms, and Human Rights   364

Preface

Those of us who regularly teach an introductory course in international politics have struggled in recent years with the content of our course and the approach we take to teach it. The end of the Cold War, the rise of globalization, the terrorist attacks of 2001, and the ensuing wars have shifted the practical agenda of international politics, and with it, our sense of what we ought to be teaching our students and how we ought to be doing it.

This book was written in the belief that we need a textbook on international politics that takes a completely fresh approach. Teaching the course immediately after the attacks of September 11, 2001, I struggled to graft a newly emerging reality onto an existing course that focused on the post–Cold War transformation of international politics. This prompted me to completely recreate my international politics course, giving expanded attention to terrorism and asymmetric conflict, to financial crises and nongovernmental actors, to health crises and transnational crime, and to constructivist and feminist theories.

As I proceeded with the notion that "everything has changed," I quickly found that this perspective did not hold true and ultimately distorted more than it revealed. Alas, not much had really changed. Competition for power continued to influence international politics, military force continued to be widely used (with mixed results), and time-tested explanatory approaches continued to have analytical value, even as their shortcomings became more apparent. Moreover, even in areas of revolutionary changes, I believed my students needed to understand where the new world had come from and how it departed from the old.

Power and Purpose

The mission for the course in international politics, as I came to see it, is to bring together traditional and innovative perspectives and to help students make the connections between the problems that have plagued the world for centuries and the revolutionary developments we see today. Therefore, *the* central goal of this text is to connect emerging problems such as terrorism, insurgency, globalization, transnational spread of disease, and economic development with traditional problems of great power politics, war and peace, free trade, and international organization.

To do this, I structure the book using two broad concepts: power and purpose. These two concepts allow us to constantly ask questions about the goals of various actors (purpose) and the means with which they pursue them (power). The breadth of these concepts allows them to be applied to a wide variety of actors, be they states, terrorist groups, businesses, or nongovernmental organizations. The concepts are not intended to be formal scientific variables, but rather provide a conceptual framework that prompts us to ask certain questions. What goals are being pursued, and why? What norms are broadly shared, and which are contested? What cultural, intellectual, economic, and military resources are used to pursue these goals? What determines how and when actors can accomplish their objectives—either achieving common goals or prevailing over others when goals are in conflict?

The field of international politics is so diverse that an attempt to cram every subject into a neat analytical framework would invariably do more harm than good. Yet if students are to make sense of the world around them, they need some way to assess connections and continuities. Traditional categories such as levels of analysis and theoretical paradigms help us do that. Yet many concrete issues do not fit easily into a single level of analysis or paradigm. The notions of power and purpose provide a very general scheme that students can use in thinking about problems of international politics.

I have chosen this scheme in part because it reflects one of the main debates in contemporary theorizing, that between rationalist and constructivist approaches. But, more significantly, I want to remind students to keep these concepts in mind when thinking about world issues. Even informed discussions of contemporary problems tend to focus on the desire to achieve a particular end, or *purpose* (such as "development"), without giving sufficient attention to the real limitations on actors' ability, or *power*, to bring about that end.

Power and purpose also provide a means for thinking about the most widely used theoretical approaches to international politics. Realism, in many people's eyes still the "dominant" approach, has always focused on power as the determining factor in international politics. Especially in its post–1945 variants, realism has not considered purpose as a question much worth pursuing. In Hans Morgenthau's formulation, power itself was assumed to be the purpose of international politics. Other schools of political thought consider power and purpose to be the most puzzling or significant factors in international politics. Liberal theories, of which there are a wide variety, tend to concentrate much more on actors' common or shared purposes, such as free trade or arms control, though some formulations still focus heavily on power. Marxists are equally varied, with traditional formulations seeing power as the driving force behind purpose (the profit motive), whereas more contemporary approaches have seen the shaping of purpose through discourse as one of the ways in which power is exercised. Feminism similarly redefines power to include domination of discourse as well as military or economic power. At the opposite end of the spectrum from realism is constructivism, an approach that has become immensely influential in recent years. In examining how notions of purpose—and especially of shared purpose—develop and influence actors' behavior, constructivism focuses less on what resources are used in pursuing those goals.

Continuity and Change

Looking at international politics through the lenses of power and purpose also allows us to consider the theme of continuity and change. Whether we talk about terrorism, globalization, resource shortages, or other issues that have burst into public consciousness in recent years, these problems have histories that sometimes go back millennia. In grappling with the ways in which the world works differently than it once did, it is essential that students and scholars understand where these problems originated. Therefore, I ask repeatedly throughout the text: in what ways is there continuity with the past and in what ways are current options constrained by the past? In what ways do today's dynamics represent a fundamental break? One way the text does this is in "The Historical Connection" boxes.

Puzzles and Problems

The approach of this text is one of questioning. The study of international politics is presented as a series of intellectual puzzles and policy problems to which there are often no clear answers. It is essential, in my view, that students understand that we have no widely shared understanding of the nature of international politics in general, or of the causes and solutions to particular problems. Focusing on questions that we seek to answer helps students to become more rigorous thinkers and more informed citizens and future policy makers. As thinkers, they are pushed to consider alternative understandings and the validity of each, and accept that uncertainty is normal in the study of politics. This approach helps them get beyond persuasion and rhetoric and begin more rigorous inquiry in political science, as imperfect as that inquiry may be. If we expect our students to become more informed citizens and future policy makers, their ability to search for and scrutinize the theories behind the arguments is essential. I have found that it is much more stimulating for me and my students when I approach the course with a spirit of inquiry, rather than operating in the mode of conveying known facts that must be mastered and memorized. My intent is to focus on the puzzles of international politics, rather than the details of various approaches to studying international politics. By necessity, however, understanding policy dilemmas requires digging into debates among competing approaches. Some of these issues are explored in more detail in "The Policy Connection" boxes in every chapter.

Cultural Connections

This book differs from most by explicitly addressing the connections between international politics and our broader culture, including music and the visual arts. The point is not to provide amusement for students but to show that international politics reaches deeply into our lives, influencing issues that would seem to be distant from the concerns of presidents and diplomats. A great deal of "high culture" as well as popular culture is influenced by international issues, and the way culture is produced and disseminated is being dramatically altered by processes of globalization. It is important to interrogate widely held conceptions about international politics. Culture, including literature, music, and film, is both a product and a promoter of these conceptions. This cultural dimension is brought out in "The Culture Connection" boxes that appear in each chapter.

Global Variation

Through the use of maps and statistics, I strive to convey to students the range of variation (and the degree of similarity) across the globe. The spatial variation in today's world is an essential component of many of the issues that concern us most. Some maps show variation across states, whereas others ignore state borders to provoke inquiry about the relative importance of intrastate versus interstate variation. Additionally, maps help students understand the historical evolution of the world we see today. Claims are constantly made about the revolutionary nature of contemporary trends such as globalization and about enduring consistencies such as the sovereign state system. Maps that show variation over time help inform us about both kinds of claims. These questions are raised where appropriate throughout the text but receive special attention in the "Geography Connection" boxes in each chapter.

Overview of the Text

Substantively, this book covers a wide range of topics and makes connections between them. After an introductory chapter, an entire chapter is devoted to the historical evolution of international politics, providing important context for much of the discussion that follows. Two chapters then examine international relations theory, one covering realism and liberalism, and the second covering economic structuralism (Marxism), constructivism, and feminism.

Moving from international relations theory to foreign policy analysis, the next section of the book consists of two chapters on the sources of foreign policy. Chapter 5 examines the state and society. It gives considerable attention to democratic peace theory because of its prominence in the contemporary literature and its use in justifying so much of contemporary foreign policy, especially that of the United States. The chapter also considers state structure, interest groups, and the influence of public opinion and the media. Chapter 6 considers bureaucratic and decision-making approaches. This book gives more attention than most to foreign policy analysis to help students understand the research findings behind the various claims made about the wide range of actors involved.

The next two chapters of the book consider international security. Chapter 7 examines the causes of war and also looks at efforts to avoid conflict, such as arms control and peacekeeping. Chapter 8 explores the use of force as a policy instrument, examining defense and deterrence. We begin with a relatively simple analysis of the relationship between political ends (purpose) and the use of force (power), then modify the framework to deal first with weapons of mass destruction, followed by terrorism. This approach allows us to address terrorism in a way that makes connections with other kinds of force but clearly shows how terrorism differs. The chapter also examines the circumstances in which nuclear weapons might strengthen or undermine deterrence and shows how transnational terrorism undermines traditional efforts at deterrence.

The following section of the text deals with international political economy. Chapter 9 provides a very short course in international economic theory. So much in international political economy is based on the theory of comparative advantage and its problems that students need to understand that theory thoroughly. Other key concepts in international political economy, such as the balance of trade and exchange rates, are also explained. The chapter then reprises the theoretical approaches from Chapters 3 and 4, showing how each of these has specific applications to international political economy. It is essential for students to understand that international political economy is not a world apart from the rest of international politics. Chapters 10 and 11 consider the related topics of globalization and development.

The final section of the book considers some of the actors and forces reshaping the contemporary international system: nonstate actors (international organizations and transnational actors) in Chapter 12; international law in Chapter 13; and the array of transnational problems creating new challenges for states, such as transnational crime, disease, and environmental problems, in Chapter 14. It asks whether these issues are likely to induce greater collaboration or intensified conflict among states. These subjects also prompt us to ask about the purposes of various actors (especially the extent to which shared purpose might emerge). More significantly, they cause us to think about alternative conceptions of power, such as those that see power in the ability to collaborate rather than in the ability to compel.

The book concludes with a look to the future. Chapter 15 asks explicitly about our ability to anticipate the future based on our understanding of the past and our understanding of how international politics works. The chapter also shows how the choices made by leaders and citizens can influence the future, and how beliefs and theories can influence those choices. The goal of this concluding chapter is to integrate themes discussed throughout the book and to reassert that the choices students and leaders make are heavily influenced by theories, whether or not those theories are explicit and well thought through.

We live in a rapidly changing world. Although we cannot predict much about the future, we can be confident that a decade or two after taking an introductory course in international politics, students will face challenges that make today's world look quaint. We can hope, however, that the concepts taught today will retain their relevance and utility well into the future. The goal of this book, then, like the goal of liberal education more broadly, is to provide the conceptual and critical skills needed to face challenges that have not yet arisen.

Student-Oriented Features

To help students grasp the material and provide them with the learning tools necessary to ensure their success, a cohesive pedagogical framework is integrated into every chapter. Each feature in the text was designed specifically to engage students in the material, address deficiencies students entering international relations may have in history, policy, culture, and geography, and to build their ability to think critically. The "Connections" boxes that were mentioned previously are described in more detail below.

- Each chapter begins with **Learning Objectives** and a **Chapter Outline**.
- **A Case-Study Approach** brings the material to life for the student. **Consider the Case** opens each chapter by introducing a real-world situation relevant to the chapter material. **Reconsider the Case** at the end of each chapter revisits the situation and presents new questions for students to consider.
- **The Historical Connection** boxes address the themes of continuity and change, asking in what ways do we see continuity with the past, and in what ways are current options constrained by the past.
- **The Policy Connection** boxes dig deeper into debates among competing approaches to the study of international politics to help understand policy dilemmas.
- **The Culture Connection** boxes take a unique look at the connection between international politics and culture, and the influence international issues have on popular culture, such as literature, music, film, and visual arts.
- **The Geography Connection** boxes use maps and statistics to help students understand the historical evolution of the world and convey the range of variation and degree of similarity on different issues across the globe.
- **Critical Thinking Questions** appear at the end of each boxed feature and at the end of each chapter, encouraging students to engage in a discussion about the material and develop their own line of questioning.
- **Marginal Definitions** reinforce key terms as they are introduced.
- Each chapter concludes with **Key Concepts**, **Study Questions**, and **Endnotes**.

New to This Edition

- Throughout the text, the cases and examples discussed have been updated where appropriate. The global economic crisis, the H1N1 flu pandemic, and the policies of various new governments around the world get repeated attention.
- Chapter 1 is largely unchanged, but it refines the discussion of power and purpose and introduces the question of whether the United States is in decline as a world power.
- In Chapter 2, coverage of the non-European world has been expanded, including a discussion of independence movements in 19th century Latin America.
- Chapter 3 puts less emphasis than in the first edition on competition between different paradigms, focusing instead on the paradigms as different tools for understanding international politics. It also includes a new discussion of the concept of "national interest."

- Chapter 4 contains a substantially revised treatment of feminism to take account of recent work in that rapidly evolving field. Like Chapter 3, it focuses more on the complementary application of different theories than on the need to choose from among them. It also contains an updated discussion of the leftist resurgence in Latin America.

- Chapter 5 picks up the discussion of national interest from Chapter 3 and puts it in the context of domestic politics. It adds a discussion of how the current economic crises have led to strengthened state roles in the economies of advanced economies. It streamlines the discussion of democratic peace theory. The discussion of democratization in U.S. foreign policy has been updated to cover the Obama administration's policy.

- Chapter 6 updates the discussion of "groupthink" to include the U.S. decision to go to war in Iraq in 2003. It also updates the treatment of efforts to reorganize intelligence and law enforcement organs to deal with terrorism. Analysis of the shift from the Bush to the Obama administration is used to evaluate the constraints faced by individual heads of state.

- Chapter 7 streamlines the section on managing the security dilemma and has relatively minor changes updating the discussions of the "military-industrial complex," the "fog of war," and "peace enforcement."

- Chapter 8 has been reorganized to simplify the discussion. It adds examination of various kinds of weapons of mass destruction and the differences among them. The analysis of counterinsurgency has been revised using the reassessment of U.S. strategy in 2010 as an example. A box addressing cyber warfare has been added.

- Chapter 9 is largely intact but contains a substantially revised discussion of China's exchange rate policy.

- Chapter 10 adds a detailed analysis of the World Trade Organization dispute resolution mechanism and a discussion about the possible erosion of the central role of the U.S. dollar in global finance. A new chapter-opening case study examines the 2010 Greek debt crisis, and a new "Policy Connection" box examines the tension between stimulating the economy and balancing budgets faced by economies in crisis.

- Chapter 11 adds considerable detail on the World Bank's lending operations.

- Chapter 12 addresses the changes brought to the European Union by the Lisbon Treaty and by acrimony over the economic crisis. It also updates the discussion of reform of the United Nations.

- Chapter 13 includes a substantially expanded discussion of human rights as well as a new "Culture Connection" box focusing on public opinion toward international law.

- Chapter 14 adds an entirely new section on population, demographic change, and migration. Other parts of the chapter have been streamlined. The discussion of environmental cooperation adds coverage of the Copenhagen summit and addresses the unintended economic and environmental consequences of the increased production of ethanol.

- Chapter 15 is revised to focus more clearly on the issues of power and purpose.

RESOURCES

For the Instructor

PowerLecture DVD with ExamView®
ISBN-10: 1-1113-4464-7 | ISBN-13: 978-1-1113-4464-1

This DVD includes two sets of PowerPoint slides (a book-specific and a media-enhanced set), a test bank in both Microsoft® Word and ExamView® formats, an Instructor's

Manual, JoinIn Clickers, and a Resource Integration Guide. The two types of PowerPoints are described in the following section.

Interactive **book-specific PowerPoint° lectures,** a one-stop lecture and class preparation tool, makes it easy for you to assemble, edit, publish, and present book-specific lectures for your course. You will have access to a set of PowerPoints, with outlines specific to each chapter of *International Politics: Power and Purpose in Global Affairs* as well as photos, figures, and tables found in the book.

The **media-enhanced PowerPoints** for each chapter can be used on their own or easily integrated with the book-specific PowerPoint outlines. Audio and video clips depicting both historic and current day events; NEW animated learning modules illustrating key concepts; tables, statistical charts, and graphs; and photos from the book as well as outside sources are provided at the appropriate places in the chapter. You can also add your own materials using both types of PowerPoints to build a powerful, personalized classroom or online presentation.

A **test bank** in Microsoft° Word and ExamView° computerized testing offers a large array of well-crafted multiple-choice and essay questions, along with their answers and page references.

An **Instructor's Manual** includes learning objectives, chapter outlines, discussion questions, suggestions for stimulating class activities and projects, tips on integrating media into your class, and suggested readings and online resources.

The **Resource Integration Guide** outlines the rich collection of resources available to instructors and students within the chapter-by-chapter framework of the book, suggesting how and when each supplement can be used to optimize learning.

CourseMate with eBook for *International Politics*
Instant Access Code
ISBN-10: 1-1113-5654-8 | ISBN-13: 978-1-1113-5654-5

The **CourseMate** for *International Politics: Power and Purpose in Global Affairs* offers a variety of rich online learning resources designed to enhance the student experience. These resources include video activities, audio summaries, case studies, simulations, animated learning modules, interactive timelines, flashcards, learning objectives, glossaries, and crossword puzzles. Chapter resources are correlated with key chapter learning concepts, and users can browse or search for content in a variety of ways.

NewsNow is a new asset available on CourseMate, which is a combination of weekly news stories from the Associated Press, videos, and images that bring current events to life for the student. For instructors, NewsNow includes an additional set of multimedia-rich PowerPoint slides posted each week to the password-protected area of the text's companion Web site. Instructors may use these slides to take a class poll or trigger a lively debate about the events that are shaping the world right now. And because this all-in-one presentation tool includes the text of the original news feed, along with videos, photos, and discussion questions, no Internet connection is required!

How do you assess your students' engagement in your course? How do you know your students have read the material or viewed the resources you've assigned? How can you tell if your students are struggling with a concept? With CourseMate, you can use the included **Engagement Tracker** to assess student preparation and engagement. Use the tracking tools to see progress for the class as a whole or for individual students. Identify students at risk early in the course. Uncover which concepts are most difficult for your class. Monitor time on task. Keep your students engaged.

CourseMate also features an **interactive eBook** that has highlighting and search capabilities along with links to simulations, animated PowerPoints that illustrate concepts, interactive timelines, videos, primary source activities, case studies, tutorial quizzes, and flash cards.

Go to **cengagebrain.com/shop/ISBN/1111344493** to access your Political Science CourseMate resources.

Instructor Companion Web Site
ISBN-10: 1-1113-0346-0 | ISBN-13: 978-1-1113-0346-4
Instructors have access to the Instructor's Manual and PowerPoints, correlated by chapter.

WebTutor™ on Blackboard® Instant Access Code
ISBN-10: 1-1114-7307-2 | ISBN-13: 978-1-1114-7307-5

WebTutor™ on WebCTTM Instant Access Code
ISBN-10: 1-1114-7293-9 | ISBN-13: 978-1-1114-7293-1

Rich with content for your American government course, this Web-based teaching and learning tool includes course management, study/mastery, and communication tools. Use WebTutor™ to provide virtual office hours, post your syllabus, and track student progress with WebTutor's quizzing material. For students, WebTutor™ offers real-time access to interactive online tutorials and simulations, practice quizzes, and Web links— all correlated to *International Politics: Power and Purpose in Global Affairs*.

International Politics Atlas
ISBN-10: 0-618-83713-2 | ISBN-13:978-0-618-83713-7

Free when bundled with a Wadsworth textbook, this atlas offers maps of the world showing political organization, population statistics, and economic development; maps highlighting energy production and consumption, major world conflicts, migration, and more; and extensive regional coverage. Students will find it useful for understanding world events and to supplement their studies with *International Politics: Power and Purpose in Global Affairs*.

The Wadsworth News Videos for American Government 2012 DVD
ISBN-10: 1-1113-4614-3| ISBN-13: 978-1-1113-4614-0

This collection of three- to six-minute video clips on relevant political issues serves as a great lecture or discussion launcher.

International Politics CourseReader: Politics in Context
ISBN-10: 1-1114-8057-5 | ISBN-13: 978-1-111-48057-8

International Politics CourseReader: Politics in Context will enable instructors to create a customized reader. Using a database of hundreds of documents, readings, and videos, instructors can search by various criteria or browse the collection to preview and then select a customized collection to assign their students. The sources will be edited to an appropriate length and include pedagogical support—a headnote describing the document and critical-thinking and multiple-choice questions to verify that the student has read and understood the selection. Students will be able to take notes as well as highlight and print content. **International Politics CourseReader: Politics in Context** allows the instructor to select exactly what students will be assigned with an easy-to-use interface and also provides an easily used assessment tool. The sources can be delivered online or in print format.

For the Student

CourseMate with eBook for *International Politics*
Instant Access Code
ISBN-10: 1-1113-5654-8 | ISBN-13: 978-1-1113-5654-5

The **CourseMate** for *International Politics: Power and Purpose in Global Affairs* offers a variety of rich online learning resources designed to enhance the student experience. These resources include video activities, audio summaries, case studies, simulations, animated learning modules, interactive timelines, flash cards, learning objectives, glossaries, and crossword puzzles. All resources are correlated with key chapter learning concepts, and users can browse or search for content in a variety of ways.

NewsNow is a new asset available on CourseMate, which is a combination of weekly news stories from the Associated Press, with videos and images that bring current events to life for the student.

CourseMate also features an **interactive eBook** that has highlighting and search capabilities along with links to simulations, animated PowerPoints, interactive timelines, videos, primary source activities, case studies, tutorial quizzes, and flash cards.

Go to **cengagebrain.com/shop/ISBN/1111344493** to access your Political Science CourseMate resources.

International Politics Atlas

ISBN-10: 0-618-83713-2 | ISBN-13:978-0-618-83713-7

This atlas offers maps of the world showing political organization, population statistics, and economic development; maps highlighting energy production and consumption, major world conflicts, migration, and more; and extensive regional coverage. You will find it useful for understanding world events and to supplement your studies with *International Politics: Power and Purpose in Global Affairs*.

International Politics CourseReader: Politics in Context
ISBN-10: 1-1114-8057-5| ISBN-13: 978-1-1114-8057-8

International Politics CourseReader: Politics in Context will enable instructors to create a customized reader. Students will be able to take notes, highlight, and print content.

ACKNOWLEDGEMENTS

I had thought for several years about writing this book, but probably would never have done so but for the encouragement of Carolyn Merrill at Cengage. She provided me not only the original encouragement to start, but support and friendship throughout the writing process, which lasted much longer than either of us anticipated. Rebecca Green and Katherine Hayes have been indispensable in developing this second edition and its ancillary program, Naomi Friedman was editor of the first edition and developed most of the graphics in the text. Many individuals read drafts of chapters or of the entire manuscript. I especially want to thank Catherine Weaver of the University of Texas. She spent a great deal of time helping me think through what to include and how to include it, and she educated me on some areas of international politics on which I was less knowledgeable than I ought to be. Laura Sjoberg of the University of Florida provided excellent advice, some of which I didn't take, about revising the discussion of feminism. Looking back, I owe a great deal to two great teachers in international politics courses I took years ago: Michael Schechter at Michigan State and Peter Katzenstein at Cornell. Finally, I thank my students. Their enthusiasm makes teaching fun; their idealism gives me hope.

I dedicate this book to my children: Jacey, Courtney, Zac, Joe, and Lily. They have taught their parents well.

LIST OF REVIEWERS

Reviewer	School
Francis Adams	Old Dominion University
Karen Ruth Adams	University of Montana
Linda Adams	Baylor University
Susan Allen	Texas Tech University
John Barkdull	Texas Tech University
Robert Bartlett	University of Vermont
Henry F. Carey	Georgia State University
Ben Clansy	College of St. Rose
David Cunningham	Iowa State University
Carrie Liu Currier	Texas Christian University
Jalele Defa	University of Nebraska-Lincoln
David Edwards	University of Texas at Austin
Ophelia Eglene	Middlebury College
Frank Fato	Westchester Community College
William Felice	Eckerd College
Ole J. Forsberg	Creighton University
Erich Frankland	Casper College
Steve Garrison	Midwestern State University
David M. Goldberg	College of DuPage
James R. Hedtke	Cabrini College
Timothy T. Hellwig	University of Houston
Uko Heo	University of Wisconsin at Milwaukee
Ian Hurd	Northwestern University
Jon Timothy Kelly	West Valley College
Soleiman Kiasatpour	Western Kentucky University
Donn M. Kurtz, II	University of Los Angeles at Lafayette
Lynn Kuzma	University of Southern Maine
Andrew G. Long	University of Mississippi
Stephen Long	Kansas State University

John Mercurio	San Diego State University
Harry Mokeba	Louisiana State University
Mark Mullenbach	University of Central Arkansas
Suzanne Ogden	Northeastern University
William M. Rose	Connecticut College
Thomas Rotnem	Southern Polytechnic State University
Stephen L. Rozman	Tougaloo College
Mark Sachleben	Shippensburg University
Kamishkan Sathasivan	Salem State College
Shalendra Sharma	University of San Francisco
Martin Slann	Macon State College
David Sobek	Louisiana State University
Patricia Stapleton	Brooklyn College
Alex Thompson	Ohio State University
Karl Trautman	Central Maine Community College
Stacy D. VanDeveer	University of New Hampshire
Rossen V. Vassilev	Ohio State University
James I. Walsh	University of North Carolina at Charlotte
Julie Webber	Illinois State University
Jeanne Wilson	Wheaton College
Wojtek Wolfe	Rutgers University
Nikolaos Zahariadis	University of Alabama at Birmingham

Focus Group Attendees

Sangmin Bae	Northeastern Illinois University
Lisa Baglione	St. Joseph's University
Ryan Baird	University of Arizona
Diggner Fiddner	Indiana University of Pennsylvania
Caron Gentry	Abilene Christian University
Patricia Keilbach	University of Colorado at Colorado Springs
Howard Lehman	University of Utah
Helen Purkitt	U.S. Naval Academy
Wojtek Mackiewicz Wolfe	Rutgers University

Author Biography

Author Biography

Paul D'Anieri is Professor of Political Science and Dean of the College of Liberal Arts and Sciences at the University of Florida. He teaches international relations and comparative politics and specializes in politics and foreign policy in the post-Soviet states. His books include *Economic Interdependence in Ukrainian-Russian Relations* and *Understanding Ukrainian Politics: Power, Politics, and Institutional Design.* He is currently studying the transnational spread of methods of political control in new democracies. He has published numerous articles in academic journals and publications on eastern European politics. A student-focused, dedicated teacher of international relations and comparative politics since 1991, Dr. D'Anieri has written this book to fill the urgent need for a text that addresses the complexities of today's newly emerging political realities while showing students how these realities are connected to problems that have existed for centuries.

INTERNATIONAL POLITICS

Introduction: Problems and Questions in International Politics

LEARNING OBJECTIVES

After completing this chapter, the student should be able to . . .

1. Identify ways in which international politics is linked to everyday life.
2. Explain the role of theory in political science.
3. Distinguish between explanatory and normative theory
4. Identify the links between theory and policy.
5. Elaborate how theories are evaluated in political science.
6. Apply the concept of levels of analysis in international relations.

◄ Chinese Democracy Protester, Tiananmen Square, 1989
AP Photo/Jeff Widener

Imagine you are president of the United States. It appears that Iran is acquiring nuclear weapons. How do you respond? Your advisors are divided. One group advocates a hard line: threaten a military attack unless Iran proves it has stopped the program. Only the threat of a U.S. assault, these advisors contend, will persuade Iran to change course. Another group counsels a conciliatory policy. The longer we can contain the problem, they say, the more likely it is that the Iranian government will either be replaced or become less hostile. Both groups warn that if you do not take their advice, you may be responsible for prompting the use of nuclear weapons against the United States. Who is correct? How can we predict the consequences of each policy option?

Imagine you are an average U.S. citizen voting for the president of the United States. The candidates have similar positions on most issues, but differ about how best to combat terrorism. One candidate argues that poverty is at the root of the problem and that, if elected, she will pursue a major program to alleviate poverty in regions from which terrorism is emerging. Another candidate asserts that terrorism is caused by the lack of democracy in many Islamic societies. She promises to bring democracy to those countries, even if it means angering authoritarian governments that are important U.S. allies. Whom do you vote for? What are the sources of terrorism? What policies can reduce the threat?

Imagine you have joined a group devoted to alleviating poverty in Africa. A philanthropist has just given the group $1 billion to reduce poverty. How should your group spend the money? Should you focus your work on educating government decision makers to make better decisions? Should you invest in primary education to reduce the illiteracy rate? Or should you spend the money on health care to reduce the drain of illness on the economy? What are the causes of global poverty? What are the cures?

These three scenarios cover a wide range of situations and viewpoints. They include issues ranging from nuclear war to economic development. But they have one thing in common. In each case, you face difficult choices that can be made wisely only if you understand how international politics works. In each case, a bad decision will be costly. These examples illustrate an important point: international politics matters to everybody, in one way or another. It affects the daily lives even of people who know nothing or care nothing about it.

Each of the preceding scenarios also illustrates why international politics is an interesting—even a dramatic—subject. International politics can be thought of as a set of puzzles, and these puzzles are often difficult to solve. They involve high stakes: Millions of lives are on the line when leaders try to avoid war or try to use war to accomplish their goals, or even when they choose policies on free trade, development aid, or environmental collaboration. International politics involves ethical quandaries, such as whether the effort to reduce terrorism justifies torture or whether it is acceptable to stand aside in the face of famine or genocide. It involves the highest aspirations of humankind, such as the dreams of ending war and eliminating global poverty. And it involves the lowest depths to which individuals and societies sink—mass murder, terrorism, starvation, and indifference to these things.

This book seeks to help students understand the puzzles that comprise international politics today. These puzzles challenge our intellects, especially because the choices we make or do not make, as citizens and as societies, will have far-reaching consequences. Wise choices may help avert wars, starvation, and environmental collapse. Poor choices can lead to disaster. That combination—difficult dilemmas and high stakes—is what makes international politics an exciting subject. That we live in a rapidly changing world only increases the risk and the challenge.

Power and Purpose

The scenarios in the previous section bring up questions of both *power* and **purpose**, two themes that run throughout this book. How can actors achieve their purposes? This is a question of *power*. **Power** is a central concept in politics, but it is extremely difficult to define, a problem we take up in more detail in Chapter 3. There are different definitions of power and different kinds of power. Moreover, what counts as power in one situation might not count as power in another one. On the battlefield, power might be measured by the number of weapons one has. Within the United Nations (UN) General Assembly, power might be measured in terms of votes. UN votes are not of much use on the battlefield, nor are guns of much use in the United Nations.

Purpose refers to the goals of political action. What are various actors trying to achieve? In this book, we consider a wide range of actors, including states, individuals, bureaucracies, firms, nongovernmental organizations (NGOs), international organizations, and terrorist groups. Regardless of the actors, we need to consider the purposes they are trying to achieve. To what extent do the actors on a given issue have shared or competing purposes? How do the purposes of states and of the international community change, and what happens when they do? These questions are central to the study of international politics.

purpose

The goals that actors pursue, including the notion of "national interest." Whether actors see themselves as having shared or competing goals is a central concern.

power

The ability of an actor to achieve its goals. Exactly what constitutes power and how to measure it are vexing problems in international relations.

Figure 1.1 Political Actors

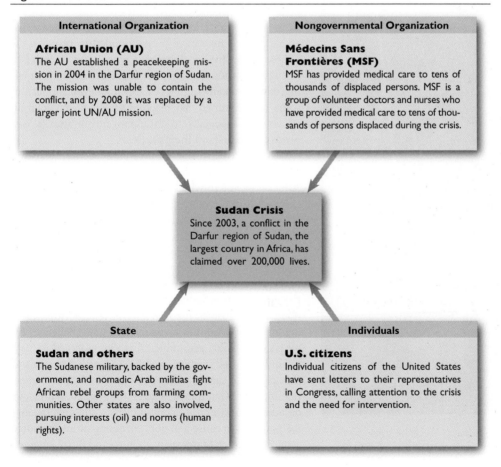

Power and purpose are central concepts in understanding political behavior, and are therefore at the center of the most widely applied theories of international politics. It is useful to come back to them again and again. Neither purpose nor power is always evident. Focusing on them prompts us to make the implicit explicit, and in doing so reveals vital characteristics of the international political process.

Power and Purpose in a Changing World

When nineteen young men hijacked four airplanes and used them as weapons to attack the World Trade Center and the Pentagon, international politics was thrown into turmoil. In the aftermath of the attack, the assertion that "this changes everything" reverberated around the world.[1] The act itself demonstrated a kind of power that few realized existed, to turn airplanes into weapons of mass destruction. Although terrorism was not new in 2001, the September 11 attacks changed our understanding of the scale of potential attacks and of the ability of terrorists to reach from bases on one side of the world to targets on the other. It revealed the power of terrorism, through a single spectacular act, to gain the attention of the entire world and to compel a massive response by the target state.

AP Photo

A bomb near Colombo, the capital of Sri Lanka, tears apart a packed passenger train. The tactic of suicide bombing was developed by the Tamil Tigers in Sri Lanka. How has the advent of suicide bombing changed the kinds of questions we ask about international politics?

The attack of September 11, 2001, struck many as "senseless," but it indeed had a purpose, even if that purpose was not entirely clear. It may have been intended primarily to get the United States to remove its troops from Saudi Arabia, as Osama bin Laden had once stated as his goal. It may have been intended to provoke the United States into a global war with Islam in order to strengthen fundamentalism. It may have been the opening salvo in a campaign to establish a new Caliphate, as some have claimed. To respond effectively to such an attack, and especially to anticipate future attacks, one needs to understand their purposes.

More broadly, the 2001 attacks demonstrated a potentially revolutionary shift in international politics. After 500 years in which the main threat to most states came from other states, and in which relations among states defined the agenda of international security, the attack on the World Trade Center raised the possibility that the main threat now came from transnational terrorist groups.

In the economic realm, we also live in times of great change and uncertainty. The dizzying pace of globalization has transformed many economic relationships, causing great opportunities for some and new challenges for others. The global economic crisis that emerged in 2008 not only induced massive hardship in North America and Europe, it also caused policy makers and scholars to question much of what they had taken for granted in previous decades. Moreover, the economic crisis, still ongoing, has the potential to cause a major reordering of international economic power. States such as China and Brazil emerged quickly from the crisis and continued to grow, while Japan, Europe, and the United States contemplated the possibility of many years of slowed growth and high debt.

The rise of the environment, and especially global warming, as a central issue is a further fundamental change. International environmental concerns are not new; nor are agreements to deal with them, but until recently, the environment was not a major domestic and international political issue—one that leaders felt compelled to deal with, and one that could vie with security and economics for a place on the agenda at major international meetings.

Terrorism, globalization, environmental degradation, and other emerging issues have raised fundamental questions about how world politics works and how it will work in the future. These questions will likely define the next several decades of international politics. They will have a major impact on the everyday lives of everyone, even those who have little interest in global affairs.

As important as these developments are, we do not understand them well enough. International politics has always been defined by ambiguity rather than by clarity, by debate rather than by certainty, and by surprise rather than by predictability. At a time when the dangers from abroad seem more immediate than ever, our understanding of those threats seems painfully inadequate. Even the most vaunted intelligence agencies in the world were unable to anticipate the upsurge in terrorism. There is a widespread perception that we must do better.

Puzzles with High Stakes

International politics today is a series of puzzles with immense consequences. A great deal— including money and lives—depends on the answers and solutions we reach. Unfortunately, we are unable to answer many questions in international politics with certainty. The problem is not that we have no answers, but rather that, for most important questions, we have two or more good answers, along with considerable debate concerning which is correct. A few of the questions that are most prominent today can be used to illustrate this point.

AP Photo/Tatan Syuflana

- **What are the sources of terrorism?** It seems that religion often plays an important role. But of all the religious people in the world, very few, even among the most fundamentalist, commit terrorism or support it. Therefore, some argue that individual frustration and alienation cause specific individuals to become terrorists. Others point to the role of poverty. Ultimately, there is no simple explanation for why one person becomes a terrorist and another does not, or why one group seems to condone terrorism while another does not. Yet governments and individuals must make decisions every day on the basis of the answers to these questions, even if those answers are tentative.

- **Are democracies more peaceful than countries with other forms of government?** It seems natural that they would be, and recent U.S. presidents of both parties have argued that this is an important consideration in their policies. Although the relationship between democracy and war is complex and is still hotly debated, important acts such as the invasion

A polluted canal runs through Jakarta, Indonesia. Gaps between the richest and the poorest are increasing worldwide. What are the causes of poverty? Does the globalization of trade and finance help or hurt?

of Iraq, intervention in the former Yugoslavia, and the provision of economic aid to Russia are justified in part by the belief that if the United States helps countries become democratic, these countries will be peaceful and war with them will be less likely.

■ **What are the causes and consequences of poverty around the world?** Many argue that global poverty is a result of the way the international economy works: competition from advanced economies makes it impossible for poor countries to succeed. Many others, however, make the opposite argument: competition, they say, increases efficiency and wealth. Poor countries would benefit from more international competition, not less. There is evidence for both arguments. For the lives of billions of people, making the right calls on this issue is essential.

■ **Is globalization inevitable, or could we halt it if we wanted to—and should we?** Is it a force to be feared or a force for good? Many people fear the consequences of globalization and argue that governments should take steps to limit it. Others argue that globalization is a natural economic and social process and that those who try to fight it will be left behind.

■ **Is the United States a declining power?** And is China's rise inevitable? What might slow or reverse the perceived decline of the United States, or sidetrack China's rise? What are the forces that lead to the rise and decline of the power and influence of different countries? And what might be the consequences when a new dominant power emerges? These are questions that have been applied to history as well as to contemporary cases. Leaders around the world are seeking to answer them, and to apply the answers successfully to their own states.

Understanding the Basis for Policies

Often we cannot delay making a decision until we have arrived at a perfect understanding of the problem. We must learn to evaluate the different arguments on a pressing question, and decide which we (as individuals or as a society) find most compelling. We base our policies on answers to questions, even when we are highly uncertain about those answers. In other words, we are forced to choose a side in key debates, even when we would rather delay. Academic debates therefore have immense practical significance.

For example, governments around the world are adopting policies to combat terrorism, even though there remains much uncertainty about the causes of terrorism. Policies range from reorganizing police forces to increasing surveillance on citizens, to waging wars abroad, and they cost a great deal in terms of lives, money, and freedom. If those policies are based on flawed understandings of the sources of terrorism, the sacrifices made may be wasted. Yet policy makers cannot wait until they have developed a better understanding of terrorism to act. They must make decisions now in considerable uncertainty.

Firms are making investment decisions. The wealth of the firms' shareholders, as well as the survival of the firms, depends on making accurate predictions of future events. Will global markets continue to open up? If so, certain kinds of investments will yield high returns. Will disputes over international trade lead to greater limits on trade? If so, a different business strategy may be appropriate. But how can firms assess the likelihood of greater or less trade openness in the future? Again, they must make decisions in the face of considerable uncertainty.

International organizations and NGOs are making decisions concerning economic aid to developing countries. Should they invest in programs to strengthen the market in poor countries, work to improve education, or focus on health care? Or should they concentrate on meeting the basic needs for food, shelter, and medical care of those in the direst circumstances? All of these goals are important. But resources are limited, and so choices must be made. If we correctly identify the causes and cures of poverty, we might

The Geography Connection

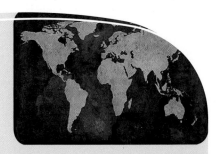

Does Size Matter?

Typical maps represent the relative land area of countries (although there are some distortions in representing a three-dimensional earth on a two-dimensional map). The map below has been changed to make each state roughly the same size.

Critical Thinking Questions

1. Compare this map to a typical representation—which countries change most and which change least? Would world politics change substantially if the world looked like this?
2. Imagine that, instead of changing the sizes of countries, we moved them around. What political or economic changes might result from changing the locations of countries?
3. What does this tell us about our thinking on the role of geography in international affairs?

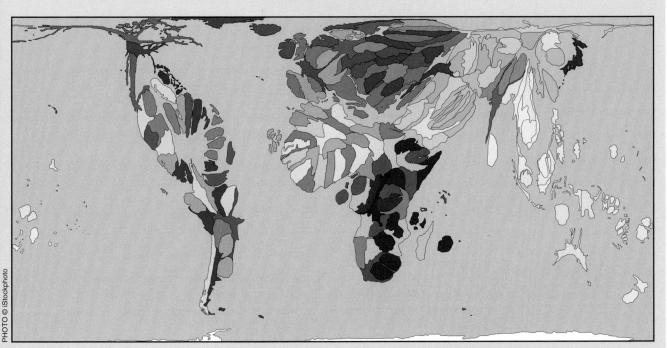

PHOTO © iStockphoto

Source: http://www.sasi.group.shef.ac.uk © Copyright 2006 SASI Group (University of Sheffield) and Mark Newman (University of Michigan), Reprinted by permission.

save many from misery. If we get it wrong, money will be wasted and children will continue to starve. Although this may sound overly dramatic, it is undoubtedly true.

Individuals are making career decisions. Should I learn to speak Chinese or Spanish? Maybe my decision will be based on my love of one language over the other. But maybe I

Figure 1.2 What does the distribution of the Homeland Security budget tell us about the U.S. government's expectations of where threats will come from?

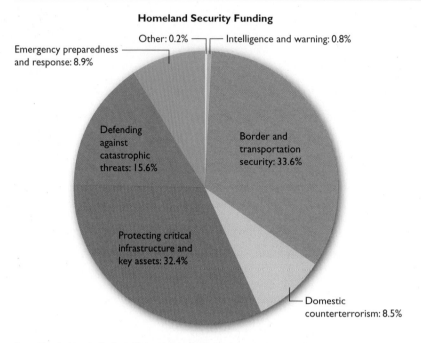

Source: Homeland Security Funding by National Strategy Mission from Homeland Securities Affairs, June 2007. Reprinted by permission of Thomas Stinson.

hope to use the language in business or in government service. If so, I want to have some expectations about the prospects for economic and political relations with the countries where these languages are spoken. I must make a prediction about international relations. Should I join the military, the Foreign Service, or an international aid organization? The answer might depend on which organizations I expect to be most influential in making policy.

Societies are making decisions about which parties and politicians to elect to office. Which parties or candidates have policies that stand up to scrutiny, and which do not? Which are based on an understanding of the world that I as a voter think is correct? In an era in which international security is subject to a variety of threats, when prosperity is more heavily influenced by international markets, and when the health of the environment depends on global action, citizens must be able to evaluate their governments' policies independently and intelligently.

There are many more examples, but the central point is this: international politics is an area in which vital decisions are made based on understandings of cause and effect that are hotly debated. As citizens, as decision makers, and as curious people, we are driven to develop our own understandings of these difficult problems.

The Goals of the Book

This book aims to help the reader evaluate everyday arguments about international politics and foreign policy. Friends, parents, teachers, bloggers, and people on the television routinely make assertions—often with great confidence—about how international politics works, and about what policies governments, groups, firms, and individuals should adopt.

Every argument about politics and policies is based on an identifiable series of assumptions. We can scrutinize those assumptions and decide whether we agree.

The Policy Connection

Academic and Policy Debates

The study of international politics and the practice of foreign policy are tightly linked. People study international politics because they hope to make better decisions concerning the real world. Every foreign policy is based on some understanding of how the world works and of what the results of different policies would likely be. For every headline one reads about a foreign policy debate, there is a corresponding academic debate. Every policy argument, boiled down to its essentials, is a causal argument: "If we do x, the result will be y." The obvious follow-up question is: "How do you know?" In the public debate, we are often not very rigorous about scrutinizing these propositions. Politicians devise clever rhetoric, or invoke simple historical analogies in support of policies they have already decided to support.

The job of the scholar, the student, and the citizen is to examine these claims more rigorously. This means understanding the assumptions and arguments behind a particular policy position, and scrutinizing them critically. Chapter 8, for example, considers efforts to combat terrorism and fundamentalist insurgency. But scholars and policy makers alike have a very weak understanding, so far, of what motivates individual terrorists and what determines that one individual will become a terrorist while many more in essentially similar circumstances will not. If policy makers believe that terrorism is caused by poverty, they will adopt a particular set of policies. If they believe that terrorism is caused by an absence of democracy, they will adopt a very different set of policies. Because resources are very limited, it is important not to waste money and effort on policies that will not work.

Chapter 10 addresses international economic crises, including the one we have been experiencing since 2008. In countries around the world, policy makers have debated how best to recover from the economic crisis. In 2010, a dominant dilemma for governments was whether to borrow and spend more to help economies grow, or whether to borrow and spend less to reduce national debts. Equally important for policy makers was how to coordinate policies with other governments, so that states did not enact policies that negated each other. These debates lead us into macroeconomics. What is the danger that reduced government spending would push economies into deeper recession? Is it bigger or smaller than the danger of debt crisis? A larger question is why traditionally strong economies (United States, western Europe) were hit harder by this crisis than developing economies we used to associate with crisis. After years of economic preaching to the developing countries, do the "advanced" economies now need to take some of their own advice?

Chapter 14 addresses international environmental problems. In the debate over the scientific evidence for global warming, we see clearly the link between scholarship, politics, and policy making. We concern ourselves in this book with the political, rather than the scientific, questions. What are the barriers to a more effective global treaty to prevent climate change? What are the economic effects of different measures? These are widely debated, and even when there is agreement on the costs, there is not agreement on who should pay those costs. Most frightening, perhaps, what are the possible international political and economic effects if little is done, and climate change begins having dramatic consequences?

Critical Thinking Questions

1. Identify a current debate (other than those mentioned here). What are the major causal arguments in favor of one policy or another?
2. Can you envision how one might design a study to assess the validity of these arguments?
3. What obstacles do you run into?

Similarly, each argument is supported by at least some evidence. We can evaluate that evidence and identify its strengths and weaknesses. For each argument, there is a competing argument, based on different assumptions and different evidence (or on a different interpretation of the same evidence). We want to be able to identify and explore the competing arguments. We want to understand where those different interpretations come from.

In sum, we want to accomplish three basic goals.

- First, we want to better our own understanding of international politics. More than learning facts, this means learning how to ask the right questions and to evaluate evidence about possible answers.

- This will allow us to achieve a second goal: to make informed evaluations about how the world works and about what choices should be made. We might use these evaluations to decide whom to vote for, where to invest, or where to volunteer.

- Third, we want to be able to engage in intelligent debate about important public policy issues. Whether the goal is to convince someone to vote for a particular candidate, to gain support for a particular policy, or simply to challenge our parents, we want to be able to bring theory and evidence together to create compelling arguments.

The Science of International Politics

Many assertions are made about international politics. Some are very general, whereas others are quite specific. In either case, however, the goal of analysis is to decide whether to accept or reject an assertion.

International politics is generally considered a part of the discipline of political science. The idea that there can be a science of politics is often regarded with skepticism. However, whether or not we admit it, all of us behave as though we can discover patterns in politics. We form generalizations about what tends to happen in certain kinds of circumstances, and about what we might do to promote some outcomes and prevent others. Without some belief that we can explain and predict political behavior, our choices would be completely random. The job of political science is to make our beliefs about causes and consequences as explicit as possible, and then to subject them to scrutiny.

How do we do this? The branch of political science known as "methodology" studies how best to verify or reject different hypotheses (assertions) about politics. However, there is profound disagreement among political scientists about which methodological approaches are best. There is equally profound disagreement about the extent to which the study of politics can be or should aim to be *scientific* in the way that term is used in the natural sciences. Rather than delve into these debates, this book uses a general model of political science, represented by the following process.

1. Begin with a question, such as "What causes wars?" The question must be clearly defined. For example, the analysis should specify whether "wars" includes both civil wars and international wars, or just international wars.

2. Identify potential answers (hypotheses). These may come from history, from political theory, from conventional wisdom, or from some observed pattern. Two prominent hypotheses about the causes of war are (1) war results from an imbalance in military power and (2) war results from the choices of aggressive leaders.

3. Determine what patterns we would observe if each hypothesis were true. What patterns would be evident if war resulted from an imbalance of power? Every time there was an imbalance of power, there would be war, and there would never be a war without an imbalance of power.

4. Decide how to define and measure the key factors. How is power defined? How is it measured? How much imbalance is supposed to matter? Issues of definition and measurement lead to a great deal of controversy about findings. Considerable disagreement as to the effects of imbalance of power on war can be attributed to the difficulty of defining and measuring "power."

5. Choose a research method. How will we link data to a hypothesis to reach a conclusion? We might look for a statistical pattern in a large number of cases: Is there a statistical correlation between the distribution of power and war? Alternatively, we might examine just a few cases in great depth to see if a link can be established between cause and effect. In this case, we might look closely at diplomatic records to see the role that an imbalance of power played in the thinking of key leaders. Or we might engage in a more interpretive approach: If the goal is to assess the role of aggressive leaders, we might analyze the rhetoric of national leaders to evaluate the subtle ways in which aggression is expressed.

6. After the evidence is collected, the investigator must evaluate the findings. In politics, researchers almost never find incontrovertible support for a hypothesis. Thus, instead of asking whether a hypothesis is true or false, political scientists ask whether it is a better or worse explanation than competing explanations. For example, there are certainly wars that were not caused by an imbalance of power. Do we, therefore, reject that hypothesis? Not if that hypothesis fits better with the data than any other hypothesis. Instead, we would accept that imbalances of power are important factors in war and continue to look for factors that might explain observed deviations from this hypothesis.

There are many variants on the research process in political science. They range from sophisticated mathematical analyses of complex data patterns, to equally sophisticated interpretations of a single case or of a pattern of discourse. The important point is that we first ask, "What is causing this phenomenon?" Then, when we have a tentative answer, we should ask, "Why is this answer more credible than another?" Skepticism about conclusions is perhaps even more important in the social sciences than in the natural sciences. Sometimes the process is frustrating, because two contradictory ideas may seem to have nearly equally convincing support. This is what makes the study of politics difficult. It is also what makes it so dramatic and compelling.

Nelson Almeida/AFP/Getty Images

Candidates for the Brazilian presidency participate in a televised debate in October 2010. Every day we hear competing claims about the nature of international politics and the best policy options. How do we evaluate which of those claims are true or even plausible?

In the natural sciences (and some social sciences), the ability to predict future events is the main criterion by which theories are judged. If a theory is valid, it ought to be able to predict future outcomes. In political science, and especially in international relations, consistently successful prediction is rare. Even reaching consensus on explanations of past patterns is elusive. Thus, the study of international relations is less about learning the accepted truths revealed by scientific inquiry than about understanding the ongoing debates among the most compelling theories. Progress is achieved more by eliminating explanations that seem plausible than by discovering scientific laws.

The Role of Theory

On the surface, academic political scientists talk about international politics very differently than do policy makers or journalists. Whereas policy makers and journalists concentrate on specific problems and look for specific answers, political scientists ask general questions about how international politics works. Despite these apparent differences, specific answers to specific questions are almost always linked to general explanations of how international politics works. These general explanations are called *theories*. Sometimes policy makers scorn the academic theories of political scientists, viewing them as too abstract to be relevant to pressing world issues.[2] Yet this superficial distinction is misleading. Even though policy makers rarely talk about theory explicitly, they use theories of international relations constantly in evaluating problems, whether they recognize it or not.

Several examples will illustrate the underlying importance of international relations theory for policy making. What is the best way to convince aspiring nuclear weapons states, such as Iran and North Korea, to give up their nuclear weapons programs? Some argue that raising the costs of such programs—through political and economic sanctions and, if necessary, military action—will persuade potential nuclear states that the cost is simply too high. Others contend that such threats only increase the perceived insecurity of the governments in question, and therefore increase their determination to get nuclear weapons. Still others look to domestic politics within the potential nuclear states, arguing that as long as their leaders get domestic political benefits from standing up to outside powers, there is little that external actors can do to dissuade them. Each of these answers is based on a general explanation—a theory—of what factors drive state behavior.

Why did the United States, after World War II, spend billions of dollars building up its former enemies in Germany and in Japan? Why did Western states contribute significant aid to their former enemies in the Soviet bloc after the Cold War? Why did the United States seek to install a democratic regime in Iraq in 2003–2004, rather than letting a new authoritarian government emerge? In each case, an underlying theory motivated these significant actions: the belief that democratic countries are much less likely to be aggressive and warlike. If this argument is true, money spent on democratization is a good investment because it will make unnecessary much larger military expenditures later.

Why did a handful of European countries form the European Community (the forerunner of today's European Union, or EU) in the 1950s? Why, over time, did they continue to lower economic barriers between the countries, culminating in the "single European market"? And why have other European states put so much emphasis on joining the European Union, so that it now has 27 members? For some of the founders of the original organization, a prime motivation was the belief that greater economic interdependence would help keep Europe from falling into another devastating war. For others, the belief that free trade leads to increased prosperity has been a primary motivation. For many of the post-communist states that have sought to join the EU in recent years, national identity may have been a driving force: being accepted into the EU meant that they were definitively part of "Europe," from which they had been isolated under

The History Connection

How History Influences Contemporary International Politics

This book, like any study of international politics, makes frequent references to historical examples—ranging in time from last year to 2500 years ago. We might ask, therefore, what connection events from the distant past have with the study of international politics today, in an age of cell phones, the Internet, and global mass culture. World leaders as well as scholars constantly look back in history to try to gain insight into the current problems they are grappling with. For some, history is a source of lessons. For others, it is a source of data. Either way, history is the primary place to look in evaluating theories. The philosopher George Santayana asserted the importance of history for leaders in his frequently quoted warning: "Those who do not know history are condemned to repeat it."

Each chapter of this book, therefore, will include a discussion showing how events in the twentieth and twenty-first centuries are not as historically unique or fundamentally new, as some believe them to be. The text will also look at the ways in which contemporary scholars and policy makers have tried to apply the lessons of the past to the problems they face today.

In one of the starkest examples in recent years, historian Robert Kaplan has argued that foreign policies today need to be based on a "pagan" or "pre-Christian" sense of ethics.[1] He contends that only by returning to an ancient set of ethical principles for conducting

foreign policy will the United States and its allies be able to achieve their goals in a dangerous world. Similarly, the fact that the United States has gained an immense amount of power has prompted many scholars, from very different perspectives, to draw parallels between the role of the United States today and the role of the Roman Empire 2000 years ago.

Do the politics and ethics of ancient Rome, at a time when wars were fought with spears and clubs and communications were written on scrolls and transmitted by messengers on foot, really provide useful lessons for modern leaders? Many people believe that the answer is yes. They contend that we have to get our expectations about the effects of different policies from somewhere, and that history is our best guide. Whether or not this argument is valid, history, of the distant as well as the recent past, continues to play an important role in debates on the contemporary world.

Critical Thinking Questions

1. Identify a current international issue. What historical examples seem most comparable?
2. Would other students in your class likely agree? If not, why not?
3. Do you think that students in Canada, China, Germany, or Russia would identify the same relevant examples? If not, why not?

[1]Robert Kaplan, *Warrior Politics: Why Leadership Demands a Pagan Ethos* (New York Random House, 2002).

communist rule. All of these theories are disputable, but they have been powerful motivators in many states' policies in recent years.

These examples demonstrate that general notions, or theories, about causes and effects, motivate all sorts of actions in international affairs. This is true whether or not policy makers recognize that their generalizations about the world can be called "theories" and whether or not those theories have been scrutinized and tested for validity. Some theories have worked out badly when applied. For example, a theory derived from the lessons of World War I, that confronting aggression could lead to unnecessary war, led to decisions that contributed to World War II.

All policy is, in one way or another, informed by theories about how international politics works. What theories might be behind the formation of the United Nations?

John Angelillo/UPI/Landov

Policy makers are concerned above all not with generalities, but with specific problems at specific points in time. However, even in the context of a single case, theory is necessary for action. Without predicting the likely results of different choices, we cannot act intelligently. Thus, any given policy can be "unpeeled" to uncover the theoretical assumptions behind it. The study of international politics aims to make those theories explicit and to subject them to scrutiny. The economist John Maynard Keynes put it rather acidly: "Practical men, who believe themselves to be quite exempt from any intellectual influences, are usually the slaves of some defunct economist."[3]

What is a Theory?

theory

A generalized explanation of a set of comparable phenomena.

In political science, the word theory is used fairly specifically: A **theory** is a generalized explanation of a set of essentially similar phenomena. Two things should be emphasized. First, a theory is an *explanation*. It answers the question "Why?" A theory specifies a particular effect that is being explained and the causes of that effect. Second, a theory is *generalized*. It seeks to explain not a single event, but a series of comparable events. Thus, political science does not advance a theory of World War I or a theory of the establishment the World Trade Organization system. Rather, political scientists develop theories of how wars occur or of trade liberalization, but not of a single event. Instead, there are *descriptions* of single events. This specific usage of the word "theory" in social science differs slightly from the conventional usage, in which a theory is sometimes used to label any conjecture about a single event, such as a *theory* of who killed John F. Kennedy or a *theory* of why a certain candidate won a certain election.

However, as this last example implies, there can often be a connection between a theory and an attempt to account for a particular event. To understand why a specific event occurred (such as the outcome of an election or the outbreak of a war), analysts almost always consider the factors that have been important in related cases. The question of why World War I occurred is related to the question, "What causes wars?" Similarly, understanding the sources of the World Trade Organization is related to understanding the general causes of trade liberalization.

Thus, theory is built on an underlying assumption that specific events are not unique and do not have unique causes. Rather, we assume that most important events are single instances of broader patterns. If we want to prevent wars, we need some notion of what causes them. This requires a supposition that different wars have something in common. When stated so starkly, this idea will appear problematical to many. For example, it might seem dubious to equate the causes of World War I with the causes of World War II. However, if the lessons of the past are to be applied to the problems of today, we must assume that events in the future are somehow related to those in the past. There is a big difference between assuming that similar events have something in common and assuming that they are identical. To develop a theory of wars, we only need assume that there are some causes in common.

Historically, there have been both successes and failures in the effort to apply theory to policy. Following World War I, the dominant theories of war focused on the absence of international law. Therefore, much effort was expended on developing the League of Nations and treaties outlawing war. The problems with this approach were demonstrated at the outbreak of World War II. After World War II, however, theories of international relations were more successfully applied with the formation of the Bretton Woods system. The Bretton Woods institutions were founded on the theory that free trade would increase prosperity, and that theory has been borne out in the post-war economic boom among the members of the Bretton Woods institutions.

Today, some of the most pressing policy issues are prompting new efforts to advance theoretical understanding of international politics. While police and military forces are working every day to intercept specific terrorist threats, scholars are seeking to better understand the underlying sources of terrorism. Is it based primarily in religion? In poverty? In political frustration? Answering these questions requires looking for the commonalities across different terrorist movements, even while acknowledging that they are all unique in some ways.

The Uses of Theory

Theory has three related main purposes: explanation, prediction, and prescription. First, theory is used to explain the common causes shared by a group of related events (explanation). Second, theory is used to apply such explanations to future events, to predict what might result from existing conditions or from some new event or policy (prediction). Third, theory is used to help policy makers and citizens choose the most effective policies for a given goal (prescription). In all of these tasks, theory becomes a means to simplify a reality that is extremely complex.

Figure 1.3 Theory has three related purposes: explanation, prediction, and prescription.

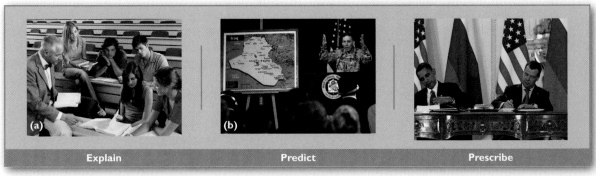

Sources: (a) Pixland/Jupiter Images; (b) AP Photo/Chris Hondros, Pool; (c) Dmitry Astakhov/AFP/Getty Images

normative theory

A theory that aims to establish the proper goals of political action.

In evaluating different theories, it is important to keep in mind that a theory deliberately abstracts from reality, leaving much detail aside. Theories identify which parts of a complex event deserve immediate attention and which are of secondary importance. Therefore, when a particular fact or a case apparently contradicts a theory, this does not mean that the theory has no utility. Rather, the theory must be evaluated on the basis of whether, overall, it provides more or less understanding than competing explanations of the same general phenomenon.

Normative Theory: The Purpose of Action

Besides increasing our ability to explain, predict, and prescribe, there is another kind of international relations theory with a very different goal: establishing what the purpose of political action should be. Such theory is called **normative theory**. While explanatory theory asks, "How does the world work?" normative theory asks, "What goals should we pursue?" and "What are acceptable and unacceptable ways to behave?" Normative theory can address a wide range of moral and ethical concerns, and these will crop up repeatedly throughout this book. Many discussions assume that certain goals are worth pursuing, and these normative arguments are often taken as self-evident and therefore are not discussed or debated. Sometimes these assumptions are noncontroversial; at other times, they warrant serious scrutiny.

For example, although much discussion in international politics centers on how to prevent wars, no theorist spends much time asserting that war is bad, because this seems self-evident. Therefore, theorists can move on to asking how to prevent war. However, in practice, we often find ourselves agonizing over whether war, as bad as it is, is worse than other possibilities. In World War II, fighting a horrendous war with millions of casualties was seen as a lesser evil than allowing Nazi Germany to rule the world. In the 1990s, many people who generally thought of themselves as opposed to military force advocated strongly for the use of military force to prevent the "ethnic cleansing" taking place in the former Yugoslavia. Although they still believed war was bad, they believed genocide was worse. Thus, even normative arguments that seem self-evident often are not. Some theorists believe that unquestioned normative beliefs often serve the interests of the powerful and that a primary goal of research should be to investigate how some normative goals come to predominate over others.

Above: National Hockey League hockey players get into a fight. Below: Adolf Hitler speaks at a rally. Are human beings inherently aggressive? Are the decisions of individual leaders responsible for different international outcomes? If so, the individual level of analysis is important.

Levels of Analysis

This book considers a variety of explanations of how international politics works and of how states behave.

At times you may find the range of theories bewildering. Unfortunately, it is not easy to reduce the number of plausible explanations down to one or two. To envision how explanations relate to one another, it is useful to group them into different schools of thought.

An initial way to categorize theories is according to their **level of analysis**. Level of analysis identifies where the analysis focuses—where the most important variation occurs. Is the main actor in the model a single individual, a larger aggregation such as a bureaucracy, or an even larger aggregation such as the state? Every analysis focuses on one aggregation and holds the other aggregations constant for the purposes of analysis. In an influential study on the causes of war, Kenneth Waltz argued that one can explain wars at any of three levels of analysis.[4] Individual-level theories are those that see the cause of war in individuals, either generally (for example, in human nature) or specifically (in the characteristics of specific leaders). State-level theories are those that locate the cause of war in the nature of states. For example, some types of governments might be more prone to war than others, or some states might have profound grievances that cause them to seek redress through war. System-level theories, which Waltz preferred, see the causes of war in the characteristics of the international system. War in this view is caused by factors that extend beyond any single state, such as the distribution of power and the number of "great powers" in the system.

Other theorists have proposed four or even five levels of analysis because they break the state level down into more than one level.[5] This book also explores explanations at a fourth level, the "substate" level, between the state and individual levels. Analyses at the substate level examine the bureaucracies and small groups that make foreign policies as well as the influence of interest groups and public opinion on foreign policy (see Chapters 5 and 6). Debating the "right" number of levels is less important than understanding the concept. Thinking about the level of analysis helps illuminate where different theories look for answers; it shows what they focus on and what they de-emphasize. More important, it helps explain why theories that are compelling sometimes tend to speak past one another. It is fairly easy, for example, for theorists who hold two different system-level theories to debate each other. It is more difficult for a theorist who prefers a system-level theory to debate one who prefers an individual-level theory because the questions they ask and the evidence they look at are different.

Following this introduction, Chapter 2 surveys the history of international politics. Chapters 3 and 4 investigate theories of international politics. With important exceptions, the main schools of thought covered in these chapters tend to seek explanations at the systemic level, bringing in theories at other levels where needed to add detail. Chapter 5 presents explanations primarily at the state level, examining the argument that democracies are more peaceful than other states, and examining the role of interest groups, public opinion, and the media. Chapter 6 presents explanations at the substate and individual levels. These include the various branches of government, bureaucracies, the small groups of advisors on whom leaders often rely, and the individual leaders themselves. The book then turns to specific issues including security (Chapters 7-8), international political economy (Chapters 9-11), international organizations and transnational actors (Chapter 12), international law and norms (Chapter 13), and transnational challenges of migration, crime, health, and environment (Chapter 14). The conclusion (Chapter 15) looks to the future in light of the theories introduced and the issues discussed.

By the end of the book, the reader will be able to see how the approaches developed in the early chapters can help address current and emerging issues. Although a goal of any such book is to teach the reader a certain amount about what the world looks like today and about the main approaches to understanding it, these are means to a greater end. The ultimate goal is to be able to tackle new and unfamiliar problems and to become critical participants, whether as citizens or as policy makers.

level of analysis
The unit (individual, state, or system) that a theory focuses on in its general explanation.

The Culture Connection

Culture and International Politics

International affairs have been one of the major influences on all aspects of culture, from ancient times to the present. Throughout the book, each chapter will examine how international affairs have shaped the themes of culture around the world, from music to art to television. Some of the most famous works of culture, those with which almost all of us are familiar, are closely connected to international affairs.

In the realm of music, for example, few melodies are more familiar than that of the *1812 Overture* by the Russian composer Peter Tchaikovsky. The 1812 in the title refers to the year that Napoleon's army invaded Russia, and the piece commemorates the triumph of Russian forces, with thundering bass drums representing the cannon of the two armies (real cannon are sometimes used in concert performances). Leo Tolstoy's great novel *War and Peace,* based on the same conflict, heads a long list of masterpieces of literature that deal with war.

In drama, Shakespeare's *Henry V,* among other plays, is about the political maneuvering to control England and France that resulted in the Battle of Agincourt in 1415. In painting, many of the great works of the twentieth century were inspired by the two world wars, including Pablo Picasso's *Guernica,* which depicts the horror of civilian casualties inflicted during an aerial bombardment during the Spanish Civil War.

Culture also helps shape international affairs, in that images of war, of peace, and of good and evil shape how we think about international affairs, and hence what we do about them. The production and manipulation of images, whether carried out by artists or by the media, can have far-reaching effects. One might speculate, for example, on how the events of September 11, 2001, would be perceived differently by people around the world if they had not been caught on videotape, broadcast again and again and again, and seared into our collective memories.

At the outbreak of World War II, the film industries in the major combating countries were charged with producing films that would lift the morale of troops and civilians, showing the courage of the countries' soldiers and justifying their sacrifices by portraying the evil nature of their enemies. Art and culture, therefore, are not only a source of insight into international politics, they are sometimes tools of international politics as well.

Critical Thinking Questions

1. Which parts of international politics do films and television tend to portray?
2. Do films and television address the actual substance of international politics?
3. How might the representation of international politics in entertainment influence your thinking?

PHOTO © ISTOCKPHOTO

Summary

International politics is a subject about which we constantly debate what we know and how we know it. These are debates with high stakes because policy making requires acting on current knowledge, even when that knowledge is imperfect. Theories of international politics are, therefore, not merely of academic interest. The study of international politics aims to make these theories explicit and to subject them to scrutiny so that they can help provide the best possible answers to the urgent questions facing governments, societies, and individuals.

Key Concepts

1. Power
2. Purpose
3. Theory

4. Normative theory
5. Methodology
6. Levels of analysis

Study Questions

1. In what ways can the study of international politics take a scientific approach?
2. What are the limitations of the "science" of international politics?
3. How do theories of international politics relate to the policies that various actors adopt?

4. What is a theory?
5. How does normative theory differ from explanatory theory?
6. How does the level of analysis we choose influence the kinds of answers we get?

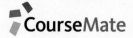

Endnotes

1 U.S. Secretary of State Colin Powell and Senator Chuck Hagel were also quoted in the immediate aftermath of the attacks using the same phrase. Karen DeYoung, *Soldier: The Life of Colin Powell* (New York: Alfred A. Knopf, 2006). "Bush vows retaliation for 'evil acts'," *USA Today*, September 12, 2001, at http://www.usatoday.com/news/nation/2001/09/11/attack-usat .htm#more

2 Harvard professor-turned member of Canadian Parliament Michael Ignatieff is one who holds this view. See "Getting Iraq Wrong," *New York Times Magazine,* August 5, 2007, pp. 26ff.

3 John Maynard Keynes, *The General Theory of Employment, Interest, and Money* (New Delhi: Atlantic Publishers, 2007 [1936]), p.351.

4 Kenneth N. Waltz, *Man, the State, and War* (New York: Columbia University Press, 1959).

5 Arnold Wolfers, "The Actors in International Politics," in W. T. R. Fox, ed., *Theoretical Aspects of International Relations* (South Bend, IN: University of Notre Dame Press, 1959), pp. 83–106; Robert Jervis, "Perception and the Level of Analysis Problem," in *Perception and Misperception in International Politics* (Princeton, NJ: Princeton University Press, 1976), pp. 13–31; and James Rosenau, "Pre-Theories and Theories of Foreign Policy," in J. Rosenau, ed., *The Scientific Study of Foreign Policy* (New York: The Free Press, 1971), pp. 95–151.

The Historical Evolution of International Politics

LEARNING OBJECTIVES

After completing this chapter, the student should be able to. . .

1. Describe the major developments in the history of international politics.
2. Understand the evolution of the international system.
3. Explain the significance of the Westphalian system.
4. Interpret the role of colonialism in transforming the international system.
5. Summarize the causes and significance of World War I, World War II, and the Cold War.
6. Identify the major developments of the post-World War II system.
7. Discuss the extent to which the international system is characterized by continuity and change.

◀ The painting *Divine Offerings Made to Captain Cook (1728–79) in the Sandwich Islands* depicts the early relationship between European colonizers and a colonized population.

Divine Offerings Made to Captain Cook (1728–79) in the Sandwich Islands (coloured engraving), Italian School (18th century)/Private Collection/The Bridgeman Art Library

Consider the Case

Past and Present in the Invasion of Iraq

Prior to and during the U.S. invasion and occupation of Iraq that began in 2003, scholars, policy makers, and individuals have continuously looked to the past to help them understand the current problems in Iraq.

For many Iraqis, history provides much of the motivation for their choice of sides in the conflict. Hostility between the three main groups, Shia, Sunni, and Kurds, is based in large part on collective "memory" of events that happened generations, or even centuries, ago. The basic split between Shia and Sunni Muslims dates from the seventh century, when the death of the Prophet Mohammed was followed by a split between those who thought that religious and political authority should pass to caliphs (elders chosen by elite consensus) and those who thought it should pass to imams (descendents of Mohammed). These two groups became known as Sunni and Shia, respectively. In 680, Mohammed's grandson Hussein was slain in Karbala by Sunnis on the day now commemorated by Shia as Ashura, and that day has come to be marked by violence in post-Saddam Iraq (and elsewhere). A series of attacks during Ashura in 2004 killed 170 Shia and wounded 500. Similarly, attacks in 2006 and in 2007 on the Shia Al-Askariya mosque, where the eleventh and twelfth imams were buried in 944, were calculated to stir up violence between Shia and Sunni.[1] A central question for those seeking to overcome these divisions is, how can hostilities that have been 1300 years in the making be overcome in a short period of time?

The U.S. public and politicians tended to invoke very different sets of historical precedents as "themes" that were shorthand for describing the nature of the conflict and the chances of success. The early rhetoric of the "global war on terrorism" cast it as similar to World War II and assumed that, as in that earlier war, the United States and its allies would triumph over evil. As the initial victory over Saddam Hussein's forces evolved into a demoralizing counterinsurgency, many viewed Iraq in light of Vietnam, a comparison that carried clear messages about the futility of increasing troop levels or committing to carrying on the war indefinitely.

For U.S. military commanders seeking to end the insurgency, history became a textbook. The U.S. army feverishly studied historic examples of successful and unsuccessful counterinsurgency operations in an effort to figure out how to defeat Iraqi insurgents. Considerable attention was given to the insurgency led by T. E. Lawrence ("Lawrence of Arabia") against Ottoman forces during World War I, to Britain's successful campaign against insurgents in Malaya from 1948 to 1960, and to the failed U.S. counterinsurgency in Vietnam, which many senior U.S. military officers had experienced 30 to 40 years earlier as young officers. For them, the question was, what lessons emerged from the history of these different conflicts?

Consciously or unconsciously, understandings of history influence the way people view problems—the grievances they perceive, the goals they set, and the policies they adopt to pursue those goals. Historical interpretation plays several different roles in Iraq and in other contemporary problems. An understanding of the historical context of international politics is, therefore, essential to comprehending today's issues.

This chapter summarizes the historical development of the international political system that exists today. The chapter does not attempt to provide a complete history of international politics. That, of course, would make for a very long book.[2] This chapter does not provide equal treatment of all events or of all parts of the world. Instead, the goal is to answer the question, how did the contemporary international system evolve?

The evolution of today's international system has been dominated by two long-term developments. The first was the development of a system of sovereign states in Western Europe. The second was the spread of that system to the rest of the world. As a result of those two processes, by the end of the 1970s the entire world was contained in a single

How does history fit into today's conflicts? In Iraq, an attack on the centuries-old Al-Askariya mosque was calculated to spur conflict between Shia and Sunni Muslims.

system of sovereign states. Today that system continues to evolve with the rise of international organizations and nonstate actors, and some argue that it is now morphing into a fundamentally new system.

The Birth of International Politics

Many histories of international politics begin with developments in the Greek **city-states** in the fifth century BCE. This Greek period is important for two reasons. First, it is one of the earliest examples of what later came to be viewed as a system of independent states. Second, this period gave rise to one of the earliest known analyses of international politics: the *History of the Peloponnesian War,* written by the Athenian general Thucydides.[3] His analysis was the first known attempt to advance a general understanding of how international politics works, and some of his fundamental assertions continue to be influential today.

In 431 BCE, Sparta and Athens, two Greek city-states, went to war. Although the details of the **Peloponnesian War** are not essential here, Thucydides' explanation of the causes is. Thucydides asserted that the war was caused by an imbalance in power between Athens and Sparta. As long as Sparta was considerably more powerful than Athens, there was no cause for war. However, as Athens' power approached that of Sparta, the Spartans feared that Athens would soon become strong enough to attack and defeat Sparta. To avoid that, Sparta attacked Athens first.

In this explanation of the Peloponnesian War, Thucydides provided an embryonic theory of international politics that has persisted to this day. The key actors were states. The key factor in international politics was the distribution of power, upon which war and peace depended.

Thucydides also argued that discussions of justice had no place in international politics. Arguments about morality, he said, were simply disguises for the ambitions of states. In a famous line, he stated that "the strong do what they can and the weak suffer what they must." For 2500 years, people have debated whether, as Thucydides says, international politics is beyond morality.

city-state

A state that centers on a single city, rather than a larger territory or a nation.

Peloponnesian War

A war between Athens and Sparta from 431 BCE to 404 BCE. Thucydides' study of this war has been influential on later thinking about international relations.

Figure 2.1 Europe in 1100 CE. For much of recorded history, global politics was not "international" politics in that it did not consist of relations between clearly delineated states. Empires were the rule, their borders were fluid, and they tended not to have extensive relations with anyone other than their closest neighbors.

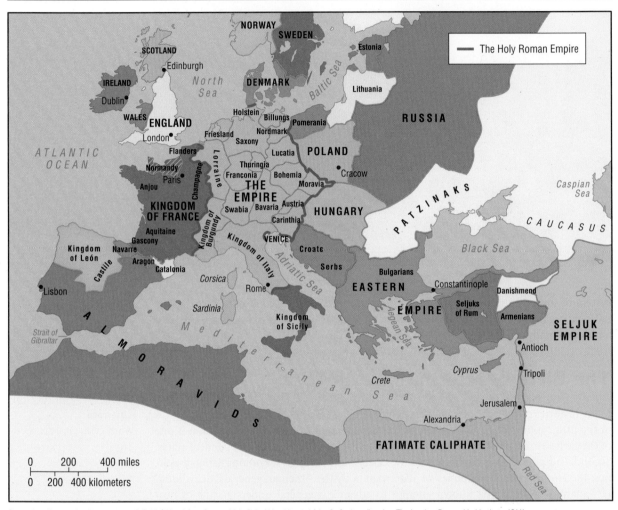

Source: http://www.culturalresources.com/MP_Muir6.html, from Ramsay Muir, *Philips' New Historical Atlas for Students* (London: The London Geographical Institute, 1911).

From City-States to Nation-States

Many histories of international politics begin in the seventeenth century. Why do they skip the preceding history? Between the fall of the Greek city-states and the rise of Western European sovereign states, a very different kind of international system existed. Initially, the Roman Empire dominated much of what Europeans considered the known world. In that system, a single empire dominated international politics. This situation contrasts sharply with the system of multiple states that later arose, and is seen as a fundamentally different kind of politics. The seemingly predominant role of the United States in the contemporary era has increased interest in the workings of systemwide empires, but by most accounts, the Roman Empire was not an international system at all.[4] Therefore, it is seen as having little relevance for understanding modern international politics.

Following the collapse of the Roman Empire, Europe was dominated by a **feudal system**. Although it was fundamentally different from the Roman Empire, in which a single government dominated all of Europe, the feudal system was also quite different from the

feudal system

A political system in which individuals within a society have obligations based on class (king, nobility, peasantry) and no single ruler has absolute authority over a given territory.

The Culture Connection

International History in Contemporary Cinema

Hollywood producers and millions of film-goers have for years been fascinated with the history of international relations. Recent years have seen a succession of highly popular movies in which the history of international politics has either played a central role in the plot or provided the backdrop for the story. Wars, not surprisingly, are a particularly popular subject. Several recent films have directly addressed U.S. involvement in Iraq and Afghanistan. Following are a few recent examples from Hollywood:

■ *Saving Private Ryan* (1998) is set largely during World War II, at the time of the U.S. invasion of occupied France. But the movie also concerns contemporary memories of that war as the generation that fought it is dying off.

■ *Fog of War* (2003) is a documentary about Robert McNamara, the Secretary of Defense who led U.S. policy on the Vietnam War. In interviews many years after the war, McNamara struggles to accept responsibility for a war in which he played a major role.

■ *Flags of Our Fathers* (2006) and *Letters from Iwo Jima* (2006) both examine the U.S. invasion of Iwo Jima in World War II, one from the perspective of U.S. soldiers and the other from the perspective of Japanese soldiers.

■ *Munich* (2005) tells the story of the Israeli assassins tasked with killing the terrorists responsible for the attack on Israeli athletes at the 1972 Summer Olympics.

■ *Charlie Wilson's War* (2007) is the fictionalized story of U.S. Representative Charlie Wilson's efforts to have the Central Intelligence Agency support Afghan militants fighting the Soviet Union after the 1979 invasion. It provides a chilling look at how the United States armed and trained the fighters who later became Al-Qaeda and the Taliban.

■ *The Hurt Locker* (2008) portrays the danger and stress experienced by a U.S. Army bomb disposal unit in Iraq.

Although all of these films depict important themes in international politics, all but the documentary *Fog of War* are fiction. To make the stories work, filmmakers sometimes quite deliberately change or misrepresent history.

Critical Thinking Questions

1. Consider an issue addressed in one of the films listed above (or some other film). How much of what you know about this issue comes from popular culture, as opposed to scholarly historical works?

2. How do television networks decide which historical events to feature in documentaries? What effect might these decisions have on our understanding of history?

3. To the extent that policies are based in part on an understanding of history, how significant is it that many people get their "history" from films and television programs rather than from history books?

sovereign state system that followed it. In a feudal system, political authority was defined personally and religiously, rather than territorially. A given territory likely had several different levels of rulers, depending on which inhabitants were being considered or what the issue was. Most notably, powers were divided among local nobles; kings, or emperors, whose power had a wider geographic scope but whose local authority was limited, and the Church of Rome, which claimed religious authority over all of Europe but whose practical power was limited. These different bases of power often clashed with one another, as each actor tried to expand its own territorial control, political power, and wealth.

The Westphalian System

Westphalian system

The system of sovereign states that was recognized by the Treaty of Westphalia in 1648.

The modern sovereign state system is often called the **Westphalian system**, after the Treaty of Westphalia, signed in 1648. The Treaty of Westphalia, which ended the Thirty Years War, is seen as enshrining the status of sovereign states, even though the process of building this sovereign state system took place gradually.

The Thirty Years War was motivated both by religious conflict and by a contest for political control over Europe. Catholic leaders sought to defeat Protestant states to restore the "true faith." States also battled to increase their power at the expense of their rivals, and several sought to conquer all of Europe in order to reestablish a single empire, as had existed under the Roman Empire. Over time, the political motive displaced the religious motive, and the conflict is thus sometimes referred to as *the last of the religious wars*. The triumph of "national interest" over religious motives is seen as one of the long-lasting effects of the war.[5]

Like many wars, the Thirty Years War lasted much longer and was much more devastating than anyone expected. In central Europe, as much as one third of the population died as a result of the war, a death rate higher than during World War I or World War II. Exhausted, the European powers gathered in Westphalia (in what is today northwestern Germany) in 1648 to make peace. The result was the Treaty of Westphalia.

The treaty established principles that defined the system from then until now. First, the treaty recognized the existence of sovereign states. Second, it defined the rights of sovereign states. The powers of Europe accepted that the dream of renewing the Roman Empire was impossible and that pursuing that goal was certain to lead to war. This meant acknowledging Europe as a system of multiple states. How would these states relate to one another? The principle of **sovereignty** answers this question. Sovereignty meant that each state had complete authority over its territory, at least in theory.

sovereignty

The principle that states have complete authority over their own territory.

Sovereignty had both internal and external dimensions. Internally, it meant that no one within a state had the right to challenge the ruler's power. Any challenges that occurred were regarded as illegitimate or unjust. This principle gave kings power over lesser nobles. The external dimension of sovereignty was that no one outside a territory had the right to say what should go on within that territory. This principle, often known as the *principle of noninterference in the internal affairs of other states*, was especially important in religious terms. In particular, the Treaty of Westphalia recognized the power of rulers to determine the religion of the people in their territory.

In territorial terms as well as in religious terms, the treaty acknowledged the reality of **pluralism**. In religious terms, pluralism meant acceptance of more than one religion, rather than an attempt to determine and enforce a single "true" religion. In political terms, pluralism meant accepting that there would be many states, rather than a single empire covering all of Europe. Europe was not going to be a single empire based on a single religion. Instead, Europe would be divided territorially, with various rulers having immense authority within their territories and none outside of them. Religious authority would also be segmented territorially, with individual leaders determining the religions of their own states but recognizing the rights of other monarchs to impose different religions in their states. This was not exactly a recipe for religious tolerance; within individual states, persecution of minorities continued to be widespread and brutal.

pluralism

The presence of a number of competing actors or ideas.

The system that emerged from this period is known by various names, including the "sovereign state system," the "Westphalian system," and simply the "state system."[6] It is based both on the acknowledgment of certain facts and on the establishment of certain principles. The key facts are that the main actors in the system are **states**, and that there are many of them. The key principle is that of sovereignty: in principle, the government of a sovereign state has complete authority within its territory but none outside of its territory. No higher (external) authority can claim authority over individual states. It must

state

An entity defined by a specific territory within which a single government has authority.

Figure 2.2 Europe in 1648. At the end of the Thirty Years War in 1648, a plurality of independent states existed in Europe. However, as this map shows, some were quite large and others were tiny. Over the ensuing centuries, borders continued to change, usually through warfare or the threat of it.

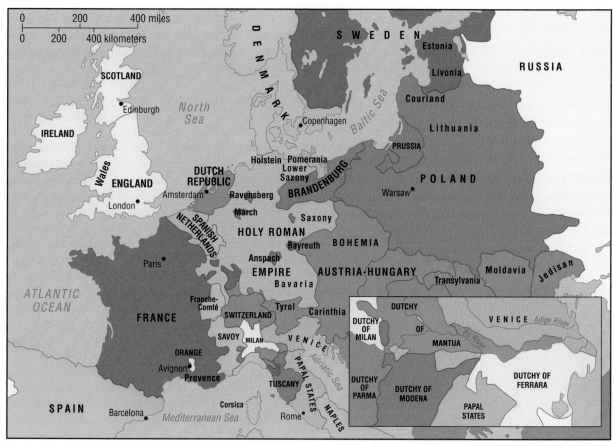

Source: http://www.lib.utexas.edu/maps/historical/europe_1648_westphal_1884.jpg

be emphasized that sovereignty is a principle, not a statement of fact. Although there have been many violations of the principle over the years, the principle itself remains the underpinning of the international system today. Moreover, sovereignty is not an objective trait of states; rather, states are treated as sovereign only when other states officially recognize their sovereignty. **Recognition** is important in this system. Political entities that are recognized as sovereign by other sovereign entities have greater legitimacy, and hence a greater chance of surviving, than those that are not recognized.

recognition
The acceptance by the international community of a state's sovereignty over its territory.

The Balance of Power System

The principles of the Westphalian system did not prevent states from pursuing their interests, and states often used war as a tool to achieve those interests. Nor did the principle that Europe would be a system of multiple states prevent periodic attempts by one state or another to assert total dominance over Europe.[7]

Sovereignty has important implications for international politics. If no higher power can tell states what to do, then there is no one to prevent states from attacking one another. Nor is there any international organization to compel or even persuade states to limit their aggression. A situation in which there is no central ruler or government above the

anarchy

A condition in which there is no central ruler.

separate actors is termed **anarchy**. Note that *anarchy* does not mean *chaos*, a term with which it is sometimes confused. A central issue in international politics is the possibility of establishing order within a system that is anarchic. This term is of central importance in understanding international politics and will be explored further in Chapter 3.

In the situation of anarchy that followed Westphalia, larger states could and often did attack and absorb smaller states, such that the number of European states declined steadily over time. In this sense, the Westphalian system was perhaps little different from what preceded it, even if the principles had changed.

Thus, the history of Europe from 1648 until the beginning of the nineteenth century was characterized by what is sometimes called the *classic balance of power system.* There was nothing to prevent states from waging war on each other, except prudence. Yet warfare in this era was in many ways more limited than it had been during the Thirty Years War that preceded it or the Napoleonic wars that followed. In part this was because of the distribution of power; although some states did seek to gain dominance over the continent, none had the ability to do so simply by conquering the others. A **balance of power**

balance of power

A system in which no single actor is dominant; also, the distribution of power in such a system, which is not necessarily equal.

meant that no one state was sufficiently powerful to defeat the others. This balance of power was both a fact and a policy. No single state could gain enough power to destroy all the others, and many states made the maintenance of a balance an explicit goal of policy.

Moreover, the nature of the states themselves placed an important limitation on the size of armies. All of these states were monarchies, in which the vast majority of the population had no rights to citizenship. There was little reason for peasants with no rights to fight for rulers of countries of which they were not citizens. Modern notions of nationalism and patriotism had not yet emerged. The only people with a "stake" in whether a territory was ruled by one king or another were the nobles, from whose ranks armed forces were drawn. This was a small group. Mercenaries were sometimes used, but this too had limiting effects on war. Mercenaries were expensive, and they tried very hard to avoid actual battle, where they might be killed. Furthermore, before modern manufacturing techniques were developed, armaments such as cannon and guns were extraordinarily expensive. There was much incentive to avoid squandering these investments. In sum, the expense of building armies and armaments kept forces small and made leaders wary of risking them in battle.

law of war

A doctrine concerning when it is permissible to go to war and what means of conducting war are permissible (and not permissible).

Finally, despite religious divisions in Europe, there existed a **law of war**, based on Christian doctrines, which raised moral objections to unlimited war, and particularly to the targeting of noncombatants (civilians).[8] These limitations, which did not apply to non-Christian groups such as the Turks, helped make war in Europe less lethal than it otherwise might have been.

Europe and the Rest of the World

What was happening in the rest of the world while the modern state system was emerging in Europe? In China in the first millennium BCE, the state varied between an empire with a single dominant leader roughly analogous to Rome during its heyday and a pluralistic system roughly analogous to the Westphalian system. Normative debates over what system should prevail helped distinguish doctrines such as Taoism and Confucianism that continue to wield influence today. For most of the past 2000 years, China has existed as a single state, although the territorial extent and the strength of that state have varied. In some periods, China expanded its political and cultural influence into adjacent regions, including Xinjiang, Mongolia, Tibet, Korea, Vietnam, and Japan. During other periods, Chinese territory was controlled by outsiders, as when the Mongol emperor Kublai Khan conquered China in the thirteenth century CE.

In the Middle East and North Africa, the rise of Islam led to the establishment of the Caliphate—a unified political area governed by Islam—the geographic extent of which varied over time. Eventually, however, various groups such as the Berbers in North Africa, the Mamluks in Egypt broke away from the Caliphate. Here, as in medieval Europe, there was a tension between a shared principal that political authority should be unified and a reality that it is was fragmented among competing societies and rulers. By the sixteenth century, the Ottoman Empire became the most powerful claimant to the authority of the Caliphate.

One marauding group, the Mongols, played a role in upending existing arrangements in three distinct regions: in China, where it ended the Song Dynasty; in the Middle East, where it ended the Abbasid Caliphate; and in Europe, where it conquered the nascent Russian state, with far-reaching effects.

In other places, such as India, feudal systems dominated, and no mutual recognition of sovereignty had emerged.[9] Most of what is today North and South America was fairly sparsely populated, so relations between distinct groups of people—international politics—were not as pressing an issue as they were in more heavily populated regions. In Africa, a great diversity of empires rose, expanded, and fell in different places at different points in time, such that the consolidation of political authority into a small number of large entities did not occur.

The period in which the modern state was emerging in Europe was also the period in which Europe was increasing its contact with the rest of the world at a rate that accelerated dramatically after the European "discovery" of North and South America in the years after 1492. Prior to that time, different systems of international relations existed largely unconnected to one another. Over the next 400 years, Europe came to dominate almost the entire globe. The rest of the world was forcibly integrated into the modern state system, first as colonies of states and then, after European powers surrendered their colonies in the twentieth century, as sovereign states.[10] For this reason, the development of the modern state system in Europe receives disproportionate attention in the study of international relations; for better or for worse, this is the system that came to dominate international politics.

How did this happen? Why were European countries able to dominate the rest of the world? Why did some other country or group or some other system of principles not become dominant? Why was resistance to European imperialism generally unsuccessful? These questions are widely debated, and there are no definitive answers.[11] Several factors likely played a role. Europeans developed superior agricultural, industrial, and, particularly, military technology. Some contend that the constant warfare among European states in the early modern period strengthened European states to compete with the rest of the world. Others point to the development of capitalism as a key source of European domination. Capitalism may have provided both the means for expansion, in terms of surplus profit to invest in overseas business ventures, and the incentive, in terms of the lust for private wealth. Finally, some point to ideology. The varieties of Christianity that predominated in modern Europe provided justification for expansion for the purpose of converting non-Christians.

European domination did not just mean that European states dominated other societies. It meant that the European system of sovereign states and subservient colonies came to dominate, and that European principles, "rules of the game," and interpretations of history dominated.

Napoleon and National Warfare

By 1800 substantial changes had taken place in European politics that would fundamentally alter the nature of international politics. These changes were embodied by the rise to power in France of Napoleon Bonaparte and by the wars he subsequently waged.[12] Napoleon sought to overthrow the Westphalian system in Europe by

The Policy Connection

Explaining the Rise of Europe and Learning Lessons from It

In 1500, Europe was neither wealthier nor more powerful than any other part of the world, but by 1900, Europe and the United States had colonized nearly the entire planet. How? The sources of Europe's rise engender debate among academics in several disciplines. For policy makers seeking to bring the "recipe" of Europe's success to the rest of the world, the debate is equally relevant.

The German sociologist Max Weber attributed Europe's success to its values. In *The Protestant Ethic and the Spirit of Capitalism* (1905), Weber argued that the adoption of Protestant religious beliefs reshaped the relationship between religion and economics in a way that promoted capitalism.[1] In non-Protestant faiths, Weber argued, religious devotion was equated with a rejection of worldly goods; hence, one could not be both pious and wealthy. Protestantism supported the notion that success on earth was an indicator of the likelihood of being "saved" after death.

More recently, in *Guns, Germs, and Steel*, geographer Jared Diamond attributes Europe's success to environmental factors that gave it an advantage in competition with the rest of the world.[2] Diamond contends that species of animals and plants suitable for domestication and agriculture were more prevalent in Europe than elsewhere. Because Eurasia stretches mostly east–west and has a roughly similar climate across its expanse, agricultural successes in one place could be adapted elsewhere. Agricultural surplus allowed cities to develop and allowed labor to be diverted into other fields. Moreover, the concentration of population in cities helped the spread of disease, such that Europeans developed resistance to many diseases that were devastating elsewhere. Concentration of population meant that the states of

early modern Europe were constantly at war, which led them to develop the superior military technology and organizations with which they then conquered the world. Diamond claims to have produced an explanation of Europe's dominance that is not based on any notion of European cultural superiority.

The sociologist Immanuel Wallerstein argues that a very small economic advantage in economic development at the beginning of the modern era allowed England and France, and subsequently other European states, to get ever further ahead than other states.[3] He contends that in a world of capitalist exchange, each exchange provides greater benefit to the wealthier. As a result, the initially small gaps between Europe and other states inevitably grew over time. This view, inspired by Marxist economics (see Chapters 4 and 9), sees Europe's advance as inseparable from, and enabled by, the spread of poverty over the rest of the planet.

These competing perspectives motivate intense debate because they lead to competing implications for two very contemporary questions: who is to blame and what is to be done?

Critical Thinking Questions

1. What different implications do the theories of Weber, Diamond, and Wallerstein have with regard to assessing blame for the relative weakness of the Third World?
2. To what extent can the sources of Europe's success cited by each theory be controlled by contemporary governments?
3. To what extent does each approach see one society gaining only at the expense of others?

[1] Max Weber, *The Protestant Ethic and the Spirit of Capitalism*, trans. Talcott Parsons (New York: Scribner, 1976).
[2] Jared Diamond *Guns Germs and Steel: The Fates of Human Societies* (New York: W.W. Norton, 1997).
[3] Immanuel Wallerstein, *Capitalist Agriculture and the Origins of the European World-Economy in the Sixteenth Century. The Modern World System*, Vol. 1 (New York: Academic Press, 1974).

taking control of the entire continent. In this he failed. However, in the process, he overthrew many of the limitations on war that had characterized the classic balance of power era.

Two important developments in European politics made possible Napoleon's rise: nationalism and democracy. **Nationalism** is the doctrine that "nations"—large groups of people who perceive themselves to be fundamentally similar to each other and distinct from other groups—are and should be a basic unit of politics. Closely linked to nationalism is the principle of **national self-determination**, the idea that each state should consist of a single nation and each distinct nation should have its own state. **Democracy** is the doctrine that the entire population of a nation, rather than a small elite or a single monarch, should control government. All of these doctrines were fairly new at this point in European history.

The French Revolution of 1789 overthrew the French monarchy and replaced it with a regime that claimed to be democratic, The combination of the doctrines of nationalism and democracy gave, in theory, every French resident a stake in the welfare and in the glory of France. In revolutionary France, every adult male (women's rights were still limited) was considered a citizen, with a voice and an interest in government. Moreover, thanks to the doctrine of nationalism, every citizen of the French state was a "Frenchman." No longer were the masses cut off from government and from each other.

Napoleon Crossing the Alps. Though he was eventually defeated, Napoleon Bonaparte harnessed democracy and nationalism in ways that overthrew the existing European order and transformed warfare.

When Napoleon Bonaparte came to power in 1799, he was able to harness democracy and nationalism for military purposes, and he sought to expand French influence across Europe and beyond. The crucial innovation in revolutionary France was the institution of a draft, known as the **Levée en Masse**, which conscripted hundreds of thousands of ordinary French peasants into the French military. Whereas the armies of his more traditional monarchical neighbors were still based on feudal principles, Napoleon was able to harness the entire French nation—both its industry and its population—behind his war effort. His tactical innovation was to develop ways of dividing and recombining forces that made the huge numbers of troops manageable on the battlefield.

By 1812, Napoleon had conquered Austria and Prussia (one of the forerunners of modern Germany), the leading European powers of the day, and had even reached Moscow, where he stabled his horses in the Kremlin. Ultimately, he failed to conquer Russia and was defeated so badly there that he was pushed all the way back to France and ultimately exiled. Napoleon was beaten partly because the Russians and others began to adopt his strategies, using the doctrine of nationalism to mobilize masses of common people into the army. Russia had even more people to mobilize than did France. Russia's armies, coupled with its vast territory and frigid winters, were more than Napoleon's armies could conquer.

Napoleon's defeat, however, did not undo the revolution in international affairs he had initiated. Gone were the days of the small professional army and of the clear distinction between the military and mass society. After Napoleon, war became *national* war, which engaged entire populations against one another. This "democratization of war," coupled with industrialization, led to a massive increase in the size of armies, the scale of combat, and the number of casualties.

nationalism
The doctrine that recognizes the nation as the primary unit of political allegiance.

national self-determination
The doctrine that each state should consist of a single nation and each distinct nation should have its own state.

democracy
The doctrine that the entire population of a nation, rather than a small elite or a single monarch, should control government.

Levée en Masse
A draft, initiated by Napoleon following the French Revolution, that allowed France to vastly expand its army.

American students can perhaps best grasp these changes by contrasting pictures of the Revolutionary War, in which small groups of soldiers faced off with muskets, to those from the Civil War, in which battles could involve over 100,000 troops. In numerical terms, 4435 U.S. soldiers were killed in the *entire* U.S. Revolutionary War, which lasted eight years. In the U.S. Civil War, which occurred after the changes of the Napoleonic era, the Confederate forces took over 5000 casualties in a single day at the Battle of Gettysburg, and war dead on the Union side totaled approximately 360,000.

The Concert of Europe

Concert of Europe

An agreement reached at the Congress of Vienna in 1815 in which major European powers pledged to cooperate to maintain peace and stability.

The Napoleonic Wars of the early nineteenth century changed not only how wars would be fought, but also how peace would be sought. At the Congress of Vienna in 1815, the victorious powers sought to put into place a mechanism to prevent a country such as France from again seeking to dominate the continent. This agreement, known as the **Concert of Europe**, was the first of its kind in modern history and is in many ways the predecessor of the League of Nations, which was formed after World War I, and the United Nations (UN), which was formed after World War II.[13]

The basis for the Concert of Europe was an understanding that the inability of Austria, Prussia, Britain, and Russia to form an early alliance against Napoleon made it considerably easier for him to succeed both politically and militarily. To prevent a similar effort in the future, the four powers agreed to work together to preserve the status quo in European international politics and to confer periodically. In contrast to later efforts, there were no formal procedures or legal documents. Instead, the Concert of Europe was a statement of intentions, and it showed an understanding on the part of the major powers that peace could be better preserved if active collaboration supplemented traditional balance of power politics.

liberal approach

Political approach focusing on the ability of actors to govern themselves without surrendering their liberty. International liberal theory focuses on the ability of states to cooperate to solve problems.

From a theoretical perspective, the Concert of Europe marks the first attempt to put into practice the emerging **liberal approach** to international affairs (explored in depth in Chapter 3). It is not coincidental that this first attempt occurred when it did; the American Revolution and the writings of European philosophers such as Immanuel Kant and Jean Jacques Rousseau, in the last part of the eighteenth century, had advanced the notion that there was another alternative to anarchy besides domination by a single dominant power.

There is considerable disagreement concerning the effects of the Concert of Europe. On one hand, the era following the establishment of the Concert was the most peaceful century in Europe's history. From 1815 to 1914, there occurred only relatively limited wars such as the Crimean War (in which Russia fought England, France, and Turkey from 1854 to 1856) and the Franco-Prussian War (in which Prussia fought France from 1870 to 1871). On the other hand, the mechanism of the Concert broke down quickly. The more authoritarian powers (Austria and Russia) wanted the Concert to preserve the domestic status quo (autocratic politics) as well as the international status quo, especially during the revolutions of 1830 and 1848. England objected to these efforts and did not participate. Skeptics assert that the Concert had little effect. In this view, deterrence through the traditional balance of power and effective diplomacy, not the Concert, dissuaded potential aggressors and preserved peace.

Nationalism and Imperialism

imperialism

A situation in which one country controls another country or territory.

The nineteenth century is also notable for the related rise of two phenomena that originated earlier: nationalism and **imperialism**. Imperialism refers to a situation in which one country controls another country or territory. This control can be achieved formally, through creation of an empire and the establishment of colonies (territories that are governed from the imperial center, rather than having their own government). Imperialism can also be less formal, when economic means or military threats are used to control the government of another country. Within Europe, the forces of nationalism unleashed a massive revision of international politics. The competition inspired by nationalism also helped justify the extension of European imperialism to cover nearly the entire globe. At the same time, nationalism among colonized peoples set the roots for the process of decolonization that would continue into the twentieth century.

Nationalism in Europe significantly altered the map. The notion that state boundaries should coincide with ethnic, linguistic, or national boundaries meant that many of the boundaries that existed in the mid-nineteenth century seemed inappropriate or even unjust. For some groups, such as Germans and Italians, nationalism implied that many states should be combined into one. In the areas that today comprise Italy and Germany, there were a large number of small, distinct states (such as Piedmont, Naples, and Veneto in Italy; or Pomerania, Bavaria, and Westphalia in Germany). The doctrine of nationalism convinced people in both regions that those smaller states should be combined into single, large, ethnically and linguistically homogeneous states. The results fundamentally altered European international politics because a unified Germany, with great industrial power, seemed to have the capacity to take over the continent, a concern that dominated the period from 1900 to 1945.

In areas where multinational empires prevailed (the Russian, Austro-Hungarian, and Ottoman Empires), nationalism created pressure to break large states into smaller parts. Each of these empires encomp assed a great number of nations that perceived themselves as deserving their own nation-states. In the Russian Empire, these included Poland, Ukraine, Latvia, Lithuania, Estonia, Georgia, and Chechnya. The Austro-Hungarian Empire likewise controlled territories that today comprise parts of the Czech Republic, Slovakia, Hungary, Ukraine, Romania, Slovenia, Croatia, Serbia, and Bosnia-Herzegovina. The Ottoman (Turkish) Empire contained much of the modern Middle East (including Israel/Palestine, Syria, Iraq, Jordan, and Lebanon) as well as parts of southeastern Europe (Bulgaria, Macedonia, Bosnia-Herzegovina, and Albania).

The doctrines of nationalism, self-determination, and democracy had profound effects in the Americas as well. In the Caribbean and Latin America, one of the first regions colonized by Europeans, nationalism led to the world's first wave of decolonization. In Haiti, an indigenous movement overthrew slavery, instituted a democratic constitution, and declared independence from France in 1804. In South America, liberation movements led by Simón Bolivar and José de San Martin led to a series of declarations of independence between 1810 and 1825. Similarly, Mexico fought a successful war of independence ending in 1821 and Brazil declared independence from Portugal in 1822. A group of British colonies in Canada formed the Canadian Confederation and became autonomous in 1867. In sum, while several territories remained colonies until the twentieth century, nearly the entire Western hemisphere became independent between U.S. independence in 1776 and the Canadian Confederation in 1867.

Nationalism helped spur a new wave of **colonialism** in the second half of the nineteenth century, driven by the idea that soon all the territory would be taken and slow movers would be forever at a disadvantage.[14] Most of Africa and Asia were colonized during this period. In most cases, colonialism took the form of direct control of a territory, along the model the Spanish had implemented in South America and the British had established in India. In some cases, such as in the Belgian Congo, this model led to brutality on a horrendous scale toward indigenous populations. In other instances, colonialism was exercised through indirect control but still achieved the goal

colonialism

A type of imperialism in which the dominating state takes direct control of a territory.

The Geography Connection

Shifting Borders, Changing Politics: Europe in 1815 and 1914

A map of the world generally shows us a static picture. But if we compare maps over time, we see that the map at any one time is just a snapshot of a changing reality

These two maps show what the boundaries of Europe looked like in 1815 and what they looked like in 1914.

Europe in 1815

Source: http://www.lib.utexas.edu/maps/historical/europe1815_1905.jpg, from http://www.lib.utexas.edu/maps/historical/history_europe.html. Courtesy of the University Libraries, The University of Texas at Austin.

Critical Thinking Questions

1. What were the causes of the differences between the two maps?

2. How has the map changed between 1914 and today, and what drove these changes?

3. How might we expect the map to change in the future, and what forces will drive those changes? Or have we reached an end to boundary changes?

Europe in 1914

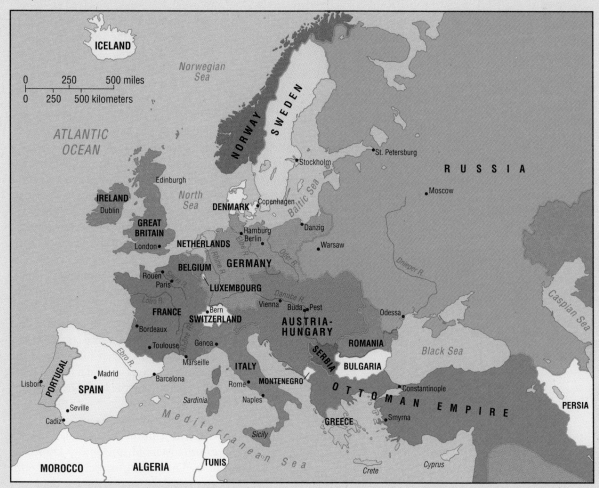

Source: http://,.lib.utexas.edu/maps/historical/shepherd/europe_1911.jpg, from http://www.lib.utexas.edu/maps/historical/history_europe.html. Courtesy of the University Libraries, The University of Texas at Austin.

of harnessing the local economy for the benefit of external powers. In the opinion of many people today, this colonial period of economic exploitation put the colonized countries in an economically disadvantageous position from which they have found it nearly impossible to recover. In China, foreign powers used military force to compel the Chinese to trade on terms that were highly favorable to the Europeans. Twice, in 1839 and again in 1856, European powers waged war on China to force its government to allow Europeans (and Americans) to sell their goods in China. The resulting "unequal treaties" created economic advantages in China for Western states without requiring them to take over the territory directly. The treaties are a source of Chinese resentment to this day.[15]

Although this last onslaught of European colonialism was partly inspired by European nationalism, it also sowed the seeds for the nationalism that was to manifest itself in many of the colonies during the twentieth century. The belief among colonized societies that they were being exploited economically helped inspire their own nationalist movements. Just as the doctrine of national self-determination undermined Europe's multinational empires, it undermined Europe's overseas empires as well. The struggles against colonial rule were, in many cases, long and brutal. Nationalism played an important role in twentieth century movements for national liberation, including the Vietnam war, the disintegration of the Soviet empire in 1989–1991, and the violent collapse of Yugoslavia in the 1990s.

The Road to World War I

Nationalism helped to erode any remaining influence of the Concert of Europe, so that by the beginning of the twentieth century there was intense competition among European powers. In part this was manifested in the rush to colonize the southern hemisphere. Competition resulted also from the belief that the increased power and ambitions of the newly unified Germany made the existing state of affairs in Europe unsustainable. Increasingly, each major European power sought to tilt the very precarious balance of power in its own favor.

The situation was made especially delicate by the erosion of two of Europe's great empires. By the late nineteenth century, the Ottoman Empire was slowly losing control of territories in what are today Bosnia-Herzegovina, Serbia, and Bulgaria, an area generally known as the Balkans. Independence movements plagued the Austro-Hungarian Empire as well. The other great powers competed to gain influence at the expense of the declining empires and each other. Many believed that the outcome of this competition would determine the long-term winners and losers in European power politics.

Russia, lying to the north and east of the Balkans, seemed most likely to gain from the disintegration of the Ottoman Empire. It sought to control the Ottoman capital, Istanbul, for both religious and geopolitical reasons. Istanbul, previously known as Constantinople, had been the traditional home of the Orthodox Christian Church until its conquest by the Muslim Turks in 1453. Through Istanbul's straits, Russia could gain year-round access to the open sea, which it otherwise lacked. Germany, however, sought to deny Russia this victory by bolstering Austria and the Ottoman Empire. France, fearing Germany after the Franco-Prussian war, saw Russia as a potential ally. Great Britain saw its place as the most powerful military and economic player on Earth jeopardized by

Table 2.1 World War I: A Guide to the Major Players

Alliance Powers	Entente Powers
Germany	Great Britain
Austria-Hungary	France
Ottoman Empire	Russia
Italy (until 1915)	Italy (after 1915)
	United States (after 1917)

the rapid rise of Germany. German weapons programs and rhetoric convinced many that Germany sought to supplant Britain as Europe's dominant country. Britain's willingness to go to war in 1914 rested on logic similar to that which Thucydides attributed to the Spartans: if war was likely, it was better to fight it before the enemy became even stronger.

The result of all these concerns was that by 1914, Europe was delicately balanced between two great alliances. The **Triple Alliance**, consisting of Germany, Austria-Hungary, and Italy, pledged the members to come to each other's aid if one of them were attacked by France or Russia. The **Triple Entente** was a similar arrangement among Britain, France, and Russia. A more complex web of alliances connected these larger powers to smaller ones, such as Serbia and the Ottoman Empire.

To the flammable situation that existed in 1914, a spark was provided by Serbian nationalists, who assassinated Archduke Franz Ferdinand, the heir to the Austro-Hungarian throne, in July 1914. In the "July Crisis" that ensued, Austria insisted that Serbia submit to Austrian control. This was unacceptable to Russia, for it would damage Russia's goals in the region. Thus, Russia backed Serbia. Germany, seeing that its position would be ruined if Russia defeated Austria, backed Austria. France, fearing its position should Germany defeat Russia, backed Russia. Finally, Britain, fearing that Germany might defeat both Russia and France and therefore rule all of Europe, backed its allies. In sum, all of Europe rushed to war as a result of the assassination of Franz Ferdinand in Sarajevo. In retrospect, many wondered why war could not have been avoided, because the quarrel was essentially between Austria and Serbia rather than among the great powers.

Contrary to expectations, World War I was not over quickly. Although the existence of railroads and automobiles meant that troops could be moved quickly, other new technologies such as the machine gun, barbed wire, and poison gas made it much easier to defend territory than to attack it. As a result, the war quickly bogged down into hellish trench warfare, and the youth of Europe were butchered in terrifying numbers. On July 1, 1916, at the Battle of the Somme, the British army took 58,000 casualties in a single day. By the end of that battle, in September 1916, total British, French, and German casualties surpassed one million.

The stalemate was broken only in 1917, when the United States intervened on the side of Britain, France, and Russia. The war ended in November 1918, but not until four major empires (German, Austro-Hungarian, Ottoman, and Russian) had collapsed, the communists had come to power in Russia, and over eight million soldiers had died.

The **Treaty of Versailles**, which officially ended World War I, was signed on June 28, 1919. It created the League of Nations, redrew Germany's boundaries, required Germany to pay substantial "reparations" for the harm it had caused in starting the war, and specified numerous limits on Germany's ability to rearm in the coming years. The aftermath of World War I saw the national aspirations of many groups fulfilled through a major wave of decolonization in Europe. Out of the rubble of the collapsed empires, the

Print Collector/HIP/The Image Works

The industrialization of warfare made World War I more destructive than its predecessors. The Battle of Verdun, shown here, lasted 10 months and claimed an estimated 700,000 lives. At the end of this longest battle of World War I, the lines of the two armies had moved only a few hundred yards.

Triple Alliance

A pre–World War I agreement by Germany, Austria-Hungary, and Italy that if one state were to be attacked, the others would come to its aid.

Triple Entente

A pre–World War I agreement by Britain, France, and Russia that if one state were to be attacked, the others would come to its aid.

Treaty of Versailles

The agreement ending World War I that set up the League of Nations.

Baltic states

Refers collectively to Estonia, Latvia, and Lithuania, which lie on the Baltic Sea in northern Europe, just to the west of Russia.

Treaty of Versailles established several countries, including Czechoslovakia, Yugoslavia, Poland, and the **Baltic states** in Europe. The granting of independence to these Eastern European countries was a major commitment of U.S. President Woodrow Wilson, who strongly supported the notion of national self-determination. Wilson believed that if free democracies could be built in a region traditionally devoid of democracy, then peace would be guaranteed there. In contrast, the Middle Eastern, African, and Asian colonies of the defeated powers were simply transferred to the control of the victors.

World War I also caused a fundamental shift in global power. Although the war had been fought in part to determine whether Britain or Germany would dominate, both were devastated. At the same time, the war demonstrated and contributed to the rise of the industrial, military, and financial power of the United States.

The Road to World War II

Table 2.2 World War II: A Guide to the Major Players

The Axis Powers	The Allied Powers
Germany	France
Italy	Great Britain
Japan	Soviet Union
	United States

Woodrow Wilson called World War I "the war to end all wars." The unprecedented destruction of that war convinced many that new ways had to be found to avoid wars in the future. It seemed that the memory of that war would motivate leaders to take the necessary steps. Yet a mere 21 years later, in 1939, World War II began, and it was to be even more brutal than World War I.[16] Why did this intense desire to avoid another war fail to prevent World War II? The reasons are complex and still debated today, but a few important factors can be identified.

Collective Security and Economic Nationalism

collective security

A doctrine nominally adopted by states after World War I that specified that when one state committed aggression, all other states would join together to attack it.

The major method by which leaders after World War I envisioned preventing war was **collective security**, whereby all states would agree that if any state initiated a war, all the others would come to the defense of the state under attack. This policy was an updated version of the liberal doctrine that inspired the Concert of Europe. With the old balance of power system having failed so miserably to prevent World War I, many states saw the need for a collaborative solution. The theory was compelling. Any state would know that if it started a war, it would face retaliation from every other country. Therefore, it could not possibly hope to gain anything from starting a war and so would not do it. If collective security worked well, the threat would never have to be carried out.

isolationism

The doctrine that U.S. interests were best served by playing as little role as possible in world affairs. From the founding of the republic until the Spanish-American War of 1898, the doctrine was largely unquestioned, but the Japanese bombing of Pearl Harbor in 1941 is widely viewed as destroying any credibility that the doctrine had left.

The problems arose in practice. After World War I, almost every state was determined to avoid another war. This was demonstrated most clearly by the United States, where the Senate refused to ratify the Charter of the League of Nations because senators sought to return to the traditional U.S. policy of **isolationism**. The U.S. participation in World War I had met serious opposition in the United States, and many sought a renewed determination to keep the country out of future wars. Collective security relied on the promise that any aggression would be countered by attacks from all the other states. With the United States and most European states reluctant to go to war, meeting the commitments of collective security became difficult in practice. For example, when Japan invaded the Chinese territory of Manchuria in 1931, the League of Nations demanded that Japan withdraw. Many saw this as the first big test of collective security, but when Japan continued the invasion, other states did nothing. Similarly, in 1935, Italy invaded Abyssinia (what is today Ethiopia). This was clearly an act of aggression. However, the major powers, working through the League of Nations, chose to impose only relatively trivial economic sanctions against Italy. Leading states again sought desperately to avoid going to war, and without their support, the League of Nations could do little. Ironically, the determination of most leading states to avoid war at all costs probably made war more, not less, likely.

When Germany began violating the Treaty of Versailles in 1936, other countries hesitated to respond with force. This reluctance made sense in light of the lessons learned from World War I. The initial violations were not extremely consequential, and no one wanted to replay World War I in response. Moreover, each country hoped that it could stand aside and let others bear the burden of keeping Germany in line. This attempt to force others to deal with Germany became more prominent in the **Munich Crisis** of 1938. This crisis was precipitated by Germany's demand that it be allowed to occupy the Sudetenland, a part of Czechoslovakia with many ethnic Germans. British Prime Minister Neville Chamberlain advocated **appeasement**, a strategy of avoiding war by acceding to the demands of rival powers (in this case Nazi Germany). Germany was given permission to occupy part of Czechoslovakia, and Chamberlain celebrated having secured "peace in our time." In later years, "Munich" and "appeasement" became synonyms for weakness in situations requiring a firm stand.

The United States, France, and Britain, all of which were hostile toward the Soviet Union, hoped that Germany would attack eastward (toward the Soviet Union). The Soviet Union signed a peace treaty with Germany in 1939, hoping to turn German aggression westward. By playing the potential allies against each other, the German leadership was able to divide and conquer. Germany was defeated only when Adolf Hitler abandoned this strategy and chose to go to war with all of these countries simultaneously. Like Napoleon's France, Hitler's Germany found Russian territory too vast and Russian winters too cold. In the United States, many leaders and much of the public opposed U.S. involvement in Europe's war, even after Hitler attacked Poland, France, and the United Kingdom in 1939 and 1940. Only after Germany declared war on the United States in 1941 did the United States join the war.

Economic Roots of World War II

World War II, by most accounts, had important economic roots as well. The 1930s was a period of economic depression around the world. As economies collapsed, most countries adopted selfish strategies to try to boost employment. A common strategy was to increase barriers to imports in order to keep more jobs at home. However, when every country took this strategy, world trade collapsed and all economies became less efficient.

Prior to World War I, Great Britain had played a leading role in organizing the world economy. Because of its considerable naval and financial power, it was able to facilitate greater trade around the world. This was seen as advantageous both to Great Britain and to other countries. The costs of World War I, however, substantially undermined Great Britain's ability to play this role. The new big player in the world economy was the United States. However, largely as a result of the doctrine of isolationism, the U.S. government declined to take up Britain's leadership role. As a result, there was no effective international collaboration to maintain trade under the stress of the Great Depression.

This lack of international economic cooperation played an important role in helping Hitler come to power in Germany. Germany after World War I was a new and unstable democracy. The war had seriously damaged its economy. The financial burden of **reparations** required by the Treaty of Versailles further undermined the German economy. Reparations were payments that Germany was forced to make as a result of losing World War I and being blamed by the victors for starting it. The payments were intended to punish Germany, to deter future aggression, and to compensate other countries for the destruction caused by German aggression. The reparations caused serious economic problems in Germany and were deeply resented by the German people. On top of these

Munich Crisis
A crisis in 1938 precipitated by Germany's demand that it be allowed to occupy part of Czechoslovakia. War was averted when Britain and France agreed to Germany's demands.

appeasement
A strategy of avoiding war by acceding to the demands of rival powers.

reparations
Payments that Germany was forced to make as a result of starting World War I. Reparations caused serious economic problems in Germany and were deeply resented by the German people.

difficulties, the Great Depression brought the German economy, traditionally one of the strongest in the world, to the brink of collapse. The failure of democratically chosen governments to avert this disaster, along with seething resentment at the economic restrictions placed on Germany by the World War I peace treaties, provided fertile ground for a fascist such as Hitler to come to power.

Fascism took nationalism, which had been growing since the late eighteenth century, to a militant extreme. As developed in Italy and Germany, the doctrine saw the strengthening of the nation, as represented by the state, as the most important political goal. In fascism, the rights or goals of individuals are subservient to those of the nation, which is viewed as a single organism. This doctrine justified political authoritarianism, economic centralization, and the belief that one nation was superior to all others. Fascism can be viewed as a mixture of the doctrines of nationalism and socialism. Although Hitler was no democrat, he was first elected Chancellor of Germany in a democratic election. A similar process had taken place earlier in Italy, where the fascist Benito Mussolini came to power.

In Japan, which had limited supplies of raw materials, the economic devastation of the Great Depression hit especially hard. Japan had started industrialization later than European powers and the United States and was striving to catch up. Like European

fascism

A doctrine in which the rights or goals of individuals are subservient to those of the nation, which is viewed as a single organism.

Figure 2.3 Japanese Expansion Prior to World War II. Japan, a relative latecomer to the practice of colonization, expanded its political and economic control in East Asia and the Pacific, threatening British, French, and U.S. colonies.

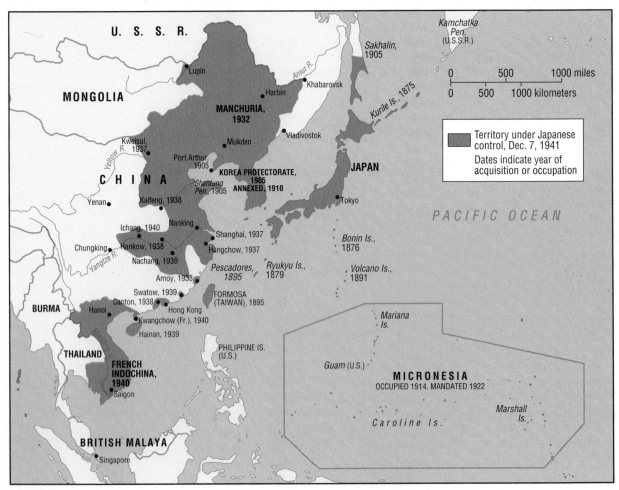

The History Connection

The Uses and Abuses of History in Foreign Policy

The nineteenth-century Prussian statesman Otto von Bismarck is reported to have said that fools learn from experience but wise men learn from other people's experience.[1] Throughout the centuries, policy makers faced with difficult choices have sought to learn from their own experience and that of prior generations. To ignore such experience would seem foolish.

However, it is difficult to know which historical experiences provide the best model for a current problem, and history is replete with examples of policy makers relying on historical analogies, only to be misled by them. Political scientist Robert Jervis has pointed out that people tend to overestimate the importance of certain types of historical events.[2] The following are among the sources of such overemphasis.

■ **Personal experience:** It appears that people give especially heavy emphasis to historical events that they experience firsthand. Because many people have only a limited knowledge of history, it makes sense that they would place disproportionate emphasis on the events with which they are familiar. Especially when such experiences are extremely negative, they can create a profound desire to avoid repeating the same mistakes. Thus, leaders in the 1930s, who had witnessed the rush to war in 1914, sought to find ways to avoid war with Germany and Japan. In the decades after the Vietnam War, many policy debates in the United States continued to be informed by the perceived mistakes made in that conflict.

■ **Generational effects:** Not only do people overemphasize their personal experience, but

experiences at a particular time in life seem to be especially salient. Thus, it is argued, many people form strong belief systems during young adulthood and maintain them for the rest of their lives. As a result, we may see "generational effects," in which a wide range of people who grew up during an especially difficult or triumphant time develop similar views. For those who came of age during the Vietnam War, for example, that conflict and the controversy that accompanied it may be especially salient. This might explain why, as that generation came to hold the key political offices in the United States, the issues of that era were debated all over again.

That policy makers would seek to learn from those events that made the biggest impression on them should probably not be surprising. But this tendency has a substantial impact on what kind of lessons can be learned. One thing is clear: people cannot learn anything at all from historical events of which they are ignorant.

Critical Thinking Questions

1. What events have had the most influence on your thinking about international politics?
2. What events had the most influence on your parents or grandparents?
3. Have you learned different lessons from those your parents or grandparents learned? Do they view current events differently than you do? Do you evaluate the events of their formative years differently?

[1]Kenneth Waltz, *Man the State, and War* (New York: Columbia University Press, 1959), p. 220; cited in Robert Jervis, *Perception and Misperception in International Politics* (New York: Columbia University Press, 1976), p. 239.
[2]Robert Jervis, *Perception and Misperception in International Politics* (New York: Columbia University Press, 1976), pp. 239-243.

imperialism, Japanese imperialism in Korea and China was motivated by economic pressures along with intense nationalism. The United States, France, and Great Britain saw Japanese expansion as a threat to their own economic and imperial interests in Asia. To weaken Japan and to impede further expansion, the United States cut off sales of key raw materials such as scrap metal. This embargo convinced the Japanese leadership that pursuing its interests would require ejecting the United States, Britain, and France from the Far East. In December 1941, Japan sought to force the United States from the Pacific region by bombing the U.S. Pacific Fleet at its base at Pearl Harbor in Hawaii.

Two related lessons were learned from World War II. First, many believed that the immediate cause of the war was the rise to power of intensely nationalistic and undemocratic regimes in Germany, Italy, and Japan. World War II thus reinforced the lesson Woodrow Wilson took from World War I: that democracy is a key underpinning of peace. Second, many concluded that democracies would be under threat if economies performed badly and that more effective governance of the global economy would be needed to prevent the sort of economic chaos that facilitated the rise of authoritarianism in Germany, Italy, and Japan.

The political and military lessons taken from World War II were almost the opposite of those taken from World War I. If World War I had shown the foolishness of going to war before diplomacy was exhausted, World War II showed the foolishness of neglecting to confront expansionist powers. It was this lesson that guided both the United States and the Soviet Union in the Cold War that followed World War II.

World War II also unleashed a new force into international politics: nuclear weapons. In August 1945, the United States dropped atomic weapons on Hiroshima and Nagasaki in Japan. The enormous power of these weapons, and the indiscriminate destruction they caused, changed how military strategists and political leaders thought about war. The advent of nuclear weapons, as much as the memory of two world wars, dominated thinking about international politics in the postwar era.

The Cold War

Cold War

A conflict between the United States and the Soviet Union during which no actual war broke out between the two superpowers. The Cold War dominated world politics from 1946 until 1991.

World War II severely weakened the traditionally powerful European states of Germany, France, Britain, and Italy and elevated to top status two relative newcomers: the United States and the Soviet Union. These two countries had been allies against Germany, but they mistrusted each other intensely and had incompatible plans for postwar Europe. The period from 1946 through 1991 is known as the **Cold War** because actual ("hot") war never broke out between the two "superpowers," despite the constant threat that it might. The Cold War conflict dominated world politics for almost 50 years.[17]

The lessons learned about the outbreak of World War II strongly conditioned how that conflict was pursued. Both the Soviet Union and the United States were intent on not repeating mistakes of the 1930s. Having learned the "lesson of Munich," both sides strived to convince the other that the slightest aggression would be countered. For example, there was a series of crises over the status of Berlin, which was surrounded by communist East Germany but had been left under joint control by the Soviet Union, the United Kingdom, France, and the United States after World War II. The Soviet Union repeatedly sought to force the Western allies out of Berlin, precipitating crises in 1948, 1958, 1960, and 1961. Berlin was nearly impossible to defend in conventional military terms, but the United States and its allies maintained that any attack on Berlin would lead to a general war.

These attempts at deterrence were strongly influenced by the development of nuclear weapons, which fundamentally changed the nature of military security and raised the potential death toll of the next major war to unimaginable levels. The "nuclear arms race" came to define Cold War security strategies, and fear that one side might seek a decisive victory through a surprise attack led to a high state of military readiness.

The Cuban Missile Crisis

The period of highest tension culminated in the Cuban Missile Crisis in 1962. Fearing that it was falling behind in the arms race, the Soviet Union began to install medium-range missiles in Cuba, less than 100 miles from the U.S. coast. The United States threatened military retaliation and blockaded Cuba to prevent the missile installations from being completed. After a tense standoff, in which U.S. President John F. Kennedy estimated the chances of nuclear war at "between one out of three and even," the Soviet Union agreed to withdraw the missiles in return for concessions by the United States.[18]

The Cuban Missile Crisis ended the period of greatest danger in the Cold War for two reasons. First, it frightened both sides into taking steps to reduce the chances of such a crisis in the future. In historical terms, the Cuban Missile Crisis forced leaders to focus a bit less on the lessons of the 1930s and a bit more on the lessons of 1914. One measure taken was the installation of a "hotline" enabling immediate communication between leaders in Washington and Moscow. The first major arms control agreement between the United States and the Soviet Union followed shortly thereafter. Second, as both sides built more and more nuclear weapons and more and more missiles and aircraft to deliver them, the chance that either side could win a nuclear war, even if it waged a successful surprise attack, diminished. This situation was known as **mutual assured destruction (MAD)**. The fact that neither country could get away with a surprise attack—and that both U.S. and Russian leaders understood this—provided increased stability. The military competition between the United States and the Soviet Union continued for three decades after the Cuban Missile Crisis, with alternating periods of increased and decreased tension, but never again did the two sides come so close to war.

mutual assured destruction (MAD)
A situation in which each side in a conflict possesses enough armaments to destroy the other even after suffering a surprise attack.

The Global Economy

Among the lessons learned from World War II was that states needed to collaborate to avert global economic crises. Although economics is often analyzed separately from politics, there were clear links between the international economic arrangements during the Cold War and the political conflict between the United States and the Soviet Union (and their allies). For the Western powers, the importance of international economic collaboration was increased by the communist challenge. The long-term fear was that international economic instability would weaken the West relative to the Soviet Union. The immediate fear in the late 1940s was that if key European states such as France and Italy did not quickly recover economically from World War II, their own domestic communist parties might be able to win power.

The United States recognized, after Japan's bombing of Pearl Harbor, that it could not remain apart from the world's problems. The failure of isolationism created a new internationalist consensus in the United States, one that emphasized not only active military confrontation with the Soviet Union but also leadership in the global economy. Taking such a role was seen as furthering general world economic interests as well as U.S. security interests. It also served the economic interests of the United States, which, as the major economy least damaged by the war, was best positioned to profit from a thriving international economy. The main institutions of international collaboration were formed at a conference in Bretton Woods, New Hampshire, in 1946, and the postwar economic system is therefore often referred to as the **Bretton Woods system**.

A central goal of the system was to foster expanded international trade in order to increase prosperity. The mechanism was the General Agreement on Tariffs and Trade

Bretton Woods system
The system that guided economic arrangements among the advanced industrial states in the post–World War II era. It included the GATT, the fixed exchange rate system, the IMF, and the World Bank. Bretton Woods was a resort in New Hampshire where the negotiations took place.

tariff

A tax on imports, used to
protect domestic producers
from foreign competition.

(GATT), which in 1995 evolved into the World Trade Organization (WTO). The GATT was a multilateral agreement on **tariff** levels. Over time, successive rounds of negotiations lowered tariffs on many categories of goods. Although some key sectors, such as agriculture and services, were left out, GATT is widely credited with having increased trade and prosperity among its members.

A second key goal of the Bretton Woods system was to provide for stability in the international financial system. This was accomplished through the development of an international currency system based on the U.S. dollar, which in turn was linked to the value of gold. This system was managed by the International Monetary Fund (IMF). Agreements on exchange rates between different currencies provided stability and predictability, and a system of IMF loans helped countries overcome short-term imbalances in their international financial positions.

The Bretton Woods system is widely credited with spurring rapid economic growth among advanced industrial states in the second half of the twentieth century, but it is important to recognize that membership in these institutions was limited to a relatively small number of wealthy industrialized states. The Soviet Union and its allies chose not to participate. Many poor countries did not meet the requirements for membership and believed that the system exploited them. Thus, for much of the period in question, the global economy consisted of three groupings. One was centered on the United States and was organized by the Bretton Woods system. A second group was centered on the Soviet Union and consisted of states with communist systems and trade largely based on bilateral agreements. The third group consisted of the developing states, which traded on whatever terms they could negotiate. These groups were known as the "First World," the "Second World," and the **Third World**, respectively. Over time, more and more states joined the Bretton Woods institutions. The "second world" vanished with the collapse of communism, and today there are a two groups, those who are members of the WTO (which now includes the majority) and those who are not (which includes many of the poorest or least market-oriented countries).

Third World

A term coined during the
Cold War to describe those
states that were neither
in the group of advanced
industrial states nor in the
communist bloc; typically it
refers to the many poor states
in the southern hemisphere.
The term is generally
considered synonymous with
"underdeveloped."

decolonization

The disbanding of nearly all
colonial relationships between
1945 and 1975.

Decolonization, Development, and Underdevelopment

Following World War II, there was a wave of **decolonization** from 1945 until 1975 that disbanded nearly all of the colonial relationships that had been established over the previous five centuries.[19] Several factors contributed to decolonization. First, the major colonial powers (especially Britain and France) had been severely weakened by World War II and were less able to resist independence movements. Second, the independence movements themselves grew stronger, as a result of the doctrine of national self-determination and the democratic ideals that were the rallying cries in World War II. This growing strength was most visible in India, where a nonviolent Indian nationalist movement led by Mahatma Gandhi used the ideals of liberal democracy to show the hypocrisy of Britain's colonial empire. In China and French Indochina (later Vietnam), Mao Zedong and Ho Chi Minh used communist ideology to bolster their independence movements. Third, the United States, which had few formal colonies but was now the leading power in the West, disapproved of colonialism and sought to undermine it.

The U.S. position on colonialism was motivated in part by the understanding that the battle with the Soviet Union would be global in scope. It was therefore crucial for the United States to gain friends and allies among the poor countries of the world, because the Soviet Union would be making similar efforts. When communist revolutionaries triumphed in China in 1949, creating the (incorrect) perception that the world's most populous country would be controlled by the Soviet Union, competition for the loyalty of

Figure 2.4 Decolonization, 1945–1975. In the decades following World War II, many of the colonies formed in the eighteenth and nineteenth centuries became independent sovereign states, a process that had occurred earlier in much of Latin America.

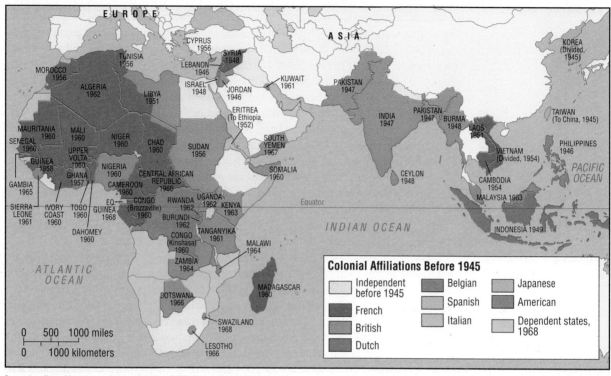

Source: http://wps.ablongman.com/wps/media/objects/262/268312/art/figures/KISH616.jpg

new states (and the remaining colonies) intensified. In some cases, this competition led to extensive financial aid, such as that which Japan and Korea received from the United States, and Egypt and China received from the Soviet Union.

In other cases, the competition took a military turn. When Vietnamese nationalists sought to gain independence from France after World War II, the United States feared that Vietnam would join China in the pro-communist camp, because the major Vietnamese independence movement had adopted a communist ideology. As a result, the United States became engaged on one side in a war between pro-communist North Vietnamese forces against anti-communist South Vietnamese forces. The Vietnam War had repercussions far beyond Southeast Asia. The fact that a nationalist movement consisting mainly of poor peasants could resist and eventually defeat the most powerful country in the world gave encouragement to other such movements. Moreover, it encouraged the belief in the Soviet Union that communist ideology combined with Soviet support could turn the tide in the developing world. It also had profound and lasting effects on the politics of Western Europe and the United States by undermining the consensus that had existed about the conduct of the Cold War and the assumption that the United States was always a force for good in the world.

The superpowers in the Cold War avoided direct combat with each other, but they often waged it through allies, or "proxies," in the developing world. In addition to the Vietnam War (1954–1975), other regional wars that emerged during the Cold War included the Korean War (1950–1953), the Ogaden War between Somalia and Ethiopia (1978), and the Soviet-Afghan War (1979–1989).

As Africa and Asia decolonized, they did not revert to precolonial territorial and political arrangements (which varied from place to place). Rather, all of these territories were integrated into the sovereign state system, a system developed and maintained by Europe. New states were formed, their borders were demarcated, and they were recognized as sovereign through membership in the UN. Possessing a sovereign state was the central goal of most nationalist movements, but integration of decolonized territory into the state system was fraught with difficulty. The sovereign state system is based on a strict territorial division of political authority. Borders had to be drawn in regions where they had not existed, in a formal sense, prior to colonialism. In many cases, borders that had served the interests of colonial administrators became the borders of new states. This created problems within countries, such as Iraq, and between countries, such as India and Pakistan, that persist today. Many of the new states were not "nation-states" at all. Some states contained multiple ethnic, linguistic, and national groups, while some groups found themselves spread across two or more states. The transition of colonies into sovereign states after World War II meant that the Westphalian state system, after 500 years of expansion and evolution, now covered almost the entire territory of the planet outside Antarctica.

Many leaders of newly decolonized states rejected the idea that they should choose sides in the Cold War. Leaders in most of these countries were much more interested in economic development, which had been ignored by the United States and the Soviet Union. In 1955, leaders of 29 African and Asian nations met in Bandung, Indonesia, to establish an agenda of collaboration for development among states hoping to avoid taking sides in the Cold War. In 1961, this group was formalized in the Non-Aligned Movement, which eventually numbered more than 100 members. Although the Non-Aligned Movement played an important role in broadening the agenda of international affairs, consensus or common interest existed only on a very limited number of issues, so these countries were rarely able to act as a single bloc.

Poverty was viewed as the major problem in the parts of the world usually identified as the underdeveloped, developing, or Third World. Because these new states' colonial history was generally seen as the cause of their poverty, there was great hope that independence would bring increased economic development and prosperity. However, the record has been very mixed, with some countries increasing their wealth dramatically since the 1950s while many others, especially in Africa, have stagnated. Which factors were responsible for the successes (and the failures) of these states has been a major source of debate to this day and remains a central concern in the study of international politics (see Chapter 11).

By the 1970s, poor countries were trying new strategies of economic development. The ability of oil-producing countries to band together into the Organization of Petroleum Exporting Countries (OPEC) to force global oil prices higher was seen as a major victory for some poor countries. For others that had no oil and needed to buy it on the world market, the price hikes were a disaster. Efforts to form cartels to boost prices of other raw material exports, such as copper, coffee, and cocoa, generally failed. Another strategy pursued was the effort to create a "new international economic order" that would change the rules of international trade to help redistribute power and wealth from the wealthy countries to the poorer ones. However, this project was largely rejected by wealthier countries, partly because they believed it was based on a faulty understanding of economics and partly because it was not in their interest.

The World Today

The Rise of Nonstate Actors

Throughout modern history, discussion of international affairs was essentially a discussion of states. States were widely viewed as the only important actors in international affairs. However, in the post–World War II era, new kinds of actors were recognized as having important impacts on international politics. Collectively, they are known as **nonstate actors**, but this is a misleading category because the variety of nonstate actors is immense. One of the first nonstate actors to gain widespread notice was the **multinational corporation (MNC)**, a company with operations in more than one country. Today, such corporations are a part of everyday life, but prior to the 1960s, they were the exception rather than the rule. Especially in relatively poor states, it often seemed as though these global corporations had more power than local governments. There was also considerable concern about the links between these large companies and their "host" governments in North America and Europe.

nonstate actor
A political actor that is not a state, such as an advocacy group, charity, corporation, or terrorist group.

multinational corporation
A company with operations in more than one country; a type of nonstate actor; also called *transnational corporation.*

Figure 2.5 Yugoslavia was formed out of several smaller independent countries and former parts of the Austrian and Ottoman Empires at the end of World War I. It fragmented in a series of conflicts beginning in 1991.

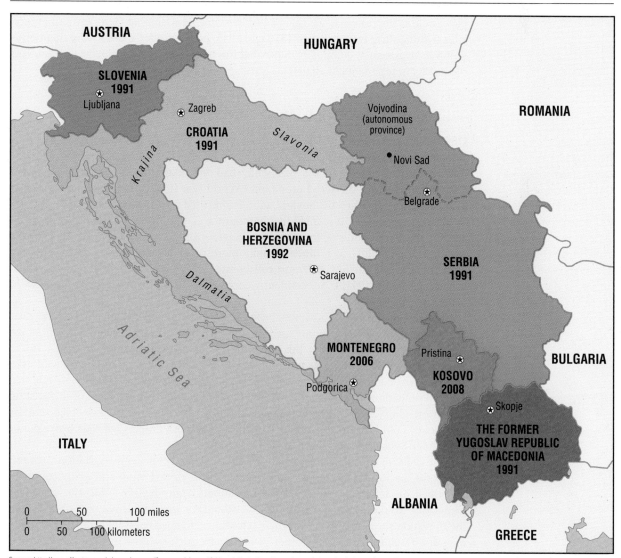

Source: http://www.lib.utexas.edu/maps/europe/fm_yugoslvia_po196.jpg. Adjusted to show dates of secession/independence. From: chttp://www.lib.utexas.edu/maps/serbia.htm. Courtesy of the University Libraries, The University of Texas at Austin.

**international
organizations (IOs)**

Organizations formed by
governments to help them
pursue collaborative activity;
a type of nonstate actor.
More specifically known as
international governmental
organizations (IGOs).

**nongovernmental
organizations (NGOs)**

A broad category of diverse
organizations, including groups
similar to domestic interest
groups but with transnational
concerns and organizational
structures, and groups that
focus not on influencing governments, but on conducting
activities in different countries.

Berlin Wall

Erected in 1961 to prevent
citizens of communist East
Germany from emigrating to
West Germany, the Berlin
Wall became a symbol both
of the division of Europe and
of the lack of freedom in the
communist-controlled areas.

Attention also became focused on **international organizations (IOs)**—organizations formed by governments to help them pursue collaborative activity. These too proliferated after World War II. The UN is perhaps the best known of these, but powerful economic IOs, such as the World Bank and the IMF, also attracted intense interest, as they were becoming very powerful actors in the world economy. More recently still, international advocacy groups, often known as **nongovernmental organizations (NGOs)**, have proliferated and taken a higher profile on many international issues.[20] Today, there is considerable debate about the relative importance of nonstate actors versus traditional states (see Chapter 12).

Perhaps the most striking development with regard to the emergence of nonstate actors was the rise of the European Union.[21] Beginning with six members in 1950, the European Union now has 27 members, including almost every state in Western and Central Europe. (Norway and Switzerland are prominent exceptions.) The members of the European Union have granted more and more political authority to common decision-making bodies based in Brussels, Belgium. The willingness of the "original" sovereign states to surrender key aspects of sovereignty has been seen as proof that IOs can play a role as important as the role played by states. The fact that Germany and France, after fighting three wars between 1870 and 1945, now consider war between themselves unthinkable is seen by some as evidence that IOs can fundamentally change the problems of anarchy in international affairs.

The End of the Cold War

On November 9, 1989, the East German government opened the **Berlin Wall** and then stood aside as its overjoyed citizens spontaneously destroyed it. Symbolically, the tearing down of the wall ended the Cold War, which had divided the Soviet-controlled regions of Eastern Europe from Western Europe since World War II. The definitive end to the Cold War came in 1991, when the Soviet Union fragmented into 15 separate states.

To some observers, it seemed that without the clash between liberal democracy and authoritarian communism, there was no longer a significant cause for conflict in the world. The possibility of a fundamentally more peaceful world was shown when the United States and the Soviet Union collaborated in forcing Iraq out of Kuwait, which it had invaded, in 1991. U.S. President George H. W. Bush declared that a "new world order" was emerging.

The rest of the 1990s, however, belied those hopeful expectations. It became clear that nationalism had been suppressed, but not extinguished, in areas under communist control. Eastern Europe went through a period of nationalist resurgence that led to the fragmentation of three states: the Soviet Union, Czechoslovakia, and Yugoslavia. This process demonstrated the tension between two important principles: national self-determination (of groups that wished to secede) versus sovereignty (of the existing countries). Only Czechoslovakia managed this process without sustained violence. After 45 years of Cold War in which there had been no war in Europe, civil wars broke out in the former Yugoslavia and in Russia (Chechnya).

The collapse of communism also led to a new wave of democratization. Around the world, authoritarian regimes were replaced with elected ones, and many countries embarked on a process called "democratization." Many believed that the spread of democracy would help to reduce conflict. Although some new democracies have made the transition successfully, many others have found themselves stuck with new variants of authoritarianism, and many other governments, such as those in China and Burma, have successfully resisted calls for greater democracy. Similarly, the hope that adopting free-market economic principles would quickly increase prosperity has worked out splendidly in some countries and poorly in others.

The 1990s also witnessed an increased willingness to tackle global problems through international collaboration. The GATT was turned into a much stronger WTO in 1995. The North Atlantic Treaty Organization (NATO) and the UN struggled to manage the conflict emerging in Yugoslavia, but eventually, when the UN could not agree on action, NATO used military force in Bosnia in 1995 and in Kosovo in 1999. A major agreement on preventing further damage to the global environment, the Kyoto Protocol, was reached. By the end of the decade, it was clear that the post-Cold War world was not going to be as simple and kind as some had hoped. At the same time, however, there was a widespread belief that the problems ahead were much less daunting than those behind.

New World Order? Or New World Disorder?

The attacks on New York City and Washington, D.C., on September 11, 2001, fundamentally changed assessments around the world about the nature of international security and challenges to it. Suddenly, a key tenet of the Westphalian system, the idea that the main challenges to state security came from other states, was undermined. Overnight, the world's attention shifted to focusing on nonstate multinational terrorist organizations such as Al-Qaeda.

Initially, the threats from terrorist groups catalyzed a new sense of common purpose among many of the world's states, for most perceived a common

On November 9, 1989, Germans in East and West Berlin breached the Berlin Wall, unifying Berlin for the first time since 1961 and symbolically ending the Cold War.

threat. However, disagreement over the best means of combating terrorism quickly undermined the emergent consensus. That acrimony was manifested intensely and publicly by the debate around the world on the U.S.-led invasion of Iraq in March 2003. Two major issues divided countries in this debate. First, what should be the relative importance of unilateral versus multilateral action in combating terrorism? Second, what is the role of traditional warfare versus less intense actions (such as policing and intelligence) in combating terrorism? Are the lessons of World War I, World War II, and the Cold War applicable to the "global war on terrorism"?

While the problems of terrorism and the Iraq war dominated headlines in the post–September 11th era, other international problems and challenges did not disappear. The outbreak of **H1N1** influenza in 2009 highlighted a new danger of global epidemic. The new strain of the flu virus, which appeared to originate in Mexico, spread quickly around the world, causing considerable economic disruption, and spurring widespread counter measures. The danger of the pandemic led to an unusual degree of international collaboration to monitor and study the virus and to impede its spread. Ultimately, it did not turn out to be as deadly as originally feared, which some saw as a sign that national and international efforts to combat the virus were a success.

The expansion of the European Union to 27 members provided renewed optimism in Europe but also raised questions about how large the organization could grow without becoming ineffective. Some have questioned whether the most powerful country in

H1N1

A new strain of flu virus (also known as the "swine flu") that spread rapidly in 2009, causing many deaths and fear of a global flu pandemic such as that which killed millions in 1918.

the world today, the United States, can or should attempt to establish global leadership, which in some ways would return the world to the pre-Westphalian dream of a single political leadership over all states. Although some view that as a dream, others see it as a nightmare.

The global economic crisis that began in 2008 further upended prevailing conceptions about international politics. The wisdom of putting more faith in the free market was thrown into doubt as governments around the world tried to rescue their economies from markets that had induced chaos and collapse. The absence of a mechanism to coordinate global economic policy was felt keenly, as countries struggled to dampen a crisis that spread rapidly around the world. The U.S. debt crisis prompted many to argue that the financial basis for U.S. global power had largely vanished.

Reconsider the Case

Past and Present in the Invasion of Iraq

As the Iraq war has progressed, more and more historical precedents have been invoked. The war is creating its own history, the lessons of which are already being debated. In 2010, the history of Turkey—which, as the Ottoman Empire, had controlled much of Iraq—was brought into the debate. The U.S. House of Representatives sought to declare that the massacre of Armenians within the Ottoman Empire at the end of World War I should be labeled "genocide." Although the events in question had occurred 90 years earlier, Armenians considered such a declaration an important step; the Turkish government, on the other hand, considered it so offensive that it threatened to withhold the considerable support it was providing to the U.S. military (especially as a transport corridor for access to Iraq).

Meanwhile, in the United States, new historical precedents were invoked in the debate over solutions to the problem of Iraq. The idea of partitioning Iraq into Kurdish, Sunni, and Shi'ite regions prompted comparison to the partition of Yugoslavia n the 1990s. People debated whether the comparison was valid and whether what had happened in Yugoslavia should be seen as a success. At the same time, the comparison to Vietnam was extended, in the debate over withdrawing troops. Opponents of a fast withdrawal pointed to the chaos and violence, including genocide in Cambodia that followed the U.S. withdrawal from Vietnam in 1975.

With the U.S. occupation of Iraq already several years old, a steady stream of books emerged evaluating the decision to go to war, the planning for the war, and the management of the occupation. Unsurprisingly, there was a great deal of finger-pointing: at the Bush administration for seeking to go to war, at the intelligence community for overstating the threat from Iraqi weapons of mass destruction, at senior military officers for not insisting on a larger invasion force, and at civilian and military leaders for not planning sufficiently for the aftermath of the conventional military phase of the operation. Already, the case of Iraq is being reconsidered in the United States and around the world.

Critical Thinking Questions

1. The "memory" of early conflicts within Islam reverberates in Iraq today. What historical memories most heavily shape thinking about the conflict in the United States, in Russia, or in France?

2. To what extent do people in different countries associate a problem such as Iraq with the same historical precedents?

3. The Iraq conflict will someday be history, and people are already drawing lessons from it. What lessons should be drawn from the 2003 invasion and its aftermath?

Summary

The system of sovereign states that we take for granted today has not always existed. It arose in Europe in the fifteenth through the seventeenth centuries and spread around the world through the processes of colonization and decolonization. Although many aspects of that system remain essentially intact, the twentieth and early twenty-first centuries have seen the state-centered model of international politics eroded both from above (through the increased role of IOs such as the UN and the European Union) and from below (through the increased role of a wide range of nonstate actors as varied as Microsoft, Greenpeace, and Al-Qaeda). Yet the importance of sovereign states remains undeniable.

Economically, global interaction has increased, sometimes at a slow pace and sometimes, as in the past decade, at a very rapid pace. The past half-century has seen the growth of free trade and growing agreement on the important role of market mechanisms in increasing wealth. Yet the benefits of those developments have been spread unevenly, both around the globe and within individual countries. Simultaneously, providing increased wealth and increased equality continues to be an elusive goal.

History influences the present in international affairs in three very distinct ways. First, history provides the background to events, helping people understand the roots of contemporary problems, the context for contemporary thinking, and the extent of change or continuity. Second, history informs attitudes and provides motivation; in other words, it helps shape understanding of the *purpose* of policies. Third, it informs peoples' understanding of the nature of international politics, providing much of the evidence used to evaluate hypotheses, arguments, and assertions about the nature of international affairs.

Looking at the events and trends discussed in this chapter, we can see how they condition the background of today's events, how they shape political purpose, and how they might provide evidence for various assertions about international politics. Conversely, we can look at any issue today to uncover the understandings of history that influence thinking about that problem. There is often much debate about what history tells us. What is indisputable is that thinking about history powerfully influences what we think about international politics, and therefore what we do.

Key Concepts

1. Peloponnesian War
2. Westphalian system
3. Sovereignty
4. Anarchy
5. State
6. Balance of power
7. Nationalism
8. Concert of Europe
9. Imperialism
10. Treaty of Versailles
11. League of Nations
12. Collective security
13. Isolationism
14. Cold War
15. Bretton Woods system
16. Nonstate actors

Study Questions

1. How did the Westphalian system differ from the medieval system that preceded it?

2. What limits on war existed in the classic balance of power system (prior to 1800)?

3. How did the system that arose in modern Europe spread to the rest of the world?

4. How did the Napoleonic wars change the way wars were fought?

5. Is the Concert of Europe best viewed as a variant of traditional balance of power politics or as a new form of international politics?

6. How did "collective security" work between World War I and World War II?

7. What role did economics play in the outbreak of World War II?

8. What were the major lessons, political and economic, that were taken from World War II?

9. What arrangements were made to govern the international economy after World War II?

10. How did the process of decolonization influence international politics?

11. What events led to the end of the Cold War?

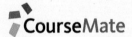

Endnotes

1. "Al-Askariya Shrine: 'Not Just a Major Temple', " *Times Online* (February 22, 2006), http://www.timesonline.co.uk/tol/news/world/iraq/article733713.ece

2. There are few, if any, comprehensive histories of international politics. Most studies focus on a particular period, a particular issue, or both. One study that begins even well before the Greek city-states is Adam Watson, *The Evolution of International Society* (London: Routledge, 1992). K. J. Holsti, *Peace and War: Armed Conflicts and International Order, 1648–1989* (Cambridge: Cambridge University Press, 1991) covers the modern era, but focuses primarily on war.

3. Thucydides, *History of the Peloponnesian War;* Donald Kagan, *The Peloponnesian War* (New York: Penguin, 2003).

4. On the Roman Empire and the *pax Romana,* see Watson, *Evolution of International Society,* Chapter 9, and Michael Doyle, *Empires* (Ithaca, NY: Cornell University Press, 1986), Chapter 4.

5. Gordon A. Craig and Alexander L. George, *Force and Statecraft: Diplomatic Problems of Our Time* (New York: Oxford, 1990), pp. 4–6.

6. See Watson, *Evolution of International Society,* Chapter 17.

7. See Craig and George, *Force and Statecraft,* Chapters 1–3.

8. See Michael Howard, George Andreopoulos, and Mark R. Shulman, eds., *The Laws of War: Constraints on Warfare in the Western World* (New Haven, CT: Yale University Press, 1997).

9. The evolution of international politics in non-European parts of the world is discussed in Watson, *Evolution of International Society.*

10. The bringing of the rest of the world into the Westphalian state system is discussed in Watson, *Evolution of International Society,* Chapter 22.

11. One compelling, though debated, explanation is that of Jared Diamond in *Guns, Germs, and Steel: The Fates of Human Societies* (New York: W. W. Norton, 1999).

12. On Napoleons revolution in warfare, see David A. Bell, *The First Total War: Napoleons Europe and the Birth of Warfare as We Know It* (New York: Houghton Mifflin, 2007).

13. See Louise Richardson, "The Concert of Europe and Security Management in the 19th Century," in Helga Haftendorn, Robert O. Keohane, and Celeste A. Wallander, eds., *Imperfect Unions, Security Institutions over Time and Space* (Oxford: Oxford University Press, 1999), pp. 48–79.

14. For a brief survey of late-nineteenth-century imperialism, see Andrew Porter, *European Imperialism 1860-1914* (New York: Palgrave Macmillan, 1996).

15. A good survey of this period is Jonathan D. Spence, *The Search for Modern China* (New York: W. W. Norton, 1999), especially Chapters 6–7.

16. On the interwar period, see Edward Hallett Carr, *The Twenty Years' Crisis, 1919-1939* (New York: Harper & Row 1964 [1939]). On the war itself, see Martin Gilbert, *The Second World War: A Complete History* (New York: Henry Holt & Co., 1989).

17. For a comprehensive history of the Cold War, see John Lewis Gaddis, *The Cold War: A New History* (New York: Penguin, 2005).

18. Despite having lasted barely two weeks, the Cuban Missile Crisis has generated an immense literature. For a participant's view, see Robert F, Kennedy, *Thirteen Days: A Memoir of the Cuban Missile Crisis* (New York: Norton, 1971). For a historical treatment, see Don Munton and David A. Welch, *The Cuban Missile Crisis: A Concise History* (Oxford: Oxford University Press, 2006).

19. John Springhall, *Decolonization Since 1945: The Collapse of European Overseas Empires* (New York: Palgrave Macmillan, 2001).

20. Margaret E. Keck and Kathryn Sikkink, *Activists Beyond Borders: Advocacy Networks in International Politics* (Ithaca, NY: Cornell University Press, 1998); Sanjeev Khagram, Kathryn Sikkink, and James V. Riker, eds., *Restructuring World Politics: Transnational Social Movements, Networks, and Norms* (Minneapolis: University of Minnesota Press, 2002).

21. Desmond Dinan, *Europe Recast: A History of European Union* (Boulder, CO: Lynne Rienner, 2004).

Theories of International Relations: Realism and Liberalism

LEARNING OBJECTIVES

After completing this chapter, the student should be able to. . .

1. Identify the major assumptions of the realist and liberal approaches.
2. Distinguish the major strands of theory within each approach.
3. Understand the normative positions of realism and liberalism.
4. Summarize the major critiques of each approach.
5. Identify ways in which each approach can be linked to policy problems.
6. Articulate and defend an argument concerning the relative merits of the different approaches.

◄ Britain's Prime Minister Neville Chamberlain and Germany's Chancellor Adolf Hitler in Godesberg, Germany, 1938
AP Images

Consider the Case

Should North Korea Obtain Nuclear Weapons?

Will North Korea be more secure if it obtains a usable nuclear weapons arsenal?[1] Many in the West argue that a North Korean nuclear arsenal would be a threat to others, but presumably the North Korean government's primary concern is making itself more secure. North Korea continues to fear a war with South Korea and the United States, and for many years has been subject to an economic embargo. The success of U.S. air power in Iraq in 1991 and in Yugoslavia in 1999 may have increased North Korea's fears that it could neither defeat nor deter a U.S. attack. North Korea probably calculates that its adversaries will be less likely to attack if they face the possibility of nuclear retaliation. This argument reflects the traditional theory of realism: in an insecure world, states gain security only by having enough power to defeat, or at least deter, their enemies. Surely North Korea cannot base its security on the hope that, if the United States were to attack, some other country or countries could or would successfully protect it. In this view, nuclear weapons are a "no brainer" for North Korea and for any other country whose leaders believe that it faces powerful adversaries.

Consider, however, the effects of North Korea's nuclear weapons program and of the fear that it has caused in other countries. North Korea has been further isolated internationally. The United States has likely developed plans for a potential attack on North Korea to destroy the weapons, either out of the blue or preemptively, in the event a war is anticipated. Two other neighbors, South Korea and Japan, might be tempted to develop their own nuclear weapons in response (and both have the resources to do so). In sum, North Korea's nuclear weapons program might mean that it faces *more* adversaries armed with nuclear weapons, not fewer, and that the United States is *more* likely to attack, not less.

Thus, North Korea faces a dilemma. If it does not build nuclear weapons, it might be attacked or threatened by more powerful actors such as the United States. But if it does build nuclear weapons, it might face additional hostile powers and increase U.S. incentives to attack. Either way, it seems difficult for North Korea to guarantee its security. Is there any way out of this dilemma? Some say there is not. Such insecurity is the essence of international politics, many believe, and the smart state procures as many weapons as is feasible to protect itself. Others say that there is a way out. If the United States threatens North Korea because it has nuclear weapons and North Korea has nuclear weapons because it feels threatened by the United States, the two could come to an agreement whereby North Korea would commit to neither attacking South Korea nor obtaining nuclear weapons and the United States would commit to not attacking North Korea. Some argue that such an agreement is impossible, either because both sides fear the other would cheat or because both seek to gain some advantage through further competition.

What are the driving forces of international politics? What underlying patterns do we see in the variety of issues and events that interest us? When we seek to explain a policy or a trend, where should we begin? These questions are answered by theories of international politics—that is, by generalized explanations of what drives states to do what they do.

Theory in international politics is characterized above all by disagreement and debate. On almost every question that matters, there is significant theoretical disagreement. Overall, the state of theory in international relations remains weak. There are virtually no theories that allow reliable predictions, and few if any theories provide explanations that satisfy a wide range of scholars or practitioners.

In this book, therefore, every important question will be addressed with more than one answer. It is essential for the student of international politics to recognize that many important questions have more than one plausible answer and that policy makers debate these answers just as much as academics do. Those who seek indisputably correct answers should study math or physics, not international politics. When we hear policy makers arguing about the best policy on some issue, we can almost always find competing theories of international politics behind the specific policy disagreement. A central goal of this text is to help the student identify the connections between theories and policy prescriptions and the corresponding links between theoretical debates and policy debates.

It is important to recognize that this multiplicity of theories is also an asset in helping us understand international politics. Different theoretical approaches provide different "lenses" through which we see events. Each "lens" brings certain aspects of international politics into sharp focus, while giving less emphasis to others. If we are able to see the same problem from multiple perspectives, we can understand it more thoroughly, and perhaps make more effective policies. Thus, although we often see different approaches as competing with one another, in practice they are often complementary.

This chapter begins an examination of theories of international politics by considering the two oldest and most widely articulated approaches: realism and liberalism. First, however, the chapter examines the ways in which compatible theories are grouped together into paradigms. Realism is an approach that focuses almost exclusively on power, viewing power as the main determinant of outcomes and the pursuit of power as the main determinant of policies. Liberalism is concerned

North Korea destroys the cooling tower of the Yongbyon nuclear complex in June 2008 as a visible symbol of its commitment to abandon its nuclear weapons program.

with power and purpose; it asserts that states have a range of goals beyond accruing power and is more skeptical of the role of power in achieving state aims.

Paradigms of International Relations

Chapter 1 introduced four levels of analysis in international relations: the system, the state, the substate, and the individual. Theories of international politics can also be categorized according to their philosophical underpinnings. Every theory makes certain simplifying assumptions in order to focus on some central concern. Scholars differ on what the central concerns are and on what matters can be set aside with these simplifying assumptions. For example, in many theories of international politics, the central concern is the behavior of states, and the actions of other kinds of actors are assumed to be relatively unimportant. This assumption allows the scholar to focus on a single problem, rather than going in ten directions at once. However, assuming that the primary actors are states naturally leads us to de-emphasize other actors.

This book discusses five distinct paradigms of international politics: realism, liberalism, economic structuralism, constructivism, and feminism. Note that these are called "theoretical approaches" or "paradigms" rather than "theories." Each paradigm is broader than a single theory and may encompass many theories. Those theories may contradict each other in some ways, but if they are based on similar philosophical assumptions, we group them together. For example, some theorists argue that the existence of many great powers in the international arena is most conducive to peace, whereas others argue that having only two great powers is most conducive to peace. In some respects, these are contradictory theories. However, because both theories view the problem of war and

The Policy Connection

What If Academics Made Foreign Policy?

The discussions of theory in this chapter might suggest that there is quite a distance between those who study international politics and those who practice it. Some might see this as a good thing. However, academics do make foreign policy when they are brought into government. In the United States alone, there are several prominent examples.

- Woodrow Wilson, president of the United States from 1913 to 1921, was a political scientist and international relations scholar. He taught at Bryn Mawr, Wesleyan, and Princeton, becoming president of Princeton in 1902. As an academic, Wilson was highly regarded for his analysis of the U.S. Congress, as well as for his work on the British cabinet system. As president, Wilson is known for putting liberal theory into practice and trying to establish international peace through democratic government, ideas developed in his earlier scholarly writings.

- Henry Kissinger was a professor of government at Harvard before becoming national security advisor under the Nixon and Ford administrations (1969–1977) and secretary of state under President Ford. As an academic, he was known primarily for his writing on realism and on balance of power as a policy. He advocated the use of "tactical linkage" of issues to yield influence and wrote about the problems of carrying out effective diplomacy in a democracy. As secretary of state, he is credited with having used tactical linkage to achieve important agreements with the Soviet Union. His mistrust of the democratic process, however, led him to be secretive to a fault, and his most important goal, extracting the United States honorably from the Vietnam War, was unachievable.

- Condoleeza Rice was a specialist on the Soviet military as a professor at Stanford before becoming national security advisor (2001–2005) and secretary of state (2005–2009) for President George W. Bush. Her most important work as an academic dealt with civil–military relations in the Soviet bloc.[1] By the time she became national security advisor, the Soviet Union was long gone, so it is hard to identify any clear link between Rice's academic writings and her policies. Interestingly, she co-authored a political science book while serving as secretary of state.[2]

- The position of national security advisor seems particularly suited to academics. In addition to Kissinger and Rice, Zbigniew Brzezinski (Carter Administration, 1977–1981) and Anthony Lake (Clinton Administration, 1993–1997) moved into it from teaching international politics. Many more academics have moved into lower levels of the bureaucracy.

- In Brazil, former sociology professor Fernando Enrique Cardoso served as minister of finance and then president from 1995 to 2003. As a sociologist, Cardoso was a central figure in the development of dependency theory, a Marxist approach to international political economy. As finance minister and president, however, he oversaw Brazil's embrace of free market economics.

Critical Thinking Questions

1. The practice of appointing academics to leading foreign policy positions is much more prevalent in the United States than in other countries. Why might this be the case?

2. What strengths and weaknesses might an academic bring to the task of devising and implementing foreign policy?

3. What kinds of traits should leaders seek in their foreign policy advisors?

[1] Condoleeza Rice, *The Soviet Union and the Czechoslovak Army, 1948–1983: Uncertain Allegiance* (Princeton, NJ: Princeton University Press, 1984).
[2] Bruce Bueno de Mesquita, Kiron Skinner, Serhiy Kudelia, and Condoleezza Rice, *The Strategy of Campaigning: Lessons from Ronald Reagan and Boris Yeltsin* (Ann Arbor: University of Michigan Press, 2007).

peace as based on distribution of power in the system, they are viewed as part of a single theoretical approach (realism).

The term **paradigm** describes an approach to a problem shared by a group of scholars. Within a given paradigm, there is agreement concerning which assumptions are uncontroversial and which are debatable. In other words, a paradigm determines which questions are asked and which questions are not asked. An issue that one group of scholars considers unimportant and ignores may be identified by another group as the central problem. Thus, it is often valuable to view a problem from more than one perspective.

Understanding the relationship among paradigms, levels of analysis, and theories is important. A *paradigm* is a set of beliefs about what should be taken for granted and what needs to be investigated, about what sorts of forces are most important in the world, and about what assumptions should begin the analysis (for example, human nature is aggressive, or states are the main actors in international politics). More than one theory can exist within each paradigm. A *level of analysis* is a "place" where the analysis takes place. Every analysis focuses on one aggregation—the individual, the group, or a collection of groups—and holds the other aggregations constant for the urposes of analysis. More than one theory can exist at each level of analysis. A *theory* is a specific statement about how international politics works. It is based on assumptions, such as what level of analysis matters most and what the most important questions are.

To clarify the relationship of these three concepts, Table 3.1 shows how different theories can be classified according to their paradigm and level of analysis. Such a classification scheme is a matter of judgment, and to put theories in boxes like this might exaggerate their differences, but this kind of exercise is useful in considering the relationship among different theories.

paradigm
A theoretical approach that includes one or more theories that share similar philosophical assumptions.

Realism

In his *History of the Peloponnesian War,* written in the fifth century BCE, Thucydides made several famous generalizations about relations between Greece's city states.

Table 3.1 Theories of International Politics Categorized by Paradigm and Level of Analysis

Paradigm	Level of Analysis			
	System	**State**	**Substate**	**Individual**
Realism	Balance of power theory; hegemonic stability theory	Revisionist versus status quo powers		Human nature as inherently conflictual
Liberalism	Liberal institutionalism; regime theory*	Democratic peace theory*	Complex interdependence theory	Human nature as inherently peaceful
Economic structuralism*	World systems theory; dependency theory	State working on behalf of the capitalist class	Firms dominating politics	
Constructivism*	Systemic norms (for example, sovereignty)	Identity politics	Transnational actors, NGOs	
Feminism*	Gendered nature of systemic international relations theory	State as a gendered construction	Effects of separating public from private	Effects of international politics on women

*Regime theory, democratic peace theory, economic structuralism, constructivism, and feminism are discussed in later chapters.

The analysis of the Peloponnesian War by the Athenian general Thucydides has influenced realist theory for nearly 2500 years.

■ "The strong do what they can and the weak suffer what they must."

■ "Of gods we trust and of men we know, it is in their nature to rule whenever they can."

■ "What made war inevitable was the growth of Athenian power and the fear that this caused in Sparta."

■ "So far as right and wrong are concerned . . . there is no difference between the two."[2]

In this ancient text, Thucydides laid out the philosophical underpinnings of the school of thought later known as realism: International politics is about the exercise of power. The first quotation indicates that the distribution of power determines the options open to states; the second asserts that ruling others is a primordial human motivation; the third contends that the distribution of power is the primary cause of war and peace. The final quotation warns that in international politics there is no shared morality, and hence, morality cannot be the basis for action. This rather bleak view of international politics continues to be influential to the present day. Some of the most prominent figures in the history of Western thought have contributed to its evolution, including **Machiavelli** and **Hobbes**.

As an approach to international politics, realism focuses on the problems of international conflict. Above all, realists seek to account for the fact that international politics over all of recorded history has seen a succession of wars. Despite progress in science and technology, the demise of monarchies and the rise of democracies, the rise and decline of colonialism, and the evolution of weaponry from spears to cannon to nuclear weapons, wars have recurred, and the possibility of war has been a constant. Why?

Niccolo Machiavelli (1469–1527)

A government official in the medieval city-state of Florence who wrote about the "laws of politics" for the "wise statesman," focusing on how the state could defend itself from domestic and foreign enemies.

Thomas Hobbes (1588–1679)

Author of the influential work *Leviathan* in which he argued that government had to be autocratic in order to prevent a slide back into anarchy.

anarchy

A condition in which there is no central ruler.

Central Assumptions

Realist theories share four central assumptions.

ANARCHY

Realism places immense emphasis on the idea that international politics is anarchic.[3] **Anarchy** is a situation in which there is no central ruler. International politics is anarchic because there is no world government to rule over the states. Thus, international politics is fundamentally different from domestic politics. Anarchy follows logically from state sovereignty and is an inherent part of the Westphalian system. For realism, anarchy predisposes international politics toward conflict.

STATES AS THE CENTRAL ACTORS

Realism sees states as the central actors in international politics.[4] Realists argue that international organizations in the contemporary era primarily reflect the interests of the states that create them. Similarly, realists assert that states can control actors such as multinational corporations when they really want to. Thus, international politics is politics between states.

The History Connection

Continuity and Change

We live in what appears to be a revolutionary time. How does our search for theories, which presume unchanging laws, relate to our understanding of history, which sees many events as unique?

The political scientist Robert Gilpin wrote in 1987 that we know little more today about international politics than Thucydides knew when he was writing in the fifth century BC.[1,2] Gilpin's point is that although much has changed, the underlying nature of international politics has not. It is still a competition for power in a dangerous world, where power determines outcomes. Even if Gilpin was right in 1987 (which many would dispute), can he still be correct today?

In contrast to this view, scholars, politicians, and commentators have argued that we live in a world that is fundamentally new. From a scholarly point of view, the influence of transnational nonstate actors and the erosion of state sovereignty are just two of many factors that undermine the Westphalian system. Popular commentators such as Thomas Friedman argue that globalization has permanently changed the nature of international economic competition.[3] And politicians have stated that since September 11, 2001 "everything has changed" in that states are no longer the primary security threat. Is international politics changing in fundamental ways, or is it changing in ways that retain the basic characteristics of a system that has always existed?

Liberal theorists, in particular, see a world that is evolving. Progress—the notion that people and societies can learn from past mistakes and develop improved solutions in the future—is part of liberalism's broad view of enlightenment.[4]

This text continuously asks about continuity and change. Even if theories can explain past events, have the "laws" of international politics changed? In particular, do the assumptions on which these theories were built still hold? What are the implications for the theories if they don't? For example, hegemonic stability theory points to the

historical pattern in which the decline of hegemonic states leads to "hegemonic war." Does this lead us to anticipate a future conflict between the United States and China?

Conversely, are some aspects of the system fundamentally new? Or do such assertions of novelty simply reflect an ignorance of history? For example, international collaboration to combat climate change appears to be a completely novel problem. But one might say that the outcome of these negotiations follows the established practices of power politics.

These questions cannot be resolved here. But the debate points to the role of history in the study of international politics. In looking to history to answer questions, there is an assumption of some continuity between the present and the past and an expectation that lessons based on the past, whether recent or distant, will be useful for the future.

And yet it is difficult to say whether more folly has been committed by those who have forgotten history or by those who have assumed incorrectly that the past offers a straightforward guide to the future. In warfare in particular, those who have assumed that the next war will be like the last have attracted as much scorn as those who have not learned the lessons of previous wars.

Critical Thinking Questions

1. What aspects of today's world seem most revolutionary—and hence least likely to follow recognized patterns? Which aspects will most likely display continuity?
2. Can you identify areas of international politics in which progress has occurred over time—where people and states have become more adept at solving international problems or avoiding them?
3. In what areas has little progress been made? Are some areas particularly resistant to efforts at improvement? Why?

[1] Thucydides, *The Peloponnesian War* (New York: Penguin, 1972).
[2] Robert Gilpin, "The Rich Tradition of Political Realism," in Robert O. Keohane, ed., *Neorealism and Its Critics* (New York: Columbia University Press, 1987), pp. 308–309.
[3] Thomas L. Friedman, *The World Is Flat: A Brief History of the 21st Century* (New York: Farrar, Strauss, and Giroux, 2005).
[4] Emanuel Adler and Beverly Crawford, eds., *Progress in Post-War International Relations* (New York: Columbia University Press, 1991).

STATES AS UNITARY ACTORS

When realists look at the state, they see a single coherent entity. This assumption has worked its way into much of the popular journalistic treatment of international politics, as well as into many history books, which treat history as a history of countries (states). When journalists or historians write "Russia did X" or "Washington believes Y," they are implicitly advancing this state-centered view.

Obviously, this is a simplifying assumption. Every country contains many individuals, and every government contains a complex array of organizations and decision-making procedures. Realists argue that in most of the important matters, states are highly constrained by their circumstances.[5] In this view, foreign policy is a rational response to external conditions, and different leaders in the same situation could be expected to behave similarly. It does not much matter if a liberal or a conservative is in power, or even if the government is democratic or authoritarian. In a commonly used metaphor, states are like billiard balls on a table. You do not need to look inside them to see how they behave; you only have to understand the external forces to which they are subject. For this reason, realism is characterized primarily as a system-level paradigm: behavior is driven by the conditions in the system, not by internal politics of the individual states.

STATES AS RATIONAL ACTORS

Realists assume that state behavior is rational. This is perhaps the most widely debated assumption of realism. Rationality does not mean that states always make the best or the "right" decisions, but rather that states "have consistent, ordered preferences, and that they calculate the costs and benefits of all alternative policies in order to maximize their utility."[6] The rationality *assumption* is not meant to be an accurate *description* of how states behave all the time; every realist understands that states sometimes make bad decisions. In practice, realists often criticize state policies as being counter to the national interest.

The notion of a state that is unitary and rational leads directly to the concept of the **national interest**—a foreign policy goal that is objectively valuable for the overall well-being of the state. The term *national interest* implies that the state is a single entity (rather than a collection of actors and interests), that it has a single interest, and that the interest can be objectively determined. Policy makers and commentators often justify particular policy prescriptions with the argument that they are in the "national interest." In practice, however, there is considerable debate as to what the national interest is, and there are frequent accusations that some interest groups are representing their group interest as the national interest in order to promote their agenda. Some argue that there is in fact no single national interest, but rather an accumulation of individual and group interests that overlap only partially (see the discussion in Chapter 5 on interest groups).

The Security Dilemma

Realism begins with anarchy, and then deduces its implications. First, anarchy leads to insecurity. Why? In anarchy, there is no one to stop one country from attacking another. In other words, realists see a "self-help world." If states are to survive, they must rely on their own means, because there is no international police force to protect them or to punish aggressors.

Second, insecurity leads states to arm themselves. States that want to survive must be able to defeat potential attackers or to deter them from attacking in the first place. The problem is that when state A arms, even if only to protect itself, states B, C, and D view the action as a threat. States B, C, and D then increase their armaments. Now state A faces a bigger threat than before, so it increases its armament. The other states then respond to this threat, and so on. The result can be an arms race, as occurred between Britain and

national interest

A foreign policy goal that is objectively valuable for the overall well-being of the state. The concept is important in realist theory and in foreign policy discussions, but some dispute that there is any single national interest.

Germany prior to World War I and between the United States and the Soviet Union during the Cold War.

The tendency for one state's efforts to obtain security causing insecurity in others is known as the **security dilemma**. If a state refrains from engaging in the weapons competition with other states, it leaves itself vulnerable to attack. But if it builds new weapons, it creates insecurity for others. The others' natural response is to arm, making the first state less secure. The dilemma is that either way, the state ends up less secure. Today, Iran's desire to obtain nuclear weapons—and the fear this causes in other states—can be understood in terms of the security dilemma. Iran seeks nuclear weapons because it fears attack, but its efforts to gain nuclear weapons may make it more likely to be attacked. Although some suggest reaching an agreement to stop building weapons (see the discussion of liberalism later in the chapter), realists contend that agreements can always be broken and that states concerned with their survival are unlikely to stake their survival on agreements with other states. Therefore, insecurity leads states to arm, but arms create more insecurity.

security dilemma
The difficult choice faced by states in anarchy between arming, which risks provoking a response from others, and not arming, which risks remaining vulnerable.

The Security Dilemma and the Prisoner's Dilemma

A branch of mathematics called *game theory* has been widely applied in efforts to understand various aspects of international politics, including the security dilemma. Simple game theory provides a provocative insight into the challenges of cooperating in a wide range of social situations. One particular model known as the **prisoner's dilemma** game has been used to represent a wide variety of social and political problems, and we shall encounter it repeatedly in this book.[7]

prisoner's dilemma
A game theory scenario in which noncooperation is the rational strategy, but leads to both players being worse of than if they had cooperated.

The basic story that gives the model its name is familiar to anyone who has watched television crime shows. The police detain two people suspected of a crime. They separate the two for interrogation and try to get each one to "rat out" the other, in return for a lighter sentence. The knowledge that the partner might implicate him or her at any moment gives each of the suspects an incentive to "defect" on the partner by confessing to the police. However, if they cooperate with each other and refuse to talk to the police, both may escape with lighter sentences.

The dilemma is represented this way: Each player's "payoff" (in this case, the sentence he or she will have to serve) can be ranked from best (4) to worst (1). In this example, "cooperate" means to cooperate with one's partner, not the police; "defect" means to defect from cooperating with one's partner by confessing to the police. The payoffs are summarized in Table 3.2.

As Table 3.2 shows, if one player cooperates and the other defects, the one who defects gets the best possible outcome (4, the benefits of a deal) while the one who cooperates gets the worst payoff (1, being ratted out by his or her partner). If both players cooperate, the police can only charge them with a lesser offense and they get the second-best outcome (3). If both defect, each gets some benefit from a lighter sentence but not as much as if the partner had

Table 3.2 Payoffs in the Prisoner's Dilemma

		Player A	
		Cooperate	**Defect**
Player B	**Cooperate**	(3, 3)	(1, 4)
	Defect	(4, 1)	(2, 2)

cooperated. The model might not perfectly capture the way criminal sentencing works, but the story is meant simply to illustrate the model, and we share it here only to explain why the model is called the "prisoner's dilemma."

What strategy should each player choose: to cooperate or defect? Analyzing the payoffs reveals a paradox that has far-reaching consequences for social interaction. At first glance, it might appear that the strategy one should choose would depend on what the other actor does, but this turns out not to be the case. Look at the problem from the perspective of player A. If player B defects, A can get the worst outcome by cooperating or the second-worst outcome by defecting, so A is better off defecting. But what if

B cooperates? Then A can get the best outcome by defecting or the second-best outcome by cooperating. *Regardless of what B does, A scores better by defecting.* Because the game is symmetric, B is also better off defecting, regardless of what A does. If both players are rational, both will defect and both will receive the second-worst outcome. But both players could be better off, at the same time, if both cooperated. This is the paradox of the model: *Individual rationality leads to collective irrationality.*

This paradox, also known as the *collective action problem*, has a direct parallel in the realist understanding of the security dilemma. For the realist, the dilemma is whether or not to arm (or to arm further). Arming is equivalent to defecting; not arming is equivalent to cooperating. Realists argue that, in anarchy, the rational state will arm, regardless of what its neighbor does. However, when both states arm, both end up less secure (because war will now be more destructive) and less wealthy. Again, individually rational behavior leads to collective irrationality. The dilemma is that the state faces diminished security whether it arms or not. For the realist, overcoming this dilemma is extremely difficult. Because there is no one to enforce agreements, cheating can leave a state that cooperates vulnerable. Therefore, prudent states consistently "defect," acquiring more and more arms.

The model embodies a great number of assumptions, including that states are unified actors, that they behave rationally, that the game is played only once, that different issues are not connected, and that payoffs are symmetric. These assumptions make it hard to apply the model to the real world, but scholars widely agree that it captures a basic problem in international politics and many other situations.

Power in Realist Theory

In the realist view, the distribution of power is the central force in international politics. The prominent realist Hans Morgenthau wrote, "International politics, like all politics, is a struggle for power."[8] Powerful states are safe; weak states are not. Relatively powerful states are able to shape the behavior of others (through threats or bribes). Because power is necessary to obtain any other goal, Morgenthau reasoned, every state's national interest boils down simply to getting more power. The alternative, Kenneth Waltz writes, is "probable suicide."[9]

Because power plays a central role in realist theories, defining and measuring power are critical.[10] These tasks have been the subject of much debate and much criticism. Morgenthau famously defined power as "man's control over the minds and actions of other men."[11] The problem with such a definition is that it does not distinguish power as a *resource* from power as an *outcome*.[12] Power can be observed only when it has successfully been exercised.

Moreover, if power is defined in this way, the outcome of conflict can be explained only in terms of power,

"But how do you know for sure you've got power unless you abuse it?"

not in terms of a better strategy or higher morale on one side or the other. If power is control over outcomes, then examples such as U.S. failure in the Vietnam War seem to indicate that power does not always matter. However, realists such as Kenneth Waltz reject this interpretation. The failure of the United States in Vietnam, Afghanistan, and Iraq, does not indicate the irrelevance of power, but rather the fact that military force is not the most appropriate tool for governing a country.[13] Therefore, it is important to specify the sources of power and to be able to measure how much power states have before they exercise it.

To John Mearsheimer, power "represents nothing more than specific assets or material resources that are available to a state."[14] A preponderance of such resources does not guarantee victory in conflict, Mearsheimer says, but states nonetheless would always rather have more assets or resources than less because, other things being equal, the more powerful state will prevail.[15] Like many realists, he defines "power" as military power, because "force is the *ultima ratio* [the last resort] in international politics."[16] For realists, therefore, the relative power of various countries is measured primarily by their military arsenals.

A-10 Thunderbolt IIs await U.S. pilots at Tallil Air Base in southern Iraq. Why has U.S. military power not triumphed in Iraq? Does power not matter, or have we not defined it well?

However, realists also stress that economic power is an essential underpinning of military power, especially in the long term. The size of a state's economy determines the potential to procure weapons. Moreover, in terms of creating threats and inducements, economics can be a power resource all by itself. There is a large literature on the use of economic sanctions to achieve goals. However, wealth does not translate directly into military power. Some countries (for example, Japan) may choose to spend a small part of their wealth on the military; others (such as North Korea) may choose to spend a great deal. Additionally, better technology may yield greater military effect for less money (although in practice, better technology often requires greater spending).

In sum, it is very difficult to define and to measure power. To the extent that power can be measured, it is clear that the most powerful do not always prevail in conflict. Despite those limitations, realists assert a larger point: states pursue power because they know it is central to their ability to pursue their interests, whether those interests are defined as survival, expansion, or acquisition of wealth.

Normative Concerns

Realism is often considered an amoral theory in two different respects. First, in its explanation of how the world works, realism finds that morality plays little or no role in the relations between states. States do what is in their interest. States that are altruistic risk being annihilated. When a leader advocates some standard of international morality, realists say, it is usually a standard that serves the interests of that leader's country. In other words, normative arguments can be just another weapon in power politics.

Second, the recommendations that realists make to leaders are often seen as amoral. Realists contend that the international system is a harsh realm and that only hardheaded pursuit of self-interest will avoid ruin. One question that often arises is whether a country should ally itself with another country that it finds morally objectionable. The realist position was captured colorfully in a quotation usually attributed to Cordell Hull, U.S. Secretary of State under Franklin Roosevelt, when considering the case of Dominican dictator Rafael Trujillo: "It doesn't matter if he's a son-of-a-bitch, as long as he's *our* son-of-a-bitch."

The Culture Connection

Realism, Cynicism, and Satire from Voltaire to Vonnegut

A central concern with all five paradigms is whether the basic circumstances of international politics can be changed or not. For realists, the laws of international politics are like laws of nature and should be treated as such. Liberals, economic structuralists, constructivists, and feminists all see transformation as possible.

The notion that international politics cannot be changed appears in literature throughout history. In Voltaire's *Candide: or Optimism* (1759),[1] the title character wanders from one disaster to another, including earthquakes, fires, and wars, all along being assured by his scholarly companion Dr. Pangloss, that despite the horror around him, this is "the best of all possible worlds." There is no point, Pangloss argues, in trying to change things, for this is the natural order. The book is a devastating satire on the doctrine that disasters brought on by human behavior, like natural disasters, result from the laws of nature and that nothing can be done about them. That doctrine, in Voltaire's view, is a self-fulfilling prophecy, because if people are convinced that things must be as they are, people will not strive to change them. Thus, war and earthquakes are seen as similarly inevitable.

A little more than 200 years later, the American novelist Kurt Vonnegut Jr. published his best-known work, *Slaughterhouse-Five* (1968).[2] The novel tells the story of the American soldier Billy Pilgrim as he survives the fire-bombing of the German city of Dresden in World War II. (Vonnegut himself was a prisoner in Dresden when the city was incinerated.) Billy Pilgrim is reminiscent of Voltaire's *Candide*, encouraged by modern science (in Vonnegut's version, Einstein's theories of space-time) to believe that nothing can be changed and that there is no point in trying. The narrator follows every mention of a death—of which there are many in the novel—with the refrain "so it goes." As horrible as it was, one character asserts, the fire-bombing of Dresden (which killed more people than the atomic bombing of Hiroshima) was necessary. Like Voltaire before him, Vonnegut is satirizing his character's views, making him look like a simpleton in order to make the opposite point: people can change the way the world works. While Voltaire had written during the Seven Years War, Vonnegut wrote during the United States–Soviet Cold War. The Vietnam War and the real possibility of nuclear annihilation were central issues, and Vonnegut appears to have been satirizing the notion that these conflicts were inevitable, that nothing could be done to resolve them, and that people, therefore, shouldn't try.

Critical Thinking Questions

1. Which international problems today seem amenable to change and which do not?
2. Can you think of a contemporary problem that has not been solved in part because people mistakenly believe that it cannot be solved?
3. Why might it be important for policy makers to recognize problems that they cannot solve?

[1]Voltaire, *Candide, or Optimism* (New York: Penguin Classics, 2005).
[2]Kurt Vonnegut, Jr., *Slaughterhouse-Five, or the Children's Crusade* (New York: Delacorte, 1969).

However, realism's position on morality is in fact a bit more nuanced. Following Machiavelli, realists emphasize that the role of a state's government is to serve the national interest of *that* state and that the government has no moral obligations to other states.[17] In this view, pursuing the national interest at the expense of other states is, in a democratic sense, moral. Realists acknowledge that policy makers often refer to common standards of behavior, but stress that they should not do so if it undermines the national interest.[18]

Realists fear that in a dangerous world, efforts to be moral can lead to immoral results, while unethical behavior might avoid much larger evils. Realists in particular point to the era between World War I and World War II, when many leaders sought to replace power politics, which was seen as immoral, with appeasement, which was seen as moral. When faced with a leader like Hitler, who rejected all standard notions of morality and had no desire for international peace, these policies, realists contend, were not moral. By failing to confront Hitler earlier, those who pursued a more "moral" solution to international conflict may have inadvertently cost millions of people their lives. In the realist view, power politics is moral because it most effectively prevents such aggressors from doing evil on a huge scale. Thus, the realist normative approach is strongly conditioned by the belief that power politics cannot be transcended.

Variants of Realism

BALANCE OF POWER THEORY

The most widely known realist theory of international politics is balance of power theory. This theory asserts that the likely result of the assumptions discussed previously will be a relatively even distribution of power between the most powerful states (the so-called great powers). Why? Although individual states will often seek to dominate, superiority will be almost impossible to achieve because states will counter each others' attempts to dominate. When many individual states strive for superiority, the likely result is balance.

Balance of power theory focuses on the most powerful states in a system because these are the states that are able to cause fundamental changes. The key process it explores is the desire of the most powerful state (or states) to rise above the rest and dominate. Historical examples include Spain under Charles V, France under Louis XIV, France again under Napoleon, and Germany in World War I and World War II. Realists consider it inevitable that powerful states will seek to dominate. But balance of power theorists consider it equally inevitable that other states strive to prevent gaps from emerging because their security depends on being able to fend off the most powerful. A balance will naturally result.

According to balance of power theory, war can begin in two ways. First, if states do not balance as they should, then power can become unbalanced, encouraging the powerful to attack. Thus, Napoleon could entertain dreams of conquering Europe because other countries failed to unify to oppose him. Second, states may initiate war in the pursuit of power, either to augment their own power, as in Germany's expansionist aims in World War II, or to prevent another state from becoming too powerful, as in Israel's attack on Iraqi nuclear facilities in 1981. This was how leaders in all the countries involved in World War I perceived the necessity of going to war in 1914: they went to war to preserve the existing balance of power.

HEGEMONIC STABILITY THEORY

In contrast to balance of power theory, hegemonic stability theory finds that stability results not from a balance among the great powers, but from unipolarity, in which one dominant state ensures some degree of order in the system. The word *hegemon* means "leader" or "dominant actor." The term *hegemonic stability* points to the main argument of the theory: stability results from a situation of hegemony, in which one great power dominates the others. Hegemony, it is argued, leads to peace because states are not irrational enough to tangle with the hegemon unless it is absolutely necessary. The hegemon, therefore, can act as the "global cop," in effect reducing the degree of anarchy in the system. The hegemon can solve the prisoner's dilemma because it has the ability to punish those who defect.

According to hegemonic stability theory, war is most likely when the dominant position of the leader erodes, giving other states the temptation to seek dominance. War can begin either if the rising second-place state seeks to assert its power or if the hegemon attacks preemptively, in order to crush the rising threat before it becomes even more powerful.

These hypotheses contradict those of balance of power theory. Where balance of power theory sees stability in balance and sees the chances of war increasing as one state seeks to dominate the others, hegemonic stability theory views stability in dominance and sees the chances of war increasing as the situation moves toward equality.

Hegemonic stability theorists interpret the history of modern Europe as a succession of hegemonies, punctuated by "hegemonic wars" that mark the fall of one hegemon and the rise of another.[19] British dominance, based on its naval supremacy, characterized the eighteenth century. At the beginning of the nineteenth century, Napoleon's France challenged British hegemony but failed, and a new era of British hegemony lasted until Germany challenged it in World War I. In that hegemonic war, both the most powerful state (Britain) and the challenger (Germany) were so badly devastated that another rising power (the United States) became the new hegemon. Many believe that U.S. hegemony is now in decline and that China is a likely successor.

Two questions arise here. First, why does the hegemon settle for leadership and not try to conquer the others, as realist theories seem to suggest? Hegemonic stability theorists would concur with balance of power theorists that if a leading state tried to conquer the others, the others would unite to defeat it, as has occurred historically. By moderating its ambition, the hegemon can make significant gains, both economically and politically, without provoking others to dig in their heels and go to war.

Second, if hegemonic states are able to order the system in a way that benefits them, why do they ever decline? A great deal of research has gone into explaining why, over

Figure 3.1 Polarity in International Politics

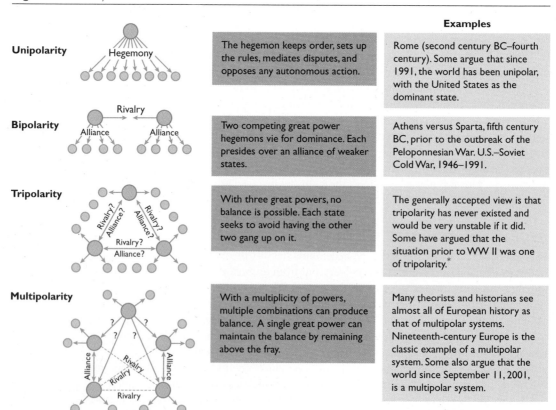

			Examples
Unipolarity	Hegemony	The hegemon keeps order, sets up the rules, mediates disputes, and opposes any autonomous action.	Rome (second century BC–fourth century). Some argue that since 1991, the world has been unipolar, with the United States as the dominant state.
Bipolarity	Rivalry / Alliance / Alliance	Two competing great power hegemons vie for dominance. Each presides over an alliance of weaker states.	Athens versus Sparta, fifth century BC, prior to the outbreak of the Peloponnesian War. U.S.–Soviet Cold War, 1946–1991.
Tripolarity	Rivalry? Alliance? / Rivalry? Alliance? / Rivalry? Alliance?	With three great powers, no balance is possible. Each state seeks to avoid having the other two gang up on it.	The generally accepted view is that tripolarity has never existed and would be very unstable if it did. Some have argued that the situation prior to WW II was one of tripolarity.*
Multipolarity	Alliance / Rivalry / Rivalry / Alliance / Rivalry	With a multiplicity of powers, multiple combinations can produce balance. A single great power can maintain the balance by remaining above the fray.	Many theorists and historians see almost all of European history as that of multipolar systems. Nineteenth-century Europe is the classic example of a multipolar system. Some also argue that the world since September 11, 2001, is a multipolar system.

*Tripolarity is discussed in theory and applied to World War II by Randall Schweller, *Deadly Imbalances: Tripolarity and Hitler's Strategy of World Conquest* (New York: Columbia University Press, 1998).

Source: Paul D'Anieri

time, the decline of a hegemon seems inevitable. Scholars have proposed three causes. First are the costs of "empire." As the hegemon's ambitions grow, so do the costs of pursuing them. Wars are especially expensive. The hegemon bears these costs, while other states invest in their economies and grow at a faster rate. Second is the potential for internal decay. If "lean and mean" states rise to hegemony, they eventually become "fat and happy," spending more and investing less. Third, technological advantages diffuse from the hegemon to other states, and new leading economic sectors may rise in other countries. All of these explanations place the underlying cause in the economic realm. Hegemony erodes when the economy underlying it becomes less productive than those of its competitors. Those who see the United States today as a declining hegemon identify all three factors at work.

Pax Brittanica? Hegemonic stability theorists believe that the economic and military power of the British Empire, including the control of the world's seas by the British Navy, played a major role in preserving peace and expanding global trade in the post-Napoleonic era.

REALISM AT THE STATE LEVEL

So far, the chapter has considered system-level theories within the realist paradigm, for which the primary characteristic of interest is the distribution of power, a characteristic of the system. However, many realists examine the intentions of individual states as well. Given a particular distribution of power, they argue, whether a state accepts the status quo or seeks to overturn it is crucial to anticipating that state's policy and to assessing the chances of war. Henry Kissinger, who was a prominent realist theorist before becoming a policy maker and then a pundit, interpreted much of the history of European politics through a lens of status quo versus revolutionary powers. When all the major powers accepted the status quo, such as after the Napoleonic wars and in the later stages of the Cold War, stability was assured. However, a revolutionary state, even one without predominant power, might be predisposed to attack other states, as in the cases of Napoleonic France and Nazi Germany.[20] A revolutionary power is particularly important in hegemonic stability theory, which expects that, as a secondary power narrows the gap with the hegemon, it might be inclined to challenge the existing order.

From this perspective, some have questioned today whether China is a revolutionary power. While system-level realists look primarily at China's growing military power and at the future potential of its economy, state-level realists ask whether China is satisfied

Figure 3.2 Hegemonic Stability Theory Timeline

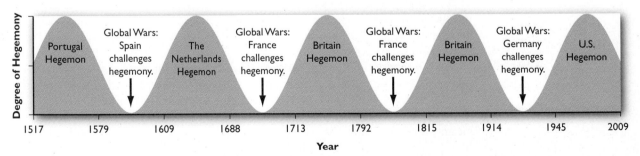

Source: Based on Modelski, George "The Long Cycle of Global Politics and the Nation-State," *Comparative Studies and History* 1978 Vol. 20, No. 2 (April, 1978): 214–235.

with the existing international order or likely to seek to overturn it. One careful analysis of China's intentions concludes that, contrary to conventional wisdom, China is not clearly a "revolutionary" power.[21]

Realist Prescriptions

Realist prescriptions follow directly from the theories. Balance of power and hegemonic stability theorists alike advocate that their governments pursue increased power and that they be especially sensitive to losses in power. For example, following the collapse of the Soviet Union, realists around the world advocated that others take steps to prevent the United States from dominating the world. Although realists see war as a useful tool of foreign policy, they may oppose it when they believe that a particular war will undermine, rather than strengthen, their country's power. Thus, John Mearsheimer and Stephen Walt, two prominent American realists, argued against the 2003 invasion of Iraq, believing that it would decrease U.S. security.[22] The concept of national interest is crucial to realist policy prescriptions, but there is often considerable debate about what the national interest is at a given point in time.

Critiques of Realist Theory

Each of the major assumptions of realism has come under fire. Whereas realists focus on anarchy as a basic condition that predisposes international relations to conflict, others see anarchy as only one of many characteristics of international politics, and as a characteristic that does not necessarily result in conflict. According to this view, there are international organizations, and an increasing amount of international law, that reduce the degree of anarchy. Similarly, many argue that the system from which anarchy emerged, the Westphalian state system, is itself evolving in a way that substantially limits sovereignty and thus the extent of anarchy. Even some scholars who agree that the system has traditionally been anarchic believe that it has changed over time. In this view, anarchy is simply an historical circumstance, which may now be replaced by another condition.

The assumption of the state as the fundamental unit of analysis has come under fire for the same reason. An increasing number of nonstate actors have influence on a wide variety of issues. If the conduct of major international wars is the focus of study, it may still make sense to regard the state as the unit of analysis. However, critics say, an increasing amount of what is interesting and important, from human rights to terrorism, concerns actors ranging far beyond the state.

Another series of critiques targets the assumptions that the state is unitary and rational. This assumption implies that, with regard to foreign policy, it simply does not matter what kind of government or society a country has. Yet many reject this assumption. We routinely assume that with a different party in power, or a different form of government, a state's foreign policy would be different.

Critics also attack realism on the basis of its usefulness, the extent to which it can be applied practically. Realism does not predict when wars will occur, critics charge. It merely tells us that when they occur, the distribution of power is the ultimate cause. To the extent that theories are evaluated on their ability to create clear, testable predictions, realism appears weak.[23]

With its fixation on power, realism is also criticized for its tendency to ignore the purposes to which power is applied. This is the central concern of constructivist theory, which is addressed in Chapter 4. However, some traditional realists also raise this concern. E. H. Carr found that without some ultimate purpose, the pursuit of power becomes meaningless.[24] Similarly, Kissinger's emphasis on revolutionary versus status quo states shows a concern with states' goals. However, most contemporary realists, in their pursuit of a rigorous scientific theory, have assumed that states' intentions can be reduced to the

Figure 3.3 What factors make a state powerful? The three tables below list the top 10 states (including the European Union as a single state) in three different categories that might be used to assess power. The Venn diagram shows which states are in the top ten in one, two, and three categories. What does this kind of analysis show us? What does it obscure? What other categories might be used to assess power? Are the different categories of equal importance? All these questions complicate efforts to assess the role of power in international politics.

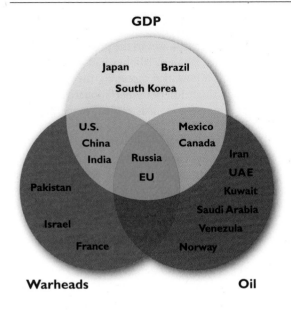

Rank	Country	T warheads
1	United States	5,521
2	Russia	5,682
3	European Union	533
4	China	~130
5	Israel	100–200
6	Pakistan	~60
7	India	~50

Rank	Country	Oil exports (bbl/day)
1	Saudi Arabia	8,900,000
2	European Union	6,971,000
3	Russia	5,080,000
4	Norway	3,018,000
5	United Arab Emirates	2,540,000
6	Iran	2,520,000
7	Canada	2,274,000
8	Mexico	2,266,000
9	Venezuela	2,203,000
10	Kuwait	2,200,000

Rank	Country	GDP (purchasing power parity)
1	European Union	$ 14,450,000,000,000
2	United States	$ 13,860,000,000,000
3	China	$ 7,043,000,000,000
4	Japan	$ 4,417,000,000,000
5	India	$ 2,965,000,000,000
6	Russia	$ 2,076,000,000,000
7	Brazil	$ 1,838,000,000,000
8	Mexico	$ 1,353,000,000,000
9	Canada	$ 1,274,000,000,000
10	South Korea	$ 1,206,000,000,000

Source: Naomi Friedman. Based on information from *CIA Factbook* and SIPRI, http://www.sipri.org/contents/expcon/worldnuclearforces.html/view?searchterm=nuclearwarheads

pursuit of power. Kenneth Waltz, recognizing that the pursuit of power could be counterproductive in the nuclear age, posited "security" as the primary state goal but did not investigate the problem of defining security.[25]

The last and most significant problem is the concept of power. Realist theory is a theory of power politics, but defining power in a meaningful way is difficult. Military capability, economic capacity, and prestige or cultural power are important components. Combining all of these factors in a way that allows researchers to determine which countries are more powerful than others is impossible, and yet realist analysis relies on the ability to do so.

Liberalism

In the eighteenth century, a new approach to politics emerged, which came to be known as liberalism. Liberal ideology took a practical form when it shaped the American Revolution and then was embodied in the U.S. Constitution. Liberal theory took hold more slowly in the international realm than in the United States, but its influence has gradually increased over time.

Both international and domestic liberalism were responses to the problem of anarchy that had been set out by theorists such as Thomas Hobbes. Hobbes had argued that in order to solve the problem of domestic anarchy, a powerful monarch, the "Leviathan," was necessary. In the international realm, since a single international "monarch" (a global empire) or a world government was viewed as impossible, realists argue that anarchy, with all its consequences, in unavoidable.

Liberal domestic theory centers on the rights (liberties) of the individual. The political theorist John Locke argued, contrary to Hobbes, that free citizens could indeed live peacefully without an authoritarian ruler. Locke and later liberals argued that individuals could freely join together to form governments that would protect them from anarchy without resorting to authoritarianism. The limitation of state power and guarantee of certain inalienable rights are still the core of liberalism (which, in contemporary usage, is often simply called *democracy*).

The central philosophical insight of liberal international theory, in whatever formulation, is that it is possible to overcome the worst aspects of the realist world. Indeed, liberals argue, because the world described by the realists is so dangerous, states and other actors have a powerful incentive to try to escape from that system, or at least to moderate its worst effects. Whereas realists are utterly pessimistic about the possibility of doing so, liberals are a bit more optimistic. They do not necessarily see people as "good" or inherently peaceful, but they do see people as being smart enough to recognize the problems created by international anarchy and to work to overcome them.

The most prominent assumption shared by all liberals is that people are rational and understand their interests. It is this faith in human reason that leads domestic liberals to believe that liberal democracy is the best form of government, and that leads international liberals to believe that efforts to overcome the problems of anarchy are not inevitably doomed.

However, liberalism is a much more diverse body of theories than is realism, and therefore it is more difficult to summarize coherently. This book will highlight three different strands of liberal theory, each of which departs from realism in a different way and each of which focuses on a different level of analysis.

None of these approaches rejects realism as completely irrelevant. Instead, they argue that the world is *contingent*. Sometimes states compete for power, and this drives international politics. But often they compete economically or join to pursue mutual goals. Additionally, actors besides states are concerned with a vast array of goals. For liberals, realist theory suffers because it does not acknowledge that various conditions exist in international affairs and that some of these create incentives to cooperate. Because realism does not take this contingency seriously, it cannot explain why international politics at some times appears conflictual and at other times does not.

One way to depart from realism is to rethink the implications of anarchy. This school, known as liberal institutionalism, agrees with realism that anarchy creates a security dilemma, in which states' efforts to gain security cause insecurity instead. According to liberal institutionalism, however, the danger of the security dilemma provides states with strong incentives to find a way out. It makes them willing to negotiate formal and informal agreements to overcome the counterproductive behaviors that result from anarchy. International institutions help increase confidence that agreements will be followed. Like the balance of power and hegemonic stability theories, liberal institutionalism operates primarily at the systemic level.

A second way to depart from realism is to discard the focus on the state as the central actor. Opening up the analysis to the whole range of actors also opens up a range of potential motivations. Firms, for example, are primarily driven not by international security motives, but by the profit motive. Focusing on multiple actors leads to a view of politics that, instead of being simple, stark, and conflictual, is complex, multifaceted, and often characterized by collaboration. Scholars Robert Keohane and Joseph Nye call this school of thought complex interdependence theory.[26] This perspective can cut across levels of analysis, but because it focuses on nongovernmental actors, much of its focus is at the substate level.

A third liberal school of thought attacks the realist notion that all states are unitary rational actors. That assumption, in realist theory, implies that a state's form of government does not affect its behavior. The democratic peace theory asserts just the opposite—that the characteristics of governments are crucial to understanding international relations. Some kinds of states—liberal democracies—are able to escape the conflictual dynamics of anarchy. This theory operates at the state level. Democratic peace theory is among the most influential schools of thought today, especially in the United States. It is so influential that Chapter 5 will examine it in detail.

A major difference between complex interdependence theory and liberal institutionalism is their view of realist assumptions. Liberal institutionalism accepts realist assumptions but contends that they do not necessarily lead to the conclusions specified by realism. Complex interdependence theory finds fault with realist assumptions and argues that if the assumptions are flawed, the theory built on them must be flawed.

As illustrated in Table 3.3, these are three very different theories. However, they are all essentially "liberal" in their belief that cooperation and order are possible in international affairs. International politics, in the liberal view, concerns the struggles to find solutions to the problems of anarchy. Liberalism is not simply naïve. It does not see collaboration as simple or unproblematic, but neither do liberals share the realist view that cooperation is inherently limited.

Liberal Institutionalism

Liberal institutionalism accepts many realist premises but arrives at different conclusions. It shares realist views on the nature of international anarchy, the problem of insecurity, and the notion that states can be seen as unitary rational actors. In adopting all these realist assumptions, liberal institutionalists want to avoid the accusation that their different conclusions stem from unrealistic assumptions. As the prominent theorist

Table 3.3 Three Strands of Liberal Theory

Variant of Liberalism	Level of Analysis	Departure from Realism
Liberal institutionalism	System; retains basic assumption of balance of power theory.	Anarchy does not necessarily lead to conflict; cooperation is possible.
Complex interdependence theory	Substate, but not exclusively; focuses on individuals, firms, nongovernmental organizations, and organizations within governments as key actors.	States are not the only important actors. Actors have diverse interests in international politics. Much of international relations has little to do with military security.
Democratic peace theory (Chapter 5)	State; focuses on what kind of government a state has.	States are not all essentially the same; liberal (democratic) states can solve disputes without war.

Robert Keohane writes, "I propose to show, on the basis of their own assumptions, that the characteristic pessimism of realism does not necessarily follow. I seek to demonstrate that realist assumptions about world politics are consistent with the formation of institutionalized arrangements, containing rules and principles, which promote cooperation."[27]

Liberal institutionalists point to the fact that the security dilemma, as portrayed by realists, offers states no good choice. Liberal theorists, however, provide a partial solution to this problem. They argue that if everyone could stop building arms at the same time, the security dilemma could be partly overcome, and everyone would be better off. If a state cannot completely escape the balance of power, perhaps it can, through agreements, help maintain a stable balance of power. In such a situation, security would be increased, and states could give more attention to other concerns, such as increasing prosperity.

LIBERALISM AND THE PRISONER'S DILEMMA

zero-sum game

A situation in which any gains for one side are offset by losses for another.

Liberal institutionalists also use the prisoner's dilemma model, and it helps illustrate how they diverge from realists. For liberals, the prisoner's dilemma demonstrates that it is possible for two states to become better off at the same time. (By moving from mutual defection to mutual cooperation, both can move from 2 to 3.) This possibility undermines the realist assumption that international politics is a **zero-sum game** in which one state can gain only at the expense of another. For liberals, states have powerful incentives to overcome the security dilemma and some ability to do so. Following is a summary of some, but not all, liberal institutionalist arguments with respect to the prisoner's dilemma.

- Shared norms or values can provide an extra incentive to cooperate. The norms of criminals, for example, create powerful incentives not to "rat out" a colleague. Liberals, therefore, study how shared norms can make it easier to solve the prisoner's dilemma in international politics.

- In interactions with more than two countries, cooperation (that is, alliances) becomes an asset to preserving security. The incentive to defect, on which realism is based, holds only for a two-player model.

- The logic of the game changes considerably if the game is played repeatedly.[28] Over time, the difference between benefits to those who cooperate and those who fail to collaborate continues to mount. In economics, for example, those who fail to collaborate will, over time, become poorer than those who solve the prisoner's dilemma. That, in turn, can leave a country weaker militarily.

reciprocity

The strategy of matching the other player's previous move.

- Playing the game over and over can increase the actors' ability to solve the prisoner's dilemma. The strategy of **reciprocity**, in which one cooperates only as long as one's partner cooperates, can persuade even selfish states to cooperate.

- Cheating is less of a problem than realists believe. States can agree on monitoring mechanisms to reduce the benefits of cheating. Moreover, a state that cheats in one area will damage its reputation as a partner across all areas, increasing the cost of defection.

Realists, of course, have responses to all of these arguments. They see the prospects for cooperation as severely limited in the real world by concerns about cheating and by concerns that one side will gain more than the other (known as the "relative gains problem").[29] They also believe that much cooperation in the world is not bargained fairly among equals, but imposed by the strong on the weak.[30]

INSTITUTIONS AND ANARCHY

institutions

Sets of agreed upon norms, rules, and practices.

The effort to use institutions to overcome the worst aspects of anarchy is, for liberal institutionalists, what international politics is all about. **Institutions** are sets of agreed upon norms, rules, and practices. They can be formal, such as those embodied in a treaty, or they can be informal, such as the annual meetings of leaders of the so-called **G-8** countries. In some cases, the institution may be an undeclared principle that is widely shared. International agreements can be supported by formal organizations (there are thousands of these, including the United Nations, the World Trade Organization, and the World Bank), or they can be carried out without any international organizational structure (as are many bilateral agreements). Some theorists use the term *international regime* to encompass the whole range of cooperative activity from formal institutions to unstated principles.[31] The historical establishment of rules of diplomacy, in which ambassadors were given "diplomatic immunity" and embassies were protected, is one example of a set of norms and practices that states found advantageous, even (or especially) when dealing with bitter rivals.

Particularly in the economic realm, collaboration among states can increase benefits without threatening survival. If states agree to trade freely, rather than to erect protectionist barriers to trade, all can become wealthier at the same time. But most liberal institutionalists contend that such cooperation can occur even among great powers and even among the most intense rivals, as between the United States and the Soviet Union during the Cold War, or the United States and China today.

INSTITUTIONALISM IN PRACTICE

Probably the first conscious attempt to put liberal theory into practice was the Concert of Europe that followed the Napoleonic Wars. This system was still anarchic and still driven largely by the balance of power, but the great powers at that time believed that the previous uncoordinated system of diplomacy had made all of them less safe. By agreeing on certain principles of engagement and meeting periodically to revise the arrangements, the states of that period were able to usher in an era of considerable peace and prosperity.[32] Skeptics point out that this system eventually degenerated and did not prevent World War I. Liberal institutionalists reply, "That is exactly our point: When collaboration broke down, everyone ended up worse off."[33]

During the Cold War between the United States and the Soviet Union, liberal institutionalists assert, it became obvious that even the most bitterly opposed and mistrusting enemies could cooperate to limit the chances of conflict. As the number of nuclear warheads rose from a few, to a few hundred, to a few thousand on each side, it became clear that the next war would be even more devastating than World War II. By the mid-1960s, neither side could gain any military or diplomatic advantage in this competition; each side could match any increase by the other side. But neither side believed that it could stop, for fear that the other would gain an advantage. This seemed to be a classic security dilemma. In a series of agreements, most notably the **SALT-I** agreement of 1972 (SALT stands for Strategic Arms Limitation Talks) and the **SALT-II** agreement of 1977, the two sides agreed to limit the building of new weapons. More significantly, they agreed to limits on certain kinds of weapons that were perceived to be especially dangerous.[34]

Perhaps an equally telling example is that of Argentina and Brazil. In the 1970s, both countries, ruled by military dictatorships, were developing nuclear weapons, largely in response to a perceived mutual threat. In 1980, however, the two countries signed the Brazilian-Argentine Agreement on the Peaceful Use of Nuclear Energy, an agreement to end their nuclear

G-8

Shorthand for the "Group of Eight" industrial countries that coordinate economic policies. Originally formed in the 1970s as the "Group of Seven" (Canada, France, Germany, Italy, Japan, the United Kingdom, and the United States). Russia was added in 1997.

SALT-I and SALT-II

Agreements between the United States and the Soviet Union to limit the building of weapons.

Liberal international relations theory finds that even adversaries under anarchy have an interest in limiting military competition. Here, U.S. and Soviet leaders Ronald Reagan and Mikhail Gorbachev at the height of the Cold War discuss limiting their nuclear arsenals.

AP Photo/J. Scott Applewhite

weapons programs, based on a mutual perception that the nuclear arms race on which they were about to embark would substantially diminish their security and undermine the economies of both countries.[35]

These examples all concern military-strategic affairs. Liberal institutionalists contend that if states find it in their interest to collaborate even on issues that have a direct impact on state survival, it makes sense that collaboration will be more extensive in other areas. They point to the ever-expanding web of economic agreements as evidence that collaboration is much more representative of international politics than is the narrow competition for power on which realism focuses. Today, major issues on which states are exploring cooperative solutions include global warming, nuclear proliferation, and traditional security dilemmas, such as those between India and Pakistan, North Korea and its neighbors, or Iran and the United States.

CHEATING AND ENFORCEMENT

One concern that often arises in liberal institutionalist theory, and in realist critiques of it, is the possibility of cheating. Especially when survival is at stake, adhering to an agreement while the other party or parties cheat can be devastating. Often, as realists emphasize, states are reluctant to agree to limit their behavior because of the fear that others will cheat. Liberal institutionalists agree that cooperation is more likely when any cheating can be detected before it threatens state security. They point out, however, that collaboration itself can make it easier to verify that states are not cheating. The SALT-I agreement included a provision that neither side would interfere with the

Figure 3.4 The graph below shows the numbers of U.S. and Soviet strategic nuclear weapons launchers over time, along with key events in the relationship. Can you assess the relative importance of arms control versus other factors in influencing weapons building?

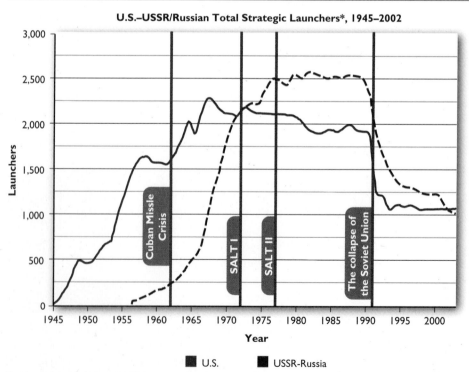

*Launchers include any vehicle capable of delivering a nuclear weapon across continents. Each single missile (land- or sea-based) or long-range bomber counts as a single launcher, even if it carries more than one nuclear warhead.
Source: http://www.nrdc.org/nuclear/nuguide/nrdcnuc.asp

other's attempts to use spy satellites to verify compliance. The United States and the Soviet Union, engaged in bitter ideological rivalry, found it in their mutual interest to facilitate spying on each other, so that they could successfully limit production of dangerous weapons. Similarly, a major point of the 1968 Nuclear Nonproliferation Treaty was verification provisions to assure all signatories that the others would not develop nuclear weapons.

A central point in liberal institutionalist theory is that cooperation does not result from altruism or trust. It results from the *rational pursuit of self-interest.* In this crucial respect, liberal institutionalist theory is similar to realism. The argument is not that cooperation can occur because states might put their interests aside in pursuit of the general interest. Rather, the argument is that sometimes the best or even the only way for a selfish state to gain its goals is to collaborate with others. In certain cases, liberals argue, it would be irrational for selfish states *not* to collaborate.

Executive-Secretary of the UN Climate Conference Yvo de Boer (L) and UN Secretary-General Ban Ki-Moon attend the plenary session at the UN Climate Change Conference in Copenhagen, December 2009.

To summarize, liberal institutionalism finds that because anarchy breeds insecurity, states have an incentive to overcome anarchy in certain areas. Although agreeing to do some things and not to do others may constitute a limitation on the rights of sovereignty, many states find it worthwhile to impose this limitation on themselves. For liberal institutionalists, the struggle of world politics is not simply the struggle for power, but the struggle for security. Although security may sometimes be increased by gaining power, it is often increased by agreeing with others to limit the unbridled pursuit of power.

Complex Interdependence Theory

According to Keohane and Nye, complex interdependence has three essential traits.

1. "Multiple channels connect societies." There is much more going on than government-to-government interaction. Bureaucratic contacts below the level of national leadership, which they label **transgovernmental relations**, are significant, as are **transnational relations** between societal actors across nation-states, including firms, NGOs, and individuals.
2. There is no clear hierarchy of issues. Security, which realists see as dominant, is not always the most important agenda item, especially in economic, human rights, or environmental relations, and especially for nonstate actors.
3. Military force is often not considered a viable tool of policy. In dealing with allies or with issues that have little to do with security (health crises, for example), military force would be inappropriate if not counterproductive.[36]

transgovernmental relations
Direct interaction between bureaucracies in different countries without going through their heads of state.

transnational relations
Interaction between societal actors across nation-states.

Complex interdependence theory rejects realism's (and liberal institutionalism's) narrow focus on the state. By defining a broader range of actors, the theory identifies a broader range of interests. In contrast to the stark simplicity of realism, a more complicated and nuanced view of the world emerges. Where realist theory sees a single actor (the state), a single goal (security), and a single driving force (power), complex interdependence theory sees multiple actors, diverse goals, and a variety of driving forces. Whether a simple or a complex theory is preferable will depend largely on the questions asked.

VARIETY OF ACTORS

pluralism

The presence of a number of competing actors or ideas.

hierarchy of goals

A clear ranking of goals.

The assumptions of complex interdependence theory are as different from those of liberal institutionalism as from those of realism. Complex interdependence assumes that international politics encompasses a wide array of actors. This array includes states, but goes far beyond them. Within states, actors such as bureaucracies, companies, political parties, interest groups, and voters are considered to be important. Beyond states, the list of actors includes international organizations and transnational actors of different varieties. This focus on multiple actors is sometimes referred to as **pluralism**.

VARIETY OF GOALS

Because complex interdependence assumes a variety of actors, it logically follows that there would be a wide variety of goals. Complex interdependence does not see security dominating all other goals. As Henry Kissinger, a noted realist, argued when he was U.S. Secretary of State in 1975, "Progress in dealing with the traditional agenda is no longer enough . . . . The problems of energy, resources, environment, population, the uses of space and the seas now rank with questions of military security, ideology and territorial rivalry which have traditionally made up the diplomatic agenda."[37] Whereas both realism's and liberal institutionalism's belief in the importance of state security means that all other goals are seen through the lens of state security, complex interdependence theory does not assume that there is a **hierarchy of goals**. States have economic, environmental, and other goals that have no substantial interaction with the pursuit of national security. In this view, when states are negotiating about banana tariffs, pollution limits, or collaboration on AIDS (acquired immunodeficiency syndrome) prevention, they are not worried about the balance of power.

Similarly, for many of the other actors involved in international politics, the goals are not primarily security. Greenpeace is concerned with environmental issues, the World Health Organization (WHO) with the spread of disease, and Toyota with selling cars. Within governments, ministries of economics and finance are primarily concerned with economic affairs, not security. It is not so much that these actors do not care about military security issues but that they leave them aside while they pursue separate goals. Moreover, to the extent that the issues they are concerned with overlap with military security issues, these other actors are likely to view military security very differently. Greenpeace, for example, might view war primarily as something that causes vast amounts of environmental damage, whereas WHO may view it as something that destroys the infrastructure needed to combat disease.

THE WEB OF RELATIONSHIPS

Realism views states as billiard balls colliding with one another. In contrast, because it sees multiple actors concerned with multiple goals, complex interdependence theory views the world as interconnected by a thick web of many relationships among many actors.

Complex interdependence theory stresses the range of actors and issues involved in international politics. In this photo, Bill Gates of Microsoft, a transnational corporation, meets with a representative of the European Union, a group of states, to discuss charges that Microsoft's software violates the European Union's competition rules

Figure 3.5 Complex interdependence theory contends that increased interaction across borders is changing the nature of international politics. One measure of increased interaction is the infrastructure that allows it to happen. This graph shows the rising number of telephone lines, Internet users, and mobile cellular subscribers worldwide.

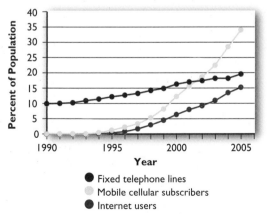

Number of Telephone Subscriptions and Internet Connections, 1990–2005

- Fixed telephone lines
- Mobile cellular subscribers
- Internet users

Source: Naomi Friedman. Based on information found at http://mdgs.un.org/unsd/mdg/Resources/Static/Products/Progress2007/UNSD_MDG_Report_2007e.pdf

The Geography Connection

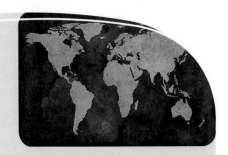

The Internet and Complex Interdependence Theory

The Internet represents the kind of connectivity that complex interdependence theory asserts is changing the nature of world politics. This map represents the relative density of Internet connectivity across the globe.

Critical Thinking Questions

1. Does the Internet actually change international politics, or just the way we talk and write about the subject? What concrete changes can you point to?

2. What is going on in the darker regions of this map? If complex interdependence depends on connectivity, will the effects of complex interdependence vary with the density of connections?

World Connection Density, February 2007

Internet Map
Connection Density

© Chris Harrison

ChrisHarrison.net

Photo © iStockphoto

Of the wide range of goals being pursued by many actors in world politics, only a very few can be attained through the exercise of military force. Rockets and bombs might determine what occurs in the realm of military conflict, but they are largely irrelevant when the goal is to limit production of polluting gases or to combat drug smuggling. Therefore, each separate issue has its own distribution of power and its own definition of what constitutes power. Russia, for example, remains powerful in the military realm, but it is less influential in financial affairs. Japan, in contrast, is much more influential in economic affairs than in security (although that is changing). Saudi Arabia is powerful in the arena of petroleum production, but not in other economic areas, such as high technology, or in military affairs.

COOPERATION

Because there are many actors concerned with much more than state security, much of international politics, according to complex interdependence theory, is not so conflictual. This position on cooperation overlaps significantly with liberal institutionalism, and places complex interdependence theory within the liberal paradigm. Where liberal institutionalism sees the possibility of collaboration even among actors with security concerns, complex interdependence sees many more actors focusing on issues less difficult than security. For the vast majority of issues, state survival is not at stake; although cheating is still a concern, it has less dire consequences and is often easy to detect. Therefore, using a logic different from that of liberal institutionalism, complex interdependence arrives at a similar conclusion in that it expects to see much cooperation in the world.

What specific predictions does complex interdependence theory make about the world? Generally, complex interdependence theory is more optimistic about the chance for peace because other goals compete with security. When seen as likely to have negative effects on other key goals, war appears more costly than when seen simply in terms of power politics. Moreover, there are many actors, in this view, who might see their interests injured through war and therefore work to prevent it.

Liberalism's Normative Position

The normative position of the liberal paradigm follows straightforwardly from its explanatory theories. If the perils and problems of anarchy can be mitigated through collaboration, liberals contend, leaders should attempt to achieve these benefits. Liberals reject the realist notion that progress in international affairs is impossible.[38] They argue that collaboration can make all participants better off and that it should therefore be a priority in international affairs. Much of the substantive discussion of issues in contemporary international politics, in security, economic, health, and environmental affairs, concerns what international collaboration should look like and how best to promote it.

The Realist Reply

Historically, realists have labeled liberal theory "idealism" and have warned that policies based on trust in international collaboration make states less secure in the face of potential aggression. This is the realist interpretation of the events that led up to World War II.[39] To the realist, anarchy is the immutable condition of international politics, and the struggle for power inevitably results. They view the belief that this can change as idealistic, or even hazardous.

Realists do not dispute that liberalism captures certain aspects of what occurs in the world. However, realists argue that liberalism fails to capture the big picture. In response to liberal institutionalism, realism accepts certain arguments about collaboration. Indeed, the concept of alliances in balance of power theory is equivalent to the liberal notion of providing security through collaboration. Similarly, the stability in hegemonic stability theory is in many respects a recognition that anarchy is more successfully dealt with in some situations than in others. In the realist view, agreements reflect the balance of power but do not alter it. In other words, international organizations and agreements are set up to serve the interests of the powerful. When power and interests change, realists argue, agreements will be abandoned or altered to reflect those changes. Ultimately, realists say, states that put their faith in institutions rather than in self-help will eventually regret it.

In responding to complex interdependence theory, realists make two arguments. First, realists accept the extensive list of actors, goals, and relationships emphasized in complex interdependence theory as a description of the world. Their goal, however, is not to provide an accurate description of the world today but to explain the major underlying dynamics that have existed for centuries. Realists say that complex interdependence

Reconsider the Case

Should North Korea Obtain Nuclear Weapons?

The question "Should North Korea get nuclear weapons?" has a strong normative underpinning. Any answer to the question requires stating what the goals are and whose goals we are talking about. North Korean leaders would likely answer the "should" question differently than U.S. leaders. Beyond this normative question, however, are the questions of what might ensue if North Korea builds its nuclear arsenal and what might convince the North Korean government that its security is better enhanced through other measures.

In February 2007, an agreement was reached at six-party talks including North Korea, the United States, South Korea, China, Russia, and Japan. North Korea agreed to stop work at its reactor at Yongbyong and to disclose all of its nuclear activities by the end of the year. The other parties agreed to supply North Korea with one million tons of fuel oil. Implementation of the first step was delayed by an argument over North Korean funds frozen in a Macau bank as a result of an unrelated dispute. By the end of 2007, North Korea had still not fully disclosed its activities, but the U.S. government appeared satisfied with progress made and chose to continue the negotiating process rather than shift back to confrontation.[40] By late 2010, the issue remained unresolved. In the meantime, Iran moved closer to developing a nuclear weapon, while commentators around the world speculated on whether the United States or Israel should or would preemptively attack to stop Iran's nuclear program.

Critical Thinking Questions

1. Imagine liberals and realists in the North Korean government. How might they frame the goals differently?
2. How would balance of power theory and liberal institutionalism explain the emergence of the 2007 agreement?
3. To what extent are U.S.-North Korean tensions driven not by the security dilemma, but by competing purposes? If the states had different goals, would the security dilemma moderate or disappear, or is it completely unavoidable?

theory, with its highly nuanced and complex view of the world, loses the big picture. The theory is not wrong, but rather answers a very different set of questions.

Second, realists are skeptical about complex interdependence theory's assertions that military security issues hold no special place above other goals. This idea may be easy to assert in times of peace, they say, but not when security is actually threatened. As was vividly demonstrated after September 11, 2001, a whole range of goals suddenly paled in comparison to the need for security. When the United States went to war with Iraq in 2003, almost no one was overly concerned with the effect of military activity on the environment or the economy. The goal on both sides was to win the war, and with security on the line, other goals took a back seat. Whether this is lamentable or not, realists argue, it remains true.

Summary

This chapter has examined the ways in which compatible theories can be grouped together into paradigms. Even though hegemonic stability theory and balance of power theory contradict each other on essential questions, both theories fit within the realist paradigm. Both see anarchy as the central condition constraining state behavior. Both see states as the fundamental actors in the system and view states as rational, unitary actors. Both argue that anarchy inexorably pushes states to seek power in order to survive. And both find that what happens in the system results from the distribution of power. The two theories share a stance of moral aloofness, arguing that it is more dangerous to make the mistake of trying to change the system than to live intelligently within its constraints.

Liberalism provides a much less pessimistic outlook on international politics than does realism. Whereas realism finds that the basic characteristics of international relations have not changed over the past 2500 years, liberalism finds that progress is possible. Liberals contend that their view is more "realistic" than realism because it helps us understand the extensive range of collaboration that exists in the world today. Realism, liberals assert, cannot account for that cooperation and therefore misses fundamental determinants of international political outcomes. Although there are no guarantees of peace or progress, liberals of different schools believe that both are attainable by intelligent and reasonable actors. Nowhere can this be seen more clearly than in the international economy. Over the past half century, increasing collaboration on free trade has yielded an enormous increase in prosperity throughout much of the world.

Key Concepts

1. Paradigms
2. Realism
3. Liberalism
4. Anarchy
5. Security dilemma
6. Prisoner's dilemma
7. Hegemonic stability theory
8. Liberal institutionalism
9. Complex interdependence theory

Study Questions

1. What is the distinction between a theory and a paradigm?
2. What common assumptions are shared by realist theories?
3. In realist theory, what are the logical links between anarchy and the balance of power?
4. What are the major critiques of realism?
5. What common assumption unites liberal theories?
6. How do realism and liberalism use the prisoner's dilemma model to advance their claims?
7. In the liberal paradigm, how does anarchy create incentives to cooperate?
8. How does complex interdependence theory differ from liberal institutionalism?
9. What are the major realist critiques of liberalism?

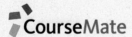 CourseMate

Endnotes

1. North Korea set off a nuclear explosion in 2006, but it was probably not an actual weapon that was detonated. In 2007, the country closed the reactor that was presumably creating the fuel needed for weapons.

2. Thucydides, *History of the Peloponnesian War.* The third quotation is from the introduction (Book I, Section 23). The other quotations are from the "Melian Dialogue" (Book V, sections 89, 105, and 97, respectively).

3. Kenneth Waltz, *Theory of International Politics* (New York, McGraw Hill, 1979), Chapter 6.

4. Waltz, *Theory of International Politics,* pp. 95–97.

5. Waltz, *Theory of International Politics,* pp. 107–111.

6. Robert O. Keohane, "Realism, Neorealism, and the Study of World Politics," in Robert O. Keohane, ed., *Neorealism and Its Critics* (New York: Columbia University Press, 1982), p. 11.

7. To see how a variety of simple game theory models can be applied to international politics, see Arthur A. Stein, "Coordination and Collaboration: Regimes in an Anarchic World," in Stephen D. Krasner,

ed., *International Regimes* (Ithaca, NY: Cornell University Press, 1983), pp. 115–140.

8. Hans J. Morgenthau, *Power Among Nations: The Struggle for Power and Peace,* 5th ed., (New York: Alfred A. Knopf, 1978), p. 27.

9. Kenneth N. Waltz, *Man, the State, and War* (New York: Columbia University Press, 1959), p. 205.

10. For an extensive treatment of the issues, see John M. Rothgeb, Jr., *Defining Power: Influence and Force in the Contemporary International System* (New York: St. Martin's Press, 1993).

11. Morgenthau, *Power Among Nations,* p. 28.

12. Keohane, "Realism, Neorealism, and the Study of World Politics," p. 11. See also Waltz, *Theory of International Politics,* pp. 191–193.

13. Waltz, *Theory of International Politics,* p. 192.

14. John Mearsheimer, *The Tragedy of Great Power Politics* (New York: W. W. Norton, 2001), p. 57.

15. Mearsheimer, *The Tragedy of Great Power Politics,* p. 58.

16. Mearsheimer, *The Tragedy of Great Power Politics,* p. 56.

17. Edward Hallett Carr, *The Twenty Years' Crisis, 1919–1939* (New York: Harper & Row, 1964 [1939]), p. 153.

18. Carr, *The Twenty Years' Crisis,* pp. 155–156.

19. Paul Kennedy, *The Rise and Decline of Great Powers* (New York: Random House, 1987).

20. Henry Kissinger, *A World Restored* (London: Wiedenfeld and Nicholson, 1957).

21. Alistair Ian Johnston, "Is China a Status Quo Power?" *International Security,* Vol. 27, No. 4 (Spring 2003): 5–56.

22. John J. Mearsheimer and Stephen M. Walt, "Keeping Saddam in a Box," *New York Times,* February 2, 2003, p. 15.

23. See John A. Vasquez, "The Realist Paradigm and Degenerative versus Progressive Research Programs: An Appraisal of Neotraditional Research on Waltz's Balancing Proposition," *The American Political Science Review,* Vol. 91, No. 4. (Dec. 1997): 899–912.

24. Carr, *The Twenty Years' Crisis,* Chapter 6.

25. Waltz, *Theory of International Politics,* Chapter 6.

26. Robert O. Keohane and Joseph S. Nye, *Power and Interdependence,* 2nd ed. (New York: HarperCollins, 1989).

27. Robert O. Keohane, *After Hegemony: Cooperation and Discord in the World Political Economy* (Princeton, NJ: Princeton University Press, 1984), p. 67.

28. There is an immense literature on the "iterated" (repeated) prisoner's dilemma. For a fun and provocative introduction, see Robert Axelrod, *The Evolution of Cooperation* (New York: Basic Books, 1984). See also Robert O. Keohane, *After Hegemony,* pp. 67ff; and Kenneth Oye, *Cooperation Under Anarchy* (Princeton, NJ: Princeton University Press, 1986).

29. See Joseph Grieco, "Anarchy and the Limits of Cooperation: A Realist Critique of the Newest Liberal Institutionalism," *International Organization,* Vol. 42 (Summer 1988): 485–508.

30. See Stephen Krasner, "Global Communications and National Power: Life on the Pareto Frontier," *World Politics,* Vol. 43, No. 3 (April 1991): 336–3 66.

31. Stephen D. Krasner, in a widely cited definition, defines regimes as "sets of implicit or explicit principles, norms, rules, and decision-making procedures around which actors' expectations converge in a given area of international relations." See "Structural Causes and Regime Consequences," in Stephen D. Krasner, ed., *International Regimes* (Ithaca, NY: Cornell University Press, 1983), p. 2.

32. Robert Jervis, "From Balance to Concert: A Study of International Security Cooperation," in Oye, *Cooperation under Anarchy,* pp. 58– 79.

33. Stephen Van Evera, "Why Cooperation Failed in 1914," in Oye, *Cooperation under Anarchy,* pp. 80–117.

34. George W. Downs, David M. Rocke, and Randolph M. Siverson, "Arms Races and Cooperation," in Oye, *Cooperation under Anarchy,* pp. 118–146.

35. See Leonard Spector, *The New Nuclear Nations* (New York: Carnegie Endowment, 1985), Chapter V; and http://www.fas.org/nuke/guide/brazil/nuke/index.html

36. Keohane and Nye, *Power and Interdependence,* pp. 21– 25.

37. Quoted in Keohane and Nye, *Power and Interdependence,* p. 22.

38. On the concept of progress in international affairs, see Adler and Crawford, *Progress in Post-War International Relations;* and Ernst Haas, *Nationalism, Liberalism, and Progress: The Rise and Decline of Nationalism,* Vol. 1 (Ithaca, NY: Cornell University Press, 1997).

39. Carr, *The Twenty Years'* Crisis. For a more modern version of the same argument, see John Mearsheimer, "The False Promise of International Institutions," *International Security,* Winter 1994/1995.

40. *New York Times,* December 7, 2007.

CHAPTER

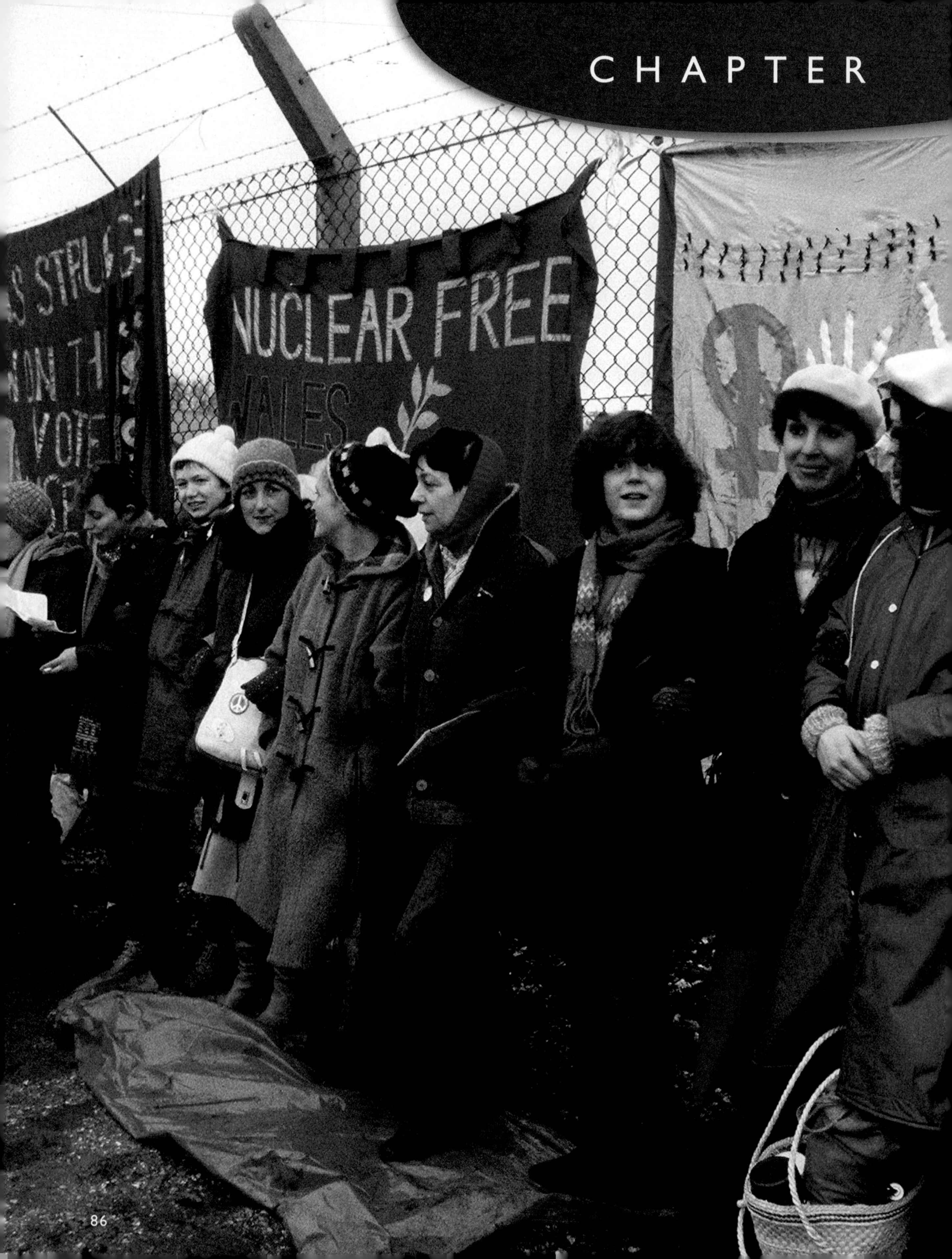

CHAPTER OUTLINE

Theories of International Relations: Economic Structuralism, Constructivism, and Feminism

LEARNING OBJECTIVES

After completing this chapter, the student should be able to. . .

1. Identify the major assumptions of economic structuralist, constructivist, and feminist approaches.
2. Distinguish the variants within each approach.
3. Understand how these approaches relate to one another and to realism and liberalism.
4. Summarize the major critiques of each approach.
5. Identify ways in which each approach can be linked to policy problems.
6. Articulate and defend an argument concerning the relative merits of the different approaches.

◄ Antinuclear protesters link hands to form a nine-mile human chain around a U.S. Air Force base in England, 1982.
© Dave Caulkin/Associated Press

Consider the Case

Resurgent Socialism in Latin America

In Latin America, as elsewhere, the 1980s and 1990s saw a turn away from socialist forms of government and economic organization and toward more market-oriented approaches. Many countries in the region adopted more democratic governing practices, and economic policies focused less on state ownership and more on private ownership and market forces. In foreign economic policy, Latin America increasingly welcomed international trade and saw the United States not only as an imperialist danger, but also as a source of economic opportunity.

In 1994, Mexico turned away from its traditional economic resentment of the United States, joining the United States and Canada in the North American Free Trade Agreement. While Cuba retained its traditional Marxist rhetoric, authoritarian rule, egalitarian economic policies, and hostility to the United States, it became increasing isolated.

However, beginning in 1998, the tide turned again in some countries.[1] Most notable has been Venezuela. Hugo Chavez, elected president in 1998, has pursued a policy he calls the "Bolivarian Revolution," after the nineteenth century anticolonial leader Simon Bolivar. Chavez has embraced socialism both in ideology and in practice. Ideologically, he has rejected previous leaders' "fetishist free-market discourse" in favor of what he calls "twenty-first-century socialism."[2] Calling U.S. President George W. Bush "the spokesman of imperialism," Chavez accused him of trying to "preserve the current pattern of domination, exploitation, and pillage of the peoples of the world . . . . The American empire is doing all it can to consolidate its hegemonistic system of domination, and we cannot allow him to do that. We cannot allow world dictatorship to be consolidated."[3] In practical terms, Chavez has established state control over Venezuela's lucrative oil industry, rejecting previous commitments to international energy firms,

on the premise that the oil represents the wealth of all the people and should be used for their benefit. He has also instituted a program of providing subsidized food and medical care in the poorest areas of a very poor country. Chavez's supporters see this as a successful attempt to achieve socialist goals; his critics view these policies as cynically spending Venezuela's oil wealth to boost his own political power.

In Bolivia, President Evo Morales nationalized the country's oil and gas industries and joined Chavez's "Bolivarian Alternative for the Americas," an attempt to form an anti-U.S. trade bloc. Morales, like Chavez, sees the involvement of foreign firms in the lucrative energy industry as exploitative. In Ecuador, President Rafael Correa echoed Chavez's call for "twenty-first-century socialism."[4] Argentina, reeling from a financial crisis, turned away from the market-oriented policies advocated by the International Monetary Fund and mainstream economists. It defaulted on its $93 billion international debt, moving away from international capital markets. Argentina was able to fully repay its debt in January 2006. This was seen as evidence that there was a genuine alternative to the international liberal economic consensus.

Why, a decade after the collapse of communism, when even China was shifting away from communism, did Venezuela, Bolivia, and Ecuador adopt explicitly Marxist doctrines and reject the accepted rules of international economic relations? Does the success of Argentina's unorthodox economic policies provide evidence that the contemporary international economic order disadvantages poor countries unfairly? Does the view of international politics put forth by leaders such as Chavez, Morales, and Correa offer an alternative to the realist and liberal approaches? Do their policies represent a revival of socialism or simply the efforts of three leaders to remain in power through populism?

This chapter continues to explore the questions raised in the previous chapter. What are the driving forces of international politics? What underlying patterns do we see in the variety of issues and events that interest us? When we seek to explain a policy or a trend, where should we begin?

This chapter will discuss very different answers to these questions by examining three approaches that critique both realism and liberalism. Economic structuralism, also known as "Marxism," focuses on the role of economic power and exploitation and sees international politics as a struggle between capitalists and workers over the profits generated by workers' labor.

Constructivism and feminism go much further than economic structuralism, liberalism, or realism in focusing their attention on *purpose* in international politics. Constructivism argues that much of the variation in the behavior of states and other actors cannot be accounted for by changes in the distribution of material power, as defined by realists, liberals, and economic structuralists. Rather, they say, change is explained by the evolution of the goals of actors, and in particular by the emergence of shared purpose in the actions of actors in the global arena. Feminism questions conventional notions of purpose as well as of power. It sees the exercise of power in the international arena as connected to the exercise of power in the domestic arena that leads to the economic and political disempowerment of women. Feminist international scholars seek to make remedying this disempowerment a central purpose of the conduct and study of international politics.

Bolivian President Evo Morales, accompanied by military forces, announces that the government is taking over the country's largest natural gas field. Does government ownership promise that citizens will benefit from the exploitation of natural resources?

Economic Structuralism

Just as liberalism was a response to realism, economic structuralism is, in many respects, a response to liberalism. Like liberalism, economic structuralism first arose as a theory of domestic politics and only later was applied to questions of international politics. Economic structuralism has its roots in the critique of liberal capitalism leveled by Karl Marx, but the label "economic structuralism" is used both because it more clearly describes the theory itself and because there are other Marxist theories that will not be covered here.[5]

Economic structuralism is a theoretical approach that focuses above all on *economics*, both as a motivation in politics and as a source of power. Wealth plays as important a role in economic structuralism as power does in realist theory, but wealth is much easier to define and measure. Where realism examines the distribution of power, economic structuralism explores the distribution of wealth (which it sees as essentially identical to power).

Economic structuralism has a strong normative component, finding that economic inequality is a double evil. In addition to creating poverty, it leads to political inequality, since political power is built largely on economic power. The economic structuralist approach is intended by its advocates not only to expose the sources and effects of economic inequality, but also to provide some guidelines as to how such inequality might be overcome. As with realism and liberalism, it is easier to see the contribution that economic structuralism makes to understanding international politics than it is to use it as a guideline for policy.

Assumptions

Economic structuralism assumes, first of all, that economics is the driving motivation behind political activity. This **economic determinism** is very compatible with the standard economics taught in every university economics department. Economic determinism assumes that political behavior is driven by economic motivations and that political

economic determinism

The assumption that political behavior is driven by economic motivations and that political outcomes are determined by economic power.

outcomes are determined by economic power. This assumption is an essential underpinning of all economic structuralist theory. This approach also assumes that wealth is a *fungible* resource. This means that it can be converted into other resources. With money, one can buy other things one needs, such as territory, bombs, or politicians.

In general, economic structuralism sees the fundamental actors in politics not as individuals or states but as *classes*. The term **classes** refers to groups of people at different places in the economic hierarchy. At the top are those who own **capital** (such as factories, stores, shares in corporations, land, and money). At the bottom are those who must sell their labor to others to earn money. This includes the majority of people, those commonly called *workers* In Marxist jargon, the owners of capital are known collectively as the **bourgeoisie** and the workers are known as the **proletariat**. According to economic structuralism, the world is divided not simply into countries, but into classes with opposing economic interests. In economic structuralist theory, a person has more in common with members of the same class in another country than with people of a different class in the person's own country. However, economic structuralists say, the workers do not always realize this, partly because the owners of capital who control the means of mass communication do not want them to. Marx saw ideas such as religion and nationalism as methods by which members of the working class were deceived about their true (class) interests. Economic structuralists have hoped, usually in vain, for an international movement of workers based on their common interests and have lamented what they see as the well-organized collaboration of the capitalist class across boundaries. For example, when World War I broke out, Vladimir Lenin, leader of the Russian communist movement, advocated and expected that workers in the various countries of Europe would see the war as in the interest of the capitalists rather than the workers and would therefore refuse to participate. As it happened, however, an upsurge in nationalist sentiment caused even the dedicated German socialists to embrace their country's war effort. Today, activists seek to build a transnational alliance of labor unions to avoid the divide-and-conquer tactics of corporations. So far, such efforts have been largely unsuccessful.

As economic structuralist theory is applied to international politics, analysis of classes and states is often blurred together such that the focus on classes loses some of its emphasis. Instead of examining poor people across the world, many analysts simplify by referring to poor *states*. This may be a less "pure" formulation, but it is essentially the same idea.

Propositions

Economic structuralism is based on the central concept of surplus value, as developed in Karl Marx's theory of economic exploitation. The main point is that when companies make a profit, the workers get a much smaller share than the owners, even though it is the workers who are actually producing the product. When a worker applies labor to some set of raw materials, value is added. Leather becomes a shoe, steel becomes a car, and so on. The difference between the value of the leather and the value of the shoe has been added by workers (using tools supplied by the factory owner). Marx called this difference the **surplus value**, and he asked a simple question: How is this "profit" divided between the person who does the work ("labor") and the person who owns the factory and tools ("capital")? Marx pointed out that the worker receives a fixed amount (a *wage*) regardless of how much value is added. Inevitably, Marx argued, the greater share of surplus value goes to the owner.[6] To many, this is obvious, logical, and fair. But Marx and others who followed this line of thinking found some disturbing implications. In particular, they concluded that in such a system, the wealthy will get ever wealthier while the poor will be left ever further behind. In recent years, this concern has been raised in debate over the issue of "sweatshops," in which workers desperate for any job accept low wages and poor working conditions. Economic structuralists often note the growing gap between rich and poor in countries such as the United States.

---

classes

In economic structuralist theory, groups of people at different places in the economic hierarchy.

capital

Resources that can be used to produce further wealth.

bourgeoisie

In Marxist jargon, the owners of capital.

proletariat

In Marxist jargon, the working class.

surplus value

In economic structuralist theory, the difference between the value of raw materials and the value of the final product; presumably this is the value added by laborers.

Economic structuralists ask how the division of profits is determined. They argue that it is determined by the relative bargaining power of the owner and the worker. In most circumstances, the theory asserts, there are fewer jobs than people looking for work. The owner or the manager can use the threat of replacing one worker with another to drive wages down. The owner of capital has what economic structuralist theorists call *structural power*. Note that this is a very different notion of power than that used by many realists, who define *power* as direct coercion through the threat or application of violence. By controlling the means by which labor is added to materials (tools, land, the factory), the owner inevitably has power to extract from the worker a disproportionate share of the profit. Economic structuralist theorists are concerned about the inequality and injustice that results.

A few implications of these propositions are worth noting. First, because the ability to extract a favorable deal from the worker depends on the worker needing the job, poverty is actually in the interest of the owner. The more desperate workers are, the more cheaply they will work. Thus, firms around the world save money by hiring economically desperate illegal aliens. Similarly, in this view, a certain level of unemployment is helpful for owners because it helps keep wages down. Economic structuralist theorists therefore see free trade as a way for owners of capital to increase their bargaining power over workers, by being able to threaten to move production abroad if wages are too high. In the contemporary world, this threat is reflected in concerns over the "outsourcing" of jobs.

Surplus Value and International Politics

What does all this have to do with international politics? When economic structuralists apply the domestic concept of surplus value internationally, it leads them to question how international politics affects the distribution of wealth in the world, which is their central concern.

To understand international politics, economic structuralists look first at the interests and actions of different economic classes, and especially at the most powerful class, the owners of capital. Economic structuralist theorists assert that behind every government is a class of owners in whose interests the government usually acts. Owners influence or even control governments through campaign contributions and lobbying and by promoting the general idea that what's good for business is good for the country. According to economic structuralist theory, owners of capital eventually exhaust the opportunities to invest profitably at home, and therefore they look abroad for further prospects. This drive for economic expansion, economic structuralists contend, drives international politics. A primary goal of governments of wealthy countries is to keep markets abroad open so that companies in those countries can invest and trade profitably.[7]

Historically, the theory argues, this goal was the impetus for colonialism. Almost every colonial arrangement had specific investment and trade provisions aimed at giving firms in the colonizing country an advantage over those in the colony. The Stamp Act and the Navigation Acts that spurred the American Revolution were but two examples. In India, the British suppressed the vibrant Indian textile industry to increase the market for Britain's own rapidly industrializing textile firms. The overall argument is that powerful states and wealthy capitalists use what power they have to gain even more, by forcing weaker actors into the parts of the production process that yield relatively little reward and saving the lucrative parts for themselves.

In this respect, economic structuralism fully agrees with the realist statement that "the strong do what they can and the weak suffer what they must." Yet there are two key differences. First, realist theories explore politics between the "great powers" because the most powerful drive the system, whereas economic structuralist theorists examine relations between the strong and the weak. Second, realists assert that the exploitation of the weak is simply a fact of life that must be accepted, whereas economic structuralist theorists consider it an unacceptable fact that must be changed somehow. Karl Marx asserted

The History Connection

The Rise and Fall of Marxism in Theory and in Practice

Today's economic structuralism has its roots in the writing of the German economist Karl Marx. Marx was disturbed at the poverty and at the growing inequality in wealth he saw during the industrial revolution in his native country, Germany, and in England, to which he emigrated. At the time Marx wrote and for many years afterward, Marxism was essentially an academic theory, although broader ideas of socialism gained popularity throughout Europe and North America in the late nineteenth century. In March 1871, following France's defeat in the Franco-Prussian War, rebelling French workers established an alternative government known as the Paris Commune. It lasted only a few months but symbolized increasing efforts among European workers to move revolution from theory to practice.

When a group of revolutionaries led by Vladimir Lenin took over Russia in 1917 and declared that they were putting Marxism into practice, the theory came to play a central role in international politics. For some, the introduction of Marxism in the Soviet Union showed that progress and revolution were inevitable, as Marx had predicted. Others saw the same possibility of revolution but regarded it as an existential threat, particularly after the Chinese Communist Party, led by Mao Zedong, took over China in 1949. For most of the twentieth century, however, almost everyone took Marxism seriously, both as a doctrine and as a set of political practices.

This was the case despite the fact that the Soviet Union and China, by most criteria, did not look anything like the communist paradise that Marx had envisioned. He certainly had not argued in favor of totalitarianism and violent state-led repression. To some, this meant that the Soviets and Chinese had perverted or digressed from the true doctrine of Marxism. To others, it indicated that Marxism could not possibly work—that it was destined to lead to dictatorship.

In the academic realm, work inspired by Marx continued to develop in new ways that moved ever further away from Marx's ideas. In Latin America, the failure to achieve economic development after World War II led

scholars to advance a new version of the theory, known as "dependency theory," which would explain how their countries continued to be underdeveloped even though formal colonialism was long gone. In Europe, Marxist thinkers sought to modify the theory to help clarify why, in conditions of "welfare capitalism," progress toward socialist revolution seemed further away than ever.

Ultimately, however, the popularity of Marxism as a doctrine hinged on the fate of the country with which it had come to be identified. When the Soviet Union collapsed in 1991 (and China abandoned much of its communist rhetoric), Marxism became widely viewed as a dead ideology, no longer worth taking seriously. Marx's words about the future of capitalism—that it would be consigned to "the dustbin of history"—were ironically applied to his own theory. As recently as the 1980s, Marx's writings were considered essential reading for undergraduates. Today, they have largely vanished from university syllabi.

After a century in which it generated both immense hopes and fears, Marxism as a prescription for how to build a society appeared to have died in 1991. And yet the theoretical descendants of Marxism remain alive and well. Many of Marx's ideas have been appropriated into mainstream thought. Marx's central concern, that growth in wealth can also lead to greater inequality, has become a central focus of economic research today. Moreover, the recent upsurge in Marxist thinking in Latin America indicates that Marx's ideas have not disappeared from policy makers' minds altogether.

Critical Thinking Questions

1. Which of the ideas connected in this chapter with economic structuralism seem most "mainstream," and which seem most radical?

2. What is your impression of how Marxism is seen today, by those outside academic circles?

3. Why did it make sense for Marx's writings to be compulsory reading for undergraduates during the Cold War? Is there any reason to read Marx today?

Chinese workers make Nike shoes at a factory in Guangdong province. When labor is added to material, the product is worth more than the material. How is this increased value divided between those who do the work and those who own the factory?

that capitalism, and the exploitation that accompanies it, would *inevitably* be overthrown in a worldwide revolution. Few theorists today believe this.

War and Peace

Although there is consensus among economic structuralist theorists that unbridled free markets lead to economic exploitation and to the expansion of wealthy states into poorer ones, there is no agreement on what this pattern means for war and peace (an issue that in general is of less interest to economic structuralist theorists).

One school of thought, advanced by the Russian revolutionary leader Vladimir Lenin, is that capitalism inevitably leads, through imperialism, to war. Lenin asserted that the pursuit of ever-increasing access to economic markets and sources of cheap labor and raw materials will inevitably lead the great powers to clash with one another. He viewed the scramble for colonies by European powers in the late nineteenth century as a prelude to World War I. After that wave of colonization, there was little territory left in the world for economic expansion. The great powers could expand only at each other's expense, so they were driven to wage war with each other.

Another school of thought fears that the opposite is true. In this view, the owners of capital and the governments of powerful states are smart enough to recognize that, rather than fighting each other, they are better off collaborating to exploit the weak. This view actually echoes the liberal institutionalist perspective, finding that, in economic terms, powerful states have many reasons to collaborate and can do so. Whereas liberal institutionalism sees this collaboration as desirable, economic structuralism sees it as paving the way for ongoing exploitation of the poor.

Today, economic structuralist theorists are skeptical of the web of collaborative institutions that is increasingly governing the world economy, such as the World Bank and WTO. They assert that these

A U.S. soldier guarding an Iraqi oil facility. To what extent is international conflict driven by the pursuit of wealth? Economic structuralists see the pursuit of economic advantage as a primary cause of war.

are sponsored by governments of wealthy countries and serve the interests of the wealthy owners of capital who influence them. Whereas liberals see these agreements as providing a level playing field on which all can compete, economic structuralist theorists point out that in the race being run on this playing field, some countries got a head start of several hundred years through colonialism. Until that initial difference in positions is resolved, they say, free trade will always favor those already ahead.

Constructivism

Constructivist approaches differ fundamentally from the realist, liberal, and economic structuralist approaches. They examine factors that those theories largely ignore, and they make much fewer categorical statements about international politics. There is a variety of constructivist approaches, but they all share a focus on how ideas influence international politics.

From the constructivist perspective, realist, liberal, and economic structuralist approaches are all essentially similar in that they are strongly *materialist*. Materialist theories are those that see *material* factors such as money, territory, and weapons as driving international politics. Realism focuses primarily on the distribution of military power; economic structuralism centers on the distribution of economic power; liberalism involves both military and economic factors. Even the liberal institutionalist explanation of cooperation is based on a material argument—that concrete incentives will lead to cooperation, even under anarchy.

In contrast, constructivism looks at the powerful role that *ideas* play in international politics. Although they do not deny the importance of material factors such as money and weapons, constructivists argue that the effects of these factors are not predetermined. Instead, the effects of these factors depend on how we think about them. In contrast to the dominant focus (especially in realism and economic structuralism) on *power* in international politics, constructivism seeks to investigate *purpose*—the goals that actors pursue with the power they have, however power is defined.

A simple illustration demonstrates this very sweeping notion. Consider the distribution of nuclear weapons. Presumably, it is important to any country that other countries have as few nuclear weapons as possible. But contrast perspectives on British nuclear weapons with the U.S. perspective on North Korean or Iranian nuclear weapons. Britain has far more nuclear weapons than either of the other two (North Korea may have as many as ten; Iran currently has zero), and yet most countries consider North Korea's tiny arsenal and Iran's potential arsenal to be more threatening than the much larger British arsenal. From a material perspective, this cannot be explained; one nuclear weapon should be just as dangerous as the next. As the constructivist theorist Alexander Wendt points out, variation in the importance of nuclear weapons can be explained only by the fact that the United States considers Iran and North Korea enemies and considers Britain a friend. Friendship and enmity, however, have no basis in the distribution of power.[8] They are *ideas*, existing only in the collective beliefs of populations and leaderships.

There is a huge variety of constructivist approaches, which are not very easily broken down into discernible "schools of thought." Nevertheless, constructivism in general focuses on three key kinds of ideas: interests, identities, and norms.

Interests

Most international relations theories connect actors' interests to their behavior. If we understand actors' interests (their goals) and the constraints they face, then we can predict their behavior. Although realist, liberal, and economic structuralist theories do not agree on who the key actors are or how their interests are derived, they all follow this simple logic. For realism, a state's interest is dictated by its place in the distribution of

Table 4.1 Constructivists assert that the identity of a country, and whether it is perceived as a "friend" or "enemy," is as important as material considerations (such as the number of weapons it possesses) in determining whether the country is seen as a threat or not. The table below shows public opinion in different countries about the threat posed by Iran. How would a constructivist interpret this data?

		Iran's Government: How Much of a Danger to the Region and the World?			
		Great Danger (%)	Moderate Danger (%)	Small or No Danger (%)	Don't Know (%)
United States	2006	46	34	11	9
	2003	26	45	21	8
Germany	2006	51	34	10	5
	2003	18	47	28	8
Spain	2006	38	26	18	18
	2003	11	31	38	20
Great Britain	2006	34	36	16	14
	2003	11	43	34	12
France	2006	31	47	21	1
	2003	11	37	48	4
Russia	2006	20	32	26	22
	2003	8	9	50	33
Japan	2006	29	41	26	5
China	2006	22	28	18	33
India	2006	8	21	35	36
Nigeria	2006	15	23	39	23
	2003	24	17	47	13
Jordan	2006	19	25	56	1
	2003	6	10	66	18
Turkey	2006	16	19	38	27
	2003	11	17	50	22
Egypt	2006	14	20	61	4
Indonesia	2006	7	29	52	13
	2003	9	18	63	10
Pakistan	2006	4	12	37	47
	2003	3	6	57	34

Source: http://pewglobal.org/reports/display.php?PageID=826. Reprinted by permission of The Pew Research Center.

power. In economic structuralism, the interests of actors (whether they are states, classes, firms, or workers) are dictated by the actors' place in the economic hierarchy.

As the example of nuclear weapons previously cited indicates, constructivists find these simple assumptions about interests highly unsatisfactory. Rather than assuming interests and then connecting them to behavior, constructivists ask *where interests come from.* Why does behavioral change often result from relatively minor changes in material factors? Constructivists posit that interests do not follow simply and automatically from material factors such as wealth or weapons. Rather, they find that **interests** are "socially constructed," meaning that groups of people together define what is good and bad and what the goals of society are. One example is the fact that during the Cold War, the United States and most European countries shifted from viewing South Africa as a friend

interests

In constructivist theory, socially constructed goals that groups of people together define for society.

Missiles on Parade in Islamabad, Pakistan. How dangerous are they? Constructivists stress that ideas of friendship and enmity are as important as weapons themselves in creating security and insecurity.

Jewel Samad/AFP/Getty Images

apartheid

A system of official discrimination in South Africa in which the African majority was controlled by the white minority.

and ally to seeing that country as a pariah. As Audie Klotz has shown for the U.S. case, interests changed because attitudes toward South Africa's **apartheid** system changed.[9] Apartheid was dismantled in the 1990s.

Another version of this problem involves how enemies become friends without much change in economic or military factors. For example, how do we explain the emergence of Franco-German friendship after World War II? The two countries had fought three wars in the space of 75 years. Yet, after World War II, leaders in both countries chose to build a fundamentally different kind of relationship. For this to happen, each country had to define its well-being as closely connected to that of the other, rather than seeing the two states' interests as necessarily conflicting. Although some degree of cooperation may be seen as driven by economic and security interests, the extent of European integration since World War II, constructivists argue, can be explained only by the salience of the *idea* of European integration, which came to have a powerful influence.[10]

Identities

identity

In constructivist theory, actors' and others' perceptions of who they are and what their roles are.

Identity, in constructivism, means who the actors are and what they and others perceive their role to be. Realist, liberal, and economic structuralist theories all take the identities of the actors as given: for realists, they are states; for liberals, they range from states to substate and nonstate actors; for economic structuralists, they are classes and states. For constructivists, a key question is how identities change. It stands to reason that as identities change, interests and behavior change as well. Theories that ignore the role of identity, therefore, will miss an important source of change. Two examples help illustrate this argument.

First is the staple of the Westphalian system, the sovereign state. Whereas other approaches take the state as a fundamental and unchanging actor, constructivists assert that, in fact, what it means to be a "sovereign state" changes over time. For example, prior to the seventeenth century, there was no widespread recognition of "state sovereignty" and the rights that accompany it. When states began recognizing each other's sovereignty and legalizing it in the Treaty of Westphalia, they then behaved differently toward each other. If the sovereign state did not always exist, there is no reason to believe that it must always exist or that it must always exist as it did then. For much of the planet, the process of being integrated (usually unwillingly) into the Westphalian system changed the identities of the actors from local, tribal, imperial, or other systems into sovereign states.

Moreover, what it means to be a sovereign state is itself changing. For example, in 1999, United Nations Secretary General Kofi Annan asserted that the doctrine of "noninterference in the internal affairs of sovereign states" was obsolete. He was concerned about the atrocities being committed by various governments against their own citizens. Preserving human rights, he asserted, took a higher priority than noninterference. This may seem like a theoretical point, but it is much easier to gain support for "humanitarian intervention" when doing so does not appear to violate important international principles. Under this new interpretation, armed interventions in Somalia, Bosnia-Herzegovina, and Kosovo in the 1990s were deemed by many to be acceptable. A change in the identity of the sovereign state altered international rules of behavior. In other words, as constructivists stress, ideas matter, and the evolution in the identity of sovereign states matters a lot.

Constructivists also explore identity in a different sense. Other approaches assume that each state has a single identity and that this identity is distinct from that of other states. Constructivists investigate the extent to which different states might develop shared identities. One prominent example is the European Union, where there may exist a "European" identity in addition to the identities of the separate states. The extent to which leaders (and voters) in different European states view themselves as "European" and essentially like one another, constructivists argue, is likely to influence policy positions. In some cases, these merged identities can be formally institutionalized. Europe, for example, has an extensive bureaucratic apparatus in Brussels. In international trade forums such as the WTO, Europe participates not as 27 sovereign states but as a single entity.

The same can be true in a region characterized by conflict. Michael Barnett has shown that alliance patterns among the Arab states are explained more completely by a focus on identity politics than by the balance of power. When identities shifted in response to evolution in the agenda of "Pan-Arabism," alliances shifted as well. Similarly, Barnett argues that the Israel–U.S. alliance is best explained neither by the balance of power nor by domestic politics but by the perception of shared values.[11]

In one of the most widely read (and widely disputed) books in recent years, *The Clash of Civilizations*, Samuel Huntington argues that identity issues are just as likely to create conflict as unity. He hypothesizes that fundamental cultural differences in different parts of the world create a permanent barrier to a further homogenization of global interests.[12] Thus, for example, the wars in the former Yugoslavia in the 1990s, as well as the Rwandan genocide, appear to be about identity conflicts between competing religious, ethnic, and linguistic groups. Moreover, he sees identity differences between Orthodox Christian, Western Christian, Muslim, Buddhist, and other cultural groupings as leading to a "clash of civilizations." Although a bit of scrutiny reveals serious problems with this hypothesis, it has gained adherents because of the seemingly fundamental nature of the conflict between "the West" and "radical Islam" (both

Figure 4.1 Constructivists emphasize the possibilities that international identities can change. This chart shows Europeans' responses to survey questions about whether they identify with Europe, their nation-state, or both. In what ways can these data be used to support or challenge the constructivist perspective?

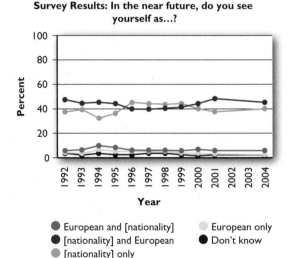

Survey Results: In the near future, do you see yourself as...?

- ● European and [nationality]
- ● [nationality] and European
- ● [nationality] only
- ○ European only
- ● Don't know

Source: Eurobarometer Interactive Search http://ec.europa.eu/public_opinion/cf/ index_en.cfm. Reprinted by permission of EB Team.

The Geography Connection

Identity and Conflict: Clash of Civilizations?

Samuel Huntington is among those scholars who argue that social identity is crucial to relations among states (although many constructivist scholars reject his arguments). The two maps below represent Huntington's assertions about the existence of distinct "civilizations" and about the affinities and tensions between them.

Critical Thinking Questions

1. Does his categorization of "civilizations" make sense? Is there an "African civilization," clearly distinguishable from a "Latin American civilization," and so on?
2. What do these maps tell us about where we should expect conflict in the future? Can they tell us anything about conflict within civilizations?
3. Mapmakers make choices about what information to include and how to present it. What are the relative merits of the two ways of demonstrating Huntington's argument?

Huntington's Map and Diagram of Conflict

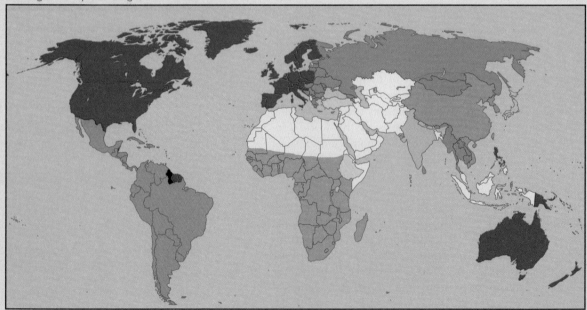

PHOTO © ISTOCKPHOTO

categories defined by identities rather than states). To the extent that Huntington's argument is correct, the source of this conflict would be difficult to understand using theories that treat identity as irrelevant.

Norms

Much of the attention of constructivist approaches has centered on the role of norms in international affairs. **Norms** are defined as shared rules or principles that influence behavior. More specifically, they can be viewed as "collective expectations for the proper behavior of actors."[13] An example of norms discussed previously is the norm of noninterference in the internal affairs of other states. Although it is clear that norms (like any other rules) are sometimes violated, constructivists contend that norms play an important role in shaping behavior, in part because those who violate shared norms pay a price in terms of losing moral influence over others. Therefore, constructivists inquire into both the effects and the causes of norms.

Eleanor Roosevelt, who campaigned for the adoption of the Universal Declaration of Human Rights. To what extent do shared norms such as human rights influence the goals that states and other actors pursue?

In terms of effects, constructivists see norms shaping the way that states define their interests, a key concern in constructivist thought. In terms of causes, constructivists ask how new norms arise and how norms change. Chapter 2 discussed how the norm of noninterference arose from the religious wars of the seventeenth century, and we might explain the decline of this norm in terms of the increasing power of a competing norm in the twentieth century: human rights. The notion of an international commitment to human rights was vaguely held prior to World War II, but the horrors of the genocide that accompanied that conflict led to a series of agreements signaling that states were willing to elevate human rights to a norm that rivaled noninterference in importance.

norms

Shared ethical principles and expectations about how actors should and will behave in the international arena, and social identities, indicating which actors are to be considered legitimate.

Implications of Constructivist Theory

Like realist, liberal, and economic structuralist theories, constructivist theory makes few unambiguous predictions about what will happen in international politics. One important criticism of this theory is that constructivism's main argument, that "ideas matter," provides no general rules about *how* they matter, *when* they matter, or *which* ideas will come to dominate a particular problem.

However, when combined with one of the other perspectives, constructivism can yield practical insights. Liberal theorists see constructivism supporting liberal arguments about the possibility of cooperation in an anarchic world. The notion that internationally shared norms or identities may arise over time would help explain why states find it easier to collaborate than realist theory indicates. Norms and identities may evolve in a way that makes interests overlap more than they have in the past. Norms can help solve the prisoner's dilemma (as when two members of a gang refuse to talk to the police), or they can change the actors' interests so that the situation is no longer a prisoner's dilemma.

Constructivism also has important implications for activists seeking to promote cooperation. If norm change can increase the likelihood of cooperation, then activists can work to promote norms that, if accepted, will likely lead to cooperation on certain issues. Examples of this in recent years include the support by a global network of activists of the **Convention on Anti-Personnel Mines** in 1997 and the movement in various countries

Convention on Anti-Personnel Mines

Also known as the Ottawa Convention. Agreement signed in 1997 and officially known as the "Convention on the Prohibition of the Use, Stockpiling, Production and Transfer of Anti-Personnel Mines and on Their Destruction."

The Culture Connection

Constructivism and Culture

Traditionally, culture was a category often used to explain states' behavior. However assertions that different societies had different "national characters" and that some were more "civilized" than others were rejected by political scientists in the latter half of the twentieth century. These assertions were criticized as biased, unscientific, thinly disguised prejudices. Moreover, because culture is generally viewed as constant, or unchanging, it did not seem well suited to explaining change.

Since the 1990s, "culture" has made a comeback in international relations scholarship, although the term *culture* has been applied in different ways. In one approach, Samuel Huntington's "clash of civilizations" hypothesis presents cultural conflict as the main source of international insecurity in the post-Cold War era. In another approach, those trying to explain the economic success of the rapidly developing economies of East Asia attributed rapid growth to "Asian values," which were alleged to be deference to authority, team versus individual orientation, and hard work.[1] Critics pointed out that, until recently, culture had been seen as a reason Asia (and other regions) did *not* develop. Max Weber's influential work, *The Protestant Ethic and the Spirit of Capitalism* (1905), argued that the Protestant values of Western Europe (including individualism) were the cultural prerequisites for economic success.

Constructivist theory has put culture front and center in scholarly discussions of international politics. A widely read collection of essays entitled *The Culture of National Security*, published in 1996, refined the concept of "culture" in the study of international politics and applied it to security issues—an area to which culture has always appeared least relevant.[2]

The central premise of cultural and constructivist approaches is that "national interests" are not "given" by structural factors, but in fact are constantly in the process of being redefined and are therefore influenced by changing cultures. "Culture," in this approach, is not a constant but rather a variable that helps explain changes in other variables. In this view, culture denotes "collective models of nation-state authority or identity, carried by custom or law."[3]

The essays in the book show that culture, norms, and identity can help explain a range of puzzles in national security affairs, such as the following:

- States tend to build advanced weapons systems that they do not really need because having the most advanced weapons (battleships 100 years ago or fighter aircraft today) helps to establish their identity as advanced states.[4]
- Cultural factors, and military culture in particular, help explain why states sometimes adopt military doctrines that turn out to be woefully inappropriate (as was France's at the outset of World War II).[5]
- A *realpolitik* (realist) approach to international affairs has predominated in China across different leaderships because "cultural realism" predominates in China, not because of anarchy in the international system.[6]

Critical Thinking Questions

1. What role does culture play in the foreign policy of your country?
2. Which (if any) of the arguments described above seem to relate to your country?
3. What important shifts in culture today might portend policy change in the future?

[1] For examples of this view, see Ezra F Vogel, *The Four Little Dragons: The Spread of Industrialization in East Asia* (Cambridge, MA: Harvard University Press, 1991); and Gilbert Rozman, ed., *The East Asian Region: Confucian Heritage and Modern Adaptation* (Princeton, NJ: Princeton University Press, 1991).

[2] Peter J. Katzenstein, ed., *The Culture of National Security: Norms and Identity in World Politics* (New York: Columbia University Press, 1996).

[3] Peter J. Katzenstein, "Introduction: Alternative Perspectives on National Security," in Katzenstein, ed., *The Culture of National Security*, p. 6.

[4] Dana P. Eyre and Mark C. Suchman, "Status, Norms, and the Proliferation of Conventional Weapons: An Institutional Theory Approach," in Katzenstein, ed., *The Culture of National Security*, pp. 79–113.

[5] Elizabeth Kier, "Culture and French Military Doctrine Before World War II," in Katzenstein, ed., *The Culture of National Security*, pp.186–215.

[6] Alistair Iain Johnston, "Cultural Realism and Strategy in Maoist China," in Katzenstein, ed., *The Culture of National Security*, pp. 216–268.

in the 1980s to promote sanctions against South Africa to overcome its apartheid system of institutionalized racism.

For economic structuralist theorists, constructivism helps explain why the exploitative system of global capitalism is so difficult to overthrow. A powerful set of ideas and norms has developed to support the notion that capitalism and international free trade are neutral and fair arrangements that effectively increase global prosperity. Economic structuralist activists fear that these beliefs, which Marx called "false ideology," help convince people that these arrangements are good, even when they cost jobs and depress wages. Therefore, a major goal of many organizations that share economic structuralist views about the global economy is to promote a norm change in order to advance the normative goals of poverty reduction and equality of wealth and to lessen support for the normative goal of free trade.

A significant literature, based in large part on the work of the Marxist theorist Antonio Gramsci, seeks to show that the capitalist system promotes a whole range of ideas that make capitalism appear normal and just.[14] In this view, purpose and power become nearly interchangeable. The ability to influence how goals are defined and what seems "normal" is seen as more powerful than the ability to coerce, because defining the purpose of activities gains the acquiescence of the exploited, without their recognizing that they are being exploited.

For some realists, constructivism is important because it helps explain state goals. These realists recognize that states often have ambitions that are not dictated simply by the distribution of power. Realists operating at the state level consider it crucial to understand whether a powerful state is a "revolutionary" or a "status quo" power. Whether a state is revolutionary- or status quo-oriented does not depend solely or even primarily on the distribution of power. One of Kissinger's crucial arguments was that as the Cold War progressed, the Soviet Union evolved from a revisionist to a status quo power, making it possible to reach agreements on key issues. The British historian E. H. Carr, one of the most prominent realist scholars of the twentieth century, insisted that power alone cannot explain international politics. Studying power, he warned, without studying the *purposes* for which states seek to use power, encourages a dangerously one-dimensional view. He stridently rejected the notion that interests are obvious, "given," or nonproblematic. His realism stems from the argument that we must deal with the world that is, rather than the world we wish to see, but he argues that we must nonetheless be motivated by the world we wish to see. Carr's views are intensely realist, but at the same time, they emphasize the questions raised by constructivists.

Feminist International Relations Theory

Feminist theory has become increasingly influential in the study of all kinds of politics in recent years, and the study of international politics is no exception.[15] Although the field of international relations has been slow to bring feminist perspectives into its mainstream, they have become important in a wide range of issue-oriented subfields, from international security to global development and the environment. Indeed, feminist approaches have had a greater impact in the practice of international politics than in the study of it.[16] Like the other approaches we have examined, feminist theory does not provide a unified, comprehensive approach to understanding international politics, but it does provide an increasingly influential "lens" through which we can examine the practice and theory of international relations. As one feminist scholar asserts: "accurate, rigorous, and ethical scholarship cannot be produced without taking account of women's presence in or the gendering of world politics."[17]

Feminist approaches to politics examine how ideas about **gender** shape political problems and our thinking about them. "Gender" is distinguished from "sex" in that sex

gender

A set of ideas that society has attached to the biological categories of male and female.

is a *biological* category, referring to genetic and physiological traits, whereas gender is a *social construction*—a set of ideas that society has attached to those genetic and physiological traits.[18] Whereas sex is generally defined unambiguously and dichotomously, gender allows for the blending or overlap of different characteristics. In one of the early landmarks of feminist scholarship, Simone de Beauvoir showed how philosophers who shaped much of modern thought, such as Aristotle and Thomas Aquinas, defined "woman" in a way that viewed women's differences from men—both biological and perceived—as imperfections.[19]

There are so many different strands of feminist theory, and they are based on such different assumptions, that it is difficult to treat feminism as a single coherent body of theory. What unites the range of feminist theories is a common belief that international politics cannot be understood without taking gender into account. Feminist theory asserts that mainstream theory is distorted by **gendered ideas**—ideas that artificially distinguish between "masculine" and "feminine" roles. Such gendered ideas, according to feminist theory, include traditional definitions of power, security, the state as a central actor, and the distinction between "high" and "low" politics. Feminist theory is concerned that this "masculinized" theory not only distorts our understanding, but guides our behavior in ways that are destructive, above all to women. All variants of feminist theory also share a normative agenda, improving the status of women, although different strands of theory differ considerably on what constitutes improvement.

Feminists question the tendency to automatically connect "feminine" traits to women and "masculine" traits to men. Moreover, they argue that "masculine" characteristics have usually been viewed as positive, whereas "feminine" characteristics have been seen as less desirable. Several problems result. First, if a set of characteristics is artificially ascribed to women and those characteristics are defined as less desirable or less important, then justification exists for putting women in a subordinate position. In political terms, this results in the widespread discrimination against women throughout history and up to the present day. In scholarly terms, it means that we tend to see those issues that are identified with women as being less important and we therefore tend to ignore them.

Second, the practice of preferring one set of traits (including autonomy, rationality, and aggression) over another (including interdependence, emotion, and pacifism) limits our understanding of international politics. Because we tend to see all actors in masculine terms (power-seeking, competitive, willing to fight), feminists contend, we underestimate the prospects for cooperative or even altruistic behavior. In practical terms, this means that war and conflict are viewed as normal, and collaboration is derided as "utopian" or "idealist." In scholarly terms, it means that international relations theory tends to be based on a series of biased masculine concepts that lead to biased analysis.

gendered ideas

Ideas that take "masculine" perspectives as "normal" and neglect "feminine" perspectives.

"How is it gendered?"

Edward Koren/Cartoonbank.com.

Third, gender distinctions lead to the artificial division of life into a "public" sphere (which is the realm of politics and policy) and a "private" sphere, which is the realm of families (which are traditionally dominated by men). This, feminists contend, causes a whole range of issues of concern to women, including abuse, women's rights, and children's welfare, to be excluded from public discussion. For example, the work women do in raising children is not "counted" in economic statistics and therefore is invisible to policy makers.

Feminist theory in general is often divided into three basic schools of thought, following a typology developed by Sandra Harding (though there are other classification schemes as well).[20] Feminist empiricism focuses on the real issues of women in the real world—including the effects of war and globalization on women—which are often ignored in mainstream scholarship. Feminist standpoint theory goes beyond "women's issues," arguing instead that every issue can be better understood if examined from a "feminine" perspective in addition to the traditional "masculine" perspective. Feminist postmodernism, like other postmodern theory, finds that all attempts to analyze politics are, consciously or not, products of a specific power position. In this view, it is necessary to constantly scrutinize the interests behind even feminist analysis, and it is important to recognize that no single theory will ever be completely valid.

Feminist Empiricism

Feminist scholars and activists note that women have tended to be "invisible" in thinking about international politics. The focus on activities traditionally dominated by males, such as war and diplomacy, has led observers to neglect how international politics profoundly influences spheres typically associated with women, such as raising a family and working low-wage jobs. This emphasis follows a pattern long observed in broader feminist theory: jobs that are identified with women, such as "housewife," are devalued and hidden compared to those associated with men, such as "businessman." Women are neglected subjects.

In one influential study, Cynthia Enloe studied the effects on local women of placing U.S. military bases in foreign countries. She found that the establishment of U.S. military bases in the Philippines changed the entire context of local women's lives. The influx of U.S. soldiers, with a new set of "needs" and the money to pursue them, changed the traditional economic roles of women.[21] In particular, the demand for sex workers skyrocketed. When NATO forces were deployed in Bosnia and then in Kosovo, many young women were led into prostitution through the combination of desperate poverty, organized crime, and high demand by the soldiers for sexual services. These women and their communities became dependent on this economy for their survival. This is but one example of how women's lives are profoundly affected by international politics in ways that few people ever consider.

A related issue is how war affects women. A great deal of attention is given to those, traditionally men, who fight war, but less attention is given to the women and children left behind to survive without those who had previously served as breadwinners. Women left in war zones encounter even greater problems, including frequently being the victims of rape. Sometimes this is an "unintended consequence" of war, but in many cases around the world rape has been used deliberately, as a tactic intended to demoralize and terrorize civilian populations in contested territories.[22] More broadly, feminist scholarship shows how women are increasingly involved in international conflict in roles traditionally assigned to men, including as soldiers, terrorists, insurgents and even war criminals.[23]

Feminist scholars have also studied the individual-level effects of global trade agreements.[24] Because women are often the primary breadwinners in their families and often work in the factories that mass-produce goods for the world market, they are disproportionately affected by changes in global trading rules. Some argue that globalization, by

Figure 4.2 Why are literacy rates different for men and women and why is the gap bigger in some cases than in others? Feminist scholarship tries to understand these differences to assess how much other inequalities (such as those in income and political rights) are linked to inequalities in education.

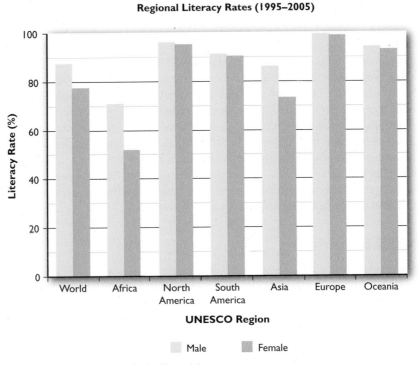

Regional Literacy Rates (1995–2005)

Source: UNESCO Institute for Statistics. Reprinted by permission.

increasing the demand for such labor, will tend to benefit women. Others fear that the competition induced by globalization, combined with weak regulations in many countries, leads to intensified exploitation of women, many of whom are desperate to earn enough to feed their families.

A broad effort in the feminist empiricist agenda is to improve the collection of data on the status of women, to render them less "invisible." One example is the "Woman Stats" project (http://www.womanstats.org), which seeks to collect detailed statistical data on the status of women around the world, and to connect that data with data on the security of states.

Feminist Standpoint Theory

A different strain of feminist theory finds that the assumptions of some theories, especially of realism, are based on gendered views of the world. In particular, they charge that views of human nature as prone to conflict are based on generalizations about "masculine" behavior and ignore "feminine" assumptions about human nature. Human nature, feminists contend, includes traits typically defined as "feminine" as well as those defined as "masculine." These "feminine" traits include nurturing and collaboration, factors that are viewed as inherent in females' roles as mothers, nurturers, and caregivers. To be clear, most feminists do not argue that women are fundamentally different from men, but rather that a group of traits has been excluded from theorizing because these traits have been *artificially* associated with women. This theoretical focus on traits artificially associated with men, feminist standpoint theorists argue, creates bias in international relations theories. "The whole theoretical approach to international relations rests on a foundation of political concepts, most of which would be far more difficult to hold together coherently were it not for the trick of eliminating women from the prevailing definitions of man as political actor."[25]

Feminists assert that, beginning with Thucydides, international relations theory has confused "human nature" with "masculine nature." For example, there is another ancient Greek view of war very different from Thucydides' view that human nature leads to conflict. In the play *Lysistrata* by Aristophanes, the women of Greece's warring city-states refuse to have sex with their husbands until the men end the Peloponnesian War. Modern feminists see this as a refutation of the notion that "mankind" is essentially warlike. Such a view, they say, focuses only on those traits artificially identified as "masculine" and ignores those traits artificially identified as "feminine."

Similarly, the division of life into a "private" women's sphere (the household) on one hand and a "public" men's sphere (the state) on the other creates the necessary basis for conventional views on war and the security dilemma. Because the private household sphere, which is often delegated to women, is excluded from the realm of power politics, the household level costs of war are rarely discussed by policy makers or international relations theory. For example, as feminist empiricists point out, casualty statistics in warfare include killed and injured soldiers, but not the battle deaths of noncombatants, the starvation of children, or the rape of women that almost always accompany war.[26] These costs can be overlooked, feminists stress, only if they are ruled out of consideration prior to the analysis. More broadly, the notion of the "state," on which so much international relations theory relies, itself relies on an artificial separation of private and public that feminists argue is gender-based and gender-biased.[27] The study of international politics therefore misses not only the violence done to women in war, but also the fact that even more violence is done to women within the everyday confines of the family, an arena that is considered "private" and therefore beyond the concern of political analysis.

We might then ask, what view of international politics would have emerged over the centuries had Thucydides written—rather than "of gods we believe and of men we know, it is their nature to rule whenever they can"—"of women we know and of goddesses we trust, it is in their nature to work together whenever they can"? Had this view been advanced in Thucydides' influential text and picked up by later theorists, feminists speculate, both our understanding of international affairs and our conduct of it might be quite different.[28]

Scrutinizing more recent literature, J. Ann Tickner shows how Hans Morgenthau's principles of realism (discussed in Chapter 3) are based on gendered notions of what is "natural." Tickner then reformulates Morgenthau's principles to show how nongendered assumptions lead to a very different kind of international relations theory.[29] Reformulating Morgenthau's definition of power as "man's control over the minds and actions of other men,"[30] Tickner provides a perspective that emphasizes context and contingency more than universal law; gives no single definition of power, viewing power as varying with context; views all action as having moral implications, rather than putting morality aside; and obscures the boundaries of what is political and what is nonpolitical.[31] To cite just one specific example, Tickner asserts that the threat to survival posed by poverty should be considered as important as the danger that arises from weapons.[32]

In contrast to the common understanding of "power" as the ability of one actor to compel another to do something he or she does not wish to do, some feminist scholars define "power" as the ability of two or more actors to work together to achieve what they cannot achieve alone.[33] In other words, the ability to solve the prisoner's dilemma—and get the higher payoffs associated with mutual cooperation—can be thought of as a form of power within a group.

A Kurdish family fleeing from Iraq to Iran. Feminist scholarship points out that the role of women in war is often ignored by casualty figures that focus only on combatants, who historically have been overwhelmingly male. What costs do women pay as they are caught on the battlefield or left behind to fend for themselves and their children?

AP Photo/Sayyad

With power viewed this way, "power politics" and collaboration do not look contradictory. This strand of thinking overlaps with liberal theories of all varieties.[34] Liberal feminists are concerned that the lack of emphasis on the possibility of collaboration becomes a self-fulfilling prophecy. If people are convinced that cooperation is limited and that they must constantly be ready for conflict, they will be less likely to put effort into cooperative solutions.

Feminist Postmodernism

Postmodernism is a broad school of thought that is skeptical of all claims to objective truth. Postmodernists find that all inquiry is biased by the questions asked (and the questions ignored), the assumptions made, and the way evidence is interpreted. Therefore, they stress that all knowledge is partial at best and that all knowledge serves someone's interest (and therefore tends to oppress someone else). Feminist postmodernism shares its basic concerns with other forms of feminist international relations scholarship: namely, a focus on the consequences of hidden gender biases and a normative concern with emancipation. However, it frames the problem in a very different way, which in important respects leads it to contradict feminist empiricism and feminist standpoint theory. Like other postmodern approaches, feminist postmodernism rejects the possibility of creating a more truthful analysis, a possibility that both feminist empiricism and feminist standpoint theory embrace.

From the postmodernist perspective, *all* claims about truth, and especially claims about truth involving social relations, are social constructions. Therefore, the goal of feminist empiricists and standpoint theorists to create a more complete or accurate

Figure 4.3 Western liberal approaches to human rights emphasize equality of the sexes. Postmodern feminists argue that this may impose Western values on other cultures, including on their women. In recent decades, Turkey's focus on secular values has led it to forbid women from wearing the traditional head scarf. Does this liberate women or oppress them? This graph shows Turkish women's responses to survey questions on Muslim dress.

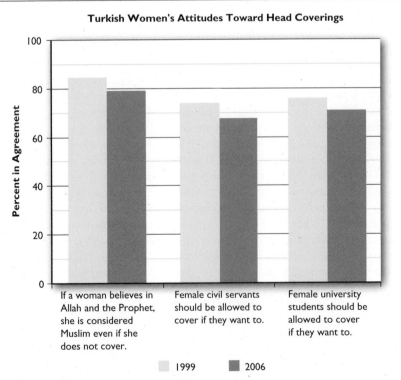

Turkish Women's Attitudes Toward Head Coverings

theory of international politics is rejected by postmodernists. Where standpoint theorists argue that our view of reality has been distorted because it focuses on the masculine at the expense of the feminine, postmodern theorists insist that the categories "masculine" and "feminine," and all other categories of analysis, are artificial constructions.

Postmodern feminists worry that analyses based on "improved" understandings of gender may themselves become part of a more subtle pattern of oppression. Two specific examples of this type of argument help illustrate this point.

Feminist empiricists and standpoint theorists agree that certain aspects of women's oppression in poor countries ought to get more attention, but cannot because of the way the discipline of international relations is constructed. Postmodern feminists raise two different kinds of concerns about these arguments. First, by dwelling on oppression based on gender, such analysis naturally gives less attention to oppression based on race, class, and colonial status. For many postmodern analysts, gender is merely one dimension in a broader pattern of oppression, and to separate it out from others is to reflect the bias of white, wealthy women from states that were colonizers rather than colonized. More broadly, Jean Bethke Elshtain cautions feminists against too ardently identifying "feminine" qualities with peace, because doing so subtly reinforces the binary categories of good and bad on which all oppression—including the oppression of women—is based.[35]

Second, and perhaps more vexing, is the assumption, implicit in feminist empiricism and standpoint theory, that clear judgments can be made about what constitutes oppression of women. For example, many feminists in Western countries take it for granted that practices such as the veiling of women, the restriction of women's political rights, and female genital mutilation are violations of women's rights and ought to be stopped. Postmodern scholars reject all universal statements about moral values and consider whether women in other cultures, with different moral codes, might be more oppressed by having to conform to Western standards of morality than by having to conform to their own culture's standards. For example, are Muslim girls in France liberated or oppressed by laws forbidding them to cover their heads in schools?

This sort of argument has led many to argue that postmodernism in general, and postmodern feminism in particular, goes too far. The notion that all truth and all moral views are socially constructed, critics point out, brings us to a situation in which we cannot say anything about truth and have no basis for deciding what we should agree upon. Most postmodernists reject this critique. They assert that greater understanding can be reached by constantly "deconstructing" claims of truth to uncover hidden biases and their potential to be used for oppression. The postmodernists' point is not that there is no truth, but that there are multiple truths. These truths depend on how questions are framed, and even more so on which issues are considered central (and therefore are "foregrounded") and which are considered less important (and therefore are left in the "background").

AP Photo/Alexander Zemlianichenko

Afghan women at a Persian New Year celebration. Many Western advocates find that laws requiring women to cover their entire bodies are discriminatory. Postmodern feminists ask whether it is not equally oppressive for Western advocates to force their own standards on women in other societies. Are universal notions of rights themselves an element of oppression?

Feminist Influence

Feminist approaches to international relations are gradually being integrated into the field. For example, in debates on two major trends in international

The Policy Connection

Women, Development, and Democratization: Applying Feminist Theory

Feminist theories of international relations remain on the edge of the mainstream, and few general policy discussions explicitly take a feminist perspective. However, feminist approaches to international politics have been influential in at least two important areas of policy: development and democratization.

In development, feminist studies have highlighted two related phenomena: the combination of economic and social exploitation that women face and the central role women play in the economic welfare of poverty-stricken populations in the world. Women are marginalized by being forced to become the primary caregivers for children. When war, disease, migration, or other causes have removed fathers from the scene, women filled the function of sole breadwinner as well as sole caregiver. At the same time, however, they tend to be excluded from many profitable areas of the economy and to be paid less than men for the work they do. The poverty of women has a disproportionate effect on children, and thus on the next generation of adult economic actors.

Feminists and development scholars have argued that if children's poverty is to be reduced and if children are to be nourished and educated in a way that improves their economic prospects, women, not men, are the best targets for aid programs. Until relatively recently, however, most programs were aimed at men, as the presumed main economic actors in societies. Two examples of programs that target women are micro-lending programs, for which Muhammed Yunus and the Grameen Bank won the 2006 Nobel Peace Prize, and the efforts to bring girls' education levels up to those of boys (efforts that have been difficult to implement in some societies with strict traditional limits on girls' education).

A second area in which women have been identified as important keys to success is democratization. Many democracy support programs led by Western states have strongly emphasized women's participation. One goal is simply to reduce the traditional disadvantages that women in every country face in political participation. In some cases, participation of women in a system previously closed to them is seen as a means to transform a system that is resistant to democratic norms. Thus, external actors insisted that women be given an increased role in the new institutions put into place in Afghanistan after the Taliban government was ejected in 2001. Such policies highlight the tensions between postmodern feminism and other variants. Postmodernists are more wary of insisting on the universality of Western notions of democracy and of the proper role of women in politics, and therefore give more credence to those women who say that they do not believe that women and men should play the same roles and who do not want to do so.

The influence of feminism on policy should not be exaggerated; women remain economically exploited and politically marginalized around the world. Still, feminism has influenced policy and served as a "practical" approach to international politics.

Critical Thinking Questions

1. In looking at public policy in general, should feminist approaches get more attention than they do now? What problems might be more effectively addressed by feminist approaches? What issues might not benefit from a greater focus on feminism?
2. What aspects of feminist thought seem most valuable in policy making?
3. Should Western countries promote universal values of women's rights or should they accept the argument that women in some countries might be more liberated by being free to choose a limited political, economic, and social role?

affairs today, democratization and development, the pivotal role of women has come to be widely accepted. Efforts to spread democracy have increasingly been premised on the notion that women, who in many respects have the most to gain from increased freedom, can be important advocates for democracy. Similarly, many development schemes have targeted the particular roles of women in developing economies. More significant is an increasing recognition that feminist approaches are not just about women—that the entire field, and all the issues it contains, are better understood when the role of gender is taken into account.

Comparing the Paradigms

To restate an important point: the five paradigms discussed in this book should be viewed as different tools for understanding international politics, not as ideological positions among which one must choose. There are important overlaps among the different approaches as well as contradictions.

Realism and Liberalism

Realism and liberalism, and particularly liberal institutionalism, share a great deal. Realism and liberal institutionalism make the same assumptions concerning the

Table 4.2 Paradigms of International Politics

	Main Variants	Essential Concepts	Key Actors	Key Processes	Normative Commitment
Realism	Balance of power theory, hegemonic stability theory	Anarchy, self-help, security dilemma	States	Changes in the distribution of power, internal and external balancing	State interest should be priority; protect the state rather than improve the world
Liberalism	Liberal institutionalism	Anarchy, security dilemma, cooperation	States	Cooperation to overcome problems of anarchy	Promote collaboration to bring peace and prosperity
	Complex interdependence theory	Multiple actors, multiple goals, nonhierarchical interests	Wide range of actors	Emergence of a complex web of cooperative relationships	
Economic structuralism		Surplus value of labor, division of gains from trade, inequality	Classes (owners of capital and workers), states	Unequal bargaining, imperialism, widening of inequality	Reduce economic and political inequality
Constructivism	Many variants, none dominant	Ideas, interests, identities, norms	States, NGOs that try to shape norms	Evolution of new interests, norms, identities	Varies; compatible with others
Feminism	Empiricism, standpoint theory, postmodernism	Gender, gender hierarchy, partial truth	Marginalized people, especially women; reproducers of gender hierarchy	Creation of gender bias; oppression; revealing of gender bias,	Liberation of women; less masculinized view of world politics

Figure 4.4 Timeline of Communism and Socialism

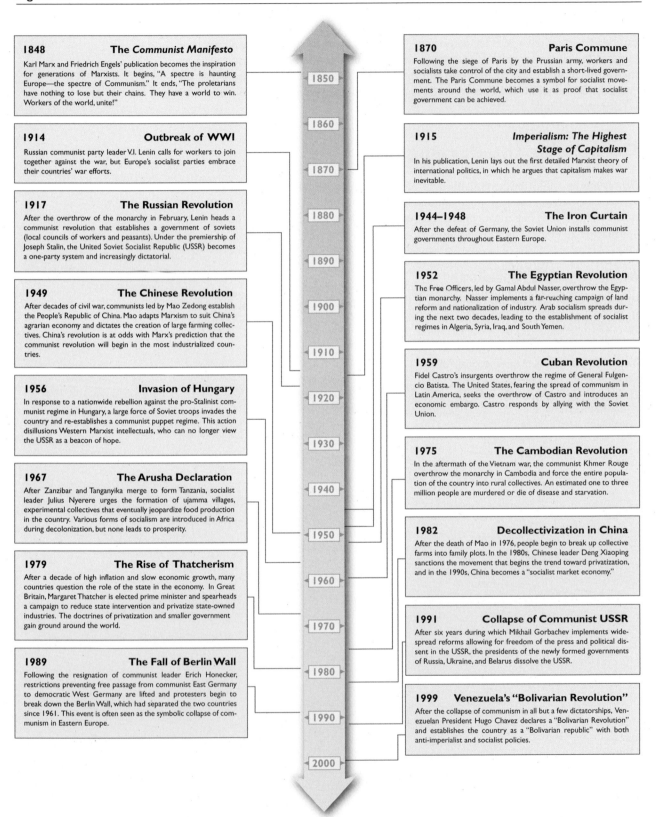

1848   **The *Communist Manifesto***

Karl Marx and Friedrich Engels' publication becomes the inspiration for generations of Marxists. It begins, "A spectre is haunting Europe—the spectre of Communism." It ends, "The proletarians have nothing to lose but their chains. They have a world to win. Workers of the world, unite!"

1914   **Outbreak of WWI**

Russian communist party leader V.I. Lenin calls for workers to join together against the war, but Europe's socialist parties embrace their countries' war efforts.

1917   **The Russian Revolution**

After the overthrow of the monarchy in February, Lenin heads a communist revolution that establishes a government of soviets (local councils of workers and peasants). Under the premiership of Joseph Stalin, the United Soviet Socialist Republic (USSR) becomes a one-party system and increasingly dictatorial.

1949   **The Chinese Revolution**

After decades of civil war, communists led by Mao Zedong establish the People's Republic of China. Mao adapts Marxism to suit China's agrarian economy and dictates the creation of large farming collectives. China's revolution is at odds with Marx's prediction that the communist revolution will begin in the most industrialized countries.

1956   **Invasion of Hungary**

In response to a nationwide rebellion against the pro-Stalinist communist regime in Hungary, a large force of Soviet troops invades the country and re-establishes a communist puppet regime. This action disillusions Western Marxist intellectuals, who can no longer view the USSR as a beacon of hope.

1967   **The Arusha Declaration**

After Zanzibar and Tanganyika merge to form Tanzania, socialist leader Julius Nyerere urges the formation of ujamma villages, experimental collectives that eventually jeopardize food production in the country. Various forms of socialism are introduced in Africa during decolonization, but none leads to prosperity.

1979   **The Rise of Thatcherism**

After a decade of high inflation and slow economic growth, many countries question the role of the state in the economy. In Great Britain, Margaret Thatcher is elected prime minister and spearheads a campaign to reduce state intervention and privatize state-owned industries. The doctrines of privatization and smaller government gain ground around the world.

1989   **The Fall of Berlin Wall**

Following the resignation of communist leader Erich Honecker, restrictions preventing free passage from communist East Germany to democratic West Germany are lifted and protesters begin to break down the Berlin Wall, which had separated the two countries since 1961. This event is often seen as the symbolic collapse of communism in Eastern Europe.

1870   **Paris Commune**

Following the siege of Paris by the Prussian army, workers and socialists take control of the city and establish a short-lived government. The Paris Commune becomes a symbol for socialist movements around the world, which use it as proof that socialist government can be achieved.

1915   ***Imperialism: The Highest Stage of Capitalism***

In his publication, Lenin lays out the first detailed Marxist theory of international politics, in which he argues that capitalism makes war inevitable.

1944–1948   **The Iron Curtain**

After the defeat of Germany, the Soviet Union installs communist governments throughout Eastern Europe.

1952   **The Egyptian Revolution**

The Free Officers, led by Gamal Abdul Nasser, overthrow the Egyptian monarchy. Nasser implements a far-reaching campaign of land reform and nationalization of industry. Arab socialism spreads during the next two decades, leading to the establishment of socialist regimes in Algeria, Syria, Iraq, and South Yemen.

1959   **Cuban Revolution**

Fidel Castro's insurgents overthrow the regime of General Fulgencio Batista. The United States, fearing the spread of communism in Latin America, seeks the overthrow of Castro and introduces an economic embargo. Castro responds by allying with the Soviet Union.

1975   **The Cambodian Revolution**

In the aftermath of the Vietnam war, the communist Khmer Rouge overthrow the monarchy in Cambodia and force the entire population of the country into rural collectives. An estimated one to three million people are murdered or die of disease and starvation.

1982   **Decollectivization in China**

After the death of Mao in 1976, people begin to break up collective farms into family plots. In the 1980s, Chinese leader Deng Xiaoping sanctions the movement that begins the trend toward privatization, and in the 1990s, China becomes a "socialist market economy."

1991   **Collapse of Communist USSR**

After six years during which Mikhail Gorbachev implements widespread reforms allowing for freedom of the press and political dissent in the USSR, the presidents of the newly formed governments of Russia, Ukraine, and Belarus dissolve the USSR.

1999   **Venezuela's "Bolivarian Revolution"**

After the collapse of communism in all but a few dictatorships, Venezuelan President Hugo Chavez declares a "Bolivarian Revolution" and establishes the country as a "Bolivarian republic" with both anti-imperialist and socialist policies.

1850 / 1860 / 1870 / 1880 / 1890 / 1900 / 1910 / 1920 / 1930 / 1940 / 1950 / 1960 / 1970 / 1980 / 1990 / 2000

centrality of states as actors and the problems created by anarchy. They disagree primarily on the extent to which states are able to transcend these problems through collaboration. Complex interdependence theorists sometimes disagree almost as much with liberal institutionalists as they do with realists. Whereas liberal institutionalism and realism both focus on the state, complex interdependence theory sees the state as only one actor among many in international politics. They also argue that divisions within the state make treating the state as a unified actor a dubious proposition.

Liberalism versus Economic Structuralism

Liberalism and economic structuralism agree to a large extent about how the world works but disagree on their normative assessment of the current system. Economic structuralism's emphasis on economic motivations is compatible with any version of liberalism. Economic structuralism and complex interdependence theory share the view that many actors have an influence over the state, although the economic structuralists' focus on large corporations is narrower than that of complex interdependence theory. Paradoxically, economic structuralism sees even more cooperation in today's world than does liberalism. What economic structuralism and all versions of liberalism disagree on is whether this cooperation is a good thing—whether it leads to increased good for everyone or to exploitation of the poor by the rich. Liberals assume that cooperation is a good thing. Economic structuralist theorists are skeptical of, and perhaps even hostile to, this cooperation. They view most international cooperation between rich states as collaboration at the expense of the poor. And when the rich cooperate with the poor, economic structuralist theorists contend, the gains from cooperation are divided disproportionately in favor of the rich.

Realism versus Economic Structuralism

In its views of relations between the strong and the weak, economic structuralism is compatible with realism. When economic structuralism identifies states rather than classes as the primary actors, or when realism analyzes strong/weak interactions rather than great power politics, the two paradigms are very compatible.[36] The primary differences are in how the paradigms define power, their assessments of whether the international system can change, and their normative prescriptions. Whereas economic structuralists hope to transform a system they see as inherently unfair, realists assert that the system cannot be changed and that efforts should be applied to winning the competition, not changing the game.

Constructivism versus Realism

Constructivism is not compatible with the dominant strands of realism today, which place a heavy emphasis on inferring interests directly from the structure of the system. Constructivism is more compatible with older versions of realism, which consider intentions, along with capabilities, to be important variables in determining how states behave. Realists of all kinds are highly skeptical of the notion that agreed upon norms can have an important effect on state behavior. Such norms will be followed, they contend, only when doing so serves other state interests. Realists assert that when vital security or economic goals are at risk, states will not be constrained by shared norms.

Constructivism versus Liberalism

In terms of specific assumptions, constructivism clashes with liberalism, and especially with liberal institutionalism. Liberal institutionalism bases its arguments on the notion that state interests can be objectively determined from the structure of the international system. This contrasts with constructivism's argument that structures do not determine interests, which must be investigated directly. Liberalism and constructivism are compatible, however, in that liberals view constructivism as supporting their arguments. Although the factors highlighted by constructivism can lead to conflict as well as to cooperation, liberals assert that the possibility that shared interests, identities, and norms can lead to cooperation further boosts their case against realism.

Constructivism versus Economic Structuralism

A strict Marxist version of economic structuralism holds that only material factors (for example, money) influence actors' behavior and that ideas and beliefs are dictated by economic interest. However, a great many theorists inspired by economic structuralism would take a less strictly materialist position and include ideologies as part of the structure of domination. This type of argument is compatible with constructivism, because it sees beliefs and ideas as contingent on many factors, and not just determined by material factors. In fact, this is the dominant strand of post-Marxist thought today. Like liberally inclined constructivists, post-Marxist constructivists seek to change ideas in order to change outcomes. In particular, they hope to help workers to overcome national identities, which, in the economic structuralist view, allow workers in different countries to be pitted against one another rather than joined in their common interest.

The Feminist Critique

It is useful to look at feminism and the other four paradigms together because some interesting connections become clear. The discussion of feminism highlighted feminist theory's rejection of the basic tenets of realism, including the anarchic nature of the system, the view of the state as an unproblematic concept, and the focus on conflict. A basic argument by many feminist standpoint theorists is that realist theory, with its masculine bias, overestimates the likelihood of conflict and underestimates the potential for collaboration. The realist definition of power in terms of compelling others, rather than cooperating with them, contributes to this bias. Therefore, feminist standpoint theorists tend to line up with liberal institutionalists in their argument that cooperation is more likely, and indeed more evident, than realists let on.[37] Similarly, the feminist insistence that theorists not dwell on one set of actors or issues to the exclusion of others fits well with complex interdependence theory.

The relationship between feminism and economic structuralism is more complex. Orthodox Marxism finds that all oppression is, at its root, economic oppression. In this view, gender bias is part of the broader pattern of economic oppression that is characteristic of capitalism.[38] Although some might debate the exact relationship of economic and gender oppression, there is considerable compatibility between most economic structuralist and feminist thought.

A great deal of feminist theory is also consistent with constructivist analysis. The idea that many categories of analysis are socially constructed is shared by both constructivist and feminist scholars; feminist scholars simply examine one particular way in which social construction leads to bias. Feminist standpoint theory in particular is in many respects a constructivist approach. Just as there are postmodern versions of feminism, there are some theorists who consider themselves both constructivist and postmodernist. Like feminist standpoint theorists, many constructivists reject the radical postmodern position that all knowledge is contingent.

Reconsider the Case

Resurgent Socialism in Latin America

By mid-2010, the three leaders of Latin America's leftward turn, Hugo Chavez of Venezuela, Evo Morales of Bolivia, and Rafael Correa of Ecuador, had all moved to strengthen their political positions by limiting political competition. But each faced increasing dissatisfaction, largely the result of economic problems. All three leaders had based generous social welfare policies on the revenues from booming global energy markets, but after petroleum prices fell and the effects of nationalization took hold, the revenue that was generated decreased.

In Venezuela, Hugo Chavez's "Bolivarian Revolution" stumbled when high oil prices, on which lavish government spending was based, collapsed in 2008. Chavez's popularity was based on a huge reduction in poverty during his presidency, but those gains were threatened. Even as the rest of Latin American rebounded from the recession, Venezuela did not, and wages in 2010 were 15 percent below their 2007 level. Critics argued that Chavez's policies quashed the private business on which the economy depended, and that, in particular, driving out international oil companies led to lower profits from the most important sector in the economy. Thus, despite Venezuela's status as a global energy powerhouse, the government had to introduce rationing in 2010.[39]

In Bolivia, Evo Morales extended nationalization of key industries, but the popularity of the measure seemed to decrease over time. By 2010, Morales' traditional supporters in the labor unions were striking to protest wage increases they saw as too small. Morales hoped that by nationalizing the electricity generating companies, he could please workers by reducing power costs. An important concern for the future will be whether nationalized power companies can increase generating capacity to feed a growing economy.[40]

In Ecuador, dissatisfaction with the government of Rafael Correa increased with economic problems. Nationalizing oil companies helped fund social spending, as did defaulting on the nation's debt, and both were popular. However, oil companies responded by reducing their investment, causing a decrease in oil output and therefore government revenues. Workers, generally Correa's strongest supporters, became frustrated at the slow pace with which wages grew. Ecuador faced the prospect of borrowing to meet its budget, and Correa's popularity plummeted from 72 to 42 percent.[41]

Despite the problems these countries have run into, many continue to support the governments' policies, finding that the efforts to reduce poverty and to distribute wealth more equitably are worth the problems they have encountered. The question for these countries (as for many more capitalistically inclined welfare states), is whether these policies will be economically and politically sustainable.

Critical Thinking Questions

1. How might a constructivist scholar or a feminist scholar interpret the case of socialism in Latin America differently than an economic structuralist?

2. How might a realist explain the international economic problems confronted by states such as Bolivia, Ecuador, and Venezuela and their policies of nationalization?

3. Which aspects of economic structuralism resonate most strongly with you? What sorts of policy prescriptions might emerge from them?

Summary

This chapter has shown that there are multiple approaches to understanding international politics. This makes it difficult for the student because almost every question has more than one answer. But it also makes international politics a fascinating subject because students, citizens, and leaders must continuously evaluate these debates and their application to the pressing issues of the day.

This book addresses five broad schools of thought, but there are other perspectives as well. Many scholars avoid altogether the very broad questions addressed in this chapter. Instead of asking about the nature of international politics, some instead ask about the nature of presidential decision making or the links between public opinion and foreign policy. Such perspectives essentially maintain that system level generalizations, such as those advanced by the approaches considered here, are of less importance than the more immediate causes of international behavior.

A favorite essay question in courses on international politics is "Which approach is best?" Similarly, students often want to pick a school of thought with which to identify. Doing so, however, to some extent misses the point. The point is not to establish a single ideology and defend it, but to understand how each of these approaches contributes distinct insight into international politics. Each provides different insights than the others, so it is more important to be able to flexibly apply different approaches to the problems one encounters than to become a die-hard advocate for any one of them.

Key Concepts

1. Surplus value
2. Class
3. Structural power
4. Capital and labor
5. Economic determinism
6. Materialist versus constructivist theories
7. Social construction
8. Interests, identities, norms
9. "Sex" versus "gender"
10. Feminist empiricism
11. Feminist standpoint theory
12. Postmodernism

Study Questions

1. How does economic structuralisms normative position differ from that of liberalism?
2. What does economic structuralism predict will happen to gaps in wealth?
3. How do economic structuralists explain the outbreak of war?
4. How do economic structuralists view the role of international organizations?
5. How does the constructivist understanding of the Westphalian system differ from the realist understanding?
6. How does the constructivist approach to interests differ from those of realism and economic structuralism?
7. How can changes in identity influence international politics?
8. In what ways can constructivism complement realist, liberal, and economic structuralist approaches?
9. In what ways do feminist approaches find conventional international relations theories insufficient?
10. What are the differences between empiricist, standpoint, and postmodern versions of feminist international relations theory?
11. What different understandings of "power" do feminist theorists offer?

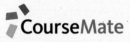

Endnotes

1. See Jorge G. Castaneda, "Latin America's Left Turn," *Foreign Affairs,* Vol. 85, No. 3 (May-June 2006): 28ff.

2. Quoted in "What Revolution?" *The Economist,* October 7, 2004.

3. "Chavez: Bush 'devil'; U.S. 'on the way down,' " CNN.com, September 21, 2006, at http://www.cnn.com/2006/WORLD/americas/09/20/chavez.un/index.html

4. "Correa's Victory, *The Economist,* October 6, 2007.

5. In some texts, this school of thought is labeled "Marxism." I do not use that label in part because it is such a politically loaded term and in part because it is somewhat meaningless to many people today. Also, there are important parts of Marxist theory that are soundly rejected by most contemporary economic structuralists, most notably the philosophy of historical materialism. At the same time, there are important contemporary theories that are Marxist but are not structural or even materialist, most notably Gramscian approaches. I have chosen the label "economic structuralism" because it simply describes the content of the approach and therefore should help readers grasp the concepts.

6. Karl Marx, *The Grundrisse,* excerpted and translated in Robert C. Tucker, ed., *The Marx-Engels Reader,* 2nd ed. (New York: W. W. Norton, 1978), pp. 247–250.

7. This thesis was developed by the English economist John Hobson, in *Imperialism* (1902), and was given an explicitly Marxist formulation in Vladimir Lenin's *Imperialism: The Highest Stage of Capitalism* (1916).

8. Alexander Wendt, "Anarchy Is What States Make of It: The Social Construction of Power Politics," *International Organization,* Vol. 46, No. 2 (Spring 1992): 391–425.

9. Audie Klotz, *Norms in International Relations: The Struggle against Apartheid* (Ithaca, NY: Cornell University Press, 1995).

10. Craig Parsons, "Showing Ideas as Causes: The Origins of the European Union," *International Organization,* Vol. 56, No. 1 (Winter, 2002): 47–84.

11. Michael Barnett, "Identity and Alliances in the Middle East," in Peter J. Katzenstein, ed., *The Culture of National Security: Norms and Identity in World Politics* (Ithaca, NY: Cornell University Press, 1996), pp. 400–447.

12. Samuel Huntington, *The Clash of Civilizations and the Remaking of World Order* (New York: Simon and Schuster, 1996).

13. Peter J. Katzenstein, "Introduction: Alternative Perspectives on National Security," in Katzenstein, ed., *The Culture of National Security,* p. 5.

14. For an example of this approach, see Mark Rupert, *Ideologies of Globalization: Contending Visions of a New World Order* (London: Routledge, 2000).

15. I am grateful to Laura Sjoberg for the detailed critique she provided on this section.

16. Laura Sjoberg, "Introduction to *Security Studies*: Feminist Contributions," *Security Studies* 18 (2009): 185.

17. Sjoberg, "Introduction to *Security Studies*," p. 186.

18. The classic exposition of this idea is in Simone de Beauvoir, *The Second Sex,* trans. and ed. H. M. Parshley (New York: Vintage, 1989) [originally published 1949].

19. de Beauvoir, *The Second Sex,* p. xxii.

20. See Sandra Harding, *The Science Question in Feminism* (Ithaca, NY: Cornell University Press, 1986). Harding's typology is applied to international relations by Christine Sylvester, *Feminist Theory and International Relations in a Postmodern Era* (Cambridge: Cambridge University Press, 1994), Chapter 1, pp. 30–67. Laura Sjoberg provides a different typology, identifying feminist approaches according to how they overlap with other perspectives (realist, liberal, constructivist, etc.). See Sjobert, "Introduction to *Security Studies*: Feminist Contributions," pp. 183–213.

21. Cynthia Enloe, *Bananas, Beaches and Bases: Making Feminist Sense of International Politics* (Berkeley: University of California Press, 1990).

22. See: Claudia Card, "Rape as a Weapon of War," *Hypatia* 11, no. 4 (Fall 1996): 5–18.

23. See Laura Sjoberg and Caron E. Gentry, *Mothers, Monsters, Whores: Women's Violence in Global Politics* (London: Zed Books, 2007).

24. See Jill Steans, *Gender and International Relations: An Introduction* (New Brunswick, NJ: Rutgers University Press, 1998), Chapter 6, pp. 130–157; and Leslie Salzinger, *Genders in Production: Making Workers in Mexico's Global Factories* (Berkeley: University of California Press, 2003).

25. Rebecca Grant, "The Sources of Gender Bias in International Relations Theory," in Rebecca Grant and Kathleen Newland, eds., *Gender and International Relations* (Bloomington: Indiana University Press, 1990), p. 9.

26. Sylvester, *Feminist Theory and International Relations in a Postmodern Era,* p. 36.

27. Steans, *Gender and International Relations: An Introduction,* pp. 46–53.

28. See Grant, "Sources of Gender Bias," p. 15.

29. J. Ann Tickner, "Hans Morgenthau's Principles of Political Realism: A Feminist Reformulation," *Millennium: Journal of International Studies,* Vol. 17, No. 3 (1998): 429–440.

30. Hans J. Morgenthau, *Power Among Nations: The Struggle for Power and Peace*, 5th Ed. (New York: Alfred A. Knopf, 1978), p. 28.

31. Tickner, "Hans Morgenthau's Principles of Political Realism" pp. 437–438.

32. Tickner, "Hans Morgenthau's Principles of Political Realism" p. 435.

33. Hannah Arendt, *On Violence* (New York: Harcourt Brace and World, 1969), p. 44, cited in Tickner, "Hans Morgenthau's Principles of Political Realism" p. 434.

34. This connection is made explicit and developed in Robert O. Keohane, "International Relations Theory: Contributions of a Feminist Standpoint," *Millennium: Journal of International Studies,* Vol. 18, No. 2 (1989): 245–253.

35. Jean Bethke Elshtain, "The Problem with Peace," *Millennium: Journal of International Studies*, Vol. 17, No. 3 (1988): 441–449.

36. The links between realism and Marxism are stressed by two prominent realists, Albert Hirschman and Robert Gilpin. See Albert O. Hirschman, "Beyond Asymmetry: Critical Notes on Myself as a Young Man and on Some Other Old Friends," *International Organization*, Vol. 32, No. 1 (Winter 1978): 45; and Robert Gilpin, *The Political Economy of International Relations* (Princeton: Princeton University Press, 1986), p. 42. Robert O. Keohane, generally regarded as a proponent of liberal international relations theory, makes a similar point in *After Hegemony: Collaboration and Discord in the World Political Economy* (Princeton, NJ: Princeton University Press, 1984), p. 44.

37. See, for example, Tickner, "Hans Morgenthau's Principles of Political Realism," and Keohane, "International Relations Theory: Contributions of a Feminist Standpoint."

38. Steans, *Gender and International Relations: An Introduction,* p. 18.

39. "Feeling the Heat," *The Economist*, May 13, 2010.

40. "Power Grab," *The Economist*, May 6, 2010.

41. "Smile Turns to Frown," *The Economist*, January 14, 2010.

5

The State, Society, and Foreign Policy

LEARNING OBJECTIVES

After completing this chapter, the student should be able to ...

1. Explain democratic peace theory and the major arguments in support of it.
2. Evaluate the arguments and evidence for and against the theory.
3. Identify the links between democratic peace theory and foreign policy.
4. Understand the influence of state structure on foreign policy.
5. Articulate different views on the role of public opinion in foreign policy.
6. Evaluate the interaction between public opinion, media, and government in making foreign policy.

◄ Students in Madison, Wisconsin, demonstrate against the Vietnam War.
AP Photo

Consider the Case

War in Iraq and Democratization in the Middle East

"The United States has adopted a new policy, a forward strategy of freedom in the Middle East. This strategy requires the same persistence and strategy as we have shown before. And it will yield the same results. As in Europe, as in Asia, as in every region of the world, the advance of freedom leads to peace."[1] In this 2003 speech, U.S. President George W. Bush linked the promotion of democracy to peace, not only in theory, but in policy. The United States had recently invaded Iraq, and at the time of the speech, many were still optimistic that the United States might soon leave a functioning democracy in place there.

In many respects, Bush's policy of democracy promotion fit into a long U.S. tradition. His predecessor, Bill Clinton, had stated: "Ultimately, the best strategy to ensure our security and to build durable peace is to support the advance of democracy elsewhere."[2] Woodrow Wilson had made democracy promotion a central goal of U.S. involvement in World War I, and the installation of working democracies in post–World War II Japan and Germany was seen as a great triumph. Democrat Jimmy Carter had increased emphasis on human rights, and Republican Ronald Reagan had started the National Endowment for Democracy. What was new, however, was the argument that the benefits of democracy were reason to use war to overthrow nondemocratic regimes.

The 2003 U.S.-led invasion of Iraq was motivated by various factors, but among the most important was the goal of transforming Middle East politics by introducing democracy to the region. U.S. leaders believed that building democracy in Iraq would provide an example that other peoples in the region would seek to follow. With democratic governments, the reasoning went, the states would be much more amenable to making peace with Israel and the United States and less likely to harbor terrorists. In 2005, Bush succinctly stated the conventional wisdom: "Democracies don't war with each other."[3]

In word, at least, the U.S. government rejected supporting authoritarian governments in return for their support of U.S. interests. Secretary of State Condoleezza Rice most directly stated that realism had been rejected: "The fundamental character of regimes matters more today than the international distribution of power."[4] Bush chided his predecessors, saying, "Sixty years of Western nations excusing and accommodating the lack of freedom in the Middle East did nothing to make us safe. . . . As long as the Middle East becomes a place where freedom does not flourish, it will remain a place of stagnation, resentment, and violence for export."[5]

In practice, the United States encountered tensions between a realist policy of finding allies based on mutual interests, and a liberal strategy of transforming autocracies into democracies to make them more peaceful. Bush stated that "the Palestinian leaders who block and undermine democratic reform . . . [are] the main obstacles to peace, and to the success of the Palestinian people." But when free elections were held for the legislature of the Palestinian Authority they were won by Hamas, a group identified by the United States as a terrorist organization. The United States was put into the uncomfortable position of refusing to deal with one of the first popularly elected governments in the region. Moreover, prisoner abuse at the Abu Ghraib prison in Iraq and objections to U.S. treatment of detainees at Guantanamo Bay undermined U.S. claims about the benefits brought by democracy.

The U.S. policy raises fundamental questions that link international relations theory to foreign policy. Is it true that democracies have different foreign policies than nondemocracies? Do democracies never go to war with one another? Should policies be based, as Rice asserted, not on the balance of power, but on the character of domestic government? In sum, do state-level variables explain international affairs better than the systemic factors?

Changing the Level of Analysis

Any analysis of international politics begins by making assumptions about where to look—about which level of analysis is the most appropriate starting point. Some theories examine the nature of the international system. If the system tightly constrains the state, then the state has a very narrow range of options. In this view, the system explains most of what states do, and we do not need to know much about the states themselves. To apply realist balance of power theory, one needs only to know a state's position in the distribution of power (whether it is strong or weak compared to other countries). To apply economic structuralist theory, one needs only to know a state's position in the global economy. In these theories, variation in the kind of state or in how the state works is not an important explanation of different outcomes.

Other theories assert that states retain a significant amount of room for choice within the constraints of the system. If states have a range of choices, how and why do states choose the policies they do? To address this question, we need more detailed theories, at a lower state and substate level of analysis, to account for behavior.

In casual usage, the word *state* is used interchangeably with the word *country*; both are inclusive terms that refer to a country's geographical territory, its population, and its government. This chapter uses **state** more specifically to mean "the government and political system of a country." This definition includes not only executives, bureaucracies, legislatures, and armed forces, but the entire *system* of government, including the constitution and laws.

State and substate approaches have in common a rejection of the systemic-level analysis, which assumes that different states will behave the same in similar international circumstances. But these approaches differ in what factors they believe to be driving state behavior. In contrast to the theories discussed in the previous chapters, state and substate approaches do not claim to offer a general theory of all of international politics. Rather than being theories of international politics, these are theories of **foreign policy**. Although the distinction may seem semantic, there is an important point here: Theories often differ in the kinds of questions they seek to answer.

Theories of international politics ask, "What is the nature of international politics?" Theories of foreign policy ask, "What explains foreign policies?" There is some overlap in these questions but a great deal of difference in the answers. Systemic theories provide answers that are presumably valid regardless of the country; state- and substate-level theories assume that countries differ from one another and that they change over time.

Are there important variations in the kinds of states that populate the world? If so, do different states behave differently? Only if the answer to both of these questions is yes do theories need to examine this level.[6]

state
The government and political system of a country.

foreign policy
Policy (actions or statements intended to change behavior or outcomes) aimed at problems outside of the policy-making state's borders.

Democratic Peace Theory

Democratic peace theory asserts that it matters profoundly what kind of states are involved in any interaction. Democratic states, it is contended, behave very differently than nondemocratic, or autocratic, states do. The argument is supported by a considerable body of evidence, but many scholars remain deeply skeptical. This is an area in which academic research has crucial implications for public policy. If democracies are truly more peaceful, then promoting democracy can be equated with promoting peace. In recent decades, this argument has been cited in support of using economic aid as well as military force to promote democracy.

Ironically, the argument that democracies are more peaceful might provide a rationale for war, because a war that installs a democracy might reduce the chances of war in

An Iraqi woman flashes the victory sign with a purple finger, indicating she has already voted, at a polling station in Az Zubayr, southern Iraq, January 2005. U.S. policy was based on the belief that elections would help make Iraq democratic and peaceful.

the long run. This logic was the basis of Woodrow Wilson's argument for involving the United States in World War I and was part of George W. Bush's justification for invading Iraq in 2003. It is essential, therefore, that we assess the validity of this theory. Whether it is worthwhile to bear the cost of building democracy in other countries, particularly if this cost involves waging war, will depend in part on whether peace is a likely result. Therefore, we must first consider the theoretical reasons why there *should* be a connection between regime type (democratic versus autocratic) and war. We then need to examine the evidence. Finally, we need to consider the implications in depth.

Democratic Peace Theory: Two Versions

It is very important to distinguish between the two versions of democratic peace theory. Only one version stands up to scrutiny, but the two are easily confused. The "simple" model, which has been discredited, argues that democracies in general are more peaceful. This model looks at the behavior of individual states. The second, "dyadic" (focusing on pairs) model holds that toward autocracies, democracies are just as warlike as autocracies but that democracies do not fight *each other*. This argument is not about individual democracies, but about *pairs* or *groups* of them. The dyadic model is considered valid by many scholars and policy makers. Both fit into the liberal paradigm, in arguing that peace is easier to attain than realists (or economic structuralists) would have us believe.

THE SIMPLE DEMOCRATIC PEACE MODEL

The "simple" democratic peace argument is intuitively plausible and normatively attractive. It is based on two notions. First, it is believed that publics are generally disinclined to go to war and will stop it if allowed. Second, it is believed that authoritarian leaders sometimes start wars to distract the public from their authoritarianism, a motivation that democratic leaders do not have.

The Cost of War and Public Opposition   The origin of the democratic peace theory is widely attributed to the German philosopher Immanuel Kant, who wrote in 1795 of the possibility of an international federation of republics that would usher in *Perpetual Peace* (as his book was titled). Kant and those following him have argued that ordinary citizens are inherently peaceful because they are the ones that have to fight the wars. In Kant's view, power-hungry governments make the choice to go to war against the wishes of their citizens.

In democracy, it is argued, the vast majority of citizens can use the vote to control politicians. Those who will suffer most from war can therefore prevent it. In autocratic regimes, the people who suffer from war have no such voice. There is some anecdotal evidence of such democratic passivity in recent years. In 2003, Spanish voters unseated a prime minister, otherwise very popular, who chose to contribute 1300 troops to the U.S. occupation of Iraq. Similarly, voter dissatisfaction with the Vietnam War in the United States led to U.S. President Lyndon Johnson's decision not to run for a second term.

War as a Distraction   A related argument asserts that autocratic regimes have a reason to go to war that democracies do not have. In democracies, the legitimacy of the ruling elite is provided by the fact that they have been elected to office in free and fair elections.

Governments in autocratic countries have no such source of legitimacy. Citizens often rally around their country's leadership in times of war, raising the popularity even of unpopular leaders. Therefore, some have argued that autocratic governments sometimes seek to use a successful military campaign to bolster their support among the public (and the elite). The cynical leader can take advantage of this **rally around the flag effect**. In 1982, for example, the unpopular and authoritarian Argentine leader Leopoldo Galtieri initiated war with Great Britain to seize the Falkland Islands, which led to a rapid boost in Galtieri's popularity. In early 2010, a North Korean torpedo attack on a South Korean ship, viewed as a highly provocative act, was attributed to the need of North Korea's ailing president, Kim Jong Il, to show his toughness to other elites, in order to ensure that his son would be chosen to succeed him. Such distractions, it is argued, are not needed in democracies because their leaders, subject to periodic elections, automatically have a certain level of popularity and a great deal of legitimacy.

rally around the flag effect
The increase in popular support often gained by leaders of a country in times of war.

THE DYADIC MODEL: DEMOCRACIES DON'T FIGHT DEMOCRACIES

Because the simple argument that democracies are more peaceful has been convincingly disproved, a more refined model has been developed. This model argues that democracies do not go to war with each other. Peace is not a characteristic of individual states, but of the relations between certain types of states. This model must explain both why two (or more) democracies are unlikely to go to war with each other *and* why democracies and nondemocracies do go to war. There are three arguments supporting this view. A structural argument focuses on ways in which democracies find it easier to reach compromises with each other. A normative argument asserts that democracies have a respect for each other that they do not have for nondemocratic states. An institutional argument, based in **rational choice theory**, finds that democracies are very successful at fighting wars and that democratic politicians are especially vulnerable if they lose a war, and that this combination makes democratic leaders fear going to war with other democracies.

rational choice theory
A theory that bases explanations of decisions on the assumption that decision makers have clear goals, calculate the costs of various courses of action, and pick the policy that will best serve their goals.

The Structural Argument   In democracies, it is argued, political disputes are resolved by compromise, and this pattern carries over into foreign relations in two ways. First, it is argued, when two democracies bargain in a dispute, they bargain the same way they do domestically, through a **politics of compromise** that searches for a mutually acceptable solution. This kind of bargaining, which rules out force as an option, cannot take place between two autocracies or even between a democracy and an autocracy, because both sides must operate in this way.[7]

politics of compromise
The tendency among democracies to resolve disputes through bargaining.

Second, some theorists point out that since policy making in democracies requires reconciliation of a range of political views, it is very difficult to adopt an extreme policy. Policies are usually watered down in the process of gaining majority support. When two democracies are negotiating with each other, even in an intense conflict, neither of them will tend toward extreme solutions, such as war. Rather, the domestic processes of democracies carry over into the international arena and lead to moderate solutions.

Third, some argue that democracies are less likely to fight not only because they can reach compromises, but also because they keep their promises. Once a commitment is made, it may be difficult to break it because democracies have institutions such as courts and legislative minorities that allow even a small minority to force a government to live up to its commitments.[8] Moreover, because leaders must publicly campaign for office, they may pay a higher penalty for reneging on their commitments. This cost of reneging is known as **audience costs**. Authoritarian leaders have low audience costs since they are less accountable to the citizenry. Because leaders of democracies understand that other democracies are more likely to honor their commitments, they are more willing to enter into agreements and make the concessions needed to avoid war.

audience costs
The costs in loss of public support paid by leaders of democracies when they renege on a commitment.

The Normative Argument   The simplest explanation of a dyadic democratic peace is that democracies do not go to war out of mutual respect. This view holds that citizens and leaders in democracies respect the institutions of democracy not only in their own country but in other countries as well.[9] They reject the idea of forcibly conquering another democracy. They expect other democracies to treat them with the same respect. In other words, both sides in a dispute reject the idea of using force, respect differences that are derived from democracy, and expect to work out problems peacefully. This is essentially a constructivist explanation based on the emergence of a shared identity among democracies and a shared norm that destroying another democracy is bad.

One strength of this normative argument is that it may explain why war between democracies and nondemocracies is more frequent than war between two nondemocracies. Although democratic states have immense respect for each other, they have disdain (not simply a neutral attitude) toward autocratic states. Therefore, a democracy in a dispute with an autocracy may be especially disrespectful of the other side and may view favorably the prospect of destroying the autocracy and replacing it with a democracy.

The Institutional Argument   Proponents of rational choice theory argue that democratic political institutions have two effects on their leaders that, when combined, make them very cautious about going to war with one another.[10] The first effect is that democratic states are more likely to win wars. This point was originally made by Machiavelli, but it has received empirical substantiation in recent research.[11] The reason, apparently, is that citizens are more likely to support their government's war efforts in a democracy. The second effect is that leaders in a democracy are more sensitive to the political costs of losing a war, because they are more likely to be turned out of office if the war fails. The combination of these two effects, it is argued, makes war between democracies especially unlikely. If democracies are hard to defeat, and democrats are especially afraid of defeat, then the combination should make democrats especially unwilling to attack other democracies. This does not mean that they do not coerce one another. When democracies are in conflict, the weaker state, being especially sensitive to possible defeat, is expected to give in.[12]

This institutional explanation, like the normative explanation, also explains why war between democracies and autocracies is more likely, and especially why democracies seem inclined to initiate war against autocracies. Democratic leaders may perceive a high likelihood of winning a war with an autocracy. They may expect that the army and/or the citizenry in an autocratic state will refuse to fight, leading to an easy victory for the attacker.

Evidence for the Democratic Peace

Much of the evidence supporting the democratic peace argument comes from statistical analyses of large data sets of all wars since the early nineteenth century. These data sets list each war (usually defined as a conflict between states resulting in more than 1500 battle deaths), data about the states involved, and the outcome of the conflict. A second kind of evidence comes from specific cases. Some scholars have looked in depth at crises between democracies and argue that there is evidence that leaders and citizens alike hesitate to initiate war with a country they recognize as a democracy and have confidence that compromise can be reached with other democracies.[13]

Scholars generally agree about two major findings.[14] First, there is *no* statistical evidence that democracies go to war less frequently than autocracies.[15] Moreover, studies that seek to determine which state is the initiator of a given war show that democracies are *not* averse to starting wars. This observation has caused the "simple" democratic peace hypothesis to be widely rejected.

The Culture Connection

Is Democracy Culturally Limited?

Over the past two decades, failed attempts to promote democracy have raised the delicate question of whether democracy is culturally limited. Are there cultural prerequisites for democracy, such that some societies simply are not "ready"? Some see the question itself as ethnocentric; others see the assumption that all countries should have the same kind of government as ethnocentric.

The collapse of communism made this a very practical question. The assumption both in the region and in the West was that any of the post-communist states could become democratic if they simply adopted the right kinds of institutions—that is, constitutions, laws, and government agencies. Skeptics pointed out that such institutions could not work—or even be adopted—in countries with no historical experience with democracy and without the societal values and practices necessary to support democracy.

The mixed record of democratization in the post-Soviet states has given some credence to the notion that some societies are not culturally ready for democracy. It would appear that democracy came most easily to those post-communist states, such as Poland, the Czech Republic, and the Baltic States, that had experienced democracy prior to World War II and had a much stronger societal commitment to it. On the other hand, scholars have not been able to identify specific cultural characteristics that democracies must have but that the struggling states lack.[1] They argue that the states that have succeeded have done so because they were given more support, in the form of prospective membership in NATO and the EU, for example.

The question comes up again when considering the spread of democracy in the Islamic world. Some have argued that Islam is incompatible with democratic government. They point out that there are few true democracies in Muslim countries, with the possible exception of Turkey, which is a secular state. If this view is valid, plans to bring democracy to Iraq and Afghanistan are doomed. Again, however, it is difficult to evaluate any such argument, since the question of whether there are such cultural prerequisites has not been settled. The general absence of democracy in the Muslim world seems to be superficial evidence that, indeed, Islam and democracy are incompatible. But the success of democracy in a Muslim country such as Turkey indicates that that is not the case.

U.S. foreign policy has in recent years assumed that there are no cultural barriers to democracy in the Muslim world, as demonstrated by the policy of setting up democracy in Iraq and encouraging it elsewhere in the region, after many years of tolerating and even encouraging authoritarianism. Secretary of State Condoleezza Rice stated in 2005, ". . . There's no culture on earth, there are no people on earth, who don't desire to be free. People in the Middle East rightly understand that for 60 years the United States, and many others, tried to trade stability for democracy. And we got neither stability nor democracy and it's not surprising to me that there are resentments about that period of time."[2]

In this debate about culture and democracy, what seems at first to be a relatively esoteric academic issue turns out to have important policy consequences.

Critical Thinking Questions

1. Are there cultural prerequisites for democracy? If so, what are they?
2. Only a few hundred years ago, there were no democracies. Now there are many. If there are cultural prerequisites for democracy, how do they emerge?

[1] See Richard Schifter, "Is There a Democracy Gene?" *The National Interest,* Vol. 17, No. 3 (Summer 1994): 121–128.
[2] National Public Radio, *Morning Edition,* May 27, 2005.

Second, there are very few, if any, cases of war between democracies in all of history.[16] Michael Doyle looked at all the wars from 1815 to 1980 and found that none were fought between liberal democracies. In a field as ambiguous as international politics, this stark result is highly unusual, and this pattern has contributed to the notion that war between democracies is practically impossible. There is disagreement about a few cases. For example, Germany had many democratic institutions prior to World War I. Therefore, World War I could be said to have involved several "democratic war" dyads (Germany vs. Great Britain, Germany vs. France, Germany vs. the United States). However, whether the number of wars between democracies is zero or very close to it, the result remains striking. One scholar has asserted, based on this evidence, that the democratic peace "comes as close as anything we have to an empirical law in the study of international politics."[17]

Critiques of Democratic Peace Theory

Although democratic peace theory been widely influential, it has attracted serious criticism as well. The critiques can be broken into three categories. Some assert that the theory is not clearly defined and that its supporters use this vagueness to misinterpret evidence. Others assert that the pattern that exists is not surprising, and in fact, does not show the powerful influence of democracy. Many have also argued that the pattern is genuine but is more plausibly explained by factors other than democracy.

DEFINING DEMOCRACY

The central critique of democratic peace theory is that the key factor, "democracy," is defined poorly and in contradictory ways. Democracy is a concept easily defined as "rule by the many," but identifying democracy in practice—what political scientists call **operationalizing** the concept—is difficult. By many definitions, Germany was a democracy prior to World War I, but if Germany is classified as such, one of the most important wars in history suddenly provides important evidence against democratic peace theory. Thus, one of the most prominent advocates of democratic peace theory, Michael Doyle, has to violate his own classification scheme to call Germany a nondemocracy.[18] One scholar has even shown that Woodrow Wilson himself considered Germany an admirable democracy when he was a scholar and changed his view only after the country became a rival.[19] But in scholarly terms, the point of objective definitions is to prevent us from interpreting the evidence to fit the theory.

A related problem is that the definition of democracy in the theory appears to change over time. No one today would consider a state a democracy if it enslaved a large portion of its population or denied half the adult citizens (women) the right to vote. But if slavery is incompatible with democracy, then the United States was not a democracy until 1863, and by the standard of universal adult suffrage, the United States was not a democracy until women were given the vote in 1920. Yet the United States is considered to have been a democracy throughout its entire history. By classifying states as democracies for more years, the period of time in which democracies did not fight each other looks much longer. This becomes important in assessing the significance of the evidence.

HOW SIGNIFICANT IS THE ABSENCE OF WAR BETWEEN DEMOCRACIES?

Critics of democratic peace theory assert that the absence of war between democracies is not surprising, for two related reasons. First, for most of recorded history, there have been very few democracies. The first state to consistently meet the definition, the United States, arose in 1789 (or perhaps much later). Using widely accepted definitions, there has been a significant number of democracies in the world only since World War II.

operationalizing

Translating a theoretical concept into attributes that can be measured.

Second, the incidence of war is also fairly rare throughout history. In any given year, only a small number of states are at war with each other. This fact, combined with the small number of democracies at most points in history, makes the likelihood minuscule that any pair of states is both at war and democratic. Thus, one critic argues that the evidence supporting the theory is "statistically insignificant," meaning that the pattern we observe is not substantially different from what we would observe if democracy and war were unrelated.[20]

OTHER EXPLANATIONS FOR THE OBSERVED PATTERN

Finally, when looking at the period in which there were more democracies in the world (after World War II), skeptics point out that there is a much simpler explanation for the absence of war between democracies: the Cold War. From 1945 until 1991, all the world's democracies were threatened by Soviet expansionism, so all were allied to combat that threat. In this view, the balance of power, not the nature of states, explains the absence of war.

In sum, although the evidence supporting the argument that democracies do not go to war with one another is compelling, the critiques of that evidence are also compelling. To some, the critiques indicate a need to reject the theory; to others, they indicate a need for caution; and to still others, the critiques are not persuasive at all. The debate, therefore, continues, and the stakes are high, because the theory has profound implications for policies involving war and peace.

Applications of Democratic Peace Theory

The idea of a democratic peace holds out a tantalizing prospect: If all the states in the world were democratic, there would be no war. In this respect, democratic peace theory is entirely at odds with realism, which sees the possibility of war as an inevitable fact of international life. Even if a world full of peaceful democracies is not possible in the very near term, many believe that a **zone of peace** already exists, consisting of North America, Western Europe, and other areas, and they hope that this zone of peace can gradually expand to include more countries. Such a process, in which a limited region of peaceful democracies gradually expands to cover the earth, is precisely what Kant envisioned in writing *Perpetual Peace* over 200 years ago.

zone of peace
A group of states that tend not to go to war with each other because they are democratic.

The idea that an existing zone of peace can be enlarged by adding new democracies has been put into practice in Western Europe since the end of the Cold War. Europe has sought to decrease instability in the post-communist region and to expand the existing zone of peace by engaging in a vigorous program to promote democracy in new states and to integrate them into the institutional arrangements that help build security in Europe, the EU and NATO.

Faced with roughly twenty states in transition in Eastern Europe (including existing communist states that were moving toward democracy and new states resulting from the collapse of the Soviet Union and Yugoslavia), both organizations have sought to put democratic peace theory into practice. Their goals are to expand the group of countries among whom war is essentially unthinkable, to increase economic influence, and to create a barrier against potential future Russian expansion.

The EU and NATO pursued these goals with roughly similar strategies of *conditionality*. Each organization has established numerous criteria for membership. In keeping with the democratic peace theory, most of the conditions for membership concern democratic governance, both generally, in terms of holding elections, and more specifically, in terms of the functioning of judicial systems, civilian control of the military, and so on.[21] The potential benefits of joining the EU and NATO, in terms of security, economics,

If Democracies Don't Fight Each Other...

Freedom House is a Washington-based NGO, funded in part by the U.S. government that assesses the state of democracy around the world. This map shows Freedom House's 2006 rankings of the level of democracy and civil liberties in countries worldwide, based on a set of criteria determined by experts selected by Freedom House.

Critical Thinking Questions

1. Consider this map in light of the democratic peace hypothesis. Are the conflicts we see today consistent with the hypothesis?

2. According to the empirical findings we have discussed, where are we most likely and least likely to see conflict in coming years?

3. Examine particular countries with which you are familiar Do you agree with the rankings? How might the map look different if it were produced in Beijing, Moscow, Nairobi, or Caracas?

Freedom House Democracy Scores, 2008

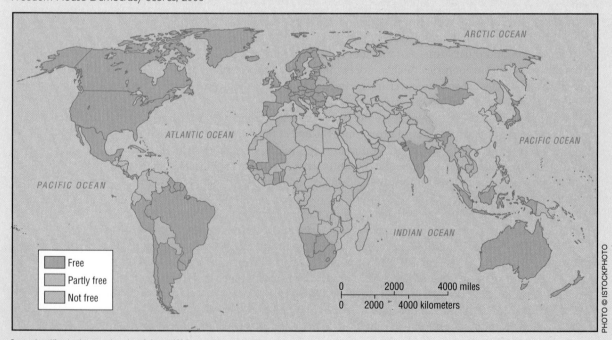

Legend:
- Free
- Partly free
- Not free

PHOTO © ISTOCKPHOTO

Source: http://freedomhouse.org/template.cfm?page=290 Reprinted by permission.

and technical assistance, are powerful motivators to many post-communist countries, creating a political will for changes that otherwise would have been difficult to promote.

The strategy appears to have worked. The EU, which had twelve members at the time of the fall of the Berlin Wall, now has twenty-seven; NATO has grown from sixteen to twenty-six members. Some of these countries are not yet fully consolidated democracies, but the new Eastern European members, who until 1989 were part of an alliance against which NATO was constantly preparing for war, are now part of a single, peaceful Europe. Those countries that have not yet been admitted to this zone of peace, including Turkey, Russia, and Ukraine, have voiced considerable resentment.

WOODROW WILSON'S WAR TO END WARS

When World War I started in Europe, most people in the United States were determined to stay out. The war was widely viewed as a quarrel among the old, nondemocratic, corrupt empires of Europe. Therefore, many in the United States perceived no real reason to go to war on either side. Woodrow Wilson (president from 1913 to 1921) took a different approach, based largely on democratic peace theory. He argued that by getting involved in the war on the side of the democratic states (Britain and France were democratic, although their ally Russia was far from it), the United States could help transform Europe into a region of peaceful democracies. In particular, Wilson contended, if Austria's empire in east-central Europe were disbanded, democracy would flourish and the states in the region would have no reason to go to war with one another. Wilson was perhaps the first to argue that war could be used to promote democracy, thereby reducing the chances for future conflicts.

In Wilson's view, an international organization to maintain the peace could work only if its members were democracies. "No peace can last, or ought to last, which does not recognize and accept the principle that governments derive all their just powers from the consent of the governed."[22] Therefore, two of Wilson's main goals, enshrined in the Treaty of Versailles, were to break up former empires to allow for "national self-determination" and to replace autocratic rule with democracy.

Ironically, the biggest democracy of that period, the United States, did not take part in the new **League of Nations** because the U.S. Senate refused to ratify the charter. However, both the entry of the United States into World War I and the diplomacy involved in ending the war were largely driven by the democratic peace theory.

League of Nations
An international organization established after World War I that aimed to maintain world peace.

POST-SOVIET RUSSIA

In 1991, following a failed coup attempt by hardline communists in the Soviet government, the Soviet Union collapsed. Russia began a massive internal transformation, with President Boris Yeltsin pledging a shift to Western-style democracy. U.S. policy makers had to decide whether to treat Russia as an enemy because of its power, which was almost as threatening as before communism's collapse, or as a friend because of its domestic reforms.

At first, the administration of George H. W. Bush (president from 1989 to 1993) and then that of Bill Clinton (president from 1993 to 2001) followed the democratic peace theory, believing that if Russia became democratic, its arsenal would be no threat to the United States. Therefore, the U.S. government (and other Western governments) initiated programs to aid Russia's transition to a market economy and democratic rule. Even though the amount of money was fairly meager compared to Russia's economy or the size of the transformation, some opposed aid to Russia. Using realist logic, they viewed Russia as a threat based on its military strength, not its intentions or form of government. Ultimately, U.S. efforts to democratize Russia failed. Russia became progressively less democratic under President Vladimir Putin, and rising oil prices increased Russian wealth, making Western economic aid unnecessary.

The Policy Connection

Building Democracy Versus Supporting Allies

In the United States, both major political parties have strongly endorsed the notion that democratic states are more peaceful than others and that it is therefore beneficial to promote the advent of democratic regimes. European states have the same view and have extended economic resources, as well as the prospect of EU membership, to the former communist states of Eastern Europe.

However, there are some cases in which governments have been very hesitant to focus too much effort on promoting democracy. What policy should be pursued when the country where one hopes to promote democracy is also an important ally? Prior to 2001, the United States and most European states had enacted sanctions against several governments in central and south Asia in response to the increasing authoritarianism of regimes there. Special attention was focused on Pakistan, where General Pervez Musharraf had come to power in a coup in 1999.

After the terrorist attacks of September 2001, when Western attention focused heavily on Afghanistan, countries that could provide access to Afghanistan's borders were essential to military success. These included not only Pakistan, which borders the region of Afghanistan where Taliban and Al-Qaeda personnel were concentrated, but also Uzbekistan, Kyrgyzstan, and Kazakhstan in central Asia. Western governments understood that they could not try to democratize the governments of these countries through the application of sanctions and gain their help in the "War on Terror" at the same time. The decision has been to mute criticism of these countries, based on in the view that prosecuting the battle against terrorism in the short term is more important than long-term goals of democratization.

In many respects, there was nothing new in this dilemma. During the Cold War, the United States and its allies championed the cause of freedom in the world. At the same time, however, they often supported authoritarian regimes in the short term, in order to fight what was seen as the biggest danger: Soviet expansionism.

A related problem is that democratic elections do not often lead immediately to pro-Western, or even pro-democratic, governments. Algeria adopted a multiparty system in 1988, but in 1992, parliamentary elections were cancelled and a state of emergency was declared when it became clear that the Islamic Salvation Front, which sought to create an Islamic state ruled by sharia law, would win a majority of seats. Similarly, the first free elections in areas controlled by the Palestinian Authority, in 2006, were won by Hamas, a group widely viewed in the West as a terrorist organization. A Saudi reformer captured the paradox, saying, "The minute you are counted on or backed by the Americans, kiss it goodbye, you will never win."[1]

In sum, the promotion of democracy in the world is not pursued simplistically. When it conflicts with other short-term goals, achieving democracy is sometimes put on the back burner. Critics of such compromises argue that in the long run, support for authoritarian governments almost always backfires.

Critical Thinking Questions

1. Is it acceptable for a society to democratically choose not to be democratic? Should outside states intervene to prevent this?
2. What kinds of constitutional provisions make it harder for democracy to be overturned by vote?

[1] Quoted in "US Backs Free Elections, Only to See Allies Lose," *New York Times*, August 10, 2007.

Implications of Democratic Peace Theory

Two implications of democratic peace theory are especially provocative. First, if democracies are more peaceful, then, as George W. Bush asserted, policies that accept authoritarian rule in return for stability are doomed to fail in the long run. This argument sharply contradicts the realist argument raised in Chapter 3 that it doesn't matter what kind of government a country has. For policy makers, democratic peace theory creates difficult dilemmas when dealing with states that are allied but authoritarian. It might seem risky in the short term to put pressure on reliable, but authoritarian, allies to change their policies. Realists point out that the result is likely to be to weaken the alliance without achieving much in the way of democracy.

A second troubling implication is that democratic peace theory, ironically, provides a rationale for democracies to wage a particular kind of war—war aimed at changing a regime from authoritarianism to democracy. Some scholars have pointed out that this temptation helps explain why democracies are not statistically shown to be more peaceful. Leaders of democracies may sometimes see it as a duty or in their countries' interest to initiate war with the goal of building a more peaceful, democratic world, as Wilson argued during World War I.

State and Substate Level Theories

Democratic peace theory has received a vast amount of attention in recent years, but it is not the only school of thought to find important variation at the level of the state. Many authors find important variations in the way that states are organized and in the way that states relate to their societies. Unlike the democratic peace theory, models of **state structure** and **state strength** have the virtue of being applicable to the whole range of foreign policy issues, not just war and peace.

For example, an influential study by Peter Katzenstein and others compared various states' responses to the oil shortages of the early 1970s. All the advanced industrial states were faced with the same external shock to their economies, but they responded in very different ways.[23] Why? Katzenstein and his colleagues found that different states had different policy instruments for influencing their economies. For example, Japan's Ministry of International Trade and Industry was set up to provide very specific, sector-level support to specific industries in Japan.[24] In contrast, the United Kingdom and the United States tend to use more blunt instruments, such as the overall level of interest rates, to govern their economies. The point is not that one type of arrangement is better than the other (although there has been much debate on this question), but rather that these different state structures will naturally lead to different policies.

Moreover, the Katzenstein study found that different states had different relationships with their societies, with some being tightly constrained and others being more autonomous. In the United States, the state was seen as "weak" because it is heavily influenced by interest groups that are given a prominent role in developing policies. In France and Japan, which are typically regarded as "strong" states, the state has a greater degree of autonomy from interest groups. In still other states, including Germany, the state negotiates major economic policies with broad associations of industry and labor groups.[25]

The issue of state strength has also received considerable attention in the literature on economic development. An important question is why certain countries, most notably the "Asian Tigers" (Hong Kong, Singapore, South Korea, Taiwan), moved from poverty to wealth while others were left behind (see Chapter 9). One argument focuses on the strength of states. These governments, it is argued, were able to raise capital for investment, funnel investment strategically, and keep labor unrest to a minimum, in order to be competitive in the global economy. Countries that developed less, in this view, had

state structure

The form and function of state institutions.

state strength

The degree to which a state is independent of societal influences.

U.S. troops intervened in Haiti in 1994 in Operation "Uphold Democracy." Although U.S. forces were able to restore basic order in Haiti, little subsequent progress was made in building a stable democracy.

Andrew Lichtenstein/The Image Works

governments that were unable to resist pressure from interest groups and thus implemented policies that served the short-term interests of those groups but undermined the economies' long-term prospects for development.[26] More recently, efforts to introduce free markets to Russia and other post-communist countries have led to a similar focus on "state capacity." Although early advice to these governments focused simply on getting the state out of the economy, experience showed that state involvement, at least in some key areas (such as combating corruption), was essential, and that where such state activity was ineffective, development was undermined.[27]

The global economic crisis that emerged in 2008 caused further focus on how different state-society arrangements affect policy. After three decades in which most states had taken an ever smaller role in the economy, the crisis seemed to show the weakness of that model. The crisis hit hardest in the most market-oriented economies, including the United States, the United Kingdom, and much of Europe. China, with its state-managed capitalism, managed well. Similarly, in Russia, the increased involvement of the state in the economy after 1999 accompanied rapid growth. Moreover, both Russia and China adopted foreign policies making extensive use of economic power. State-society relations therefore remain an important influence on foreign policy.

What Is the National Interest, and Who Says So?

Theories that link foreign policy to citizen and societal influence typically explore the roles of organized interest groups, public opinion, and the media in determining foreign policy. They examine the relationship among the media, public opinion, and official policy. They ask, how is the *purpose* of the state's foreign policies determined, and what is the *power* of different actors (including governmental actors) in formulating these goals? Put differently, when the phrase "national interest" is used to justify a policy, the questions become, *who* defines the national interest this way, and *how* is that definition of national interest chosen over others?

The **national interest** is a central topic in many discussions of foreign policy. Realist theory in particular assumes that each state has a single set of interests, and that policy makers ought to recognize these interests and pursue them. Much daily debate concerning foreign policies around the world concerns what a state's national interest is and how it ought to be pursued. Typically, elements of the national interest are viewed as wealth, power, and prestige. However, there are two important objections to the concept of "national interest," as well as to its application. First, even if we assume that there is a single national interest, it seems that people never agree on what it is. Even experts who share a commitment to advancing the interests of a particular country often disagree on what those interests are, and these disagreements are the fodder of political conflict.

Second, and more fundamentally, many would argue that the concept of "national interest" is in fact a myth, or a concept that a variety of special interests invoke to promote their goals. This view is visible in complex interdependence theory, with its emphasis on multiple actors with multiple interests, and with economic structuralism, which sees different corporations and classes pursuing their interest and trying to use the state to promote them. It is also visible in theories of interest group politics that are widely applied to the study of domestic politics. In this view, societies are made up of multiple interests that are not easily reconciled. Different groups may genuinely see their interest as the national interest, or they may cynically try to use the label "national interest" or "vital national interest" to gain particular benefits. For this reason, it is essential to consider the role of interest groups in foreign policy making.

Interest Groups in Foreign Policy

The role of interest groups is consistently emphasized in analyses of politics and policy making. Generally speaking, however, the role of interest groups has received less attention in the study of foreign policy than in the study of domestic politics. In fact, interest groups have a powerful stake in various aspects of foreign policy. Because many interest groups are primarily motivated by business and are centered on particular industries, we see interest groups most clearly in the making of foreign economic policy. Given the vast sums of money spent on defense in most countries, we see a great deal of interest group involvement on security issues as well. However, the kinds of foreign policy issues that are the subject of interest group activities vary from country to country. In some countries, immigration is a major concern of industrial and labor groups. In other countries, the pervasive influence of cultural products (such as films, television shows, music, and fashion) from abroad drives organized groups to try to change policies. In most countries, interest groups contest their states' relationship with the world economy.

To understand the role of interest groups, we must focus on three questions, each of which is very broad. First, what do interest groups want? Second, how do they go about getting what they want? Third, how successful are they at getting it?

WHAT DO INTEREST GROUPS WANT FROM FOREIGN POLICY?

The goals of interest groups are as diverse as the interest groups themselves, so it is difficult to generalize. However, interest groups can be divided into three broad categories, based on their motivations. The first category consists of interest groups that support foreign policies that have very predictable economic benefits for the group. A typical example is an interest group of automobile producers lobbying for increased tariffs on foreign automobiles. Such tariffs decrease competition and allow domestic producers to sell more cars at higher prices.

Worldwide, two economic interest groups that have most consistently, and most successfully, lobbied governments for protection from foreign competition are the steel industry and agricultural interests. In both these industries, there has tended to be a consistent surplus of production in the world, which drives prices down. Although lower prices are good for consumers, they are bad for producers, who consequently band together to pressure governments for protection.

A second category of interest groups consists of those seeking revenue directly *from* the government. Most prominent here are groups hoping to sell their goods or services to the government. In many countries, the most significant actors within this group are military contractors. Military budgets generally dwarf all other foreign policy spending (such as foreign aid), and a significant portion is spent on every kind of good used by the military, from air mattresses to aircraft carriers. Military contracts are often highly lucrative, and foreign policy choices or military strategy can significantly influence the level of a government's demand for a particular product. Recognizing the influence of outsiders on procurement decisions, India recently prohibited agents of arms manufacturers from visiting its defense ministry in an effort to reduce their influence on procurement, but the ban seems to have had little effect, as firms find ways around it.[28]

A third category of interest groups is not interested primarily in money, although this may be one of their goals. These groups are formed by people and organizations with particular concerns about some aspect of foreign policy. Some of these groups would probably rather be labeled NGOs, but for our purposes they are not fundamentally different from interest groups (see the discussion of NGOs in Chapter 12). Some focus on policy toward a particular country; others are concerned with policy on a particular issue, such as immigration or global warming.

HOW DO INTEREST GROUPS INFLUENCE FOREIGN POLICY?

Interest groups pursue their goals in a number of ways, depending on the resources available to them and on the governmental system in the country in which they are operating. Interest groups that have a large number of members, for example, can seek to convince politicians that supporting the groups' goals will be rewarded at the next election. Thus, labor unions have sometimes been effective in lobbying for greater barriers to trade because their large memberships and their effectiveness in getting their members to vote make them valuable to politicians. In South Africa, for example, the ruling African National Congress (ANC) has been forced to resist calls by business leaders for greater economic liberalization because of the ANC's significant dependence on trade union members, who oppose liberalization.[29]

Another resource available to interest groups in varying amounts is money. Money can obtain influence in a number of ways. First, although politicians routinely deny that campaign contributions influence the decisions they make, interest groups make significant contributions to political campaigns on the assumption that contributions do indeed create influence. If campaign contributions do not influence policies, then many of the smartest business leaders around the world are wasting a great deal of money.

Money can also be influential when used indirectly. Interest groups can influence policies by shaping public opinion—by going directly to the people through advertising. The opinion and editorial pages of leading newspapers and news/talk shows on television are preferred locations for advertising aimed at the politically active portion of the public. They may also conduct research on a specific issue and share the results with politicians, bureaucrats, and the public.

Finally, interest groups influence foreign policy by hiring lobbyists. Lobbyists are individuals who make a profession out of their connections with policy makers. Their access to policy makers can, in effect, be sold to their clients. For this reason, individuals who have recently served in key areas of the foreign policy bureaucracy are especially sought after as lobbyists, and such individuals command high fees for their work. In the United States, many former high-ranking government officials, including secretaries of state and defense, directors of the Central Intelligence Agency, generals, and members of Congress have left office and moved into lobbying for interest groups, which are willing to pay them hefty fees to return to where they worked in the public interest and work instead for the private interest. A similar process takes place in many other countries.

In Germany in 2005, for example, Chancellor Gerhard Schröder ardently supported an important agreement with the Russian gas monopoly Gazprom to build a new pipeline to bring Russian gas to Germany. Two months later, after leaving office, Schröder took a lucrative position as chairman of the board of the consortium formed to build the pipeline.[30] Observers wondered whether Schröder's access to the top levels of the German government, rather than his ability as a businessman, was his main job qualification. The role of prominent former public servants in lobbying firms raises some interesting questions. Henry Kissinger, for example, is a former U.S. national security advisor and secretary of state who went on to form Kissinger Associates, Inc., a lobbying firm. Yet he is also a frequent guest on public affairs television programs and an author of columns on the opinion and editorial pages of leading newspapers. When a former government official recommends a particular policy position, is he or she speaking as a private citizen, as a former government official, or as a businessperson who gets paid to disseminate a particular point of view in the press?

TO WHAT EXTENT DO INTEREST GROUPS DRIVE FOREIGN POLICY?

It is difficult to generalize about the success of interest groups in determining foreign policy, especially given all the other factors that might influence policy. Moreover, there is likely to be significant variance across states. Whereas the United States has a political system that is especially open to influence by interest groups, many other states have fewer channels through which interest groups can operate. In addition, although there are cases in which interest groups have had an obvious impact on foreign policy, there are other cases in which it is difficult to detect their effect.

Governments have sought to devise ways to resist pressure from groups seeking protection. Many see the WTO as a broad effort to make governments less susceptible to lobbying. Similarly, many see the formation of the EU's "single European market" as a means of shifting trade policy decisions from national capitals to EU bureaucrats, presumed to be less subject to interest group pressures. However, an immense lobbying establishment has now built up in Brussels (administrative home of the EU), so that any respite from the influence of lobbying will likely be temporary.

Public Opinion

Public opinion is an important consideration in almost all policy decisions, even in nondemocratic societies, and foreign policy is no exception. Unfortunately, despite the global spread of public opinion polling, most analysis of the influence of public opinion on foreign policy has concerned one country, the United States.[31] Ironically, research on public opinion and foreign policy has violated one of the cardinal rules of polling, that a poll must be conducted using a **representative sample.**

- Research on public opinion and foreign policy has focused on four separate issues: What does public opinion "look like"? Are people well informed, or not? Are their attitudes stable or unstable? Is foreign policy important to them or not?

- What effect *should* public opinion have on policy? This is a normative question. Should public opinion play an important part in leaders' considerations, either because of democratic values or because "the people know best"? Or should foreign policy be the domain of experts, who have more knowledge and better judgment than the average citizen?

- What effect *does* public opinion have on foreign policy? This question is central in understanding the sources of foreign policy. Do decision makers limit their policies to what they think will be popular? Can public opinion force leaders to adopt new policies or change unpopular ones?

■   What influences public opinion on foreign policy? Where does the public get its information, and who or what is influential in shaping and changing public attitudes? Can leaders actively shape public opinion? What about the news media?[32]

WHAT DOES PUBLIC OPINION LOOK LIKE?

A great deal of research has focused on the relatively simple question: What do people think about foreign policy? Researchers have tried to measure popular support for various actual or potential foreign policies. They also assess the extent to which people disagree with each other or the government. For example, during much of the Cold War, many scholars wrote of a "Cold War consensus" that referred to agreement across most of the U.S. political spectrum on the need to contain communism and on the best ways to do it. A similar consensus exists today in Pakistan regarding relations with India.[33]

In all the research on public opinion and foreign policy, a few facts consistently emerge. First, most citizens do not pay much attention to foreign policy, except in times of crisis. Most of the time, only 20 to 30 percent of citizens in democracies are interested in foreign affairs.[34]

Second, and related, most citizens know very little about foreign affairs. Surveys show repeatedly that citizens (especially in the United States) know little about the geography, history, or current leadership of other countries. Moreover, sometimes what citizens "know" is manifestly wrong. A majority of U.S. citizens vastly overestimates the amount of foreign aid that the United States gives to poor countries. The public can be misinformed even on issues to which it is paying close attention. A study of multiple polls taken before and after the U.S.-led invasion of Iraq in 2003 showed that 20 to 25 percent of Americans incorrectly believed that Iraq had been directly responsible for the 2001 terrorist attacks in the United States.[35]

These basic facts—citizens care little, know little, and sometimes harbor significant misperceptions—have led many to lament, "How can a country be expected to have a wise foreign policy if the voters are apathetic and uninformed?" Private foundations and the government (not to mention college professors) thus expend considerable resources trying to get people more engaged. Others find public ignorance "rational." They argue that because citizens have many issues to focus on, it makes sense that they pay little attention to foreign policy. They can always learn more when a situation merits it.[36]

Contrary to earlier studies that found that public opinion was highly volatile, changing quickly based on events or on attempts at persuasion, recent research has found that individuals tend to have a structured set of beliefs about foreign policy that are linked to one another, are mostly consistent with one another, and are relatively stable over time.[37]

SHOULD PUBLIC OPINION MATTER?

Some people argue that the public should have extensive influence over foreign policy, for several reasons. The first is simply democratic theory. The point of democracy is to give the governed control of the government, and foreign policy should be no exception. Moreover, some hope that public opinion will have a positive effect on foreign policy.

In general, our view of the desirability of a strong public influence on foreign policy is partly related to our level of trust in the government to do the right thing by itself. Which is more dangerous, an irresponsible government or an uninformed public? For those who mistrust leaders, the public check on foreign policy is crucial. For those worried about the influence of interest groups on foreign policy, an involved public provides a necessary counterweight. However, for those concerned that the public is uninformed or subject to irrational passions, leaving foreign policy to the experts is more desirable.

The History Connection

Press and Public Opinion in the Spanish-American War

In perhaps no episode in history has the role of the press and public opinion been more controversial than in the run-up to the Spanish-American War (1898), in which the United States seized from Spain territories including Cuba, Puerto Rico, and the Philippines.

The push toward war was strongly supported in the United States by two competing New York newspapers, the *New York World,* owned by Joseph Pulitzer, and the *New York Journal,* owned by William Randolph Hearst. The two papers, competing to be the first to reach a circulation of one million, ran increasingly sensationalist stories throughout the 1890s about Cubans' struggle for independence from Spain, riots in Havana, and Spanish repression of the populace.

As Cuba slid toward conflict, Hearst, in particular, saw the opportunity to increase circulation. He sent reporters and artists, including author Stephen Crane and sculptor Frederick Remington, to capture the scene in Cuba for his readers. When Remington wrote to Hearst that there was no war in Cuba to report on, Hearst responded, "Please remain. You furnish the pictures. I'll furnish the war." Pulitzer and Hearst competed to print the most gripping stories of the mistreatment of Cubans by the Spanish. Coverage of the situation in Cuba occupied as many as eight pages in some issues of the *Journal,* and competing papers sought to avoid being outdone. Overall, the effect was that the U.S. news media saturated readers with calls for war.

When the U.S. battleship *Maine* exploded in Havana harbor in February 1898, the *Journal* blamed the explosion on Spain (a claim for which there was little evidence) and openly called for war against Spain. On April 4, 1898, a special issue of the *Journal* dedicated to war with Spain was published in a million copies, a huge number at that time.

U.S. President William McKinley initially opposed going to war to seize Cuba, preferring instead that Cuba gain autonomy from Spain. However, pressure from public opinion and Congress constrained his choices. On April 11, 1898, McKinley sought permission from Congress to intervene in Cuba, and Congress quickly passed what was effectively a declaration of war. By

Hearst's *New York Journal* left little doubt that the *Maine* had been sunk by Spain.

all accounts, the attention given to the events by the New York newspapers was indispensable in convincing Americans to support war with Spain and in convincing McKinley that it would be politically devastating for him to oppose it.

Hearst and Pulitzer were memorialized in different ways. Ironically, Pulitzer, who was credited with inventing "yellow journalism," became the namesake of a prestigious prize for journalism. Hearst, who sought to surpass Pulitzer, was the model for the title character in *Citizen Kane,* regarded as one of the finest films ever made.

Critical Thinking Questions

1. Can you think of recent events where sensationalist press helped drive a particular foreign policy?
2. Can citizens take some role in making the press more responsible? How?

PHOTO © ISTOCKPHOTO

Topham/The Image Works

DOES PUBLIC OPINION INFLUENCE FOREIGN POLICY?

This question is difficult to answer, because it is so hard to detect influence. If a change in public opinion is followed by a change in policy, can we conclude that the change in public opinion caused the change in policy? Not necessarily. It might be that some third factor (a crucial event or a campaign by some group) causes both public opinion and policy to change. Or, it may be that leaders first decide to change policy and then promote a change in public opinion. Even if public opinion does have an effect, it might not be possible to detect. If policy makers consider a change in policy but reject it because they are afraid of the public's reaction, then public opinion has had an influence—but unless we can listen in on discussions at the highest levels of government, we will never see evidence of that influence.

Historically, public opinion has undoubtedly played a role in some foreign policies. A frequently cited case in the United States is the opposition to the Vietnam War. The U.S. Congress voted overwhelmingly to give President Lyndon Johnson authority to send ground forces into Vietnam in 1964. That Congressional vote reflected public opinion, which supported the troop deployment to halt the spread of communism in Southeast Asia. By 1967, large demonstrations against the war broke out, primarily on college campuses. By 1968, public opinion had shifted dramatically, and support for the war within Johnson's Democratic Party eroded. Johnson chose not to run for reelection, recognizing that he probably could not even win his own party's nomination. Almost every account of that conflict finds that public opinion played a decisive role in altering government policy. A similar process seemed to be underway in 2006, when many voters cited dissatisfaction over the U.S. war in Iraq in an election that saw significant reversals for the ruling Republican Party. Olympia Snowe, a Republican Senator from Maine, commented immediately after the election that policy on the war "absolutely has to change."[38] Public opinion can get a country into a war as well as out of it, as the case of the Spanish-American war shows (see History Connection box).[39]

Public opinion can be equally important in motivating change in economic policy. In Mexico, for example, shifting public opinion, which increasingly came to view Mexico as a "developed" rather than "developing" country, enabled President Vicente Fox to pursue a free trade-oriented policy after his election in 2000. In addition, scholars have perceived shifts in Mexican attitudes toward the United States, with closer ties to the United States seen as a way of improving the lot of average Mexicans.[40] At the same time, however, outcry against the war in Iraq forced Fox's government to oppose the war.

The Case Against the Importance of Public Opinion   Do the examples from U.S. and Mexican policy demonstrate that public opinion has a powerful effect on foreign policy? Most scholars and policy makers are skeptical, seeing the cases as notable exceptions. Because most people take little interest in foreign policy and know little about it, they are disinclined to take an active role in shaping it. The vast majority of foreign policy is carried out in relative obscurity, beyond the front pages (or even the inside pages) of the newspapers. On most issues, most of the time, therefore, leaders can ignore public opinion.

However, the exceptional cases raise two questions. First, when do exceptions arise, and how? Second, if leaders know that exceptions are possible, how does this knowledge affect their policies? The concept of *latent public opinion* helps answer both these questions.

Latent Public Opinion   Although the public may be passive and apathetic about most foreign policy questions most of the time, the knowledge that the public can become very active at any time does influence foreign policy decision making.[41] Thus, public opinion might have a *latent* effect. Leaders try to anticipate which issues or policies are likely to turn public opinion from a latent to an active factor.[42]

Figure 5.1 Looking at the graph, what hypotheses might one advance about the influence of public opinion in this case?

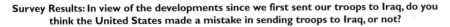

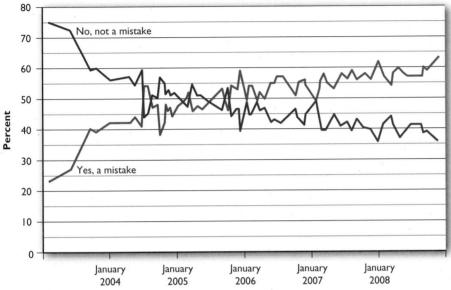

Survey Results: In view of the developments since we first sent our troops to Iraq, do you think the United States made a mistake in sending troops to Iraq, or not?

Source: http://www.gallup.com/poll/106783/Opposition-Iraq-War-Reaches-New-High.aspx. Used by permission of Gallup.

If public opinion is usually latent (inactive), what determines when and for which issues it becomes active? One finding in research is that public opinion becomes more important when leaders disagree. When there is debate within a government or among the broader "foreign policy elite" that includes experts and nongovernmental research institutions, the opposing sides are likely to turn to the public to gain support for their positions. This can occur even in authoritarian societies. In Iran, for example, there has been public disagreement between "hardliners" and "liberals" concerning, among other things, the country's policies toward nuclear weapons and toward the West. In the Soviet Union, foreign policy debates, including debates over the possibility of winning a nuclear war, emerged in public on several occasions.

Another factor that increases public interest is military casualties. In many military conflicts, public support erodes when casualties rise. This phenomenon has had an important constraining effect on the planning of military operations. Whether force will be used—and how operations are planned—is strongly influenced by leaders' desire to keep casualties at nearly zero.

Figure 5.2 In 2002, only 4% of the U.S. public believed Iraq had anything to do with the terrorist attacks on September 11. As President Bush began mentioning Iraq more often when speaking about the "global war on terrorism," more people began to associate Iraq with 9/11. By January 2003, 44% believed that most or some of the 9/11 terrorists were from Iraq. In fact, none of the terrorists were Iraqi. This is an example of the ability of a popular leader to sway the public's beliefs.

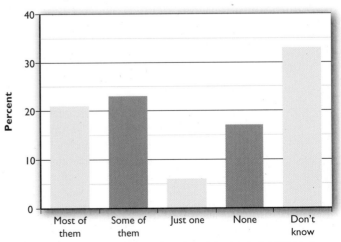

Survey Results: As far as you know, how many of the September 11th terrorist hijackers were Iraqi citizens?

Source: Knight Ridder poll conducted by Princeton Survey Research Associates. Jan. 3–6, 2003, http://www.pollingreport.com/iraq17.htm. Reprinted by permission of The Polling Report.

Such considerations influenced the first Bush administration's decision not to push on toward Baghdad to eject Saddam Hussein during the first U.S.-Iraq war in 1991 and prompted the Clinton administration's determination to rely only on bombing, and not on ground troops, to force Serbian troops out of Kosovo in 1999. So worried was Clinton about public opposition to U.S. casualties, which would have been inevitable in a ground invasion, that he did not even want to threaten an invasion or prepare for it as a way of pressuring the Serbian government. More recently, Vice President Joseph Biden and others have advocated an increased use of air strikes to fight the war in Afghanistan in order to reduce U.S. casualties. The possibility that such air strikes increase civilian casualties on the ground has made them controversial.

WHAT DETERMINES THE CONTENT OF PUBLIC OPINION?

The study of the effect of public opinion on foreign policy has been informed by broader research on the sources of political attitudes in general. The predominant school of thought today sees public opinion as being structured and consistent, if not deeply informed. But to the extent that the public does have views, where do they come from?

Much of the content of public opinion seems to be determined by elite views, because these are generally what the public is exposed to. In other words, rather than public opinion influencing political leaders, often the opposite occurs. As Seymour Martin Lipset, a prominent scholar of public opinion, puts it, "The president makes public opinion, he does not follow it."[43] Citizens hear opinions on foreign policy issues primarily from government officials, publicly recognized "experts," and leading journalists. It makes sense that the range of public opinion would therefore reflect the range of elite opinion.

However, much depends on the degree of elite consensus. Consensus among elites creates a **mainstream effect**, whereby only one view is expressed by leaders and people get only one view from the media. In such an atmosphere, people are likely to adopt this "mainstream" view.[44]

mainstream effect

The tendency for the public to follow political leaders and the media when those actors have consensus on an issue.

Competition over Public Opinion   When there is a lack of consensus among elites, however, there is likely to be a battle over public opinion.[45] This battle often takes the form of an effort to frame the issue in a way that will lead people toward a particular conclusion. For example, a political party that opposes immigration will try to frame the issue in terms of lawbreaking or diminished security, whereas a proimmigration party will try to frame the issue in terms of the gains to society from the increased labor supply. Whether a particular conflict is labeled "genocide" or whether a particular practice is called "torture" often is part of an effort to shape attitudes. The people who specialize in political communication are experts at producing words and visual images that establish their preferred frames in the minds of citizens and other elites.

To Whom Does the Public Listen?   Many actors—including interest groups and NGOs, political parties, and individual leaders—seek to frame issues, but research indicates that some actors have much more influence over public opinion than do others, and hence have a disproportionate ability to frame issues and sway public opinion.

Research on the U.S. case shows that elected officials do not generally have much sway over public opinion. Citizens appear to recognize that these officials are partisan and hence not objective observers. A low level of trust for elected officials in general might also explain this lack of influence.

However, there is one important exception to the weak influence of public officials: Popular heads of government can have a significant effect on public opinion.[46] The more people approve of the job the head of government is doing, the more likely people will be to trust his or her judgment on foreign policy issues.

Popularly recognized "experts" are also shown by research to have influence over public opinion. These experts are sometimes former government officials, such as former

AP Photo/Vahid Salemi

Iranian President Mahmoud Ahmadinejad at an anti-Israel rally in Tehran, Iran. Research shows that popular leaders can sway public opinion on foreign policy. Does Mahmoud Ahmedinijad's popularity in Iran make it more likely that citizens will embrace the nuclear programs he supports?

ministers of defense or foreign affairs. On military matters, former senior officers are often viewed as experts. Occasionally, even college professors are accorded this status. These experts' opinions are transmitted to the public through a variety of avenues. Experts are often sought out for interviews by journalists, and they often are guests for longer discussions on television talk shows. These experts are influential for two related reasons. First, they are introduced as experts. Second, they are viewed (often incorrectly) as being nonpartisan and unbiased. However, many of these experts are paid by special interest groups or even foreign governments to promote specific policies.

Finally, prominent journalists may also influence public opinion. They are widely recognized, and people often trust these journalists to give them most of their information about the world. And whereas most of the news they report is presented as "objective," journalists have a great deal of latitude concerning which stories get covered and how they are framed.

The Media in Foreign Policy

The news **media** play an important role in determining the agenda of public debate. Even if news sources do not always tell people what they should think, they do indicate, simply by what they choose to cover, what issues people should think *about*. When a network news program decides to do its one international story on a particular issue, or when that issue is the only international story on the front page of a newspaper, this suggests to the viewer or the reader that the issue is an important one. Thus, it is important to understand how this agenda is formed.

media

The different means through which news and entertainment are conveyed.

WHAT DETERMINES WHICH ISSUES THE MEDIA COVER AND HOW THEY ARE COVERED?

How do editors and journalists decide what the public needs to know, and what other pressures do the media face? One pressure that helps determine what gets covered is the business side of journalism. Most news outlets around the world are owned by people hoping to make a profit. Therefore, journalists and editors have strong incentives to give their audience not just what they *need*, but what they *want*. Many journalists might believe

"I'm still undecided—I like Leno's foreign policy, but Letterman makes a lot of sense on domestic issues."

that citizens need a deeper understanding of the sources of terrorism, the problems of poverty in Africa, or the foreign policy views of the Japanese government. But do viewers *want* to read about those issues or see them covered on a television program? Or would people rather watch an exclusive interview in which a movie star discusses her battle with substance abuse? In an environment in which profits are driven by the ability to sell advertising, and advertising revenue is driven by the number of viewers, there are strong incentives to assume that what viewers will watch is what they need.

In 2009, only two international stories (the war in Afghanistan and election protests in Iran) were among the top ten stories (in terms of minutes of coverage) on U.S. network news. The death of Michael Jackson earned more coverage than any international story except Afghanistan. Iraq, where the United States was still heavily involved, was not among the top twenty stories.[47]

EFFORTS TO INFLUENCE MEDIA COVERAGE

Journalists and their editors do not make their decisions in a vacuum. Many people and organizations seek to influence what journalists cover and how. Just as lobbyists seek to persuade legislators to address certain issues, lobbyists also try to get journalists to cover certain issues. They may do this by calling journalists on the phone and explaining why their issue is important or by staging a newsworthy event.

One factor that determines when and if an issue gets covered is whether the issue has an identifiable "angle" or a "story" to it. Issues that evolve slowly over time, such as poverty, may never present a single event that makes journalists or editors believe that the issue should be covered that very day.

Those seeking to get their stories into the news, therefore, compete to devise events that are worthy of news coverage and provide exciting footage for television. An NGO might sponsor a particularly spectacular rally or public display. Legislators may schedule hearings and require well-known people or executive branch officials to testify in those hearings in order to create good video or photo opportunities. Such events are timed carefully so that they are less likely to coincide with other events that might "bump" them off the front page or the evening news.

In getting a particular issue on the agenda, the executive branch of the government has powerful advantages over other groups. First, because foreign policy is chiefly the responsibility of the executive branch, the activities of a head of government, the secretary of state or foreign minister, and the defense minister are inherently newsworthy. If the head of government simply gives a speech expressing concern about an issue, it is immediately important news. High-ranking government officials thus have immense power to shape the news agenda.

In many countries, leaders have more direct means of controlling the media. In Mexico, prior to political reform in the 1990s, most media outlets were controlled by or allied with the ruling party, the PRI (Institutional Revolutionary Party). Moreover, most newspaper advertising revenue came from the government, so newspapers had powerful incentives to keep the leaders happy. This allowed leaders to shape news coverage and to avoid coverage of difficult issues. As the political process in Mexico became more democratic, media became more independent. This independence led to a period of "high politicization," in which the media were controlled by political and economic elites.[48] More recently, Russia and Venezuela have seen successful efforts by governments to increase control over media.

MEDIA POWER

Despite being subject to the influence of advertisers, lobbyists, and others, the media can nevertheless place items on the agenda that governments then are forced to deal with. This ability is sometimes called the **CNN effect**, referring to the nearly instantaneous worldwide news coverage that was pioneered by CNN (Cable News Network) in the early 1990s.[49] The news coverage that led up to the U.S. intervention in Somalia in 1992 is a classic case. News outlets began giving increasing coverage to a serious famine in Somalia that had resulted from civil war. Images of starving people halfway around the world confronted Americans on their living room television screens and in their morning newspapers. There was an increasing sense that "something must be done," and shortly before leaving office, George H. W. Bush deployed U.S. forces to provide enough civil order to allow food to be distributed. Secretary of State Lawrence Eagleburger later recalled, "I will tell you quite frankly, television had a great deal to do with President Bush's decision to go in the first place; and I will tell you equally frankly, I was one of those two or three that was strongly recommending he do it and it was very much because of the television pictures of the starving kids."[50]

However, the CNN effect may well be exaggerated, and the Somalia case may be an exception. There are few similar cases and many counterexamples, such as the case of Darfur. Even in Somalia, the U.S. government intervened in large part because it believed that the costs of intervention would be low. Moreover, since the Somalia episode in 1992, most newspapers and television networks have drastically cut back on overseas staffing in order to save money, reducing their ability to provide detailed accurate coverage.

CNN effect
The ability of the media to draw attention to an issue and force policy makers to address it.

AP Photo/Roberto Borea

When U.S. Special Forces landed on the beach in Mogadishu, Somalia, in December 1992, TV cameramen were there to meet them. What effects do the media have on the conduct of foreign policy?

The Media, Public Opinion, and the State

Although it is possible to identify the media, the public, and the state as three primary actors shaping foreign policy, it is difficult to state conclusively which of these three actors is "driving" the other two. There are three models of influence, as shown in Figure 5.3. In the real world, all of these processes may be happening simultaneously, with interest groups, lobbyists, and public relations firms competing to shape the outcome of the process.

The first model focuses on the ability of the executive branch of government to shape the public agenda through the media. By getting the media to focus on particular issues and by using its access to media to frame those issues, the executive can create public demand for the very policies it favors. In this model, the public is a "captive" of the executive branch (and the media). In fact, some proponents of this model argue that government responsiveness to public opinion is a myth created by the government itself. The executive branch has the ability to bring an issue to the public's attention not only through rhetoric, but also through action. Deployment of military force, signing a new agreement, or attending a "summit meeting" with foreign leaders can focus attention on a particular issue.

In the second model, the media lead, as in the CNN effect. This model assumes that the media have an independent notion of what ought to be on the agenda, and perhaps even what ought to be done about it. In this view, media coverage of an event raises public concern, and the public demands that the government "do something" about the problem in question. Alternatively, the government, anticipating the concern being generated by media attention, may take steps even before the public demands them.

In both of these models, the public is largely passive, which reflects much of the research on public opinion. In the third model, the public may be passive, but its role as consumers of advertising forces the media to cater to it. News providers figure out what kinds of stories the public will pay attention to—which ones will prompt them to buy newspapers or tune in to television programs—and then provide those kinds of stories. Political leaders then seek to show that they are doing something about the issues the public cares about. For example, knowing that the public is very willing to consume news reports about death and violence, the media give prominent coverage to the deaths of soldiers in war. This coverage puts considerable pressure on governments, given public sensitivity to casualties.

There is some truth in all of these models. Different forces seem stronger at different times and on different issues. Rather than creating simple models relating public opinion, the media, and foreign policy makers, it may be more helpful to devise *contingent generalizations,* in which we make one generalization about what tends to happen in

Figure 5.3 Three Models of Influence

Executive leads	Executive sets agenda	Media cover executive	Public opinion follows media
Media lead	Media set agenda	Public opinion follows	Executive follows public opinion
Public leads	Public sets agenda	Media cater to public opinion	Executive follows public opinion

Source: Paul D'Anieri

one set of circumstances, but a different generalization about what will happen in other circumstances, and so on.

Four contingent generalizations about public opinion in foreign policy are worth noting. First, when there is consensus among leaders, the public tends to follow this "mainstream" view and there tends to be consensus in public opinion. Second, when there is dissent among leaders, the potential role of the media and of public opinion expands considerably. Third, extraordinary issues, most notably those related to war and peace, seem most likely to shift the public from passivity to activity, and in this regard, public opinion is especially sensitive to casualties in military actions (and those resulting from terrorism). Fourth, when public opinion does become active, political leaders are often very sensitive to it, especially if elections are near.

Reconsider the Case

War in Iraq and Democratization in the Middle East

The Bush administration policy of using force to introduce democracy to the Middle East was widely seen as a failure. Not only did democracy not thrive in Afghanistan and Iraq, but various abuses associated with those wars discredited, in the eyes of many, the agenda of democracy promotion. At the same time, however, some argue that the introduction of elections has changed the nature of debate in the region. In 2009, rigged presidential elections in Iran were met with widespread street demonstrations by a population that expected better. In Saudi Arabia, one of the most illiberal states in the world, the royal family began slowly introducing some limited steps to opening society, including a discussion of the ban on women driving automobiles.

When Barack Obama was elected president of the United States in late 2008, U.S. policy itself began to change. The Obama administration distanced itself from the democracy promotion agenda, focusing more on "concrete" results of policy. Obama supported the democracy agenda in principle but recoiled from the idea of using force: "It [democracy] is one of our best exports, if it is not exported simply down the barrel of a gun." Obama was skeptical of the narrow focus on elections as the primary indicator of democracy, saying that "in a lot of countries… the first question is freedom from want and freedom from fear. If people aren't secure, if people are starving, then elections may or may not be able to address those issues." Obama's secretary of state, Hilary Clinton, similarly changed emphasis. In her confirmation hearings, she discussed a wide number of issues,

but said relatively little about democracy promotion. She discussed "three D's" of foreign policy (defense, diplomacy, and development) but did not include a fourth—democracy.[51]

Democracy advocates in both major parties were dismayed by Obama's turn toward realism. They emphasized that although Bush had taken a particularly militant approach to promoting democracy, the policy had deep roots in U.S. foreign policy under Democratic as well as Republican presidents. Jennifer Windsor, executive director of Freedom House, stated: "To see democracy as a particularly Republican or Bush policy is to misunderstand our country's foreign policy history."[52]

Several analysts pointed out that although Obama's policy seemed an abrupt change from that of George W. Bush, the focus on concrete interests resembled that of earlier republicans, including George H. W. Bush and Richard Nixon.[53] Oddly, the Republican president had adopted a strongly liberal policy, while the Democratic president took a more traditional realist position.

Critical Thinking Questions

1. How confident are you that the democratic peace theory is essentially correct? What limits might you place on it?

2. How has the debate on democracy promotion shifted in recent years?

3. How would you weigh the relative importance of democracy promotion compared with other foreign policy goals?

Summary

This chapter has considered two related questions about the role of state and society in foreign policy making. First, how does the nature of the state influence the substance of foreign policy? We explored two different answers. At a general level, the state structure argument asserts that the form of state institutions influences the kinds of tools a government is most likely to employ. Moreover, the focus on "state strength" finds that some states are more open to societal influence than others. A much more specific theory is the democratic peace hypothesis, which holds that democracies do not resort to war when dealing with each other.

Both the state strength and democratic peace arguments prompt us to look more closely at the role of interest groups and public opinion. If democracies are less likely to go to war with one another, what role does public opinion play? In the second half of the chapter, we explored these questions, finding that both interest groups and public opinion play an important role at times, but that no simple generalization can capture the complexity of these relationships. Ultimately, many analysts are convinced that it is less important to focus on society, and more important to focus on the government officials that are closest to actual policy making, and we turn our attention to them in the next chapter.

Key Concepts

1. The state
2. Democratic peace theory
3. "Simple" versus "dyadic" models of democratic peace theory
4. Structural, normative, and institutional explanations of the democratic peace
5. State structure
6. State strength
7. Interest groups
8. Lobbying
9. Public relations
10. Latent public opinion
11. Mainstream effect
12. "CNN effect"

Study Questions

1. How are theories of foreign policy different from theories of international politics?
2. How do different theoretical approaches view the role of the state in foreign policy?
3. What are the hypothesized links between democracy and peace in democratic peace theory?
4. What two historical patterns must democratic peace theory account for?
5. How strong is the evidence supporting democratic peace theory?
6. What are the major criticisms of democratic peace theory?
7. What are the policy implications of democratic peace theory?
8. How does state structure influence foreign policy?
9. What kinds of interest groups are involved in the making of foreign policy?
10. What strategies and resources do interest groups use to influence foreign policy?
11. Research on public opinion and foreign policy focuses largely on the United States. Would you expect to find similar or different patterns in other countries? Why or why not?

12. Why do people disagree about how much influence public opinion should have on foreign policy?

13. In what ways might public opinion influence foreign policy, and what are the limits on such influence?

14. What advantages does the executive branch of government have in defining the agenda of the news media?

 CourseMate

Endnotes

1. President Bush Discusses Freedom in Iraq and Middle East," remarks by the president at the twentieth anniversary of the National Endowment for Democracy, Washington, D.C., November 6, 2003.

2. "Bill Clinton, "Address Before a Joint Session of the Congress on the State of the Union *January 25, 1994*" at http://www.gpoaccess.gov/sou/index.html

3. President and Danish Prime Minister Rasmussen Discuss G8, Africa," White House Press Release, July 6, 2005.

4. Condoleezza Rice, "The Promise of Democratic Peace: Why Promoting Freedom Is the Only Realistic Path to Security," *Washington Post,* December 11, 2005, p. B7.

5. "President Bush Discusses Freedom in Iraq and Middle East," remarks by the president at the twentieth anniversary of the National Endowment for Democracy, Washington, D.C., November 6, 2003.

6. Robert Jervis, *Perception and Misperception in International Politics* (Princeton, NJ: Princeton University Press, 1976), pp. 14–15.

7. Bruce Russett, *Grasping the Democratic Peace* (Princeton, NJ: Princeton University Press, 1993), pp. 3–40.

8. James Fearon, "Domestic Political Audiences and the Escalation of International Disputes," *American Political Science Review,* Vol. 88, No. 3 (September 1994): 577–592.

9. Russett, *Grasping the Democratic Peace,* pp. 30–38; Zeev Maoz and Bruce Russett, "Normative and Structural Causes of Democratic Peace, 1946–1986," *American Political Science Review,* Vol. 87, No. 3 (September 1993): 624–639.

10. Bruce Bueno de Mesquita, James D. Morrow, Randolph M. Siverson, and Alastair Smith, "An Institutional Explanation of the Democratic Peace," *American Political Science Review,* Vol. 93, No. 4 (December 1999): 791–807.

11. David A. Lake, "Powerful Pacifists: Democratic States and War," *American Political Science Review,* Vol. 86, No. 1 (March 1992): 24–37; Dan Reiter and Allan C. Stam III, "Democracy, War Initiation, and Victory," *American Political Science Review,* Vol. 92, No. 2 (June 1998): 259–277.

12. Bueno de Mesquita et al., "An Institutional Explanation," p. 801.

13. John M. Owen, "How Liberalism Produces Democratic Peace," *International Security,* Vol. 19 No. 2 (Fall 1994): 87–125.

14. Bueno de Mesquita et al. list eight "empirical regularities" that they associate with the democratic peace.

15. Zeev Maoz and Nasrin Abdolali, "Regime Types and International Conflict, 1816–1976," *Journal of Conflict Resolution,* Vol. 33, No. 1 (March 1989): 3–35.

16. Michael Doyle, "Kant, Liberal Legacies, and Foreign Affairs," *Philosophy and Public Affairs,* Vol. 12, No. 3 and No. 4 (Summer and Fall 1983): 205–235, 323–353; Maoz and Abdolali, "Regime Types and International Conflict," pp. 4–6.

17. Jack S. Levy, "The Causes of War: A Review of Theories and Evidence," in Philip Tetlock, Jo L. Husbands, Robert Jervis, Paul C. Stern, and Charles Tilly, eds., *Behavior, Society, and Nuclear War,* Volume I (New York: Oxford University Press, 1989), p. 270.

18. See the critique of Doyle's categorization of World War I in David Spiro, "The Insignificance of the Liberal Peace," *International Security,* Vol. 19, No. 2 (Fall 1984): 50–86. Doyle's justification is in "Kant, Liberal Legacies, and Foreign Affairs," footnote 8.

19. Ido Oren, "The Subjectivity of the 'Democratic' Peace," *International Security,* Vol. 20, No. 2 (Fall 1995): 147–184.

20. Spiro, "The Insignificance of the Liberal Peace," p. 51.

21. The process of expansion of the zone of peace in Europe is discussed in detail in Jan Zielonka and Alex Pravda, eds., *Democratic Consolidation in Eastern Europe, Volume II: International and Transnational Factors* (Oxford: Oxford University Press, 2001).

22. Address of the President of the United States to the Senate, January 22, 1917, at http://www.lib.byu.edu/~rdh/wwi/1917/senate.html

23. Peter Katzenstein, ed., *Between Power and Plenty: Foreign Economic Policies of Advanced Industrial States* (Madison: University of Wisconsin Press, 1978).

24. T. J. Pempel, "Japanese Foreign Economic Policy: The Domestic Bases for International Policy," in Katzenstein, ed., *Between Power and Plenty,* pp. 139–190.

25. Peter Katzenstein, "Conclusion: State Structure and Strategies of Foreign Economic Policy," in Katzenstein, ed., *Between Power and Plenty,* pp. 295–336.

26. Joel Migdal, *Strong Societies, Weak States: State-Society Relations and State Capabilities in the Third World* (Princeton, NJ: Princeton University Press, 1988).

27. See, for example, Nils Boesen, *Enhancing State Capacity—What Works, What Doesn't, and Why?* (Washington, DC: World Bank, 2004).

28. *The Economist,* October 21, 2006, p. 54.

29. Ian Taylor, *Stuck in Middle GEAR: South Africa's Post-Apartheid Foreign Relations* (Westport, CT: Praeger, 2001).

30. *Washington Post,* December 10, 2005.

31. Douglas Foyle, "Foreign Policy Analysis and Globalization: Public Opinion, World Opinion, and the Individual," *International Studies Review,* Vol. 5, No. 2 (June 2003): 165. For one exception, see Thomas Risse-Kappen, "Public Opinion, Domestic Structure, and Foreign Policy in Liberal Democracies," *World Politics,* Vol. 43, No. 4 (July 1991): 479–512.

32. For an excellent review of the literature on public opinion in U.S. foreign policy, see Philip J. Powlick and Andrew Katz, "Defining the American Public Opinion/Foreign Policy Nexus," *Mershon International Studies Review* 42 (1998): 29–61.

33. Mohammad Waseem, "The Dialectic between Domestic Politics and Foreign Policy," in Christophe Jaffrelot, ed., *Pakistan: Nationalism without a Nation?* (London: Zed Books, 2002), p. 264.

34. Risse-Kappen, "Public Opinion, Domestic Structure, and Foreign Policy in Liberal Democracies," p. 481.

35. Program on International Policy Attitudes, "Misperceptions, the Media and the Iraq War," October 2, 2003, at http://www.worldpublicopinion.org/pipa/articles/international_security_bt/102.php?nid=&id=&pnt=102&lb=brus.

36. Robert Shapiro and Benjamin Page, "Foreign Policy and the Rational Public," *Journal of Conflict Resolution,* Vol. 32, No. 2 (1988): 211–247. John Aldrich, John L. Sullivan, and Eugene Borgida, "Foreign Affairs and Issue Voting: Do Presidential Candidates 'Waltz Before a Blind Audience?' " *American Political Science Review* 83 (1989): 123–142.

37. Ole R. Holsti, "Public Opinion and Foreign Policy: Challenges to the Almond-Lippman Consensus," *International Studies Quarterly* Vol. 36, No. 4 (December 1992): 448–449.

38. Robert Toner, "A Loud Message for Bush," *New York Times,* November 8, 2006.

39. Luis Carlos Ugalde, "U.S.-Mexican Relations: A View from Mexico," in Luis Rubio and Susan Kaufman Purcell, eds., *Mexico under Fox,* (Boulder, CO: Lynne Rienner, 2004), pp. 123,132.

40. Andrés Rozental, "Fox's Foreign Policy Agenda: Global and Regional Priorities," in Rubio and Purcell, *Mexico under Fox,* pp. 96,109.

41. Powlick and Katz, "Defining the American Public Opinion/Foreign Policy Nexus," pp. 33–35.

42. Powlick and Katz, "Defining the American Public Opinion/Foreign Policy Nexus," p. 33.

43. Seymour Martin Lipset," The President, the Polls, and Vietnam," *Transactions* 3 (1966): 20, quoted in Powlick and Katz, "Defining the American Public Opinion/Foreign Policy Nexus," p. 29.

44. Powlick and Katz, "Defining the American Public Opinion/Foreign Policy Nexus," 35; John Zaller, *The Nature and Origins of Mass Opinion* (Cambridge: Cambridge University Press, 1992).

45. Powlick and Katz, "Defining the American Public Opinion/Foreign Policy Nexus," pp. 34-35; Benjamin I. Page, *Who Deliberates? Mass Media in American Society* (Chicago: University of Chicago Press, 1996).

46. Benjamin I. Page and Robert Y. Shapiro, "Presidents as Opinion Leaders: Some New Evidence," *Policy Studies Journal* 12 (1984): 649–661.

47. These statistics are from the Tyndall Report, "Top 20 Stories of 2009," (http://tyndallreport.com/yearinreview2009/). The analyses cover week-night newscasts. Up-to-date weekly analyses of network coverage can be found at http://www.tyndallreport.com

48. Daniel C. Hallin, "Media, Political Power, and Democratization in Mexico," in Myung-Jin Park and James Curran, eds., *De-Westernizing Media Studies* (New York: Routledge, 2000), pp. 97, 99, 108.

49. Research on the CNN effect is reviewed in Eytan Gilboa, "Global Television News and Foreign Policy: Debating the CNN Effect," *International Studies Perspectives* (August 1995): 325–341.

50. "The CNN Effect: How 24-Hour News Coverage Affects Government Decisions and Public Opinion," a Brookings/Harvard Forum: Press Coverage and the War on Terrorism, at http://www.brookings.edu/events/2002/0123media_journalism.aspx

51. Peter Baker, "Quieter Approach to Spreading Democracy Abroad," *New York Times*, February 22, 2009.

52. Baker, "Quieter Approach to Spreading Democracy Abroad."

53. Michael Freedman, "Barack Obama Is No Jimmy Carter. He's Richard Nixon," *Newsweek International Edition*, May 4, 2009.

CHAPTER

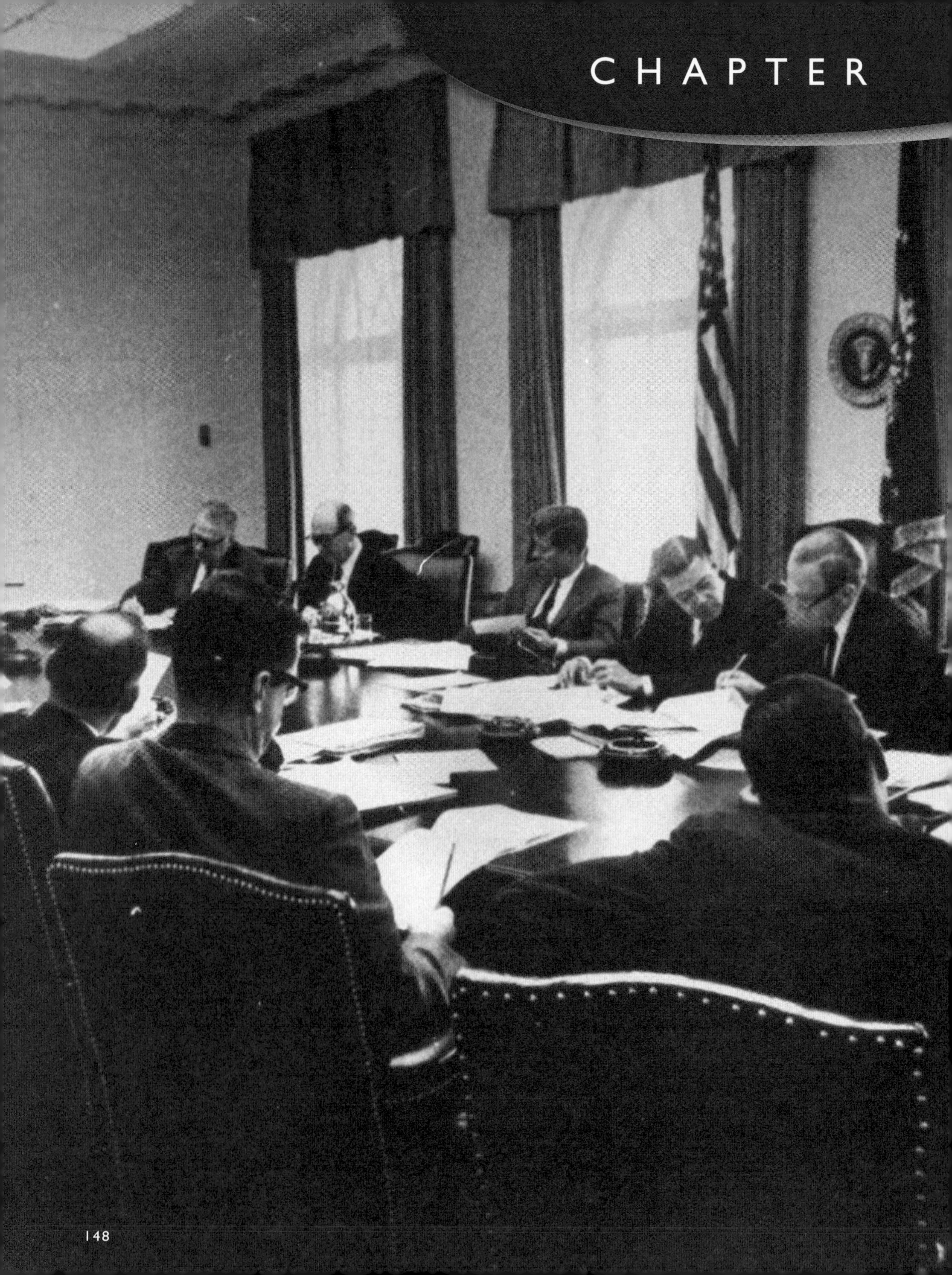

6

Bureaucracies, Groups, and Individuals in the Foreign Policy Process

LEARNING OBJECTIVES

After completing this chapter, the student should be able to . . .

1. Identify the major points of the rational action, bureaucratic politics, and organizational process models of foreign policy making.

2. Understand the arguments for and against the importance of individual decision makers in foreign policy making.

3. Weigh the influence of group dynamics on decision making.

4. Identify the range of sources of misperception in foreign policy making.

5. Understand prospect theory and its implications for decision making in international politics.

◀ John F. Kennedy meets with his closest advisors, the "ExCom," during the 1962 Cuban Missile Crisis.
Cecil Stoughton/Time Life Pictures/Getty Images

Consider the Case

Israel's Invasion of Lebanon, 2006

In the summer of 2006, **Hezbollah**,[1] a group operating in Lebanon with support from Syria and Iran, began attacking towns in northern Israel with mortars and Katyusha rockets. Hezbollah soldiers then crossed the border to kidnap two Israeli soldiers, killing three others in the process. Israel responded with a ground invasion of Lebanon, supported by air strikes. After a month of intense fighting, a cease-fire was brokered.

Many Hezbollah fighters were killed and many of the group's weapons were destroyed, severely diminishing its capacity to fight. But by withstanding Israel's attack, Hezbollah temporarily gained immense prestige in the region. Israeli casualties were low, but the absence of a decisive victory against a poorly equipped and much smaller foe, combined with the considerable collateral damage caused in Lebanon, led many in Israel and in the international community to view the invasion as a failure.

A subsequent inquiry in Israel faulted the prime minister, the defense minister, and the army chief of staff for deciding to invade without collecting sufficient information.

"The decision to respond with an immediate, intensive military strike was not based on a detailed, comprehensive and authorized military plan, based on careful study of the complex characteristics of the Lebanon arena . . . . Consequently, in making the decision to go to war, the government did not consider the whole range of options, including that of continuing the policy of 'containment', or combining political and diplomatic moves with military strikes below the 'escalation level', or military preparations without immediate military action, so as to maintain for Israel the full range of responses to the abduction."[2]

Why did Hezbollah not anticipate that its kidnapping of the Israeli soldiers would prompt Israel to invade Lebanon? Or was that the response Hezbollah hoped to provoke? And why did Israel go to war without first considering other alternatives or the likely consequences of the invasion? More broadly, why, historically, do countries so often have similar regrets after decisions to go to war? When the stakes are so high, and with so many experts available to consult, why are decisions to use force so often made without thorough weighing of costs, benefits, and alternatives?

Hezbollah

A military and political force in Lebanon. It operates as a parliamentary party in Lebanese politics and is also a transnational terrorist movement, conducting attacks in Israel as well as in Lebanon.

In Chapter 5, we focused on the nature of the state as a source of foreign policy behavior. In this chapter, we make two related shifts. First, we are again changing our level of analysis. The theories discussed in Chapters 3 and 4 tend to focus on the system level, and those discussed in Chapter 5 focus on the state level. In this chapter, we look inside the state for sources of foreign policy, beginning with several levels that might be labeled "substate" and working all the way down to the level of the individual. In contrast to the approaches we have examined so far, the understanding of international relations discussed in this chapter assumes that foreign policies "bubble up" from within a government, and so are not "made" at the top or imposed by circumstances.

Second, we change our focus from *structure* to *process*. In the previous chapter, we focused on the *structure* of the state, and in Chapters 3 and 4, we emphasized the *structure* of the system. Structural approaches see outcomes determined by a set of unchanging constraints (structures) such as the distribution of power or the type of government. The approaches discussed in this chapter stress process as a distinct source of variation in state behavior.

AP Photo/Jeff Riggins/NBC Newswire

Israel's invasion of Lebanon in 2006 was seen, in retrospect, as poorly planned and executed. What accounts for the decisions that state leaders make?

Foreign Policy Analysis

In Chapter 5, "foreign policy" replaced "international politics" as the subject of analysis. In considering the influence of factors *within* the state and society, we are shifting from the question "How does international politics work?" to the question "What determines foreign policies?" Obviously, there is a great deal of overlap in these two questions, but they contain different emphases and are likely to yield different answers.

Since the early 1960s, the field of **foreign policy analysis** has grown rapidly. It includes scholarly research as well as much of the analysis undertaken by government intelligence agencies and foreign ministries around the world. In seeking to predict what other governments do, these actors put a lot of effort into understanding how different governments make foreign policies and what might influence a change in these policies.

Foreign policy analysis is not, however, important only to governments. It is also important to anyone who hopes to influence a government's foreign policy. If a group of citizens wants a government to change its policy and the group has a limited amount of time and money, where should it aim its effort? At the foreign ministry? At the head of government? At the legislature? How might the answer change depending on whether the target government is that of Germany, the United States, Mexico, or Nigeria?

Foreign policy analysis can be divided into three areas of study. The first concerns the workings of *bureaucracies*. Presidents and prime ministers love to complain about bureaucracies, but governments cannot function without them. Based largely in the disciplines of management and organizational behavior, the study of bureaucracies gives important insight into why leaders feel constrained and frustrated by them. The second approach examines the process of *decision making*, not only in large bureaucracies, but also in small groups, such as a leader's immediate advisors. A third school of thought considers the *psychological* characteristics of leaders themselves and draws on insights from the field of psychology to help explain the many ways in which the idea of rationality seems to provide a poor explanation of behavior. The reader will notice, however, that all three of these schools of thought focus on the executive branch of government. Why do we not consider the judicial branch, or, especially in democracies, the legislative branch? This question must be answered prior to considering the bureaucratic, decision-making, and psychological approaches in detail.

foreign policy analysis
Analysis that attempts to understand states' behavior in terms of actors and processes at the domestic (state and sub-state) level.

Branches of Government

The role of the different branches of government varies across countries, and across time and issues within countries. Most foreign policy analysis, however, focuses on the executive branch for three reasons. First, in many countries, the constitution or legislation specifies that the head of government shall be responsible for making foreign policy. In the U.S. Constitution, for example, Article II, Section 2, stipulates that the president shall be commander-in-chief of the armed forces and has the right to sign treaties and appoint ambassadors (subject to Senate confirmation).

Second, there is often (although not always) agreement within a country that the country needs to have a single voice abroad and that the head of government should be that voice. Thus, international "summit meetings," such as those held by the G-8 countries, are attended by heads of government, not groups of legislators. There is a perceived need to speak with a single, united voice on the international stage and to play down internal disagreements on policy. There are certainly exceptions to this general rule, such as when legislators, citizen groups, or opposition politicians seek to make foreign policy themselves or to undermine the authority of the head of government, but these cases are relatively rare. Most of the time, a single individual is allowed to lead in the area of foreign affairs. This notion is captured by the phrase "politics stops at the water's edge," meaning that no matter how much disagreement on policy there is within a country, the country's politicians strive to present a "united front" abroad.

Third, heads of government tend to control the making of foreign policy because they control the executive branch of government. Most foreign policy is made not through legislation, but through negotiation, implementation of laws, and sometimes war. The conduct of diplomacy, the gathering of intelligence, or the waging of war are functions carried out by agencies of the executive branch.

In the United States, the constitution makes the president commander-in-chief of the armed forces, and these forces can be sent into combat on the president's orders. Congress has the constitutional authority to declare war but has not used it used since the outbreak of World War II. In practice, the president can initiate war whether Congress approves or not. After the Vietnam War, Congress passed a resolution known as the **War Powers Resolution** to reassert congressional control over decisions to go to war, but it is not clear that the resolution has had much effect. The resolution requires that if the president puts U.S. troops into a combat situation, the troops must be removed after sixty days unless Congress passes legislation allowing the operation to continue. U.S. presidents have consistently held that the law is unconstitutional but have generally behaved according to its provisions, so its constitutionality has yet to be tested in a court challenge.

The same situation often occurs in other countries. Ukraine, for example, sent a contingent of troops to take part in the occupation of Iraq in 2003, despite a resolution against such a deployment passed by that country's parliament. Because the Ukrainian constitution, like the U.S. Constitution, states that the president is the commander-in-chief, he was able to deploy the troops against parliamentary opposition. In contrast, German forces cannot be sent into combat without the prior approval of the German Parliament.

Legislatures in Foreign Policy

Although in many respects foreign policy is the domain of the executive branch, there are significant ways in which legislatures influence policy. This legislative influence has increased in many countries that have become more democratic in recent years. The most

War Powers Resolution
A 1973 law that limits the U.S. president's ability to go to war without permission of Congress.

World leaders gather at the Nuclear Security Summit in Washington, D.C., April 2010. Gatherings of heads of state are considered important events. Meetings of legislators or judicial branch officials are less common and are generally ignored.

Jewel Samad/AFP/Getty Images

significant source of legislative influence is the power of the budget. In most democracies, all government expenditures must be approved by parliament. This gives the parliament power to block measures it opposes. Although the U.S. Congress found it difficult to persuade the president (first Johnson, then Nixon) to negotiate a settlement in Vietnam, it found that the "power of the purse" was an effective means to enforce its will. The Congress passed a resolution forbidding the expenditure of public money on the prosecution of the war. Essentially, this resolution said "you, as commander-in-chief, can do what you wish with the military, but you cannot pay for it with public funds." The cutoff of funding was effective in forcing the withdrawal of U.S. troops from Vietnam. After the majority in the U.S. Congress shifted to the Democrats in 2006, congressional efforts to limit the Iraq war by restricting funding took center stage in the debate about the war, although such a measure did not pass.

The same tactic has been used to influence U.S. policy in a wide range of areas. Congress can prohibit the funding of projects in countries toward which it determines the United States should take a tougher policy (such as countries in which there are human rights problems). For example, in 2010, the leadership of the House Foreign Affairs Committee held up an appropriation of $100 million in military aid to the government of Lebanon, due to concerns about the Lebanese army's connections to Hezbollah. The committee chair, a Democrat, was blocking the policy of a Democratic administration, which supported the appropriation as a way to support a friendly government and promote stability in the region.

However, the power of the legislature varies across countries. Steven Philip Kramer contrasts the French system sharply with that of the United States, arguing that the French National Assembly "has little say in foreign policy" and that the French Senate "has even less."[3]

In countries with a parliamentary, rather than a presidential, form of government, there is likely to be much less tension between the executive branch and the legislature because in parliamentary systems, the parliamentary majority chooses the prime minister (and the rest of the ministers). Thus, a situation in which the executive branch is controlled by one party and the legislature by another is impossible. Instead, when a majority coalition is made up of multiple parties, there may be difficult bargaining over foreign policy within the ruling coalition. In some cases, disagreement over foreign policy may prompt a governing coalition to collapse, forcing new elections. In Israel, for example, the need to keep a coalition intact has been a significant constraint on nearly every government's foreign policy.[4]

Members of the Israeli legislature debate during a special session called to address increased conflict with the Palestinians that followed the failure to reach an accord at Camp David in 2000. A no-confidence vote in the Israeli legislature can topple a government.

Pentagon Papers

A series of secret Defense Department reports on the origins of the Vietnam War that raised serious questions about U.S. involvement in the war.

Courts in Foreign Policy

Traditionally domestic courts have been involved in foreign policy only in isolated instances. Courts' jurisdiction is generally limited to domestic affairs, and foreign policy questions are very rarely the subject of lawsuits. Hence, the courts' role has been minimal. However, there are signs that the courts' role may be growing in response to recent developments. One example of domestic courts playing a prominent role was in the case of the "Pentagon Papers" in 1971. The **Pentagon Papers** were a series of secret Defense Department reports on the origins of the Vietnam War that raised serious questions about U.S. involvement in the war. They were leaked to the *New York Times* by a Defense Department employee. The *Times* planned to print the reports, but the administration of President Richard Nixon sued, arguing that they were secret. The U.S. Supreme Court ruled that the constitutional guarantee of a free press outweighed the government's interest in secrecy. The subsequent publication of the papers played an important role in undermining public support for the war. Although the Supreme Court decision was based on the principle of domestic free speech and was not in its substance about foreign policy, it had a significant effect on foreign policy.

More recently, U.S. courts have become involved in foreign policy through a series of lawsuits challenging the government's policies of detaining suspected terrorists without trial. The most noted case so far has been *Hamdan v. Rumsfeld* (2004), concerning the legal rights of Yasir Hamdan, who has dual U.S. and Saudi Arabian citizenship, was captured in Afghanistan, and was alleged by the U.S. government to be an "unlawful combatant." The Supreme Court was eventually asked to evaluate what kind of legal rights Hamdan had, and the case was seen as having wide repercussions for how the "war on terror" might be pursued. The Court ruled that Hamdan did indeed have legal rights as a U.S. citizen that needed to be protected and that the war powers of the executive branch did not limit the jurisdiction of the courts in the matter. The ruling was seen as placing limits on how terrorism suspects could be treated by the government.

In Spain in 1998, Judge Balthazar Garzon issued an arrest warrant for former Chilean dictator Augusto Pinochet for the alleged murder by Pinochet's government of Spanish citizens. Pinochet was vacationing in Britain at the time, and Garzon issued a Europe-wide arrest warrant, which obligated the British to arrest Pinochet and hand him over. The British courts then had to rule on whether the extradition was legal. Thus, the Spanish and British courts got involved in a major diplomatic tussle that primarily concerned the conduct of Chilean politics. Pinochet asserted that he was immune from prosecution, while victims of his regime supported putting him on trial. Ultimately, the diplomatic crisis was avoided by a British court's ruling that Pinochet was too ill to be put on trial. This allowed him to be released without setting any precedent about putting former dictators on trial abroad.

Since the Pinochet case, prosecutors and judges have appeared increasingly willing to seek to bring to trial former state leaders who have committed abuses and then have traveled outside their own countries. Garzon later caused another diplomatic panic when he sought to investigate the role of former U.S. Secretary of State Henry Kissinger in political violence in Latin America. In 2004, former Ukrainian Prime Minister

Pavlo Lazarenko was tried and convicted in the United States on money laundering charges stemming from allegations of corruption when he was prime minister. Incidents such as these almost always spill out of the legal arena into that of foreign policy because the "home" governments of these individuals almost always take a strong interest in what becomes of them. In the case of the Ukrainian Lazarenko, Ukraine's government cooperated with the U.S. prosecution team because Lazarenko was viewed as a political rival to then-president Leonid Kuchma.

The Executive Branch in Foreign Policy

Both courts and legislatures play an important role from time to time in the making of foreign policy. This is truer in democratic political systems, in which legislatures and courts generally play greater roles than they do in nondemocratic systems. Nonetheless, the vast majority of foreign policy decisions are made and implemented within the executive branch, so it is this branch on which the remainder of this chapter focuses.

The Rational Action Model

Discussions of how foreign policy decisions are made by governments almost always compare actual decisions to some ideal abstraction of how decisions should be made. This ideal is often referred to as the **rational action model**, although there is also a more explicit version of the rational action model known as "expected utility theory."

In trying to explain any decision, people implicitly assume that it is based on some underlying rationality. For example, an explanation of why Iran has sought to acquire nuclear weapons generally poses the question "What did the Iranian government hope to gain by that?" In framing the question that way, we presume that the Iranians' action is a logical attempt to achieve an identifiable goal. We do not ask whether they are trying to achieve some foreign policy goal; we simply assume it. The answer is arrived at by working backward: What goal would this policy most obviously serve? The pursuit of that goal must explain the policy. The alternative is to assume that actors do things for no reason, an assumption that defies reason and would make explanation impossible.

To say a decision was arrived at rationally does not mean that it turns out well. Sometimes even the best choices turn out badly for unpredictable reasons. But arriving at a rational decision does require making a conscious attempt to calculate the best choice. Figure 6.1 illustrates the four-step process of the rational choice model.

Expected Utility Theory

Economists and some international relations scholars have refined the general rational action assumption to derive **expected utility theory**, which is especially useful in

rational action model

A model that bases explanations of decisions on the assumption that decision makers have clear goals, calculate the costs and benefits of various courses of action, and pick the action that will best serve their goals.

expected utility theory

A variant of the rational action model. The theory asserts that leaders evaluate policies by combining their estimation of the utility of potential outcomes with the likelihood that different outcomes will result from the policy in question.

Figure 6.1 Rational Choice Model

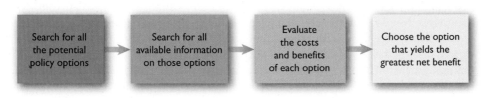

Search for all the potential policy options → Search for all available information on those options → Evaluate the costs and benefits of each option → Choose the option that yields the greatest net benefit

Source: Paul D'Anieri

thinking about decision making under uncertainty, when not all conditions are known and the results of a particular policy cannot be perfectly predicted. Expected utility theory focuses on two factors: payoffs and probability. *Payoffs* are the benefits (economists refer to these as the *utility*) of various outcomes. *Probability* is the chance that a particular outcome will result from a certain policy. Thus, expected utility theory views rational decision making not as seeking the highest payoff because there might be a one-in-a-million chance of gaining that. Instead, expected utility theory predicts that actors will choose the policy that has the greatest value when both payoffs and the probabilities of obtaining them are taken into account.

In mathematical terms, expected utility is equal to the value of an outcome times the probability of obtaining it. For example, when playing the lottery, the expected utility is the payoff times the odds of winning. If there is a one-in-a-thousand chance of winning $900, the expected utility is the chance of winning (.001) times the payoff ($900), or $0.90. Using the expected utility approach, it is rational to buy a ticket for such a lottery only if the ticket costs less than the expected utility of $0.90.

One problem with expected utility theory is that experience with lotteries indicates that people are either unable to calculate expected utility or are irrational in other ways; millions of people play lotteries in which their expected utility is negative. Lottery payoffs can be very high, but the odds against winning them are even higher, so that the expected utility of buying a ticket is always negative. Yet millions of people buy tickets every day. The theory cannot explain these decisions without stretching the definition of rationality considerably (by assuming that there is "utility" in playing the game itself). Likewise, many scholars and practitioners contend that in foreign policy, decision making deviates considerably from the ideal of rationality. Various approaches have been used to account for this.

Alternatives to the rational action model do not assert that policy making is *irrational*, but rather that the process by which foreign policy is made leads to important deviations from strict rationality. In a highly influential work published in 1969, political scientist Graham Allison applied two alternative approaches to the 1962 Cuban missile crisis to show how and why policies deviate from what would normally be regarded as "rational." Allison's "bureaucratic politics" model focused on how the struggle for influence among bureaucracies affects the policies that they create and prevents them from arriving at the ideal policy. His "organizational process" model looks at how the routines that bureaucracies follow produce policies based on the implementation of procedures, rather than on the search for the ideal policy.

Bureaucracies in Foreign Policies

Most foreign policies are conceived of and carried out by bureaucracies. This fact has led to a focus on bureaucracies as an important source of foreign policies. Understanding the role that these organizations play, however, is not easy, and there is some disagreement about how to interpret their role in foreign policy.

The words *bureaucracy* and *bureaucrat* have taken on a fairly negative connotation in popular political discourse, but governments cannot work without them. Legislatures and heads of state can make policy decisions, but they cannot implement anything by themselves. Nor do they have the time to collect the information needed to make policies or to monitor closely the implementation of policies. All of these tasks are delegated to various parts of the executive branch. Even in China, a country with a highly centralized political system, the expanding range and complexity of foreign policy issues require that specialized bureaucracies be given an expanded role in foreign policy development and implementation.[5]

The Culture Connection

Dr. Strangelove and the Rationality of Nuclear Deterrence

A critique of the rationality assumption as it applies to nuclear war might not seem like an entertaining basis for a movie plot, but in the film *Dr. Strangelove, Or How I Learned to Stop Worrying and Love the Bomb* (1964), the implications of rational deterrence theory are satirized. Besides being a hilarious movie and the only feature-length comedy by famed director Stanley Kubrick, *Dr. Strangelove* is perhaps the best way to get an idea of the level of paranoia that characterized the height of the Cold War

The film considers what could happen if an American general decided by himself to initiate war on the Soviet Union. The general does so because he is concerned that plans to add fluoride to drinking water, ostensibly to improve dental health, are actually a communist plot. He launches the attack, and the rest of the movie follows a B-52 pilot trying to carry out the attack and the efforts of the U.S. president and his military advisors to stop it. They know that if one bomber gets through, the Soviet Union will respond with a devastating nuclear strike.

In the course of the movie, the Soviet leadership reveals that it has built a "Doomsday Machine"—an automatic system that will detect the explosion of a nuclear weapon on Soviet territory and automatically launch a massive counterstrike. The twisted American strategic genius (Dr. Strangelove) points out that this

is not only possible, but perfectly rational. If the United States knows that a strike on the Soviet Union will automatically lead to the destruction of the world, it can never initiate such a strike. The fatal problem is that unless the Americans *know* about the Doomsday device, they cannot rationally modify their behavior. Thus, the lack of information leads to a disastrous policy.

In a related vein, the Americans are horrified to learn that the Soviets have developed an extensive system of nuclear shelters, built deep underground in mine shafts, so that they will survive the ensuing holocaust better than the Americans. This revelation causes much consternation among the Americans about a "mine shaft gap," Kubrick's way of satirizing the panic over a much-hyped (but nonexistent) "missile gap" in the early 1960s. Overall, the point of the movie is to show that somehow, what is perfectly rational at each step leads to a catastrophic result.

Critical Thinking Questions

1. In what ways do policy makers' behaviors routinely reject strict rationality?
2. Is it possible to base policy on the assumption that our partners or adversaries are irrational? How?
3. In what ways did policy in the Cold War differ from the satirical picture Kubrick paints in *Dr. Strangelove?*

PHOTO © ISTOCKPHOTO

Every country has a roughly similar set of executive branch institutions (bureaucracies). In most countries these are called **ministries** (in the United States, they are called "departments"). The two most important bureaucracies with respect to foreign affairs are the ministry of foreign affairs and the ministry of defense (or the Department of State and the Department of Defense, respectively, in the United States). A third key organization is one that collects and analyzes information, or "intelligence," on other countries. In the United States, this mission is divided among several organizations, including the Central Intelligence Agency (CIA) and the National Security Agency (NSA). In Britain, this mission is given to an organization known as MI6, which is most famous in fiction for employing James Bond. Russia's intelligence service is known as the Foreign Intelligence Service. China's is called the Ministry of State Security.

ministries

The main institutions of the executive branch of government. In the United States, these institutions are called "departments."

Russia's Foreign Ministry Building in Moscow. Around the world, ministries of foreign affairs are given primary responsibility for foreign policy. How does the process affect the outcome?

In addition to these organizations that are primarily concerned with foreign and security affairs, other ministries and agencies have important foreign affairs concerns as part of broader missions. Ministries of economics (in the United States, the Department of Commerce) have a great deal of oversight of foreign economic policy. Some countries have separate ministries of foreign trade. Thus, the question of who makes foreign policy in the executive branch becomes complicated very quickly. Depending on the issue, almost any ministry or agency can have a role in foreign policy. Coordination and competition among these different agencies and within them is an important challenge for every government in the world.

Those who focus on bureaucracies in foreign policy agree on one central point: the ways in which bureaucracies work deviate substantially from the notion of the unified rational state assumed by many theories and by popular news accounts. Although a news account or a realist analysis may say that "Russia" took an action or "Germany" enacted a new policy, those actions are usually implemented by agencies within those governments, and the decisions to enact those policies are heavily influenced by those agencies.

The Bureaucratic Politics Model

The bureaucratic politics model of foreign policy asserts that different bureaucracies have distinct, and often competing, interests. Policy often results from the messy process by which these bureaucracies fight for their interests, rather than from a search for the most "rational" policy for the country. To simplify, this perspective sees foreign policy making as influenced by a giant case of "office politics," in which policies may be chosen according to how bureaucrats and organizations pursue their own political needs rather than foreign policy needs. Thus, a study of China finds that "competition for turf and influence by rival bureaucracies appears to pervade the Chinese foreign policy system."[6]

BUREAUCRATIC INTERESTS

Why do different bureaucracies have different interests? Are they not all concerned with serving the national interest? Bureaucracies may promote different policies for two primary reasons: role and budget. First, because each agency has a particular notion of its "mission," it will tend to promote solutions that fit with that role. For example, the role of foreign ministries is to conduct diplomacy, solving problems through negotiation; defense ministries' role is to wage war, solving problems through the use of force. It is to be expected, then, that because these two bureaucracies have different roles and different tools at their disposal, they are likely to propose different solutions to foreign policy problems.

A second reason bureaucracies conflict over policy is that they are in competition over budgets, which will in turn affect the scope of their mission. Bureaucracies tend to seek larger budgets; to justify them, they need to show that what they do is more important than what other bureaucracies do. Hence, any bureaucracy will tend to support the foreign policies that put it in charge, use its solutions, and place a premium on its resources. Being in charge of policies and resources increases the importance of the organization, justifies a larger budget and more missions in the future, and increases the prestige associated with that organization.

These role and budgetary concerns of bureaucracies lead many to assert that in discussions over policy making, "where you stand depends on where you sit." In other words, top bureaucrats' positions on policy issues are determined by the interests of the organization they head, not just the government they serve. In many respects, the bureaucratic politics model looks like the realist balance of power theory applied to relations between bureaucracies rather than to those between states.

An important historical illustration is found in the career of Winston Churchill, who is most famous for having been Prime Minister of Britain during World War II. Prior to that time, Churchill served in several positions in the British government. As President of the Board of Trade, he argued against greater spending on the navy. Just a few years later, as First Lord of the Admiralty, in charge of the navy, he ardently asserted the need to substantially increase the budget in order to build more ships. Later, as Chancellor of the Exchequer (finance minister) in the 1920s, he again advocated reduced spending. Similarly, as Minister of Colonies in France in the late nineteenth century, Théophile Delcassé advocated that France send an expedition to the Nile River to challenge Britain's position in that region. Later, as Foreign Secretary (in charge of diplomacy), Delcassé sought to recall the expedition.[7] Examples like these are cited as evidence that bureaucratic politics strongly influence policy positions.

COMPETING PRIORITIES

In the United States, much is written about the struggle over foreign policy between the Department of State, which is viewed as tending to advocate diplomatic solutions, and the Department of Defense, which is seen as putting a greater emphasis on military solutions to problems. In his study of the **Cuban missile crisis**, Allison shows that military leaders advocated a surprise attack on Cuba from the very outset and continued to advocate that position. The State Department, in contrast, feared that a military response might spiral out of control and advocated holding off on military action until efforts at negotiation had been exhausted.

Cuban missile crisis
A crisis that arose in 1962 when the United States discovered Soviet missile bases in Cuba. The crisis nearly precipitated a nuclear war between the United States and the Soviet Union.

It is important to note that the bureaucratic politics model does not imply that all military leaders are "warmongers." Rather, these leaders see their primary mission as prevailing in a military conflict, should one occur. In the case of Cuba, military leaders viewed the crisis in those terms, and from a military perspective, it appeared that an early strike, before the Soviet missiles could be made operational, was safer. Delaying a strike would make it less likely that such a strike would succeed.

More recently, the State Department and the Defense Department disagreed profoundly concerning the best way to deal with Iraq prior to the war in 2003. The State Department, led by Colin Powell, sought to continue the diplomatic process as long as possible and to work within the United Nations Security Council where possible. The State Department was concerned about the diplomatic consequences of going to war and the difficulties involved in occupying Iraq afterward. The Defense Department, led by Donald Rumsfeld, showed disdain and impatience for the diplomatic process and the efforts to work through the UN Security Council. Because its primary goal was winning the war, the Defense Department considered the diplomatic wrangling to be interfering with planning the timing of the attack.

Pakistan has seen a different kind of problem in its efforts to combat the Taliban and Al-Qaeda along its border with Afghanistan. For many years, Pakistan's Directorate for Inter-Services Intelligence (ISI) supported many of the Al-Qaeda and Taliban training camps in the region because both groups supported Pakistan in its conflict with India over the territory of Kashmir. Although the Pakistani government, at least outwardly, shifted emphasis away from Kashmir and sought to close the camps, the ISI retained its commitment to the earlier goal and thus limited its efforts against the insurgents.[8] As a result, Pakistan's allies (notably the United States) complained that the country was not doing enough to combat terrorism.

The Policy Connection

Organizing to Fight Terrorism

Many governments have reorganized their intelligence and law enforcement agencies to deal with the rise of transnational terrorism. In the United States, review of the September 11, 2001, attacks revealed that various U.S. government agencies had had evidence that Al-Qaeda was planning a major attack involving hijacked airplanes.[1] However, the information was scattered among different organizations and was never put together in such a way as to present a clear picture of the danger. Prior to 2001, the organizational mission of the FBI included catching criminals after the fact, but not preventing crime. The CIA and other intelligence agencies were not tasked with threats on U.S. soil. Following the attacks, there was a far-reaching overhaul of security and intelligence services that included the creation of the Department of Homeland Security, to put many functions in one organization, and the Director of National Intelligence, to coordinate the 16 different intelligence service organizations. These changes in *structure* were intended to create changes in *process*.

In practice, there is uncertainty over the benefits of the changes. In December 2009, a Nigerian man boarded a flight from Amsterdam to Detroit with a bomb that failed to detonate. Afterward, it emerged that there had been considerable evidence that the man was a danger, but again, it had not been brought together. Moreover, bureaucratic infighting continuously undermined the newly created position of Director of National Intelligence, who was never able to gain budgetary or operational control over the CIA, which continued to report directly to the White House. Turnover was high, with four directors in five years.

Germany faced a different problem. In its federal system, there is no national police or intelligence service akin to the FBI or Britain's MI5. Instead, each of the *Länder* (states) has its own police force.

Coordination among these sixteen separate forces on terrorism and other national and international problems is difficult. For example, efforts to create a single nationwide database on terrorism are hindered by the fact that each state collects different data and organizes it differently.[2]

Pakistan encountered a different problem still. Its counterterrorism policy was largely handled by its intelligence organization, the ISI. Prior to September 11, 2001, the Pakistani government had actually supported the Taliban movement in Afghanistan, because that movement was seen as extending Pakistani influence. However, the Taliban's sheltering of Al-Qaeda, and Al-Qaeda's attacks on the United States, meant that Pakistan now had an interest in helping the United States combat those organizations. However, simply changing the internal practices of the ISI and the sympathies of ISI personnel has not been easy, and many observers continue to assert that ISI pursuit of Al-Qaeda and Taliban forces in Pakistan is halfhearted. As Taliban insurgents began attacking Pakistani government installations as well as U.S. targets in Afghanistan, Pakistani forces attacked them more directly, but the issue remained tense, both within Pakistan and between Pakistan and the United States.

Critical Thinking Questions

1. To what extent were U.S. intelligence failures prior to September 11, 2001, and prior to the Iraq war the result of organizational structure and process, as opposed to other factors?
2. Why has it been difficult to address the problems through reorganization?
3. What other kinds of decision-making problems are likely to complicate efforts to combat terrorism?

---

[1] See *The 9/11 Commission Report Final Report of the National Commission on Terrorist Attacks Upon the United States, Official Government Edition* (Washington, DC: U.S. Government Printing Office, 2004), Chapters 3, 8, and 11 (pp. 71–107; 254–277; 339–360). The report is available online at http://www.gpoaccess.gov/911/ index.html

[2] "Immune No More," *The Economist* (August 26, 2006), p. 43.

Critics of the bureaucratic politics model point out that disagreements among bureaucrats are not always determined by the relative influence of their respective bureaucracies. In Mexico, prior to the U.S. invasion of Iraq in 2003, there was profound disagreement *within* the Foreign Ministry between Ambassador to the United Nations Adolfo Zinser, and Foreign Ministe, Jorge Castañeda. Zinser refused to discuss policy with Castañeda and instead dealt only with President Vicente Fox.[9]

EFFECTS OF BUREAUCRATIC POLITICS

A crucial conclusion of the bureaucratic politics model is that the policies that emerge from bureaucratic conflict are often policies that *nobody* intended. When two or more organizations fight it out, often the result is unpredictable. In the case of the Cuban missile crisis, there was a dispute between the Air Force and the CIA over which entity would fly U-2 spy planes over Cuba to monitor the situation. Each side sought to carry out the mission. The eventual result was a compromise: Air Force pilots flew CIA planes. However, while this dispute was being resolved, neither organization made any flights for several days. Neither side advocated delaying flights, but that was the result. The consequence was that the missiles were discovered much later, and much closer to operational readiness, than otherwise would have been the case. This intensified the crisis by reducing the amount of time that Kennedy and his advisors had to find a solution.

To summarize, the bureaucratic politics approach sees foreign policy as the result of an internal battle, not as a decision agreed on by all the actors. The result may be a decision preferred by one of the bureaucratic actors, it may be a compromise between competing bureaucratic parties, or it might be something that none of them would have advocated.

CRITIQUE OF THE BUREAUCRATIC POLITICS MODEL

Critics of the bureaucratic politics approach assert that this portrait of "where you stand depends on where you sit" is a gross oversimplification. There are many examples of bureaucracies' advocating positions opposite what this approach would have predicted. In the United States during the administration of Ronald Reagan in the 1980s, the State Department was widely seen as advocating the use of the military to counter leftist insurgents in Latin America; the Defense Department resisted this approach. During the first Bush administration and again during the Clinton administration, the State Department sought to have the United States take an active role in stopping "ethnic cleansing" in the former Yugoslavia, using military force if necessary. It was the military that opposed such intervention, fearing that it would be bogged down in a conflict whose goals were unclear and from which there was no easy way out.

Further, some analysts are skeptical about the power of bureaucracies to escape the control of the head of government, who generally has a large staff dedicated to managing policy. Thus, such critics point out that, although President John F. Kennedy and Secretary of Defense Robert McNamara quarreled with leaders of the armed forces during the Cuban missile crisis, Kennedy prevailed.[10] An even more notorious case was the disagreement between President Harry S Truman and General Douglas MacArthur during the Korean War (1950–1953). When MacArthur, a charismatic figure and World War II hero, advocated extending the war to China, Truman simply fired him. Similarly, in June 2010, Barack Obama fired General Stanley McChrystal, the top commander in Afghanistan, after McChrystal and his staff expressed their lack of confidence in the civilian leadership.

The Organizational Process Model

The organizational process model stresses how the *procedures* by which bureaucracies make decisions influence the *content* of those decisions. This approach stresses the fact that bureaucracies make policies not by weighing the costs and benefits of all alternatives, but rather by applying similar procedures to the wide variety of questions that arise.[11]

Bureaucracies are created in large part to deal with an immense number of essentially similar situations. They create **standard operating procedures** to organize their work. These can range from the standard procedure used at a department of motor vehicles for issuing a driver's license to the standard procedure used at a ministry of foreign affairs to manage new information coming in from its embassies abroad. These procedures can be thought of as the bureaucratic equivalent of a computer program, which always performs the same function in response to the same input. If every time a foreign citizen wanted to enter Mexico, the Foreign Ministry had to figure out from scratch whether to issue a visa, the process would be incredibly inefficient. Instead, standard procedures are put in place to indicate what documents are required, what questions are asked, and what rules are applied in making the decision. Similarly, intelligence agencies bring in an immense amount of data and could not possibly manage all of it unless there were established practices for categorizing the data, filing it for later retrieval, synthesizing it into reports, and deciding which findings are important enough to be brought to the attention of higher authorities. In the military realm, armed forces cannot wait until they are at war to decide how they will fight a battle. Instead, they develop standard procedures, known as *doctrines*, which cover everything from how to wage tank warfare in the desert to how to cook the soldiers' dinner. In sum, procedures allow large organizations to function.

But just as a computer cannot do something it is not programmed to do, organizations can have great difficulty performing tasks that are outside their typical responsibilities or that require departing from standard operating procedures. Almost everyone has had the frustrating experience of dealing with a bureaucracy that invokes a narrow set of rules and procedures in response to a situation that is, in fact, unique. This happens in the realm of foreign policy as well. Standard operating procedures work well at handling large numbers of similar problems. But by their nature, they are not tailored to unusual situations. This limitation can lead to undesirable outcomes and to outcomes that deviate from the rationality assumption. A good example of this is German war plans prior

standard operating procedures

Procedures that bureaucracies adopt to deal efficiently with a large number of similar tasks.

Figure 6.2 Diagram of the Intelligence Process. Intelligence agencies around the world follow a standard process in gathering, analyzing, and disseminating information. Especially important is the feedback by which current findings inform planning for future information gathering. What kinds of problems might surface when this process breaks down?

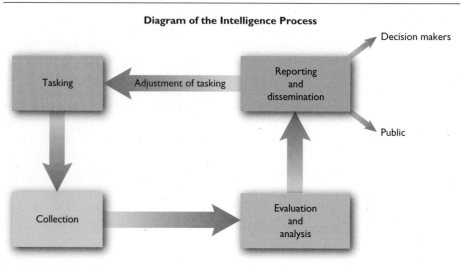

Diagram of the Intelligence Process

to World War I, as discussed in the History Connection box. This problem is inherent in the process of collecting and assessing intelligence, especially as it relates to terrorism. Collecting and sifting through vast amounts of data requires standard operating procedures, but the threats that one is seeking to identify are by their nature unique, and not standard.

Organizational Process versus Bureaucratic Politics

The organizational process model is quite distinct from the bureaucratic politics model. The bureaucratic politics model focuses on organizations struggling against one another for power and budgets. In contrast, the organizational process model examines the problem-solving procedures adopted by organizations and how they sometimes lead to unintended results. According to the bureaucratic politics model, what comes out of the process is a result of a battle. In the organizational process model, what comes out is an "output" of a defined process.

The point of both schools of thought, however, is the same. Both indicate that the rational model of decision making, which is typically applied to governmental policy making, is flawed. Both find that a significant amount of variation in policy can be explained by examining the workings of bureaucracies and small groups.

Small Group Decision Making

Although to a great extent foreign policy is made and executed by bureaucracies, many observers remain convinced that on issues that are important, key decisions are made by the head of government and his or her closest advisors. Therefore, much attention has been focused on the small groups of advisors that help heads of state make their decisions. The goal of such research is both to explain foreign policy and to offer advice on how to improve that process.[12]

Several pathologies of small group decision making may have particularly profound effects on foreign policy, leading policy to deviate significantly from "rational" decision making. Most important among these pathologies is a phenomenon whereby a group very quickly arrives at a single solution and closes off debate. This phenomenon, dubbed "groupthink" by one prominent analyst, means that in crucial situations, groups of decision makers often do not make an effort to examine a wide range of options.[13] Instead, members of the group are under a great deal of pressure to reach a consensus on policy. This need for consensus often leads decision makers to quickly agree on the option that first seems optimal.

There are several reasons why a group may dismiss certain options before they have been thoroughly assessed. First, in many groups, teamwork is highly valued, which often leads a group member to fall in with the preferences of the team even when he or she disagrees. Because all the members are expected to support the group's decision, members hesitate to criticize an option that appears to

"All those in favor say 'Aye.'"
"Aye."
"Aye."
"Aye."
"Aye."
"Aye."

The History Connection

The Schlieffen Plan and World War I

Among the best known cases in which the implementation of predetermined plans led to unintended (and disastrous) results was the German army's war plan prior to World War I. Known as the *Schlieffen Plan*, after the general who devised it, the strategy was to avoid having to fight simultaneously on two fronts: against France to the west and against Russia to the east. To prevent this, Schlieffen developed a plan whereby at the outset of war, the bulk of German forces would strike rapidly at France by passing through Belgium and Holland (thus bypassing the strongest French defenses). In the meantime, a much smaller force would keep Russia in check. Because Russia was a huge country with a somewhat underdeveloped military and transportation infrastructure, it would take several weeks for Russia to prepare to attack. The idea was to defeat France while Russia was still mobilizing. Then, as Russia became stronger, forces could be shifted to the east.

The military merits of the plan are debatable, but the diplomatic effects were profound. Germany's war plans depended on moving to war as rapidly as possible once a crisis occurred. To the extent that Belgium and Holland prepared to slow the German advance or that Russia began mobilizing its forces sooner than anticipated, the plan's success was imperiled.

Thus, during the July Crisis in 1914, the German army put immense pressure on German civilian leaders and diplomats to begin the war before its enemies could prepare. In particular, once Russia began its mobilization,

the clock was ticking. Unless France could be defeated by the time Russia was ready to fight, Germany would be doomed. The existence of a standard, predetermined plan for war removed any potential diplomatic flexibility Germany might have sought.

The situation in 1914 was exacerbated by the nature of military transportation. Mobilization was carried out primarily by rail, and extremely precise schedules had been worked out to move troops to the front and return rail cars to the rear. These precise schedules did not allow for a "lull" or a halt in mobilization once it had begun. Such a halt would have led to logistical chaos and severely delayed further mobilization. Hence, the train schedules themselves made it extremely risky, in military terms, for diplomats to agree on a halt in mobilization.

The Schlieffen plan, slightly modified, was carried out and narrowly failed. Belgian troops delayed German forces longer than expected and were reinforced surprisingly quickly by British forces, allowing France to regroup. The Russian army was able to mount an initial attack on the eastern front much more quickly than expected. The tragedy was not in the plan's failure, but in the fact that implementing the plan made it almost impossible to let diplomacy run its course before the initiation of war

Critical Thinking Questions

1. Given what you know about the outbreak of World War I, what other strategic options might Germany

PHOTO © ISTOCKPHOTO

be favored by the rest of the team. Hence, when one option begins to emerge as a favorite, there tends to be a rush to support it rather than to scrutinize it. Second, getting along with colleagues often requires refraining from subjecting their proposals to serious criticism, yet such criticism is exactly what the rational action model assumes will take place. These tendencies exist in a wide variety of groups, and those making foreign policy are no exception.

In foreign policy, however, a third factor may lead to even greater restriction of debate. A single individual (the head of government) is in charge of making the decision and is

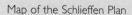

Map of the Schlieffen Plan

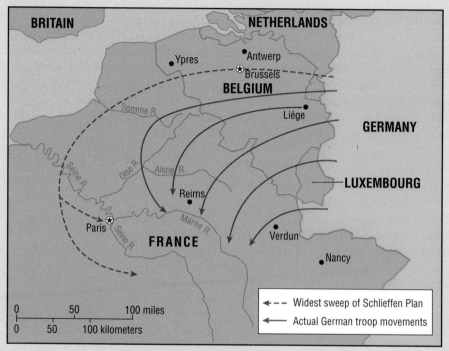

Source: http://encarta.msn.com/media_681500236_761569981_-1_1/schlieffen_plan_and_actual_troop_movements.html. Reprinted with permission from Microsoft Corporation.

have devised? How much blame for the war should be placed on the Schlieffen Plan versus other factors?

2. Contrast diplomacy efforts during the July Crisis that led to World War I with those made during the Cuban missile crisis. How was diplomacy related to military strategy in the Cuban case?

3. Can the models in this chapter be used to analyze the 2003 U.S.-led war with Iraq? How did beliefs about how the war would proceed influence U.S. and Iraqi diplomacy prior to the war?

also responsible for the career success of everyone else in the room. Once it appears that the leader favors a particular choice, there are strong disincentives to raise criticisms of that policy. Criticism may be regarded as disrespectful at best and as disloyal at worst. Access to the leader and influence, which ambitious political officials value most, are at stake.

In some instances, disagreeing with the leader does not lead to negative consequences. However, announcing that one does not share the views of the head of government may make it less likely that one will be consulted on future problems. Thus, disagreement can lead to reduced access and influence. In still other cases, it can cost the individual his or her job in the inner circle. In the most extreme cases, such as in the Soviet Union under Joseph Stalin (who ruled from 1922 to 1953), such disagreement could result in the advisor's imprisonment, exile, or execution.

For these reasons, there is a tendency on the part of a head of state's advisors to try very hard to figure out ahead of time what policy the leader will support and then to support that view. Once a policy is favored, there are strong incentives to support it rather than to scrutinize it or to put other options on the table. In this way, one of the most important requirements of rational decision making—an even-handed evaluation of all the options—may be very unlikely in the real world of small-group decision making.

Many analysts of the decision making leading the U.S. decision to invade Iraq in 2003 pointed to groupthink in the U.S. intelligence community. A bipartisan report by the U.S. Senate Select Committee on Intelligence, published in 2004, found that: "IC [intelligence community] personnel involved in the Iraq [weapons of mass destruction] issue demonstrated several aspects of groupthink examining few alternatives, selective gathering of information, pressure to conform within the group or withhold criticism, and collective rationalization."[14] The report went on to point out that several standard procedures specifically intended to avoid groupthink, such as "'red teams,' 'devil's advocacy,' and other types of alternative or competitive analysis," were neglected.[15]

Individual Decision Making

So far, we have "unpeeled" the layers of decision making from the level of the state down to bureaucracies and to small groups. Ultimately, some scholars point out, many of the most important policy decisions are made by a single decision maker, the head of state. If this individual has some latitude for action and if different leaders do not all behave identically, then it follows that the particular characteristics of the individual leader will have a substantial effect on what kind of policies are made. This is why the media spends so much effort analyzing a new leader who has come to power in an important country. At the level of the government, it explains why intelligence agencies spend so much effort collecting clues to the psychology or leadership style of foreign leaders.

In several important historical cases, the characteristics of individual leaders appeared to play a crucial role in determining policy. Germany under Adolph Hitler is one such example. Many believe that under a different leader, Germany would not have pursued the policies that it did. Ironically, many also believe that if not for Hitler's leadership, Germany might have won World War II, or at least been able to fight much longer. Most people, when considering elections such as for a new president, believe that different leaders will have very different foreign policies. In the case of the United States, people in the United States and around the world believe that different individuals would make dramatically different foreign policies, whether the choice is between Bush and Gore or Obama and McCain. In all of these cases and in general, then, individual leadership seems to matter. But how? How is the "personality" or "style" of one leader different from that of another, and how do individual traits guide leaders to different responses to the same situation or challenge?

Skeptics wonder whether individual leaders really make that much of a difference. Leaders may be subject to so many international and domestic political constraints that they often feel that they have little freedom of action. For example, Barack Obama came to power in the United States committed to getting U.S. troops out of Afghanistan and to closing the U.S. detention facility in Guantanamo Bay, Cuba. When he took office, and had to face the options and their consequences, he chose to increase the U.S. force level in Afghanistan, and as of July 2010 had not come up with a plan to close Guantanamo Bay, largely because there were no palatable alternatives for dealing with the detainees held there. In practice then, Obama's policy did not differ dramatically from Bush's."

Perception and Misperception

Ambiguity and uncertainty are inherent characteristics of international politics. How leaders resolve such uncertainty will help explain policy choices, and different ways of resolving ambiguity may explain why different leaders might respond differently to the same situation. A great deal of research has been conducted on the sources of perception and misperception in international politics. Most of this research marries psychological research on cognition to historical evidence gathered from case studies. The amount of research conducted is extensive, and the number of theoretical approaches used is vast, so here we will merely sample some of the more prominent approaches and try to stress some key concepts.

One key distinction to keep in mind is that between "unmotivated" and "motivated" bias. **Unmotivated bias** is bias that results from the simplifications and categories that every decision maker uses to make sense of a complicated world. **Motivated bias**, on the other hand, is bias that is driven by some psychological or emotional need.

UNMOTIVATED BIAS

Unmotivated bias naturally creeps into the way that people grapple with large amounts of information and simplify highly complex problems. Central to the idea of unmotivated bias is the notion that decision making is characterized by "bounded rationality." The theory of **bounded rationality** posits that decision makers are trying to be rational but that they face several inherent limits on their ability to do so. People are limited in how much information they have access to and in their ability to effectively process all the information. Time limits further reduce the ability to acquire and process information. People therefore take a number of "shortcuts" to make timely decisions in a world of bewildering complexity and limited information. In this view, decision making is not irrational but rather is *imperfectly* rational. Several approaches from the cognitive psychology literature have been applied to the study of international politics to show how unmotivated bias is a product of humans' cognitive limits.

Attribution Theory   Attribution theory offers one explanation of how misperception often results from unmotivated bias. Attribution theory sees decision makers as "naïve scientists," actively working to understand the world accurately.[16] In this view, the key process is **attribution**, whereby individuals attribute the behavior of others to one cause or another. The simplified models that result from the effort to understand how the world works are used to explain behavior. According to this perspective, new evidence can and does change existing understandings (and hence policies), but often imperfectly.

Attribution theory focuses on how decision makers' theories about how the world works are shaped and how they change. Of particular interest are generalized findings in the field of psychology about how preexisting beliefs shape the interpretation of new information. What people already believe strongly shapes their interpretation of new information. According to attribution theory, this tendency is driven by the way in which individuals with limited time and information are forced to take shortcuts. Rather than going through a full scientific process, as implied by the rational decision making model, individuals instead look around until they come up with an explanation that is fairly plausible, and they often stop there. Thus, those explanations that we already have are likely to be used first to explain new events.

One particular finding of psychological research is especially relevant to the study of international politics: the **fundamental attribution bias**. The fundamental attribution bias is people's tendency, when looking at actors they mistrust, to attribute those actors' negative behaviors to "bad" or aggressive intentions and to attribute the actors' positive behaviors to circumstances beyond their control. People tend to apply the opposite set of biases to themselves. When people do something that might be criticized, they attribute

unmotivated bias
Bias that occurs as a result of the simplifications inherent in the process of perceiving an ambiguous world.

motivated bias
Bias that occurs as a result of some psychological need, such as the need for all of one's beliefs to be consistent with each other ("cognitive consistency") or the need to believe that a good solution to a problem is available.

bounded rationality
A theory that decision makers try to be rational but face several inherent limits on their ability to do so.

attribution
The process whereby individuals attribute the behavior of others to one cause or another. Attribution can create unmotivated bias in decision makers.

fundamental attribution bias
The tendency to believe that if an adversary makes a concession, they were forced to, but if they make an unwelcome move, they did so freely due to bad intentions; and the tendency to have the opposite bias about ourselves.

their behavior not to "bad" intentions but to circumstances that left them little choice. People tend to see their own positive behaviors as the results of their own good will.

The fundamental attribution bias lends important insight to the workings of the security dilemma. In an anarchic world, each actor is faced with uncertainty about others' intentions. Actors are therefore concerned about the abilities of others to hurt them. If one state makes a move to expand its influence, does the act arise from aggression or from a desire to protect itself? The fundamental attribution bias indicates that actors are more likely to mistake a peaceful state for an aggressive one rather than vice versa. Other things being equal, this tendency will make it more likely that a security dilemma will spiral toward higher levels of armament, mistrust, and conflict. Moreover, actors tend to believe strongly that their own moves are unthreatening to others and that others can easily see this. Hence, if others respond negatively to their policies, actors tend to conclude that others are hostile, not that they genuinely feel frightened.[17]

This problem may have played an important role in the early years of the Cold War.[18] U.S. leaders interpreted a variety of Soviet actions as proof of the Soviet Union's aggressive designs to expand as far as possible into central Europe. The installing of pro-Soviet governments in Poland, Czechoslovakia, and East Germany was seen as prime evidence of Soviet expansionism. Much less attention, however, was given to the Soviet withdrawal from Austria, which it had also occupied at the end of World War II. It is difficult to build trust in situations in which concessions are not noticed.

Today, the same phenomenon may be occurring in a variety of conflicts around the world. For example, states that have possessed nuclear weapons for a long time consider it obvious that their own weapons are not threatening to others, whereas they perceive efforts by other states to gain nuclear weapons as a sign of aggression. The states seeking nuclear weapons probably see their own efforts not as acts of aggression but as acts of deterrence, preventing others from attacking them. Iran, for example, has seen two of its immediate neighbors, Afghanistan and Iraq, invaded in recent years, and Iran itself was attacked by Iraq in 1980. A similar phenomenon takes place in international trade negotiations. Countries tend to regard their own barriers to trade as necessary and justifiable economic, environmental, or safety policies. At the same time, they tend to view other states' trade barriers as deliberate efforts to "cheat" in international trade. Thus, the United States sees EU loans to Airbus as illegal subsidies but does not see U.S. military contracts to Boeing as subsidies. The EU sees it the other way around, and there has been a series of conflicts over the two companies' competition in the market for commercial airliners.

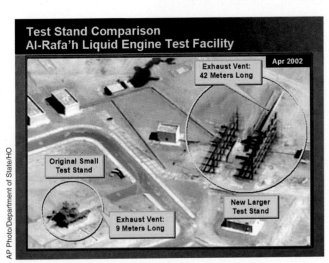

AP Photo/Department of State/HO

What is in this photo? U.S. leaders claimed that it showed sites of Iraqi weapons of mass destruction. Leaders as well as citizens based their support for the invasion of Iraq on that belief. The belief turned out to be wrong.

Historical Lessons and Analogies   Another example of unmotivated bias that results from bounded rationality is the use of lessons or analogies from the past to interpret present circumstances. Psychologists note that people tend to develop mental categories over time and to try to fit new people or events into these already familiar categories. Historians point out that leaders repeatedly use decisive events from early in their adult lives as the basis for categories with which to interpret later phenomena.

An example of fitting people into standard categories was illustrated by James F. Byrnes, who was U.S. Secretary of State in the early Cold War period (1945–1947). He had to deal with the Soviet leader Joseph Stalin, whose motivations were unclear.

Having served in the U.S. Senate, however, Byrnes believed he knew how to deal with the Soviets, saying "It's just like the U.S. Senate. You build a post office in their state, and they'll build a post office in our state."[19]

The Lesson of Munich More often noted is how leaders compare new crises with old ones. One of the most common scenarios over the past sixty years has been to assume that authoritarian leaders whose countries are aggressive are just like Hitler. The reasoning that usually follows is that, since Hitler was stopped only through war and since the delay in confronting Hitler was costly, this new leader must be stopped immediately. Those who advocate negotiation in such situations are then sometimes accused of "appeasement," the strategy pursued by British Prime Minister Neville Chamberlain, who mistakenly believed that giving concessions to Hitler would satisfy him.

The **lesson of Munich**, referring to British attempts to appease Hitler at the 1938 Munich peace conference, has influenced policies repeatedly since World War II. The decision to confront the Soviet Union after World War II was motivated in large part by the belief that, had Hitler been confronted sooner, World War II could have been avoided. The British Prime Minister at the time, Neville Chamberlain, has been criticized since for "appeasement," but he himself was acting on the basis of the lesson of a previous war: the horrors of World War I, it was believed, could have been avoided if the July 1914 Crisis had been resolved through concessions rather than confrontation. In responding to the North Korean invasion of South Korea in 1950, U.S. President Harry Truman explicitly compared the situation to events prior to World War II: "Communism was acting in Korea just as Hitler, Mussolini, and the Japanese had acted ten, fifteen, twenty years earlier. . . . If this was allowed to go unchallenged, it would mean a third world war, just as similar incidents had brought on the second world war."[20] When communism was gaining popularity in Vietnam in the late 1950s, U.S. leaders believed that it must be stopped or that it would gain in momentum and power, just as Hitler had.[21] The lesson was invoked again by President George H. W. Bush in 1990 when Iraq invaded Kuwait. Bush explicitly compared Saddam Hussein to Hitler.

After September 11, 2001, comparisons of current events with those before World War II again became popular. During the debate over invading Iraq in 2003, British Foreign Secretary Jack Straw warned that hesitating in the conflict with Iraq would be equivalent to the reluctance to confront Hitler in the late 1930s. The cover of an issue of *Time* magazine showed Saddam Hussein with a red X painted over his face, directly mimicking the cover the magazine had run after the fall of Hitler in 1945.[22] In 2006, George W. Bush compared Osama bin Laden to Hitler, referred to Islamic terrorists as "fascists," a term widely applied to Nazi Germany, and equated criticism of his policy in Iraq with "appeasement."[23] Bush stated further that today's terrorists are "the successors to fascists, to Nazis, to communists and other totalitarians."[24] Secretary of Defense Donald Rumsfeld asserted that terrorism presents the same kind of threat as Nazi Germany's invasion of Poland in 1939. "I recount this history because once again we face the same kind of challenges in efforts to confront the rising threat of a new type of fascism."[25] It is debatable whether the equating of today's issues with those of 1939 was actually influencing the Bush administration's policy or whether this rhetoric was merely a way of justifying that policy. Even if the latter is true, it shows the leaders' belief that the analogy would be compelling to listeners.

The Lessons of Vietnam Although the lesson of Munich has been widely influential, the Vietnam War also taught "lessons" to subsequent generations, although not everyone learned the same lessons from that conflict. To those who came of age during the Vietnam conflict, that war provides a point of view from which to evaluate every subsequent military conflict. The lessons taken from that war by many, especially those in the military, are that starting wars is much easier than ending them, and that what starts as a small intervention can grow into a conflict of massive proportions if the alternative is to admit defeat.

lesson of Munich
The lesson learned from British attempts to appease Hitler at the 1938 Munich peace conference, namely, that costly wars can be avoided by confronting hostile leaders promptly.

Powell Doctrine

A set of criteria guiding
military engagement, including
establishing clear goals and
using overwhelming force.

Thus, U.S. national security advisor (and later Secretary of State) Colin Powell, who experienced Vietnam firsthand as a young officer, developed a set of criteria collectively known as the **Powell Doctrine** to guide the use of force. The criteria included being clear about goals and using "overwhelming" force, rather than starting small and then raising force levels. When asked about the possible use of "surgical" bombing to compel Serbian forces to refrain from attacks against Bosnians, Powell replied, "As soon as they tell me it is 'limited,' it means they do not care whether you achieve a result or not. As soon as they me tell me 'surgical,' I head for the bunker."[26]

In a similar vein, U.S. military leaders sought to gain approval for as large a force as possible for the 2003 invasion and occupation of Iraq, hoping to crush opposition quickly. When resistance to U.S. occupation increased after the war, newspapers and leaders alike raised the question of whether the United States was again getting into a Vietnam-like "quagmire."

Generational Change Working from the lessons of history does not always or necessarily lead to bad decisions. Indeed, almost everyone would agree that being informed by history is essential to good decision making in foreign policy. What an immense amount of research has shown, however, is that decision makers are very uneven in their use of history. Most individuals view current problems in light of only a few historical events and are unable to conduct a broad, open-minded search for the historical lessons that apply best to any particular circumstance.

One possible result of the simplistic use of history is that there may be generational change in foreign policy attitudes. When an entire generation is seared by a particularly traumatic or triumphant foreign policy experience, such as a war, there is some tendency for people whose political attitudes were formed at that time to see future problems in light of that formative experience. That does not mean that everyone in the same generation will see the same thing. In the United States, for example, many people of a certain age tend to look at current events in light of the Vietnam experience that shook a generation, but now, as then, there are deep and bitter divisions over the lessons of that experience. Some view that conflict as a mistake from the beginning, which was halted through the commitment of domestic protestors. Others regard it as an honorable war that was abandoned because of the treachery of domestic protestors. An earlier generation was influenced primarily by World War II, and an even earlier generation was influenced by World War I. Today's college students, with few exceptions, remember none of those conflicts but came of age during the wars in Afghanistan and Iraq that followed the terrorist attacks of 2001. It remains to be seen what lessons will be taken from those conflicts or if they will spawn as much disagreement as Vietnam has.

Prospect Theory   One of the more exciting developments in decision making theory in recent years has been "prospect theory," for which Daniel Kahneman won the Nobel Prize in economics in 2002.[27] **Prospect theory** contends that how individuals weigh options is heavily influenced by how the choices are framed. To anyone who has seen politicians attempt to "spin" a discussion to their favor, this point may seem obvious. But prospect theory is more precise, is supported by experimental evidence, and leads to some very important generalizations that are relevant to international politics.[28]

Among prospect theory's most important findings is that individuals are much more willing to take risks to avoid a loss than to achieve a gain. For example, research subjects are willing to take a greater risk to avoid the loss of a dollar than to gain a dollar. In terms of expected utility, there is no difference between losing a dollar and failing to win one, but prospect theory shows that psychologically the difference is significant and that it has a measurable impact on people's behavior.

In international politics, one important lesson is that leaders will take considerable risks to protect what they have (to avoid a perceived loss). In other words, there is a strong **status quo bias** in international affairs. Intuitively, this appears to make sense:

prospect theory

A theory that contends that
how individuals weigh options
is heavily influenced by
whether a particular outcome
is seen as a gain or a loss.

status quo bias

The tendency of leaders to
take considerable risks to
avoid a perceived loss.

the inhabitants of an invaded territory would be expected to fight harder to defend their land than the invaders would fight to conquer new territory. U.S. experience in the Vietnam War or the Russian experience in invading Afghanistan in 1979 seems relevant in this respect. A territory should be of equal value to any two states, but prospect theory leads us to expect that the state that controls a territory will exert more effort to keep it than another will to take it.

Prospect Theory and Coercion Prospect theory may help explain why smaller, weaker states sometimes refuse to bow to threats from larger, more powerful actors. If it is protecting something it believes already belongs to it, the small state may have a high sensitivity to loss and may therefore be willing to accept higher-than-normal risks of going to war. This tendency is something that decision makers could learn to take into account.[29]

For example, when the United States and its NATO allies sought to coerce Serbia to withdraw from Kosovo in 1999, there seemed to be good reason to believe that the threat of force, or the application of moderate force, would be enough to do the job. Only a few years earlier, when the territories under threat were Bosnia and Herzegovina, a limited bombing campaign was sufficient to induce concessions from Serbia. In the Kosovo case, however, an extensive and highly destructive bombing campaign was necessary. Why were the two cases different and could the resistance in the Kosovo case have been predicted?

Figure 6.3 According to standard rational choice theories, each increment of change in payoff is worth the same amount. If that were true, the line in the graph would be straight. Prospect theory finds that whether a change in payoff matters a lot or a little depends on whether one is on the "loss" or the "gain" side of the status quo. Note that the "gain" side is not a mirror image of the "loss" side: on the loss side, value goes down more steeply and further than on the gain side.

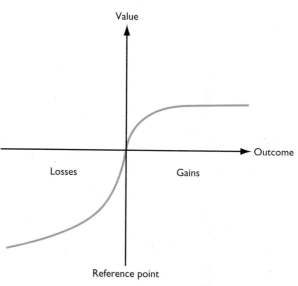

Prospect Theory Value Function

Source: http://en.wikipedia.org/wiki/Prospecttheory

Prospect theory might help us understand why Serbia behaved differently in the two situations and might have helped anticipate the problems in Kosovo. Derek Chollett and James Goldgeier point out that whereas Bosnia and Herzegovina had not traditionally been controlled by Serbia, Kosovo had been controlled by Serbia for many years. It was predictable, these analysts therefore contend, that Serbian President Slobodan Milosevic would pay higher costs to avoid the loss of Kosovo than to achieve the gain of Bosnia.[30]

A particular problem arises when both sides perceive the status quo to be on their side. If both sides see giving in as a loss of an existing territory (or principle), both might be quite willing to accept risks to avoid the loss. This may be what occurred in 1914, when both Austria and Russia believed that the status of Serbia could not be maintained and that losing influence there would do substantial damage to their position. Austria saw Serbia's support of separatists within Austria as a threatening departure from the status quo, while Russia saw Austria's efforts to limit Serbian autonomy as an equally threatening departure. Because both sides feared a loss if they did not prevail, diplomacy, rather than war, was seen as especially risky. A similar danger presented itself in the Cuban missile crisis. From the U.S. perspective, a Cuba without nuclear weapons was the status quo, and any change from that was a loss. But with the missiles already partly installed, would the Soviet Union view this as a *new* status quo and be equally ready to take risks to defend it? Apparently not, or at least not so much that Khrushchev was willing to risk nuclear war.

Prospect theory applies as well to other issues as to security concerns. In negotiations over trade liberalization, actors (not only states, but interest groups as well) often react much more negatively to the specific losses that some economic sectors might endure from a reduction in trade barriers than to the likely overall gains that occur from such agreements. Prospect theory finds that it is easier to agree on how to divide up gains than to agree on how to divide up losses.[31] Therefore, even states that can agree on how to distribute the benefits from a trade deal may find it much harder to agree on how to share the losses because they are much more sensitive to the losses.

Prospect theory also has interesting implications for cooperation on environmental problems. The theory implies that once actors clearly perceive a tangible loss from further environmental degradation, they will take risks to avoid those losses. Thus, when scientific evidence on the depletion of the ozone layer became clear and the health consequences of this situation were fully understood, an international agreement on limiting ozone-depleting chemicals was reached fairly quickly. Although the issue of global warming is complex (and the perceived economic costs of limiting production of greenhouse gases are quite high), prospect theory implies that if the high costs of global warming become more clear, leaders will be more likely to take risks to avoid them.

In the broadest sense, prospect theory confirms something we already knew—that people are very sensitive to how a particular issue is "framed." In a narrower sense, however, it illuminates a new and useful principle. Leaders are likely to take much bigger risks to avoid losses than they are to achieve gains. When the importance of the status quo is recognized, this knowledge can induce caution in those who would revise the status quo. But when the importance of the status quo is not recognized or when the status quo is itself ambiguous, leaders can make important miscalculations.

MOTIVATED BIAS

As noted previously, motivated bias is bias that is driven by some psychological need. The actor subject to motivated bias tends to see what she or he *wants* to see. There is a range of potential sources of motivated bias, from personal insecurities that may result from childhood issues to the fear created by the prospect of war. The distinction between motivated and unmotivated bias is useful not just for categorizing psychological theories but also for thinking about how to reduce misperceptions.

cognitive dissonance theory

A theory that holds that individuals tend to construct internally consistent views of the world and that psychological discomfort, or "cognitive dissonance," results when some new piece of information does not fit with an individual's existing beliefs.

Cognitive Dissonance   Much early research on misperception among leaders focused on **cognitive dissonance theory**, which addresses a classic type of motivated bias.[32] The theory holds that individuals tend to construct internally consistent views of the world and that psychological discomfort results when some new piece of information does not fit with an individual's existing beliefs. This discomfort is known as "cognitive dissonance." The theory holds that because cognitive dissonance is uncomfortable, new information is unlikely to cause a change in views, even when it should. (We often refer to this state of mind as "being in denial.") More specifically, new information that contradicts existing views will either be discredited or will be interpreted to confirm rather than challenge existing beliefs. Similarly, new information that reaffirms existing beliefs tends to be more readily believed and more heavily emphasized than information that calls those beliefs into question. This argument has led to a great deal of research on "belief systems," in the view that leaders have consistently structured beliefs and that if analysts understand these belief systems, they can understand and predict how leaders will react to new information.

In international relations, cognitive dissonance seems to be especially prominent in antagonistic relationships, in which evidence that an adversary is making a concession is likely to be rejected and evidence of an unfriendly move is likely to be readily accepted. In the Cold War, both Soviet and U.S. leaders adopted views of each other that were wholly negative, and both sides therefore had a very difficult time admitting when the other side had made a concession or perhaps become less belligerent. Evidence that the other had made a concession did not fit with existing beliefs, emphasizing that the other side was totally hostile and unwilling to compromise.

Thus, when Mikhail Gorbachev initiated a much more conciliatory line in Soviet foreign policy in the late 1980s, many in the United States warned that Gorbachev's goal

The Geography Connection

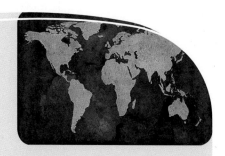

Maps and the Framing of Problems

This chapter explores how perceptions of issues can influence decisions. Consider the maps of the Middle East conflict, which show boundaries at different points in time.

Critical Thinking Questions

1. Which map might a Palestinian be likely to see as the "normal" situation that a peace agreement should achieve? Which map might an Israeli see as "normal"?

2. Now consider these maps in light of prospect theory. Considering Palestinians' and Israelis' different perspectives on the "baseline" for assessing a division of territory, what difficulties arise for negotiators?

Palestinian and Israeli Land

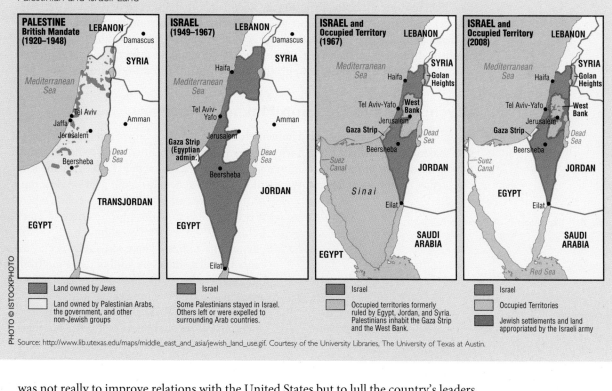

PHOTO © ISTOCKPHOTO

Source: http://www.lib.utexas.edu/maps/middle_east_and_asia/jewish_land_use.gif. Courtesy of the University Libraries, The University of Texas at Austin.

was not really to improve relations with the United States but to lull the country's leaders into complacency in order to achieve a long-term Soviet victory. Evidence that the Soviet Union was changing from within and was seeking international stability did not fit with the views of many Americans that the Soviet Union was implacably hostile and could not change. As cognitive dissonance theory indicates, new evidence did not change the existing view, but rather was reinterpreted to support it. Even after the opening of the

Berlin Wall in 1989, which effectively ended communism in Eastern Europe, prominent American leaders cautioned against assuming that a fundamental change in Soviet foreign policy was under way.

Today, some people label leaders who reject the need for international collaboration on global warming as suffering from cognitive dissonance. These leaders, critics argue, find ways to dismiss increasingly compelling evidence of global warming while exaggerating the significance of data that cast doubt on the existence of the problem.

Cognitive dissonance theory is especially useful in explaining why foreign policies do not change in light of changed circumstances or new evidence. Because it only explains continuity, however, it is less useful at explaining how foreign policy changes. Nor does it explain where a particular belief system came from in the first place.

bolstering

The tendency of decision makers facing a difficult decision to increase their certainty once a decision is made.

Bolstering   A concept related to cognitive dissonance is **bolstering**, whereby decision makers facing a difficult decision tend to increase their certainty once a decision is made.[33] Before making a close call, a decision maker might keenly perceive the pros and cons of different choices. He or she might agonize over the decision. However, after making a decision, individuals can experience a psychological drive to convince themselves that they have made the correct choice. The knowledge that they have chosen a policy that might not work and that another policy might be better causes psychological stress that leaders avoid by subconsciously convincing themselves that they really have chosen a very good policy, even going so far as to reinterpret the evidence to support the decision that has been taken. Exaggerating the benefits of the chosen policy is then likely to reduce the search for better alternatives. Moreover, overconfidence may result, leading to a lack of preparedness if things turn out badly. By losing the uncertainty that preceded the original decision, a leader may also reduce his or her ability to continue to question the policy. There is a tendency for bolstering by individuals, groups, and societies following almost every decision to go to war. Once such a decision is made, there is immense psychological and social pressure to believe that war is not only the best policy, but also the only real choice.

Psychology and Decision Making: Summary

The study of psychology has added immensely to our understanding of foreign policy decision making. It has helped explain why foreign policy makers often seem to deviate from the standard tenets of rational decision making. However, although psychological theories can predict the results of laboratory experiments, they generally do not provide clear predictions in the real world of foreign policy, where it is impossible to control for a variety of other influences.[34] In particular, although all of the phenomena addressed here sometimes occur, we cannot predict when one kind of deviation from rationality rather than another will occur. None arises in a constant or predictable way.

Regardless of these limitations, psychology offers lessons for analysts as well as practitioners of foreign policy. For students and scholars, one lesson is that the rationality assumption cannot perfectly describe or explain what happens in the real world. For those who make foreign policy, a lesson is that they should not base their policies on the expectation that others will behave perfectly rationally. For example, if a policy maker's strategy for resolving a crisis

Table 6.1 Explanations of Decision Making

Level of Analysis	Explanations
State/system	Rational action model Expected utility theory (a variant of the rational action model)
Bureaucracies	Bureaucratic politics model Organizational process model
Small groups	Groupthink
Individual: Unmotivated bias	Attribution theory Bounded rationality (example: use of historical lessons and analogies) Prospect theory
Individual: Motivated bias	Cognitive dissonance theory Bolstering

depends on an adversary's abilities to correctly perceive the message sent and to weigh costs and benefits in a rational way, then the policy maker had better come up with an alternative strategy. A second, perhaps equally important, lesson is that our *own* perceptions, understandings, and policy choices are not "rational" in any objective sense but rather are influenced by our experiences, our beliefs, and our personalities.

Reconsider the Case

Israel's Invasion of Lebanon, 2006

Why do states make decisions that appear, in retrospect, not only to be unwise, but to have been made without sufficient input, analysis, and debate? This chapter began with an examination of Israel's invasion of Lebanon in 2006. The Israelis' own investigation into the Lebanon invasion shows that Israel experienced many of the problems referred to in this chapter. Specifically, the inquiry found that:

- Despite repeated alerts that soldiers along the border might be abducted, the army was unprepared when it actually happened. When the abduction occurred, the army chief of staff responded "impulsively," short-circuiting existing decision-making procedures.

- The army did not warn the political decision makers that it was unprepared for a large-scale ground invasion. The political leaders, therefore, could not properly assess risks and benefits.

- The minister of defense did not sufficiently consult experts outside the military and did not pursue the reservations that were raised. Because he was not an expert in military affairs, the minister could not challenge information coming from the military.

- There was debate within the military concerning whether the planned actions could achieve the stated goals, but this debate was not shared with the political leadership.

- "The prime minister made up his mind hastily despite the fact that no detailed military plan was submitted to him and without asking for one."[35]

An explanation of *why* these shortcomings occurred must await a much more in-depth analysis of the decision process. The pathologies of decision making discussed in this chapter might offer some clues that would help explain the problems that arose in this case. How might these approaches explain, for example, why the Israeli army might have hesitated to tell the political leadership that it was unprepared for

an attack that had long been anticipated by its military intelligence? What information about Hezbollah's decision-making process would be needed to understand its decision to attack Israel when it did?

In May 2010, another Israeli military action yielded new questions about decision making. Israeli commandos boarded a Turkish ship that was bringing aid to Gaza, despite an Israeli (and Egyptian) blockade of the territory. Nine members of NGOs that were accompanying the aid were killed. The deaths created an enormous diplomatic cost for Israel. The incident caused a split with Turkey, one of Israel's few Muslim allies, and led to intense criticism around the world. The United States, which routinely vetoes UN Security Council resolutions that criticize Israel, refrained from doing so. Ultimately, the action may have undermined the blockade by creating international pressure on Israel to ease it. It quickly emerged that the Chief of Staff of the Israel Defense Forces (IDF) was not present at headquarters when the operation took place, which appeared to violate established procedure. Again, Israel set up a panel to investigate the incident.[36]

Critical Thinking Questions

1. How might each of the decision-making problems identified in the Israeli invasion of Lebanon be explained in terms of the dynamics explored in this chapter?

2. Are the problems that Israel encountered exceptional, or are they a normal part of foreign policy making? What are the implications of concluding that good foreign policy making is an exception?

3. Is it possible that both Hezbollah and Israel acted rationally? What arguments about their goals and their alternatives could be used to make the case for rational action?

Summary

The theories examined in previous chapters held that understanding the details of the internal workings of a government is not necessary to explain its decisions in the international arena. The approaches covered in this chapter and summarized in Table 6.1 reject this assumption. These approaches make one fundamental point—but make it many different ways. The fundamental point is that what goes on *inside* the government can have a great impact on what kinds of foreign policy come *out* of the government. Determining the purpose of foreign policy, as well as the best means to pursue that purpose, is a complicated process. This point becomes clear when we go below the state level of analysis to several lower levels, working all the way down to the level of the individual decision maker. The chapter examined how large bureaucracies work, how small groups interact, and how individual psychology affects decision making. In doing so, the chapter showed that to understand what foreign policies come out of a state or a bureaucracy, we need to understand how decisions are being made.

Key Concepts

1. Foreign policy analysis
2. Expected utility
3. Bureaucracy
4. Standard operating procedures
5. "Groupthink"
6. Bounded rationality
7. Motivated versus unmotivated bias
8. Prospect theory

Study Questions

1. How do the various branches of government influence foreign policy making?
2. Why does foreign policy analysis tend to focus on the executive branch?
3. How does the expected utility approach explain foreign policy?
4. Why are bureaucracies necessary for policy making?
5. What factors lead bureaucracies to disagree about the best policies?
6. Why are standard operating procedures necessary for policy making?
7. In what kinds of situations do standard operating procedures appear to be especially inappropriate?
8. What potential hazards arise in small-group decision making?
9. What does prospect theory imply about foreign policy decision making?
10. What policies might improve the content of foreign policy by improving the process by which it is made?

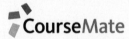

Endnotes

1. Hezbollah is difficult to characterize. It maintains a significant military force in Lebanon. It also operates as a parliamentary party in Lebanese politics. It is also a transnational terrorist movement, conducting attacks in Israel as well as in Lebanon. It receives funding and support from both Syria and Iran, although the extent to which those two governments control Hezbollah is disputed. For an overview of Hezbollah and a review of recent literature, see Adam Shatz, "In Search of Hezbollah," *New York Review of Books*, April 29, 2004, at http://www.nybooks.com/articles/archives/2004/apr/29/in-search-of-hezbollah/

2. Israel Ministry of Foreign Affairs, "Winograd Commission Submits Interim Report," April 30, 2007, at http://www.mfa.gov.il/MFA/Government/Communiques/2007/ Winograd+Inquiry+Commission+submits+Interim+Report+30-Apr-2007.htm

3. Steven Philip Kramer, "French Foreign Policy: The Wager on Europe," in Ryan K. Beasley, Juliet Kaarbo, Jeffrey S. Lantis, and Michael T. Snarr, eds., *Foreign Policy in Comparative Perspective* (Washington, DC: Congressional Quarterly, 2002), p. 60.

4. See Juliet Kaarbo, "Power Politics in Foreign Policy: The Influence of Bureaucratic Minorities," *European Journal of International Relations,* Vol. 4 (March 1998): 67-97.

5. Brian Ripley, "China: Defining Its Role in the Global Community," in Beasley et al., *Foreign Policy in Comparative Perspective,* p. 132.

6. Ripley, "China: Defining Its Role in the Global Community," p. 132.

7. Both of these examples are from Robert Jervis, *Perception and Misperception in International Politics* (Princeton, NJ: Princeton University Press, 1976), p. 26.

8. "The Trouble with Pakistan," *The Economist,* July 6, 2006.

9. Andrés Rozental, "Fox's Foreign Policy Agenda: Global and Regional Priorities," in Luis Rubio and Susan Kaufman Purcell, eds., *Mexico under Fox* (Boulder, CO: Lynne Rienner Publishers, 2004), p. 105.

10. Stephen D. Krasner, "Are Democracies Important? (Or Allison Wonderland)" *Foreign Policy 7* (Summer 1972): 159–172.

11. See John D. Steinbrunner, *The Cybernetic Theory of Decision* (Princeton, NJ: Princeton University Press, 1974).

12. See, for example, Alexander L. George, *Presidential Decisionmaking in Foreign Policy: The Effective Use of Information and Advice* (Boulder, CO: Westview Press, 1980).

13. Irving L. Janis, *Groupthink: Psychological Studies of Policy Issues and Fiascoes* (Boston: Houghton Mifflin, 1982).

14. United States Senate, Select Committee on Intelligence, "Report on the U.S. Intelligence Community's Prewar Intelligence Assessments on Iraq," July 7, 2004, p. 28.

15. "Report on the U.S. Intelligence Community's Prewar Intelligence Assessments on Iraq," p. 35.

16. See Richard E. Nisbett and Lee Ross, *Human Inference: Strategies and Shortcomings in Social Judgment* (Engelwood Cliffs, NJ: Prentice Hall, 1980).

17. Jervis, *Perception and Misperception in International Politics,* pp. 354–355.

18. Deborah Welch Larson, *Origins of Containment: A Psychological Approach* (Princeton, NJ: Princeton University Press, 1985), p. 38.

19. Larson, *Origins of Containment: A Psychological Approach.* p. 194.

20. Harry S. Truman, *Memoirs Volume 2: Years of Trial and Hope* (Garden City, NY: Doubleday, 1956), pp. 332–333.

21. See Yuen Foong Khong, *Analogies at War: Korea, Munich, Dien Bien Phu, and the Vietnam Decisions of 1965* (Princeton, NJ: Princeton University Press, 1982).

22. The two covers can be viewed at http://www.time.com/time/covers/0,16641,19450507,00.html (Hitler) and http://www.time.com/time/covers/0,16641,20030421,00.html (Saddam).

23. "Bush compares Bin Laden to Hitler," British Broadcasting Company, September 5, 2006, at http://news.bbc.co.uk/2/hi/americas/5318204.stm. Janadas Devan, "How Appeasement Became a Bad Word," *The Straits Times,* September 3, 2006. For a defense of the term "Islamic fascism," see Victor Davis Hanson, "It's Fascism—and It's Islamic," *Baltimore Sun,* September 8, 2006, A13.

24. Bush speech at the 2006 American Legion convention, reprinted in "The President's Speech," *New York Times,* August 31, 2006, at http://www.nytimes.com/2006/08/31/washington/31text-bush.html

25. CNN.com, August 29, 2006, at http://www.cnn.com/2006/POLITICS/08/29/ rumsfeld.ap/

26. *The Guardian,* September 29, 1992, p. 7.

27. The classic work in this field is Daniel Kahneman and Amos Tversky, "Prospect Theory: An Analysis of Decision Under Risk," *Econometrica* 47 (1979): 263–291.

28. See Jack S. Levy, "An Introduction to Prospect Theory," *Political Psychology* 13 (1992): 171–186; and Levy, "Prospect Theory, Rational Choice, and International Relations," *International Studies Quarterly,* Vol. 41, No. 1 (March 1997): 87–112.

29. See Jeffrey D. Berejikian, "A Cognitive Theory of Deterrence," *Journal of Peace Research,* 39 (2002): 165–183.

30. Derek H. Chollett and James M. Goldgeier, "The Scholarship of Decision Making: Do We Know How We Decide?" in Richard C. Snyder, H.W. Bruck, and Burton Sapin; with Valerie M. Hudson, Derek H. Chollett, and James M. Goldgeier, *Foreign Policy Decision-Making (Revisited)* (New York: Palgrave MacMillan, 2002), p. 160.

31. Levy, "Prospect Theory, Rational Choice, and International Relations," p. 93.

32. On cognitive bias in international affairs, see Jervis, *Perception and Misperception in International Politics,* Chapter 11 (pp. 382–408). The classic work in psychology on cognitive bias is Leon Festinger, *A Theory of Cognitive Dissonance* (Stanford, CA: Stanford University Press, 1957).

33. See Richard Ned Lebow, *Between Peace and War: The Nature of International Crisis* (Baltimore, MD: Johns Hopkins University Press, 1981), p. 110; and Irving L. Janis and Leon Mann, *Decisionmaking: A Psychological Study of Conflict, Choice, and Commitment* (New York: The Free Press, 1977), pp. 74–95.

34. These problems of "external validity" are summarized in Levy, "Prospect Theory, Rational Choice, and International Relations," pp. 98–100.

35. This quotation and the other criticisms in this section are from Israel Ministry of Foreign Affairs, "Winograd Commission Submits Interim Report," April 30, 2007, at http://www.mfa.gov.il/MFA/Government/Communiques/2007/ Winograd+Inquiry+Commission+submits+Interim+Report+30-Apr-2007.htm

36. "IDF Chief Was Not in Command During Onset of Gaza Flotilla Raid," Haaretz.com, June 13, 2010. http://www.haaretz.com/news/diplomacy-defense/idf-chief-was-not-in-command-during-onset-of-gaza-flotilla-raid-1.295846

7

International Insecurity and the Causes of War and Peace

LEARNING OBJECTIVES

After completing this chapter, the student should be able to . . .

1. Identify the range of explanations of the causes of war and evaluate the strengths and weaknesses of each explanation.

2. Articulate and defend an argument concerning the causes of war.

3. Connect explanations of war to appropriate foreign policies.

4. Understand the role that arms control can play in ameliorating the security dilemma.

5. Evaluate the policy of collective security and its weaknesses.

6. Analyze peacekeeping as a means of limiting conflict.

◀ A Vietnamese woman flees a napalm attack, Trang Bang, South Vietnam, June 8, 1972.
AP Photo/Nick Ut

Consider the Case

The Defenestration of Prague and the Thirty Years War

On May 23, 1618, a group of Protestants, enraged at efforts to curtail their religious freedom, seized two officials of the King of Bohemia at Prague Castle and threw them out the window. Miraculously, neither was seriously hurt, as a result of intervention by angels, according to some accounts, and according to other accounts, by the fact that they landed in a pile of manure. The event, known as the Second Defenestration of Prague, touched off the Bohemian Revolt, the first stage of the Thirty Years War. By 1648, central Europe had been despoiled and roughly a quarter of the population had been wiped out. The system of sovereign states, as enshrined in the Treaty of Westphalia, was consolidated.

How could the early equivalent of a world war be caused by throwing a few bureaucrats out of a window, not even killing them? Most historians would argue, of course, that the Second Defenestration of Prague did not really *cause* the Thirty Years War. Rather, some would argue, religious strife that had been flaring up since the Protestant Reformation

made conflict inevitable. Others would stress the competition for territory among the great powers of the day: Spain, France, Sweden, and the Holy Roman Empire. In either view, the Second Defenestration of Prague was only a spark, and given the underlying impetus toward war, any spark could have set it off. Put differently, absent a situation primed for war, the incident might have had little effect (or might not have occurred at all).

Similar arguments can be made about the origins of other wars, such as World War I or the 1969 "Football War" between El Salvador and Honduras. Was World War I caused by Gavrilo Princip's assassination of Archduke Francis Ferdinand, or by underlying power politics or imperialism? Was the "Football War" caused by the violence surrounding the World Cup qualifying matches between Honduras and El Salvador, or was it caused by the underlying tensions between the two countries that had been building for years? These questions illuminate one of the central quandaries scholars face when developing theories of war and peace.

---

defenestration

The ejection of someone from a window.

What causes war? Conflicts over the balance of power? Imperialism? The absence of democracy? Innate human aggression? Unjust patriarchal power relations? Random events, such as **defenestrations**, assassinations, and soccer matches? After centuries of analysis, the question of the causes of war remains at the center of the study of international politics.

The question attracts such great attention because avoiding war is such a high priority for governments, organizations, and individuals. People cannot take effective steps to avoid war, the reasoning goes, if they do not know what causes it. Stopping the practice of throwing people out of windows in anger will probably not do it. Nor will halting soccer matches. But what will? This chapter will examine different approaches to understanding the causes and prevention of war.

The Causes of War

The history of international politics is replete with warfare, and the prospects of this changing seem remote. Because war is so destructive and causes so much suffering, the search for ways to prevent it has been a primary motivation for the study of international politics for centuries. Although it is logical that if we seek to prevent war, we must understand what causes it, this is more easily said than done. There are more theories about the causes of war than can possibly be reviewed here, and there is no consensus among scholars about which theory is best, or even where to begin. There are multiple causes of war, at multiple levels of analysis, and these causes interact with one another.[1] War is almost never an end in itself, but rather a means to other ends. Leaders in every state that goes to war believe that they did not want to choose war but did so because there was no better option. Therefore, in considering why states go to war, it is necessary to consider the range of goals that can bring states into conflict with each other.

System-Level Theories

REALISM

The predominant realist explanation of the causes of war focuses on the system level. As discussed in Chapter 3, the realist view is based on the anarchic nature of the system. Simply put, the world is a dangerous place. States or groups can attack each other, and can be attacked, with immense violence. They can also threaten attack if certain conditions are not met, or they can

"You see, we have to build our navy up to what the other nations said they would build theirs up to, if we built ours up."

be the subject of those threats. How do states deal with these unfortunate facts? States in a "self-help" system arm to defend themselves, and this makes other states less secure. The result is competition for military dominance.

War breaks out, in this view, "because there is nothing to prevent it."[2] This system-level version cannot explain why any *particular* war breaks out. Rather, it explains why wars in general break out: "The origins of hot wars lie in cold wars, and the origins of cold wars are found in the anarchic ordering of the international arena."[3] Accordingly, even states that do not have expansionist agendas will initiate war if they expect it to make them safer in the future. An example of this sort of war might be the Soviet Union's attack on Finland in 1940, which was intended to give the Soviet Union a greater territorial buffer to protect Leningrad, a major Soviet city (now known as St. Petersburg), which was located very close to the prewar border. Furthermore, even peaceful states may have to start wars to increase their security. This rationale was how the U.S. government justified its decision to go to war against Iraq in 2003.

In the systemic realist view, any number of **proximate causes** can ignite a war: the assassination of the Archduke Franz Ferdinand (World War I), Germany's unquenchable desire for conquest (World War II), or the Bush administration's mistaken assessment of intelligence on Iraq (the U.S. invasion of Iraq in 2003). In all cases, realists would contend, these proximate causes resulted from international anarchy and were able to set off wars because of international anarchy. Critics of this approach argue that anarchy by itself cannot cause war: if all states were satisfied with their positions, there would be no war, even under anarchy.[4] To the extent this is true, we need to look to lower levels of analysis to understand the outbreak of particular wars.

Realists debate what distribution of power (bipolar or multipolar; balanced or unbalanced) is most likely to lead to war, but they agree that anarchy is the underlying cause.

proximate cause

An event that immediately precedes an outcome and therefore provides the most direct explanation of it.

The Policy Connection

Preventive War

In the months following the September 2001 terrorist attacks on the United States, U.S. President George W. Bush outlined a series of foreign policy principles that came to be called the "Bush Doctrine." Among those principles was the argument that the United States might wage preventive war on a country that was in the process of gaining weapons of mass destruction. In other words, it might be necessary to attack a country that was not attacking the United States if that country was seen as hostile and was gaining nuclear capability. A group of advisors known as "neoconservatives" had been advocating such a policy since the early 1990s, but the terrorist attacks of 2001 strengthened the view that such a policy was both justifiable and necessary.

Bush elaborated the argument for preemption in several speeches. In his 2002 State of the Union address, he said, "The United States of America will not permit the world's most dangerous regimes to threaten us with the world's most destructive weapons." He identified three potential targets—Iraq, Iran, and North Korea—calling them the "axis of evil." In a speech at the U.S. Military Academy at West Point later the same year, he said, "Our security will require all Americans to be forward-looking and resolute, to be ready for preemptive action when necessary to defend our liberty and to defend our lives."[1]

The same issue had arisen immediately after World War II, when the United States possessed nuclear weapons and the Soviet Union did not. Some in the U.S. military advocated preventive strikes on Soviet facilities to prevent the Soviets from gaining nuclear weapons. However, such a policy was dismissed because of the perceived unacceptability of deliberately starting a war and the large number of civilian casualties that would likely result. The United States again rejected preventive war during the Cuban missile crisis.

The attractions of the policy of prevention were clear: by dealing with potential nuclear proliferation through military attack, major dangers could be averted without the delays, complications, and fallibility of the diplomatic process. Following Bush's 2002 identification of Iran as a potential target, U.S. leaders continued to state that preventive war was among the possible options for dealing with Iran's nuclear weapons program.

However, critics of preventive war pointed out several problems with the strategy. First, there was a danger that any war started for such reasons would get out of control or drag on much longer than intended. Second, there was the question of whether preventive war was legal under international law. Some policy analysts were concerned that if the United States were perceived as waging illegal war, it

Statistical studies on these questions give unclear results. One author of a statistical attempt to study the balance of power and war concludes, "No particular distribution of power has exclusive claim as a predictor of peace or war either in theory or in the empirical record of the period 1816–1965."[5] Others argue that *change* in the distribution of power, especially rapid change, increases the chance of war.[6]

CAPITALISM AND WAR

Economic explanations of the causes of war have been offered at the system level as well as at the state level. At the system level, the most familiar explanations of war are those offered by economic structuralism. Economic structuralists find that capitalism inevitably produces the need for states to expand. Declining returns on investment at

Iran's Nuclear Reactor at Bushehr, Iran. Some have advocated attacking Iranian nuclear facilities before they have produced nuclear weapons. What is the logic behind such a strategy, and what are the risks?

AP Photo/Vahid Salemi, file

would lose the moral leadership that was so important in the war on terror. Third, there was the danger that the strategy might cause what it was intended to prevent: that states feeling threatened by U.S. attack might respond, not by backing down, but by accelerating efforts to procure nuclear weapons and systems to deliver them on the United States. This appears to have been the response of North Korea and Iran.

Critical Thinking Questions

1. In what circumstances, if any, is preventive war a good policy? What criteria should be used in evaluating this question?
2. How do terrorism and weapons of mass destruction alter the security dilemma and the incentive to strike first?
3. How might states behave in a world in which preventive war was considered legal?

[1]Both Bush quotes are from the Public Broadcasting System, *Frontline*, "Chronology: The Evolution of the Bush Doctrine," at http://www.pbs.org/wgbh/pages/frontline/shows/iraq/etc/cron.html

home, the need for more labor and raw materials, and the need for expanded markets in which to sell goods all lead capitalist states to expand. Scholars have attributed the surge in European imperialism in the late nineteenth century and the outbreak of World War I to these dynamics. Later, Marxist scholars called attention to the United States' economic motivations for playing a prominent global role after World War II, including its involvement in the Vietnam War.[7] Some today fear that China's growing need for raw materials to satisfy its economic growth will make it more aggressive.

FREE TRADE AND PEACE

Liberal theorists have a view of the relationship between economics and war that is nearly opposite that of economic structuralists. Many have argued that there is a connection between economics and war but that economics can be the route to peace as well as to conflict. Since the early nineteenth century, liberal theorists have argued that free trade reduces the likelihood of war, and that the absence of free trade makes war more likely. This is a system-level theory because the amount of free trade is not a characteristic of one state but of a system of states. This view concurs with the Marxist perspective that war has often been fought for economic gains but finds that the tendency toward war can be overcome through trade. There are two primary arguments in support of this claim.

First, if the major cause of war is the acquisition of some raw material or another, free trade offers the possibility of getting the same materials much more cheaply. War is an expensive business. The costs of outfitting armies, sending them to war, and occupying a conquered country are extraordinary; it is much cheaper, liberals assert, to buy needed supplies on the free market than to acquire them through conquest. Therefore, it is concluded, war should occur for economic reasons only in the absence of an open market.

Second, the interdependence of economies and the spread of firms around the world ought to blur the economic distinction between "them" and "us" for both populations and firms. If another country is a major market for exports and a major source of desirable inputs, destroying that country through war is likely to wreak economic havoc on the country that initiates hostilities. The costs might be especially high for multinational firms with factories and offices in many countries. Skeptics dispute both the theory and evidence in this argument.[8] With regard to the theory, philosophers as far back as the eighteenth-century French writer Jean-Jacques Rousseau argued that interdependence is often unequal and therefore leads to economic coercion and from there to conflict. He advised smaller states especially to become *autarchic* (economically self-sufficient) to avoid conflict.

Empirically, the same kinds of statistical studies used to test the democratic peace hypothesis have been applied to the economic interdependence hypothesis and have found little support for this claim. The reason for this lack of support becomes evident when considering the role of geography in trade and war. States tend to trade most with their neighbors. They also tend to go to war most frequently with their neighbors. Therefore, there is some tendency to go to war with trading partners, even if trade does have some benefits. The case against free trade leading to peace is exemplified by World War I. Trade among the European powers was at an all-time high in 1914, but this did not prevent them from fighting the most destructive war that had been waged up to that point in history.

State-Level and Substate-Level Theories

REGIME TYPE

As noted in Chapter 5, some have argued that a country's form of government has an important impact on whether the country is peaceful or not. To summarize, it is widely argued that democracies tend not to fight each other, but that otherwise there is no persuasive relationship between regime type and war. (Even those who assert the validity of the democratic peace theory, it should be noted, do not assert that authoritarian states are the *cause* of wars. Democracies have not been found to be more peaceful than nondemocratic states. Rather, they tend not to go to war *with each other*.) Thus, promotion of democracy is viewed by many as an important means to reduce conflict.

An intriguing argument developed more recently contends that although democracies may be more peaceful in general, *new* democracies are especially prone to waging war because they do not yet have the institutionalized tendency toward compromise that constrains the incentive to build public support through assertive foreign policies. "Using the same databases that are typically used to study the democratic peace theory, we find considerable statistical evidence that democratizing states are more likely to fight wars than are mature democracies or stable autocracies."[9]

The Geography Connection

Poverty, Wealth, and War

The map shows relative wealth in countries around the world as well as places where conflicts have occurred in recent years.

Critical Thinking Questions

1. Can you judge from this map whether conflict is in some way linked to wealth and poverty? Where does the relationship seem to hold? Where doesn't it?

2. What other maps might you want to study to understand the geography of war?

Economic Development and Conflict

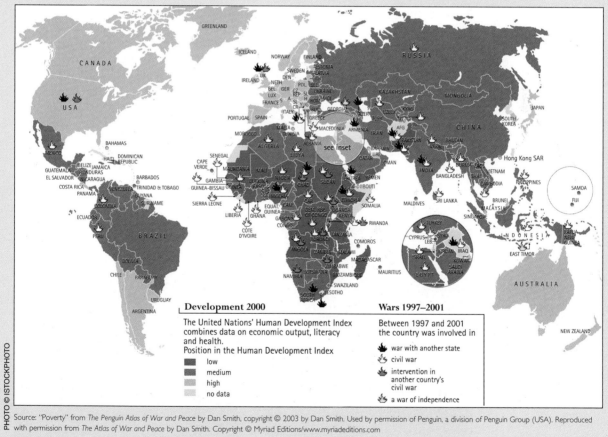

Development 2000

The United Nations' Human Development Index combines data on economic output, literacy and health.
Position in the Human Development Index

- low
- medium
- high
- no data

Wars 1997–2001

Between 1997 and 2001 the country was involved in

- war with another state
- civil war
- intervention in another country's civil war
- a war of independence

Source: "Poverty" from *The Penguin Atlas of War and Peace* by Dan Smith, copyright © 2003 by Dan Smith. Used by permission of Penguin, a division of Penguin Group (USA). Reproduced with permission from *The Atlas of War and Peace* by Dan Smith. Copyright © Myriad Editions/www.myriadeditions.com

EXPECTED UTILITY THEORY

expected utility

A variant of the rational
action model. The theory
asserts that leaders
evaluate policies by combining
their estimation of the utility
of potential outcomes with
the likelihood that different
outcomes will result from the
policy in question.

Expected utility theory predicts that states will choose the available course of action that
has the highest **expected utility**. If, at a given time, war has a higher expected utility than
peace for a given state, then that state will start war. In practice, it is of course difficult
if not impossible to measure the expected utility of different policies. Such a judgment
must be subjective. But conceptually, expected utility theory makes a crucial point: a state
initiates war when leaders believe it is in the state's interest to do so. This logic underpins
the policy of deterrence through retaliation. The goal of deterrence is to raise the costs of
going to war in an effort to influence another state's expected utility. If the other state's
expected utility of war can be driven down below the expected utility of some other
policy, then war might be averted.

Expected utility theory might help explain one of the historical puzzles about the initiation of wars. Many wars, it seems, are started by states that then go on to lose. In World
War I, World War II, the Arab-Israeli wars, and many others, the states that started the
wars lost, sometimes with devastating consequences. On the surface, it seems that this
is inherently irrational. Similarly, why do states with weak armies sometimes choose to
resist more powerful states, rather than make concessions to avoid an attack? Why, for
example, did Saddam Hussein in 1991 not withdraw Iraqi troops from Kuwait rather
than face certain defeat by the U.S.-led military forces? Perhaps war is always based in
irrationality, as some assert.

Expected utility theory offers an explanation of why it might be considered rational
to fight a war, even if the odds of winning are low. The theory emphasizes that states
will not necessarily choose a *successful* strategy, but that they will choose the one with
the *highest expected utility*. Especially for a weak state that believes it is backed into a
corner, a long shot at winning a war may have greater utility than the certainty of being
occupied. In 1991, for example, Saddam Hussein was concerned above all with maintaining power within Iraq. He may have believed that he was better off losing a war
with the United States, if it left him in power and allowed him to claim to have fought
off the superpower, than making concessions that might have weakened him and led to
his overthrow. The fact that Saddam Hussein ruled Iraq for another twelve years after
being defeated in the 1991 war indicates that losing did not necessarily undermine his
interests.

Was Saddam Hussein
irrational in accepting war
with the United States
in 2003 (and 1991)? Or
was going to war with the
United States less certain
to cause his downfall than
giving in to U.S. demands?

AP Photo/Iraqi TV via APTN

Expected utility theory also offers an explanation of World War I. The empires that are generally regarded as initiating World War I, Germany and Austria-Hungary, not only lost—they ceased to exist. The monarchies were abolished in both countries, and both lost territory, especially Austria-Hungary. How can this have been rational? Expected utility theory raises the question "What alternatives were available?" From the Austrian and German perspectives, the problem with avoiding war was that during peacetime, their position in Europe seemed to be slipping away. In other words, they perceived a choice between a *certain loss* (if peaceful events kept evolving according to trends) and a *possible victory* (if the war could be won).

This analysis offers an important policy lesson: if you want to avoid war, be sure that your opponent has a better alternative. Even a country in a dominant position may be attacked if its adversary cannot find a better alternative. John F. Kennedy was widely seen as having been uncommonly wise when, in the Cuban missile crisis, he insisted on giving Soviet leader Nikita Khrushchev a way to "save face." If making a concession on the Cuban missiles meant complete humiliation for Khrushchev personally and for the Soviet Union as a state, war might have seemed the better alternative for them. Kennedy promised to remove U.S. missiles from Turkey and to refrain from attacking Cuba. This promise allowed Khrushchev to claim that the Soviet Union had accomplished its goals.

Although expected utility theory holds that states go to war because they see it as being in their interest, the theory says very little about what those interests might be. What goals of states are so important that they might provide sufficient motivation to accept the inherent risks of going to war? Several other theories seek to explain these state level motivations.

AGGRESSIVE STATES

Chapter 3 noted that some variants of realist theory have a strong state-level component. This is consistent with the view that anarchy is the *permissive* cause of war, but that some more positive cause is required to actually start a war.[10] Aggressive states provide one explanation. States can be aggressive simply because their leaders believe that the prevailing arrangements (in territory, economic affairs, or other matters) do not suit their interests. Revisionist states—states that reject the status quo—might see war as one means of achieving a more favorable situation. According to **power transition theory**, a state that has gained power over time might seek a reordering of affairs that recognizes its power and provides it more benefits. This is one explanation for German policy leading to both World War I and World War II. There are two motives that might cause states to reject the status quo: imperialism and nationalism.

IMPERIALIST STATES

State-level economic theories of war focus on how individual states pursue military conquest for economic reasons. Generally, imperialist arguments focus on **economic imperialism**, the efforts of states to improve their economic situation through military expansion, usually to gain better control of resources and markets. This view plays a prominent role in economic structuralist theory. Many (and not only economic structuralists) attributed the colonial conquests of the sixteenth through the nineteenth centuries to economic imperialism. The desire to gain control of important natural resources was also seen in World War II, in Japan's expansion into Southeast Asia, and in Germany's attacks on Poland and then the Soviet Union through which it gained territory, or "living space" (*Lebensraum*) and oil, which were important goals of war.

In one form of this argument, a politically powerful **military industrial complex**, linking military contractors and armed forces, lobbies governments for continuously increasing defense spending. Some believe that the military industrial complex

power transition theory
A theory that postulates that war occurs when one state becomes powerful enough to challenge the dominant state and reorder the hierarchy of power within the international system.

economic imperialism
Efforts by states to improve their economic situation through military expansion, usually to gain better control of resources and markets.

military industrial complex
A term made popular by President Dwight D. Eisenhower that refers to a group consisting of a nation's armed forces, weapon suppliers and manufacturers, and elements within the civil service involved in defense efforts.

exaggerates security threats or even helps create them in order to drive up profits. This concern was made famous by the warnings of U.S. President (and retired five-star general) Dwight Eisenhower in his farewell address in 1961. More recently, former Secretary of State Colin Powell warned of the emergence of a "terror-industrial complex."[11] A related academic argument contends that coalitions of domestic actors that will benefit from expansionist foreign policies propagate "myths of empire" to justify imperialism. When these coalitions are able to prevail domestically, aggression is likely to result.[12]

NATIONALISM

At different times in history, nationalism and ethnic strife have been viewed as central sources of international conflict.[13] This cause is placed at the state level because it is the nationalism of existing nation-states or nationalism in the effort to create new nation-states that is the source of conflict. As noted in Chapter 2, the rise of nationalism increased the ability of governments to mobilize their populations for war. World War I, World War II, and the wars in the former Yugoslavia have all been blamed on nationalism, as have several incidents of genocide (in Rwanda in 1994 and in Armenia in 1915–1918) and terrorism (the Irish Republican Army in Britain and Basque separatists in Spain).

nationalism

The doctrine that recognizes the nation as the primary unit of political allegiance.

Nationalism can be defined as the doctrine that recognizes the nation as the primary unit of political allegiance. The nation, in turn, can be defined as the largest group that people define as their "in-group." Traditionally, national identity was viewed as somehow linked to genetics, such that there was a fundamental identifiable difference between people of one nationality and another. Some still hold that view, but most scholars view a "nation" as something that is perceived rather than based in physical reality. In other words, nations are socially constructed, or, as in the title of an influential book on the subject, *Imagined Communities*.[14] In its most virulent forms, nationalism can by itself lead to conflict. When one group of people (Nazi Germany is the best example) believes that it is so superior to others that it has the right (and perhaps the duty) to rule over or even exterminate other groups, it is easy to see how violence can result. That sort of doctrine was widespread in the era before World War II.

More broadly, however, nationalism has led to conflict when combined with a related doctrine, "national self-determination." The doctrine of national self-determination holds that every nation should rule itself by having its own state. This doctrine is based in democratic theory, which asserts that each group of people should rule itself. However, basing the notion of the "body politic" on ethnic and national criteria, rather than on territory, sows the seeds for innumerable conflicts. The "nation-state" is an abstraction; almost no state in the world is ethnically or nationally homogenous.[15] National groups are often mixed together and often cross established political boundaries.

As a result, the drive for national self-determination invariably involves giving one group control over a territory and either reducing other groups to second-class status or ejecting them from the territory altogether. It may also involve trying to conquer territory belonging to other states in order to bring an ethnic group under one government. Thus, the doctrine of national self-determination can lead directly to violence.

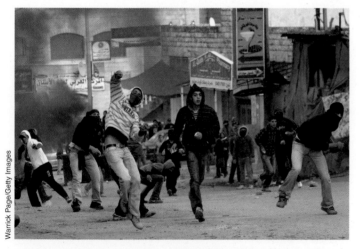

Palestinian youths throw rocks at Israeli border police in Shuafat refugee camp, in Jerusalem, Israel, March 2010. Religion and nationalism play important roles in this conflict.

Warrick Page/Getty Images

There can be little doubt that nationalism has been an important component in the origins of some wars. Since the end of the Cold War, ethnic conflict has played a role in civil and international wars in nearly every region of the world. However, nationalism does not appear to be the sole cause of war, since some wars lack an ethnic dimension

Figure 7.1 Ethnic Division in Iraq. If nationalism requires that each distinct group have its own state, what are the prospects for peace in Iraq? How did the country stay together for most of the twentieth century?

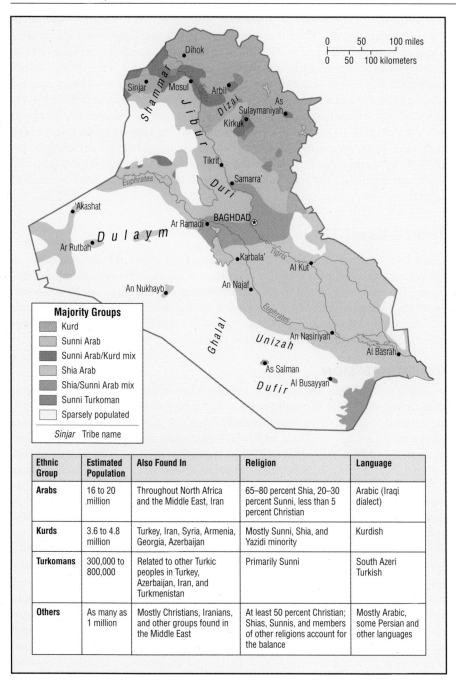

Ethnic Group	Estimated Population	Also Found In	Religion	Language
Arabs	16 to 20 million	Throughout North Africa and the Middle East, Iran	65–80 percent Shia, 20–30 percent Sunni, less than 5 percent Christian	Arabic (Iraqi dialect)
Kurds	3.6 to 4.8 million	Turkey, Iran, Syria, Armenia, Georgia, Azerbaijan	Mostly Sunni, Shia, and Yazidi minority	Kurdish
Turkomans	300,000 to 800,000	Related to other Turkic peoples in Turkey, Azerbaijan, Iran, and Turkmenistan	Primarily Sunni	South Azeri Turkish
Others	As many as 1 million	Mostly Christians, Iranians, and other groups found in the Middle East	At least 50 percent Christian; Shias, Sunnis, and members of other religions account for the balance	Mostly Arabic, some Persian and other languages

Source: http://www.lib.utexas.edu/maps/middle_east_and_asia/iraq_ethno_2003.jpg. Courtesy of the University Libraries, The University of Texas at Austin.

(the U.S. Civil War is one example). Moreover, although war is an age-old phenomenon, nationalism and the idea of the nation-state are relatively modern phenomena, dating roughly to the period of the French Revolution. If war is caused by nationalism, there should have been little war prior to the era of nationalism. At best, therefore, nationalism can only provide a partial explanation of war.

WAR AS A DIVERSION

The diversionary theory of war holds that wars are sometimes initiated to distract the public from other, more troubling issues. Thus, Vyacheslav Plehve, Russian interior minister at the time of the Russo-Japanese War (1904–1905), is reported to have advocated going to war, saying, "What this country needs is a short, victorious war to stem the tide of revolution."[16] The same effort to influence public opinion has been linked to other decisions to go to war, including those of Germany in 1914, Argentina in invading the Falklands/Malvinas islands in 1982, and the United States in attacking suspected terrorist bases in Afghanistan and Sudan in 1998. Indeed, historian Geoffrey Blainey claims that the argument that war is a "foreign circus staged for discontented groups at home . . . was invoked to explain individual wars from the Hundred Years war, which began in 1328, to the Vietnam War more than six centuries later."[17] Although diversionary wars have traditionally been viewed as a policy of autocratic leaders who had no democratic legitimacy for their rule, the theory has been applied more recently to democracies as well.[18]

Individual-Level Theories

Individual-level explanations of war find the causes of war either in human nature or in the psychology of individual leaders. An important distinction between theories at this level is whether or not they assert that the shortcomings of individuals can be overcome. For example, if genetics determines that we are all aggressive, there may not be much that can be done. But if wars are caused by the mistakes, either of people in general or of particular individual leaders, better education may reduce conflict.

HUMAN AGGRESSION

Some scientists argue that war is simply another form of aggression, which is "hardwired" into human beings through genetics. According to this view, some tendency toward aggression is innate in many species of animals. Scientists study the sources of violence in the animal kingdom, which include disputes over food, mates, and territory, as well as differences between groups. Scientists also study variations in patterns of violence, including those based on sex, age, and population density, among other factors. Moreover, research has shown that violence can be conditioned by experience.[19]

This research implies that human beings have the same predispositions toward violence as other animals. Furthermore, humans are only narrowly removed, in evolutionary terms, from an environment that truly was anarchic and in which the weak were at the mercy of the strong, just as is still true today among many animal species in the wild. Stronger, more aggressive individuals were better able to protect and feed their young, and hence were preferred by mates. In such an environment, the aggressive were more likely to reproduce, and the passive less likely. Thus, it is argued, **natural selection** favored aggression in human beings.[20] Psychologist Sigmund Freud found aggression inherent in human nature: "It is a general principle, then, that conflicts of interest between men are settled by the use of violence."[21] Others agree that people are inherently aggressive, but they rely more on religious or philosophical beliefs to support that assertion. Christian theologians from Augustine of Hippo in the fifth century to Reinhold Niebuhr in the twentieth

natural selection
The tendency for traits that increase the likelihood of individual survival to become more common in future generations of a species.

have made this argument, as have philosophers such as Benedict de Spinoza.[22] Both religious and scientific arguments lead to the conclusion that conflict is the inevitable outcome of human aggression.

Evidence to counter the thesis that people are inherently aggressive has been sought by anthropologists, who have scoured the world to find nonviolent primitive societies. The existence of societies with no violence would undermine the idea that violence is innate in human beings and instead support the idea that violence is learned through socialization. Several peaceful societies have been identified, although they are small and geographically isolated.[23] However, it is not clear whether conflict and violence were genuinely absent from these societies, or whether they have used powerful socialization effects (such as ostracizing those who commit acts of violence) to deter violence.

Is aggression inherent in all animals, including humans? Is this the root cause of war? If people are inherently aggressive, what accounts for peace?

The notion that people are aggressive or power-hungry has been adopted by a wide range of political and international relations theorists. As Thucydides stated: "Of gods we believe and of men we know, it is in their nature to rule whenever they can."[24] Similarly, Hans Morgenthau states, "Human nature, in which the laws of politics have their roots, has not changed since the classical philosophies of China, India, and Greece endeavored to discover these laws."[25]

The problem with the innate aggression hypothesis is that it cannot explain *variation* in the amount of conflict observed. The human genome is more or less constant, yet the level of war and peace varies greatly over time and across space. This is true whether we consider violence between states or between street gangs. The biological explanation, even to the extent that it is true, does not get to the key question of why violence happens at some times and not others.

Moreover, there is a powerful counterargument, also based on natural selection. This approach points out that because individual human survival in the wild is a very uncertain proposition, humans who cooperate in groups are more likely to survive and reproduce. Therefore, natural selection would favor those individuals who could collaborate with their fellows instead of killing them. This view resonates with the feminist critique of a masculine definition of "power" as the ability to coerce or injure, rather than as the ability to collaborate.

INDIVIDUAL LEADERS: MADMEN AND MEGALOMANIACS

Chapter 6 devoted considerable attention to biases that can cause misperceptions on the part of state leaders. In a state where a single leader can be highly influential in the choice to go war, such misperceptions can be seen as the proximate cause of war. Thus, World War II in Europe is explained largely by the pathological aggression of Adolph Hitler, and it is difficult to explain the Napoleonic Wars that ravaged Europe in the early nineteenth century without looking at the remarkable ambition and leadership of the man for whom these wars are named, Napoleon Bonaparte. This approach seems to fit well with the democratic peace theory, which would find that in democracies such leaders would be unable to bring their countries to war single-handedly. Many theorists, however, find this view of war unconvincing, in part because such explanations seem closely linked to the wartime propaganda that every state produces to portray its adversaries as evil aggressors, bent on conquest for its own sake. Moreover, scholars find that behind many of these "madmen" lie genuine conflicts of interest. Thus, Germany's involvement

Turkmen President Saparmurat Niyazov (r) had massive statues of himself build around the country, including one in Ashgabat that rotates so that it always faces the sun. Iranian leader Mahmoud Ahmedinejad denies that the Holocaust happened. Do individual leaders' characteristics heavily influence foreign policies?

in World War II, for example, is seen as driven less by Hitler alone than by the distribution of power that developed in Europe in the 1930s.[26]

MISPERCEPTION

The views of expected utility theory are sharply contested by those who focus on the processes of misperception. According to this perspective, war is almost always the result, not of rational calculations, but of *irrational* calculations and of psychologically driven misperceptions. Such misperceptions lead states to begin wars that they later regret and that later seem idiotic.

Problems of misperception are likely to be strongest when leaders are under psychological stress, such as when they find themselves in a crisis, possibly headed to war.[27] In other words, misperception is likely to be worst when accurate perception matters most. Some fear that expected utility theory will convince leaders that they can calculate the expected utility of their adversaries and use deterrence very precisely, when in reality it might be incredibly difficult to anticipate what an adversary might do in a crisis.

Several examples of misperception leading to war were discussed in Chapter 6, including Germany's belief in 1914 that Britain would not join the war. Soviet ruler Joseph Stalin calculated in 1939 that signing a nonaggression pact with Hitler would protect the Soviet Union from attack. By all accounts, Stalin went into denial when Germany attacked and did not speak publicly for a week while German troops demolished the Soviet army. American leaders never took seriously the notion that Japan would attack Pearl Harbor. The Japanese, in attacking Pearl Harbor, expected the United States to withdraw from the Pacific, rather than resolving to destroy Imperial Japan. In the early 1960s, the United States believed that a few of its military advisors could easily help the South Vietnamese army defeat a poorly armed peasant communist movement in Vietnam, and in 1979, Soviet leaders believed they could quickly conquer Afghanistan (they were still there a decade later). Saddam Hussein believed in 1990 that no one would do anything about his invasion of Kuwait.

The belief that war often results from misperception has led to a search for ways to prevent such misperceptions. This was an especially important theme during the Cold War, when the stakes were particularly high. But the stakes remain high now, whether in considering a nuclear war between India and Pakistan or a war involving other countries, where levels of conventional armaments are already increasing. Avoiding misperception is seen as an important means of avoiding war.

"THE FOG OF WAR"

fog of war

A phrase coined by Prussian strategist Karl von Clausewitz to characterize the difficulties in controlling war once it starts.

Expectations about war that turn out to be wrong are not simply the result of misperceptions or stupidity. War is an immensely complex endeavor, and its path and consequences are inherently unpredictable. The inability to predict how a war will go and the difficulty in controlling it once it starts, are problems that have been studied for centuries. The Prussian strategist Karl von Clausewitz coined the phrase "the **fog of war**" to characterize the difficulties in controlling war once it starts. The phrase was prominent more recently as the title of a 2003 documentary film about the Vietnam War, and about the lessons that Robert McNamara, the U.S. Secretary of Defense during the war, learned from it. Many of these lessons concerned the unpredictability of war and the need to constantly question one's assumptions and beliefs.

The difficulty of predicting how war will proceed is a particular case of a broader problem discussed in Chapter 3: the difficulty of defining power. Even if we focus on military power, numbers of weapons and soldiers tell only a small part of the story. Technology, tactics, morale, geography, economics, and sometimes luck all play roles in how a conflict will actually turn out.[28]

For this reason, expected utility theorists contend that misperception does not really undermine their theory, for misperception only reveals itself in hindsight. Given what they know *at the time,* expected utility theorists contend, leaders of two states will go to war when both calculate that the expected benefits of going to war exceed the benefits of making the concessions needed to avoid war. War, therefore, can be seen as being caused by disagreement over the distribution of military power and as ending when warfare clarifies the distribution of power.[29]

Why is it so difficult to predict how war will turn out? Even wars in which the winner is correctly predicted from the onset rarely turn out as expected. For example, no one doubted that the United States could prevail in the U.S.-Iraq war that began in 2003, but few predicted that the defeat of the Iraqi army and the dismantling of Saddam Hussein's state would lead to an insurgency that the United States would struggle for years to defeat. Neither the speed of the original victory nor the dragging on of the ensuing insurgency was widely anticipated.

Every war is unique, not only in the circumstances and in the combatants, but also in the technology used and its effects. This makes it difficult to predict how a war will be fought and who will prevail. Germany's wars with France (and others) from 1870 through 1945 illustrate this point. The Franco-Prussian War of 1870 was over in six weeks. Prussia (a state that later united with others to become Germany) was able to use a new technology, railroads, to move its troops very rapidly to outmaneuver the French forces. Because Prussia was able to win through maneuver, there were no major battles and casualties were low. In preparing for war in the following decades, military planners in all countries assumed that the next war would be the same. In 1914, the willingness of all sides to go to war was fed by the belief that the war would be over quickly and that casualties would be low. However, several technological innovations whose effects had not been anticipated changed the nature of war. Barbed wire and machine guns, among other factors, made defense very easy, and attack was nearly suicidal. As a result, the war rapidly stalemated into trench warfare, and huge numbers of soldiers were sacrificed in futile efforts to break through opposing lines.

In the years leading up to World War II, the French learned the lessons of defense from World War I and devised a series of fortresses, known as the *Maginot Line,* to help keep out Germany. However, another new technology had emerged: the tank. German tacticians figured out how to form separate tank forces that could move through or around enemy lines and rapidly cut them off from behind. These tactics made the French fortifications utterly useless. Germany never attacked the Maginot Line when it invaded France in 1940. Instead, German forces went around them and were in Paris within weeks. Thus, in each of these three wars, the relative strengths of offense and defense were completely different. States whose leaders anticipated these strengths correctly had an advantage, but especially in World War I, the costs were enormous. Germany was defeated in World War II only when Russian generals learned the German tactics and deployed them with devastating effect against Germany's overstretched forces at the Battle of Stalingrad (1942–1943) and afterward.

The course of war can also change fundamentally when the goals change. In 1991, the United States devised a brilliant war plan to defeat Iraq with almost no U.S. casualties. A long air campaign combined with rapid tank movements (and overwhelming superiority in weapons) quickly ejected Iraq's army from Kuwait. In 2003, the same tactics were applied with roughly similar success, except that in this case the goal was to occupy the country and govern it. Because the new war plan made few provisions for occupying Iraq after the main military campaign, the United States quickly ran into problems. Whether better planning would have led to a better outcome or whether the task was essentially impossible remains a matter of debate. However, the point is that the change in goals required a change in strategy that did not take place.

To summarize, it is often difficult to anticipate how a war will proceed. Each war is different in terms of the combatants and in terms of the military objectives. At the same time, military technology is changing over time, and the effects of these changes can rarely be anticipated until the technology is actually used in war.

The Search for Scientific Explanations

Despite the massive amount of research on the subject, there remains little consensus on the causes of war. As the expected utility and misperception approaches both assert in different ways, the decision to go to war is based on the perception that war is the best alternative available. To the extent that this is true, however, the theories do not say much about the broader causes—about the roles of economics, domestic politics, nationalism, the distribution of power, and other factors that contribute to the belief that war is the best option. All of these factors can be plausible explanations, especially when applied to one or a few cases. However, none provides a satisfying explanation of variation in the outbreak of war—of why wars occur in some cases, but not in others.

Why, with all of the data collected on wars and all of the sophisticated methods of analysis available, are scholars unable to definitively determine the causes of war? Does the evidence not support some explanations better than others? In some cases, it does, but different paradigms conceptualize the problem differently and therefore are difficult to compare directly or to evaluate using a single body of evidence.

Note, however, that the lack of conclusive answers about the causes of war should not obscure the fact that several very plausible explanations have been discredited, helping advance the search for valid explanations. Statistical analyses of data have shown that several of the most plausible-sounding and widely held understandings of war do not hold up to scrutiny. Neither balance of power nor imbalance of power is closely associated with war. Economic interdependence does not reduce the likelihood of war and may increase it. A democratic form of government does not reduce the likelihood of a state being involved in war. By eliminating these plausible explanations, scholars can focus more attention on other potential causes.

Evidence associated with the democratic peace theory indicates that democratic dyads are less likely to go to war than other dyads,

Figure 7.2 War: The Funnel of Causation. Explanations of war operate at different levels of generality, from showing why it is possible, to hypothesizing about what makes it more likely and what causes the final decision to attack.

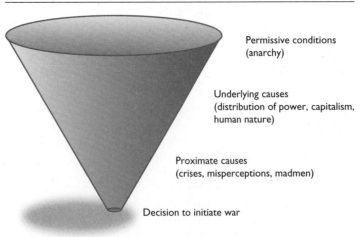

Permissive conditions
(anarchy)

Underlying causes
(distribution of power, capitalism, human nature)

Proximate causes
(crises, misperceptions, madmen)

Decision to initiate war

Source: Paul D'Anieri

although both the evidence and the implications are disputed. It is also clear that states that are close to one another geographically are more likely to go to war. This finding is so self-evident that it does not seem impressive. Moreover, it is questionable whether this pattern will continue to hold as technology continues to "shrink" the globe.

OBSTACLES

Despite the vast amount of research on the subject, there are several obstacles to progress toward a scientific explanation of the causes of war. Some obstacles are conceptual and some have to do with the nature of evidence and data collection. One conceptual problem has to do with different ways of defining the "causes" of war. This discussion so far has referred to at least three different views of the causes of war.

- Permissive conditions—reasons why war is *possible*—as causes. This understanding of "cause" is especially prominent in realist theory.

- General sources of conflict as causes; also known as the *underlying* causes of war. This notion of cause is found in many theories at the system and state levels.

- *Decisions* to initiate war as causes, a definition especially prominent at the state and individual levels.

Unless there is agreement on which kind of cause matters most, there can be no agreement on exactly what question to ask or what kind of evidence is relevant to answer it.

A related problem is that, by all accounts, the road to war is a complex process. Many factors contribute, making explanations focusing on one or a few factors insufficient. War is also complex in that some causal factors occur prior to others. In other words, before the decisions of individual leaders can cause a war, other conditions (such as underlying conflicts) have to exist. Even if there were agreement on the "list of ingredients" of war, figuring out how they fit together would still be problematic.

Moreover, there may be *multiple pathways* to war, meaning that no single cause will explain all wars. Some wars may concern territory; others might concern national self-determination; and still others may involve neither. We actually have a good general understanding of what makes wars more or less likely, and therefore, we are rarely surprised when one breaks out. We know the warning signs. But a broad model that predicts exactly which combinations of circumstances will lead to war and which will not is beyond our current understanding.

Table 7.1 Summary of Causes of War

	System Level	State Level	Individual Level
Theories that assert that war is inevitable	Realism (war is caused by anarchy) Economic structuralism (war is caused by capitalism)		War is caused by human aggression
Theories that assert that war is avoidable	Economic liberalism (free trade leads to peace)	Democratic peace theory Expected utility theory Realism (war is caused by aggressive states) Economic structuralism (war is caused by capitalism)	War depends on the psychology of individual leaders War is driven by psychological misperceptions

The History Connection

Underlying versus Proximate Causes of War: Sarajevo versus Cuba

One of the most difficult questions for scholars as well as policy makers is whether to focus on the underlying causes of war or the proximate causes. This is the question raised at the outset of this chapter concerning the Thirty Years War. Underlying causes refer to the long-term buildup in tensions that lead countries to believe that they may go to war with each other and to prepare for such a war. Proximate causes are the crises that move countries from a situation of hostility to one of outright conflict. Those who advocate focusing on each perspective point to history to make their case.

Those who focus on underlying causes see these as more fundamental, both for explaining why wars happened in the past and for explaining why they might happen again in the future. In this view, if there is a long-term buildup toward war, any number of proximate causes can set it off, and the particular incident does not really much matter. This view does not put much stock in the claim that World War I was caused by the assassination of the Archduke Franz Ferdinand, even though that statement is in some sense true. The major powers of Europe had been planning for war with each other for some time; all were expecting it to happen sooner or later, and some even welcomed war. Thus, it did not matter that the Bosnian crisis of 1912 did not lead to the war, and it would not have mattered if the 1914 July crisis had somehow been resolved. Sooner or later, the war would have occurred. In this view, it was the underlying problems in the distribution of power and the alliance system that caused the war. Or, from an economic structuralist view, it was the underlying working of the capitalist system.

Others reject this view, arguing that war is never inevitable and that if crises can be managed successfully

for long enough, the tensions underlying them might eventually diminish. Had World War III broken out over the Cuban missile crisis, future historians (if there had been any) could easily have argued that the war was inevitable; that if war had not occurred over the 1961 Berlin crisis or the 1962 Cuban crisis, it would have broken out later over something else. In retrospect, however, it is now clear that war between the Soviet Union and the United States was not inevitable. The Cold War ended and the Soviet Union collapsed without World War III happening. Therefore, some scholars and policy makers see the proximate causes of war as the most crucial.

For this reason, a great deal of research has gone into studying crisis resolution. Research has focused on how the stress of crisis influences individual psychology and group decision making. Research has also been directed at improving crisis decision-making procedures—everything from ensuring that a country's top leaders can gather in one place quickly to ensuring that they can contact leaders in other countries rapidly.

Critical Thinking Questions

1. Consider two of the wars of the twenty-first century, those in Iraq and Afghanistan. To what extent can these conflicts be attributed to underlying versus proximate causes?
2. How does your answer to the previous question influence debates over whether these conflicts could have been or should have been avoided?
3. Looking into the future, would focusing on the underlying or proximate causes of war seem to offer a more promising strategy?

PHOTO © ISTOCKPHOTO

In addition to conceptual problems, there are data problems. It is relatively easy to obtain data on many states over many years on such basic characteristics related to war as population, national wealth, military spending, government type, and the like. But it is much harder, if not impossible, to collect data on other factors, such as the nature of the decision-making process within a government, or the evaluations of risks, payoffs, and alternatives discussed in expected utility models. Most governments work hard to keep these matters secret. Finding large amounts of comparable data on a variety of conflicts is, and probably will remain, impossible. The available data are sometimes sketchy and therefore subject to multiple interpretations. For all of these reasons, a considerable amount of work needs to be done before we fully understand the causes of war.

Managing the Security Dilemma

States sometimes pursue security not by trying to win the competition for power, but by seeking to escape or manage the security dilemma. As noted in Chapter 3, the liberal school of thought considers this both desirable and possible. It is difficult to point to any easy techniques for resolving international conflict, but security dilemmas can ease, either by themselves or through diplomatic efforts.

Arms Control

Arms control aims to make war less likely and less destructive. Arms control agreements can help prevent the outbreak of war by reducing uncertainty about states' capabilities and intentions. Thus, arms control is of particular use in situations in which states do not have a powerful desire for expansion but might initiate war out of the fear of what will happen if their enemy strikes first. Historically, a substantial number of wars seem to have started this way. World War I is an example. The Cuban missile crisis, which at the time seemed to have the potential to lead to World War III, is an example of a situation in which this did not happen.

An early arms control agreement was the 1922 Washington Naval Agreement, which limited the size of the fleets of the five signatories (France, Italy, Japan, the United Kingdom, and the United States), in order to maintain the prevailing distribution of power in the Pacific. The goal was not to undo the logic of deterrence or to equalize the size of the states forces, but rather to make the existing deterrence more robust and stable.

ARMS CONTROL AND CRISIS STABILITY IN THE COLD WAR

The great fear during the Cold War was that during a crisis, both states would want to avoid war but that one would attack anyhow. Thomas Schelling, an early proponent of nuclear arms control, demonstrated the problem. During a crisis, both superpowers would have to worry about what would happen if war started. Although neither would want to go to war, the essential goal would be to avoid suffering a first strike. The superpower that struck first would decimate the other country and perhaps wipe out enough of its nuclear forces to reduce the impact of the inevitable retaliation. Not only would each country have a strong incentive to go first, Schelling argued, but each would know that the other side had a similar incentive. Schelling envisioned a U.S. or Soviet leader thinking, " 'He thinks we think he thinks we think . . . he thinks we think he'll attack; so he thinks we shall; so he will; so we must.' "[30] To put it more generally, where offensive weapons are perceived to have a large advantage, the knowledge that war is possible can become a self-fulfilling prophecy.[31] Arms control agreements are intended to reduce such dangers.

In the 1972 SALT-I treaty, the United States and the Soviet Union agreed to limit the number of offensive weapons. Keeping a rough balance in offensive weapons presumably reduced the chance that one side could hope to attack first and win a war.

Moreover, the two sides agreed not to interfere with each other's spy satellites. Only through mutual surveillance could the two sides be satisfied that the agreements were being obeyed.

A second example from the Cold War was an effort to avoid conventional war in Europe. The United States and the Soviet Union had huge numbers of troops and weapons facing off against each other in central Europe, in a line running roughly north/south between **East and West Germany**. Because of the nature of modern tank warfare, there was a widespread belief that the side that attacked would have a huge advantage. Added to this was the fact that both sides periodically held huge military exercises to practice for a future war. The fear was that one of these exercises would be mistaken for a real attack and would thus initiate World War III. In 1975, the two sides agreed to limit the size of such exercises so they would be small enough that neither side, seeing the other's force moving, would feel compelled to initiate a counterattack. The two sides also agreed to notify each other of any significant exercises well in advance. These agreements were never violated because to do so would have gained no advantage for the violating state and would have perhaps spurred an attack due to misperception.

The Scrapping of a Backfire Bomber in Ukraine. The United States and the Soviet Union, despite being locked in an intense ideological and geopolitical conflict, found it in their interest to reduce or eliminate certain categories of weapons.

AP Photo/Efrem Lukatsky

THE NUCLEAR NON-PROLIFERATION TREATY

A final example goes beyond the Cold War and the U.S.-Soviet conflict. One of the most difficult challenges today is the limitation of the spread of nuclear weapons. A significant number of countries have the economic and technological ability to build nuclear weapons but do not want to. However, these countries can only refrain from building nuclear weapons as long as most other countries do the same. Without very detailed and intrusive inspections, it is impossible to tell a peaceful nuclear energy program from a nuclear weapons program. The danger is that some countries will build nuclear weapons not because they really want them, but because they fear that others might be getting them and therefore believe that they need some deterrent. Thus, following North Korea's nuclear test in 2006, there was considerable speculation that South Korea and Japan might decide they needed nuclear weapons as well.

This problem has been addressed through the **Treaty on the Non-Proliferation of Nuclear Weapons** (NPT). Signed in 1968, the NPT is an agreement that states without nuclear weapons will refrain from getting them and will allow detailed inspections in order that other states can be certain that they are fulfilling their obligations. To make this work, the International Atomic Energy Agency (IAEA) maintains a large staff of expert scientists who travel around the world conducting inspections and notifying the world of violations. The NPT is far from foolproof. It does not prevent proliferation by states that are determined to proliferate. It only prevents proliferation by those states that do not want nuclear weapons but might acquire them because of the security dilemma.

Arms control agreements are also intended to limit the destructiveness of war, should it occur. An important early effort to reduce the horror of war was the 1925 Geneva Protocol banning the use of poison gas in war. Poison gases such as mustard gas and chlorine had been used during World War I, and the world had been shocked at their horrific effects on soldiers. An agreement banning them was reached in 1925, and they were not used in World War II, although after World War II, both the United States and the Soviet Union built enormous stocks of more lethal chemical weapons.

East and West Germany

From the end of World War II in 1945 until 1990, there were two German states, the Federal Republic of Germany, or "West Germany," allied with the United States, and the German Democratic Republic, or "East Germany," allied with the Soviet Union. A year after the decision to bring down the Berlin Wall in 1989, Germany was reunited.

Treaty on the Non-Proliferation of Nuclear Weapons

An agreement that states without nuclear weapons will refrain from getting them and that they will allow detailed inspections in order that other states can be certain that they are fulfilling their obligations.

THE CAMPAIGN TO BAN LAND MINES

The 1997 Ottawa Treaty prohibits the deployment of antipersonnel mines, and requires destruction of existing stockpiles. Unlike previous arms control efforts, this one was primarily promoted not by states, but by NGOs. Land mines are very effective and cost-effective military weapons, providing a cheap, easy, and long-lasting way to deny a particular territory to an enemy's troops. But land mines are viewed as especially inhumane weapons not so much for what they do to soldiers, but because they are very indiscriminate killers. Once land mines are laid, they are rarely removed, and long after a war is over, civilians are still killed and maimed by land mines. Land mines are cheap and effective, but despite this, 156 countries had agreed to the treaty.

LIMITS TO ARMS CONTROL

Skeptics argue that arms control works only when it is not needed—that only countries that are peaceful are willing to reach agreements, and that that states only agree not to do things that they did not intend to do anyway. In 1934, as Japan grew more assertive, it simply renounced the Washington Naval Treaty. Critics of the SALT-I and SALT-II treaties point out that they did not really slow the arms race. The SALT-I treaty, for example, limited the number of missiles, but both sides were allowed to add as many warheads as they could to those missiles. Hence, the treaty actually ushered in a large growth in the number of warheads. Similarly, those countries most interested in acquiring nuclear weapons either simply refuse to sign the NPT (Israel, India, Pakistan, and North Korea) or violate it (Iran).

A more basic problem is that the two goals of arms control sometimes conflict. Some weapons may help prevent wars but increase destructiveness. There is no doubting the horrendous effects of land mines on civilians around the world. But because they are stationary weapons, mines can only be used to defend territory and not to attack. They are one of a few weapons that do not exacerbate the security dilemma. They are also one way to protect territory in a way that makes a first strike by an adversary much less of a threat and hence reduces the mutual first-strike dilemma that many arms control agreements are intended to address. The United States, for example, relies heavily on land mines to help defend South Korea from a possible invasion by North Korea. Using land mines reduces the number of troops or other weapons that would need to be deployed, thus decreasing North Korea's fear of an impending attack (and saving a lot of money in the process). As a result, the United States has been unwilling to sign the international land mine ban, a policy for which it has been criticized. Unfortunately, the destructiveness of war is still one of the main deterrents to initiating war. So agreements that lower the cost of war might accidentally increase the likelihood of war occurring

Figure 7.3 The Nuclear Fuel Cycle. The key difference between the nuclear material used as fuel in producing nuclear energy and nuclear material used in nuclear weapons is the level to which it is enriched (the concentration of the isotopes of uranium, U-235, and plutonium, Pu-239, in the fuel). Therefore, IAEA representatives focus on monitoring the enrichment process and on ensuring that all uranium and plutonium is accounted for.

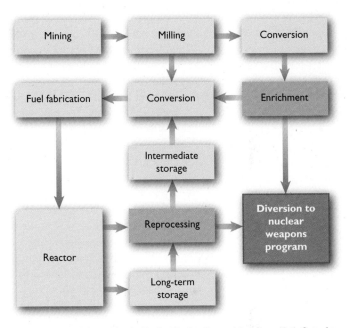

Source: http://cns.miis.edu/research/wmdme/flow/iran/. Reprinted by permission of James Martin Center for Nonproliferation Studies, Monterey Institute of International Studies.

Collective Security

For generations, people have held the hope that war would be prevented not only by the actions of the potential combatants, but by the intervention of other disinterested states, whose primary goal would simply be to prevent war. The goal of the League of Nations, formed after World War I, was to reduce international aggression: if one state committed aggression, all other states would join together to attack it. This doctrine is known as **collective security**. The threat of collective retaliation, it was reasoned, would make it irrational for any state to ever initiate an attack. In the 1930s, however, disinterested states generally put the goal of avoiding war ahead of the principle of collective security. When Japan invaded Manchuria in 1931 and Italy invaded Ethiopia in 1935, the targeted states appealed to the League of Nations to implement collective security, but other states chose not to go to war to punish the attackers. Thus, some argue that collective security works worst when it is needed most.[32]

More recently, the principle of collective security seemed to re-emerge after the Cold War. When Iraq invaded Kuwait in 1990, many countries agreed that the invasion was an act of aggression that must be reversed. More significantly, as the Cold War was ending, the United States and the Soviet Union could agree to use force to eject Iraq from Kuwait. The United States provided most of the force for the subsequent attack, but the war had the support of a very wide range of states and was sanctioned by the UN Security Council.

However, hope for a "New World Order" based on collective security did not survive the decade. When war broke out in the former Yugoslavia, the powerful states of western Europe were determined not to get involved. Instead, they initially tried to insulate themselves from the conflict by tightening policies preventing refugees from entering their countries. Later, when several states increased their resolve to intervene to stop aggression by Serbian forces, they did not receive unanimous support from the UN Security Council. NATO-led interventions in 1995 and again in 1999 can perhaps qualify as successful applications of the doctrine of collective security, but they proved divisive.

collective security

A doctrine nominally adopted by states after World War I that specified that when one state committed aggression, all other states would join to attack it.

Peacekeeping and Peace Enforcement

Peacekeeping and *peace enforcement* are based on very different logics. Peacekeeping has been more frequent historically and works much like the arms control agreements that are aimed at preventing war. Traditional **peacekeeping**, also known as "first-generation peacekeeping," is the introduction of foreign troops or observers into a region in order to increase confidence in a situation when conflict is absent, either because a cease-fire has taken place or because hostilities have not actually broken out. Such missions require the consent of the conflicting parties, and are usually authorized under Chapter VI of the Charter of the United Nations, which concerns "Pacific Settlement of Disputes."

Peacekeeping can only begin when two sides have agreed that they want to stop fighting (or avoid going to war). States or groups at war sometimes want to stop fighting but believe they cannot do so for fear that their adversaries will take advantage of their stopping by rearming and then starting the war from a stronger position, by launching a surprise attack, or by continuing attacks covertly while claiming to have stopped. Arriving at an agreement to verify a truce can be impossible when the two sides do not trust each other.

Peacekeeping provides outside forces to monitor a truce or peace agreement. The role of peacekeeping is rarely to physically prevent two sides' forces from attacking each other (which would be more akin to *peace enforcement*). In fact, peacekeeping missions are usually lightly armed, and if one side does decide to attack, the peacekeepers may be incapable of stopping the attack (or even of protecting themselves). Instead, the role of

peacekeeping

The introduction of foreign troops or observers into a region to increase confidence that states will refrain from the use of force.

The Culture Connection

The Music of War

For centuries, composers and songwriters have been inspired by the horror or glory of war to compose some of the most famous music in history. The music of war has reflected changing public attitudes about wars. It may also be that the music itself actually influences attitudes about war.

Perhaps the most well-known piece of music about war is Tchaikovsky's *1812 Overture,* which celebrates the Russian triumph over Napoleon in 1812. The overture conveys Tchaikovsky's perception of the glory of that war and of the patriotism that was surging throughout Europe at the time of the composition 70 years later. Interestingly, the overture is now a staple at American Independence Day concerts.

Another famous classical piece on war is Gustav Holst's "Mars: The Bringer of War," part of his composition *The Planets,* which was written during the early years of World War I and conveys anguish rather than glory. It has been widely influential in recent years, having been adapted as the basis for the scores of the films *Star Wars* (1977) and *Gladiator* (2000).

Whereas World War I was widely seen as a waste, World War II was viewed by many as a glorious struggle of good against evil. In the popular music of that era, there are positive songs about soldiers and their girlfriends and the hope of returning home soon. The seriousness of the war is avoided in songs such as "Praise the Lord and Pass the Ammunition." Later, the darker side of the war was addressed as well. "Babi Yar," the opening movement of the Symphony No. 13 by the Russian composer Dmitri Shostakovich, provided haunting music for Yevgeny Yevtushenko's poem about a ravine in Kyiv, Ukraine, where thousands of Jews were murdered.

Initially, the Vietnam War was greeted with the same sort of patriotic music that characterized World War II. In 1966, "The Ballad of the Green Berets" by Barry Sadler, an American army sergeant, became a hit. Quickly, however, the popular music of Vietnam became explicitly antiwar. Examples are too numerous to mention, but John Lennon's "Give Peace a Chance" (1969) is a classic in the genre.

During the later years of the Cold War, in the 1980s, fears of nuclear war led to another round of antiwar songs, including U2's "War" ("It takes a second to say goodbye/push the button and pull the plug") and the German star Nena's "99 Red Balloons," which told of a nuclear war accidentally started by the release of a bunch of balloons. The aftermath of the September 11, 2001, attacks saw a return to prowar music, with Toby Keith proclaiming ". . . we'll put in a boot in your ass/ It's the American way." After the 2003 invasion of Iraq, antiwar music again made a resurgence, with songs like Pearl Jam's "Worldwide Suicide."

Critical Thinking Questions

1. In addition to reflecting attitudes about war, how might popular music actually influence attitudes?
2. Are songs about war interesting merely as aspects of popular culture, or do the attitudes expressed in these songs have relevance for policy debates?
3. Are musicians a credible source of opinion on issues of war and peace? If so, to whom might their opinions be of interest?

the peacekeepers is to provide two kinds of reassurance to the two sides in the conflict. First, peacekeepers monitor the agreement and provide each side with reliable, unbiased reports on whether the other side is meeting its commitments. Second, peacekeepers are often placed physically in territory between the two sides, and sometimes in the territory that the two sides are fighting over. This positioning creates a situation in which both

Table 7.2 Active UN Peacekeeping Missions, December 2009

Mission	Countries	Year of Origin	Police/Military Forces
UNTSO	Egypt, Israel, Jordan, Lebanon, Syria	1948	151
UNMOGIP	India/Pakistan	1949	43
UNFICYP	Cyprus	1964	921
UNDOF	Israel, Syria	1974	1043
UNIFIL	Lebanon	1978	11,862
MINURSO	Western Sahara	1991	232
UNMIK	Kosovo	1999	17
MONUSCO	Congo	1999	20,509
UNMIL	Liberia	2003	10,947
UNOCI	Cote d'Ivoire	2004	7536
MINUSTAH	Haiti	2004	9057
UNMIS	Sudan	2005	10,259
UNMIT	Timor-Leste	2006	1552
UNAMID	Sudan (Darfur)	2007	19,949
MINURCAT	Central African Republic/Chad	2007	2773

Source: http://www.un.org/peace/bnote010101.pdf. Reprinted by permission of United Nations.

sides know that before attacking their enemy, they must inevitably attack an international peacekeeping force (often containing soldiers from countries with a powerful capacity to attack). The incentive to attack is reduced considerably, but even the need to overcome foreign troops cannot stop a determined attacker.

Peacekeeping is not meant as a permanent solution (although, in fact, some peacekeeping missions have gone on for decades). Rather, it is intended to end the fighting on relatively neutral terms and to provide for enough stability that peaceful negotiations can take place. Eventually, in theory, an agreement should end the dispute and allow the peacekeepers to be withdrawn.

peace enforcement

The application of force (or the threat of force) to compel states to stop fighting.

Peace enforcement can be defined as the application of force (or the threat of force) to compel states to stop fighting. The logic is simple: Military intervention by an external actor (usually a very powerful state or group of states) can force warring parties to stop fighting. The U.S.-led attack in Iraq in 1991 was seen by some as a peace enforcement move: Iraq attacked Kuwait, and the U.S.-led coalition then attacked Iraq to reverse its aggression. The international interventions in the former Yugoslavia (in Bosnia in 1995 and over Kosovo in 1999) are other prominent recent cases. In contrast to peacekeeping, peace enforcement operations do not require the consent of the conflicting parties. They are generally authorized by Chapter VII of the UN Charter, which allows the UN to "take such action by air, sea, or land forces as may be necessary to maintain or restore international peace and security."[33]

In the 1990s, "second-generation peacekeeping" emerged to deal with crises in places such as Somalia, Cambodia, and the former Yugoslavia. Second-generation peacekeeping goes beyond monitoring missions and may provide humanitarian assistance, help countries carry out elections, and protect civilians, with armed force if necessary. Like

Reconsider
the Case

The Defenestration of Prague and the Thirty Years War

The Second Defenestration of Prague, which led to the beginning of the Thirty Years War, is one of many events that provide evidence to answer the question "What causes war?" and it reflects as well the ongoing debate over the relative importance of underlying versus proximate causes of war. However, knowing the specifics of the Thirty Years War does not tell us much about the causes of war in general. Many of the factors in that case, such as the defenestration, the combatants, and the weapons of that historical era, were specific to that conflict.

In developing generalized explanations of war, we look for factors that occur in many cases of war but that are not present when war does not occur. The Defenestration of Prague may have been unique, but the "triggering event" or a "proximate cause" is present in many cases. Is a triggering event necessary, or not? Similarly, the specific distribution of power present in Europe in 1618 may not be replicated in other

cases, but the intense concern over the distribution of power seems to recur in many cases.

A central question in all kinds of social science explanations is whether a particular cause is a *necessary* condition for an effect (meaning that the effect cannot occur without that cause) or whether it is a *sufficient* condition (meaning that this cause, by itself, can cause the effect in question). The simplest explanations are those with a single cause that is both necessary and sufficient..

Critical Thinking Questions

1. Can we identify any factors that by themselves are sufficient to cause war?
2. What factors or combination of factors are necessary to cause war? Is there some necessary "ingredient" such that if people controlled that factor they could limit war?

peace enforcement missions, second-generation peacekeeping missions do not require the consent of all parties. To capture the idea that these missions blur the distinction between traditional peacekeeping and peace enforcement, they are sometimes called "Chapter VI ½ missions."

Summary

This chapter has examined explanations for wars and strategies by which wars might be prevented. The examination began with a survey of theories of war at various levels of analysis. Although scholars have learned a great deal about the sources of war, a single unified explanation has been elusive, given the complexity of the problem and limited data. Despite these obstacles, efforts to overcome the security dilemma through agreements, negotiation, collective security, peacekeeping, and peace enforcement have achieved some success. Yet no theory has produced a prescriptive formula for avoiding war. In the immediate future, both agreements and armaments are likely to be pursued as means of protecting state security.

Key Concepts

1.   Security dilemma
2.   Human aggression
3.   Imperialism
4.   Nationalism
5.   "Fog of War"

6.   Permissive conditions
7.   Underlying causes
8.   Collective security
9.   Peacekeeping
10. Peace enforcement

Study Questions

1.   How can the realist paradigm explain a country's decision to strike first?

2.   How does expected utility theory explain a country's decision to go to war?

3.   What claim about war and free trade is advanced by the liberal paradigm? What evidence supports or refutes this claim?

4.   How do economic structuralists explain war?

5.   Which type of explanation of war do you find most compelling?

6.   What obstacles are there to a definitive explanation of war?

7.   How do arms control agreements seek to overcome the security dilemma?

8.   How is collective security intended to preserve peace? What obstacles does it face?

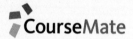

Endnotes

1.   Greg Cashman and Leonard C. Washington, *An Introduction to the Causes of War: Patterns of Interstate Conflict from World War I to Iraq* (Lanham, MD: Rowman and Littlefield, 2007), p. 3.

2.   Kenneth N. Waltz, *Man, The State, and War: A Theoretical Analysis* (New York: Columbia University Press, 1954), p. 188.

3.   Kenneth N. Waltz, "The Origins of War in Neorealist Theory," *Journal of Interdisciplinary History*, Vol. 83, No. 4 (Spring 1988): 620.

4.   Randall Schweller, "Realism's Status Quo Bias: What Security Dilemma?" *Security Studies* Vol. 5, No. 3 (1995/1996): 90–121.

5.   Bruce Bueno de Mesquita, "Risk, Power Distributions, and the Likelihood of War," *International Studies Quarterly*, Vol. 25, No. 4 (December 1981): 541–568.

6.   Daniel S. Geller, "The Stability of the Military Balance and War among Great Power Rivals," in Paul F. Diehl, ed., *The Dynamics of Enduring Rivalries* (Urbana: University of Illinois Press, 1998), pp. 165–190.

7.   See, for example, Harry Magdoff, *The Age of Imperialism* (New York: Monthly Review Press, 1969).

8.   A historical overview and critique of the view that free trade leads to peace can be found in Geoffrey Blainey, *The Causes of War*, 3rd ed. (New York: The Free Press, 1988), Chapter 2, pp. 18–32, "Paradise Is a Bazaar."

9.   Edward D. Mansfield and Jack Snyder, "Democratization and the Danger of War," *International Security*, Vol. 20, No. 1 (Summer 1995): 302.

10. See Schweller, "Realism's Status Quo Bias," pp. 90–121.

11. Walter Isaacson, "GQ Icon: Colin Powell," *GQ*, October 2007, p. 2, at http://www.gq.com/news-politics/newsmakers/200709/colin-powell-walter-isaacson-war-iraq-george-bush

12. Jack Snyder, *Myths of Empire: Domestic Politics and International Ambition* (Ithaca, NY: Cornell University Press, 1991).

13. See John L. Comaroff and Paul C. Stern, eds., *Perspectives on Nationalism and War* (Amsterdam: Gordon and Breach, 1995).

14. Benjamin Anderson, *Imagined Communities: Reflections on the Origins and Spread of Nationalism*, rev. ed. (London: Verso, 1991).

15. Walker Connor, "Nation-Building or Nation-Destroying?" *World Politics*, Vol. 24, No. 3 (April 1972): 319–355.

16. See David Walder, *The Short Victorious War: The Russo-Japanese War, 1904–1905* (New York: Harper & Row, 1974).

17. Blainey, *The Causes of War*, pp. 72–73. Blainey, it should be noted, is quite critical of this view (pp. 74–84).

18. See Alistair Smith, "Diversionary Foreign Policy in Democratic Systems," *International Studies Quarterly* 40 (March 1996): 133–153.

19. Konrad Lorenz, *On Aggression* (New York: Harcourt Brace Jovanovich, 1966). See also Raymond Aron, "Biological and Psychological Roots," in Lawrence Freedman, ed., *War* (Oxford: Oxford University Press, 1994), pp. 77–81.

20. This theory was portrayed graphically in the opening sequence of Stanley Kubrick's film *2001: A Space Odyssey* (1968), in which an ape involved in a

dispute realizes that it can destroy its adversaries by using a stick instead of just its bare hands to attack.

21. Sigmund Freud, "Why War?" in Melvin Small and J. David Singer, eds., *International War: An Anthology*, 2nd ed. (Chicago: The Dorsey Press, 1989), pp. 176–181. Freud's essay was part of a correspondence with Albert Einstein on the causes of war.

22. Waltz, *Man, the State, and War*, pp. 20–22.

23. David Fabbro, "Peaceful Societies: An Introduction," *Journal of Peace Research*, Vol. 15, No. 1 (1978): 67–83.

24. Thucydides, *History of the Peloponnesian War*, Book V, section 105.

25. Hans Morgenthau, *Politics Among Nations: The Struggle for Power and Peace*, 5th ed. (New York: Knopf, 1978), p. 3.

26. See Randall Schweller, *Deadly Imbalances: Tripolarity and Hitler's Strategy of World Conquest* (New York: Columbia University Press, 1998).

27. Richard Ned Lebow, *Between Peace and War* (Baltimore, MD: Johns Hopkins University Press, 1981).

28. Two examples of luck illustrate the point. If winter had not come early to Russia in 1941, Moscow might have fallen, perhaps allowing Germany to defeat Russia. At the Battle of Midway, the turning point of the Pacific part of World War II, a Japanese scout plane running behind schedule was precisely the plane that would have discovered the U.S. fleet; the delay helped sway a battle in which Japan lost the core of its fleet of aircraft carriers.

29. This view is expressed through a historical argument in Blainey, Chapter 8, and in formal rational choice terms by James D. Fearon, "Rationalist Explanations of War," *International Organization*, Vol. 49, No. 3 (Summer, 1995): 379–414.

30. Stephen Van Evera, "Offense, Defense, and the Causes of War," *International Security*, Vol. 22, No. 4 (1988): 5–43.

31. Richard K. Betts, "Systems of Peace or Causes of War: Collective Security, Arms Control, and the New Europe," *International Security*, Vol. 17, No. 1 (Summer 1992): 5–43.

32. Thomas Schelling, *Strategy of Conflict* (Cambridge, MA: Harvard University Press, 1960), p. 207.

33. Charter of the United Nations, Chapter VII, Article 42.

8

The Use of Force

LEARNING OBJECTIVES

After completing this chapter, the student should be able to . . .

1. Define "force" and understand the link between the threat of violence and the actual use of violence.

2. Distinguish the policy of defense from that of deterrence.

3. Explain the effects of WMD on deterrence, defense, and crisis stability.

4. Define "terrorism."

5. Summarize the competing explanations of the causes of terrorism and evaluate each.

6. Link different explanations of terrorism to possible policy responses.

◄ Russian troops move into Abkhazia, Georgia's breakaway province, August 2008.
AP Photo/Vladimir Popov

Consider the Case

Military Force as a Response to Terrorism

On September 11, 2001, nineteen men boarded planes in three American cities. They were armed only with box cutters and perhaps pepper spray. But they were also armed with knowledge of airline security procedures and of how to fly Boeing 757 and 767 airplanes. They had an ingenious plan and were willing to die carrying it out. These nineteen men were able to kill nearly 3000 people, destroy several huge buildings, shut down the U.S. and trans-atlantic air transport systems, create lasting fear, and spur conflict between the United States and Muslim populations in the Middle East and central Asia.

The United States, Great Britain, and their allies responded to the 2001 attacks in part through very conventional application of military force: they used regular armed forces to attack Afghanistan, which had harbored the group behind the attack. The allies then went to war against Iraq, based on the contention that it might be a threat in the future. Although both of those campaigns were quickly victorious in conventional military terms, neither had achieved its political goals by 2010. When the US declared the end of combat operations in Iraq in August 2010, it had been in combat in Iraq longer than in World War II.

Why has the most powerful military the world has ever seen been unable to defeat the various groups of insurgents in Iraq and Afghanistan? The states involved in these conflicts have spent years trying to answer this question, in the hope of devising a way of putting their immense military power to more effective use.

A far broader group of states than those involved in Iraq and Afghanistan is seeking to prevent terrorist attacks in their own countries or to fight insurgent groups within their borders. In some states, the military is the primary tool used. Elsewhere, terrorism is treated more as a law enforcement issue. How does a law enforcement strategy differ from a military one and which strategy is more appropriate to various kinds of threats?

Recent terrorist attacks, the military campaigns that have followed, and the protracted insurgencies that have resulted have raised several vexing questions for policy makers and academics alike. Why are the most technologically advanced armies in the world unable to defeat much more poorly equipped adversaries? Why are some states pursuing nuclear weapons even as terrorism and insurgency are proving so effective? What explains why some people are willing to become suicide bombers? What convinces some individuals in some societies to view terrorism as an admissible means of waging conflict, while others see it as unacceptable? How are terrorism and WMD related to more traditional applications of force? Questions like these are reshaping debates about international security in the contemporary world.

There are many forms of power in international politics, including economic, cultural, and military power, but military power is commonly viewed as the most fundamental. Different theoretical perspectives disagree on just how important military power is, but all agree that it plays a central role, and many see military power as the last resort available to states seeking to prevail in a disagreement. Many analysts therefore identify the contest to accumulate military power, and the ability to use it effectively, as the central problem in international politics. Because of the expense of acquiring military power and its destructiveness, the question of purpose is central in considering the political use of military power. The central premise of this chapter is that conventional weapons, weapons of mass destruction (WMD), insurgency, and terrorism are all employed as a means to achieve particular ends. Each operates according to a different logic. Each incurs different costs. But each is intended to achieve purposes that cannot be achieved through other means. This point is captured in the oft-cited assertion that "war is the continuation of policy by other means."[1] The implication is that to be useful, war must have a purpose, and that purpose must be achievable through war and valuable enough to offset the incredible costs of war. **Carl von Clausewitz**, the Prussian strategist responsible for that famous assertion, further stressed that state purposes are often best served by *avoiding* battle.[2]

But for what purposes do states and others employ violence? Only the most important goals are worth the costs of acquiring and using military force. The terms *international security* and *national security* identify a primary purpose: security. The goal of most actors who acquire and use military force, most of the time, is to *prevent* the use of military force by others. The definition of "security" has been broadened in recent years to include security from environmental, health, and economic threats, as well as from traditional military dangers. However, the traditional notion of security—

Taliban Militants Fighting in Ghazni Province, Afghanistan, in 2008. U.S. and allied forces were able to quickly topple the Taliban government in 2001 but then found themselves unable to consolidate control against lightly armed insurgents.

safety from the threat of attack—remains at the top of the agenda of international politics. When states, groups, or individuals are threatened with physical violence, other issues become secondary. The security dilemma provides one simple explanation for why states arm: They fear that if they do not, they will be vulnerable to attack or the threat of attack. Simply scanning the headlines of a newspaper shows that the use of military force and the desire for protection against it remain constant concerns for states and citizens around the world.

Around the world, not only states but many other actors consider the use of force and the threat of force to be useful tools of policy. Violence and the threat of it are used not only to prevent others from using violence, but to obtain a range of other goals, such as the removal of a regime considered especially odious, the revision of territorial boundaries, or a change in rights for a group of people. This chapter analyzes how state and nonstate actors use force to achieve their goals in international politics.

Military Force and Its Purposes

What does it mean to say that someone used *force* rather than *persuasion*? **Force** can be defined as the use of violence or the threat of violence to achieve a political goal. There are two things to notice about this deceptively simple definition.

First, the word "force" is a euphemism for the word "violence." Whether employed by a small gang or a large army, the use of force involves violence: killing, wounding, and starving people, and destroying property. Thus, how much force a state has at its disposal is equivalent to how much capacity it has to kill and destroy and how much capacity it has to defend its own citizens and property. These two abilities do not always go together.

Second, the *threat* of violence can also be considered the use of force. The ability to commit an act of violence often has an effect by itself, even if actual violence is not committed. Indeed, states often seek to acquire sufficient military capability that others can be frightened into making concessions. Gaining concessions without ever going to battle has been a major theme in strategic writings at least since the sixth century BCE, when the Chinese military strategist Sun Tzu wrote his *Art of War*.[3] The threat of force remains as important as the actual use of violence.

force

The use of violence or the threat of violence to achieve a political goal.

The Policy Connection

The Emergence of Cyber Warfare

In May 2007, the Estonian government decided to move a Soviet-era monument to World War II soldiers out of the center of Tallinn, Estonia's capital, to a less central spot. Ethnic Russians and the Russian government were enraged by what they saw as an insult to Russian soldiers. Within days, Estonian government Web servers experienced "distributed denial of service attacks," in which huge numbers of "zombie" computers are used to generate so much traffic to a Web site that it closes the Web site down. The attacks, it appears, originated from within Russia, although the zombie computers were spread around the world. It was unclear whether the Russian government orchestrated the attack or whether Russian hackers acted spontaneously.[1] To many, this was the first genuine instance of cyber warfare. In 2008, just before Russian forces invaded Georgia, Georgia too experienced a cyber attack, and many of its government Web sites were shifted to U.S. government servers to keep them running. In early 2010, Google revealed that a sophisticated Chinese attack had penetrated Google's networks, allowing the Chinese government to collect information on Chinese dissidents.[2]

Cyber warfare and cyber terrorism involve using various techniques to degrade computer systems, to sabotage systems that rely on computers, or to conduct espionage. Possible examples include hacking power or financial systems in order to induce economic chaos in a target society, degrading an opposing military's information technology (IT) systems in order to reduce its fighting capacity, attacking air traffic control systems to create airline crashes, and penetrating IT systems in order to gain valuable information. Speaking in 2009, U.S. Director of National Intelligence Mike McConnell warned that "a coordinated attack from a remote location by a small group on our electric grid, transportation network, and banking system could create damage as potentially great as a nuclear weapon over time."[3]

For policy makers, the advent of cyber warfare poses several challenges. First, territory provides no defense. The extensive use of the Internet in all aspects of our lives means that nearly everything we do can be attacked by hackers or governments anywhere in the world. Second, many vulnerabilities may

Coercive Diplomacy

coercion

The use of a threat to change another actor's behavior.

Coercion occurs when an explicit or implicit threat is used to persuade another actor to change its behavior. In some cases, as in the Cold War between the United States and the Soviet Union, threats are explicit and readily apparent. In other cases, threats may remain implicit. Simply possessing the means to destroy creates a threat that others are aware of, whether a threat is intended or not. There is a common perception that threats and negotiation are fundamentally different policies: A threat implies an unfriendly action aimed at gaining an unfair advantage, whereas negotiation appears to be a more friendly way to reach a mutually acceptable agreement. In fact, however, every negotiation entails an implied threat in the form of a question: "What happens if we do not arrive at an agreement?" Depending on the answer to this question, one side may have much greater incentive than the other to reach a deal. Implicitly, then, there is the threat that if concessions are not made and the situation remains unchanged, one state will be in an unfavorable position.

It is equally true that every threat is an offer to negotiate. Even a coercive threat ("If you do not do what we say, we will attack") is an attempt to bargain. Sometimes, a threat

not be apparent until they are exploited. Although defenders must identify and fix all possible vulnerabilities, an attacker need only find one to succeed. Second, cyber attacks may be difficult to deter because it is often not clear where they originate, meaning that the target for retaliation is not clear. Many of the "zombies" used to attack Estonia were actually in the United States, where they had been taken over by viruses spread by hackers. One can imagine a government (or a terrorist group) in one country arranging an attack from computers in a second country on the assets of a third country. The goal might not just be to disguise the attack but to spur conflict between the two target states.

Third, to combat potential cyber warfare, governments need to be actively involved in monitoring Web traffic and managing the Internet. This causes great concern for privacy advocates and civil libertarians. As the Chinese example shows, authoritarian governments have an interest in controlling the Internet.

To meet the emerging challenge from cyber warfare, governments and militaries around the world are organizing new units to address the problem directly, including the U.S. military's U. S. Cyber Command. Clearly, however, such organizations are not merely figuring out how to protect their own assets; they are also trying to figure out how to wage successful attacks on potential adversaries. Thus, even though cyber warfare is still considered an emerging threat, there have already been proposals for "arms control" agreements to limit the danger.

Critical Thinking Questions

1. Are cyber attacks likely to be useful in deterring or coercing an adversary? What characteristics of them make them similar or different to armed attacks?
2. How useful will the threat of retaliation using conventional or nuclear weapons be in deterring cyber attacks?
3. In the long run, is the offense or defense likely to dominate cyber warfare?

---

[1]BBC, "Estonia Hit By Moscow Cyber War," May 17, 2007, at http://news.bbc.co.uk/2/hi/europe/6665145.stm
[2]The attack is described by Jack Goldsmith, "The New Vulnerability," *The New Republic*, June 7, 2010, at http://www.tnr.com/article/books-and-arts/75262/the-new-vulnerability
[3]Quoted in Goldsmith, "The New Vulnerability."

---

may be necessary to begin a bargaining process because without it, a country that regards the status quo as beneficial may have no incentive to negotiate. A threat is only convincing, of course, to the extent that it would be rational to carry it out.

Credibility is an essential concern in applying threats of force to gain concessions. Credibility can be defined as the extent to which an actor making a threat has both the *will* and the *capability* to carry out the threat if concessions are not forthcoming. Thus, military capability helps make the threat of force credible and, therefore, provides benefits even if it is never employed on the battlefield. In general, states with larger military capabilities are likely to be in a better bargaining position.

credibility

The ability and will to carry out a threat.

Defense versus Deterrence

If some countries seek to use the threat of force to coerce others, all countries seek to use the threat of force to avoid being the victims of such coercion. If a state can convince others that an attack would be unwise, it can reduce the credibility of the

The Great Wall of China is an example of a purely defensive structure. It was powerful in defense but nearly useless in attack.

threat of such an attack and therefore reduce its vulnerability to coercion. There are two ways in which the potential use of force is leveraged to prevent another country from attacking: defense and deterrence. The distinction is essential. States shift their reliance on defense and deterrence depending on the technology and tactics available to them and their perceived power relative to states they perceive as potential adversaries.

The simplest way to provide security is to be able to repel an attack. This has been the traditional means of defense, and it involves building fortifications, buying weapons, and training soldiers to fight off a potential attacker. Around the world, the remains of such preparations are visible almost everywhere. The Great Wall of China, Moscow's Kremlin, the castles of medieval Europe, and the "battery" (now Battery Park) at the southern tip of Manhattan were all built to protect against attacks. A second goal of these preparations, equally important, is to convince an opponent that an attack will fail and therefore should not be attempted. This has the additional effect of rendering coercive threats less effective.

However, in some cases, it may either be difficult or exceedingly expensive to actually defend territory and assets. How can a country then protect itself from attack? An alternative to defense is **deterrence**, which entails convincing a potential opponent not to attack by raising the costs of attack so that they are higher than the perceived benefits. Even if it is impossible to defeat a very powerful enemy on the battlefield, it may be possible to cause enough destruction in the course of the war to convince the potential attacker that it's simply not worth it. In its purest form, deterrence does not consist of actually repelling the attack. U.S. and Soviet strategies in the Cold War exemplified a pure deterrent strategy. Neither side could hope to repel an attack by nuclear-armed missiles. Both sides sought, instead, to convince the other that such an attack would be met with a devastating response. The nuclear strategies of other countries are based on the same logic. Similarly, insurgent strategies, discussed later, do not aim to defeat an army in battle, but to raise the costs of an occupation unbearably high.

Historically, defense and deterrence strategies have often overlapped. From early history to World War II, the measures taken to defeat an attack also served to raise the cost of an attack. However, the advent of the airplane in the early twentieth century raised the possibility a pure deterrence strategy based on aerial bombing of an enemy's cities. The emergence of WMD further increased the possibility of "pure" deterrence. These weapons are very difficult to use in offensive operations but can be used to raise the costs of an attack, either as a defense against an invading force or as a deterrent aimed at the civilian population.

deterrence

A policy aimed at convincing a potential opponent not to attack by raising the costs of attack so that they are higher than the perceived benefits.

Table 8.1 Defense/Deterrence Continuum

Pure Defense	Mixed	Pure Deterrence
Walls, fortifications	Most conventional weapons including ground troops, aircraft, navies, tanks	Strategic nuclear weapons, most insurgent strategies

Table 8.2 Potential Arms Race as a Prisoner's Dilemma

		State A	
		Cooperate (refrain from further arming)	**Defect (build more weapons)**
State B	**Cooperate**	(3, 3) Neither state arms further, so they continue to deter each other with their existing armaments, but the costs of preparing for war and fighting it stay level.	(1, 4) State A has more weapons, is more secure, and can threaten State B.
	Defect	(4, 1) State B has more weapons, is more secure, and can threaten State A.	(2, 2) Both states arm, so they continue to deter each other, but they have spent money and war will be more costly if it occurs (see the "Prisoner's Dilemma" in Chapter 3).

The Security Dilemma

The discussion so far has given the impression that states should expend considerable resources to acquire as much military capability as possible. Indeed, through much of history, this is what many states have done. However, obtaining the capacity for violence is not without its problems. If nothing else, it is expensive. But the **security dilemma** creates an even bigger challenge to a policy of unrestrained procurement of military capabilities. Military capability is seen by others as a threat even if no threat is ever stated. The more powerful a state becomes, the more other states will perceive it as a threat and begin to treat it accordingly. This behavior is sometimes not readily apparent, but it is, in fact, pervasive. When one country gains new capabilities, those around it consider adding to their own arsenals, or even attacking preemptively. In 1981, Israel attacked Iraq to destroy a facility that Israel feared would be used to produce nuclear weapons. One justification for the U.S. attack on Iraq in 2003 was to prevent it from gaining WMD. Iran's nuclear program, which itself might be seen as a response to perceived threat from others, has provoked speculation that a similar preemptive attack would be forthcoming. The decision to arm or not arm can be viewed as another version of the prisoner's dilemma discussed in Chapter 3.

security dilemma
The difficult choice faced by states in anarchy between arming, which risks provoking a response from others, and not arming, which risks remaining vulnerable.

Actors compete not only in the quantity of weapons they amass, but in the technological sophistication of those weapons and the ways they are used. New developments in technology and strategy create new challenges for international security. How is the nature of military power changing? How can states defend themselves against both old and new threats? In an attempt to answer these questions, this chapter analyzes how defense, deterrence, and coercive diplomacy are influenced today by modern military strategies and weaponry. In particular, this chapter examines the use of WMD, high- and low-tech weaponry, and terrorism and considers how effective policies can be pursued given the current level of understanding of these phenomena. Weapons of mass destruction shifted the focus from defense to deterrence, but low-tech weapons and terrorism are shifting the focus back toward defense.

Contemporary Competition for Military Advantage

The contemporary competition for military advantage is characterized by the military preponderance of the United States, the acquisition by a few states of high-tech weaponry that reduces the cost of war, and the proliferation of low-tech weapons that are used as deterrents. In addition, a recent increase in sensitivity to casualties plays a considerable role in the ability of many states to leverage their military strength to their advantage.

Military Preponderance

The most striking way in which the contemporary military situation differs from previous eras is the extraordinary disparity between the United States and other states in conventional weaponry. Not only in the quantity of weapons, but in their quality, a few states, first and foremost the United States, have advantages in conventional weaponry rarely seen in history. U.S. weaponry is the most advanced in the world, and the United States has more weaponry in almost every category than any other country (although several other countries have more soldiers). Included in that weaponry is the air and naval capacity to put troops on the ground and sustain them in almost any part of the world. Only a few states possess advanced weapons, and only the United States possesses the ability to deploy them around the world for prolonged periods. Not surprisingly, the United States spends vastly more money on the military than any other country (see Figure 8.1).

However, as conflicts in Afghanistan and Iraq (and in Vietnam before them) have shown, a preponderance of force does not guarantee the achievement of state goals. The overwhelming superiority of U.S. conventional forces has led many states and other actors to conclude that it is hopeless to compete with the United States in terms of conventional weapons. As a consequence, the incentive to build up nonconventional capabilities has increased; the spread of WMD, insurgency, and terrorism is a direct result of the fact that most other states and groups have no hope of competing with the United States in terms of conventional weapons. Therefore, these nonconventional strategies will likely become increasingly popular options.

precision-guided munitions

Weapons with guidance systems and maneuvering capability that allow them to strike individual targets with a high degree of accuracy. Also known as "smart bombs."

The Role of High-Tech Weapons

Recent decades have witnessed a technological revolution in conventional weaponry. Most widely known, because of their visibility in recent conflicts, are unmanned aircraft (drones) and **precision-guided munitions**, which include bombs and missiles with a variety of guidance systems providing a high degree of accuracy (many such systems can deliver weapons with 10 feet of a target). Even the cannons on tanks, with high-velocity projectiles and computerized aiming systems that take into account the movement of both the tank and its target, are becoming much more accurate. Militarily, the significance of such weapons is their ability to destroy a given target with a high degree of reliability. Politically, precision-guided munitions have been important not only for what they hit, but for what they generally

U.S. Air Force Predator Unmanned Aerial Vehicle (UAV) at Tallil Air Base in Iraq. How might the advent of UAVs change the strategies of military forces that possess them and those that do not?

Figure 8.1 Measured by how much different countries spend on their militaries, power in the world today is grossly imbalanced, probably more so than at any other time in history.

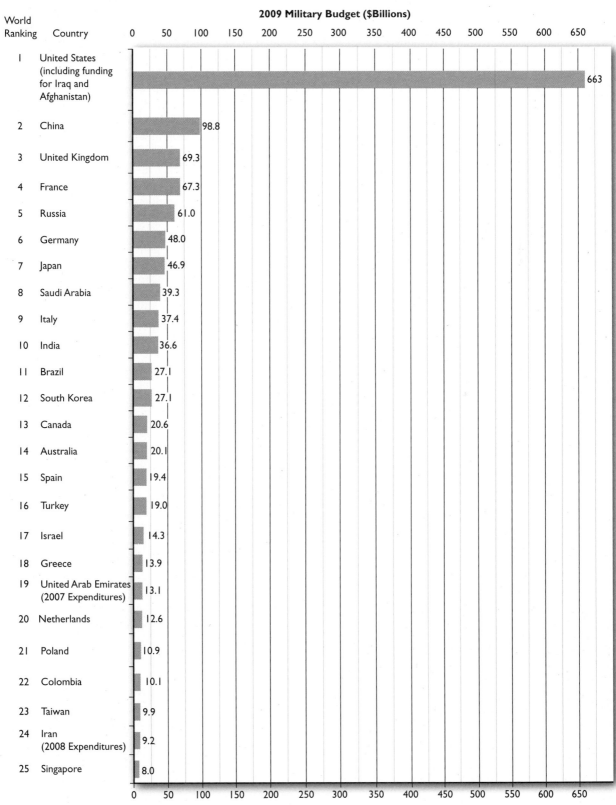

2009 Military Budget ($Billions)

World Ranking	Country	Budget
1	United States (including funding for Iraq and Afghanistan)	663
2	China	98.8
3	United Kingdom	69.3
4	France	67.3
5	Russia	61.0
6	Germany	48.0
7	Japan	46.9
8	Saudi Arabia	39.3
9	Italy	37.4
10	India	36.6
11	Brazil	27.1
12	South Korea	27.1
13	Canada	20.6
14	Australia	20.1
15	Spain	19.4
16	Turkey	19.0
17	Israel	14.3
18	Greece	13.9
19	United Arab Emirates (2007 Expenditures)	13.1
20	Netherlands	12.6
21	Poland	10.9
22	Colombia	10.1
23	Taiwan	9.9
24	Iran (2008 Expenditures)	9.2
25	Singapore	8.0

Source: Based on the Stockholm International Peace Research Institute (SIPRI) Military Expenditure Database 2009.

do not hit: unintended targets, including civilians. This potential has allowed military planners to contemplate "surgical" use of these weapons to destroy certain targets yet incur low "collateral damage," or civilian deaths. Presumably this reduction of collateral damage makes it easier to contemplate using these weapons for coercion. This is exactly what happened in Kosovo, where U.S. forces were able to strike at targets important to Yugoslavia's government and military while causing relatively few civilian casualties (although the Chinese embassy in Belgrade was accidentally bombed). Paradoxically, these might also increase expectations that civilian casualties will be avoided, thus increasing resentment when they occur. There has been considerable outrage, both internationally and in Afghanistan, about civilian casualties from U.S. air strikes, and this outrage has undoubtedly undermined the effort to win "hearts and minds." New weapons also hold out the hope that meaningful military results can be achieved with very low risk of casualties in the attacking force. The ability to minimize the risk to soldiers and to innocent bystanders makes war much more politically palatable. Whether this is a good thing is, of course, debatable.

The Proliferation of Low-Tech Weapons

Although high-technology weapons have changed the capabilities of the most powerful states in the system, lower-technology weapons have proliferated in vast numbers around the world. Low-tech weapons include everything from assault rifles and grenade launchers to antiaircraft missiles. The ultimate low-tech weapon in recent years, the "improvised explosive device" (IED), has played a prominent role in the conflicts in Iraq and Afghanistan. These weapons make use of widely available and inexpensive materials and production techniques to create huge tactical problems for their makers' adversaries. Intense competition in the global arms industry has increased supply and driven down the price of low-tech weapons.

Although none of these weapons kills immense numbers of people at once, the huge numbers of such weapons means that they can kill many thousands of people, just as nuclear weapons can. In by far the most lethal conflict of the 1990s, approximately 800,000 Rwandans were killed with little more than rifles, machetes, and improvised weapons. In Sudan, roughly two million people have been killed with low-tech weapons in a civil war that began in 1983. The insurgencies that have bedeviled the United States and its allies in Iraq and Afghanistan are armed almost exclusively with such weapons. The proliferation of low-tech weapons has made them readily available to various nonstate actors, such as terrorist groups, separatist movements, and criminal organizations. The result is that security threats no longer come only from states and are no longer aimed only at states.

Sensitivity to Casualties

A factor that has been increasing in salience since World War II has been the sensitivity to casualties in many countries. Most societies still have a high tolerance for casualties suffered to defend their homeland, but the willingness to have soldiers dying abroad has decreased considerably. Research on the United States finds evidence of this trend as far back as the Korean War (1950-1953), and by 1965,

Figure 8.2 Arms proliferation around the world is driven by the sale of a few large suppliers.

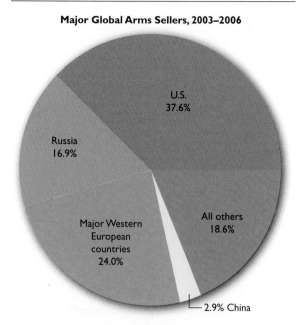

Major Global Arms Sellers, 2003–2006

U.S. 37.6%

Russia 16.9%

Major Western European countries 24.0%

All others 18.6%

2.9% China

Source: "Arms Transfer Agreements Worldwide," http://www.fas.org/asmp/resources/110th/RL34187.pdf. Used by permission.

Undersecretary of State George Ball produced data predicting that public support for the Vietnam War would decline as casualties increased.[4]

In many countries, public opinion will support military intervention abroad only as long as casualties remain very low. As casualties mount, policy makers and citizens alike will come to oppose the use of force. For military and political planners, such a loss of support can be devastating. As a result, which fights get fought and how they get fought are heavily influenced by perceptions of what will lead to a minimal number of battle deaths. The advent of precision-guided weapons has made reducing battle deaths easier for the few states that possess them, but it has also increased the public's expectations in many countries that war can be fought with few casualties. However, the prolif-

Sensitivity to casualties was so high that, after 2003, the U.S. government refused to allow the press to photograph the return of the bodies of soldiers killed in combat.

eration of low-tech weapons and the spread of insurgency techniques have made it possible in some cases to offset the effects of high-tech weaponry and raise casualty rates even for powerful armies.

Different levels of sensitivity to losing soldiers can be an important aspect of power relations between countries. Deterrence and coercion rely on being able to raise the costs of a given course of action higher than the benefits. Some countries may be comparatively weak in their ability to inflict such costs on others, but comparatively strong in their ability to withstand such pain. Other countries may be the opposite. This was the case in the Vietnam War: North Vietnam lost at least a million people in that war, while the United States lost roughly 58,000. Yet the United States found the cost intolerable before North Vietnam did. This does not mean that the Vietnamese do not value human life, but rather that they valued what they were fighting for much more than the United States did. Ultimately, Vietnam's advantage in sensitivity to casualties outweighed the U.S. advantage in the ability to inflict casualties.

To summarize, the post–Cold War era has been defined, in military terms, by a set of unprecedented developments whose interacting effects are not often appreciated. Oddly, the effects of different developments seem to cancel out each other in some ways. More than at any time in history, one country is vastly predominant in the means of waging war. However, this imbalance has prompted some states to seek WMD, while other actors have turned to terrorism and still others to insurgency. Similarly, high-tech weaponry has created the ability to wage war in a more precise and less destructive way. Yet this advantage has been eroded by a corresponding increase in sensitivity to casualties. And although the great fear has been and continues to be the employment of WMD, proliferation of low-tech weapons has made mass death possible without WMD.

Weapons of Mass Destruction (WMD)

In many respects, the advent of nuclear weapons changed the fundamental rationale governing the use of force. Among the nuclear-armed states and their allies, the emphasis

"World War III? Hmm. O.K., but , remember, nobody gets hurt."

shifted from defense to deterrence. Defeating an adversary on the battlefield made less sense when a nuclear war might kill a huge part of the populations of the warring states. Instead, the goal of policy was to create fear of *any* war on the grounds that it might lead to a nuclear response.

The shift from defense to deterrence began almost immediately with the annihilation of Hiroshima and Nagasaki. These attacks did not contribute meaningfully to defeating the Japanese military. Instead, the Japanese government, seeing the terrible destruction that could be wrought by these weapons, quickly surrendered; in other words, they were deterred from further resistance. The apparent lesson was that nuclear weapons could be used to coerce adversaries, especially if they did not have nuclear weapons of their own. It quickly became evident, however, that nuclear coercion would not be so simple.

Types of WMD

There are five categories of WMD:

- Nuclear weapons, which create an explosion from nuclear fission or fusion. They can be thousands of times as powerful as those dropped on Japan in World War II. In addition to blast effects, they create extreme heat, blinding light, radiation, and radioactive fallout.

- Chemical weapons, which include:
  - Choking agents: These primarily attack the lungs, causing them to fill with fluid. Important examples include the chlorine and phosgene gases that were used in World War I.
  - Blistering agents: These cause chemical burns on the skin, in the eyes, and in the lungs, as well as various secondary effects. A prominent example is mustard gas, which was used in World War I.
  - Nerve agents: These chemicals, often absorbed through skin, interfere with the transmission of nerve signals that control breathing. Some, such as VX and Sarin, are highly lethal. This is where much of the focus was in the Cold War and today.

- Biological weapons, which use various infectious agents, including anthrax botulism, pneumonic plague, and smallpox.[5]

radiological weapons

Weapons that use conventional explosives to distribute radioactive material, which has long-lasting poisonous effects. Also known as "dirty bombs."

electromagnetic pulse weapons

Weapons that use a powerful burst of energy to damage electronic circuits.

- **Radiological weapons**, which use various radioactive materials, some of which are also highly poisonous. Radiological weapons can be based on a broader range of materials than can nuclear weapons, and can use smaller amounts. They rely on a conventional explosion (creating a so-called "dirty bomb"). For these reasons, they are much easier to build than nuclear weapons.

- **Electromagnetic pulse weapons**, which use a powerful burst of energy to damage electronic circuits. The most powerful such weapons are driven by nuclear explosions, but nonnuclear variants also exist.

The attractiveness of nonnuclear WMD (and of chemical and biological weapons in particular) is that they are much easier and cheaper to produce than nuclear weapons.

Therefore, states or groups that do not have the resources or materials to acquire nuclear weapons can pursue other WMD. Chemical weapons are especially easy to produce. On the other hand, these weapons are not very easy to deploy with massive effect. Chemical and biological weapons have to be delivered in mass quantities to have mass effects. Moreover, distribution of these weapons is a challenging task. Chemical weapons were of limited use in World War I in part because shifts in winds sometimes brought them back on the forces that discharged them. Anthrax, although deadly, is very difficult to produce in a form that hangs in the air and is therefore likely to be inhaled.

Moreover, for any of these weapons to be useful as retaliatory deterrents (or as offensive weapons), the deterring country must be able to deliver the weapons to the homeland of the potential adversary. Therefore, the quest for WMD has been accompanied by the quest for long-range delivery systems (generally long-range missiles). Consequently, along with efforts to reduce the proliferation of WMD, states are also trying to reduce the proliferation of long-range missiles.

Even if chemical, biological, and radiological weapons do not automatically have massive destructive effect, they would likely have a massive *disruptive* effect, for example, by causing large population groups to avoid going outside, or to get preventive medicines, or simply to live in great fear. In the 2001 anthrax attacks in the United States, only a few people died, but much of Washington, DC, was disrupted. To capture this distinction, the U.S. Department of Homeland Security now refers to "weapons of mass destruction, disruption, and effect."

Nuclear Deterrence in the Cold War

The nuclear relationship that developed between the United States and the Soviet Union was driven by two puzzles that faced strategists on both sides. Despite the end of the Cold War, both these puzzles recur in different ways even today. First was the problem of **crisis stability**, discussed in the previous chapter. Both sides feared a surprise attack that would destroy their weapons before they could be launched. Therefore, even from a defensive perspective, there was an incentive to strike first—to "use 'em or lose 'em," as the saying goes.[6] As the number of weapons grew into the thousands, it became much less likely that one side could execute a first strike that wiped out all of the other side's weapons. Even after a massive attack, each side would retain a "second-strike" capability. This situation came to be known as "mutual assured destruction" (MAD). Stability stemmed from the assurance that there was little advantage in going first. However, in the post-Cold War world, in which countries are developing relatively small nuclear arsenals, the hope (and fear) of a successful first strike has re-emerged. This is a problem that today confronts India and Pakistan, Israel and Iran, and North Korea and the United States. Low numbers of nuclear weapons create high crisis instability.

The second puzzle was how to make nuclear weapons politically useful. Contrary to early expectations, nuclear coercion did not prove very easy, largely because the threat was not perceived as variable. A paradox of nuclear weapons is that even if their use might be irrational, the *threat* of using them might have substantial utility and might deter a potential aggressor. Because the potential aggressor cannot be certain that the response to an attack will be rational, that state cannot safely assume that a conventional attack would not lead to a nuclear response. One strategist of the Cold War era thus referred to "the threat that leaves something to chance."[7]

Proliferation

In the Cold War, the two states with the most nuclear (and chemical and biological) arsenals were also the two states with the most powerful conventional forces. Thus, the

crisis stability
The likelihood that a crisis, once it begins, will have dynamics that tend to lead toward war.

Table 8.3 Estimated Total Nuclear Warheads Worldwide, 2010[8]

Country	Warheads
Russia	12,000
United States	9600
France	300
China	240
United Kingdom	225
Israel	80
Pakistan	70–90
India	60–80

distribution of nuclear weapons paralleled the distribution of conventional forces. But Britain, France, and China also procured nuclear weapons. None of those countries could hope to defeat the United States or the Soviet Union in either conventional or nuclear combat. However, their nuclear weapons would allow any of those states to raise the costs of an attack unbearably high for any opponent. Just a few French nuclear weapons delivered on the Soviet Union, or Chinese nuclear weapons delivered on the United States would outweigh whatever benefit one of those states might have gained in initiating an attack.

Today, this logic is driving the proliferation of WMD. As the United States gets further ahead of other countries in terms of conventional weapons, deterrence through defense becomes increasingly impossible for weaker states. U.S.-led campaigns against Iraq (1991, 2003) and in the former Yugoslavia (1995, 1999) demonstrated that the United States could use high-tech weapons to soundly defeat an adversary at little cost in U.S. lives. Many states, such as North Korea and Iran facing the United States, Pakistan facing India, or Israel facing the Arab states, fear that they may not be able to defend themselves against a conventional attack. Instead of (or in addition to) increasing their defense capabilities, therefore, these states are focusing increasingly on retaliation, which is accomplished most effectively through WMD. At the same time, terrorist groups seeking to maximize the effects of their attacks are naturally interested in developing WMD.

WMD as a Deterrent

Do weapons of mass destruction really deter attack? Many have viewed nuclear deterrence as the essential source of peace during the Cold War, a peace that Winston Churchill called "the sturdy child of nuclear terror."[9] However, it is difficult to know when deterrence has worked. If a country did not attack, was it because it was successfully deterred or because it did not intend to attack in the first place? It seems that WMD are very successful. They apparently prevented the Soviets from attacking western Europe, Pakistan from assailing India, and the Arab states from striking Israel, among other cases. But it may be that none of these states ever *intended* to attack, or that the anticipated cost of conventional war has been a sufficient deterrent. Thus, the absence of war is not necessarily a sign that deterrence was working.[10] On the other hand, the fear that many states express over their adversaries gaining nuclear weapons indicates that they do have a powerful political effect. States fear Iraqi, Iranian, or North Korean nuclear weapons in part because they would make it much more costly to attack those states and therefore easier for those states to get away with behavior that others consider seek to prevent.

Table 8.4 Chemical and Biological Weapons Programs Worldwide, as of 2002[11]

Country	Chemical Weapons	Biological Weapons
China	Probable	Suspected
Cuba	Suspected	Probable research program
Egypt	Probable	Suspected
Ethiopia	Probable	
India	Discontinued	Research program
Iran	Known	Suspected
Iraq	Probable	Suspected
Israel	Probable	
Libya	Known	
Myanmar	Probable	
North Korea	Known	
Pakistan	Probable	Suspected
Russia	Known	
Syria	Known	
Taiwan	Probable	Suspected research program

WMD and Crisis Stability

A prominent realist theorist of international politics, Kenneth Waltz, has argued that proliferation of nuclear weapons will likely make the world more, rather than less, safe. This argument applies realist analysis in a way that challenges the conventional wisdom that nuclear proliferation is a threat to international security. Waltz's argument, simply put, is that by making it easier to deter an attack than to wage an attack successfully, nuclear weapons increase stability. "If countries with nuclear weapons go to war, they do so knowing that their suffering may be unlimited. Of course, it also may not be, but that is not the kind of uncertainty that encourages anyone to use force."[12]

Others dispute this view on several grounds.[13] First, the argument that nuclear weapons contribute to deterrence relies on the assumption that leaders are rational, a view that many analysts find questionable. Second, it assumes that civilian leaders, even if rational, have effective control over militaries. As weapons spread to less stable countries, some believe, it is more likely that weapons will be controlled by military organizations not fully in tune with their countries' national interest. There is also fear, especially concerning Pakistan, that a government might be toppled by radical groups with connections to terrorists or with extreme ideologies that might motivate use of nuclear weapons. There is also concern that some governments might be less able to protect nuclear weapons or

Estimated Radius of a Nuclear Weapons Blast in New York City. The concentric circles show various levels of blast damage.

materials from possible theft. This problem of "loose nukes" has led to ongoing concern about Russia, with its vast number of nuclear installations and high level of government corruption and organized crime.

Even if leaders are rational and in control, however, crisis stability will continue to depend on mutual confidence in a secure second-strike capability. This is especially problematic for new nuclear powers, which are likely to have small arsenals deployed in a limited geographic area and a single means of delivering the weapons. These states, and their weapons, may be tempting targets for a first strike, not only by another nuclear power, but also by a well-armed conventional power. A potential attacker might believe that it could completely eliminate a small arsenal with a first strike, and that doing so might be safer than enduring the chance that the arsenal will grow or become more securely defended. The state with the small arsenal of WMD faces the "use 'em or lose 'em" dilemma. The result, therefore, is that as WMD spread (as they almost certainly will), the temptation to wage preventive war and the challenges of maintaining crisis stability will increase in importance.

WMD and the Security Dilemma

In sum, the dynamics of the proliferation of WMD are not fundamentally different from those of conventional weapons. States that perceive a security threat can be expected to respond by increasing their own military capabilities. When it is easier to prevent an attack by threatening retaliation than by building the capacity to win on the battlefield, states can be expected to do this. Those states that build powerful military capabilities can anticipate that others will arm against them, with WMD if necessary. This is the classic security dilemma.

WMD more clearly separate the defensive and deterrent functions of weapons. WMD are particularly effective at strengthening deterrence by increasing the damage that can be inflicted on an attacker. The deterrent power of WMD explains why states make such costly efforts to gain them, and why few states that have them wish to give them up. States seeking to gain WMD capabilities are generally experiencing intense security dilemmas. In particular, those that face rivals with whom they cannot compete in terms of conventional weapons have a strong incentive to obtain WMD. And although the spread of WMD may induce some states to be more cautious in their policies, it also creates the potential for a high level of crisis instability. Moreover, in recent years, the problem of WMD proliferation has meant that states must prepare not only for the possibility that other states will acquire WMD, but also for the possibility that terrorists will gain access to these weapons.

Insurgency, Guerilla Warfare, and Counterinsurgency

insurgency
An effort to overthrow the political power in a territory through violence.

guerilla warfare
Warfare in which tactics of harassment and ambush are favored over direct battle.

In terms of the scale of destruction, insurgency and guerilla warfare seem quite different than deployment of WMD, but they share the same logic. Like deterrence, **insurgency** and **guerilla warfare** focus not on defeating the enemy on the field of battle, but on raising the costs of conflict so that they are higher than any possible benefit to the attacker.[14] In contrast to nuclear deterrence, however, insurgency may be more difficult to employ as a strategy in advance of an attack. Rather, it is used to deter the continuation of an invasion or to compel an invader to leave.

Weak actors use insurgent tactics to change the rules of the game to minimize their weakness and maximize that of their adversaries. As the gaps between powerful militaries and weaker ones have grown, and as more armed conflicts have involved nonstate actors incapable of conventional defense, insurgency has become a more widely used tactic.

Examples of insurgent warfare in recent decades include wars in Vietnam, Iraq, and Afghanistan (where the Soviet Union faced this strategy in the 1980s and the United States has confronted it since 2001). Earlier cases that have been widely studied include the case of Malaya, where local insurgents sought independence from Britain; China, where communists led by Mao Zedong opposed Chinese nationalist forces and the Japanese military from the 1920s through the 1940s; and Saudi Arabia, where Britain instigated a local insurgency against Ottoman rule during World War I.

A general set of lessons has emerged about the successes of insurgency and counterinsurgency. Insurgency is chosen by forces too weak to defeat an opponent's army in open battle. Rather than wage open warfare, insurgents seek to strike quickly through ambushes and then disengage before a larger battle emerges. Similarly, they seek to avoid standard "lines of battle," instead, crossing into territory ostensibly held by the enemy to attack areas that should be safe. Thus, Mao Zedong stated that, "the guerrilla must move amongst the people as a fish swims in the sea." When insurgents try to hold a territory, the opposing army can bring its superior forces to that area and force the insurgents either to fight a battle they will likely lose or to abandon the territory. Thus, insurgency is less well suited to holding territory than to raising the enemy's costs. The insurgent force does not try to match the strength of an established power, but rather seeks to take advantage of its own weaknesses, such as controlling no territory, and having no large force concentrations that can be attacked. For this reason, insurgency it is often labeled **asymmetric conflict**.

asymmetric conflict
A conflict between actors with very different strengths, vulnerabilities, and tactics.

Most analysts agree that winning the "hearts and minds" of noncombatants is crucial to the outcome of an insurgency/counterinsurgency conflict.[15] Only when the general public supports the insurgents can they move freely behind enemy lines and prepare attacks without being discovered. When the public opposes the insurgency, counterinsurgent forces can more easily locate insurgent forces. Moreover, counterinsurgent sympathizers can provide intelligence that helps counterinsurgent troops avoid traps and ambushes. For example, a key goal of U.S. forces in Iraq has been to persuade local Iraqis to provide warning of IEDs. If the counterinsurgent forces cannot win the support of the population, they will likely be forced either to give up or to wage war on the population itself, as the United States did in attacking villages that supported insurgents in Vietnam, or as Russia did in depopulating areas of Chechnya in the 1990s.

The challenge for both insurgents and counterinsurgents is determining how to carry out day-to-day operations in a way that does not undermine support from the population. As an insurgent leader, Mao Zedong instituted a set of rules (such as not stealing from people, being courteous to them, and returning borrowed items) intended to ensure that his forces did not alienate the population among whom they operated. For the United States in Vietnam, Iraq, and Afghanistan, short-term efforts to eliminate insurgents (by arresting many people and taking them away for interrogation, for example) had the long-term effect of angering local populations and increasing support for the insurgents. The fact that foreign troops fighting an insurgency often do not speak the language or understand the culture in which they are operating puts them at a huge disadvantage relative to locally based insurgents. Many analysts looking back on the Vietnam War have pointed out that U.S. forces rarely, if ever, lost a battle. But in fighting an insurgency, winning battles is insufficient, and sometimes irrelevant, to strategic victory because insurgents can raise costs intolerably high without ever winning head-to-head battles.

The U.S. and NATO-led counterinsurgency in Afghanistan are good illustrations of the challenges of insurgency. The United States and its allies possess immense capability to find and destroy insurgent forces, but that is not enough. General Stanley McChrystal, commander of NATO forces in Afghanistan in 2009-2010, stated: "The Russians killed 1 million Afghans, and that didn't work."[16] He recognized that every civilian casualty caused several more people to join the insurgency. Therefore, he implemented very strict rules of engagement to prevent civilian casualties and other offenses that set back the battle for "hearts and minds." Afghan insurgents did not face the same constraints. They had an enemy that was easily located and attacked, did not face the same criticism for killing noncombatants, and were not limited by restrictive rules of engagement. U.S. soldiers feared that the restrictions placed on them prevented them from winning battles with Taliban forces, but using too much force might win the battle while losing the war. "Right now we're losing the tactical-level fight in the chase for a strategic victory," one officer pointed out. "How long can that be sustained?"[17] When General McChrystal was fired in June 2010, U.S. and NATO leaders were still struggling to find a strategy that would succeed both tactically and strategically.

The Power and Purpose of Terrorism

The advent of cross-border terrorism by well-funded and well-organized nonstate organizations causes scholars and policy makers alike to rethink the fundamental questions of power and purpose. The ability of these small nonstate actors to drive the global security agenda has called into question traditional conceptions of international power, which have been based on size of territory, economic resources, and arsenals.

Because these actors are pursuing goals that have little to do with state interests, a great deal of debate has focused on understanding the purposes of terrorists. Historically, terrorists have had a variety of objectives. Some appear to have far-reaching messianic goals, such as bringing down the capitalist economic system or waging a holy war. Others appear to have very limited local goals, such as driving an unwelcome political power out of a particular territory.

Terrorism has become a central focus in popular discussions of international politics today. Terrorist attacks in the United States in September 2001, in Madrid in 2004, in London in 2005, in Bombay in 2008, and repeatedly in Moscow, have brought to major cities a level of violence and fear from which they had been immune in recent decades. As a result, in many societies, fear of attack by terrorists has replaced fear of attack by other

Bombed Train Cars, Madrid, March 11, 2004. A coordinated set of bombings on Madrid's trains killed 191 and injured over 1700 people.

AP Photo/Paul White, File

states as the primary external security threat. Although terrorism is not new, the role it is now playing in the politics of international security is new. Consequently, scholars and policy makers are racing to assess the impact of terrorism on international politics and to gauge how radical a change it actually represents. A central point emerges: terrorism is difficult for states to deal with because the two traditional approaches to security—defense and deterrence—are less effective against terrorists than against states.

Defining Terrorism

Because the words "terrorism" and "terrorist" are so laden with emotion (they have become nearly synonymous with the word "evil"), it is difficult to use the words analytically in a way that makes it clear what is *terrorism* and what is not and who is a *terrorist* and who is not. **Terrorism** is the use of violence, or the threat of it, by nongovernmental actors in an effort to change government policies by creating fear of further violence. This definition—and it is not the only one possible—stresses three key points.

First, terrorism is a method, not a goal. Although some may perceive terrorism as senseless violence, most experts agree that terrorism is almost always a means to achieve particular goals. Walter Laqueur, a leading scholar on terrorism, emphasizes that terrorism "is not an ideology or a political doctrine, but rather a method—the substate application of violence or the threat of violence to sow panic and bring about political change."[18] Similarly, Robert Jervis defines terrorism as "the use of violence for political or social purposes that is not publicly authorized by leaders of recognized political units, including acts that are sponsored and supported by states, but not publicly avowed."[19] In contrast, violence that is committed only for monetary gain or for the sake of killing is generally not defined as terrorism. Hence, there is a difference between terrorism and organized crime or psychopathic violence.

As a tactic or method, terrorism works quite similarly to any kind of coercive diplomacy or deterrence. The goal is to raise the costs of certain policies so that states will choose other policies. For example, the Irish Republican Army (IRA) bombed innocent civilians in British cities to raise the cost of British control of Northern Ireland. Al-Qaeda commits its attacks in order to raise the cost of various policies it opposes, including U.S. support for Israel and the stationing of U.S. troops in Saudi Arabia.

For as much fear as it creates, terrorism is a weapon of the weak. Like insurgency, terrorism is adopted by actors who do not stand a chance of competing with a government in conventional terms. Terrorism is adopted by a group only when its cause is not popular enough to prevail through normal political channels. Terrorism presents a weapon with which the weak can "sting" the powerful, but it is important to recognize what terrorism cannot do: It cannot take control of a territory or govern a society. Thus, terrorist groups that accomplish the goal of rising to power have to adopt different strategies in order to govern.

Second, violence committed by a government is generally not labeled "terrorism."[20] By this definition, a government that bombs another country's population, even with WMD, is not terrorist, regardless of how evil it might be. During the Cold War, a prominent nuclear strategist described the mutual threats against the populations of the United States and the Soviet Union as a "delicate balance of terror." Yet few people would have called the United States or the Soviet Union terrorists for employing this threat. Similarly, today, when a state's military force uses bombs to kill people or to coerce a government, its actions are not generally called terrorism. When a nonstate group uses bombs to kill people, this behavior *is* called terrorism. This difference makes clear that in deciding what terrorism is, it is important not only what is done and to whom, but *by whom* it is done. Some see this distinction as hypocritical, but there may in fact be a good reason to distinguish violence used by states from violence used by

terrorism
Use or threat of violence by nongovernmental actors to change government policies by creating fear of further violence.

A Brief History of Terrorism

The term *terrorism* is at least 200 years old, and the phenomenon is much older than that. The words *zealot*, *thug*, and *assassin* all come from the names of premodern terrorist groups. During the Roman Empire, a group of Jewish people known as the Zealots fought an armed struggle against Roman rule in Israel. A subset of that group, the *Sicarii* ("Daggers"), carried out a campaign of murder against other Jews who did not support the Zealot movement.[1] From the eleventh through the thirteenth centuries in Persia, a group known as the Assassins developed a secret force of trained killers who murdered their victims, usually prominent political figures, in public.[2] This practice of killing in public to maximize publicity, and of accepting certain death, has certain echoes in today's terrorism.

In nineteenth-century Russia, terrorism took on what might be called its first "modern" incarnation, as an act of the weak against the state. A group known as *Narodnaya Volya* ("The People's Will") conducted a series of attacks on leading Tsarist government officials, including the assassination of Tsar Alexander II in 1881. This movement is relevant not only because of its political influence, but because it developed the "cell" organization—in which no member knows the identity of more than a few others—that is still used by terrorist organizations today. The successors to *Narodnaya Volya* popularized the use of terrorist tactics among politically extreme groups in the late nineteenth and early twentieth centuries. These groups tended to target major political figures. In the United States, anarchist Leon Czolgosz assassinated President McKinley in 1901. In 1914, a Serbian nationalist group assassinated the heir to the Austro-Hungarian throne, Archduke Franz Ferdinand, touching off World War I.[3]

In recent decades the conflict between Palestinians and Israel has been a source of much terrorist activity. In 1972, Palestinian terrorists invaded the athletes' village at the Olympic games in Munich, Germany, killing several Israeli athletes and taking several others hostage. As a result of satellite television transmissions, which were new at the time, events in Munich could be seen around the world as they happened. Since the goal of terrorism is to make an impression on as many people as possible, the advent of live television coverage has dramatically increased terrorism's power. This process reached its zenith in 2001, when images of the World Trade Center burning and then collapsing, were shown repeatedly on television around the world.

PHOTO © ISTOCKPHOTO

nonstate groups (just as both of these are distinguished from the violence committed by ordinary criminal gangs).

Finally, the target of terrorism is usually not the immediate victims (those killed or maimed), or even their close relatives, but rather the broader society and the government.[21] Most of the time, terrorists are not concerned with exactly whom they kill. Rather, the dramatic way in which people are killed conveys the desired message. Especially when targeting democracies, the "mechanism of influence" seems to be to kill innocent people, either to get the broader population to pressure governments for change in policy or to undermine government credibility. There are exceptions. In some cases, terrorists seek to directly attack state leaders or military forces. By killing innocents, or particularly visible individuals, terrorists seek to achieve political effects that are disproportionate to the amount of violence used.

The "terror" of terrorism comes only in part from the number of people killed, which is often quite small. In 1996, for example, a person was 33 times more likely to die from

A second set of conflicts that erupted in a great deal of terrorism was between governments and leftist or anarchist movements in the 1970s and 1980s. These echoed the Russian leftist terrorist movements of the nineteenth and early twentieth centuries. Germany, Italy, Greece, and Japan all had homegrown movements that carried out substantial violence in protest against their own governments' policies. These groups were largely crushed in the 1980s, through infiltration by law enforcement and because they never had many members to begin with. Similar movements in the United States, including the Weather Underground and the Symbionese Liberation Army, quickly faded on their own.

A third set of terrorist campaigns has occurred during conflicts over national self-determination. The IRA sought to end British control over Northern Ireland and set off bombs around Britain for several years before agreeing to a truce in 1998. In Spain, the Basque separatist group ETA has engaged in a campaign of bombings and intimidation in an effort to gain an independent Basque territory. Similarly, in Turkey, the Kurdish Workers' Party (PKK), a group fighting for Kurdish independence, was responsible for a series of bombings for many years before the arrest of its leader led to a decrease in attacks. In Sri Lanka, the "Tamil Tigers," fighting for an independent homeland for the Tamil ethnic group, pioneered the use of suicide bombers in their struggle with the Sri Lankan government.

Critical Thinking Questions

1. Throughout history terrorism has been used by a wide range of groups and has been invoked to support a wide array of causes. Is there anything fundamentally new about the terrorism in recent years?

2. Does examining the long history of terrorism offer significant insight into its causes, or would it be better to focus on recent years?

3. Are there useful lessons to learn from terrorist movements in history that were either defeated or simply faded away?

[1] David C. Rapaport, "Messianic Sanctions for Terror," *Comparative Politics*, Vol. 20, No. 2 (January 1988): 195.

[2] Rapaport, "Messianic Sanctions for Terror," p. 195.

[3] Anna Geifman, *Thou Shalt Kill: Revolutionary Terrorism in Russia, 1894–1917* (Princeton, NJ: Princeton University Press, 1993).

meningitis than from terrorism, 822 times more likely to die by murder, 1200 times more likely to die by suicide, and 1833 times more likely to die in a car accident.[22] Yet none of these inspire the fear that results from terrorism. Rather, the terror and the political effect are a result of the *way* people are killed, which is violent, sudden, public, and seemingly random.

STATES, NONSTATE ACTORS, AND TERRORISM

As the preceding discussion shows, the concept of terrorism is based on the belief that certain acts are acceptable if undertaken by states, but unacceptable if undertaken by others. This raises the question of who is regarded as a "legitimate" actor in international politics, a question of the sort pursued by the constructivist approaches. To put this idea in different language, terrorists are *private* actors who use violence for *public* goals. Thus, terrorism can be contrasted with state violence, which is public violence for public goals, and common crime, which is private violence for private goals.[23]

Since the Treaty of Westphalia, a norm shared by states internationally has been that the use of armed force is reserved for sovereign states. That norm is enforced internally by states on their own citizens, but it has also generally been observed internationally. Most definitions of "the state," therefore, focus on its monopoly over the legitimate use of force. Although other actors (bank robbers, street gangs, or terrorists) might use force, only states can use force *legitimately,* in the generally accepted view. This explains why threats of violence against civilians by nonstate actors are seen as less legitimate, and having less moral standing, than those by states. Some see this conception of terrorism as hypocritical, but these distinctions are widely accepted.

TERRORISM AS ASYMMETRIC CONFLICT

Terrorism, like insurgency, is a form *asymmetric conflict,* a term that emphasizes that terrorism involves a conflict between different kinds of actors with very different strengths, vulnerabilities, and tactics. This view of terrorism contrasts starkly with the traditional conception of war, in which combat takes place between similar actors (states).

It is essential in any analysis to acknowledge two differences between states and terrorist groups.

- States control territories and populations, among other things. Therefore, they can potentially be deterred. Terrorists, because they do not control territory and are not responsible for populations, have nothing of value against which to make deterrent threats.

- Terrorists can choose when and where to strike states, whereas states often cannot locate and engage terrorists. If states cannot locate terrorists, then conflict takes place on terms determined by the terrorists.

The first point shows why states have a difficult time deterring terrorists. The second explains why states have a difficult time defending against them. Neither of the two strategies on which states rely to prevent attacks from other states works effectively against terrorists. For this reason, many advocate addressing terrorism not with acts of war, but through the implementation of law enforcement.

Causes of Terrorism

In recent years, combating terrorism has become one of the most important policy challenges for many governments. However, the task of designing effective counterterrorism policy is hampered by our limited understanding of the causes of terrorism.

Why does terrorism emerge in some cases but not in others? Why do some individuals become terrorists while others, in seemingly similar circumstances, do not? There is a wide variety of theoretical approaches to explain terrorism. As in the literature on the sources of war, that on terrorism varies from system-level approaches (such as the argument that terrorism is an inherent result of globalization) to individual approaches, which seek to identify the specific psychological characteristics of the individuals who carry out attacks. In between are societal-level explanations, which ask why some societies seem willing to give terrorists the cover they need to avoid capture. As in the literature on war, some approaches to terrorism view it as inherently irrational and try to explain the pathologies behind it. Other approaches view terrorism as rational and seek to explore the goals being pursued by terrorists and the choice of terrorism rather than some other method. Power and purpose remain at the center of the discussion. So far, no explanation of terrorism has gained wide support among scholars. This subject will likely be one of the main lines of research in international relations in coming years.

RATIONAL CHOICE EXPLANATIONS

From the rational choice perspective, the problem of explaining terrorism becomes an attempt to answer the question "To what set of circumstances is terrorism a rational response?" The key, from this perspective, is to understand the options open to very weak actors in combat with powerful governments. For a group that considers itself to be at war with a vastly more powerful adversary, engaging in conventional war would guarantee defeat.

This point is perhaps more easily understood if we return to our distinction between defense and retaliation. When an actor believes that it cannot muster enough force to defeat an adversary on the battlefield, it can instead adopt a policy of retaliation: raising the cost of a particular policy in an effort to force the adversary to adopt a different policy. At one end of the military spectrum, this results in efforts by states to gain WMD. At the opposite end, this results in a shift to "low-intensity" tactics, such as insurgency and terrorism.

For the IRA, for example, terrorism against the British government was intended to raise the cost of British control of Northern Ireland. Palestinian attacks against Israelis are similarly seen as aimed at raising the cost of Israeli occupation of territory claimed by Palestinians. Attacks by Chechens against civilians in Russia are aimed at forcing the Russian government to grant the territory of Chechnya autonomy or independence.

To the extent that terrorism is a tool, how can we explain groups such as Al-Qaeda, which are not focused on territorial goals? Al-Qaeda, at least originally, had a clearly announced goal of its terrorism: to force the United States to remove forces stationed in Saudi Arabia. More broadly, members of the group share a sense of grievance against American policies in the Middle East, including U.S. support for Israel against Palestinians and support for authoritarian allies such as Saudi Arabia and Egypt. Al-Qaeda has also sought to deter other states from collaborating with the United States in Iraq and Afghanistan.

The rhetoric of some groups, however, is more difficult to reconcile with a rationalist explanation of terror. Some Islamic groups expound the goal of establishing a region-wide Islamic government to recreate the Caliphate of the medieval era. It is difficult to see how terrorism is a means to such a goal. Thus, although terrorism can raise the costs of certain policies, it does not appear useful in achieving positive goods such as control of a territory or of a government.

Terrorism can also be a means of communicating outrage to the general public as well as to governments. Many interpret much of the anticapitalist terrorism in western Europe during the 1970s as an attempt to call attention to the injustice of the prevailing system. The Oklahoma City bombing of 1995 can also be seen as a protest against the U.S. government's treatment of far-right groups. In both cases, there is no sign that the terrorists had any notion that their actions would lead to a change in the system of government or even a change in policy. Rather, the actions were meant to attract global attention to the terrorists' cause.

POVERTY

Some see poverty as an underlying cause of terrorism. In this view, the poverty that is endemic in so much of the world creates a sense of desperation and alienation that makes people willing to tolerate or even to participate in terrorism against the wealthy and powerful societies that control the world economy. A cursory look at the areas from which terrorism is emerging today appears to support the plausibility of this approach. The Palestinians who commit suicide bombings against Israelis live in grinding poverty. The young Afghanis who support the Taliban and Al-Qaeda live in one of the poorest countries in the world. The influential author and *New York Times* columnist Thomas Friedman contends that although poverty does not directly cause terrorism, "poverty is great for the terrorism business because poverty creates humiliation and stifled aspirations and forces many people to leave their traditional farms to join the alienated urban poor in the cities—all conditions that spawn terrorists."[24]

Obviously, not all poor people are terrorists. Very few are. Therefore, if there is a connection between poverty and terrorism, it must be an indirect one. Many have argued that poverty in some parts of the world contributes to terrorism by creating a large number of young men with no hope of advancement through education or good jobs. Such hopelessness might have several effects that contribute to terrorism. First, it might make people more susceptible to radical political or religious doctrines. Those who see no hope on earth might be more likely to subscribe to extreme religious beliefs that promise rewards in the afterlife. Second, it might make individuals more hostile toward the existing political and economic system and therefore more interested in overthrowing it. To the extent that poverty occurs in societies with corrupt and authoritarian governments, that tendency may be strengthened. Third, hopelessness gives individuals less to lose. People with good prospects of advancing economically are less likely to want to sacrifice that to terrorism.

These arguments make intuitive sense, but there is little evidence showing a link between poverty and terrorism.[25] Although many terrorists come from poor backgrounds, many others come from relatively wealthy backgrounds. Most notable in this regard is Osama bin Laden, who came from a family of multimillionaires to lead the Al-Qaeda organization. Many of his initial supporters also came from well-to-do Saudi families. The individuals who actually conducted the attacks of September 11, 2001, all had university educations, and by entering the United States, they had gained access to an economy in which any of them could have thrived.

Similarly, the anticapitalist terrorists who plagued Europe in the 1970s and 1980s generally came from upper-middle class backgrounds and were reacting, to some extent, against that background. In the United States, the few homegrown terrorist movements (such as the Weather Underground and the Symbionese Liberation Army of the early 1970s) sprang from the educated and wealthy, not the masses of urban poor. More broadly, there is relatively little organized terrorism in many of the poorest countries of the world. If poverty leads directly to terrorism, terrorism should predominate in sub-Saharan Africa, where it is largely absent. In sum, there seems to be little identifiable relationship between poverty and terrorism.

RELIGION

The obvious religious agenda of much recent terrorism has led some to argue that religious extremism is itself the cause of terrorism.[26] Some argue that any religion, if it is adhered to strongly enough, can produce the kinds of beliefs that seem to justify terrorism. Religion may contribute to extremism by fostering the belief that God's will justifies whatever measures are taken to achieve it. This notion justified the torture to which Catholics and Protestants subjected each other throughout history, and it appears in the rhetoric of some Muslim terrorist groups today. The notion that God's will provides an absolute commandment to action helps undermine any tendency toward compromise that otherwise might emerge in a situation. These arguments are quite controversial and are difficult to discuss because they engage powerful emotions.

Islam And Terrorism　　Particularly widespread in the world today is the contention that followers of Islam are especially prone toward religious violence and terrorism because of various concepts in the Qu'ran (such as jihad, or holy war), which can be used to justify such violence. Because many Islamic terrorist groups assert that the Qu'ran commands them to undertake holy war, it is easy to reach the conclusion that the Qu'ran indeed does so. Scholars and students should be careful, however, about reaching such a conclusion for several reasons.

First, although some of the most violent terrorists have claimed Qu'ranic sanction for their actions, many more Muslim scholars and practitioners recognize no such commandment. In fact, many scholars point to sections of the Qu'ran that offer clear statements against such violence. Fundamentalist Islam "represents only a small niche in the spectrum of Islamic views of political theology. Its beliefs and its actions fly in the face of doctrines of warfare that run widely and deeply in the Islamic tradition: a prohibition of the direct intentional killing of innocents; the requirement of justly constituted authority; a restrictive understanding of who is an aggressor that would thoroughly reject Osama bin Laden's assessment of the United States."[27]

Second, the tendency for religious extremists to claim divine or scriptural support for their actions is not unique to Islam. Hindu hardliners in India and Jewish extremists in Israel make similar claims, as did Christian Crusaders for centuries. These extremists may be no more representative of anything inherent in their faiths than Islamic fundamentalists are of theirs. Until recently, the conflict between Catholics and Protestants in Northern Ireland, which constituted terrorism by Christians against Christians for essentially religious reasons, was by far the greatest terrorist threat to the United Kingdom. Speaking in New York in 2002, Malaysian Prime Minister Mahatir Mohamad complained that "only Muslim terrorists are linked to their religion . . . . When Muslims in Bosnia-Herzegovina were being slaughtered by the Serbs, there was no mention of Christian Orthodox terrorists. These Christian Orthodox terrorists killed far more people than were killed on September 11. The world did not mobilise to fight Christian Orthodox terrorists even when they terrorised the Kosovars."[28]

Similarly, there is no clear connection between religion or religious intensity and suicide attacks. Suicide bombing was developed as a technique by the Tamil Tigers in Sri Lanka, whose members were neither Muslim nor highly religious. Tamils in general are Hindu, but the Tamil Tigers were a communist group and hence tended toward atheism, giving them no hope of religious salvation for their acts.

Third, the religious sources of terrorism warrant skepticism for the same reason that simple explanations based on poverty do: Much terrorism throughout history has not been religiously motivated. Only in the past two decades does religion appear to have become the major motivation for terrorism. Prior to that time, nationalism and ideology (anarchism, socialism, and the like) were the most common motivators of terrorism. Even today, a good deal of terrorist activity is not wrapped up in religious conflict, as shown by the Basque terrorist group ETA (Euskadi Ta Askatasuna, or "Homeland and Freedom") and the Kurdish PKK (Kurdish Workers' Party), both of which share the religions of those whom they attack.

Just as it is an oversimplification to equate poverty with terrorism because terrorism seems to occur in poor countries, it is an oversimplification to equate terrorism with Islam, simply because much terrorism in recent years has emanated from Islamic societies. There is no doubt that religion and poverty can be powerful sources of grievance, as can the desire for national self-determination or the desire to change a form of government. But although all of these factors can be motivations for terrorism, all are dealt with by most people most of the time without recourse to terrorism. So none of them, by itself, provides a sufficient explanation for terrorism.

The Culture Connection

What Impact Is Terrorism Having on Popular Culture?

As the focus of global politics—and of the public—shifts to the "global war on terror," what impact is terrorism having on popular culture? Conversely, how is popular culture influencing perceptions of and policies on terrorism?

In the realm of film, Hollywood had perfected the evil genius well before Osama bin Laden came along. A great many films pitted international terrorists against a hero who saved the day. Examples include the *Die Hard* series as well as several James Bond movies, but there are many, many more.

The film industry responded initially to the 2001 attacks by moving away from the subject of terrorism, rather than toward it. Several movies were scrapped, modified, or delayed because they dealt in one way or another with the World Trade Center or New York. In one notable case, producers deleted a scene from a trailer for *Spiderman*, which showed Spiderman catching a villain's helicopter in a web strung between the Twin Towers. A film featuring Jackie Chan as a window washer at the World Trade Center who combats a terrorist attack was scrapped altogether.[1]

More broadly, it appears that there was a deliberate content shift in Hollywood's movie offerings after September 11. Fantasies and comedies became the order of the day, and movies that treated more serious issues appeared to be much less popular. Over time, however, popular entertainment began to address the subject directly. Michael Moore's film *Fahrenheit 911* questioned much about the U.S. government's policies toward terrorism and the Iraq war. And in 2006, the film *United 93* sought to realistically portray the events on one of the planes hijacked on September 11, 2001, and perhaps ended whatever taboo there may have been on terrorism as a theme in popular entertainment. Films such as *Body of Lies* (2008) dealt directly with intelligence efforts aimed at combating terrorism.

PHOTO © ISTOCKPHOTO

THE INDIVIDUAL LEVEL

What makes a person a terrorist? There appears to be a range of motives for terrorism and a range of historical and economic conditions that give rise to terrorism. The best conclusion, then, is that terrorism results when powerfully felt agendas cannot be advanced through other means. That is only a partial explanation, however, because for the vast majority of individuals, such grievances do *not* lead to a decision to murder innocent civilians. Why, given a situation in which their agendas cannot be met through other political channels, do some people continue to work nonviolently, whereas others give up, and yet others resort to terrorism?

From this perspective, the question shifts from people's grievances, which may be shared by many, to the decision to adopt violence, which occurs only among a tiny subset of the aggrieved. A great deal of research is currently being conducted on the psychological sources of terrorism. Here the question is not "Why is there terrorism?" but "Why are there terrorists?" or rather "Who becomes a terrorist?"

Research such as this may have important implications for combating terrorism. Just as domestic law enforcement officials attempt to develop "profiles" of serial killers, an ability to "profile" potential terrorists could be very useful in combating terrorism. Thus far, there have been few conclusive findings on the subject. But just as the adoption of psychological

In the United States, the television show *24* portrayed intelligence agent Jack Bauer combating terrorism in real time. Running from 2002 until 2010, the show took advantage of the preoccupation of the time. Over time, however, the plotlines and events became increasingly absurd, including scuba divers under the White House seeking to assassinate the president.

Presumably, this was all harmless entertainment, and yet there was some evidence that Bauer's fictional exploits were actually shaping debates on antiterrorism policy. In a 2007 presidential debate, candidate Representative Tom Tancredo, asked about interrogation methods, stated, "I'm looking for Jack Bauer at that time, let me tell you." One critic of the program pointed out that the Bauer character never tortured the wrong person or elicited false information through torture, and wondered if this helped explain why polls showed many Americans believing that torture was often justifiable.[2]

Do Americans get their attitudes about terrorism and torture from television shows? There is no evidence of that. It is equally likely that the show's popularity, like that of much popular entertainment, stemmed from its suspense and from its comforting simplicity about difficult moral issues about torture.

Critical Thinking Questions

1. Has the content of films and television or their attitude toward terrorism shifted since 2001? What about the treatment of law enforcement?
2. Have film and television shows played a noticeable role in influencing attitudes? Would your answer change if you included television news programming in your consideration?
3. How could you empirically test your answers to these questions? What would a good study look like?

---

[1] "Judging the Mood of a Nation," *PBS NewsHour Extra*, October 24, 2001, at http://www.pbs.org/newshour/extra/features/july-dec01/culture.html
[2] "Agent Improbable," *The Economist*, May 29, 2010, at http://www.economist.com/node/16219301?story_id=16219301

---

models brought a great deal to the understanding of foreign policy making, it promises to bring a great deal to our understanding of terrorism.

"PROFILING" TERRORISTS

Sociological studies have indicated that terrorists tend to be young (in their twenties), male (over 80 percent), college-educated, and from upper-class or middle-class backgrounds.[29] However, there are important exceptions to these findings. In Northern Ireland, terrorists on both the Catholic and the Protestant sides were overwhelmingly from working-class backgrounds. The same is true for the PKK in Turkey.

More recently, research has focused on identifying a profile for suicide bombers. Because the identities of these

© Nasser Ishtayeh/HO/Associated Press

Palestinian suicide bomber Dareen Abu Aisheh blew herself up near an Israeli checkpoint in 2002. What makes a few individuals willing to conduct suicide bombings, while many others with the same grievances choose other tactics, or simply give up?

The Geography Connection

Combating Terrorism Through Social Network Analysis

This "map" shows the links among the 9/11 conspirators, as generated through a technique known as "social network analysis." The idea is to gather data on interactions among members of a group of people in an effort to understand the nature of a network. Important data might include phone calls, e-mail messages, or electronic transfers of funds. Even if the messages are encrypted, the amount of traffic can establish a pattern. The pattern of communications might indicate who the key actors in a network are or whether the structure of the network resembles that of a terrorist group.

Critical Thinking Questions

1. What pattern does this diagram show that might have helped warn governments about the 9/11 conspirators?
2. How might information such as this be used to render a group less effective?

Social Networks Analysis Map

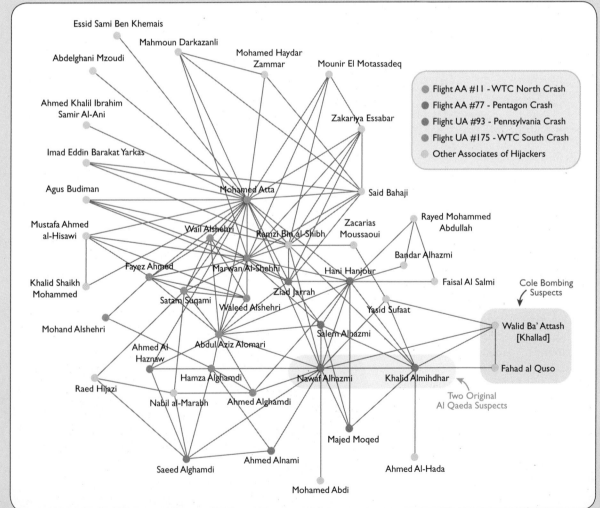

PHOTO © ISTOCKPHOTO

individuals are usually discovered after the attacks, it may be possible to research their backgrounds and to draw some conclusions about what they may have in common. The hope is that building such a profile may enable law enforcement agencies to more effectively prevent suicide attacks. However, findings so far are insufficient to yield straightforward lessons. One of the most thorough reviews of research on profiling terrorists concludes, "People who have joined terrorist groups have come from a wide range of cultures, nationalities, and ideological causes, all strata of society, and diverse professions. Their personalities and characteristics are as diverse as those of people in the general population. There seems to be general agreement among psychologists that there is no particular psychological attribute that can be used to describe the terrorist or any 'personality' that is distinctive of terrorists."[30]

One study found that the poverty rate among suicide bombers in Palestine was lower than the rate in the overall Palestinian population (13 percent versus 32 percent), and their education level was higher. Although suicide bombers are obviously willing to take their own lives, psychologists have found evidence that they do not exhibit the standard risk factors for suicide, such as mood disorders or other mental illness.[31]

The most famous group of suicide bombers, those who carried out the attacks of September 11, 2001, seemed not to fit any identifiable "profile" of a terrorist or suicide bomber. These men were older, well-off financially, well educated, and not obviously loners. Some of them had little difficulty integrating into American life. They traveled around Europe and the world meeting each other and a wider network of operatives and patiently prepared for years, learning to fly commercial airliners and devising a plot of astonishing ingenuity.

GROUP DYNAMICS AND TERRORISM

The inability—so far—to identify a psychological profile of a suicide bomber has led some researchers to argue that the key factor is not the individual, but the organization. In this view, some organizations are both willing to promote the tactic and able to motivate individuals with different psychological backgrounds to carry out the attacks. In some respects, this is a frightening finding: it implies that a wide range of people are potential suicide bombers, given the right circumstances.

To the extent that this is true, a far different conclusion concerning prevention emerges: The mission is not to profile individuals, but to profile groups. Why do some groups use this tactic whereas others do not? Does the reason have to do with the strength of their grievance or the level of desperation perceived by the group? Or is the decision tactical, based on what kind of effect suicide bombing is expected to have on the population being targeted for influence?

A key factor in the utility of suicide bombing may be whether or not the population from which the bombers emerge is sympathetic to the tactic. From this perspective, the question shifts from the individual and group levels to the societal level. Why do some societies support suicide bombings whereas others do not? In a society sufficiently angered or aggrieved, suicide bombing may come to be seen as more legitimate. Moreover, suicide bombers might be viewed as heroes, which should make recruiting much easier. One researcher argues that the tactics used to recruit suicide bombers and to get them to carry through with their missions are not fundamentally different from standard military recruitment and training around the world, which focus on the value of the unit over the individual and on the virtues of sacrifice.[32]

Sociological and psychological approaches to explaining terrorism may yield significant fruit, but for now we must admit that we have a lot of questions and very few reliable answers. Thus, this discussion cannot reach a firm conclusion. We can elaborate a set of grievances that might lead to terrorism, but the set of grievances is very broad, and most people cope with such dissatisfactions through means other than terrorism. Terrorism can be viewed in rational terms as a means of promoting change undertaken when all other means seem to fail. This prompts us to explore the range of grievances that groups around the world feel and the varying capacities of different countries for peaceful resolution of political conflict. But terrorism, in some cases, seems aimed more at expressing frustration and outrage than at actually changing anything. To the extent that this is true, psychological explanations may help us better understand terrorism.

Our limited understanding of terrorism has important implications for efforts to combat it. Because the underlying sources of terrorism have not been clearly identified, it is difficult to reliably design policies to address it. As a result, there is intense disagreement as to how to think about combating terrorism, with some seeing the task falling within the realm of law enforcement and others viewing it as falling within the realm of warfare.

Reconsider the Case

Military Force as a Response to Terrorism

The most visible response by the United States to the September 11, 2001, attacks was the invasion of Afghanistan. However, in mid-2007, after nearly six years of U.S.-led occupation of Afghanistan, a National Intelligence Estimate (NIE), an official statement of findings by sixteen U.S. intelligence agencies, asserted that Al-Qaeda had regrouped and presented a "heightened threat environment" for the United States.[33] An earlier 2006 NIE found that the war in Iraq was "fueling the spread of the jihadist movement."[34]

Assuming that such assessments have some validity, what can we learn from them about the sources of terrorism and the best policies to combat it? This question, of course, is intensely politicized, which makes it even more difficult to address objectively. Although much remains unclear about the causes of terrorism, the intelligence estimates referred to previously did reach conclusions that many people find valid. Collaboration among governments in combating terrorism grew dramatically after September 11, 2001, and helped put pressure on Al-Qaeda, but the 2007 NIE voiced fears that such collaboration will wane "as 9/11 becomes a more distant memory and as perceptions of the threat diverge."[35]

The 2006 NIE noted other causes of terrorism, including "entrenched grievances, such as corruption,

injustice, and fear of Western domination . . . ; the slow pace of real and sustained economic, social, and political reforms in many Muslim majority nations; and . . . pervasive anti-U.S. sentiment among most Muslims."[36] If the intellectual challenge in devising counterterrorism policy is figuring out the relative weight of these different factors, the policy challenge is how to pursue various strategies without having one set of policies undermine the goals of another. For example, can Western states conduct war in Iraq and Afghanistan and reduce anti-American sentiment at the same time?

Critical Thinking Questions

1. Why are the most technologically advanced armies in the world unable to defeat much more poorly equipped adversaries?

2. How might efforts to combat terrorism strengthen terrorist groups? Is it possible to avoid such negative effects without seriously weakening counterterrorism efforts?

3. How might military force and coercive diplomacy be used differently to achieve goals such as those that prompted the U.S.-led invasion of Afghanistan?

Summary

It became a cliché to say that the attacks of September 11, 2001, changed the world, just as it was a cliché of an earlier generation to say that the advent of the atomic bomb changed everything. In part, the change is perceptual. The world may not be more dangerous now than it was five minutes before the first plane hit the World Trade Center, but our perception of the danger has been dramatically heightened. Around the world, people quickly changed their notions of what "foreign policy" is about.

The relative newness of the topic of terrorism and the powerful emotions the topic engenders make it difficult to deal with analytically, as just another intellectual problem. And yet that is how it must be treated, at least by scholars and students. Treating the problem of terrorism analytically will allow us to see several points that will be useful in very practical terms. Most important among the points raised in this chapter is that terrorism has again shifted the calculus of defense and deterrence that evolved before and during the Cold War. The strength of terrorists derives from their weakness. Because they control little, they have little to destroy and cannot easily be deterred. Hence, states need to return to some combination of defense and preemption to deal with the problem. But defense and preemption are different too in that states are now dealing with asymmetric, rather than state-to-state, conflict. Understanding the nature of this asymmetric conflict and understanding the sources of terrorism are two of the main tasks that will face today's generation of students.

Key Concepts

1. Security dilemma
2. Coercive diplomacy
3. Defense versus retaliation
4. Sensitivity to casualties
5. Precision guided munitions
6. Weapons of mass destruction (WMD)
7. WMD proliferation
8. Preventive war
9. Crisis stability
10. Terrorism
11. Asymmetric conflict

Study Questions

1. What is the relationship between coercive diplomacy and deterrence?

2. What did von Clausewitz mean when he wrote that, "War is merely the continuation of policy by other means"?

3. How are threats and negotiation connected to one another?

4. How is a threat of retaliation meant to deter a potential attacker, and how does this threat differ from defense?

5. In what sense are India and Pakistan, or the United States and Iran, involved in security dilemmas?

6. Why do some countries seek WMD? Why do other countries not do so?

7. What factors have increased the potential for nuclear proliferation in recent years?

8. How might nuclear proliferation affect crisis stability?

9. How might missile defense affect crisis stability?

10. Define terrorism. What difficulties are involved in defining this term?

11. What does terrorism have in common with other uses of force in international politics?

12. What are the hypothesized causes of terrorism? What problems arise with the various explanations?

13. How does terrorism undermine the traditional strategies of defense and deterrence?

14. How does the "war on terror" differ from traditional war between states?

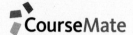
CourseMate

Endnotes

1. Carl von Clausewitz, *On War,* edited and translated by Michael Howard and Peter Paret (Princeton, NJ: Princeton University Press, 1984), p. 87.

2. von Clausewitz, *On War,* p. 96.

3. Many translations of Sun Tzu's *Art of War* are available, including those with applications to business and other fields.

4. For evidence on public opinion and casualties in Korea and Vietnam, see John E. Mueller, *War, Presidents, and Public Opinion* (New York: Wiley, 1973); George Ball's views are cited in Ole R. Holsti, "Public Opinion and Foreign Policy: Challenges to the Almond-Lippman Consensus," *International Studies Quarterly,* Vol. 36, No. 4 (December 1992): 446.

5. U.S. Centers for Disease Control, "Bioterrorism Agents/Diseases," at http://www.bt.cdc.gov/agent/agentlist-category.asp

6. See Thomas Schelling, *Strategy of Conflict* (Cambridge, MA: Harvard University Press, 1960), Chapter 9. pp. 207–229.

7. Thomas Schelling, "The Threat That Leaves Something to Chance," in *Strategy of Conflict* , Chapter 8, pp. 187–206.

8. Stockholm International Peace Research Institute, "World Nuclear Forces Table," http://www.sipri.org/contents/expcon/worldnuclearforces.html

9. On the importance of nuclear weapons in deterring war between the United States and the Soviet Union, see Robert Jervis," The Political Effects of Nuclear Weapons: A Comment," *International Security,* Vol. 13, No. 2 (Fall 1988): 80–90.

10. John Mueller," The Essential Irrelevance of Nuclear Weapons," *International Security,* Vol. 13, No. 2 (Fall 1988): 55–79.

11. Data from the Center for Nonproliferation Studies (CNS), "Chemical and Biological Weapons: Possession and Programs Past and Present," at http://cns.miis.edu/cbw/possess.htm. States listed by the CNS as having "possible" programs or as "likely" to have programs are listed here as "suspected." Precise status of many countries is unknown.

12. Kenneth N. Waltz, "More May Be Better," in Kenneth N. Waltz and Scott D. Sagan, *The Spread of Nuclear Weapons: A Debate* (New York: W. W. Norton, 1995), p. 7.

13. For a good summary, see Scott D. Sagan, "More Will Be Worse," in Waltz and Sagan, *The Spread of Nuclear Weapon,* pp. 47–91.

14. See T. X. Hammes, "Fourth Generation Warfare Evolves, Fifth Emerges," *Military Review* (May-June 2007): 14–23.

15. Growth in the literature on insurgency and counterinsurgency has been spurred by the current conflicts in Afghanistan and Iraq. See John A. Nagl, *Counterinsurgency Lessons from Malaya and Vietnam: Eating Soup with a Knife* (Westport, CT: Praeger, 2002); and *FM 3-24: Counterinsurgency* (the latest U.S. Army/Marine Corps counterinsurgency manual), at http://www.fas.org /irp/doddir/army/fm3-24.pdf

16. Quoted in C. J. Chivers, "General Faces Unease among His Own Troops, Too," *New York Times,* June 23, 2010, p. All.

17. Quoted in Chivers, "General Faces Unease.," p. A11.

18. Walter Laqueur, "Left, Right and Beyond: The Changing Face of Terror," in James F. Hoge, Jr., and Gedeon Rose, eds., *How Did This Happen? Terrorism and the New War* (New York: Public Affairs, 2001), p. 71,

quoted in Lisa Anderson, "Shock and Awe: Interpretations of the Events of September 11," *World Politics* 56 (January 2004): 312.

19. Robert Jervis, "An Interim Assessment of September 11: What has Changed and What Has Not?" in Demetrios James Caraley, ed., *September 11, Terrorist Attacks, and US Foreign Policy* (New York: Academy of Political Science, 2002), p. 180.

20. Beginning with the origin of the term in revolutionary France, all the way through the Soviet Union under Joseph Stalin, the word "terrorism" was generally applied to states that used terror to control their population. Only more recently has the meaning of the word been reversed, so that it refers to attacks by nonstate actors or individual citizens on states or on other citizens.

21. Audrey Kurth Cronin, "Behind the Curve: Globalization and International Terrorism," *International Security,* Vol. 27, No. 3 (Winter 2002/03): 32.

22. Richard Falkenrath, "Analytical Models and Policy Prescriptions: Understanding Recent Innovation in U.S. Counter Terrorism," *Studies in Conflict and Terrorism* 24, 3 (2001): 170, cited in Peter J. Katzenstein, "Same War—Different Views: Germany, Japan, and Counter terrorism," *International Organization* 57 (Fall 2003): 734.

23. Jervis, "An Interim Assessment," 182–183.

24. Thomas L. Friedman, "Connect the Dots," *New York Times,* September 25, 2003, at http://www.nytimes.com/2003/09/25/opinion/25FRIE.html

25. See Michael Mousseau, "Market Civilization and Its Clash with Terror," *International Security,* Vol. 27, No. 3 (Winter 2002/03): 6.

26. A good example of a religious explanation for terrorism is Daniel Philpott, "The Challenge of September 11 to Secularism in International Relations," *World Politics* 55 (October 2002): 66–95.

27. Philpott, "The Challenge of September 11 to Secularism in International Relations," p. 84.

28. "Islam, Terrorism and Malaysia's Response," Remarks by Mahatir Mohammed, the Asia Society, New York, February 4, 2002, at http://www.asiasociety.org/policy-politics/international-relations/intra-asia/islam-terrorism-and-malaysias-response

29. Congressional Research Service, "Sociological Characteristics of Terrorists in the Cold War Period," at www.fas.org/irp/threat/frd.html

30. Rex A. Hudson, *The Sociology and Psychology of Terrorism: Who Becomes a Terrorist and Why?* (Washington, DC: Library of Congress, 1999).

31. Michael Bond, "The Making of a Suicide Bomber," *New Scientist* (May 15, 2004): 34.

32. See Bond, "The Making of a Suicide Bomber," p. 34.

33. National Intelligence Council, "The Terrorist Threat to the US Homeland," July 2007, at http://www.dni.gov/press_releases/20070717_release.pdf, p. 6.

34. U.S. Director of National Intelligence, "Declassified Key Judgments of the National Intelligence Estimate. Trends in Global Terrorism: Implications for the United States dated April 2006," at http://www.dni.gov/press_releases/Declassified_NIE_Key_Judgments.pdf, p. 2.

35. National Intelligence Council, "The Terrorist Threat to the US Homeland," p. 6.

36. U.S. Director of National Intelligence, "Declassified Key Judgments of the National Intelligence Estimate," p. 2.

9

Fundamentals of International Political Economy

LEARNING OBJECTIVES

After completing this chapter, the student should be able to . . .

1. Explain the benefits of trade in terms of the theory of comparative advantage.

2. Define "exchange rates" and the "balance of trade" and explain how the two interact.

3. Define "protectionism" and identify different barriers to trade.

4. Show how economic structuralists and realists evaluate the gains from trade differently than liberals.

5. Describe constructivist and feminist approaches to international political economy and show how they depart from other approaches.

6. Connect theoretical arguments about international political economy to contemporary policy discussions.

7. Articulate and defend an argument concerning the relative merits of different approaches to international political economy.

◀ Exports loaded onto a cargo ship in Singapore.
Jonathan Drake/Bloomberg/Getty Images

Consider
the Case

Protesting the World Trade Organization

In December 1999, representatives of the more than 100 members of the WTO gathered in Seattle to lay the groundwork for a new round of global trade **liberalization** (reduction of the barriers to trade). Rather unexpectedly, thousands of protesters who opposed further liberalization rioted in the streets of Seattle, smashing windows and disrupting the talks, which ended up in disarray. Earlier that year, a French farmer named José Bové had destroyed a McDonald's restaurant under construction to oppose

South Korean farmers offer flowers to a memorial altar of dead compatriot farmer, Lee Kyung-hae, before an anti-World Trade Organization (WTO) protest at the Victoria Park in Hong Kong.

"what the WTO and the big companies want to do with the world."[1]

At another WTO meeting in Cancun, Mexico, in September 2003, a Korean farmer named Lee Kyung-hae, wearing a sign reading "the WTO kills farmers," stabbed himself to death in public. Rice farming plays an essential role in Korean culture and history, perhaps akin to the role of the family farm on the American prairie. Like the U.S. government, the South Korean government protected its farmers from global competition. However, with other states threatening to reduce South Korea's access to their markets for valuable industrial goods, South Korea had recently agreed to reduce agricultural subsidies, and South Korean farmers found themselves competing unsuccessfully against cheaper imported rice. Many went out of business, and Lee himself lost his farm to foreclosure.[2]

A few days after Lee's suicide, delegations from 22 developing countries walked out of the talks, effectively ending them. Why did many world leaders (and most economists) believe that further liberalization was an important goal? Why did so many other people find that goal reprehensible? And what are the prospects for further liberalization in this increasingly combative environment?

Lee Jae-Won/Reuters/Landov

liberalization

Reducing barriers to trade (increasing free trade).

International economics affects every aspect of our contemporary lives, from the trivial to the profound. So widespread are the effects of international economics and world trade that it is easy to take them for granted. But if we stop to examine our clothes, our computers, our cars, and our food, we recognize that international trade is responsible for much of the way we live our lives. In news reports, international trade and financial disputes arise so frequently that they no longer seem novel. But while international trade is becoming so commonplace that it may seem unimportant, the opposite is true—as rising oil prices, trade protests, and immigration debates indicate. The increasing flow of goods, services, money, people, and ideas across state borders promises immense opportunity for mutual benefit. But because the stakes are increasing, international commerce also contains the potential for mutual damage and for dispute. This mixture of opportunity and hazard makes international political economy an increasingly important part of the field of international politics. And although many dispute the claim that economics has displaced security as the primary issue in world politics, few deny that it is more important now than ever before.

The Importance of International Economics

International political economy (IPE) is the two-way relationship between international politics and international economics. The links between politics and economics run in both directions: events in the international economy often have political consequences. When the importing of automobiles from Japan causes job losses at U.S. manufacturers, for example, U.S. citizens appeal to politicians to address the problem. The reverse is also true: policies made by individual states often affect the international economy. For example, a decision by the U.S. government to increase subsidies for ethanol production is intended to reduce dependence on petroleum and to enrich farmers. But it has the effect of reducing the amount of crops available for food, which drives up prices around the world. Similarly, a debt crisis in one country can cause economic havoc in many others. The links between economies mean that even policies that are intended solely for domestic purposes (such as farm subsidies) have international repercussions.

The study of IPE encompasses a variety of economic and political questions. All these questions concern the movement of goods, money, people, and ideas across borders. States are only partly able to control economic processes that occur entirely within their borders. Individual governments are even less able to influence the activities that cross borders. Trade creates the potential for conflict, but because it is so lucrative, there are also powerful incentives to work out differences through compromise and negotiation. Because the amount of cross-border movement of goods, money, people, and ideas is increasing rapidly, a process widely known as **globalization**, the conflicts and pressure for negotiated solutions have increased in recent years and can be expected to increase even more in the future.

Trade and Domestic Policy

For states considering their economic relations with others, several practical issues arise. To what extent should free trade be the state's primary economic policy? What are the benefits and dangers of such a policy? How does increasing exposure to the international economy affect the state's ability to govern its own domestic economy? If economies are mutually dependent, to what extent do states need to coordinate their domestic economic policies? Most troubling, perhaps, how can interdependence be managed when states disagree either on the goals or on the best policies? Can economic sanctions provide an alternative to the use of military force?

Beneath all these questions lies one certainty: economics has become central to contemporary politics. U.S. President Bill Clinton captured this notion famously when, running for the presidency in 1992, he made a mantra of the line, "It's the economy, stupid." Despite the popular notion that the economy functions best without interference from the government, Clinton understood clearly that in contemporary democracies, people hold governments accountable for the workings of economies. When times are bad, governments are expected to take measures to remedy the situation or risk being voted out (or, in less stable countries, overthrown). When the economy is strong, voters seem content to return incumbents to power.

This notion that the government is responsible for the economy is relatively recent, dating in the United States to the New Deal of President Franklin Roosevelt.

international political economy

The two-way relationship between international politics and international economics.

globalization

A process in which international trade increases relative to domestic trade; in which the time it takes for goods, people, information, and money to flow across borders and the cost of moving them are decreasing; and in which the world is increasingly defined by single markets rather than by many separate markets.

The Wealth of the World

Typically, the size and shape of countries on a map are determined by the land area of the country. In this map, the size of each country is determined by the size of its economy.

Critical Thinking Questions

1. How does the world look different on this map than on a map based on land area?

2. What does this map show that a map based on land area does not?

3. How might scholars from different theoretical schools view this map? What points would they make? For example, what might a theorist who believes that wealth equals power say about how Africa looks in this map?

World Showing States by Size of GDP

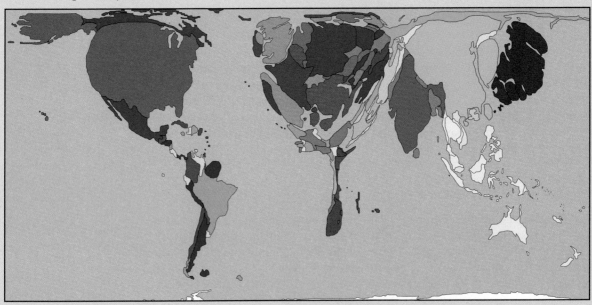

PHOTO © ISTOCKPHOTO

Source: http://www.sasi.group.shef.ac.uk. © 2006 SASI Group (University of Sheffield) and Mark Newman (University of Michigan). Reprinted by permission.

Prior to that time, economic difficulties were seen as natural calamities, no more in the government's ability to prevent or fix than a drought. Since that time, economists as well as politicians have accepted that certain government **fiscal and monetary policies** can influence the economy. As economies become more closely linked, however, one government's economic policies have increasingly significant effects in other countries, which may provoke a response from adversely affected countries. Political leaders face the challenge of trying to govern economies that are increasingly out of their control. Welfare now rivals warfare as the main foreign policy concern for many states.

Key Economic Concepts and Theories

For the student or scholar of international politics, there are three basic questions: Why do states trade? What are the benefits of trade? Who gets the benefits of trade? These fundamental questions must be answered in order to understand contemporary debates about international trade, finance, and globalization. This chapter examines the concepts and theories developed to address the questions.

Why do states trade? The answer seems obvious: people buy things from abroad because they are cheaper, and people sell things abroad to make more profits. This answer is basically true, but it obscures several issues that go to the heart of IPE. It is essential to understand the benefits of trade in order to understand states' motives in preserving trade despite the trouble it often causes. Therefore, a brief economics lesson is in order. Although they may seem a bit technical, a few key concepts from economics capture the essence of political debates about international economy. First, this chapter explores economists' answers to the question "Why do states trade?" Later, the chapter examines the concepts of the balance of trade, exchange rates, and protectionism, which are frequently discussed but rarely understood.

fiscal and monetary policies
The two major ways in which governments can influence their economies. In fiscal policy, a government uses a budget deficit or surplus to stimulate or slow economic growth. In monetary policy, a central bank raises or lowers interest rates to stimulate or slow economic growth.

The Theory of Comparative Advantage

Developed by the English economist David Ricardo in the early nineteenth century, the **theory of comparative advantage** goes beyond intuitive understandings of trade to show logically how and why trade is beneficial to both partners. The theory has crucial implications for our understanding of international trade and the political debates that surround it. The basic point is that by specializing and trading, states and individuals can increase overall consumption and efficiency.

Like most economic models, the theory of comparative advantage uses a few simple assumptions to derive more profound conclusions and sets aside many real-world complexities for the sake of clarity and simplicity. A simple example will illustrate the theory. Imagine a world with two countries, China and the United States, and two goods, wheat and textiles. Imagine also that the only factor in the production of these two products is labor. Imagine, finally, that labor can move between production of wheat and production of textiles (but not between countries) and that the cost of transportation is negligible.

Suppose that in the two countries, the amount of wheat and textiles that can be produced by one person working for one day is as shown in Table 9.1. In this example, labor is more productive in China than in the United States—both wheat and textiles are made with less labor in China than in the United States. Why would China import anything from the United States when both products can be made with less labor in China? The key to the answer lies not simply in comparing China's productivity to that of the United States, but also in comparing productivity *across* sectors *within* the two countries. The key question is, "How much labor must be diverted from one sector to produce more in the other?" In China, wheat and textiles are produced at a rate of 300:1200, or 1:4. For every extra bushel of wheat the Chinese wish to produce, they must forgo four yards of textiles. In the United States, wheat and textiles are produced at a ratio of 100:200, or 1:2. In the United States, producing an additional bushel of wheat requires surrendering only two yards of textiles. In effect, wheat is more expensive in terms of textiles in China than in the United States. Similarly, the Chinese must give up only one-quarter of a bushel

theory of comparative advantage
A theory developed by the English economist David Ricardo to show logically how and why trade is beneficial to both partners.

Table 9.1 Production Conditions

	Wheat (Bushels per Day of Labor)	Textiles (Yards per Day of Labor)
China	300	1200
United States	100	200

of wheat to get a yard of textiles, whereas those in the United States must give up one-half of a bushel. Textiles are twice as expensive in terms of wheat in the United States as in China.

It is this *difference in relative prices* that creates the basis for profitable trade. Consider what is possible in trading one bushel of American wheat for 3 yards of Chinese textiles (note that this price of 1:3 falls between the domestic prices of 1:2 in the United States and 1:4 in China). For the Chinese, trade with the United States makes it possible to get a bushel of wheat for only three yards of textiles, rather than four as in the domestic economy. For the Americans, trade makes it possible to receive three yards of textiles for each bushel of wheat, rather than only the two yards obtained by shifting labor from wheat to textiles in the domestic economy. Both countries receive more goods for the same cost.

To illustrate the overall effects of such trade, we can calculate the consumption possible in each country with trade and without it. Suppose that each state has twenty workers and that labor initially is divided evenly between sectors (ten workers producing wheat and ten producing textiles). Part A of Table 9.2 shows the overall outputs, based on the labor productivity specified in Table 9.1. Part B of Table 9.2 shows the overall production that can be achieved through specializing (the United States totally, China partially). In the United States, all twenty workers are working in wheat production; in China, one-third of the workers are working in wheat and two-thirds are working in textile production. *Overall production increases by 2000 yards of textiles with no additional labor and with no reduction in wheat production!* Part C of Table 9.2 shows the overall production that can be achieved by both specializing and trading, exchanging 1000 bushels of wheat for 3000 yards of textiles (at the price of 1:3). By specializing and trading, both states are able to increase their consumption of textiles without using additional labor or reducing consumption of wheat.

Two important conclusions can be drawn. First, with specialization, the overall amount of production and consumption increases *without* any increase in inputs. In this example, total textile production has increased from 14,000 to 16,000 yards, with no reduction in wheat production. Second, specialization and trade lead to increased consumption in *both* countries. Each country can increase its consumption of textiles by 1000 yards (or shift more workers back into wheat) through trade. Trade increases overall consumption without any cost. This example shows in technical terms what people experience practically every day. By buying shoes made in China and watches made in Taiwan (and selling U.S. software there), we can consume more than we otherwise would be able to afford.

Table 9.2 Overall Output With and Without Specialization and International Trade

		Wheat (Bushels per Day)	Textiles (Yards per Day)
A. No specialization and no trade	China	3000	12,000
	United States	1000	2000
	Total	4000	14,000
B. Specialization but no trade	China	2000	16,000
	United States	2000	0
	Total	4000	16,000
C. Specialization and trade	China	3000	13,000
	United States	1000	3000
	Total	4000	16,000

The answer to the original question, therefore, is that states trade because trading allows them to produce and consume more and because it leads to greater overall efficiency. Both states can benefit simultaneously. As long as the two states have different ratios of productivity from one sector to the next, this result holds. Adding real-world factors, such as the cost of transportation, the large number of countries that engage in trade, and the large number of goods traded, complicates the analysis but does not undermine this fundamental logic.

Comparative Advantage and Liberalism

The previous discussion of comparative advantage is closely linked to the liberal approach to international relations theory. The finding that trade makes both partners better off and increases overall efficiency underpins liberal trade theory and liberal international relations theory more broadly. Indeed, the liberal international theory introduced in Chapter 3 was in large part inspired by economists such as Ricardo and Adam Smith. The theory of comparative advantage establishes in the economic realm what liberals claim more broadly: that when states cooperate, both can benefit simultaneously. The theory of comparative advantage proves that both sides can gain simultaneously through trade. In this way, the theory powerfully contradicts the realist view that international affairs is a **zero-sum game** in which one side can gain only at the expense of another.

In contemporary international politics, the theory of comparative advantage is still used, implicitly or explicitly, to justify increased international trade, decreased barriers to trade, and international economic integration. The growing integration of the EU, the development of the North American Free Trade Agreement (NAFTA), and the lowering of tariffs through the WTO all make sense in terms of comparative advantage. By making trade easier, these institutions allow states to specialize in the areas in which they are most efficient, leading to greater overall production and consumption.

However, realists and economic structuralists do not simply give in to the logic of comparative advantage. They criticize the goals implied by the liberal model and focus on other potential effects of trade. Much of the political discussion of free trade—for example, between those who support and those who oppose NAFTA—pits followers of the liberal economic model against those who reject that model in favor of realism or economic structuralism (although proponents of these views rarely use those labels). These critiques will be discussed later.

zero-sum game
A situation in which any gains by one side are offset by losses for another.

The Balance of Trade

Every month, governments around the world release statistics on their country's balance of trade. These statistics are reported in major newspapers and are announced on most newscasts. In recent years, the statistics have usually shown that the U.S. trade deficit is increasing. So what? What is the "balance of trade," and what about it is important enough to make the news month after month? This term is widely used in news reports but rarely understood.

First, it is important to recognize that the balance of trade often is not balanced at all. In economic terms, the **balance of trade** is simply exports minus imports (measured in dollars or another currency). In other words, it is a net accounting of how much in the way of goods and services is exported from a country compared to how much is imported. When the trade balance is zero, the economy is importing exactly as much as it exports. When the "balance" is negative (a "trade deficit"), the economy in question is importing more than it exports, such that exports minus imports is a negative number. The balance is positive (a "trade surplus") when the country is exporting more than it imports. News reports give the distinct impression that a surplus is good and a deficit bad. Why is this so?

balance of trade
Exports minus imports (measured in dollar value); a net accounting of how much in the way of goods and services is exported from a country compared to how much is imported.

The Culture Connection

Attitudes Toward Economic Globalization

Footage on television of protests against globalization, as well as much of the rhetoric about the downside of globalization, might suggest that most people around the world are opposed to it. Surprisingly, perhaps, that does not appear to be the case. A 2002 survey by the Pew Research Center found that in nearly every

Global Trade's Impact on Country

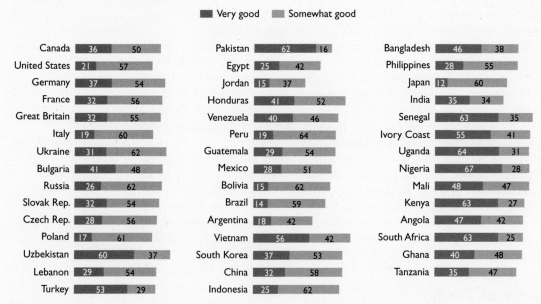

■ Very good   ▨ Somewhat good

Country	Very good	Somewhat good
Canada	36	50
United States	21	57
Germany	37	54
France	32	56
Great Britain	32	55
Italy	19	60
Ukraine	31	62
Bulgaria	41	48
Russia	26	62
Slovak Rep.	32	54
Czech Rep.	28	56
Poland	17	61
Uzbekistan	60	37
Lebanon	29	54
Turkey	53	29
Pakistan	62	16
Egypt	25	42
Jordan	15	37
Honduras	41	52
Venezuela	40	46
Peru	19	64
Guatemala	29	54
Mexico	28	51
Bolivia	15	62
Brazil	14	59
Argentina	18	42
Vietnam	56	42
South Korea	37	53
China	32	58
Indonesia	25	62
Bangladesh	46	38
Philippines	28	55
Japan	12	60
India	35	34
Senegal	63	35
Ivory Coast	55	41
Uganda	64	31
Nigeria	67	28
Mali	48	47
Kenya	63	27
Angola	47	42
South Africa	63	25
Ghana	40	48
Tanzania	35	47

Source: http://www.people-press.org/reports/display.php3?ReportID=185. Reprinted by permission of The Pew Research Center.

PHOTO © ISTOCKPHOTO

Trade deficits are viewed not in isolation, but with reference to their implications for the rest of the economy, and especially for employment. A trade deficit implies that goods that otherwise might be produced domestically are being produced abroad. If that is true, then the shift of production from the "home economy" to other countries decreases the demand for labor at home, which, other things being equal, implies that wages and employment levels will go down. In a modern democratic country, these are two of the most sensitive political issues. In contrast, a surplus is seen as being beneficial because it implies that the country, by selling goods abroad, can employ more workers at higher wages than if production and sales were limited to the domestic market.

Trade surpluses are seen as beneficial for other reasons, too. When an economy is exporting more than it imports, the demand to buy that state's currency will be higher

one of the forty-four countries surveyed, a majority of respondents believed that increased international ties were good for their country and their family. There was some limit to this enthusiasm—many respondents viewed international ties as "somewhat good," rather than "very good."

These attitudes were voiced even though many also expressed serious concerns about their own economic situations. This finding implies that most people do not hold globalization responsible for their economic problems. Rather, they appear to blame factors within their own countries. The attitudes were expressed by respondents in countries that are not thought of as bastions of capitalism or free trade. In Vietnam, 56 percent of respondents viewed international trade as "very good" and 42 percent thought of it as "somewhat good." In Uzbekistan, the figures were 60 percent and 30 percent, respectively. Surprisingly, the percentages were much lower in Japan, a leader in global trade, where only 12 percent of respondents viewed trade as "very good" and 60 percent said it was "somewhat good." This difference may have been a response to the fact that Japan was in the midst of a major economic downturn in 2003.

When asked about the role of large international corporations, responses were again generally positive, although there was some interesting regional variation. International corporations were viewed most favorably in Africa, with countries in the Middle East less enthusiastic. Europe and North America, where most of the firms are based (and where they create a great deal of wealth), viewed them most negatively. It is difficult to explain these results.

Among these generally positive attitudes toward economic globalization, there was one issue about which respondents around the world were almost uniformly negative: migration. Majorities in nearly every country surveyed supported increased restrictions on migration into their countries.[1]

Critical Thinking Questions

1. Would people's attitudes toward free trade change if they understood the theory of comparative advantage better?
2. What factors might make public opinion more or less supportive of free trade?
3. Why do you think multinational corporations are more popular in Africa than in Europe or North America?

[1] All data are from The Pew Research Center for People and the Press, "Views of a Changing World 2003," at http://peoplepress.org/reports/display.php3?ReportID=185

than the need to sell, and the value of the currency will increase, which many believe is beneficial to the economy. Overall, however, the key point for many analysts is that the balance of trade crucially affects key state goals: economic prosperity in general and the level of employment in particular.

The concern over trade deficits has led some to advocate "fair trade" rather than simply "free trade." The distinction, advocates of fair trade claim, is that under **fair trade**, action would be taken against states that pursued a trade surplus as a means of stimulating their economies. This view sees trade imbalances as the result of cheating on free trade rules, which, in fact, is only one possible source of imbalance.

However, it should be clear that a focus on balance of trade turns the IPE into a zero-sum game. It is mathematically impossible for two states both to have a surplus relative to

fair trade

A narrower approach to free trade that advocates retaliation against states that are perceived as "cheating" on free trade.

Figure 9.1 The graph shows the emergence of the U.S. trade deficit and its growth. What are the sources of the deficit, and how much of a policy concern should it be?

U.S. Trade Deficit

Source: http://www.census.gov/foreign-trade/statistics/historical/gands.pdf

the other. One state can obtain a greater benefit (trade surplus) only if its partner suffers a corresponding loss (trade deficit). For this reason, the balance of trade becomes the cornerstone of the modern realist analysis of trade. For the same reason, liberals tend to reject its importance, arguing that trade imbalances are usually offset by surpluses in financial transactions or that trade imbalances will remedy themselves if the market is left to work on its own. Some argue that a trade deficit is simply a result of being wealthy and is not to be feared. It is natural, in this view, that the wealthy United States buys more from China than relatively poor China buys from the United States, and therefore, trade deficits are not anything to worry about. However, states often work intensively at maximizing their exports and reducing their imports, which leads inevitably to conflict. To the extent that states focus on the balance of trade, conflict rather than cooperation will define international economic relations.

Exchange Rates

Currencies are often labeled "strong" or "weak," and they are said to "rise" or "fall." These vague terms all relate to the price of a currency. Like potato chips or computers, currencies can be bought and sold. And like the price of anything else, the price of a currency depends on supply and demand. So, when the dollar is "strong," it is relatively expensive for others to buy, and other currencies are relatively cheap in terms of dollars. For example, between July 2007 and July 2008, the value of the U.S. dollar dropped by about 15 percent, from .74 to .63 euros. That may seem a trivial decline, but it would add $3400 to the U.S. price of a $20,000 Volkswagen.

Why do these prices change? There are many reasons, but a simplified explanation is that **exchange rates** change because supply and demand change. One reason people buy and sell currencies is to use them in importing and exporting. If importers want to buy goods made in Germany, they need to pay the German suppliers of the goods in euros. If all they have is dollars, they must trade dollars for euros. As demand for European goods increases, the number of people wishing to sell dollars and buy euros will increase. The supply of dollars for sale will go up, the supply of euros for sale will go down, and the price of euros (in terms of dollars) will increase. The value of the dollar thus declines. Trade is only one factor that changes the value of currencies.

exchange rate

The price of one currency in terms of another.

Differences in interest rates also influence the demand for currency, and hence exchange rates. If interest rates are higher in Europe than in the United States, investors can make more money investing in Europe and will convert some of their dollars into euros in order to do that, again raising the price of euros. Similarly, if a government issues more currency to stimulate its economy, the supply of that currency increases relative to other currencies and its value decreases. Billions of dollars worth of currencies are traded on world markets every day, as investors speculate on future currency fluctuations and try to hedge other risks.

Why do exchange rates matter? Exchange rates affect trade just as trade affects exchange rates. If the dollar decreases in value against the euro, it will take more dollars to buy the same number of euros. This means that goods whose prices are determined in terms of euros will become more expensive for Americans paying in dollars. If a dollar buys one euro, then a Volkswagen that costs € 20,000 can be bought in the United

States for $20,000. If the value of the dollar falls by 20 percent, so that $1 = € .80, the German supplier must increase the U.S. price of that Volkswagen to $25,000 in order to make the same profit (in euros) as before.

This price fluctuation will likely have two effects. First, to the extent that the imported goods have no domestic substitutes, the increased prices paid for them cause inflation in the domestic economy and divert purchasing power away from other goods. If a consumer spends an extra $5000 to buy an automobile, she will spend $5000 less on other things. Second, domestically produced goods will become more competitive. A car manufactured in the United States that costs $22,000 would be more expensive than the $20,000 Volkswagen, but cheaper than the Volkswagen after the exchange rate change caused its price to rise to $25,000. This is bad for the foreign exporters, who lose business, and good for the U.S. manufacturer, who will see demand for its cars rise (and may even be able to raise prices slightly). Because exchange rates have powerful effects on the prices of goods and therefore on the success of different countries' manufacturers, they are the subject of intense political attention. In sum, for those who compete with imported products, a weak currency can be helpful and a strong currency destructive.

Table 9.3 Effect of Exchange Rates on Import Prices: Hypothetical Cost of Volkswagen

Price in euros	Price in Dollars July 2007 ($1 = € .74)	Price in Dollars July 2008 ($1 = € .63)	Price Increase
€14,800	$20,000	$23,400	$3400

The Interaction of Exchange Rates and the Balance of Trade

Combining the discussions of exchange rates and the balance of trade raises two key points. First, in theory, these factors should balance each other. If the United States has a trade deficit with Germany, there will be more demand for euros than for dollars. The price of the euro will go up, leading to an increase in the prices of German goods in the United States, and a decrease in the prices of U.S. goods in Germany. In theory, this self-regulating process will continue until a new equilibrium is reached with balanced trade at a different exchange rate. In practice, this rarely happens completely, because so many other factors affect exchange rates and trade flows. This process is illustrated in Figure 9.2. For example, for many years, a falling U.S. dollar was accompanied by rising, rather than falling, U.S. imports. The willingness of other countries to lend the U.S. government and consumers vast sums of money meant that normal constraints on purchasing were loosened.

The second key point about exchange rates and the balance of trade is that if states put a high priority on achieving a trade surplus, they can manipulate their currency price to boost trade. By lowering interest rates, printing more money, or selling reserves of its own currency, a government can deliberately reduce the value of its currency (or *devalue* the currency) relative to others. Imports become more expensive, and hence decrease. At

Figure 9.2 The Interaction of Exchange Rates and the Balance of Trade

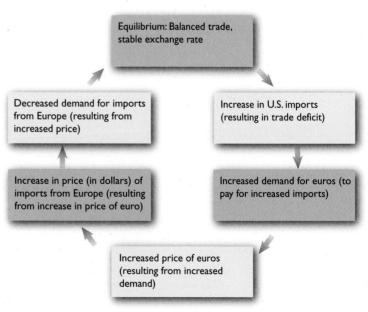

Source: Paul D'Anieri

The Policy Connection

China's Strong Currency Policy

As China's exports have grown, the Chinese government's policy of keeping the value of its currency, the yuan, artificially low has caused concern and even anger in the United States and in Europe.[1] China has sought to maintain a weak currency in order to ensure that its exports remain very cheap in dollar and euro terms. By using China's enormous export earnings to buy U.S. bonds (essentially lending money to the U.S. government), the government was increasing the demand for dollars relative to the yuan, suppressing the yuan/dollar exchange rate. By 2010, China held over 2 trillion U.S. dollars.[1]

U.S. manufacturers complained bitterly that by making Chinese exports cheaper, the cheap Chinese currency was wiping out U.S. firms and jobs. The economist Paul Krugman called China's policy "predatory."[2] European governments were also concerned. In May 2005, the U.S. government hinted that if China did not "revalue" its currency, the United States would classify China as a "currency manipulator," and Congress threatened trade sanctions if steps were not taken to revalue the yuan. Beginning in 2005, China slowly allowed the yuan's

value to increase, but only slowly. Even so, by 2008, the yuan had increased its value relative to the dollar by 20 percent, and China again fixed the exchange rate. In June 2010, following a renewed effort in the U.S. Congress to take action against China, the Chinese government announced it was removing the formal "peg" between the yuan and the dollar, but it continued to intervene in the market, allowing the yuan to rise only slightly. It appeared that China was doing just enough to avoid a strong reaction from the United States.

The yuan/dollar exchange rate has far-reaching economic and political implications. For China, revaluing the yuan might have several negative consequences. Increases in the prices of Chinese exports would make them less competitive in foreign markets. This would likely cut profits for exporters and increase unemployment, which the Chinese government feared might lead to social unrest. The Chinese Commerce Ministry, dedicated to the interests of exporting firms, strongly objected to a change in the policy. Moreover, any decrease in the value of the dollar would diminish the

PHOTO © ISTOCKPHOTO

[1] Paul Krugman, "China's Dollar Trap," *New York Times*, April 3, 2009, p. A29.

the same time, the devaluing country's products become comparatively cheaper and exports increase. This has been a major issue of contention between the United States and China. China maintained a policy of keeping the value of its currency, the yuan, low compared to the dollar. The United States, deeply concerned with its increasing trade deficit with China, has pressured the Chinese government, with limited success, to allow the yuan to appreciate (increase in value) to help moderate the deficit (see the Policy Connection box).

States have considerable temptation to compete to have the lowest-valued currency in order to boost their domestic employment. This behavior is called **competitive devaluation**. Competitive devaluation, which took place during the Great Depression, leaves everyone worse off by undermining the stability needed for trade to take place. Exchange rates, therefore, are not as abstract as they seem; nor are they merely financial indicators. Their ability to affect world trade and employment levels makes them a tempting but dangerous tool for governments trying to improve their trade position.

competitive devaluation
Competition between states to have the lowest-valued currency in order to boost domestic employment.

value of China's vast holdings of dollars. Finally, many Chinese see the issue as one of national sovereignty, and strongly objected to China adjusting its policy under pressure from the United States. It appeared that the Chinese leadership hoped to revise the policy, but was constrained by nationalist public opinion.[3]

There were dangers for the United States as well. The U.S. government continued to run large deficits, requiring massive borrowing. If China reduced purchases of U.S. bonds, decreasing the demand, interest rates would rise. This would dampen economic growth during a recession and increase the price of financing the massive debt. Finally, U.S. consumers benefits immensely from the low prices of Chinese goods. A weakening of the dollar relative to the yuan would create inflation (price increases) that further inhibit economic growth. The Obama administration resisted a harder line toward China for other reasons: it was hoping for China's help on security threats from Iran and North Korea.[4]

There was nothing fundamentally new about the U.S.-China currency conflict. The same kinds of issues have arisen ever since the fixed exchange rate system ended. Although it appears that the United States has become heavily dependent on borrowing money from China, China is also dependent on the United States because it relies on exports to the United States to fuel economic growth and to honor its debts. Two powerful countries, accustomed to independent action, have become increasingly interdependent.

For the EU, the dollar-yuan exchange rate also creates huge problems. The yuan's price is determined primarily in relation to the dollar, so as the dollar has declined against the euro, so has the yuan. This has made it more difficult for European manufacturers to compete with Chinese producers, and the EU's trade deficit with China has grown.

Critical Thinking Questions

1. When two states disagree on what their currency exchange rate should be, who should bear the costs of solving the problem?

2. In the case of the United States and China, what sources of economic power does each side have that help it to force the other to deal with the problem?

[1]"What Do Yuant from Us?" *The Economist Global Agenda*, May 18, 2005.
[2]Paul Krugman, "Chinese New Year," *New York Times*, December 31, 2009.
[3]Keith Bradsher, "Spotlight Complicates Chinese Steps on Currency," *New York Times*, April 13, 2010.
[4]"Yuanimpressed," *The Economist*, July 1, 2010.

Protectionism

The previous section discussed the possibility that states might want to limit their imports. States can do so through a variety of measures, collectively known as **protectionism**. The primary goal of protectionism is to protect domestic producers against competition from foreign firms. Protection can be aimed at specific industries or at the entire economy. In some cases, an industry is protected because it employs so many people that unemployment would rise considerably were the industry to fail. The U.S. auto industry is an example. In other cases, an industry is protected because it is seen as essential for broader economic growth. In the twentieth century, the auto industry was regarded as such an industry; today the computer and programming sector is viewed that way. The United States, for example, has shown concern over becoming too dependent on foreign supplies of microchips. Other industries might be seen as essential for national defense. For this reason, many countries protect arms manufacturers and their suppliers.

protectionism

Measures taken by states to limit their imports.

quota

A numerical limit on the
amount of a certain item that
can be imported.

tariff

A tax on imports, used to
protect domestic producers
from foreign competition.

subsidies

Direct payments to producers
to help them remain
profitable.

Protection of a specific industry can be accomplished through a variety of means. Perhaps the simplest is the **quota**, a numerical limit placed on the amount of a certain item that can be imported. In the 1980s, a quota was placed on Japanese automobiles imported into the United States in order to protect U.S. auto firms. One of the most widely used protectionist measures is the **tariff**, which is simply a tax on imports. By adding to the cost of imported goods, the tariff makes it easier for domestic producers to compete. Also widely used are **subsidies**, which are direct payments to producers to help them remain profitable. Subsidies are often implemented for other policy reasons, but they reduce foreign competition, whether they are intended to or not. The extensive subsidies to farmers in the United States and Europe are often cited by developing countries as barriers preventing them from competing more successfully in the global marketplace.

Finally, almost any type of regulation (such as environmental or health regulation) can serve as a protectionist measure if, in practice, it creates more difficulty for importers than for domestic producers. European Union restrictions on genetically modified crops, viewed in Europe as a health measure, are viewed as trade barriers by U.S. farmers and agribusinesses because U.S firms produce more genetically modified crops and seed than EU farmers do and are therefore disproportionately hindered by the restrictions. Argentine beef ranchers make the same complaint about U.S. health regulations.

In addition to measures aimed at individual industries, protectionism can target the overall economy. In this case, the goal of the measure is generally to create a favorable balance of trade by providing some level of protection to every domestic producer. Two measures can be used to protect an entire economy: a general tariff that applies to every good and a currency devaluation.

Five Approaches to International Political Economy

Realist, liberal, economic structuralist, constructivist, and feminist theories seek to explain the IPE as much as they do other aspects of international relations. Indeed, in important respects, the economic theories of liberals and economic structuralists

Table 9.4 Protectionist Measures: Who Pays and Who Benefits

	Who Pays?	Who Gets the Money?	Who Wins?	Who Loses?
Quotas	No payment	No payment	Domestic producers, who can charge higher prices and innovate less	Consumers, who must pay higher prices for less innovative goods; producers in other countries
Tariffs	Exporting firms	Government	Domestic producers, who can charge higher prices and innovate less	Consumers, who must pay higher prices for less innovative goods; producers in other countries
Subsidies	Governments (taxpayers)	Domestic producers	Domestic producers, who can make the same profit charging a lower price	Producers in other countries, who have to charge full price
Regulations that discriminate against imports	Governments (pay for enforcement)	Bureaucrats (especially if they can take bribes to help firms avoid regulations)	Domestic producers, who face reduced competition and so can charge more	Consumers, who must pay higher prices; producers in other countries, whose costs are higher

predate their theories of international relations. Examining these five approaches to IPE serves two purposes. First, it extends our understanding of the theories. Second, and more important, it helps us understand the fundamental debates about economic policy that we hear every day. Policy disagreements are often debated in terms of economics. In many cases, however, policy disagreements are actually rooted in different normative assumptions (different values about what goals are most important).

Liberalism

The liberal approach to IPE has already been discussed in some detail, in the section on comparative advantage. The theory of comparative advantage shows that through trade, various states can all increase their welfare at the same time. Because welfare is an essential goal of contemporary states, states will (and should, liberals argue) pursue more free trade. Liberals argue that protectionism, although tempting for certain actors within states, leads to overall inefficiency and loss for almost everyone. The main challenge of international trade politics, in the liberal view, is to resist the temptation to seek selfish advantage through protectionism and instead to seek mutual advantage through trade. "Probably the most important insight in all of international economics is the idea that there are *gains from trade*—that is, that when countries sell goods and services to one another, this is almost always to their mutual benefit. . . . The single most consistent mission of international economics has been to analyze the effects of . . . protectionist policies—and usually, though not always, to criticize protectionism and show the advantages of freer trade."[3]

For example, economists predicted that the institution of the WTO, a new free trade agreement in 1995, would lead to efficiency gains of $270 billion per year.[4] The gains of protection, liberals hold, are an illusion: protectionism diverts resources from efficient uses and impedes economic growth. Liberals attribute the duration and depth of the Great Depression to the policies states adopted to shield themselves from trade, and they credit the emergence of a free trading system after World War II with the incredible increases in wealth seen throughout the developed world. They have been deeply concerned that the current economic crisis will lead to a resurgence of protectionism, although so far free trade has held up.

Anticipating the criticisms from economic structuralists, liberals assert that the extreme poverty present in much of the world is not a result of free trade but the result of *not enough* free trade. When Third World countries try to protect their domestic economies through tariffs, quotas, and the like, liberals argue, they shut themselves off from an important engine of efficiency and growth: the international market. Especially in terms of wages, liberals find that free trade helps the poorest nations. In countries where poverty makes people willing to work cheaply, goods produced with a lot of labor can be produced relatively cheaply. As more firms move their manufacturing facilities to such countries, the demand for these workers will rise, and so will wages. Theoretically, this will continue until Third World wages equal those of the First World. China is seen a case in point. China's opening to world trade has led to hundreds of millions of people being lifted out of poverty.

THE REALIST AND ECONOMIC STRUCTURALIST CRITIQUE

Realists and economic structuralists do not completely reject liberal analysis, but by exploring several questions that liberalism neglects, they arrive at very different conclusions about the nature of IPE. Rather than focusing on the overall benefits of trade, they ask about the distribution of those gains. Economic structuralists argue that the increased wealth created by trade tends to accrue to the wealthier side, such that trade widens the gap between rich and poor. Realists agree, and examine how power allows some states to exploit others economically. Realists are also concerned with how economic power can lead to political and military power.

The example of wheat and textile trade between the United States and China can be used to illustrate the problems that both economic structuralists and realists have with liberalism. By specializing and trading, the United States and China could increase overall textile production by 2000 yards. The liberal analysis stops here, concluding that since trade increases production at no extra cost, it is good for everyone. Realists and economic structuralists, however, ask, "How are these gains from trade divided?" The question is impossible to answer without making further assumptions, but for many the answer is crucial. If China and the United States trade textiles for wheat, at what price do they trade? In our example, the benefits from trade were split equally: the price of one bushel of wheat for three yards of textiles falls neatly halfway between the Chinese domestic price and the American domestic price, and as a result each side gains the same: 1000 yards of textiles. But how was this price established? It was chosen arbitrarily to simplify the math in the example.

Suppose China said to the United States, "We will trade with you, but not at the price of one bushel for three yards. We will only trade at the price of one bushel for 2.1 yards." What would happen? At that price, the international price of wheat is substantially less than the Chinese domestic price (4:1), but the international price of textiles is only slightly cheaper than the American domestic price (one bushel gets 2.1 yards in trade, versus two yards domestically). China gains a lot (1.9 yards of textile per bushel of wheat), and the United States gains little (0.1 yard of textile per bushel of wheat). Why would the United States agree to such a deal? Because it would still be marginally better off trading internationally at 1:2.1 than trading domestically at 1:2. Some might argue that the United States could refuse to trade unless China negotiated a fairer price. Would China give in? That would presumably depend on who needed the trade more. This, economic structuralists and realists emphasize, has to do with *power*. As long as one country needs trade more than the other, the gains from trade will be distributed unequally. Or, if one side can use other means (such as military threats or colonial control) to influence trade, then the benefits of trade are likely to be distributed unequally. The question of the distribution of the gains of trade becomes the focus of economic structuralist and realist analyses. It is a question not emphasized by liberal analysis. In this respect, the theories do not directly conflict, but rather ask different questions.

Realism

Realist analysis of IPE, like realist analysis more broadly, deals with the interests of the state, not with the interests of individuals within the state or with economic efficiency. This emphasis on state economic interests underlies variants of realism such as **mercantilism** (prominent in the sixteenth through the nineteenth centuries), economic nationalism (nineteenth and twentieth centuries), and protectionism, or neomercantilism (twentieth and twenty-first centuries). All of these doctrines share a focus on state goals, a concern with the distribution of the gains from trade, and an emphasis on the conflictual nature of international trade. To see why a focus on distributive questions leads inevitably to a conflictual view of IPE, examine again the comparative advantage example. When liberals consider the overall gains from trade, they see that the level of production goes up, so both states can gain simultaneously. But when realists examine how the gains from trade are divided, they see that one side can gain only if the other loses. The situation is now a zero-sum game. In our U.S.-China example, the gains from trade consist of 2000 additional yards of textiles. For China to increase its share of the gains (say, to 1200 yards of textiles), the U.S. share must correspondingly decline (to 800).

mercantilism
A trading doctrine that focused on state power in a conflictual world. It was based on the idea that the overall amount of wealth in the world was fixed by the amount of precious metals. Therefore, international trade was a zero-sum game, in which one state could gain only at the expense of another. The goal of every state was to run a trade surplus in order to accumulate more money. Adam Smith and David Ricardo effectively demolished the notion on which mercantilism was based, that the amount of wealth in the world was fixed.

Why do realists take this particular perspective rather than the liberal view? Traditionally, the answer returns to realists' central focus on state survival, three aspects of which emphasize distribution rather than overall wealth. First, states seek self-sufficiency, especially in the industries critical to war efforts. If a state becomes too dependent on other states for key military inputs such as steel, it faces the prospect of being cut off in a time of need. In the contemporary world, many states expend considerable resources to maintain a high degree of self-sufficiency in food, oil, and most defense industries. Thus, economic efficiency does not always contribute to the state's ability to survive. In such cases, realists argue, states will put survival first and spend more money to maintain self-sufficiency.

Second, even seemingly mundane trade relations have important power consequences in the realist view. "The interdependence of national economies creates economic power, defined as the capacity of one state to damage another through the interruption of commercial and financial relations. The attempts to create and to escape from such dependency relationships constitute an important aspect of international relations in the modern era."[5] Economic wealth can be converted into political and military power (most directly by paying soldiers and purchasing bombs and bullets). If one state can gain more wealth from a given transaction, it can potentially increase its military power vis-à-vis the other state. This problem of **relative gains** implies that even if both sides gain, the side that gains more may increase its power over the side that gains less.

Third, realist theory of IPE has more recently focused on prosperity and employment. Contemporary citizens expect their governments to ensure some degree of economic security. To the extent that prosperity and high employment become state goals, realists assert that these goals too will be placed above the pursuit of overall economic efficiency. The establishment of prosperity and high employment as state goals makes the balance of trade a primary concern of contemporary realist analysis. The doctrine of focusing trade policy on the balance of trade is known as **neomercantilism**. If the United States runs a large trade deficit with Japan, for example, the implication is that employment, wages, and profits are higher in Japan and lower in the United States than they would be without such an imbalance. In the realist view, the U.S. government can be expected to try to change that balance of trade, even if it emerged in the free market and even if the efforts to change it reduce overall economic efficiency. In this way, the realist view of IPE has moved well beyond traditional concerns with military power and survival to the issue of domestic prosperity.

Whereas in previous centuries many realists who focused on self-sufficiency would have found trade beneficial only in a very limited range of circumstances, contemporary realists agree with liberals that trade provides benefits for all states involved. But because realists emphasize distribution, the key to the game for realists is to trade, but only to the extent that the terms are favorable (or at least not unfavorable). When two states that share this viewpoint trade with each other, bargaining can be expected to be intense. Realists point to recent disputes among the United States, the EU, and China, among others, to support their argument that conflict over the gains from trade is the dominant characteristic of the IPE.

Economic Structuralism

Economic structuralism shares realism's concern with distribution, but takes it in a different direction. For economic structuralists, the fundamental actors in politics are not states, but classes. Economic structuralism therefore asks about the effects of the international economy on different classes, spotlighting its effects on the poor. For this reason, much of the practical agenda of economic structuralist international political economics has involved issues of underdevelopment and poverty in the Third World.

relative gains

A problem with free trade arising from the fact that if one state can gain more wealth from a given transaction, it can potentially increase its military power vis-à-vis the other state. This implies that even if both sides gain, the side that gains more may increase its power over the side that gains less.

neomercantilism

The belief that states should seek a trade surplus. This focus on the balance of trade makes trade a zero-sum game, as it was for traditional mercantilists.

Figure 9.3 The liberal view differs from the realist and economic structuralist views on the effects of free trade on preexisting inequalities. Following neoclassical economic theory, liberals see a trend toward equilibrium, in which gaps in wealth shrink while everyone gets richer. Realists and economic structuralists see gaps in wealth growing as a result of free trade.

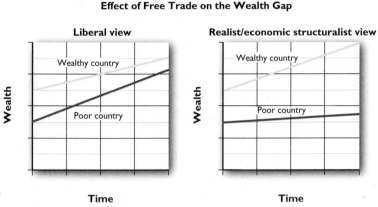

Effect of Free Trade on the Wealth Gap

Source: Paul D'Anieri

Economic structuralists, like realists, ask, "What determines how the gains from trade are divided?" Like realists, economic structuralists emphasize that power determines how the gains from trade are divided, and in this sense, their international argument replicates their domestic argument. When rich and poor countries trade or when rich First World companies hire impoverished workers in the Third World, the poorer actor is always more desperate than the richer one. The richer actor is able therefore to bargain for a disproportionate share of the gains. As the Russian revolutionary V. I. Lenin put it, "The uneven and spasmodic character of the development of . . . individual countries, is inevitable under the capitalist system."[6]

In recent years, this perspective has gained much visibility in the movement to improve working conditions in Third World factories that manufacture goods for First World consumers. Activists have been successful in showing, for example, how little of the price paid for a pair of name-brand athletic shoes accrues to the workers who made them, and how those workers often work long hours in difficult and unhealthy conditions to earn these meager wages. Although not presented in Marxist terms, such analyses are good examples of economic structuralist thought.

A second focus of economic structuralism has been the issue of child labor. For example, the use of children in Pakistan to assemble many of the soccer balls used throughout Europe and North America has received much attention. Liberals tend to view this employment pragmatically, pointing out that if children could not work these jobs, their families would be even poorer and more desperate than they are now and that denying children jobs would not put them in school. Economic structuralists respond that this is precisely the point: the economic desperation of such people makes it rational for them to take any work offered at any wage. The response, they say, should be to alter the balance of power between workers and employers so that employers have greater incentive (or are required by law) to pay a reasonable wage and children have enough economic security that they do not feel compelled to pass up school for work. In the developed world, economic structuralists contend, this balance is provided through the bargaining power of labor unions and through the establishment of minimum wage laws, which do not exist in many developing countries.

Economic structuralism examines closely how the dynamics function over time. If one actor starts out wealthier than another, then the wealthy actor, being less desperate, will be able to bargain for a greater part of the gains from trade. Because the rich actor gains more, the gap between the two actors' wealth is larger after the transaction than before. When the same two actors meet again, the increased disparity in wealth makes the bargaining position of the wealthy actor even stronger, and it bargains for a still bigger share of the gains from trade. Over time, therefore, economic structuralist analysis predicts that the gap between the wealthy and the poor will widen, rather than narrow.

Two important points emerge from this analysis. First, the assertion that gaps in wealth increase over time puts economic structuralist analysis in direct opposition to liberal analysis. Where liberal analysis shows how economic disparities tend toward

The History Connection

The Great Depression

On October 28, 1929, subsequently known as "Black Monday," U.S. stocks lost 13 percent of their value. They fell another 12 percent the following day. Thus began the Great Depression, which impoverished much of the United States, and spread around the world. Within a few years, roughly a quarter of American workers were unemployed and GDP had fallen by nearly 30 percent.

How did a stock market crisis in New York lead to a global depression? Because many people and financial institutions had borrowed heavily in order to invest in the growing stock market, the collapse of 1929 left many people and firms unable to repay loans. As a result, banks came under severe financial stress. A bank panic ensued, in which people withdrew their money from banks, out of fear that the banks would collapse and take people's savings with them. With cash in extremely short supply, banks sharply curtailed lending activity. Because both businesses and consumers depended on credit for purchases, the collapse in credit led to a collapse in consumption. As demand fell, so did prices—a condition known as *deflation*.

Although deflation of prices might seem like a good thing, it can start a devastating cycle. Once potential buyers anticipate that prices will fall, they have an incentive to delay purchases until prices go lower. As a result, consumption drops further. As producers were unable to find buyers, they laid off workers. Unemployed workers were unable to buy, so overall demand in the economy fell even further.

The depression spread around the world in part because of protectionism. In 1930, the U.S. Congress passed the Smoot-Hawley Tariff Act, a huge increase in tariffs intended to let fewer imports into the United States, and thereby to increase demand for U.S. goods and labor. This led to a collapse in demand in countries that supplied the United States. They responded with tariffs against the United States. The collapse in trade, a sort of deglobalization, exacerbated the depression around the world.

In financial terms, the fact that most countries still fixed the price of currency to gold (the "gold standard") meant that the supply of money contracted. As banks and individuals hoarded money, taking money out of the financial

system, there was no way for governments to inject more money into the economy to maintain the supply of credit. This contributed to deflation and to the crisis of credit.

Governments responded in different ways. In the United States and United Kingdom, politics turned to the left. Franklin Roosevelt, elected in 1932, introduced the "New Deal," which substantially increased government involvement in the economy. By borrowing vast sums of money and spending it on public works projects, the government sought to put people back to work, and by putting money in workers' pockets, to increase demand for consumer goods. The United States also passed legislation strengthening the power of labor unions and introducing the Social Security system, among other things. Other countries turned to the right, however. In Germany, the depression made the Communist Party more popular, but fear of the communists led many to support the right wing Nazi Party, led by Adolf Hitler.

The economist Ben Bernanke, writing 70 years later, stated that "To understand the Great Depression is the Holy Grail of macroeconomics."[1] By 2008, Bernanke was Chairman of the Federal Reserve Board, and the depression was no longer just an academic subject. The United States was again surprised by a collapse of credit and of asset prices (including stocks and housing). Again the crisis quickly spread around the world. The threat of a new deflationary spiral and a long-term depression led many to look back to the Great Depression for lessons. In contrast to 1930, however, there was no illusion that disaster might be averted without intervention, and governments leapt into action to avoid economic collapse, debating all the way what causes depressions to start and to spread.

Critical Thinking Questions

1. In what respects do the events of 1929–1930 resemble those of 2008–2009?
2. What changes since the Great Depression might make it easier or harder to avoid a repetition today or in the future?

PHOTO © ISTOCKPHOTO

[1] Ben S. Bernanke, *Essays on the Great Depression* (Princeton, NJ: Princeton University Press, 2000), p. 5.

equilibrium in a free market, economic structuralist analysis predicts that disparities will widen. Second, in the economic structuralist view, once a disparity is established, it tends to be self-perpetuating. From this perspective, even where colonialism ended decades or centuries ago, the effects of the colonialism are still being felt and will not go away by themselves over time.

Constructivism

Constructivist approaches to IPE address the profound disagreements among the three views discussed previously. A key determinant of international economic policies, constructivists find, is the understanding of the nature of IPE held by citizens, state leaders, and global policy makers. Whereas the three schools of thought that have been outlined assume that states have certain goals, constructivists hold that actors' goals vary and therefore those goals must be a central subject of research. Some actors might subscribe to liberal views; others might hold economic structuralist views. Moreover, actors may have strong interests in promoting one view over the others. Over time, the views of various actors can change, such that shared understandings emerge and dissipate. As these understandings of interests change, policies can be expected to change as well. In other words, rather than adopting one or another of these broad approaches, constructivists ask which approach to a problem was adopted by the actors in a given situation. In particular, constructivists explore the extent of normative agreement on key issues. As normative agreement develops between states, it becomes much more likely that the states will agree on policy coordination. Several examples will help illustrate how constructivist theory is applied to IPE.

In one of the earliest and most influential constructivist studies, John Ruggie showed that the international trading system that encompassed the Western world after World War II was the result, above all, of a normative commitment (value judgment) that came to be shared by the key countries. This commitment, which Ruggie labeled **embedded liberalism**, was essentially liberal in its recognition of the benefits of free trade, so the major focus of the postwar trading system was the reduction of tariffs. However, leaders also recognized that free trade would be politically unsustainable if it caused excessive disruption or hardship to domestic economies (interests of concern largely to realists and economic structuralists). So, the postwar system included important exceptions to a pure free-trade approach. In this view, it was an idea—the compromise between free trade and protection—rather than a concrete factor, such as money or power, that led to agreement.[7]

This approach can be applied to a wide variety of issues in IPE. For example, in trying to explain why a certain "recipe" for economic stability was attempted in a wide variety of developing and postcommunist countries in the 1990s, constructivists would show how a set of prescriptions known as the "Washington consensus" came to dominate thinking on economic policy.

Today, one the most potentially far-reaching developments is a widespread shift in thinking about the role of governments in the economy. The notion that that economies function best when governments are least involved was never fully accepted globally, but the concentration of the post-2008 economic crisis in those countries most dedicated to the free market doctrine (especially the United States and the United Kingdom), has contributed to the view that state intervention is important, and the markets left to themselves will induce crisis.

The constructivist approach makes no sweeping statements about the nature of the IPE, focusing instead on the argument that what we collectively think about the international economy goes a long way to explaining policies. Nor does constructivism make any predictions about how the world is likely to develop. Rather, this approach finds

embedded liberalism

According to John Ruggie, the normative consensus that guided international economic arrangements after World War II. It combined a commitment to expansion of free trade with acceptance that states would have to intervene domestically to protect themselves from some of the effects of free trade.

prediction difficult because of the complexity of anticipating how actors' understandings of their interests will evolve. In fact, it should be noted that all of the perspectives discussed have had limited success in clearly and correctly predicting future developments.

Feminism

The basic feminist critique of the four IPE approaches described previously is that by ignoring women and issues of gender, these approaches fail to fully understand how the IPE works, and they cause harm to women by ignoring their role in it. Understanding the role of women in IPE, feminists contend, is essential to understanding the dynamics of the global economy. Conventional analyses fail to see how the IPE contributes to the economic and political oppression of women, especially the poorest and most vulnerable women. Moreover, many development economists as well as feminists assert that women play an underappreciated role in the economic growth of developing nations.

DIFFERENTIAL EFFECTS OF THE ECONOMY ON WOMEN

Feminist scholars argue that the IPE has particular effects on women, because women often are assigned specific (disadvantageous) roles in the economy. In addition, feminists assert, women often play multiple roles, some of which are excluded from analysis because of an artificial analytical distinction between "public" and "private." "Women's and girls' ability to participate in educational, productive, and civic activities and thus to empower themselves economically and politically is often limited by a household division of labor that assigns to women and girls the bulk of the responsibility for everyday household maintenance tasks."[8] In the developing world, some of these household tasks impose enormous burdens: collecting firewood takes the average woman over an hour per day in some countries, and collecting and managing water is a further burden. Underdeveloped public transport systems increase the time these chores require and therefore are particularly burdensome on women.[9]

Whereas liberal economists propose that free trade will make everyone better off, once adjustment to new conditions takes place, feminists ask how costs and benefits will be distributed across genders (just as economic structuralists ask how the costs and benefits will be distributed across classes). The work that women do in factories in return for wages is included in standard economic analysis. But the "domestic" work they do, raising children, finding and preparing food, and maintaining a household—and the fact that these tasks prevent women from seeking wage labor—is often ignored. Similarly, informal production by women, whether in maintaining household garden plots or doing piecework in the home for the international market, is often not accounted for. Thus, feminists claim, women's work is systematically undervalued.

Feminists also find that the costs of globalization are unevenly distributed, in part because the costs to women are not visible in standard analyses based on macro-level statistics. Measures of gross domestic product (GDP) per capita and income inequality are calculated without regard to differences between women and men, and this approach can obscure critical gender inequities. Statistics that take gender into account show significant gender inequities that are otherwise obscured. For example, in the wealthiest industrialized countries, where men and women have roughly equal access to education, there is a remarkable disparity in the estimated earned income of women and men. In the United States, for example, women in 2004 on average earned $30,581, while men earned $49,075—38 percent more. In Ireland, men on average earn 49 percent more than women, and in Japan, they earn 66 percent more.[10] In many countries, education, which is demonstrated to have an important influence on earning power, is less available to girls than to boys.[11] In the poorest countries, the effects of economic discrimination can be dramatic: "In India alone, among children aged one to five, girls are 50 percent more likely to die than boys—meaning that 130,000 Indian girls are mortally discriminated against every year."[12]

Aspects of globalization that are generally viewed as beneficial can have very negative effects on women. For example, cheap international travel and the Internet facilitate "sex tourism," the practice of traveling to places primarily in order to engage in sexual exploitation without the fear of punishment (for further discussion, see Chapter 14). The Internet makes it easy for those who offer such services to make themselves known to potential customers around the world. Cheap international travel makes it economically viable for many in developed countries to participate. The phenomenon is widespread in various countries in Southeast Asia and Latin America, and in some countries sex tourism plays a major role in the economy.[13] Women and especially girls under age eighteen are the predominant targets. The U.S. State Department estimates that over one million children are victimized every year.[14] By vastly increasing the demand for such "services" and therefore the profits to be made by those organizing them, cheap travel and the Internet have increased the incentive to exploit girls and women.

WOMEN AS AGENTS OF DEVELOPMENT

Whereas some view women as victims of international economic processes, others point out the crucial role that women can play in solving broader problems. Indeed, some feminists reject the idea of women as "victims," stressing instead the ways in which women actively work to transform their economic circumstances and, by extension, the international economy.

The argument that women have a special role to play in international development is the feminist argument that perhaps has had the widest influence beyond the feminist movement. Because women play a disproportionate role in childrearing, for instance, they play a crucial role in reducing children's poverty. Studies have shown that women tend to use a much higher proportion of their earned income on household expenditures, including higher quality food, home maintenance (including sanitation), and clothing and school fees for children, whereas men are somewhat more likely to spend money on entertainment, drugs, and prostitution.[15] Likewise, the human development indicators monitored by the United Nations Development Programme indicate that the children of women who receive higher levels of education and earned income in turn attain higher levels of literacy and life expectancy. Women's overall development is strongly correlated with overall human development, particularly for children.

Based on such findings, development aid programs since the 1970s have increasingly targeted women. One of the most significant innovations was the development of microlending programs for women. Mohammed Yunus and other microlending pioneers recognized that the key obstacle to women's economic development was their lack of access to credit that could be used to invest in entrepreneurial activities. Social customs that deny property rights (necessary for collateral for loans) to women effectively choked off an important path to increased earning. Even a very small loan can make a significant difference in a woman's earning power.

For example, women sewing garments by hand can realize a huge increase in productivity if they are able to purchase a sewing machine with funds from a microloan. A woman can pay off the loan and then continue to be much more productive, and therefore earn more, well into the future. Similarly, a woman who cooks and sells food

Zahra Dehghani milks cows she bought through a microloan program in Bam, Iran. She sells the cow's milk to provide an income for her family.

John Sanmeyer/VII/Associated Press

in her neighborhood can also vastly increase her productivity with a small investment in equipment. Women, therefore, represent an untapped source of economic development.

Moreover, although some reject the notion that women behave differently than men, women's behavior is seen as one of the reasons that microlending has been so successful. Women, it turns out, have a much higher rate of repaying loans than do men. This is important because microlending organizations can only make new loans as old ones are repaid. Women's higher repayment rate is thought to be based not on individual differences between women and men, but rather on the nature of the cooperative groups formed by women to manage the loans; such groups exert a strong normative pressure to repay the loan so that the next woman can benefit.

Comparison of the Approaches

The key characteristics of each approach to IPE are summarized in Table 9.5. Note that there is some overlap as well as some degree of contradiction among the approaches. Realists and economic structuralists agree on the vital importance of distributive issues. But while realism looks at national interests, economic structuralism focuses on class interests, which in many analyses means the interests of the capitalist class, which is assumed to be dominant both economically and politically. When economic structuralist analyses equate rich and poor states with rich and poor classes, or when realism takes up the issue of underdevelopment, the two schools become nearly indistinguishable analytically, but they still differ on their normative commitments. Economic structuralism and liberalism disagree on the key issue of whether, left to themselves, free markets reduce or increase inequality. The two approaches agree, however, that substate actors such as firms and classes, rather than states (the focus of realism), are the key actors and that arguments about "national interest" usually disguise the interest of some powerful actor seeking government protection. Finally, realism and liberalism also disagree about whether international trade is a positive-sum or a zero-sum game. On much of the basic economics,

Table 9.5 Summary of Major Approaches to International Political Economy

	Key Actors	Key Processes	Key Questions	Value Commitment
Liberalism	Individuals and firms	Trade, which increases wealth	What factors lead to more open international trade?	Economic efficiency, overall wealth, free trade
Realism	States	Conflict over the gains from trade	How does power affect the distribution of gains from trade? How does trade affect the distribution of power?	State power, domestic employment, self-sufficiency
Economic structuralism	Classes, multinational corporations	Unequal distribution of the gains from trade	How does international trade contribute to poverty? How can that be changed?	Equality (both domestic and international)
Constructivism	States, state leaders, intellectual leaders	Diffusion of new ideas, development of new values	What understandings of international political economy are dominant?	Varies
Feminism	Individuals (especially women), NGOs	Gender-based exploitation, gender-based development programs	How does international political economy affect women? How can gender-based programs promote development?	Recognition of influence of gender, equality for women

Source: Paul D'Anieri.

they agree: neither realists nor economic structuralists contradict most of liberal economic theory, and they accept the theory of comparative advantage. But they have a very different notion of who the important actors are and of whether free trade is beneficial to all or only to some.

To a large degree, the last column of Table 9.5 is the most important one. The analytical disagreements among the various schools often reflect different goals. For example, two analysts might agree that NAFTA increases overall efficiency and will make Canada, Mexico, and the United States all wealthier, and that many workers in each country will have to find new jobs as tasks are moved to more efficient producers. One analyst might argue that the overall efficiency gains are worth the disruption caused to workers needing to readjust and that NAFTA is therefore beneficial. Without disagreeing about the facts, the other could argue that the costs imposed on workers who must find new jobs are too high a price to pay and that NAFTA therefore is a bad idea. The disagreement here is not theoretical—it does not stem from disagreement over how the world works. The disagreement is normative, concerning values as each gives a different answer to the question, "How much inequality is acceptable in the effort to gain greater overall wealth?"

In contemporary international politics, actors are concerned with both efficiency and distribution of gains. There is relatively little disagreement with Ricardo's finding that trade leads to economic gains. But the distribution of those gains is a sensitive political issue, whether to those concerned with power or to those concerned with welfare and equality. In this sense, international trade can be characterized as a

mixed-motive game (similar to the prisoner's dilemma), in which actors have incentives that partially overlap with and partially contradict those of their partners. There can be no general statement concerning how sensitive actors are to the distributive issues—this varies across actors and over time. However, the more sensitive actors are to distributive issues, the more difficult it will be to achieve the mutual gain of free trade.

Moving from theory to the real world, these mixed motives are visible in operation every day. The United States uses its considerable power to attempt to decrease its trade deficit with China, and China uses its power to maintain its surplus, while at the same time both states take care not to let the dispute completely ruin the relationship, which on balance is profitable. The same story can be told about the United States and the EU, or the EU and China, or many other relationships.

mixed-motive game
A situation in which actors have incentives that partially overlap with and partially contradict those of their partners. The prisoner's dilemma is one representation of a mixed-motive game.

Reconsider the Case

Protesting the World Trade Organization

Since the walkout of developing countries from the Cancun talks in 2003, the WTO has continued to be hamstrung by fundamental disagreements concerning the agenda for world trade. The Doha Round of negotiations, which began in 2001, remained stalled in 2010. A meeting scheduled for 2006 was canceled by the WTO's director general because there was so little prospect for progress. An effort to achieve agreement among four key actors— the United States, the EU, Brazil, and India—failed in 2007. Essentially, the United States and the EU seek lower tariffs on manufactured goods in developing countries such as India and Brazil, while developing countries seek less protection for agriculture in developed states (for example, tariffs in the EU countries and subsidies in the United States). A U.S. offer to reduce its maximum agriculture subsidies to $17 billion did not impress the developing states, since U.S. subsidies had been only $11 billion in 2006.[16]

In South Korea, barriers to agricultural imports continued to fall, driven by deals with other countries to increase access to their markets for industrial goods. In 2005, the government agreed to double the proportion of imported rice in the South Korean market by 2014.[17] Overall, South Korea's economy relies much more heavily on manufactured goods than on agriculture, so the tradeoff was seen as a good move for the country as a whole. But as with

many trade deals, benefits and costs are not distributed equally

In 2008–2009, international trade fell by as much as a third. The decrease was driven in large part by the overall economic contraction around the world, but increasing protection likely had an effect as well. Many leaders announced their intention to resist protectionism during the economic crisis, but domestic pressure to aid ailing industries was powerful, and complaints that other states were violating WTO agreements increased.

Critical Thinking Questions

1. How should the overall benefits provided by free trade be weighed against questions of distribution and equality raised by various schools of thought?

2. What kinds of measures might deal with the concerns raised by opponents of further liberalization? Would such measures need to be adopted by international agreement or could they be implemented primarily through domestic policy?

3. If liberalization creates winners and losers, will the pattern of winners and losers in the future look like that in the past? Which countries and what kind of individuals are likely to find their interests in liberalization changing in coming years?

Summary

Because domestic economic prosperity has become one of the most salient political issues in most countries and because international trade has increased, the effects of international economics on domestic economics are becoming more central to international politics and foreign policy. The ability of one state's domestic policies or problems to harm or benefit other states transforms the domestic economy of each state into an international concern. Put differently, because each state's economy is increasingly affected by influences from abroad, it is less affected by its own government's policies. Therefore, governments that seek to promote domestic prosperity need to be more concerned with the policies of other states. Some predict that this interdependence will lead to greater cooperation; others see it leading to greater conflict. Either way, these trends put IPE at the center of contemporary international politics.

The same approaches that are used to understand international politics in general, or to explain international conflict, can also be applied to the problem of IPE. The focus of Western nations on free market economics makes the liberal view the most widely held view of IPE, but crisis in the Western economies has led to more focus on state control domestically, and on economic realism internationally. Economic structuralist and feminist analyses also often work their way into policy debates as well as academic discussions. Disagreements over particular economic policies such as tariffs, free trade, and development are often traceable either to the different analyses based on these theories or to the different normative goals of the theories.

Key Concepts

1. Liberalization
2. Barriers to trade
3. Fiscal policy
4. Monetary policy
5. Zero-sum game versus positive-sum game
6. Balance of trade
7. Exchange rates
8. Distribution of gains from trade
9. Protectionism
10. Neomercantilism
11. Embedded liberalism
12. Gendered economic roles

Study Questions

1. What is international political economy?
2. How does the theory of comparative advantage explain international trade?
3. What are the benefits of free trade and who gets them?
4. What are the costs of free trade and who pays them?
5. How are international politics and international economics interrelated?
6. In what respect does liberal trade theory see trade as a positive-sum game?
7. In what respect do realist and economic structuralist theories see trade as a zero-sum game?
8. What is the perceived importance of the balance of trade?
9. What effects do changes in exchange rates have?
10. How do people's views of international trade depend on whether they focus on overall efficiency or on the distribution of gains?
11. What differences exist in male and female economic roles and how do these differences influence global development?

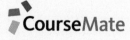
CourseMate

Endnotes

1. Quoted in "The Early Pioneers," *The Economist*, July 26, 2007.

2. *New York Times*, September 16, 2003; Luis Hernandez Navarro, "Mr. Lee Kyung Hae," at http://www.globalexchange.org/campaigns/wto/1123.html

3. Paul R. Krugman and Maurice Obstfeld, *International Economics: Theory and Policy*, 3rd ed. (New York: HarperCollins, 1994).

4. *Sunday Times* [London], July 24, 1994.

5. Robert Gilpin, *U.S. Power and the Multinational Corporation: The Political Economy of Direct Foreign Investment* (New York: Basic Books, 1975), p. 38.

6. V. I. Lenin, *Imperialism: The Highest Stage of Capitalism* (New York: International Publishers, 1939), p. 62.

7. John G. Ruggie, "International Regimes, Transaction, and Change: Embedded Liberalism in the Postwar Economic Order," *International Organization*, Vol. 36, No. 2 (Spring 1983): 379–415.

8. UN Millennium Project, *Taking Action: Achieving Gender Equality and Empowering Women* (London: Earthscan, 2005), p. 7.

9. UN Millennium Project, *Taking Action*, pp. 7–8.

10. United Nations Development Programme, *Human Development Report 2006* (New York: United Nations, 2006), p. 367.

11. UN Millennium Project, *Taking Action*, pp. 4–6.

12. Nicholas Kristof, "Wretched of the Earth," *New York Review of Books* (May 31, 2007): 34.

13. U.S. Department of Justice, "Child Sex Tourism," at http://www.usdoj.gov/criminal/ceos/sextour.html

14. U.S. Department of State, Office to Monitor and Combat Trafficking in Persons, "The Facts About Child Sex Tourism," August 19, 2005, at http://www.state.gov/g/tip/rls/fs/2005/51351.htm

15. UN Millennium Project, *Taking Action*, pp. 88–89. See also L. Haddad, J. Hoddinott, and H. Alderman, *Intrahousehold Resource Allocation in Developing Countries: Methods, Models and Policy* (Baltimore, MD: Johns Hopkins University Press. 1997); and Kristof, "Wretched of the Earth," p. 35.

16. *The Economist*, July 28, 2007.

17. *International Herald Tribune*, December 12, 2005.

CHAPTER

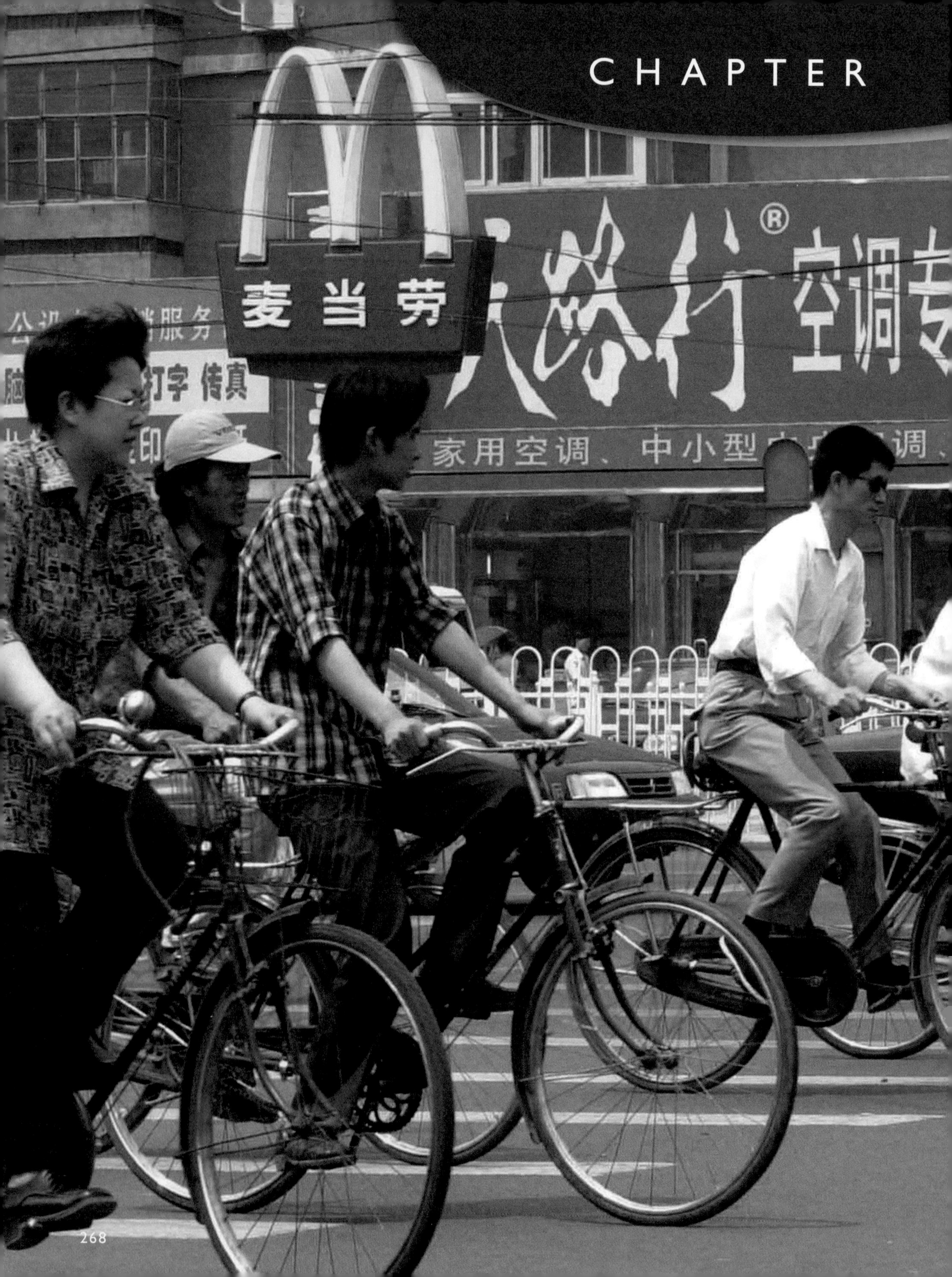

10

The Globalization of Trade and Finance

LEARNING OBJECTIVES

After completing this chapter, the student should be able to . . .

1. Distinguish between quantitative and qualitative changes in global interactions.

2. Describe the historical evolution of the post-World War II trading system.

3. Identify the major issues surrounding the World Trade Organization.

4. Analyze the competing goals of international monetary arrangements and the tensions between these goals.

5. Describe the evolution of the international financial system since the nineteenth century.

6. Analyze the sources and mechanisms of crisis in the contemporary international financial system.

7. Evaluate competing arguments about the benefits and problems of contemporary globalization.

◀ McDonald's in Beijing.
AP Photo/Chien-min Chung

Consider the Case

Europe's Debt Crisis: From Local to Global

In early 2010, it appeared that the government of Greece might default on its debt. By May, people were questioning whether Europe's single currency, the euro, could persist, and stock markets around the world fell because of the uncertainty in Europe. Fears about governments' ability to repay their debts extended to other European countries as well as to the United States, where the size of the budget deficit became a major economic concern and political topic. Why was Greece unable to pay its debt and how did that threat spread much more widely?

Greece's difficulty paying its debt resulted in part from the broader factors driving the economic crisis. Prior to 2008, interest rates were low, and the Greek government borrowed extensively to fund generous pensions and public services. Like many other countries, Greece spent more than it raised in taxes. As long as borrowing remained within limits, lenders were confident that Greece could meet its obligations. However, when the economy shrank beginning in 2008, and tax revenues decreased, the gap between government income and spending widened, to the point where lenders feared that the government would not be able to pay its debt. Lenders compensate for increased risk by charging higher interest rates. Increased interest rates made paying Greece's debts even harder, in a vicious cycle characteristic of debt crises.

Normally, a country in such a situation might address the problems through monetary policy: Printing more money would help pay debts and would devalue the currency (leading to higher exports). But as a member of the Euro zone, Greece had no independent control of monetary policy. Critics of the EU pointed out that this inflexibility was devastating, and some predicted that Greece would be forced to leave the Euro zone.

The Greek crisis spread to the rest of Europe through two mechanisms. First, the banks and investors that had lent money to Greece were based in many other countries and often owed money to others. If Greece failed to pay its debts, the banks that lent them the money would be unable to *their* debts, and so on, in a chain reaction of default. Second, the crisis spread through fear. As Greek default loomed, investors began looking more critically at other states' ability to repay their debts. Attention focused initially on Spain, which had problems comparable to those of Greece. Spain, as a much larger economy, presented a much larger danger to the system.

Greece's partners in the Euro zone had to choose between two potential contagions. On one hand, if Greece defaulted, the crisis would quickly spread around Europe. On the other hand, if Greece were bailed out, what incentive would others have to be more responsible? Many thought that Greece had created its own problems through excessive spending and dishonest accounting. Greece, in this view, had to enact a severe austerity package and accept real pain before it should be bailed out.

Throughout the spring of 2010, a game of chicken ensued. The likely funders of a bailout, especially Germany, insisted that Greece enact a harsh austerity policy. German voters were angry that they were being asked to fund a bailout so that the Greek government could provide its workers with a lower retirement age than German employees received. Greek workers demonstrated in the streets against proposed austerity measures. Meanwhile, Greece's interest rates rose, Greece moved closer to default, and Spain and others looked increasingly shaky. Finally, in May, EU governments agreed to a bailout package of nearly $1 trillion. The hope was that such a massive commitment would create "shock and awe" that would restore investor confidence that no European state would default. Markets around the world quickly responded positively, but confidence about states' ability to pay their debts was shaken. In subsequent weeks, markets stumbled as people took a harder look at the long-term prospects for presumed pillars of the global economy like the United Kingdom and the United States. Can crises such as this one lead to a reversal of globalization or can states learn to handle such international crises more effectively?

The roots of the current world financial crisis lie in the globalization of trade and finance systems in recent decades. Increasing freedom to move money across borders has led to a vastly increased scope for investment in foreign countries, which can be a boon both to investors and to the economies in which they are investing. But because this money can move very quickly and because the amounts of money in the global marketplace dwarf those in any one domestic market, domestic markets can now quickly be overwhelmed by currency movements. Governments now have less ability to control domestic and international finance than at any time in history. A defining question today is whether it is possible to gain the benefits of financial globalization while avoiding the dangers.

Three Characteristics of Globalization

The term *globalization* is used by many people to mean many different (and sometimes contradictory) things. For the purposes of this text, **globalization** refers to a process in which international trade increases relative to domestic trade; in which the time it takes for goods, people, information, and money to flow across borders and the cost of moving them are decreasing; and in which the world is increasingly defined by a single market rather than by many separate markets.

globalization
A process in which international trade increases relative to domestic trade; in which the time it takes for goods, people, information, and money to flow across borders and the cost of moving them are decreasing; and in which the world is increasingly defined by single markets rather than by many separate markets.

First, perhaps the most basic aspect of globalization is the growing importance of international trade to local and domestic economies. For almost every country in the world, foreign trade is growing much faster than the domestic economy. The logical result is that over time, the portion of each country's economy that either is sold as exports or is bought as imports is growing. This is apparent not only at the level of economies, but even at the level of individuals. Anyone reading this book can simply look at his or her clothes,

Greeks protest austerity measures enacted in 2010 as a result of Greece's debt crisis.

Aristidis Vafeiadakis/Alamy

phone, or even food, and see from the labeling how much we all rely on imports today. Figure 10.1 shows that trade makes up an increasing share of many countries' economies.

Second, the cost and the time it takes to move almost anything around the world are falling. Lower transportation costs mean that price differentials in distant places can be exploited more easily than before. This is especially true of differential labor costs. Fifty years ago, it was difficult to take advantage of cheap labor located overseas because much of the savings in labor costs would be eaten up in the costs of transporting finished goods to markets. As transport costs fall relative to labor costs, it becomes easier to produce even low profit–margin goods wherever labor is cheapest. This accounts for the massive consumption by Americans of goods manufactured in Asia. In some cases, electronics components are manufactured with high-wage, high-skill labor in one country, shipped across the ocean for assembly in low-wage areas, and then shipped back across the ocean for consumption.

Not only goods and people, but money and investment also flow across borders in sums vastly larger than only a few years ago. The third and most far-reaching aspect of

Figure 10.1 For most countries, foreign trade comprises an ever-increasing share of the overall economy.

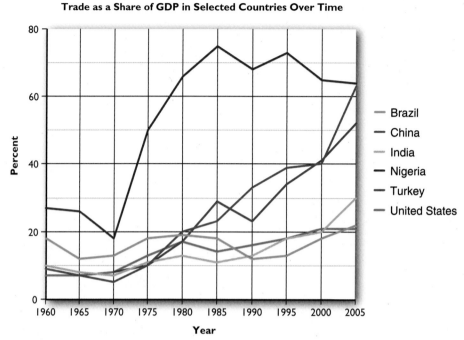

Trade as a Share of GDP in Selected Countries Over Time

Source: World Bank. http://ddp-ext.worldbank.org/ext/DDPQQ/member.do?method=getMembers&userid=1&queryId=135. Data collected into document.

globalization in the past two decades has been in financial flows. As recently as 1980, the amounts of currency being traded by private actors (banks and investment firms) were relatively small compared with those controlled by governments. As a result, governments had much influence over exchange rates. By the 1990s, trading by private actors exceeded the total currency reserves of governments. Currency trading now dwarfs foreign trade: In 2001, global exports were $5.7 trillion for the *year,* whereas currency trading averaged $1.25 trillion per *day.*[1] In this area, a change in amount (quantitative change) led to a change in the nature of the system (qualitative change). The role of states in setting foreign exchange rates was significantly weakened and that of markets was strengthened.

Those who view globalization as qualitatively new point to several developments as evidence.

- Private international financial transactions now dwarf the financial resources controlled by states, displacing states' ability to influence financial markets.

- States have much less ability to limit the movement of money and goods in and out of their territories, decreasing states' influence over their own economies.

- Firms can move resources and production around the world to find the most favorable conditions, maximizing their leverage over less mobile actors, such as states, local governments, and workers.

- Comparative advantage today is increasingly based not on natural resource endowments, but on factors such as technology, education, and network effects that can shift from one country to another, and on regulatory environments.

Together, these trends indicate that states have lost control over globalization. In previous eras, states could choose whether to decrease barriers to commerce. Today, the elimination of such barriers is a fact states must deal with, whether they like it or not.

Globalization of Trade

The Historical Context

International trade increased steadily in the decades leading up to World War I. However, there was no agreed-on international framework to facilitate international trade. Instead, trade agreements were made on a bilateral basis. World War I destroyed many of these trading relationships, as trading partners became military adversaries.

Efforts to rebuild international trade after World War I were hampered by a variety of factors, but most prominent was the **Great Depression**, which began just a decade after the war's end, in 1929, and was spurred in part by the policies adopted to cope with the aftermath of the war. Most states at the time responded to the decline in their economies by enacting protectionist measures, such as tariffs. The goal of these measures was to get consumers to purchase domestically produced goods rather than imports, thus providing business for domestic firms and workers. However, when every country followed this same policy, any gain in domestic consumption was outweighed by losses in export sales. Moreover, the overall efficiency of each economy suffered, as the gains from trade were forgone. As a

Figure 10.2 The flow of money across borders is rapidly increasing. The amount of money moved dwarfs the amount of goods and services, and the amount of money moved by private actors surpasses that controlled by governments.

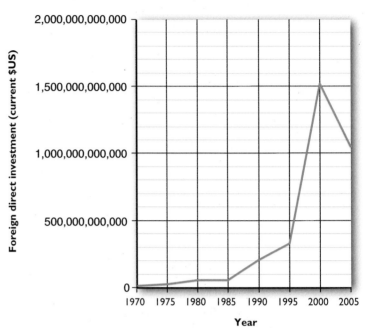

Source: World Bank. http://ddp-ext.worldbank.org/ext/DDPQQ/member.do?method=getMembers&userid

Hong Kong became a thriving port city within the British Empire in the nineteenth century.

Great Depression

The global depression that lasted from 1929 until World War II, during which the economies of the United States and Europe declined by as much as 25 percent. In economics, a decline in output of less than 10 percent is referred to as a "recession," while a deeper contraction is called a "depression."

Bretton Woods system

The system that guided economic arrangements among the advanced industrial states in the post-World War II era. It included the GATT, the fixed exchange rate system, the IMF, and the World Bank. Bretton Woods was a resort in New Hampshire where the negotiations took place.

General Agreement on Tariffs and Trade (GATT)

The main trade provision of the Bretton Woods system.

result, the measures taken to combat the depression made matters worse. It was difficult to see what any individual state could do to solve this problem. If one state chose to keep its markets open to foreign products, while others did not, the open state would face the worst of both worlds: loss of overseas markets without an increase in share of the domestic market. Thus, the prisoner's dilemma applies to trade policy. Prior to World War I, Great Britain had been so powerful that it could use its influence to prod others to lower barriers to trade. However, its financial and trading position was so weakened by World War I that this was no longer possible. In addition, the rise of nationalist doctrines tended to emphasize the competitive side of international trade at the expense of mutual gain.

ORIGINS OF THE BRETTON WOODS SYSTEM

Following World War II, conditions changed in important ways. The leading economic powers broadly agreed on the *purpose* of improving trade cooperation, and the United States had the *power* to push toward that end. First, leaders in many states perceived that rebuilding free trade was critical. Second, World War II had enormously shifted world economic power in favor of the United States. At the same time, U.S. attitudes toward international leadership had changed. The policy of isolationism, which had led the United States to shun the League of Nations and to stay out of World War II until the Pearl Harbor attack, had been discredited. Pearl Harbor had shown that isolationism would not protect the United States from attack, and the perceived menace of the Soviet Union convinced most Americans that a strong global actor was needed and that only the United States could play that role.

For these reasons, the United States and its allies met in 1944 to set up a new trading and financial system. The **Bretton Woods system** consisted of both trade and financial provisions, which were intended to promote free trade and increase wealth around the world. These were seen not only as worthwhile goals in general, but also as a way of defeating communism and promoting peace. The main trade provision was known as the **General Agreement on Tariffs and Trade (GATT)**. Initiated in 1946, the GATT lasted until 1995, when it was replaced by a stronger version embodied in the World Trade Organization (WTO).

The economic power of the United States played an important role in formation of the Bretton Woods system. Not every country agreed to all the provisions that the United States proposed. Skeptics (and realists) argue that free trade was not in the interest of everyone, but was supported by the United States because it served by U.S. interests The United States was in a favorable competitive position, and would gain economically and politically from greater free trade. Because the United States controlled half of the world economy, it could provide strong incentives to do things its way. Any country that was excluded from the system or that chose not to participate would find itself disadvantaged in U.S. markets and investment.

THE PRINCIPLE OF NONDISCRIMINATION

The mechanism of the GATT was simple. First, members agreed that they would use tariffs rather than other methods (such as quotas) as their primary means of protection. Second, they would work over time to

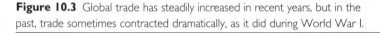

Figure 10.3 Global trade has steadily increased in recent years, but in the past, trade sometimes contracted dramatically, as it did during World War I.

World Exports, 1870–1998

Source: From http://www.treasury.govt.nz/publications/research-policy/wp/2007/07-05/03.htm

slowly decrease the level of those tariffs. These reductions were carried out in nine "rounds" held over the succeeding decades.

The revolutionary aspect of the GATT was that it produced an entirely new principle guiding tariff levels. Prior to World War II, trade agreements were conducted bilaterally (between two states) and were based on the principle of **reciprocity.** Reciprocity meant that two states would agree to have the same tariffs on each other's goods. That seemed fair enough. However, it meant that any country might have many different tariffs for the same good, depending on where that good came from. This was economically inefficient because it meant that the firms seeking to sell a particular good in a particular country were not all competing on the same terms. This undermined competition, removing an important impetus to increased efficiency. Competition to negotiate more advantageous terms led to intense competition.

The GATT was based on the principle of **nondiscrimination**, rather than reciprocity. Nondiscrimination meant that a given state's tariff on a particular good would be the same for all GATT members. Giving one state a better deal than others, in return for some mutual concession, was no longer permitted. If a state lowered a tariff for one GATT member, it was obliged to lower the tariff for all members. This principle was also known as the "most-favored-nation" principle, meaning that every GATT member would be treated as well as the "most-favored nation." The key achievement of the GATT was that it put all foreign producers on equal footing. This facilitated competition according to comparative advantage and hence improved overall efficiency. Moreover, it tended to produce, over time, a decline in tariff levels, slowly bringing foreign and domestic producers ever closer to an equal footing.

"EMBEDDED LIBERALISM"

Why were tariffs not eliminated completely, if this was the ultimate goal? Why were some states (notably the United States) willing to allow nonreciprocity, which meant that their markets were more open to others than others' markets were to them? The short answer is that the deviations from free trade were viewed as politically necessary in order to cushion its effects.

To open up all markets in the GATT countries to unlimited international competition was seen as being too disruptive for domestic economies, and in particular to those who would lose their jobs to competition from overseas producers. Today we see a similar issue in debates concerning the "outsourcing" of jobs and the movement of industries from rich countries to poorer ones.

Especially in the aftermath of the Great Depression, and in an era in which socialist and communist political parties were quite popular in Britain, France, and Italy, the responsibility of

Figure 10.4 Overall, tariffs have steadily been eliminated since World War II. Many see this decline in tariffs as largely responsible for increases in global trade and overall wealth.

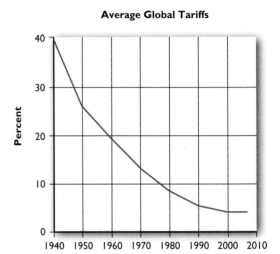

Average Global Tariffs

Source: Charles W. Kegley, *World Politics, Trends and Transformations* 11th ed. (Boston: Wadsworth, 2006). p. 324.

reciprocity

An arrangement whereby two states agree to have the same tariffs on each other's goods.

nondiscrimination

A principle guiding tariff policy that requires a country to apply equal tariffs on all of its trading partners; also referred to as the "most-favored-nation" principle.

Workers at GM's Opel automobile factory in Bochum, Germany, protest GM's plans to cut its workforce in Germany. The cuts were part of GM's efforts to regain profitability.

the government to ensure that workers had jobs was taken much more seriously than it is today. One lesson of the Great Depression had been that the market will not always fix itself if left alone. The modern welfare state represented a new social contract in which government was expected to intervene in the economy to ensure prosperity. Thus, the arrangements of the Bretton Woods system, including the GATT, were a compromise between economic liberalism (letting the market work to increase wealth) and state intervention to soften the impact that the market might have on domestic economies in general and on specific industries. This compromise came to be labeled "embedded liberalism" because it placed liberalism within the broader goals of governments.[2] Expanding trade and fostering economic efficiency were never the sole purposes of the Bretton Woods system.

FROM THE GATT TO THE WTO

The GATT was widely seen as a success, but it had problems that led to an increasing desire to fundamentally revise the agreement and to strengthen some parts. In 1995, after more than a decade of haggling, the GATT was replaced by the WTO. The advent of the WTO has not only *not* solved all the problems with the GATT, it has also provoked some new dissatisfactions.

A central problem with the GATT was that it only covered certain classes of products. Agriculture was left entirely out of the original agreement and was treated only in a limited way in subsequent rounds. The reasons for this were political. In many countries, agricultural interests are extremely powerful politically, and agriculture is seen as being essential not only to the food supply, but to an entire way of life. Thus, the shared purpose on freeing trade did not include agricultural products.

The GATT did not cover trade in services, such as insurance, banking, and consulting. As the service economy increasingly displaced the manufacturing economy in the last quarter of the twentieth century, an ever-larger part of international trade was not covered by the GATT. Leading service firms put pressure on governments to reduce discrimination in services. This issue was pushed primarily by the United States, where many leading service firms were located.

States increasingly enacted "nontariff barriers" to trade. Although a guiding principle of the GATT was to channel protection into tariffs, other measures persisted. Moreover, as tariff levels dropped, nontariff barriers that might not have been noticed previously became relatively more powerful. Almost every country succumbed to the temptation to protect its producers in one way or another. There are a variety of nontariff barriers to trade—such as health regulations—to circumvent the intent of the GATT without technically violating it.

- Quotas (limits on the number of an item that can be imported)

- "Voluntary export restraints" (VERs), adopted when one country threatens restrictions on trade and an exporting country "voluntarily" agrees to limit exports, in order to avoid the imposition of more stringent limits

- Domestic content laws, popular in the automobile industry, which state that to be sold as a "domestic" product (and therefore be exempt from tariffs), a certain percentage of the components in a final product must be assembled domestically

Bdb/ImageStste/Jupiter Images

The Swiss government is one of many that spends great sums on agricultural subsidies to preserve its rural villages. Agriculture as a sector has been highly resistant to efforts to reduce barriers to trade.

- Health and environmental regulations, which can easily be written in ways that give an advantage to domestically produced products over imports

What could be done when one country enacted a nontariff barrier that others claimed violated the agreement? The dispute resolution mechanism under the GATT was slow and contained weak enforcement measures. This frustrated smaller countries, which found that the United States had much more leverage in making them accept its position on various matters. But it also frustrated the United States because, as a leading exporter, it found itself the main target of nontariff barriers around the world. Some of these could be removed through political pressure, but doing so took considerable time and effort. As disputes over nontariff barriers increased, so did frustration with the weakness of enforcement mechanisms.

THE WTO

To address the problems inherent in the GATT, 117 states signed a new agreement in 1994 founding the WTO. The main provisions of the GATT were incorporated into the WTO, and a General Agreement on Trade in Services (GATS) was added. In return for greater protection of intellectual property rights in the developing world, the advanced economies agreed to eliminate protection for their textile industries by 2005. Agriculture was the main sticking point in the negotiations, with the United States, the EU, and Japan reluctant to open their markets to international competition. Only limited cuts were made in agricultural tariffs, which continue to be the main area of dispute.

The main change in moving to the WTO was the development of an enforcement mechanism that allows states to challenge each other's laws. If the laws are found to be barriers to trade that violate the agreement, then the WTO can assign penalties against the offending states. These penalties consist of countertariffs that the injured state can enact to offset the damage. To supporters of free trade, this was an essential development, providing a means to fight back against the increasing use of various domestic regulations as nontariff barriers. However, many were concerned that the new measures would undermine state sovereignty and could be used to overturn important environmental, health, and labor legislation.

DISPUTE RESOLUTION IN THE WTO

The WTO dispute settlement process is intended not simply to judge right and wrong, but to mediate conflict. The first step, therefore, is consultation, to see if the parties can reach an agreement. If they cannot, the case is then referred to a panel, the members of which are chosen with the approval of the parties (or, if they cannot agree, by the larger Dispute Resolution Body). The findings of the panel are then provided to the parties and to the Dispute Resolution Body, where they can be overturned only by a unanimous vote. This is the most important contrast with the GATT, where only a single vote, even from the accused party, could reject the panel's findings. The expectation is that once a panel finding has been accepted, the offending state will change its behavior. If it doesn't, however, there are provisions for the aggrieved party to levy trade sanctions, both to compensate it for its losses and to encourage the offender to comply with the ruling. This process does not work quickly, and cases sometimes take years, but the same is true in many lawsuits in domestic courts.

A famous case is that between the EU and the United States concerning the competition between the airline firms Boeing (based in the United States) and Airbus (based in Europe). The United States brought a complaint against Europe, arguing that low-interest loans and other subsidies reduced Airbus's cost, and constituted an unfair barrier to free trade. The EU brought a case in return, claiming that U.S. military contracts with Boeing provided an unfair indirect subsidy, both financially and in technology development. In 2010, WTO dispute resolution panels found both sides' accusations valid and the dispute continued.

The History of Globalization

Skeptics about globalization point out that in historical context, much of this phenomenon is not new. If globalization is viewed as a process in which the costs of transport and communication decrease and the division of labor widens geographically, then the process has been in place for centuries. "Essentially, the basic motivations that propelled humans to connect with others—the urge to profit by trading, the drive to spread religious belief, the desire to exploit new lands, and the ambition to dominate others through armed might—all had been assembled by 6000 BCE to start the process we now call globalization."[1] From this perspective, the scope of the "global" economy has been spreading for centuries. Several examples help illustrate this perspective.

■ **Migration:** *Homo sapiens* originated in Africa and spent the next 50,000 years spreading out to inhabit almost the entire globe. The waves of migration that brought the Huns, Magyars, Mongols, Goths, and others out of the plains of Asia into Europe in the first millennium wrought extraordinary political,

economic, and cultural changes. The history of the western hemisphere is, in many respects, a story of successive waves of migration from Asia, Europe, and Africa.

■ **Trade:** Much early interaction was driven by the desire to trade more profitably, just as it is today. The Silk Road, connecting Europe to China via Central Asia, was an important commercial route from the eleventh through the fourteenth centuries. Made famous in particular by the Venetian Marco Polo (1254–1324), the Silk Road first brought Chinese noodles to Italy, where they would be called spaghetti. A primary impetus of the Age of Exploration was the desire to find a quicker, cheaper trade route from Europe to East Asia. Trade continued to grow nearly constantly up until World War I. Some scholars, therefore, see the most recent boom in international trade not as a new development, but as a return to the normal course of affairs that was interrupted by the great conflicts of the twentieth century.

PHOTO © ISTOCKPHOTO

The United States is both the most common filer of complaints and the most common target of complaints by others. In late 2009, Brazil won a ruling that U.S. subsidies to cotton farmers unfairly hurt Brazilian exports. The ruling allowed Brazil to retaliate by imposing tariffs against U.S. exports, proportional to U.S. cotton subsidies. Brazil targeted not only U.S. cotton exports, the source of its complaint, but also U.S. automobiles, and threatened to target software as well in an effort to increase domestic pressure on the U.S. government to change its policies.[3]

Contemporary Challenges

The WTO agreement has achieved many of the major goals advanced by its supporters. Global trade has continued to grow, and nontariff barriers have come under attack. States have eagerly sought membership in the WTO, and no state has ever left the group. As of mid-2010, the WTO had 151 members, and many other states were seeking to become members.

However, a great deal of dissatisfaction remains concerning the international trading system, leading some to question whether the agreement will continue to play an influential

- **The Food Economy:** Genetically modified crops and shopping mall Chinese food are only the most recent in a long line of agricultural transplants with far-reaching consequences. Some argue that a key source of the industrial revolution in Europe was that labor was freed up by the importation from South America of the potato, which could provide more calories per unit of land than existing crops. The transplant of the rubber plant from Brazil to Southeast Asia made possible the automobile boom of the twentieth century (by providing rubber for tires). The importation of strains of wheat from Central Europe enabled the Great Plains of the United States and Canada (previously known as the "Great American Desert") to become the world's breadbasket.

- **Speed of communication:** The most far-reaching shift in communication in history may not have been the emergence of the Internet but the invention of the telegraph, which introduced nearly instant communication in the mid-nineteenth century. From this point on, the price of stocks in the New York market could be monitored around the country, leading to the rapidly moving financial markets we are familiar with today. In 1858, New York and London were connected by telegraph, spurring a celebration that nearly burned down City Hall in New York. The increase in speed of communication that occurred with the move from the hand-delivered letter to the telegraph was as dramatic as the increases later provided by the emergence of faxes and the Internet.

Critical Thinking Questions

1. Do you agree with the argument that globalization is not really new?
2. What key factors make globalization today fundamentally different from what occurred in the past?
3. What component of globalization (trade, migration, culture, and so on) do you see as being most important in the coming decade?

[1]Nayan Chanda, as quoted in William Grimes, "The Rise of Globalization, A Story of Human Desires," *New York Times*, May 30, 2007, p. B6. The quotation is from Chanda's book *Bound Together: How Traders, Preachers, Adventurers and Warriors Shaped Globalization* (New Haven, CT Yale University Press, 2007).

role in the future. Among the problems facing the WTO is the continuing impasse over agricultural protectionism. An important WTO meeting in Cancun, Mexico, in late 2003, broke up prematurely when 22 developing states walked out, dissatisfied with the lack of progress on agricultural tariffs. This disagreement has prevented further progress on other issues. Having given advanced industrial economies access to their markets for manufactured goods and services, developing countries are increasingly unwilling to tolerate what they see as an unequal arrangement in which North American and European governments subsidize their agricultural producers, undermining the competitiveness of developing countries' agricultural exports. Many scholars and policy analysts have argued that reduction of agricultural subsidies by wealthy states is the single most important policy that can be used to promote Third World development.

THE DIFFUSION OF ECONOMIC AND POLITICAL POWER

As the preceding discussion indicates, poorer countries are now playing a prominent role in negotiations over world trading arrangements, largely due to the diffusion of economic power. The U.S. share of global GDP has declined from roughly 50 percent when the GATT was formed to roughly 20 percent today. Many scholars invoke hegemonic stability theory to explain the growth in free trade after World War II. In this view, barriers to increased free trade can only be overcome when a single state is powerful enough to persuade (through threats and incentives) other states to go along.[4] Since the 1980s, adherents of this view have fretted about what would happen in an era in which the United States power eroded.[5] Today, the United States is still the largest economy in the world, but it now controls only a relatively small percentage of global GDP and only one vote of over 150 in the WTO.

Critics of hegemonic stability theory point out that most of those advocating this theory happen to be Americans. From the perspective of developing countries, the diffusion of power is good in that they may now be able to force the leading economic states to make some concessions, specifically in regard to agriculture. To the extent that economic power matters, there is no doubt that it is more evenly distributed than in the past. Whether or not this situation will inhibit further collaboration remains to be seen.

REGIONALIZATION: FREE TRADE AREAS

Regional trading agreements have proliferated in recent years. The model for all such agreements is the enormously successful European Union, although most regions do not envision such extensive political integration. The NAFTA between the United States, Canada, and Mexico, which took effect in 1994, is a significant example of such agreements. Within a free trade area (FTA), there are no tariffs at all, and efforts are made to limit other barriers to trade. As a result, members of the FTA have an advantage over those outside, even if those outside are members of WTO. In other words, barriers may be low for WTO members, but they are even lower or nonexistent for partners in an FTA.

Attempting to build on the success of NAFTA, the United States has supported expanding that group into a Free Trade Area of the Americas (FTAA), which would include Latin America, one of the fastest growing economic regions in the world. In Asia, there has been talk of expanding the Asian-Pacific Economic Cooperation (APEC) group into some sort of regional FTA. However, the fact that at least two states in the region (China and Japan) are regarded as potential security threats to the others inhibits willingness to collaborate, as does the wide range of forms of government. In the former Soviet Union, Russia has sought to build an FTA around the Commonwealth of Independent States, but the hesitation of key states (most notably Ukraine) has hampered that effort.

Supporters of free trade have mixed opinions on the virtues of regional FTAs. To some, regional trade agreements, because they represent more free trade than the status quo, are a step in the right direction and may be a stepping stone to increased global trade cooperation. Others fear that regional FTAs are a poor substitute for greater global liberalization. In this view, regionalism is fragmenting the global trading system. Some fear the rise of a series of regional trade blocs, each dominated by a large wealthy country that has privileged access to the less developed countries in that region and a strong bargaining position relative to them. This might resemble the system two centuries ago, when the leading economic powers in Europe carried on much of their trade, not with each other, but within the colonial empires they had constructed.

COMPETING INTEREST GROUPS

The debate over the WTO, free trade, and globalization pits those who follow liberal trade theory, as described in Chapter 9, against those who support economic structuralist and realist views. Yet, on another level, the debate takes place within interest group politics, setting those who stand to gain from freer trade against those who stand to lose. As discussed in Chapter 5, interest groups are often involved in lobbying on foreign policy, and especially on foreign economic policy. Decisions on tariff levels and FTAs can mean billions of dollars in gains or losses for different economic actors, whether they are firms, industries, workers, or even localities.

It is misleading, therefore, to think about trade politics only in terms of what national governments want, for every government is subject to competing domestic interests, pushing and pulling it in different directions. For example, a wide range of actors lobbied the U.S. government prior to its 2001 decision to raise tariffs against imported steel. American steel firms lobbied strongly for increased tariffs, which would allow them to sell steel at higher prices. Workers and labor unions also supported the tariffs because protection from foreign competition would protect their jobs and wages. The automobile industry and other industries that use steel as an input lobbied against higher tariffs, since they would be paying a higher price for steel. Tariff increases were also opposed by a broad range of economic actors who saw free trade in general as being in their interest. They were concerned not only that the principle of free trade would be undermined, but also that other countries would retaliate against the United States.

Economists have developed a general theory to explain which economic actors tend to seek protectionism and which tend to support free trade. Actors who control inputs that are plentiful locally (such as labor, land, or capital) tend to support free trade. Because such inputs are plentiful locally, they are likely to be cheap, and free trade will open markets for these cheap inputs. Actors who control inputs that are locally scarce tend to oppose free trade. The local scarcity of these inputs allows those who control them to charge premium prices, and competition from abroad would reduce those prices. In the United States, where capital is plentiful but cheap labor is relatively scarce, financial interests support free trade, as do manufacturers who can move production overseas. Labor and those industries that cannot easily move production tend to oppose free trade. In contrast, in countries where land is scarce, such as Japan, agricultural interests oppose free trade. In much of the Third World, where labor is plentiful, labor and industries that rely on abundant labor support free trade. Although this simple rule does not explain all trade preferences, it provides a general idea about how free trade can affect different economic actors within the same country differently.

One group of actors rarely gets mentioned in discussions of free trade: consumers. This group plays an insignificant role in trade politics of trade, despite the fact that consumers benefit massively from free trade in the form of lower prices for the goods they buy. Because consumers are a diffuse group, they are not as well organized as "special" interests. Protectionism preserves the jobs of a relatively small number of workers (and the profits made by their companies) at the expense of an increase in cost to a vast number of consumers. Each threatened worker or firm has a huge incentive to lobby for protection, while each consumer has a smaller interest, even if the total damage done to consumers is great.

Free trade advocates cite statistics indicating that every job saved by protectionism costs consumers far more in lost savings. According to the **U.S. Federal Reserve System**, "Even when they temporarily stave off job losses, trade barriers are costly. For example, trade protection saved 216 U.S. jobs in the production of benzenoid chemicals, used in suntan lotion and other products—but at a cost of nearly $1.4 million per worker. Because the chemical workers earn a fraction of the protectionist toll, it would cost far less to simply pay them not to work!"[6] A more efficient policy, in this view, is to allow

Irish farmers protest against reduced agricultural tariffs outside the European parliament in Strasbourg, France.

U.S. Federal Reserve System

The central bank of the United States. The "Fed," as it is known, controls interest rates and the supply of currency to promote economic growth while preventing inflation.

the market to do its job but to use taxing and social policy to compensate and retrain displaced workers.

How much harm should be done to consumers and taxpayers in order to protect workers and firms? This was the central question in debates over protecting U.S. car companies as they faced bankruptcy in early 2009. The Obama administration was concerned that the demise of U.S. car firms would cause the failure many other firms, such as suppliers, driving unemployment up permanently. The fact that auto workers provide a historically strong democratic voting bloc in pivotal states also likely played a role in the administration's thinking. This is the kind of challenge that comes between the theory and practice of free trade.

TRADE POLICY AS A "TWO-LEVEL GAME"

For national level policy makers considering trade agreements, therefore, two sets of negotiations take place simultaneously, one with other countries and one with domestic constituents. A popular metaphor for this process is the "two-level game," in which a solution must be found that works at both levels simultaneously.[7] This is often difficult—and sometimes impossible. Leaders cannot always find a solution that satisfies both international partners and domestic constituents. In such cases, domestic constituents nearly always win out because they will determine whether the politicians in question remain in office. In many cases, domestic interests themselves are in conflict. The cagey negotiator can try to convince trade partners that he or she cannot make further concessions because domestic actors (such as the legislature) will not permit them.

Globalization of Finance

Compared with changes in the international trading system, changes in the international financial system have been much more far-reaching. The international financial system has experienced two revolutions in recent decades. First, in 1971, the United States single-handedly ended the system of fixed exchange rates that had prevailed since 1946. Second, in the 1980s and 1990s, governments lifted limits on capital movements, paving the way for the massive international flows of capital today. In quantitative terms, the growth in the movement of money around the world has reached astonishing levels. In foreign exchange markets, nearly two *trillion* dollars worth of currencies are traded *every day*. It is now easy for firms and individuals to buy stock in foreign countries and to sell it just as quickly. Thus, the amount of cross-border **portfolio investment**—investing by purchasing stocks rather than physical assets—has skyrocketed. These changes bring the risk of financial crises, such as the one that occurred in Asia in 1997, that can spread quickly from one country to another.

portfolio investment
Investments made by purchasing stocks rather than physical assets.

The Monetary "Trilemma"

In deciding how to approach international monetary policy, states historically have had three goals.

- **Predictable exchange rates:** Fixed exchange rates facilitate free trade and investment by eliminating the risk that fluctuations in exchange rates will destroy anticipated profits. Stability and predictability are accomplished most precisely by fixing exchange rates.

- **Free movement of capital:** Free capital movement allows investors to invest where returns are greatest and provides poor economies access to much-needed foreign investment.

■ **Autonomous monetary policy:** Governments use monetary policy to respond to changes in their domestic economies (raising and lowering interest rates to regulate growth and inflation), without regard for policy choices in other countries or international markets.

It is a fundamental rule in international finance that it is impossible to attain all three goals simultaneously because economies are dynamic and always changing. This inability to attain all three goals is sometimes referred to as a *trilemma*, because states, and groups of states, must decide which one of the goals to forsake when they devise different exchange rate mechanisms and international financial practices.[8]

It is possible, for example, for states to fix their exchange rates and to have complete capital mobility. But the only way to maintain fixed exchange rates, if currencies can move freely, is to alter domestic monetary policy according to the dictates of the international market, rather than according to domestic policy goals. As demand for currencies varies, states must raise and lower interest rates or buy and sell currency in order to maintain the fixed exchange rate. In such a system, interest rates cannot be used to control domestic economic growth and inflation, as they generally are today. Such a system existed prior to World War I and was known as the gold standard.

Alternatively, it is possible to maintain free international flows of capital and domestic monetary autonomy if exchange rates are allowed to float. Essentially, that is the system in use today in most of the world. The price paid for domestic monetary autonomy is that fluctuations in exchange rates can seriously undermine international trade and cause other problems as well.

Who Pays the Costs of Adjustment?

In every system, the central question is how imbalances in currency flows are addressed. What happens when, in response to imbalances in imports or differences in investment opportunities, the demand for one country's currency rises relative to others? In a floating exchange rate system with free capital flow, imbalances are corrected through changes in the currency exchange rates. Some countries will see their currencies rise or fall in value, with predictable effects on importers and exporters. In a system in which capital movement is limited, the inability to move huge sums of capital helps limit instability, but currency imbalances continue to occur as a consequence of trade, so that states must alter domestic policies and limit trade to achieve balance. In a system without domestic policy autonomy, domestic economies are forced to absorb the changes emanating from the international system. Each system puts the burdens of adjustment on different actors. Much of the politics of international finance concerns states' desire to force the **costs of adjustment** onto others.

costs of adjustment
Financial burdens that are imposed on a country as a result of changes in the international economic system.

Evolution of the International Financial System

Since the late nineteenth century, three different international financial systems have existed, separated by two long intervening periods in which states struggled to create a new system after the previous one had collapsed.[9] These five periods are summarized in Table 10.1.

THE CLASSICAL GOLD STANDARD, 1870–1914

In the system that prevailed until World War I, every major currency was valued in terms of a certain weight of gold. Because currencies were fixed to gold, there was great stability in their exchange rates. This stability facilitated the steady increase in trade and international investment prior to World War I. In terms of the "trilemma" of policy choices, the

The Geography Connection

The World Is Flat. Or Is It Spiky?

Many maps (including almost all of those in this book) consider country-level statistics because these are easiest to find and to map. However, this perspective misses a great deal of variation that is evident when statistics are presented using other scales. Consider these maps, which measure different aspects of economic and scientific activity.[1]

Critical Thinking Questions

1. What issues arise when you look at data aggregated by square kilometer rather than by country?
2. How does "globalization" look different from this perspective?
3. How concerned should people be about the vast differences in conditions displayed in these maps?

Population

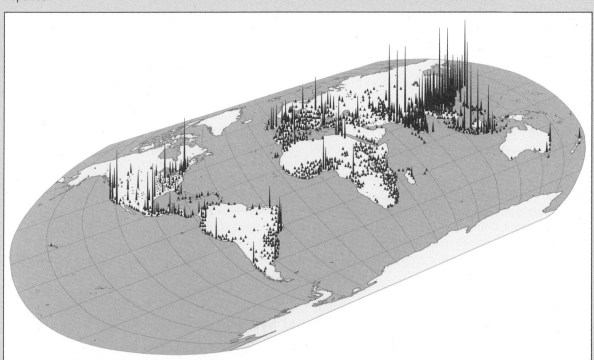

Source: From October 2005 *Atlantic Monthly*

[1] The argument that the world is "flat" can be found in Thomas Friedman, *The World Is Flat: A Brief History of the Twenty-First Century* (New York: Farrar Straus and Giroux, 2005). For a competing analysis, see Pankaj Ghemawat, "Why the World Isn't Flat," *Foreign Policy* No. 159 (March/April 2007), pp. 54-60.

PHOTO © ISTOCKPHOTO

Light Emissions

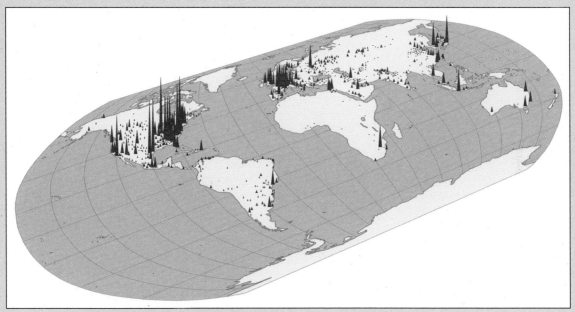

Source: From October 2005 *Atlantic Monthly*

Patents

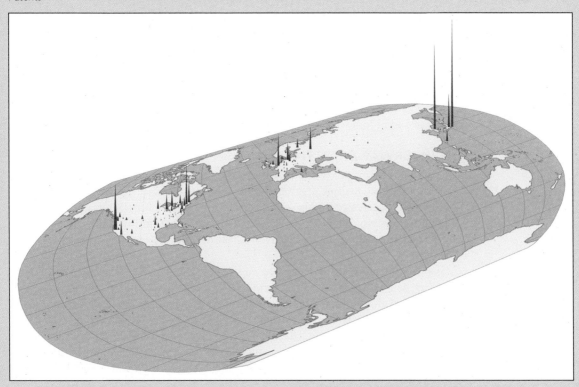

Source: From October 2005 *Atlantic Monthly*

Table 10.1 Systems of International Financial Arrangements

System	Goals Emphasized	Goals Sacrificed	Who Maintained the System, and How?	Who Adjusted?
System I: Classical Gold Standard (1870–1914)	Fixed exchange rates to facilitate trade	Domestic autonomy	Great Britain; through trade and financial dominance	States whose currencies deviated from established rates; all adjusted to Great Britain
Intervening Period: Interwar Era (1914–1944)	Domestic economic autonomy	Exchange rate stability, capital mobility	No one; system crashed in Great Depression	States and firms; states dominated markets
System II: Bretton Woods (1946–1971)	Stable exchange rates to facilitate trade; domestic autonomy (embedded liberalism)	Capital mobility	Bretton Woods institutions, especially the IMF backed by U.S. power	States whose currencies deviated from established rates; all adjusted to the United States
Intervening Period: Post–Bretton Woods (1971–1980s)	Maintain some exchange stability with greater domestic autonomy; increasing capital mobility	Pursuit of all goals simultaneously meant none were fully achieved	Negotiations between major trading states (G-7); maintenance depended on agreement	States sought to force each other to adjust; the United States could no longer avoid adjustment; states dominated markets
System III: Global Capital Mobility (1980s–)	Capital mobility	Domestic autonomy	No one; markets are expected to provide equilibrium	States and firms; markets dominate states

gold standard

A system in which each currency represents a specific weight of gold. This facilitates stability but is highly inflexible.

gold standard prioritized fixed exchange rates and the free flow of capital, at the expense of domestic monetary autonomy.

The strength of this system was its stability and predictability. But because each country's currency was linked to gold, there was no capacity at all to devise domestic monetary policy. The gold standard functioned as well as it did, most agree, because of the leading role played by the British government and British banks. The government of Britain was willing to lend money to governments that were experiencing short-term imbalances in their payments. By acting as "lender of last resort," Britain ensured that small crises did not spread and become big ones.

THE INTERWAR ERA, 1914–1944

The economic demands of World War I caused all the major countries to abandon the gold standard and instead to print large amounts of currency to finance the war effort. Moreover, the war severely weakened Britain's financial position. Both of these factors undermined the gold standard system. The solution, in the eyes of many, was for the United States, which had become the dominant financial player, to take over Britain's role in financing the world economy.

The United States, however, embraced isolationism instead. When German inability to pay debts associated with World War I threatened other countries' financial systems, the United States refused to finance a new loan to avoid crisis. Moreover, citizens and governments were no longer willing to endure economic recession and depression as the price for international financial stability. Shared purpose no longer existed. The major economic powers sought to force the costs of economic adjustment onto one another. The result was financial instability, which exacerbated the Great Depression.

THE BRETTON WOODS SYSTEM, 1946–1971

Following World War II, the United States had the power and the will to lead a new international financial system. It embraced internationalism, aimed both at avoiding the mistakes that had led to World War II and at heading off competition from the Soviet Union. However, the purpose of economic policy had changed in favor of state intervention in the economy for the purposes of creating economic stability and guaranteeing welfare. There would be no return to the gold standard. Instead, the United States and its partners pursued "embedded liberalism," a compromise between the desire to facilitate international trade and the need to give domestic governments latitude to govern their economies.

In terms of the trilemma of policy choices, the Bretton Woods system opted for fixed exchange rates and domestic monetary autonomy at the expense of the free flow of capital across borders. The system had several key components.

Children play with blocks made from German currency, 1923. Hyperinflation made the currency nearly worthless.

- The price of the U.S. dollar was fixed to gold at $35 per ounce. In some respects, this was a return to the "gold standard," but there was a key difference: the United States continued to issue more dollars in order to facilitate economic expansion.

- The prices of other currencies were fixed to the U.S. dollar. This provided the stability of fixed exchange rates. It also meant that other states had to adjust to changes in world economy (for example, some economies growing faster than others), while the United States, as the standard setter, never had to adjust.

- All countries placed limits on the import and export of capital. Imbalances in financial flows would occur primarily as a result of trade imbalances, which limited the size of the potential problem.

The IMF was created to help the system overcome imbalances. Shorter-term imbalances were handled with loans. IMF aid for longer term balances came with strings attached: states were forced to alter domestic economic policies to reduce monetary imbalances. These "strings" were widely resented because the austerity they required could throw a domestic economy into recession, and because all of the cost of adjustment fell onto states running a current account deficit. The virtue of the Bretton Woods system was that it found a compromise that allowed for the expansion of international trade (facilitated by stable exchange rates) while allowing an extensive degree of domestic autonomy (facilitated by limited capital movement, IMF adjustment assistance, and periodic changes in exchange rates). However, strains inherent in the system eventually led to its demise.

In the Bretton Woods system, adjustment to imbalances was forced largely onto states running trade and current account deficits. As long as the states in question were willing to adjust, and the amount of adjustment needed was limited, this worked. But by the 1960s, the biggest problem in the system was the United States. U.S. spending on fighting the Cold War sent large amounts of U.S. currency flowing out of the country. The number of dollars held in foreign hands grew much faster than the supply of gold backing them. In return for the U.S. military and political role in facing off against the Soviet Union, key U.S. allies agreed to hold those dollars, rather than redeeming them and diminishing U.S. gold reserves. As this "dollar overhang" increased, it became clear that all dollars could never be redeemed at $35 per ounce of gold. Implicitly then, those holding dollars abroad were subsidizing the U.S. economy and foreign policy. In other words, the costs of adjustment, which were typically forced onto the deficit country, were not forced onto the United States when it was the deficit country.

In the late 1960s, three developments brought the problem to a crisis. First, the combination of the Vietnam War and the "Great Society" antipoverty programs increased the U.S. budget deficit substantially and pushed the current account deficit even higher. Second, as the "dollar overhang" grew, investors and governments abroad became less willing to finance it. Finally, international objections to the Vietnam War undermined U.S. moral authority, and other states saw less reason to hold dollars as "payoff" for the U.S. role combating the Soviet Union. By the early 1970s, redemptions of dollars from abroad for U.S. gold increased, as others sought to force adjustment back onto the United States.

In 1971, U.S. President Richard Nixon announced that the United States would no longer redeem dollars for gold, and that henceforth the dollar would be allowed to float against other currencies. The Bretton Woods era was over. Without the U.S. commitment to the price of the dollar in terms of gold, the fixed exchange regime was dead. Since that time, currency prices have fluctuated according to the supply and demand for each currency.

THE POST-BRETTON WOODS SYSTEM, 1971–1980s

With no agreed-on mechanism to determine who would bear the costs of adjustment, there was a danger in the post-Bretton Woods era that each state would try to force the costs onto others and that the result would be the sort of mutually defeating policies that had existed in the 1930s. Moreover, the ability of the various states to conduct independent domestic economic policies was now threatened. One country's decisions on interest rates and on monetary policy could now substantially affect exchange rates, which in turn could create negative economic effects in other countries.

As a result, the leaders of the biggest economies tried to agree on what exchange rates they would aim for and what measures they would take to achieve them. These discussions became institutionalized in the form of the Group of Seven leading economies, called the "G-7." Augmented now by Russia to form the G-8 (and by many others in the G-20) the group still meets to coordinate economic policies.

The post–Bretton Woods international monetary system was a mixture of coordinated government interventions, unilateral government policies, and market forces. In terms of the trilemma of policy choices, it included partly floating exchange rates, limits on capital movements, and a moderate degree of domestic policy autonomy. Exchange rates were "partly fixed" because they were only partly controlled by markets. When exchange rates were within ranges that governments found acceptable, they were left alone. But when a particular currency was viewed as too weak or too strong, governments sometimes intervened in markets (buying and selling currencies) to alter the price.

GLOBAL CAPITAL MOBILITY

In the 1980s and 1990s, an increasing number of states removed the restrictions on capital flows that had been part of every state's policies since World War II. These shifts in policy to allow capital to flow freely were not made as part of any international agreement. Rather, they have occurred as individual states have decided, one by one, to drop their capital controls. Why have states removed controls on capital movement?

First, in terms of interest group politics, actors who controlled a lot of capital (investment banks and corporations hoping to invest abroad) put pressure on governments to allow freer movement. For states in which finance was an important business, liberalization was seen as an economic opportunity (think of the economic benefits to New York City of being a leading financial center). The export of financial services, and of

The Policy Connection

Stimulus versus Debt Reduction: Domestic Policy and International Politics

Globalization has made it increasingly difficult for states to maintain completely independent economic policies. Policy changes in one country cause economic effects that spill over into others. These connections become particularly worrisome in economic crises, where disaster can spread from one economy to the next, and where one state's anticrisis measure can undermine others' economies. In 2010 a dispute emerged among major Western countries concerning the relative importance of stimulating their economies out of recession and containing the growth of their debt. Economic stimulus packages, like those enacted in the United States and many other countries in 2009, are based on fiscal policy: if the government spends more than it takes in through taxes, the net effect is to inject money into the economy, helping end recession. But to spend more than it takes in, the government must borrow. In 2009, many leading industrial states (Japan, the United Kingdom, the United States) agreed that a fiscal stimulus was necessary, while Germany, historically more conservative, was less convinced. Those favoring stimulus argued that for it to work, governments needed to join together. Globalization meant that the effects of any state's stimulus would "spill" outside its borders, diluting the effects on the home economy. Thus, if only one or a few states adopted stimulus packages, the effect might be insufficient.

In 2010, however, the tension sharpened as the Greek debt crisis made two things clear. First, financial markets were beginning to doubt the ability of governments to pay back their debts. This could undermine recovery, increase borrowing costs, and lead to debt crisis, as Greece experienced. Second, such a crisis could severely damage the economies even in countries that did not overborrow, since their banks held many of the loans.

In the United States, there was a fierce debate, with President Barack Obama and many liberals worried that a deflationary spiral would lead from recession to depression, and fiscal conservatives worried more about growing debt. But, in contrast to past debates, the United States also found itself under considerable international pressure to limit deficit spending. In Germany, the conservative government of Angela Merkel sided with those who saw debt as the major danger. In the United Kingdom, an election shifted power from the Labour Party to a coalition of Conservatives and Liberal Democrats, which also focused on debt and quickly adopted a massive budget cutting program. Both the United Kingdom and Germany put pressure on the United States to bring its deficit under control.

Why did Germany and the United Kingdom care about U.S. fiscal policy? As the largest economy in the world, any crisis in the United States would have a powerful effect on almost everyone else, and especially with major trading partners like the United Kingdom and Germany. Moreover, increased borrowing by the United States was likely to drive up interest rates even if it did not lead to crisis. With a fundamental disagreement about which threat to the U.S. and global economies was greatest—debt crisis or recession—it was impossible to agree on coordinated policy.

The danger emerged that the different policies would cancel each other out. If the United Kingdom and Germany were, through austerity packages, taking demand *out* of their economies, it could offset U.S. efforts to increase demand in its economy. Similarly, the sacrifices that U.K. citizens were going to make through reduced government services might achieve less affect if U.S. borrowing created a debt problem anyway.

Globalization has created increased need for policy coordination, especially in times of crisis, but no way of achieving it. Economies with contradictory policy needs, and societies with contradictory policy preferences, have much less freedom to behave independently of one another.

Critical Thinking Questions

1. Why were different governments able to reach some consensus in 2009, but none in 2010, over the merit of further economic stimulus?
2. Can new international rules or institutions facilitate greater coordination of domestic economic policies?
3. Is the case discussed here exceptional or will this problem be inherent in a globalized economy?

money itself, can be highly lucrative, so countries with leading financial sectors, such as the United States and Great Britain, were among the first to drop restrictions on capital movement.

Second, a new shared purpose emerged, an ideology of liberalization. The post-World War II emphasis on state intervention in economies eroded, beginning with the Thatcher government in Great Britain (1980–1990) and the Reagan administration in the United States (1981–1989). The belief that markets were better than governments at allocating economic resources gained influence and made these two governments willing to surrender control. Thus, the earliest liberalizers were motivated by a combination of ideology and economic interest. Other countries then followed in order to avoid losing investment and to participate in the increase in the global financial services industry.

Finally, for countries that sought to bring in investment to promote economic development, allowing capital mobility provided access to massive amounts of international capital. Global investors were much more willing to invest in economies where they had the freedom to move money in and out at will. For countries in Asia, this was a particularly important motivation. Opening up to global capital made it possible for developing states to bring much more money into their stock markets, providing investment that they badly needed and could not accumulate domestically.

For investors, the ability to invest in stock markets around the world was a great opportunity, allowing them to spread their risk and to invest their money wherever rates of return were highest. Developing countries that had been starved of investment in the past were now seen as offering important opportunities—to the benefit of both investors and the receiving countries. In contrast to the traditional form of overseas investment—building or buying "bricks and mortar" assets—investing in the stock market (portfolio investment) allowed foreign investors to sell their assets quickly and move the money elsewhere as economic opportunities changed.

TOWARD A POST-DOLLAR ERA?

Even after the decline of the Bretton Woods system, the global financial system revolved around the dollar. The dollar was the largest currency in the world in total value, and was widely viewed as the most solid, because it had the power and credibility of the U.S. government and the U.S. economy behind it. Therefore, most international transactions are carried out in dollars, and many governments maintain large reserves of dollars.

In recent years, however, various factors have undermined the role of the dollar as the main currency of international commerce and as a reserve currency. The founding of the euro created another highly stable currency, backed by an economy larger than that of the United States. Many governments and firms shifted some reserves into euros in order to spread their risk. Moreover, the steady strengthening of the euro relative to the dollar in the euro's early years provided an advantage to those holding euros and furthered the notion that the dollar was receding as the dominant currency. Concerns over U.S. government debt, which many thought implied a future devaluation of the dollar, contributed to flight from the dollar. Throughout Europe, it made increasing sense to determine international trade in euros rather than dollars. Even though the dollar remains the dominant global currency today, that position looks less certain than in the past.

What are the alternatives to a dominant dollar? One possibility is a world of multiple major reserve currencies. The dollar might be joined by euro and the Chinese yuan, if it were made freely convertible. An advantage might be that the issuing governments would compete to have the most stable, freely accessible currency and transparent markets and policies. A disadvantage would be that without policy coordination among the reserve currencies, changes in values could cause serious disruptions in the global economy. A different option would be to create a new global currency, managed by an international organization. It seems unlikely that there will be sufficient will (and common purpose) to establish such a common currency anytime soon, but in fact a prototype already exists. The IMF has a "quasicurrency" called the "Special Drawing Right," (SDR) which is based on "basket" of leading currencies (dollar, euro, yen, pound). The SDR, then, is already a stable multicurrency system, but it is limited to use as an accounting mechanism within the IMF. Thus, although it seems like the dominant position of the dollar will erode, there is no good alternative yet available.

The Perils of Financial Globalization

Flows of capital around the world are now so large that not even the biggest governments can control them. As long as markets work well, there is no problem. But markets do not always work well. Markets can sometimes spiral out of control, with dire consequences for governments, investors, and average citizens alike. Within domestic economies, governments use a large range of regulatory mechanisms to prevent the kind of economic crises that occurred at the beginning of the Great Depression and in the housing and banking sectors in 2008–2009. As bad as those crises were, governments had some tools at their disposal to minimize the damage. At the international level, no such regulatory apparatus exists. Therefore, when domestic crises become international crises, as they often do in a highly globalized economy, there are few policy levers readily available. The current wide-open international financial system has been subject to both debt crises and exchange rate crises. Currently, the ability of governments to solve these, either individually or together, is limited.

DEBT CRISES

Debt crises have repeatedly threatened the stability of individual countries and of the international financial system since the 1980s. The most significant crises, such as those that took place in the early 1980s in Latin America, in Mexico in 1994, and in Asia in 1997, have essentially similar roots. The crisis that struck the United States and Europe beginning in 2008 had slightly different sources.

First, developing countries often do not have enough extra money in their economies to finance both investment and current consumption. Yet without such investment, they cannot increase their efficiency to catch up with advanced economies. So, they borrow internationally. If the investment is successful, the increased earnings will allow the borrower to pay off the debt and interest and still make a profit. At the same time, those who have excess capital are often looking for places to invest it profitably. The more excess capital there is in the system, the more desperate investors are in their search for investment targets. This factor was especially prominent in the 1970s: increases in oil prices left Middle Eastern oil exporters with enormous supplies of capital, and they were looking for places to invest it. Much of this money was lent to Latin American economies through U.S. banks. Today, huge increases in oil prices again leave oil-exporting states looking for places to invest their vast profits.

In the United States, and several European countries in the past decade, the debt crisis began not primarily with government borrowing, but with debt in the housing and investment markets. In these countries, borrowing was driven not by the needs of economic development, but by a combination of factors. On the demand side, consumers incurred debt to buy goods and homes, especially given the perception that home values were certain to increase. On the supply side, loose monetary policies kept interest rates low, enticing actors to borrow. In contrast to earlier crisis, the initial inability to pay came from firms and individuals, not states, but by 2010, states such as Greece were in danger

Figure 10.5 International Debt Crisis

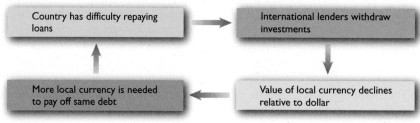

Source: Paul D'Anieri

of default as recession decreased tax revenues and increased spending on unemployment benefits and stimulus measures.

debt crisis

A crisis that occurs when a debtor country is no longer willing or able to make the scheduled payments on its debts.

A **debt crisis** occurs when the debtor is no longer willing or able to make the scheduled payments on its debts (see Figure 10.5). Sometimes a debtor is able to continue payment but sees the costs of defaulting on the loans as lower than the cost of sacrificing domestic goals in order to continue making payments. If a government fears domestic unrest, it may default, causing a debt crisis. The Latin American debt crisis arose in 1982 when Mexico announced that it could no longer make payments on certain loans. Two rapid increases in oil prices in the 1970s inhibited economic growth both within Mexico and around the world, decreasing demand for Mexican imports. So while obligations to repay debts remained constant, the supply of income with which to repay them declined.

Most international loans are denominated in dollars. Borrowers borrow dollars, not their local currency, and must pay back dollars. Therefore, any debt crisis can be exacerbated by a loss in the value of the debtor's currency relative to the dollar. If that occurs, the borrower must raise even more of its own currency in order to make the fixed payment (in dollars) on the loan. This problem hit homeowners in Hungary especially hard in 2009–2010. Many had borrowed money in euros because interest rates were lower, but the fall in the value of the Hungarian forint meant that debt payment in forints increased as the value of the currency dropped. It took IMF intervention to stabilize the forint and head off the crisis.

There are two ways in which debt crises can fall into a spiral that makes them much harder to solve. First, uncertainty over a country's ability to repay its loan will lead investors to withdraw their investments. That causes them to sell the currency of the country in question, reducing its value. It then becomes even harder to repay debts, so that more investors leave, continuing the downward spiral.

A second mechanism that exacerbates debt crises is the need to "roll over" debt—to replace old loans with new ones. If interest rates increase for any reason, the new debt will require more money to repay than the old debt. When confidence in a country's ability to repay its debts decreases, lenders require a higher interest rate to compensate for the increased risk. As old debt is rolled over into new debt at a higher interest rate, the crisis deepens.

Who is to blame for debt crises? This question arises not only internationally, but also in domestic debt crises such as the one that emerged in 2008 in the United States. Lenders sometimes use bad judgment in making loans; borrowers sometimes use bad judgment in borrowing. Sometimes loans are not bad in principle, but economic mismanagement can undercut a state's ability to repay. Sometimes changes in the global financial situation undermine even loans that were originally sensible. Typically, international lenders and organizations such as the IMF, which is often called in to help resolve crises, put the responsibility on the borrower rather than on the lender, a practice that has engendered considerable resentment.

MONETARY CRISES

Monetary crises can arise independently of debt problems, although the two problems are sometimes connected. A **monetary crisis** emerges when investors anticipate that the value of a particular currency is likely to fall. In ideal circumstances, the markets will simply adjust as people sell the currency, and a new, lower price for the currency will be established. However, in an era with a great deal of cross-border stock investment and instant movement of capital, a "panic" is possible, which will send the value of the currency crashing downward and the entire economy with it. Most often this happens when a government is trying to hold the value of its currency at a particular price, and currency traders doubt its ability to do so.

Today, there is a great deal of foreign investment in stock markets. Therefore, when the value of a currency drops, the value of stocks priced in that currency drops as well. This may prompt investors to sell stocks, and thus the currency. This drives the value of the currency down further, prompting even more investors to sell, and so on, until the value of both the currency and the stocks valued in that currency is greatly reduced. Because investors with other kinds of debts (for example, building loans) might be relying on their stock assets to pay off those other loans, the crash of the stock market can cause repercussions throughout the economy (as it did in the United States in 1929). This cycle is represented in Figure 10.6.

monetary crisis
A crisis that emerges when rapid sales of a particular currency cause its value to collapse.

CONFIDENCE AND CONTAGION

In both debt crises and monetary crises, a manageable downturn turns into an unmanageable panic when investors lose confidence in the ability of the markets to right themselves. The belief that the value of a currency or asset will decrease prompts people to sell, creating a self-fulfilling prophecy. Worse still, the ability of investors to move capital so quickly leads to a contagion effect—a spreading of the crisis from one country to another. When Thailand's economy began to spiral downward in 1997, investors began withdrawing their money from other Asian economies. When Greece threatened default in 2010, confidence in Spain, Portugal, the United States, and the United Kingdom decreased as a result. The central policy question of the contemporary international financial system is whether some mechanism can be developed to halt international financial crises before they turn into panics and spread around the world.

In domestic economies, there is a relatively simple solution: The government acts as a "lender of last resort." A **lender of last resort** is an actor that is committed to continuing to lend money to stressed economic actors when market institutions would refuse to do so. Because investors know the government will back up banks rather than letting them fail, they maintain confidence that a crisis will not spread, and panic is averted. In the United States, for example, a government agency, the Federal Deposit Insurance Corporation (FDIC), guarantees people that they will receive their savings back even if their bank goes bankrupt. In the EU, the European Central Bank played a similar

lender of last resort
An actor that is committed to continuing to lend money to stressed economic actors when market institutions would refuse to do so.

Figure 10.6 International Monetary Crisis

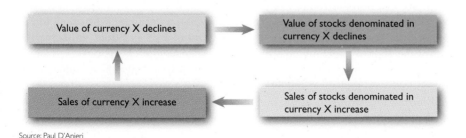

Source: Paul D'Anieri

role in 2007, injecting over $100 billion into the financial system when problems with "mortgage-backed securities" threatened several investment firms.[10] The U.S. government similarly headed off a collapse of the domestic banking system in 2008–2009, and the EU (primarily Germany) played that role for Greece in 2010.

Previous international monetary systems had a mechanism to provide a lender of last resort. Under the classical gold standard system, the Bank of England played that role. Under the Bretton Woods system, the United States played the same role. The United States continued to play that role informally in the post–Bretton Woods system. The 1980s Latin American debt crisis and the 1994 Mexican crisis were managed largely through solutions organized and funded by the U.S. government.

In the current system of capital mobility, it is not clear how the role of lender of last resort will be fulfilled. In the 1997 Asian financial crisis, a set of measures to stem the panic and stabilize the situation was negotiated by the IMF. The IMF, however, did not itself have enough money to restore confidence in the markets. A solution required contribution by IMF member countries. This recent history leaves much uncertainty about solving future crises. The United States still seems committed to playing some role, but confidence in its commitment and ability is diminished because of its own much weaker international financial position after its own financial crisis beginning in 2008.

Economists and political scientists genuinely disagree about what sorts of measures should be taken in future economic crises and about who should be authorized to take them. Many people object to giving the IMF a leading role because it tends to focus on solutions that put most of the cost of adjustment on the economies in crisis. To some, this emphasis absolves investors from the developed countries that fund the IMF of their responsibilities and protects their economic interests at the expense of the poorest people in the countries, where difficult adjustments must be made.

Some economists object to the current ad hoc system, not on grounds of fairness, but on grounds of effectiveness. Given the amounts of money moving around the world and the size of a panic that can occur in such situations, some fear that a financial crisis might arise that is simply too big and fast-moving for the IMF to solve "on the fly." The fear is that a global financial crash, worse than any ever seen, is now possible.[11]

The Debate over Globalization

The rhetoric we hear today concerning globalization tends to be rather strident in one direction or another. Some see globalization as wholly positive, bringing the economic benefits of markets to rich and poor alike. Others see it as mostly negative.

Does Globalization Aid the Poor or the Rich?

Those who support globalization in trade and finance argue that the biggest beneficiaries are poor workers in poor countries. This view is rooted in standard liberal economic prescriptions: The market produces wealth, and interfering in the market makes everyone poorer. Liberals argue that when governments or other forces intervene in the economy, it is usually politically motivated and does not serve the interests of the poor. By opening up opportunity, especially for cheap, unskilled labor, globalization allows the poor to participate economically in ways they could not do so before. Moreover, globalization, by making poor countries wealthier, allows them to spend more money on education, health care, and other services that are essential to further reducing poverty. Liberals argue that protectionism has a poor track record of aiding economic development. A great deal of evidence supports this view. Poor

"I totally agree with you about capitalism, neo-colonialism, and globalization, but you really come down too hard on shopping."

The New Yorker

countries that participate in the global economy tend to grow more quickly than those that remain isolated. Thus, supporters of globalization argue that if countries remain poor, it is because they have too little exposure to international markets, not too much.

Critics of globalization argue that it puts more power in the hands of those who are already the most powerful and wealthy. By reducing barriers to the movement of capital, it allows those who control capital (wealthy corporations and investors in the developed states) to have more power over workers and governments to coerce workers to accept lower wages. Clearly, those in advanced economies who have their jobs "outsourced" pay the costs of adjusting. But opponents of globalization do not believe that poor workers in developing countries benefit as a result. Focusing on the work conditions in "sweatshops" (see Chapter 11), they do not see workers in these places rising into the middle class. Rather, these critics believe that workers' economic desperation is being exploited: Because they are desperate to feed their families, they work long hours, with dangerous chemicals and machinery, with no ability to unionize, and for a pitiful wage that shows no promise of increasing.[12] In sum, opponents contend that the money that is saved when First World workers are fired and Third World workers are hired goes not to Third World workers, but rather to First World corporations and to their executives and investors, who are already the wealthiest people in the world.[13]

There may be some truth in both views. Whether workers benefit or lose from globalization probably depends on how much education they have. Whether they are in the United States or Sri Lanka, workers with little education or skill tend to be relatively poorly paid. However, disagreement remains on whether globalization increases opportunity for these workers, decreases it, or whether that still depends on what country they are in.

The Culture Connection

The Globalization of Culture: Homogenization or Hybridization?

Perhaps no aspect of our lives is as heavily influenced by globalization as culture. It sometimes seems as if American culture is spreading beyond the United States, such that the world is slowly losing its diversity of cultures and instead gaining a single American-centered culture. This spread is apparent in the global distribution of American films and television shows, for example.

However, there is another process going on as well. As American culture is adopted around the world, artists in other countries add something to it and change it. Often those changed cultural forms return to the United States. Thus, the spread of American culture is changing American culture quite dramatically. The result is hybrids of different cultures' artworks, rather than simply a one-directional expansion.

The history of rock music illustrates this vividly. Rock music, as it developed in the 1950s, was essentially an American phenomenon, which was exported to much of the world. The 1960s, however, witnessed the "British invasion," in which the driving creative forces in music were British artists such as the Beatles, the Rolling Stones, the Who, and Eric Clapton. All of these artists were steeped in the American blues and rock traditions, but they fundamentally changed the music, and American artists were in turn influenced by the British scene. In recent years, U.S. pop music—which continues to be hugely influential—has adopted styles and instruments from Latin, Caribbean, African, and Asian music.

A second example of this cross-cultural hybridization is in film animation. The spread of cartoons by Disney and others around the world represents homogenization. Not only has the production of animation been globalized (much of the actual animation work is done in Asia or Eastern Europe), but the content has become more homogeneous. However, other cultures are altering this art form and sending back fundamentally new genres to the United States.

A particularly salient example is the influence of the Japanese *anime* style of animation on U.S. animation and films. Anime emerged stylistically out of Japanese *manga* comic books, which themselves were inspired by their American counterparts. In the late 1960s, anime crossed over into American popular culture when the anime series *Mach Go Go Go* became the popular cartoon *Speed Racer*. Since the 1990s, anime series aimed at children, such as *Yu-Gi-Oh!* and *Pokemon*, have become icons among American children.

Anime influences more serious films as well. The popular film *The Matrix* (1999) was based on the anime film *Ghost in the Shell* (1995) and sought to translate the visual style of anime into live action film. The trend came full circle in 2008 with *Speed Racer*. As the trend has spread, anime has had a major influence on the visual style of American films. The result is complex cultural blending that is neither fully Japanese nor fully American.

Critical Thinking Questions

1. If global culture is becoming both more homogenous and more hybridized, what effect will that have on international politics? Could a common popular culture bring about greater understanding and agreement in the political realm?

2. What might be the significant political effects if the dominance of the United States in production of global popular culture were to give way to a world with many cultural "leaders"?

3. Are there signs that cultural production is an area of competition among states? If so, what are they?

Does Globalization Cause a Regulatory "Race to the Bottom"?

Critics of globalization also focus on the pressure that globalization puts on governments, and on the ways that it increases the power of global corporations at the expense of governments. Critics are particularly concerned that globalization helps corporations pressure governments to reduce protections for health, environment, workers, and so on. According to this view, countries must now compete for investment more than before, and the only way to win it is by making more and more concessions to corporations. This means not only reducing health, labor, and environmental standards, but also lowering taxes on corporate profits. Neither local workers nor small businesses have the ability to make the same threats, because they have less freedom to move elsewhere. As a result, tax burdens are likely to be shifted from corporations to citizens. Anyone who has followed the debates about financing sports stadiums in U.S. cities, where city governments are told to provide public financing or risk having their team move, has seen an example of this phenomenon. Thus, many fear that globalization creates a "race to the bottom" in which governments are forced to eliminate all kinds of protections in order to attract investment. In many countries, such criticisms come from both the right and the left.

Some researchers have questioned whether the race to the bottom actually occurs, despite a few notable examples. Foreign investment is still highest not in poor countries with very few regulations, but in wealthy countries that are the most heavily regulated in the world.[14] Moreover, supporters of free trade argue that since governments and interest groups are so good at inventing nontariff barriers to trade disguised as labor, environmental, and health regulations, some limits on these barriers are not bad. Nonetheless, even supporters of globalization recognize that the perception of the "race to the bottom" must be dealt with if the benefits of globalization are to be maintained. U.S. President Bill Clinton noted this following the violence at the 1999 WTO meeting in Seattle.

Reconsider the Case

Europe's Debt Crisis

As the Greek debt crisis unfolded in 2010, it raised some very big questions for policy makers around the world on at least three different levels. At the level of individual countries, policy makers had to weigh two competing threats: If governments borrowed more money to stimulate their economies, they might in the future be more likely to run into a debt crisis like that experienced by Greece and other countries before it. But if governments moved quickly to deal with debt by reducing spending, they might push their fragile economies back into recession. Doing so would not only be wildly unpopular, but would reduce the tax revenues needed to make debt payments. Because the boom years had left these

economies with high costs, and therefore uncompetitive, it remains unclear whether economic growth can stay ahead of the growth in debt or whether default, with all its consequences, is eventually inevitable.

At the level of supranational organizations, the EU faced something of an existential crisis. Countries cannot easily share a single currency if they do not face similar economic circumstances. Otherwise, the monetary policies appropriate for one economy might be the opposite of those needed by another. Greece's inability to use monetary policy made a bad situation worse. Although some speculated that Greece might be forced to leave the Euro zone, others speculated that Germany might do so to escape the tight connection to the policies of less frugal governments. Dismantling the Euro zone would be exceedingly disruptive, and many pointed in the opposite direction. To have a single currency, they argued, Europe needed a single government, able to impose a single fiscal policy, and to effectively transfer wealth when that was needed.

For the broader international community, the European crisis helped shift attention from the short-term economic crisis to the longer term potential for debt crisis. Meeting at Toronto in June 2010, the G-20 states agreed to halve their deficits by 2013 and to stabilize their debt/GDP ratio by 2016. The statement left some wiggle room on the timetable, however, in recognition that some states might need to continue to stimulate their economies through borrowing to avert a prolonged recession. U.S. President Barack Obama pointed to the problem that deficit reduction

could make debt repayment harder, not easier, if it led to economic contraction: "We must recognize that our fiscal health tomorrow will rest in no small measure on our ability to create jobs today."[15]

Critical Thinking Questions

1. To what extent can a single, large state provide the financial resources to head off a developing financial crisis?

2. Does the crisis of 2008 mark a fundamental turning point in the history of international political economy? If so, what are the defining characteristics of the new era?

3. Is it possible for one state to insulate itself from bad economic decisions in other states or does globalization make that impossible?

Summary

There is substantial disagreement about whether globalization is good or bad, whether it is a choice or an inevitable development, and whether it is fundamentally new or not. However, there is no dispute that the globalization of trade and finance is among the most important developments in international politics today. Globalization is causing, for better or worse, huge shifts in economic activity around the world and is creating new challenges both within states and between them. In trade, the transition from the GATT to the WTO proceeded rather smoothly, but it is not clear whether free trade will continue to expand on a global scale, or whether states will pursue trade bilaterally and regionally. In finance, globalization has proceeded in a much less controlled fashion since the demise of the Bretton Woods system in 1971. States are still learning to cope with the effects of globalized finance, and international mechanisms to manage the dangers inherent in such an arrangement have not developed as fast as financial movements have grown. The struggle against further crises will, therefore, be an important story in the coming decades.

Key Concepts

1. Globalization
2. Bretton Woods system
3. General Agreement on Tariffs and Trade (GATT)
4. World Trade Organization (WTO)
5. "Most-favored-nation" principle or "nondiscrimination"
6. Nontariff barriers to trade
7. Regionalization
8. Two-level games
9. Internationalization of finance
10. Costs of adjustment
11. Gold standard
12. Debt and monetary crises

Study Questions

1. What makes globalization today different from past expansions in international trade?

2. How was the formation of the Bretton Woods system motivated by the "lessons" of the interwar period?

3. How does the principle of nondiscrimination differ from the principle of reciprocity?

4. How did nontariff barriers undermine the GATT?

5. How does the WTO differ from the GATT?

6. What are the major arguments for and against the WTO?

7. How do domestic and international factors interact in producing trade policies?

8. What is the "trilemma" of international monetary policy?

9. Why have controls on capital movements been reduced over time?

10. What are the dangers of freely flowing global capital?

Endnotes

1. Thomas D. Lairson and David Skidmore, *International Political Economy,* 3rd ed. (Belmont, CA: Thomson Wadsworth, 2003), p. 109.

2. John G. Ruggie, "International Regimes, Transactions, and Change: Embedded Liberalism in the Postwar Economic Order," *International Organization,* Vol. 36, No. 2 (Spring 1983): 379–415.

3. "Picking A Fight," *The Economist,* March 9, 2010.

4. A seminal work in this field was Charles Kindleberger, *The World in Depression 1929-1939* (Berkeley: University of California Press, 1973).

5. Robert Keohane, *After Hegemony: Cooperation and Discord in the World Economy* (Princeton, NJ: Princeton University Press, 1984).

6. Federal Reserve Bank of Dallas, *2002 Annual Report,* at http://www .dallasfed.org/fed/annual/2002/ar02f.html

7. Robert Putnam, "Diplomacy and Domestic Politics: The Logic of Two- Level Games," *International Organization,* Vol. 42, No. 3 (1988): 427–460.

8. See Benjamin Cohen, *The Geography of Money* (Ithaca: Cornell University Press, 1998); and Barry Eichengreen, *Globalizing Capital: A History of the*

International Monetary System (Princeton, NJ: Princeton University Press, 1996).

9. On the evolution of the international monetary system, see Eichengreen, *Globalizing Capital.*

10. *International Herald Tribune,* August 14, 2007.

11. See Paul Krugman, *The Return of Depression Economics* (New York: W. W. Norton, 1999).

12. PeterS. Goodman and Philip P. Pan, "Chinese Workers Pay for Wal-Mart's Low Prices," *The Washington Post* (February 8, 2004); A1, at http://www .washingtonpost.com/ac2/wp-dyn/A22507-2004Feb7?language=printer

13. Mark Rupert and M. Scott Solomon, *Globalization and International Political Economy* (Lanham, MD: Rowman & Littlefield, 2006).

14. Geoffrey Garrett, "Global Markets and National Politics: Collision Course or Virtuous Circle?" *International Organization,* Vol. 52, No. 4 (Autumn 1998): 787–824.

15. Quoted in "G-20 Leaders Agree to Halve Budget Deficits," *New York Times,* June 28, 2010, p. B7.

The Problem of Global Inequality

LEARNING OBJECTIVES

After completing this chapter, the student should be able to . . .

1. Identify different ways of defining and measuring poverty, and articulate the implications of using different definitions and measurements.

2. Discuss the UN Millennium Development Goals.

3. Explain the problem of late development and the challenges faced by late developers.

4. Identify strategies for late development, and analyze the strengths and weaknesses of these strategies.

5. Contrast competing explanations of the success of the "Asian Tigers."

6. Evaluate the role of foreign aid in economic development.

◀ A young boy brings food to his family members, who work at a garbage dump in New Delhi, India.
AP Photo/Gurinder Osan, File

Consider the Case

India: From Riches, to Rags, to . . . What?

In 1700, prior to British colonization, India controlled roughly the same share of the world economy as did all of Western Europe.[1] By the time India became independent in 1947, its share of the world economy had fallen to roughly 4 percent, and it was one of the poorest countries in the world. How did colonialism produce this result? What kinds of policies would reverse this trend? Since independence, reduction of poverty and establishment of consistent economic growth have been central issues for India's governments. A variety of strategies have been pursued.

At the time of independence, India's leadership believed that colonial connections were the main source of poverty and that disconnecting from the global economy would bring development. The initial development strategy, therefore, focused on achieving national independence, which had political benefits as well. Moreover, in keeping with the predominant thinking of the time, the state took a prominent role in the economy, controlling the largest industries in an effort to allocate resources strategically, while leaving smaller sectors to the market. By 1980, however, not much progress had been made.

India remained mired in poverty and was growing much more slowly than other Asian economies.

In 1991, India undertook a major change of course, ending restrictions on foreign investment and reducing state control of various parts of the economy, a trend that has continued since. Recently, India has experienced a technology and services boom as both Indian and Western firms have sought to take advantage of the country's comparatively cheap but well-educated workforce. After growing at an annual rate of only 0.8 percent from 1900 to 1950 India's economy grew at an annual rate of 6 percent from 1980 to 2002 and 7.6 percent from 2002 to 2006.[2] At the same time, although poverty has been reduced, it is widespread, and inequality is high.

What factors explain India's success after centuries of poor economic performance? Can the policies adopted since 1991 continue to create growth or must other measures now be taken? Can India reduce inequality as its overall wealth grows? These questions remain unanswered, even as the country is poised to become one of the world's largest economies in coming decades.

Even though overall world wealth has increased dramatically since World War II, poverty remains widespread in the world today and inequality continues to grow steadily. The gap between the wealthiest and the poorest societies continues to widen, as shown by the following statistics:

- Between 1980 and 2000, many countries, including Russia and most of Latin America, actually moved backward in terms of their relationship to the average world GDP.[3]

- Between 1990 and 2000, poverty *increased* in thirty-seven of sixty-seven developing countries for which data were available.[4]

- Since 1960, annual per capita income in the world's twenty poorest countries has increased only slightly, from $212 to $267, while the economies of other countries have boomed.[5]

- Of the roughly 6 billion people in the world, 2.5 billion live on less than $2 per day, and 1.2 billion (roughly four times the population of the United States) live on less than $1 per day.[6]

The grinding poverty of the world's poorest countries stands in stark contrast not only to the vast wealth of the wealthy countries, but also to the progress made in many other formerly poor countries that are now closing the gap with the wealthiest. These glaring statistics raise three fundamental questions: Why is poverty so persistent? Why is inequality growing? What can be done to reduce poverty and inequality? There are no simple answers, as the rest of this chapter will demonstrate.

Ethics and Self-Interest in Combating Poverty

Why should we address poverty in the world? The answer seems self-evident, but different actors—states, international organizations, NGOs, individuals—have a range of motives with regard to this issue. The way different actors think about poverty and inequality will influence the priority they attach to the problem and the strategies they adopt.

Perhaps the most obvious reason to seek to reduce poverty is normative—it seems immoral or unethical not to try to do something. Nearly every religious credo in the world places considerable value on the willingness of the wealthy to aid the poor. On a less doctrinal level, nearly everybody who sees pictures of starving children with bloated bellies feels that something ought to be done to help. Professional ethicists also provide detailed philosophical arguments showing that the wealthy have an ethical duty to help alleviate poverty.[7]

Self-interest is also a motive in efforts to stem poverty. Poverty has global effects that the governments of rich countries perceive an interest in fighting. First, poverty is viewed as an underlying factor in a much broader range of political problems that affect wealthy countries. Although there is considerable doubt about whether there is a direct link between poverty and terrorism, it is still widely believed that reducing poverty would decrease the supply of recruits to terrorist groups and would reduce the willingness of societies to support or tolerate terrorism. More broadly, the hostility toward the West that seems to grip some societies is at least in part linked to resentment over gaps in wealth and might be moderated by economic development.

Second, poverty is seen as a source of a wide range of problems that spill over from poor to rich countries, including immigration, crime, and health threats. Much migration, historically and today, is motivated by the desire to escape conflict, but much more, not only today but throughout history, has been driven by the desire of immigrants to go where economic opportunities are greatest. In North America and Western Europe, where illegal immigration is a major policy problem, reducing poverty in the "sending" countries is a potential solution.

Poverty also has an effect on the level of transnational crime. Economic desperation clearly makes individuals more willing to break the law in order to get by. For example, in South America and in Central and South Asia, it is very difficult to convince impoverished peasants to stop growing crops for drug production when they cannot feed their families any other way. The result is a ready supply of drugs for customers in wealthier parts in the world, which fosters social problems there.

Poverty also makes it much harder to combat environmental problems.[8] Very few people would choose to starve to save an acre of rainforest or an endangered species, but that is, in effect, the choice that many people face every day. It is much easier to save the environment from a position of wealth.

Third, poverty actually undermines economic growth in rich countries. Poor people do not buy much. This keeps overall consumer demand lower than it otherwise might be.

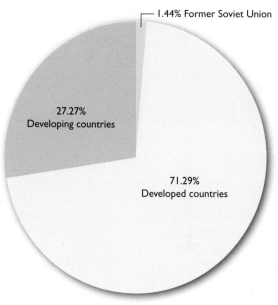

Figure 11.1 Percentage of World GDP, 2007

1.44% Former Soviet Union

27.27% Developing countries

71.29% Developed countries

Source: http://www.ers.usda.gov/Data/Macroeconomics

The Culture Connection

Pop Stars and Global Poverty

Since the 1980s, a small number of pop stars have become increasingly vocal advocates for fighting world hunger. They strive to use their personal popularity and visibility to get their fans to be more concerned about world hunger and to bring pressure to bear on politicians to do more.

The pioneer in this movement was George Harrison, the Beatles guitarist, who in 1971 organized a concert at New York's Madison Square Garden to raise money to fight hunger in Bangladesh, which was suffering famine after its war for independence with Pakistan. The "Concert for Bangladesh" featured Harrison's friend Eric Clapton, fellow ex-Beatle Ringo Starr, and Bob Dylan, among others.

This movement was rekindled in 1984 by the Irish singer Bob Geldof, lead singer of a band called the Boomtown Rats. With famine threatening millions in Africa, Geldof organized "Band Aid," a group of nearly forty British rock stars, including David Bowie, Paul McCartney, and Sting, to record "Do They Know It's Christmas?" The song and its accompanying video became enormous hits in both Europe and the United States. American stars, led by Michael Jackson and Quincy Jones, then joined the cause. Their group, called USA for the World, included Ray Charles, Bob Dylan, and the six Jackson siblings, and produced the song "We Are the World," which also became a number-one single. In July 1985, two concerts were held simultaneously, one at Philadelphia's JFK Stadium and the other at London's Wembley Stadium, to raise money to fight global hunger. After a time, however, the efforts of rock stars and their fans to combat hunger waned.

More recently another Irish rock star, Bono (Paul Hewson), of the band U2, has been the most vocal and visible celebrity focusing attention on global poverty and hunger. Bono has even been included in meetings of world leaders on the issue. He has become a regular at gatherings such as the World Economic Forum in Davos, Switzerland. In February 2005, the *Los Angeles Times* argued in an editorial that Bono should be chosen to run the World Bank.[1] That seemed entirely unlikely (George Bush chose Deputy Defense Secretary Paul Wolfowitz), but it demonstrated Bono's emergence as a serious player in discussions of global poverty.

Bono with former British Prime Minister Tony Blair and Liberia's President Ellen Johnson-Sirleaf at the World Economic Forum in Davos, Switzerland.

Critical Thinking Questions

1. Can popular musicians have an important influence on shaping the behavior of states with regard to matters such as global poverty?
2. What long-term effects might efforts such as massive rock concerts have on efforts to reduce global poverty?

[1]"Bono for the World Bank," *Los Angeles Times*, February 25, 2005, Section B, p. 12.

Moreover, because poverty generally prevents people from becoming highly educated, it leads to lower worker productivity. The health problems and political instability that come with poverty further inhibit overall productivity. In sum, poverty is bad for the economy.

U.S. President George W. Bush captured the range of motivations for combating poverty in a 2002 speech: "We fight against poverty because hope is an answer to terror. We fight against poverty because opportunity is a fundamental right to human dignity. We fight against poverty because faith requires it and conscience demands it. We fight against poverty with a growing conviction that major progress is within our reach."[9] For all these very practical reasons, the wealthy countries often perceive a self-interest in helping the poor. It is often easier to justify spending taxpayers' money to pursue national self-interest than to pursue the ethical agenda of poverty reduction. However, the pursuit of poverty reduction based on self-interest often has bizarre effects on who gets helped and how.

Defining and Measuring Poverty

Despite the previously cited statistics showing the persistent problem of poverty in the world, there are also statistics that show a much less dire situation. This different view results in part from the different comparisons being made. The poorest countries continue to lag behind, but another group of countries has made steady progress in income growth. To make sense of the barrage of statistics, which often seem contradictory, it is necessary to understand differences in what is being measured.

Poverty versus Inequality

Traditionally, **poverty** was defined in absolute terms, as a condition characterized by comparatively low income, a definition referred to as "income poverty." However, many economists, such as the Nobel Prize-winning poverty scholar Amartya Sen, reject that definition in favor of one that focuses on relative capabilities—on the range of choices open to an individual.[10] Thus, the UN Commission on Human Rights defines poverty as "a human condition characterized by the sustained or chronic deprivation of the resources, capabilities, choices, security and power necessary for the enjoyment of an adequate standard of living and other civil, cultural, economic, political and social rights."[11]

In this view, poverty is defined in relative terms. However, poverty is often measured in *absolute* terms, such as income, in part because such data are more readily available. In contrast to poverty, *inequality* is inherently comparative; in measuring inequality, the question becomes, "How much wealth or income does one person have compared to someone else?" It is very possible that a person's income is growing, but more slowly than that of others. As a result, income is increasing but so is inequality. Does this mean poverty is increasing or decreasing? Questions like these make it essential to evaluate the nature of the statistics.

When examining individual welfare, analysts and policy makers are often concerned with absolute poverty: Do individuals have enough income to avoid malnutrition, to get basic health care, housing, and education? Politics, however, is also deeply concerned with issues of equality (both within and between countries). In many discussions, therefore, simply preventing people from starving or freezing to death is rarely considered the goal of economic policies. Reducing inequality in the population and keeping people moving upward economically are also important goals.

poverty
The lack of sufficient income, which is often accompanied by insufficient nutrition, housing, and other necessities. Poverty can be defined in absolute terms as "income poverty" or in relative terms, with a focus on the range of choices open to individuals.

per capita GDP

The average income of the people in a country.

purchasing power parity (PPP)

A measure used to calculate GDP that takes into account that goods cost different amounts in different countries.

Human Development Index (HDI)

A measure of poverty, produced by the United Nations Development Programme, that supplements per capita GDP (at purchasing power parity) with measures of life expectancy, literacy rates, and average years of schooling.

Gini coefficient

A statistic developed by Italian statistician Corrado Gini to compare the incomes of the top and bottom fractions of a society.

Gender Development Index

A measure, published by the UN, of the economic equality of men and women.

MEASURES AND STATISTICS

Several different methods of measuring poverty and inequality are in widespread use.

■ **Average income: Per capita GDP** refers to the *average* income of the people in a country. It is calculated by dividing the overall annual income of the country by the population. It is probably the most widely used statistic because it is among the easiest to determine. However, it is also one of the most misleading, especially in societies where there is considerable inequality. In such a society, for every millionaire whose income is far above the average, there must be thousands of others whose income is far below the average. So to the extent that a country has a small number of wealthy people who make a disproportionate share of income, per capita GDP tends to underestimate poverty.

■ **Average income adjusted for cost of living:** One problem with traditional GDP figures is that they do not take into account that goods cost different amounts in different countries. Thus, it is difficult to imagine how anyone survives in a country with a per capita GDP of $500. However, $500 goes further in many poor countries than it does in rich countries. Calculating GDP at **purchasing power parity (PPP)** takes this fact into account by figuring in the different cost of goods. The difference can be significant: in 2007, for example, China's per capita GDP was measured at $2360 using normal methods, but at $5370 using the PPP method.[12] Purchasing power parity is widely considered a better statistic by economists but is less frequently used because calculating it requires a great deal of data on comparative prices.

■ **Basic human needs approaches:** Some measurements have tried to get away from reliance on income figures and to focus on what actually matters—people's living conditions. This change in measurement approach accompanies shifts to policies that aim at providing for these basic human needs. One widely used measure is the **Human Development Index (HDI).** Produced by the United Nations Development Programme, the HDI supplements calculations of per capita GDP (at purchasing power parity) with measures of life expectancy, literacy rates, and average years of schooling.

■ **Inequality:** Some analysts seek to focus solely on the question of inequality within a society. To do this, they often use a statistic known as the **Gini coefficient**, which compares the incomes of the top and bottom fractions of society. The coefficient ranges from zero to one, with one representing a situation in which one person has all the income and everyone else has none and zero, representing a situation in which everyone has equal income.

■ Gender equality: The **Gender Development Index**, published by the United Nations Development Programme, measures the economic equality of men and women. It is similar to the Gini coefficient, but it compares men and women rather than the poorest and richest. High-ranking countries include Norway, Iceland, Sweden, Australia, and the United States

Table 11.1 Gini Coefficients of Various Countries

Highest (Most Inequality)	Lowest (Least Inequality)	Selected Other Countries
Namibia, 0.743	Denmark, 0.247	China, 0.469
Lesotho, 0.632	Japan, 0.249	Mexico, 0.461
Botswana, 0.630	Sweden, 0.250	United States, 0.408
Sierra Leone, 0.629	Czech Republic, 0.254	Russia, 0.399
Central African Republic, 0.613	Norway, 0.258	India, 0.368
Botswana, 0.605	Slovakia, 0.258	United Kingdom, 0.360
Bolivia, 0.601	Bosnia/Herzegovina, 0.262	Australia, 0.352
Haiti, 0.592	Finland, 0.269	Canada, 0.326

Source: Data are from UN Human Development Programme, "Human Development Indicators," *Human Development Report 2007/2008*, pp. 281–284, at http://hdr.undp.org/en/media/HDR_20072008_EN_Indicator_tables.pdf

(at .94). Low-ranking countries include most of the countries of sub-Saharan Africa, such as Niger (.28), Burkina Faso (.32), Mali (.33), and Burundi (.33). Women are especially disadvantaged in countries where poverty is harshest.

Given all these different ways of measuring poverty and inequality and the trends in the world today, it is possible to reach very different conclusions about the overall state of affairs.

- Many countries in Asia and in Central Europe that were formerly poor are now reducing the gap with the wealthiest countries. These countries provide evidence that both overall poverty and inequality are decreasing.

- Another group of countries, mostly in Africa, have made almost no progress at all, and in some cases are worse off than they were in 1980, even in absolute terms. This group of countries suggests that there has been no improvement in the worst cases of poverty and that overall inequality (defined as the gap between the richest and poorest) has increased.

- In nearly every country, gaps between the wealthiest and the poorest are growing, after a century in which they tended to narrow.

- There are major gender gaps in wealth, especially in the poorest countries. Many economists now believe that the economically disadvantaged status of women harms not only the women, but also the overall economy.

The UN Millennium Development Goals

In 2000, the United Nations established the **UN Millennium Development Goals**, a set of goals with accompanying targets to achieve in the coming years and decades. One aim of establishing these goals was to create a greater sense of urgency and a greater claim on resources. In other words, one goal was to get wealthy states to acknowledge that addressing poverty and inequality is important for development. The specific targets were intended to provide some concrete standard against which to measure change in the coming years. Consider a few examples.

UN Millennium Development Goals
A set of goals and accompanying targets set by the UN, aimed at addressing poverty and inequality.

- Goal 1: Eradicate Poverty and Extreme Hunger
  - Target 1. "Halve, between 1990 and 2015, the proportion of people whose income is less than $1 a day."
  - Target 2. "Reduce by half the proportion of people who suffer from hunger."
- Goal 8: Develop a Global Partnership for Development
  - Target 2. Develop further an open trading and financial system that is rule-based, predictable, and nondiscriminatory and includes a commitment to good governance, development, and poverty reduction—nationally and internationally.
  - Target 5. "In cooperation with the private sector, make available the benefits of new technologies—especially information and communications technologies."[13]

Some targets are more easily measured than others. Progress on daily income levels can be assessed by statistical analysis as shown in Figure 11.2. But it is much harder to determine whether the international trading system has been reordered according to the stated goals. By mid-2007, halfway through the fifteen-year timeline for achieving the goals, it appeared that few goals would be achieved on time. Perhaps this should not be surprising, since inequality has been centuries in the making. Whether the targets are met is only part of the point.

Figure 11.2 Percentage of People Living on Less Than $1 a Day, 1990–2002

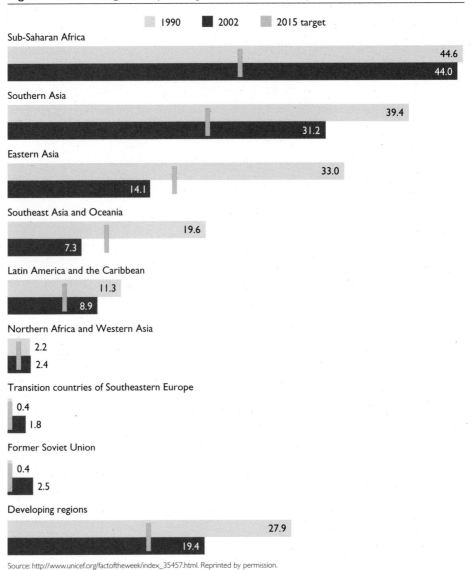

Source: http://www.unicef.org/factoftheweek/index_35457.html. Reprinted by permission.

The Historical Roots of Inequality

Global poverty and inequality are not recent developments. Rather, they have emerged over time. In their search for solutions, different schools of thought place different emphasis on the significance of poverty's historical roots. Economic structuralists tend to argue that inequality was produced by colonialism and will persist unless specific steps are taken to reverse the effects of colonization. Many others believe that, whatever the roots of poverty, the solutions lie simply in the adoption of sound economic policies today.

Economic inequality has not always been as pronounced as it is today. At different points in history, civilizations around the world flourished and outperformed other regions. The fantastic tombs of the Egyptian pharaohs were built at a time when Europe and North America had rather primitive societies. The Muslim world achieved great advances in mathematics while Europe was mired in the Dark Ages. Until the middle of the last millennium, there was a relatively low level of inequality across states.

In 1750, the countries that are today considered the developing world produced 73 percent of global manufacturing output, while the United States and Europe together produced only 23.3 percent. By 1900, the figures were practically reversed: The United States and Europe produced 85.6 percent and the developing countries only 11 percent.[14] Similarly, per capita incomes in Europe and Asia were roughly equal in 1800, but by 1900, the wealthier European states had average incomes 10 times those in Asian countries.[15] As Herman Schwartz put it, "One of the great peculiarities of history is that an economically marginal, technologically backward set of religiously fractionalized and fanatic peoples 'governed' by virtually no administrative apparatus managed to conquer most of the world in about 300 years."[16]

How did this happen? Generations of scholars have tried to answer this question. Several explanations, not all mutually exclusive, have emerged. One school of thought contends that European societies developed political systems that encouraged innovation and investment, which are crucial to growth. Because of the advent of the sovereign state and capitalism in early modern Europe, in this view, governments had some incentives to let commerce flourish rather than controlling it. Moreover, the development of capital markets facilitated the investment needed to discover more productive technologies and put them to use. These factors, it is argued, led to the industrial revolution in Europe, and not elsewhere. In this view, Europe's domination of the rest of the world was not a cause of Europe's wealth, but a result of it: Once Europe had moved ahead economically, it was easy to dominate.

This view is rejected by various economic structuralists and by other historians as well, who see the European colonial conquest of the world as central to Europe's economic development and to the impoverishment of the rest of the world. By shipping gold and silver from Mexico and Peru, for example, Europeans forcibly transferred wealth directly from Latin America to finance European development. Control over trading relationships ensured that raw materials would be extracted from colonies and that manufacturing, where most of the money was made, would be carried out in Europe. The U.S. colonies broke out of this relationship through the American Revolution, but by the time most other colonies gained their independence, they were in a position of poverty and political weakness relative to Europe. In other words, decolonization provided political independence but not economic independence.

There are other views as well, but these two broad perspectives underline the key debate today. Did Europeans discover the secrets of wealth generation and surpass other countries, or did Europeans conquer and exploit others to achieve development at the expense of the underdevelopment of their colonies? The answers to these questions are linked not only to notions of responsibility for global poverty, but also to proposed solutions. Those who believe that Europeans simply discovered the best economic system tend to contend that the key to development today is for others to develop the same kinds of systems—democratic and market-oriented—that prevail in the developed economies. Those who see development and underdevelopment as essentially linked tend to believe that some restructuring of economic relations between rich and poor is required.

The Problem of Late Development

Even if Europe got ahead of the rest of the world simply by developing better economic and political institutions, it does not necessarily follow that other states can take the same path. The **problem of late development** is that those states that are developing later have to contend with something that the first developers did not: economic competition from more advanced states.[17]

Early developers enjoy what economists call **first-mover advantages**, three of which are especially relevant.

problem of late development

The economic challenge faced by developing states because of economic competition from more advanced states.

first-mover advantages

Advantages enjoyed by firms or countries that first enter a new industry, including advantages gained from economies of scale, network effects, and access to investment funds.

The History Connection

The Opium Wars

In the early nineteenth century, British merchants were buying increasing amounts of goods (much of it tea) in China for resale in Britain. To achieve a balance of trade, the British hoped to sell goods in China as well. Then, as today, China was seen as a potentially lucrative market. (There were over 400 million people in China in the mid-nineteenth century.)

Although many British goods did not sell well in China, the British did succeed in selling opium (a powerful narcotic, derived from poppy plants, from which heroin is made). The British produced opium in their colony in India, and its sale in China became an increasingly important source of revenue. The Chinese sought to limit the trade, in part because of the negative influence on their balance of trade, and in part because of the social havoc created by widespread drug addiction. By 1839, Britain was selling over 4.5 million pounds of opium extract in China.

When, in 1840, the authorities in the city of Guangzhao (formerly Canton) seized and destroyed British opium shipments, the British Navy attacked Guangzhao and several other cities. British military superiority was decisive, and in 1842, the Chinese were compelled to sign the treaty of Nanjing, which handed control of Hong Kong to Britain (Britain controlled Hong Kong until 1997) and opened Guangzhao and other port cities to unlimited British imports of opium and other goods. Other powers such as France and the United States were then able to force identical concessions from China. The Chinese again sought to end the opium trade in 1856, and a second opium war led to another Chinese defeat and to further concessions to European states.

The great care China has taken in opening itself to trade in recent years and the resentment that sometimes seems to characterize Chinese attitudes toward the West have their roots in the humiliation China suffered in the Opium Wars.[1]

Critical Thinking Questions

1. To what extent is force used today to promote international trade?
2. How might memories of the colonial era lead to different perspectives on free trade in countries that were colonized and in colonizing countries?

[1] See Timothy Brook and Bob Tadashi Wakabayashi, eds., *Opium Regimes: China, Britain, and Japan, 1839–1952* (Berkeley: University of California Press, 2000).

- **Economies of scale:** In almost every industry, goods and services can be produced more cheaply when they are produced in bulk. Those who enter an industry first can be first to build a good on a large scale. Later developers have to start small, just as the first developers did. Later developers, producing on a smaller scale and therefore at higher cost, struggle to compete with the early developers, who by then are producing on a large scale at lower cost.

- **Network effects:** When a particular industry begins to succeed in a certain location, other firms related to that business tend to locate in the same area in order to reduce costs. Having related firms nearby gives established businesses two advantages over new entrants. First, transportation costs are decreased. Second, the concentration of many people and firms in a particular area leads to greater innovation, by existing firms and new ones. Detroit (in automobiles) and Hollywood and Bombay (in film) are prominent examples. More recently, the location of a few early firms in the area around Palo Alto, California, led that region, known as Silicon Valley, to dominate the global market for computers and software during the late-twentieth-century technology boom. Many other cities around the world have sought to emulate Silicon Valley's success, but building a second such center is inherently difficult because of competition from the first.

■ Investment funds: In both direct and indirect ways, investment is crucial to economic development. Directly, the ability of firms to invest in new technology or to build more efficient plants will determine their success. Indirectly, those societies that invest in public goods such as education, infrastructure, and efficient administration will provide a more favorable environment for business. But where do the funds for such investment come from? They come from the profits of earlier economic activity. Therefore, those who succeed early on will have more money to invest and hence will be more likely to succeed later on.

Access to investment funds may be more available to late developers today than in past decades. The globalization of financial markets (see Chapter 10) has made it much easier for profits earned in one country to be invested in another country. Therefore, investment capital is increasingly available to developing countries that can provide promising opportunities. However, although foreign direct investment in developing countries has increased, it tends to focus on a few of the most promising countries and to ignore the neediest.

Declining Terms of Trade

A problem related to late development is that of **declining terms of trade**. The terms of trade refer to the relative prices of the goods a country imports and exports. Many developing countries have relied on exports of commodities, including agricultural products, fuels, and minerals. However, as a result of technological advances, raw materials (especially agricultural products) tend to take up an ever-smaller portion of the cost of manufactured goods. Raw materials were the costliest portion of key nineteenth-century manufactured goods such as locomotives. Today, however, the raw materials in a computer or a cell phone make up a tiny part of the overall cost. Some lucrative businesses, such as software, insurance, and banking, involve no raw materials at all. For states whose economies rely primarily on exports of raw material (including agricultural products),

declining terms of trade Conditions of international trade that force countries that primarily produce raw materials to export ever-increasing amounts of raw materials to earn the revenue needed to buy the manufactured goods they require.

this fact of modern life creates a losing battle. They must export ever-increasing amounts of raw materials to earn the revenue needed to buy the manufactured goods and the services they require. In recent years, commodities, and oil in particular, have increased in price, but the overall historical trend is downward. Because colonial policies often forced colonies to abandon manufacturing and concentrate on raw materials production, many poor countries came to rely primarily on raw materials exports. They therefore suffer from this problem in addition to the broader problems of late development.

To avoid declining terms of trade, countries (as well as firms) strive to move from exporting raw materials and goods produced by unskilled labor to exporting manufactured goods and goods created by skilled labor, for which profit

Table 11.2 Internet Users Per 1000 People, 2008

Highest	Lowest	Other Countries of Interest
Netherlands, 868	Burkina Faso, 9.2	Germany, 757
United Arab Emirates, 857	Burundi, 7.3	United States, 712
Denmark, 849	Niger, 5.4	Australia, 568
United Kingdom, 799	Congo, 4.5	Italy, 494
Antigua and Barbuda, 785	Central African Republic, 4.3	China, 223
Faroe Islands, 777	Ethiopia, 4.2	Mexico, 216
South Korea, 775	Sierra Leone, 2.3	South Africa, 86

Source: World Resources Institute, "Population, Health and Human Well-being -- Access to Information: Internet users per 1000 people" at http://earthtrends.wri.org/searchable_db/index. php?theme=4&variable_ID=554&action=select_countries

margins are highest. This transition is sometimes difficult. For example, whereas businesses in the United States and Europe now have access to cloud computing through ultra-fast Internet connections, aspiring competitors in Africa are still hoping to get reliable electricity 24 hours per day to keep their computers operating. If the Internet is the key to the future, then the rich look poised to extend their lead.

Historical Strategies for Overcoming Late Development

Ever since Britain began industrializing in the eighteenth century, those states that have followed have been seeking strategies to overcome late development. Important successes in the nineteenth century were the United States and Germany. In the twentieth century, Japan and the "Asian Tigers" managed to achieve development. Are there lessons that can be learned from these cases that are applicable today?

The United States' strategy toward competing with Britain was developed in Alexander Hamilton's "Report on Manufactures," in which he advocated protectionism against imports as a means to development. By creating steep barriers to imports from other countries, the United States gave its firms the opportunity to develop without competition from established firms in other countries. The United States also had at least two advantages that others could not easily match. The first was an enormous amount of cheap capital in the form of land that was taken from Native Americans. The second was a close historical connection with Britain, which provided much of the investment that financed the growth of U.S. industry, and of railroads in particular.

Like the United States, Germany used protectionism to help protect its "infant industries." Unlike the United States, Germany did not rely primarily on private capital markets but rather used taxation to accumulate capital, which it then invested in the economy. Germany's efforts were bolstered by a first-rate education system focused on science and technology, which directly contributed to industrialization. Japan also combined protectionism against imports with government-driven accumulation of capital for investment. After World War II, the Japanese government identified key economic sectors for investment, such as electronics, which Japan came to dominate in the late twentieth century.

These three success stories all relied heavily on protectionism in the early stages; the countries opened up markets to international competition only after their firms could compete successfully against others. The later cases, including Germany and Japan, also relied heavily on state direction of the economy. This model, therefore, became the dominant model in the decades after World War II. By the 1990s, however, it was seen as a failure and was largely abandoned. The policies that succeeded for the "late developers" may not succeed for the "late, late developers." The debate over development strategies therefore continues.

Strategies for Development Today

Different development strategies are linked to the different interpretations of the historical roots of inequality, to broader views of international political economy. Realists and economic structuralists tend to believe that Europe (especially Britain) developed at the expense of its colonies, and those who hold this view are more skeptical of free trade as a solution. They see the keys to Germany's and Japan's success in protectionism and in the role of the state. Liberals tend to see U.S., German, and Japanese success resulting from their focus on exports and embrace of free markets.

Views on development today are also conditioned by the lessons learned from the successes and failures of recent decades. In the second half of the twentieth century, three broad strategies of development dominated: import substitution (which predomined in Latin America, India, and parts of Africa), state socialism (which dominated the Soviet bloc in eastern Europe but was tried on other continents as well), and export-led growth (which predominated in East Asia). Of the three, only export-led growth retains a wide degree of credibility today, simply because the other strategies did not succeed. However, it has been difficult to figure out exactly *why* export-led growth succeeded and whether it can be replicated for "late, late, late developers."

Import Substitution

The term **import substitution** refers to the strategy of producing domestically those goods that a country has been importing. It is based on the model that succeeded for the first round of late developers, including the United States, Germany, and Japan (although it also appealed to followers of Marx). This model was widely in Latin American during and after World War II, as well as in India. In many countries, the strategy was aimed at breaking disadvantageous relationships with former colonial powers.

import substitution

The strategy of producing domestically those goods that a country has been importing.

The central strategy was to shift from the production of raw materials (which has become relatively less profitable over time) to manufactured goods. Initially this would be done by replacing goods that were being imported from developed countries with substitutes produced domestically. Because these goods were already being consumed in the country, the market was established. By limiting imports, domestic producers could capture these markets. The hope was that their technology would catch up with international producers and that over time barriers to trade could be lowered. This was known as "infant industry" protection. A second perceived advantage of import substitution was an improvement in the balance of payments. By producing domestically goods that were formerly imported, states could import more technology without creating a current account deficit.

Despite this model's success in earlier cases, it did not fare well in the late twentieth century for several reasons. First, the timing was unfortunate. Just as these countries shifted out of agricultural production into manufacturing, a substantial increase in global agricultural prices in the 1970s put food importers at a disadvantage. In addition, a dramatic increase in world oil prices penalized countries where industrialization was based on cheap energy.

Second, despite protection from international markets, domestic production in most import-substitution countries did not become competitive in international markets. In the small consumer markets of a relatively poor country, production of important goods (such as automobiles) could never reach the economies of scale to make the goods competitive with those produced for much larger domestic markets or for international markets.

Third, reducing competition from foreign firms reduced the incentives for domestic firms to innovate and become more efficient. Instead of preparing firms for the international market, protection allowed them to remain inefficient. There was little incentive for technological improvement. Poor-quality or obsolete goods might succeed in a protected domestic market, but they could not compete internationally.

Fourth, because protected firms became powerful politically, politicians were hesitant to reduce their protection. As a result, protection from competition tended to become permanent instead of temporary. In many cases, protectionism became a source of cronyism and corruption, which enriched elites at the expense of economic development. For example, by maintaining protection against a particular import, a corrupt politician could provide an opportunity for a local business controlled by supporters or relatives. Or the politician could build the basis for a lucrative smuggling enterprise.

Import Substitution. When India started making automobiles, it began by copying the British Morris Oxford model, which was already sold in India. Although Britain's Morris ceased production in 1984, the Hindustan Ambassador is still manufactured today and widely used as a taxi in India.

As time went on, these less efficient producers did not become more ready for the global market. Instead, protectionism allowed them to remain less efficient and led to higher prices domestically than in the world market. This took money out of consumers' hands, which, if saved, might have yielded more funds for investment.

State Socialism

state socialism

A strategy for development in which the state rather than the market allocates resources.

State socialism, an alternative strategy for development, emerged with the establishment of the Soviet Union in 1917 and spread after World War II to eastern Europe, China, and Cuba. State socialism was a mix of two kinds of ideologies. Most prominent was economic structuralism: the notion that market capitalism and private property led inexorably to the exploitation of one class by another. Less prominent ideologically, but perhaps more prominent in practice, was state economic planning, which provided an alternative to market-based distribution.

The Soviet Union, beginning in the late 1920s, developed a series of "five-year plans," which outlined detailed economic goals, including the quantities of different kinds of inputs and final products to be produced. These plans led to a substantial transformation of a largely peasant society into an industrial juggernaut. If one looks only at the increases in industrial production, state socialism provided remarkable results in the Soviet Union. However, a high human cost was paid: To coerce people into making the changes dictated by state planners, the government executed millions and imprisoned others in wretched conditions in Siberia. Millions more starved to death during collectivization of agriculture in the early 1930s.

Eventually, the Soviet model failed on economic as well as human grounds. As long as the central task was shifting resources from agriculture into industry, state planning was reasonably effective, if brutal. As more resources were put into industry, production increased. However, state planners could not "plan" innovation. Economic gains in the Soviet system generally came from using more resources, not from devising innovative ways to use resources more efficiently. By the 1970s, when there was no additional pool of unused labor or untapped natural resources to bring into production, the Soviet economy began to stagnate. The story in the other state socialist economies was the same. Over time, these economies grew much more slowly than those in the West, leaving their citizens much poorer.

Export-Led Growth

export-led growth

A development strategy that focuses on exporting to the global market.

In part as a response to the failures of import substitution, a group of countries in East Asia developed a strategy known as **export-led growth**. The leader in this strategy was Japan, which shifted from import substitution after World War II. But the countries that made it a model to study and to emulate were the so-called Asian Tigers. These countries—Korea, Taiwan, Singapore, and Hong Kong—used this strategy to move from being among the world's poorest countries to being among the world's richest in about a half century. This different strategy was feasible in part because the Asian states conceived of the *purpose* of development differently. They placed less emphasis on self-reliance and on severing ties with former colonial masters, and saw integration with international markets as acceptable and even desirable.

The central insight in the strategy of export-led growth is to "go where the money is." Rather than building industries to serve domestic markets, which for most poor countries are relatively small, this strategy focused on the markets in developed countries with larger and wealthier populations. In the second half of the twentieth century, going where the money was meant exporting primarily to the U.S., European, and Japanese markets.

Initially, the strategy was not to out-compete firms in the leading technological sectors of these economies, but rather to produce mass-market goods better and more cheaply. Because workers in the Asian Tigers were, at the beginning of this process, much poorer than workers in the countries with whom they were competing, wages tended to be much lower. Initially, then, much of the focus was on low-cost production based on abundant cheap labor, the strategy pursued by China today. Japanese and other Asian manufacturers recognized that the huge U.S. market could yield more sales and profits than an import-substitution strategy would allow.

Export-led growth used the profits generated and expertise gained in producing such "low-end" goods to "move up the food chain." Like Germany and Japan before them, the Asian Tigers had very high domestic savings rates, which provided the investment needed for technological advancement. In the 1960s and 1970s, the primary virtue of Japanese cars for the American buyer was that they were *cheaper* than American brands. By the 1990s, Americans were willing to pay more for Japanese cars because they were *better*. In the 1970s, Taiwan was associated in the United States with cheap radios and televisions, but by 2000, it was the world's leading producer of laptop computers, computer motherboards, and scanners.[18]

The Toyota Toyopet was the first Japanese automobile exported to the United States (1957).

Bettmann/CORBIS

Planners in export-led economies adopted an attitude toward the world market opposite to that of import substitution and state socialism, and this attitude apparently yielded opposite results. In the 1980s and 1990s, other Southeast Asian countries, including Malaysia, Thailand, and the Philippines, began following the Asian Tiger model, with various levels of success. In post-communist Europe, many states also adopted the position that free trade is preferable to closed markets as a development strategy.

Prescriptions for Success

The astounding economic success of the Asian Tigers led scholars and politicians alike to seek to understand their approach better, in the hope that those countries' success could be replicated elsewhere. After two decades of debate, there has been some movement toward consensus on the key determinants of the Tigers' success and the relevant lessons for other economies. Unfortunately, it is not clear that the conditions that led to their success still exist for those coming behind them.

THE WASHINGTON CONSENSUS

Liberals have argued that the success of the Asian Tigers is evidence that a free market approach—both domestically and internationally—is optimal. In particular, their success is seen as real-world evidence that even poor countries benefit when they follow the laws of comparative advantage and of market economics. The Asian Tigers embraced the global market, rather than retreating from it. They acknowledged that they could not compete in every sector, but rather let the market determine the niches they targeted. They were willing to import the necessary inputs and technology. By producing where they could succeed, these countries had sufficient income to import what they needed. The World Bank produced a well-known analysis of the Asian Tigers, praising the cases as a triumph of the liberal model. It stressed that state intervention in those economies was tangential to their success.[19]

This interpretation became part of what was known as the **Washington consensus** on development strategy. By the late 1980s, leaders in donor countries and in donor organizations, most importantly the IMF and the World Bank, agreed on what was required for successful development. Internationally, the Washington consensus embraced the virtues of open economies and free trade. Domestically, it focused on minimizing the

Washington consensus

A development strategy favored by leading donor countries and organizations that advocates open economies, free trade, and minimal interference by the state in the economy

The Policy Connection

Child Labor and the Sweatshop Dilemma

Much of the clothing and other consumer goods that Americans buy are manufactured in developing countries under conditions that many consider unacceptable. Hours are long, wages low, and workers' rights limited. Moreover, in some countries, children as young as five years old work in these factories. Worldwide, one child in every six between ages five and seventeen works, and the proportion is much higher in developing countries.[1]

A number of organizations have taken up the task of combating child labor and sweatshop conditions. One, the Fair Labor Association (FLA), has over 200 U.S. universities and colleges as members. These institutions became involved when students protested the fact that much of the clothing bearing their school's name was made in sweatshop conditions.

The FLA "Workplace Code of Conduct" states that, "No person shall be employed at an age younger than 15 (or 14 where the law of the country of manufacture allows) or younger than the age for completing compulsory education in the country of manufacture where such age is higher than 15."[2] The code also contains less specific provisions on wages, safety, and workers' rights. Members of the FLA commit to using contractors who are certified by the FLA as following the Code of Conduct.

A boy taking a break from sorting. He is one of an estimated 50,000 Brazilian children who work at garbage dumps. Are sweatshops bad if the alternative is picking through garbage? How can the range of alternatives be expanded?

AP Photo/Dado Galdieri

PHOTO © ISTOCKPHOTO

state role in the economy, inspired by the policies of the Thatcher administration in Britain and the Reagan administration in the United States in the 1980s. This view dominated the advice given to developing states, and implementing free market policies became a central condition of receiving aid and loans in the 1990s.

THE ROLE OF THE "DEVELOPMENTAL STATE"

Others, however, strongly dispute the view that the East Asian states were textbook examples of a liberal development strategy. Doubters emphasize three key deviations from that

However, there is another perspective on the problem, a view that might be called "economic realism." This view argues that in conditions of poverty that are unlikely to end anytime soon, child labor and sweatshop conditions might be better than the alternatives.

Columnist Nicholas Kristof of *The New York Times* traveled to Cambodia to report on the large number of people who work in the city garbage dump. People brave the filth and stink to collect things such as plastic bags and scraps of metal that they can then sell, earning roughly seventy-five cents per day. Working conditions are undoubtedly bad in many factories, he says, "But the primary problem in places like this is not that there are too many people being exploited in sweatshops, it's that there are not enough."[4]

The International Labor Organization (ILO) disputes the idea that child labor is economically efficient. The ILO produced a study showing that although it would take $760 billion over twenty years to put all children in school and to replace the income that they would make working, the payoff would be as much as seven times that figure.[5]

Critical Thinking Questions

1. What kinds of sacrifices should people in wealthy countries be forced to make in order to end child labor in the poorest countries?

2. Should child labor be banned, even if that labor provides an important source of income for families? If it should be allowed in poor countries, why not for poor people in wealthy countries?

[1]"Economics Focus: Sickness or Symptom," *The Economist*, February 5, 2004.
[2]Fair Labor Association, "Workplace Code of Conduct," at http://www.fairlabor.org/all/code/index.html
[3]Nicholas D. Kristof, "Inviting All Democrats," *The New York Times*, January 14, 2004.
[4]Nicholas D. Kristof, "Realities of Labor," Op-Ed Audio Slide Show, NYTimes.com, January 14, 2004.
[5]"Economics Focus: Sickness or Symptom," *The Economist*, February 5, 2004.

model. First, in the early years of their development, none of these states were democracies. South Korea, Taiwan, and Singapore were essentially authoritarian; Hong Kong was still a British colony. The authoritarian governments in these countries suppressed labor unions, sometimes violently, which kept wages much lower than they otherwise would have been. Low wages were an essential ingredient in the industrial competitiveness in these states. Only in the 1990s, when their economic success was already established, did Taiwan and South Korea become genuine democracies. In Singapore, democracy remains limited, and Hong Kong has been transferred from colonial British control to authoritarian Chinese control.

Second, in each country, the government took an active role in accumulating capital for investment and in directing that investment into particular industries. Governments picked industries in which they believed their firms could compete, such as shipbuilding in South Korea and microprocessors in Taiwan, and channeled investment into those sectors, rather than letting the market determine investment decisions. Close connections between governments and leading firms helped favored firms get access to cheap, state-subsidized capital for investment. Domestic competition was squelched so firms could concentrate on the international market. Moreover, through various mechanisms, the East Asian states provided "infant industry" protection to those industries identified as priorities for development.

Third, the state did not merely stand aside from the economy, but helped build the legal and bureaucratic infrastructure needed for capitalism to thrive. Financial markets will not automatically lead to development if insider trading and cheating are rampant, as Russia found in the 1990s. The state must do certain jobs, and do them very well. Among these jobs is investing in public education, which has been a hallmark of success in each of the Asian Tiger countries. Math and science education in these countries is far better than in the United States, and the steady supply of engineers and scientists produced by state-run universities has been essential to the continuation of earlier successes.

This more statist interpretation of the East Asian economic miracle gained currency after the Asian financial crisis of 1997–1998. That crisis helped expose the close connections between firms and the government, which in some cases were corrupt. The phrase "crony capitalism" suddenly replaced "Asian Tigers" in discussions of the region.

developmental state

A state that takes an active role in economic development by fostering the accumulation of capital to invest in particular industries and building the legal and bureaucratic infrastructure necessary for capitalism to thrive.

An alternative model of East Asian development, emphasizing the positive role played by the **developmental state**, emerged. Those who focused on the developmental state did not reject the importance of export-led growth or the role of the market domestically. However, they believed that the state plays an essential role in accumulating capital, directing investment, and providing legal, administrative, and educational infrastructure. In recent years the success of China has increased the credibility of the notion that a strong state is as important as embracing the free market, and is more important than democracy. The economic crisis in the United States and Europe beginning in 2008 further undermined the influence of the Washington consensus.

The Post-Communist Experience

The importance of the state gained renewed attention in the 1990s in light of the experiences of the post-communist states, and Russia in particular. The post-communist states were not as poor as many other developing states, but their economies were stagnating, largely because of state control. Therefore, most of the aid and advice given to post-communist governments centered on getting the government out of the economy and introducing the "invisible hand" of the market. A particular emphasis was on privatizing state-owned businesses. In the spirit of the free market, many advisors asserted that it did not matter how privatization was achieved, or who bought the firms; what mattered was getting the firms out of the hands of the state as quickly as possible. Exposing the firms to the competitive pressures of the market would achieve several objectives: align supply and demand, weed out weak and inefficient firms, direct investment and labor toward the most productive sectors, and attract foreign investment.

However, because state apparatuses were weak and corrupt, privatizing state companies worth billions of dollars became a bonanza for those well connected enough, or corrupt enough, to rig the privatization process. As a result, governments lost billions of dollars' worth of revenue, much of the economies came under the control of a small number of oligarchs, and bribery became a way of life in the government, especially in the post-Soviet states. Democracy and the free market, greeted with enthusiasm throughout the former Soviet Union in 1991, were viewed much more skeptically a decade later. By 2007, Russia and several other states had adopted a version of capitalism that preserved a major role for the state in determining economic priorities.

The central problem in the post-Soviet cases was the absence of a state authority strong enough, competent enough, and honest enough to ensure that people and firms competed fairly in the free market. The New York Stock Exchange works so well in large part because of the effective regulation of the Securities and Exchange Commission, the government agency charged with preventing fraud, insider trading, and manipulation of the market. Without such regulation, the market could not be expected to work—yet this is essentially what was expected to happen in most of the post-Soviet economies.

Assassination of Andrei Kozlov, Deputy Director of the Russian Central Bank, in 2006. Days earlier, Kozlov had advocated harsher penalties for financial crimes.

Emerging Consensus?

Today, much scholarship and many international organizations such as the World Bank are arriving at a view of development strategy that embraces both the free market and the developmental state. Although important differences of emphasis remain, most specialists acknowledge that both a competent and honest state and a willingness to embrace the market are necessary to produce economic development.

The World Bank, for example, continues to advise states to increase their openness to the global economy and to minimize market-distorting policies such as protectionism, but it is also giving increasing attention to issues of "good governance" and corruption. **Good governance** refers to government that is transparent, controlled by the rule of law, accountable, and effective. Interestingly, it now seems much easier to achieve economic openness than good governance. Once a state decides to open itself to free trade, the changes are relatively easy to implement from above. However, rooting out governmental overregulation, corruption, and incompetence requires thorough transformation, and government officials who profit from corruption may have little interest in such change.

good governance
Governance that is transparent, controlled by the rule of law, accountable, and effective.

The Changing International Environment

Even if there is increasing consensus on the best strategies for development, two significant barriers remain. The first is that domestic transformation is very difficult to accomplish. In much of Africa, for example, it is impossible to think about serious governmental reforms in countries that are plagued by civil wars, health crises (such as AIDS), corruption, and authoritarian regimes with little interest in such reforms.

However, even for those states that adopt sound strategies, it is not clear that the path followed by the East Asian states is still open. The East Asian economies developed during the Cold War, and this timing substantially influenced their access to markets. For Korea and Japan especially, the strategic importance of the region made the United States willing to tolerate significant trade deficits because the United States had a security interest in helping them develop. Today, there is no such strategic impetus, and every country has become much more sensitive to trade deficits. Although the WTO agreement has lowered many barriers to trade, many of the poorest states are not eligible for these benefits because they are not WTO members. Moreover, the WTO is weakest in the area in which developing countries are most competitive: in agricultural exports. For example, some of the poorest countries in the world, including Benin, Burkina Faso, Chad, and

Women and Development

Examine these maps of GDP per capita and women's educational levels.

Critical Thinking Questions

1. Where are the greatest disparities in educational level between men and women?

2. Do you see a correlation between overall levels of wealth and women's education?

3. If so, which of these factors is causing the other? Is it possible to tell this from the maps?

GNP per Capita Growth Rates

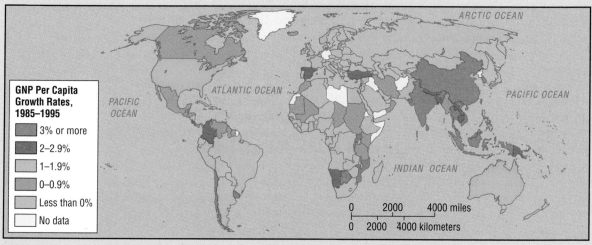

Source: http://www.worldbankorg/depweb/beyond/global/chapter4.html. Reprinted by permission of World Bank via Copyright Clearance Center.

Gender Equality and Empowerment of Women: Eliminating Differences in Education

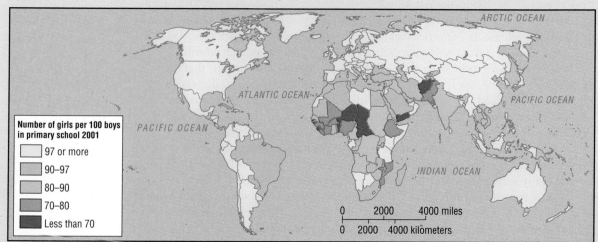

Source: http://maps.grida.no/go/graphic/gender_equality_and_empowerment_of_women_education_status

Mali, rely heavily on cotton for export earnings. They must compete not only with producers in developing countries such as China and India, but with firms in wealthy countries such as the United States, which receive large subsidies from their governments.[20] This protectionism is the source of considerable resentment in the developing world, but interest-group politics in the wealthy countries make it difficult to abolish.

A separate, and perhaps more daunting, challenge is the increasingly competitive nature of the world economy. When the Asian Tigers were thriving in the 1970s, there were few countries using their strategy of low-wage, high-technology production for the export market. Today, many developing countries are trying this strategy, including not only the technologically advanced countries of post-communist Europe, but China and India. With over two billion people willing to work at low wages and with increasing technological sophistication, there seems to be little room for other competition on this basis. American labor has often complained that its low-wage jobs are moving to Mexico—but even Mexican workers, cheap by American standards, are finding their jobs outsourced to even cheaper labor in China.

The Role of Foreign Aid in Development

Whether out of altruism or self-interest, states, individuals, and international organizations have taken a strong interest in combating poverty and reducing inequality. Even those who are generally skeptical about the role of governments in the economy often advocate for foreign aid. The World Bank, at the height of the Washington consensus on free markets, continued to advocate and coordinate development aid. Historically, the crucial role of aid was demonstrated by the reconstruction of Europe after World War II, where the World Bank got its start. Similarly, the success of the U.S. Marshall Plan aid in rebuilding Europe (and in reducing support there for communism) provided both altruistic and self-interested justification for aid.

Over time, the approaches and strategies for international development aid have shifted as the prevailing thinking about the purposes of aid and the most effective programs has shifted. In much of the post–World War II period, development aid focused on infrastructure, technical know-how needed for development, and the investment funds that could build these things. Such projects were essential for further growth but were unlikely to be funded by private investment, either because of their public character (roads, dams, ports) or because the payoffs were of such a long-term nature that private investors would not be interested. Because private capital was in short supply, having wealthy state governments raise capital and distribute it through international organizations was seen as a solution. The hope was that by allowing states to build infrastructure, aid would create a better environment for smaller-scale private investment to succeed. That strategy characterized the post-war construction era up through the 1960s.

Under the presidency of Robert McNamara (1968–1981), the World Bank shifted from infrastructure projects to a **basic human needs approach** aimed at short-term alleviation of poverty. The belief was that if basic problems of food, shelter, and health care were not addressed, individuals and societies could not make longer term decisions and investments.

In the 1980s and 1990s, the goal of aid shifted again, to structural adjustment. **Structural adjustment** refers to efforts to strengthen the financial basis of a country's economy. The strategy was inspired by the focus on the free market and the role of monetary policy then ascendant in Western states (the Washington consensus). The strategy was to improve the investment climate by reducing government budget deficits and by stabilizing the value of the currency. Funding from the World Bank and the IMF was often

basic human needs approach

A development strategy focusing on the short-term alleviation of poverty as a prerequisite for further progress.

structural adjustment

A strategy adopted by the World Bank in the 1980s and 1990s aimed at strengthening the financial basis of a country's economy.

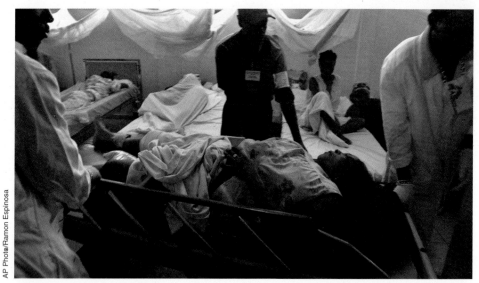

Members of Médecins Sans Frontières (Doctors Without Borders) work to save those wounded in a clash between Haitian gang members and UN Peacekeepers at this aid-funded clinic. Basic human needs approaches to development aim at directly addressing the problems of poor people, rather than on macro-level economic growth.

used to help states through the most difficult part of this process, and structural adjustment programs were often made a requirement for other kinds of international support.

Most recently, aid has focused on good governance. The current wisdom is that markets cannot function in the absence of a competent and honest government and that corruption plays a major role in undermining investment in particular and economic growth in general. Additionally, a focus on the UN Millennium Development Goals, with their emphasis on human development, signals a partial return to the basic human needs approach.

International aid has also played an important role in addressing emergencies and humanitarian crises around the world. Food aid has repeatedly been used to reduce starvation when food supplies have fallen short for one reason or another. International aid to refugees displaced by war or natural disasters has been important, as has immediate help to countries in times of natural disaster, such as after the Haitian earthquake of January 2010.

Shortcomings of International Aid

There is considerable debate on whether and how aid actually contributes to development. One problem with most international aid is that it goes primarily to governments. In general, this makes sense because it is governments that are generally charged with getting economies to function better. For example, the central goal of structural adjustment aid is to shore up weaknesses in a government's financial position. However, the government may be a central part of the problem, through some combination of corruption or incompetence, and even when a government is competent in general, it may be ill suited to carrying out the tasks envisioned by the aid.

If governments cannot or will not spend aid effectively, the money may be wasted. When the money in question is lent, rather than donated outright, the society faces a financial burden that it must repay. International organizations and governments have been widely criticized for lending money to corrupt Third World governments, which sometimes simply funnel the money into offshore bank accounts or into the hands of their supporters. Regardless of what happens to the money, the citizens of that country are left to pay it back through tax payments, sometimes long after the corrupt government in question is gone (along with the money). For countries that have a difficult time earning enough hard currency to fund investment, having to spend that money to pay back debts incurred by previous governments for projects that yielded no benefits is especially frustrating.

Another problem is that aid sometimes flows out of a country as quickly as it flows in. What economists call the "multiplier effect" of aid then may accrue to the donor rather than to the recipient. The **multiplier effect** refers to the fact that when money is spent (for example, on goods), the person or firm receiving the money often spends all or part of it on something else, and the recipient of those purchases does the same, and so on. Thus, a single donation has its effect multiplied as it flows through an economy, yielding profit to a succession of firms or individuals. If the money flows immediately out of the country, the multiplier effect goes with it.

This is especially true of so-called **tied aid**, which must be spent on goods or services from the donor country. Especially when tied aid comes in the form of loans, the receiving country may get little of the benefit of the aid, but be responsible for paying back the entire loan. For example, the Freedom Support Act, through which the United States provided aid to the post-Soviet states after 1991, required that much of the money be spent on U.S. grain and farm equipment, both of which were more cheaply available in Russia. The benefit to U.S. firms was obvious, but it is not clear that this provision of the act provided a substantial benefit to the Russian economy. In a similar vein, the World Bank has been faulted for requiring that significant portions of its aid be spent on technical assistance, which generally comes in the form of costly consultants from developed states.

Some analysts support the idea of aid but believe that the shortcomings of aid are so common, and so difficult to combat, that in practice aid does more harm than good. Economist William Easterly charges that "one of the best economic ideas of our time, the genius of free markets, was presented in one of the worst possible ways, with unelected outsiders imposing rigid doctrines on the xenophobic unwilling."[21] For example, if it is true that aid can only be implemented wisely by competent governments, it is also true that countries with competent governments are among the least likely to need aid. Many would take exception with this view, arguing that substantial aid packages make it much easier for competent governments to pursue economic reforms.

A more strident school of thought disagrees with aid in principle, based on a belief in the primacy of markets. To those who believe that any interference with the market inhibits reform, aid makes the problem worse, not better. It is hard to test this theory for two reasons. First, to withhold aid altogether would be considered inhumane by many. Second, interference with market forces is practiced by every government in the world and is provided for in international agreements such as the WTO, and it is unlikely that the "pure" market would be adopted in this one area.

multiplier effect

An economic effect whereby an increase in spending (for example, of funds provided to a country by a donor) produces an increase in national income and consumption greater than the initial amount spent. When aid flows out of a country, the benefit of aid may accrue to the donor rather than to the recipient.

tied aid

Aid that must be spent on goods or services from the donor country.

Multilateral Aid and the World Bank

Multilateral aid pools donations by multiple states and then distributes the aid through international organizations. There are various international organizations engaged in providing multilateral aid, including the World Bank, the IMF, and the UN Development Programme.

Among these organizations, the World Bank, based in Washington, D.C., is widely considered the most important because it is the primary vehicle for multilateral aid in terms of the amount of money disbursed. It also influences other donors. Individual governments and private lenders routinely rely upon the World Bank's evaluations in making their own decisions about aid and lending. Moreover, it has widely recognized expertise in the area of development (although many disagree with its views). As a result, the World Bank has played a leading role in defining the "best practices" in development aid for the past six decades. More fundamentally, the World Bank has shaped the very definition of "development," which is often taken for granted but which shapes the purpose of all aid activities.[22] Because it plays this central role, the World Bank has been a primary target for criticism by those who question the dominant practices.

STRUCTURE OF THE BANK

The World Bank consists of two main structures and several smaller ones. The two main structures are the International Bank for Reconstruction and Development (IBRD) and the International Development Association (IDA).

The IDA focuses on the poorest countries, those who may have considerable difficulty paying back any aid. It averages roughly $14 billion per year in new loans, over half of which is spend in sub-Saharan Africa and almost another third of which is spent in South Asia. In 2009, the top five borrowers were Nigeria, Pakistan, Ethiopia, Vietnam, and Bangladesh. Its loans have a ten-year grace period on repayment of the principle; in 2009, however, 18 percent of loans were grants, meaning they do not need to be repaid. The main program areas are infrastructure (35 percent), social sector such as education and health services (26 percent), and public administration (19 percent). One sees in this funding a mix of development strategies: infrastructure development, basic human needs, and improved governance.[23]

The IBRD focuses its lending on middle-income countries and poorer countries considered to be a good risk in terms of repaying loans. South Asia and Africa each receive about a quarter of the bank's loans, with Latin American, Eastern Europe, and Asia receiving between 15 and 20 percent each. The two largest areas of focus are public administration and law enforcement (22 percent) and transportation (20 percent). Other areas of emphasis include water and sanitation, health, and education.[24]

Two smaller World Bank agencies seek to foster private investment in developing economies. The International Finance Corporation finances private investment in developing countries. The Multilateral Investment Guarantee Agency provides political risk insurance for private investors, helping protect them against political turmoil in developing countries, and therefore reducing the danger of investing.

Whereas voting on policy is based on "one state/one vote" within most international organizations, voting in the World Bank (and in the IMF) is based on the financial contributions each member makes to the Bank's lending resources. In 2009, the United States had 16.4 percent of the votes, followed by Japan with 7.9 percent, Germany with 4.5 percent, and France and Britain with 4.3 percent each. The remaining 182 World Bank member states each have less than 1 percent of the vote. Moreover, the president of the World Bank is, by tradition, always an American.

The voting structure of the World Bank is based on pragmatism. It would be impossible to get the wealthy countries to put significant resources into an organization they did not control. However, this structure is one source of dissatisfaction with the World Bank. The developing countries have little influence at the Bank. This leads to accusations that the Bank remains a semicolonial organization, in which the wealthy countries decide what will happen to the poor ones.

Table 11.3 Voting Shares at the World Bank, June 2010

Country	Percent of Votes
United States	16.40
Japan	7.87
Germany	4.49
France	4.31
United Kingdom	4.31
Canada	2.78
China	2.78
India	2.78
Italy	2.78
Russia	2.78
Saudi Arabia	2.78
Netherlands	2.21
Brazil	2.07
Belgium	1.80
Spain	1.74
Switzerland	1.66
Australia	1.52
Iran	1.48
Venezuela	1.27
Mexico	1.18
Argentina	1.12

The rest of the World Bank's 187 members have less than 1.12 percent of the vote.

Source: World Bank, "International Bank for Reconstruction and Development Subscriptions and Voting Power of Member Countries," at http://siteresources.worldbank.org/BODINT/Resources/278027-1215524804501/IBRDCountryVotingTable.pdf

Figure 11.3 World Bank Project Cycle

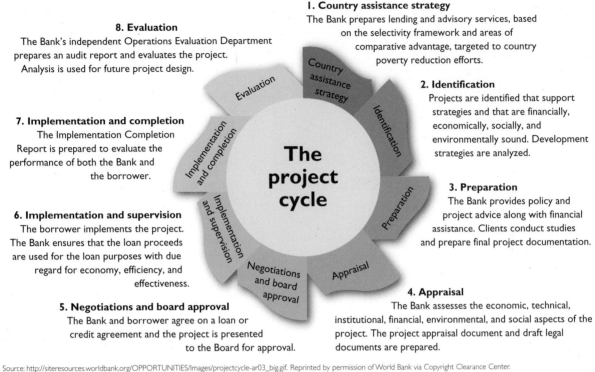

1. Country assistance strategy
The Bank prepares lending and advisory services, based on the selectivity framework and areas of comparative advantage, targeted to country poverty reduction efforts.

2. Identification
Projects are identified that support strategies and that are financially, economically, socially, and environmentally sound. Development strategies are analyzed.

3. Preparation
The Bank provides policy and project advice along with financial assistance. Clients conduct studies and prepare final project documentation.

4. Appraisal
The Bank assesses the economic, technical, institutional, financial, environmental, and social aspects of the project. The project appraisal document and draft legal documents are prepared.

5. Negotiations and board approval
The Bank and borrower agree on a loan or credit agreement and the project is presented to the Board for approval.

6. Implementation and supervision
The borrower implements the project. The Bank ensures that the loan proceeds are used for the loan purposes with due regard for economy, efficiency, and effectiveness.

7. Implementation and completion
The Implementation Completion Report is prepared to evaluate the performance of both the Bank and the borrower.

8. Evaluation
The Bank's independent Operations Evaluation Department prepares an audit report and evaluates the project. Analysis is used for future project design.

Source: http://siteresources.worldbank.org/OPPORTUNITIES/Images/projectcycle-ar03_big.gif. Reprinted by permission of World Bank via Copyright Clearance Center.

ACTIVITIES OF THE BANK

The World Bank has three important functions.

- Conducting research on development issues
- Making policy recommendations to specific governments
- Lending money

In practice, these three activities are closely linked. Policy recommendations are often linked directly to loans provided by the IBRD and IDA. In a practice known as **conditionality**, states wishing to receive loans from the World Bank must agree to certain conditions, which generally take the form of a set of policies that the World Bank believes will help promote development. Countries often resent these conditions—but when they are desperate for a loan, they feel they have little choice but to accept them. In many cases, the terms of those loans are *concessionary*, meaning that the interest rates and repayment schedules are more generous than what could be obtained in private financial markets—but in all cases the loans must be repaid whether the recipient's economy improves or not. A developing country that defaulted on loans from the World Bank would find virtually every other source of credit cut off as well. Therefore, it is important that loans are made wisely and programs implemented effectively, but that has not always been the case.

conditionality

The requirement that an aid recipient agree to a set of conditions that the donor believes will help promote development in the country.

CRITIQUES OF THE WORLD BANK

The World Bank has been the target of sustained criticism, from policy experts and social activists alike. The joint meetings of the World Bank and the IMF, held every year in Washington, D.C., are routinely the target of protests by thousands of people, and much of central Washington is shut down in order to keep protestors from gathering at the Bank's headquarters.

Protesters outside the World Bank in Washington, D.C., in 2007.

The World Bank has its own version of the rational action model of decision making and has been widely criticized for deviating from the model in various ways.

Some of the criticisms of the World Bank echo the general criticisms of development aid. Others are specific to the World Bank. The following are among the most significant criticisms of the World Bank:

- The voting procedure disenfranchises the poor countries that have the most at stake.

- Lending, unless it is highly effective, may leave recipients with debts but without much benefit.

- Conditionality undermines the sovereignty of recipient governments.

- Conditionality often requires harsh economic policies, which hurt the poorest people in the recipient countries most.

- Conditions that produce hardship can lead to unrest, destabilizing the very government the Bank is trying to help and undermining the basis for reform.

- Development projects supported by the World Bank have been focused only on narrow economic performance, and in some cases have had severe environmental consequences.

- The Bank's analysis and its conditionality policies seem to be driven by an ideology, economic liberalism, that many believe is too simplistic for the problems it addresses.

Despite the frequently bitter criticisms leveled at the World Bank, it remains one of the few available sources of investment, advice, and credibility for the development efforts of poor states. Despite the dissatisfaction with it, therefore, the rich states continue to support it financially, and poor states continue to look to it for aid.

Bilateral Foreign Aid

Bilateral foreign aid, defined as aid given by one government directly to another, is almost as controversial as World Bank aid. Although there are important historical successes, bilateral foreign aid is criticized both within the donor countries and internationally.

In the United States, many politicians have criticized the amount of funding spent on foreign aid projects. Others, however, believe that U.S. aid levels are too low. Respondents to a 1995 public opinion survey estimated, on average, that U.S. foreign aid was 15 percent of the national budget. In fact, aid at that time made up less than half of 1 percent of the U.S. budget.[25] The gross overestimation of how much is being spent may have some effect on how unpopular that aid is and therefore on the likely political support for such aid. Since 1960, U.S. foreign aid has decreased from 0.52 percent of GDP to 0.24 percent.[26] As Figure 11.4 shows, the United States is the largest donor in terms of absolute dollars but is far behind in terms of aid as a percentage of GDP.

There are two main arguments against bilateral aid. First, bilateral aid is often seen as serving the geopolitical needs of the donors more than the development needs of the recipients. Thus, the single largest recipient of U.S. foreign aid in recent years has been Iraq. For the past few decades, the top recipient was not a developing country at

Figure 11.4 Aid in U.S. Dollars and as a Percentage of Gross National Income (GNI). The total net official development assistance in 2009 was about $119 billion.

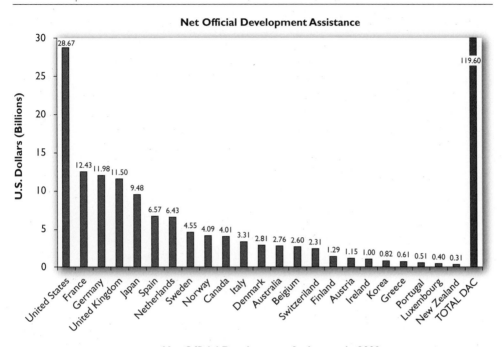

Net Official Development Assistance

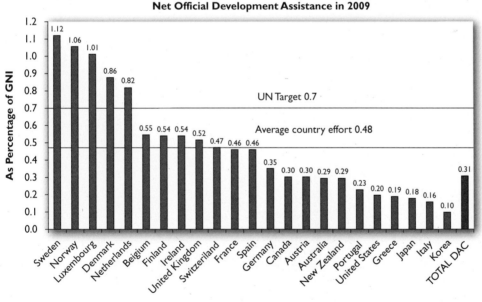

Net Official Development Assistance in 2009

Note: DAC refers to the Development Assistance Committee, an organization of major aid-providing countries.
Source: http://www.oecd.org/dataoecd/23/14/37955301.pdf. Reprinted by permission of OECD.

all, but rather Israel, a key ally in the Middle East. Following Israel, the second biggest U.S. aid recipient is Egypt, in return for its role in the Middle East peace process. Figure 11.5, showing U.S. aid in 1994 and 2004, gives some indication as to how priorities have shifted.

Second, a great deal of bilateral aid is tied aid, which must be spent on goods and services from the donor country, such that much of the economic benefit accrues to firms in the donor states. In particular, critics point out that much bilateral aid is in the form

Figure 11.5 Top U.S. Aid and Grant Recipients in 2008 and 2000

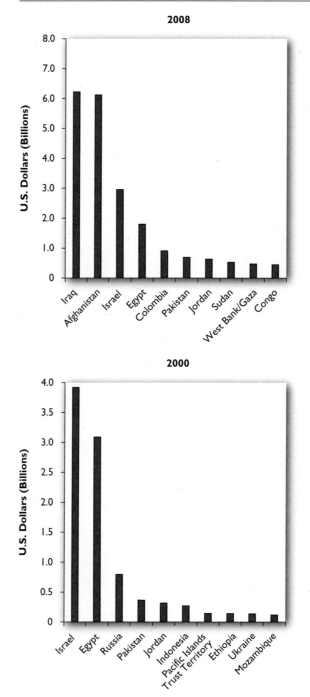

Source: Curt Tarnoff and Larry Nowels, "Foreign Aid: An Introductory Overview of U.S. Programs and Policy," U.S. Congressional Research Service, April 2004, p.13.

of loans to buy military equipment from the donor. Such purchases contribute nothing to the economy of the aid recipient and may make the region in question less secure.

Nonetheless, foreign aid remains an important foreign policy tool, even if it is not a significant development tool for the poor countries of the world. Shifting patterns of aid programs show that countries tend to contribute where they have the most immediate foreign policy aims. In the 1990s, for example, the EU concentrated its aid efforts on the post-communist states of eastern Europe, the stability and prosperity of which were considered essential to the security and economic interests of the EU. In the past decade, China has taken on a larger foreign aid role, especially in countries in Africa with important natural resource supplies.

After the attacks of September 11, 2001, aid from various governments shifted to the states of Central Asia, which are viewed as crucial in dislodging the Taliban movement in Afghanistan and in preventing the spread of militant Islamic fundamentalism. That the governments are neither democratic nor following accepted economic development strategies was less important than that they are willing to ally themselves with the West in the "global war on terror." From the perspective of economic development, this may not make much sense, but from the perspective of national security, it makes a great deal of sense. Thus, bilateral aid is best thought of as a foreign policy tool, not as a development tool.

Reconsider the Case

India: From Riches, to Rags, to . . . What?

India's poverty at the time of independence could be blamed in large part on colonialism, but the end of colonialism did not automatically put the country on the path to rapid growth. Since then, India experimented first with an import-substitution model of development, which after several decades was viewed as a failure. Later, a model that combined export-led growth with domestic liberalization yielded better overall results, and for many, India's high-tech industries make the country a new global powerhouse to be admired and feared.

However, when examining the question of poverty, India's recent experience looks more mixed. Eighty-six percent of Indians live on less than $2 per day.[27] Twenty-nine percent of Indians live below the government-defined poverty line. Forty-seven percent of children under five are malnourished.[28]

Is India's glass "half full" or "half empty?" Clearly, most of the trends are moving in the right direction. But whether this is good news or not depends on how progress is defined. Overall, India's growth rate is faster than that of many developing and developed states. But given where it is now, it will take a very

long time for India to match European standards of living, even if current trends prevail. Similarly, although the poverty rate is being reduced, inequality in India is actually growing.[29] Is it possible to devise economic development strategies that reduce not only the poverty rate, but the gap between rich and poor? This is not just a question for international economics, but for policy makers who must try to steer their countries along the uncertain path of economic development.

Critical Thinking Questions

1. How has India's recent economic strategy compared to that of the Asian Tigers?
2. Given the measures India took in 1991 to open up its domestic market to free trade and reduce government controls, what factors do you think will determine whether India's reforms will be a success?
3. How might it be possible to devise development models for countries such as India that close gaps between poor and rich as well as lifting people out of poverty?

Summary

There remains considerable debate about the causes and potential cures of global inequality and of the poverty that pervades much of the world. Does the international system breed inequality, or is free trade the route to wealth? The uneven pattern of success and failure across states indicates that neither of these arguments is always true. Recent findings indicate that what goes on in the international system is not nearly as important as domestic policies within poor countries.[30] If so, what domestic factors seem to inhibit and which seem to promote wealth creation? The debate has evolved in recent years, and there is increasing agreement on a combination of previously accepted views. Socialist approaches, in which the state makes most of the decisions in the economy, have been discredited among scholars but have made a minor comeback among governments such as that of Venezuela. To a large extent, import substitution has also been discredited. There is broad agreement that the market is essential to economic growth. However, there remains considerable disagreement on the proper role of the state. Some see the state as doing more harm than good; others see the "developmental state" as a key actor in creating and maintaining a strong market and in building internationally competitive business. After the 2008 economic crisis, state intervention also appeared useful for limiting the tendency for free markets to spin out of control

Increasingly, analysts and policy makers are coming to believe that international trade promotes economic development, as the experience of the Asian Tigers seemed to demonstrate, but many continue to argue that trade is fundamentally unfair and will lead to increasing gaps between rich and poor. Foreign aid is equally controversial. The funds allocated for it remain miniscule, and much bilateral foreign aid is aimed at political goals rather than economic development. Despite the lofty pronouncements often made about substantially reducing global poverty, it will quite likely remain a serious problem for decades to come.

Key Concepts

1. Human Development Index (HDI)
2. Gini coefficient
3. Late development
4. Economies of scale
5. Network effects
6. Import substitution
7. Export-led growth
8. Washington consensus
9. Developmental state
10. World Bank
11. Tied aid
12. Good governance

Study Questions

1. What are some different ways of defining and measuring poverty?
2. What challenges do late developers face that early developers did not?
3. What have been the major strategies adopted by late developers?
4. What contrasting explanations are there for the success of the Asian Tigers?
5. What are the main arguments for and against foreign aid?

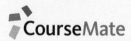
CourseMate

Endnotes

1. Manmohan Singh, "Of Oxford, Economics, Empire, and Freedom," *The Hindu,* July 10, 2005, p. 1.

2. These statistics are from Gurcharan Das, "The India Model," *Foreign Affairs* 85.4 (July/August 2006): p. 2.

3. UC Atlas of Global Inequality, at http://ucatlas.ucsc.edu/income/rtioppp.html

4. UN Development Programme (UNDP), *Millennium Development Goals: A Compact Among Nations to End Human Poverty* (New York: UNDP, 2003), p. 3.

5. Steve Schifferes, "Can Globalization Be Tamed?" BBC, February 24, 2002.

6. World Bank, *World Development Report 2000/2001* (New York: Oxford University Press, 2001), p. 3.

7. Henry Shue, *Basic Rights: Subsistence, Affluence, and Foreign Policy,* 2nd ed. (Princeton, NJ: Princeton University Press, 1996).

8. See UNDP, *Human Development Report 2007/2008: Fighting Climate Change: Human Solidarity in a Divided World* (New York: UNDP, 2007).

9. George W. Bush, remarks at United Nations Financing for Development Conference, March 22, 2002, at http://www.pbs.org/newshour/updates/march02/bush_3-22.html

10. See Amartya Sen, *On Economic Inequality,* expanded ed. (Oxford: Clarendon Press, 1997 [1973]), pp. 164ff.

11. UNCHR, "What Is Poverty?," at http://www.unhchr.ch/development/poverty-02.html

12. World Bank, "GNI Per Capita 2007, Atlas Method and PPP," at http://siteresources.worldbank.org/DATASTATISTICS/Resources/GNIPC.pdf

13. See http://www.un.org/millenniumgoals/. In the text, the wording of some of the goals has been edited for the sake of brevity.

14. Thomas D. Lairson and David Skidmore, *International Political Economy: The Struggle for Power and Wealth,* 3rd ed. (Belmont, CA: Wadsworth, 2003), p. 246.

15. Herman Schwartz, *States versus Markets: History, Geography, and the Development of the International Political Economy* (New York: St. Martin's 1994), p. 10.

16. Schwartz, *States versus Markets,* p. 10.

17. The classic exposition of the theory of late development is Alexander Gerschenkron, *Economic Backwardness in Historical Perspective* (Cambridge, MA: Belknap Press, 1962).

18. Lairson and Skidmore, *International Political Economy,* p. 268.

19. The World Bank, *The East Asian Economic Miracle: Economic Growth and Public Policy* (New York: Oxford University Press, 1993).

20. See Kym Anderson and Ernesto Valenzuela, "The World Trade Organization's Doha Initiative: A Tale of Two Issues," *The World Economy* Vol. 30, No. 8 (2007): p. 1282.

21. William Easterly, "The Ideology of Development," *Foreign Policy* (July/August 2007): p. 31.

22. For a short critique of the World Bank, see Easterly, "The Ideology of Development"; for a longer and more radical critique, see Arturo Escobar, *Encountering Development: The Making and Unmaking of the Third World* (Princeton, NJ: Princeton University Press 1995).

23. Data in this paragraph are from the IDA Web page, at http://go.worldbank.org/ZRAOR8IWW0

24. Data in this paragraph are from the IBRD Web page, at http://go.worldbank.org/SH36X77BF0

25. Lairson and Skidmore, *International Political Economy,* p. 315.

26. Theodore Cohn, *Global Political Economy: Theory and Practice,* 2nd ed. (New York: Longman, 2002), p. 405.

27. World Resources Institute, "Economic Trends: India," at http://earth-trends.wri.org/pdf_library/country_profiles/eco_cou_356.pdf, p. 2.

28. World Bank, "India at a Glance," at http://devdata.worldbank.org/AAG/ind_aag.pdf

29. "Sensex Nicks 9000, But What About Gini Coefficient?" *The Indian Express,* December 4, 2005, at http://www.indianexpress.com/res/web/pIe/columnists/full_column.php?content_id=83241

30. Several recent books that make this case are also excellent overviews of the problems of global development and underdevelopment. See Robert Calderisi, *The Trouble with Africa: Why Foreign Aid Isn't Working* (New York: Palgrave Macmillan, 2006); Paul Collier, *The Bottom Billion: Why the Poorest Countries Are Failing and What Can Be Done About It* (New York: Oxford University Press 2007); William Easterly, *The White Man's Burden: Why the West's Efforts to Aid the Rest Have Done So Much Ill and So Little Good* (New York: Penguin Press, 2006); and David Ellerman, *Helping People Help Themselves: From the World Bank to an Alternative Philosophy of Development Assistance* (Ann Arbor: University of Michigan Press, 2006).

International Organizations and Transnational Actors

LEARNING OBJECTIVES

After completing this chapter, the student should be able to . . .

1. Define "international governmental organization," "international nongovernmental organization," "transnational corporation," and "transnational advocacy network."

2. Describe the structure of the United Nations and the functions of its various agencies, programs, funds, and commissions.

3. Evaluate different arguments concerning the significance of the United Nations.

4. Describe the structure of the European Union and the functions of its various branches and institutions.

5. Analyze the challenges facing the European Union.

6. Assess the influence of transnational corporations on governments.

7. Identify the ways in which international nongovernmental organizations and transnational advocacy networks influence international politics.

◀ United Nations Headquarters in New York City
AP Photo/Osamu Honda

Consider the Case

Sudan: Who Can End the Genocide?

Genocide in the Darfur region of Sudan emerged in 2003 out of a civil war. When government forces were unsuccessful in defeating rebels among Darfur's local tribes, the government switched instead to a policy of genocide, using a combination of its own forces and *janjaweed* militia, which it armed and supported. The United Nations estimates that 300,000 people have died in Darfur, and over two million were displaced.

Around the world, there was widespread agreement that intervention was necessary to counter what was widely viewed as genocide. But the question was, Who should conduct the intervention? Initially, the Sudanese government and the international community agreed on a force of 7000 troops from the African Union (AU), a regional organization. These troops began operations in 2004. However, the AU forces were lightly armed and were charged only with observing a cease-fire. They had no power to actually stop the violence, which continued unabated.

In August 2006, the United Nations Security Council agreed to send a UN force of 17,000 troops to the region to replace the AU troops, a plan to which the Sudanese government strongly objected. Some, frustrated with the inefficacy of the AU forces and the delay in deploying a UN force, advocated that a third international organization, NATO, intervene: "Who besides NATO has the requisite size of forces, the logistical and transport capacity, the essential interoperability, and the experience to mount such a protection operation?"[1]

In 2009, the International Criminal Court (ICC) indicted Sudanese President Omar al-Bashir on charges of war crimes. Bashir was the first sitting head of state to be indicted by the ICC. The debate surrounding the decisions to indict Bashir helped keep the international focus on Darfur. However, no one was willing to apply the force needed to eject Bashir from power or to bring him to justice.

In the meantime, a broad array of NGOs was involved in bringing relief to Darfur, including Oxfam, the International Crisis Group, and Médicins Sans Frontières (Doctors Without Borders). They faced difficulties delivering aid because they were subject to attack and detention, but it was these NGOs—not the UN or any outside governments—that were primarily responsible for ensuring that even more people did not die.

International efforts to deal with the conflict in Darfur raise important questions about who the key actors will be in the future. Individual nation-states (outside of Sudan) played a relatively minor role. Rather, states pursued their goals largely through international organizations such as the AU, the UN, or the ICC.

As the situation dragged on, the question remained: Who could successfully intervene to stop the genocide? Could the AU develop the necessary capacity? Could the UN persuade the Sudanese government to allow its troops in? Would NATO step up, as it did in the former Yugoslavia? Or would a solution depend on stronger intervention by nation-states, such as the United States and China? Would the ICC's indictment of Bashir on genocide charges galvanize an international reaction? So far, individual states have chosen not to intervene. The preference has been for intervention by international organizations, but they too have failed to stop the violence. Only the NGOs have been able to accomplish anything concrete.

The case of Darfur epitomizes both the hopes and the frustrations that IOs elicit. Many people express skepticism about the ability of individual states and traditional, established international institutions, such as the UN and the World Bank, to solve difficult international crises. Where these older institutions are failing, regional IOs and new international NGOs are intervening to provide solutions.

This trend raises several important questions. In what ways can international governmental organizations (IGOs) solve problems that states, or temporary alliances between

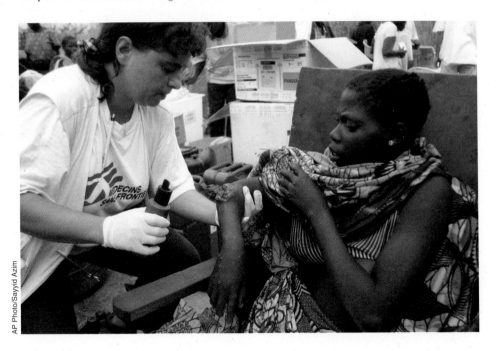

A medic with Médecins Sans Frontières (Doctors Without Borders) treats a young woman injured as tribal militias clash in the Congo.

AP Photo/Sayyid Azim

states, cannot? What is the function and future of transnational NGOs? How are these organizations infringing on state sovereignty, and is their rise an indication of the end of the Westphalian system? This chapter will address these questions by examining the structure and function of the UN, the EU, and other IGOs and by exploring the rise of NGOs and other transnational actors and their impact on the state.

Types of International Organizations

International governmental organizations (IGOs) are generally defined as organizations whose membership consists of three or more nation-states.[2] In such organizations, representatives of states gather to discuss issues that are of mutual interest to the member states. IGOs are also generally defined as having permanent secretariats or bureaucracies (so while the UN and WTO are IGOs, the G-8 is not). Today, there are thousands of IGOs. Some, like the UN, have universal or nearly universal membership, meaning that every state is a member. Others have some subset of states as members, based on either a particular interest or a particular region. The Association of Southeast Asian Nations (ASEAN), as its name implies, has as members states located in Southeast Asia and concerns itself with regional issues. The Organization of Petroleum Exporting Countries (OPEC) has members around the world and is concerned with promoting the interests of oil exporters. Some IGOs are more obscure and are concerned with more mundane issues. The mission of the International Postal Union, for example, is to coordinate the delivery of mail across state borders. All of these organizations, however, share a common characteristic: They are formed by states and have states, rather than individual citizens, firms, or other actors, as their members.

Why do states form IGOs and why do they work through them? Different theoretical perspectives have different answers to this question. Liberal institutionalism provides the standard explanation: States form IGOs because it is in their interest to do so. Some problems can be solved more easily and less expensively with IGOs than without them. In particular, liberal institutionalism focuses on collective action problems (prisoners'

international governmental organizations (IGOs)
Organizations whose membership consists of three or more nation-states.

dilemmas), such as the security dilemma, the temptation to enact competitive tariffs, and the difficulty in agreeing to protect the environment.

To address many of these problems, states need to coordinate their activities and monitor other states to make sure they are living up to their commitments. For example, in the case of the security dilemma, states that seek to avoid nuclear proliferation needed to form the IAEA to monitor the agreement and to help states complying with it to legally exploit nuclear energy. In the case of free trade, the WTO was formed to coordinate the negotiation of tariffs and to provide a mechanism for resolving disputes. In the case of the environment, the Intergovernmental Panel on Climate Change has been established to collect data and provide scientific analysis of climate change. Some of these tasks might be vastly more complicated and expensive to implement without the mechanism of IGOs. Others would be impossible. For example, without the reliable information on various countries' nuclear programs provided by the IAEA, the security dilemma,

Table 12.1 Types and Examples of International Organizations[3]

International Governmental Organizations (IGOs)		
Global IGOs	Security	UUN Security Council
	Trade	World Trade Organization
	Finance	International Monetary Fund
		Bank for International Settlements
	Development	World Bank
		UN Conference on Trade and Development
	Human rights/	UN High Commission for Refugees
	Humanitarian aid	UN Relief and Works Agency
	Environment	UN Environment Program
Regional IGOs	Security	North Atlantic Treaty Organization
		African Union
	Trade	Economic Community of West African States (ECOWAS)
		ASEAN
	Finance	European Central Bank
	Development	Asian Development Bank
		African Development Bank
	Human rights/	European Human Rights Commission
	Humanitarian aid	
	Environment	International Commission for Protection of the Danube River Mediterranean Commission for Sustainable Development
Transnational Actors		
TNCs		Coca-Cola, Mitsubishi, Royal Dutch Shell, Novartis, many others
INGOs	Security	International Committee of the Red Cross Campaign to Ban Landmines
	Trade	International Trade Union Confederation
		Global Exchange
	Finance	Jubilee Debt Campaign
	Development	OxFam
		Save the Children
	Human rights/	Human Rights Watch
	Humanitarian aid	Amnesty International
		Médecins Sans Frontières
	Environment	Greenpeace
		World Wildlife Fund

combined with uncertainty about other countries' programs, would likely compel far more countries to pursue nuclear weapons.

IGOs are sometimes created not to solve specific collective action problems, but to provide a forum for discussion. This is the primary function of the UN General Assembly. It has no predetermined agenda, but it provides a forum in which states can discuss and debate issues that arise. The UN Security Council has a narrower agenda but is also primarily a forum. Similarly, one primary goal of the WTO is simply to organize meetings at which states negotiate to solve problems.

There are thousands of IOs less prominent than the UN, each playing some role in linking governmental decision making in one particular area. There remains considerable disagreement about the significance of states' growing reliance on IOs. To some, the result is an increasingly important web of "global governance." The word *governance*, rather than *government*, emphasizes that norms are being established and affairs regulated in the absence of an overarching government. A single government need not be established to achieve global governance.

Transnational actors, in contrast, are organizations that work across national boundaries, but whose members are not states. These too are proliferating today. One of the most prevalent categories of transnational actors is **transnational corporations (TNCs)**—corporations that have operations in more than one country (also known as multinational corporations, or MNCs). A second broad category of transnational actors is transnational **nongovernmental organizations (NGOs)**. NGOs are so diverse that a simple characterization is difficult to devise. The category includes groups, such as Greenpeace, that are similar to domestic interest groups but have concerns and organizational structures that are transnational in scope. It also includes groups that focus not on influencing governments, but on conducting activities in different countries. This would include many humanitarian organizations, such as the International Committee of the Red Cross, pro-democracy groups such as the International Renaissance Foundation, or health care providers such as the International Planned Parenthood Federation. Most large organized churches, which conduct activities in many countries, can also be thought of as transnational actors. The key characteristic of all these is that their members may be individuals or national-level organizations but are not states.

transnational corporations (TNCs)
Corporations with operations in more than one country; also called multinational corporations (MNCs).

nongovernmental organizations (NGOs)
A broad category of diverse organizations, including groups similar to domestic interest groups but with transnational concerns and organizational structures, and groups that focus not on influencing governments, but on conducting activities in different countries.

A Tale of Two IGOs

In the years following World War II, many IOs were formed, including the UN (1945) and the EU (originally formed as the European Coal and Steel Community [ECSC] in 1951). The UN was born fully formed with a wide range of institutions, and many had great hopes that it would foster peace and economic development. In contrast, the ECSC was formed around a relatively narrow issue and had a similarly limited institutional apparatus. The UN, in the eyes of many, has failed to fulfill the high expectations of 1945, whereas the EU has achieved broader and deeper collaboration than anyone thought possible. Although the UN has seemed powerless to limit conflict, the EU has helped to make war among European states seem inconceivable after centuries in which it was considered normal. And whereas the relevance of the UN is often questioned, the EU has come to be seen as the standard for a regional IGO. A discussion of these two IGOs, therefore, reveals the potential and the limitations of IGOs.

The United Nations System

The UN was formed at the end of World War II to provide a means by which the great powers of the day could join forces to promote peace and development. It is the most visible IGO and the one with the broadest scope. Its membership is universal. Indeed, membership in the UN is generally seen as the main criterion by which a state can be said to be a recognized sovereign state in the modern system. The UN General Assembly has a mandate that allows it to address nearly any area of international relations, and its vast array of specialized organizations addresses a great number of issues, as Figure 12.1indicates.

The UN is important symbolically because it is the nearest thing there is to a body that represents the international community. Some see the UN as the hope of mankind, as providing a way to solve global problems effectively and without force. Others see it as a potential threat to national sovereignty and as interfering with states' domestic matters. Most, however, recognize that the UN is unlikely to play either of these roles. States are too jealous of their sovereignty, and too diverse in their interests, to allow the UN to become a dominating global government, either for good or for ill.

PURPOSES AND PRINCIPLES OF THE UN

The UN Charter embodied a set of principles (purposes) and created a set of institutions, and both were controversial. In terms of principles, the goal of effective international action competed with the goal of preserving state sovereignty. Nearly every state was concerned that no statement in the UN Charter could be interpreted as undermining or taking priority over the individual states. Thus, Article 2 of the UN Charter states, "The Organization is based on the principle of the sovereign equality of all its Members." As international security problems have increasingly emerged from instability within states, rather than conflict between them, the tension between promoting international security and respecting state sovereignty has increased.

A second area of tension, both in principle and in terms of the UN organization, was the relative rights of large and small states. U.S. President Franklin Roosevelt, who played a major role in setting up the UN, recognized that the organization would never work if the "great powers" could be outvoted by the small ones, so five countries deemed to be **great powers** (Britain, China, France, the Soviet Union, and the United States) were given permanent seats on the Security Council and the right to veto any Security Council measure. Giving these states special status contradicted the principle of sovereign equality. In some measure, this arrangement was compensated for by the **one state, one vote** voting scheme in the General Assembly, where the smallest state has the same rights as the most powerful.

ORGANIZATION OF THE UN

The General Assembly   Today, the UN General Assembly has 192 members, from the largest states in the world to microstates like Nauru. In the General Assembly, all states, regardless of size, have equal rights, and each has a single vote. Superficially, the UN General Assembly looks like a legislature in that representatives from the states of the world gather to debate and pass resolutions on the issues of the day. However, the main purpose of the General Assembly is not to pass laws, but rather to provide a forum for debate on global issues and to express, when possible, international consensus.

The General Assembly differs fundamentally from national-level legislatures in two significant ways. First, although the General Assembly has the right to consider almost any issue it chooses, its resolutions are not considered law and therefore no state is compelled to comply. The UN Charter gives the General Assembly the power to "discuss any questions or any matters within the scope of the present charter," but the General Assembly's only clear power is over the UN budget.[4] In part, the power of the General Assembly was limited out of respect for the doctrine of sovereignty. It was also limited in response to the interests of the most powerful states, which refuse to be bound by an organization they do not control.

great powers
The UN Charter ascribed this status to Britain, China, France, the Soviet Union (Russia), and the United States.

one state, one vote
A voting system in which each state has one vote, regardless of its size, population, or other characteristics. Used in the UN General Assembly and many other international organizations.

Figure 12.1 The United Nations System Principal Organs

Security Council

Peacekeeping Operations
UN Peace-building Commission
Counter-terrorism Committee
International Atomic Energy Agency

General Assembly

Subsidiary Bodies

Main Committees
Standing Committees
Human Rights Council

Programs and Funds

UNCTAD (UN Conference on Trade and Development)
UNDCP (UN Drug Control Program)
UNEP (UN Environmental Program)
UNDP (UN Development Program)
UNIFEM (UN Development Fund for Women)
UNICEF (UN Children's Fund)
UNFPA (UN Population Fund)
UNHCR (UN High Commissioner for Refugees)

Economic and Social Council

Specialized Agencies

ILO (International Labor Organization)
FAO (Food and Agricultural Organization)
UNESCO (UN Education, Cultural, and Scientific Organization)
WHO (World Health Organization)

World Bank Group

IMF (International Monetary Fund)
ICAO (International Civil Aviation Organization)
IMO (International Maritime Organization)
ITU (International Telecommunication Union)
IPU (International Postal Union)

Functional Commissions

Narcotic Drugs
Crime Prevention and Criminal Justice
Science and Technology for Development
Sustainable Development
Status of Women
Population and Development
Statistical Commission

Regional Commissions

Africa
Europe
Latin American and the Caribbean
Asia and the Pacific
Western Asia

International Court of Justice

Secretariat

Departments and Offices

Office of the Secretary General
Office of Internal Oversight Services
Office of Legal Affairs
Department of Political Affairs
Department of Peacekeeping Operations
Office for the Coordination of Humanitarian Affairs
Office of the High Commissioner for Human Rights
Department for General Assembly and Conference Management
Department of Public Information
Department of Management

Source: http://www.un.org/aboutun/chart.html

Electronic boards display voting results on a human rights resolution in 2006. To many, the UN General Assembly represents the collective opinion of all the nations of the world.

Second, the budget authority ("power of the purse") that makes domestic legislatures so powerful is not available to the General Assembly. The UN budget is small (the regular budget was just over $2 billion in 2009) because it depends on dues payments from members, who are unwilling to make large payments. During the 1980s, the ability of the UN to carry out its basic tasks was hampered when the United States, the largest contributor to the budget, withheld payments because it had various complaints about the organization. Today, over 80 percent of UN members fail to pay their dues in full and on time.[5]

This does not, however, mean that the General Assembly is irrelevant. On the contrary, it is quite important as an arena in which issues are debated and discussed, and its resolutions, although not binding in a legal sense, have a great deal of influence in terms of agenda setting—in expressing the shared purpose of the international community. The General Assembly has the ability to put issues at the top of the international agenda. By defining certain standards for dealing with problems, the General Assembly often shapes subsequent agreements that are reached within other organizations. The Millennium Development Goals discussed in Chapter 11 are a case in point. When some group sits down to work out international standards on some problem, an existing General Assembly resolution setting out a standard is likely to have a significant influence because symbolically, if not legally, the General Assembly is seen as expressing world opinion.

The Secretariat The various UN agencies are supported by a Secretariat with roughly 8900 employees, which performs organizational, budgetary, translation, research, and other support services and administers decisions. Unlike delegates to the General Assembly and the Security Council, personnel of the Secretariat are employed by the UN, not by their home governments, and they take an oath not to take instructions from their home governments. Nonetheless, governments engage in considerable political maneuvering to have their candidates chosen for particular posts. The Secretariat has been a target in recent years of accusations of corruption, most notably in administering the **oil-for-food program**, part of the pre-2003 sanctions against Iraq, whereby Iraq was allowed to sell oil to purchase humanitarian supplies. Secretariat employees were accused of taking bribes in return for steering contracts toward certain firms.

The UN Secretariat is headed by a **secretary general**. The power of the secretary general stems less from his or her role as the head of the UN bureaucracy than from his or her role as the personification and public face of the UN. The position of the secretary general thus carries immense prestige. To the extent that any individual can presume to speak for the international community, it is the UN secretary general. UN secretaries general have, over the years, played an important role in mediating conflicts as well as in promoting new norms and publicizing neglected problems. Since its founding, the UN has had eight secretaries general:

- Trygve Lie (Norway), 1946–1952
- Dag Hammarskjöld (Sweden), 1953–1961

oil-for-food program
Part of the pre-2003 UN sanctions against Iraq, whereby Iraq was allowed to sell oil to purchase humanitarian supplies.

secretary general
The head of the UN bureaucracy and the personification and public face of the UN.

- U Thant (Burma, now Myanmar), 1961–1971
- Kurt Waldheim (Austria), 1972–1981
- Javier Pérez de Cuéllar (Peru), 1982–1991
- Boutros Boutros-Ghali (Egypt), 1992–1996
- Kofi A. Annan (Ghana), 1997–2006
- Ban Ki-moon (South Korea), 2007–

The UN Security Council   In questions of war and peace, the UN **Security Council** is the most important component of the UN, but it has rarely been able to fulfill the hope placed in it. According to Article 24 of the Charter, the members of the UN "confer on the Security Council primary responsibility for the maintenance of international peace and security, and agree that in carrying out its duties under this responsibility the Security Council acts on their behalf." The Security Council has 15 members, five of which are the "permanent five" with veto powers. The 10 nonpermanent members are elected to two-year terms by the General Assembly. The Council is chaired by a president; the presidency rotates among the members, in alphabetical order, from month to month. The Security Council's purpose is to help to avoid conflict in the international arena by performing deterrent, peacekeeping, and negotiating functions.

Security Council
The fifteen-member council within the UN in charge of dealing with threats to international security.

Deterring and Countering Aggression The UN Charter provides two statements on the use of force that are in constant tension with each other. Article 2 provides that "all members shall refrain in their international relations from the threat or use of force against the territorial integrity or political independence of any state, or in any other manner inconsistent with the purposes of the United Nations." Article 51, however, states that "nothing in the present Charter shall impair the inherent right of individual or collective self-defense if an armed attack occurs against a member of the United Nations, until the Security Council has taken measures necessary to maintain international peace and security." This exception for self-defense is routinely invoked by those using force to justify their actions.

The UN Security Council met in May 2010, in response to an incident in which nine people died when Israeli commandos stormed a fleet of ships carrying aid to Gaza, which Israel had blockaded.

For example, when the United States attacked Iraq in 2003, the U.S. government invoked the right of self-defense as a legal basis for the attack. Some argued that because Iraq had not actually attacked the United States, there was no legal basis to claim self-defense. Others countered that self-defense can include a preemptive attack on a hostile power.

The deterrent function of the Security Council is based on the model of collective security established in the League of Nations. The idea is that all states agree to join forces against any state that commits an act of aggression. Presumably, any state would be deterred from using force if it could expect retaliation by all or most other states. If this deterrent is credible, collective force should rarely have to be used. In theory, this model is straightforward, but in practice it has rarely worked.

There are three barriers to the simple application of UN-sponsored force to retaliate against aggression. First, it is rarely very clear which state in a conflict is the aggressor. In many cases, all states involved can plausibly claim that they were responding to another's aggression (thus justifying their use of force). Second, states will rarely condemn their friends and allies and are sometimes unwilling to come to the aid of their rivals. Third, even when all agree on what the problem is and what ought to be done, states are often unwilling to commit their forces to action in a conflict that might be of only limited interest to them. In every country, there are often strong domestic constituencies opposed to war, especially when the issue at stake does not appear to be vital interest.

Peacekeeping One of the most important contributions made by the UN over the years has been in peacekeeping, which was discussed in detail in Chapter 7. Peacekeeping helps solve the security dilemmas that can prevent warring parties from agreeing to stop fighting even when they want to. More recently, "second-generation" peacekeeping has given UN forces a more active role, including providing humanitarian relief, protecting civilians, and running elections.

The UN has sponsored many peacekeeping missions around the world. Some of these have been relatively brief; others have lasted decades. As Table 7.2 indicates, some missions are now over fifty years old. Although the long durations of these deployments may seem to be a problem, they perhaps indicate that peacekeepers are still needed to prevent conflict (and are succeeding). Most recent deployments have been responses not to conflict between countries, which was the trend through the 1980s, but to civil wars within collapsing states.

peace enforcement

The use of military force to compel an actor to cease or avoid some activity viewed as a threat to peace and security.

UN peacekeepers have been seen, in some cases, as ineffective or worse. The most troubling case arose in the former Yugoslavia, where lightly armed peacekeepers were assigned several missions, including creating "safe zones" for refugees and monitoring arms stockpiles to ensure that the weapons were not used in the conflict. In several key cases, peacekeepers had to stand aside as Serbian forces with superior capability did exactly what the peacekeepers were supposed to prevent. This failure resulted in part from the blurring of the line between traditional peacekeeping and **peace enforcement**. The UN forces were lightly armed and had very constraining rules of engagement, but they were put in a situation in which they might be confronted by a large and well-armed hostile force.

However, the fact that UN peacekeeping efforts sometimes fail does not indicate that peacekeeping is not an important tool. Peacekeeping cannot succeed when states or groups are determined to go to war. Rather, it succeeds when states or groups hope to avoid conflict but might be afraid that others will take advantage of them.

AP Photo/APTV

Peacekeeping forces are lightly armed, and therefore, they cannot repel a determined effort to break the peace. These Dutch peacekeepers were captured and held hostage by Serb forces in Bosnia.

The Geography Connection

UN Peacekeeping Missions

Examine the distribution of UN peacekeeping missions in this map, noting the dates.

Critical Thinking Questions

1. What patterns do you notice in the location of the missions? How has the pattern shifted over time?

2. What might explain the geographic distribution of missions? Why do conflicts in some areas receive peacekeeping missions, whereas those in other areas do not?

UN Peacekeeping Missions

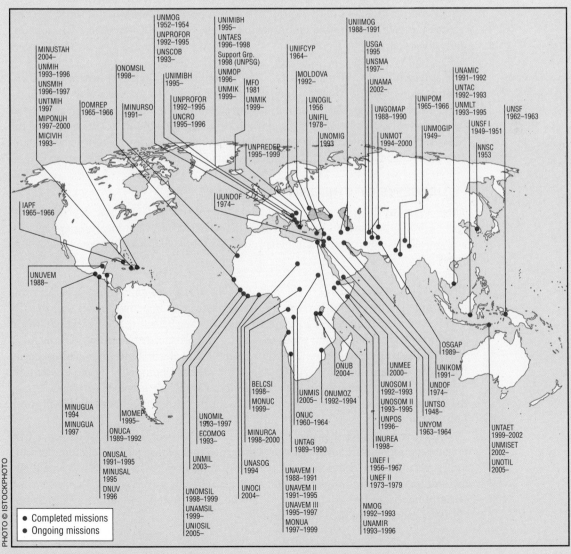

PHOTO © ISTOCKPHOTO

Source: Charles W. Kegley, *World Politics: Trend and Transformation,* 11th ed. (Boston: Wadsworth, 2007), p. 560.

Even when states are willing to contribute forces to peacekeeping missions, the question remains of how to pay for them. When a mission is sponsored by the UN, it would seem reasonable that the cost should come out of the UN budget. However, states have resisted the formation of a separate UN peacekeeping budget that would require an ongoing contribution from each country sufficient to meet peacekeeping needs. Therefore, UN peacekeeping operations are almost always underfunded. The countries that provide the troops (which are usually smaller states perceived as neutral, rather than the permanent Security Council members) often have to provide a disproportionate share of the funding as well, decreasing the willingness of countries to participate.

Economic and Social Council (ECOSOC)

The UN council that oversees work on economic and social issues.

The Specialized Agencies   When it was founded in 1945, the UN included an **Economic and Social Council (ECOSOC)** to oversee work on matters of development and related issues. Today, this council has been supplemented by a wide array of related programs, funds, commissions, and specialized agencies. Some of these are well known, such as UNICEF (the United Nations Children's Fund[6]); the IAEA, charged with monitoring compliance with the Nuclear Non-Proliferation Treaty; the World Bank Group, which plays a central role in economic development (see Chapter 11); and the WHO, which coordinates policies on disease prevention (see Chapter 14). Other agencies are more obscure, such as the World Meteorological Organization and the Statistical Commission. UN organizations are essential to international collaboration on some matters of great importance to the states of the world. In some respects, it is the work of the specialized agencies, rather than the General Assembly or the Security Council, that has concrete daily effects around the world.

International Court of Justice (ICJ)

Also known as the "World Court," the body that adjudicates disputes that arise over treaty obligations.

The International Court of Justice   The **International Court of Justice (ICJ)**, also known as the "World Court," adjudicates disputes that arise over treaty obligations. Many treaties stipulate that if there is disagreement over the terms of the treaty or over what constitutes a violation, the dispute will be resolved by the ICJ. More generally, the ICJ is also acknowledged as the authority on what the body of international law says and how it should be interpreted. This agency is discussed in more detail in Chapter 13.

FOUR VIEWS OF THE UNITED NATIONS

There are many different ways of evaluating the role of the UN. These depend in large part on which purposes of the organization are singled out, what measures are applied, and especially, which theoretical perspective is adopted. This section summarizes four views.

UN as World Government   The notion of the UN as an embryonic world government provokes two opposite reactions. Some place great hope in the idea that the UN may become a genuine world government because they believe that only through world government can fundamental issues of security and prosperity be resolved. At the theoretical level, this view follows the realist analysis that derives international insecurity from international anarchy. Optimists see the UN as potentially ending anarchy by becoming a single, democratic, global sovereign. Few people involved with the UN take the idea of the UN as world government seriously; rather they focus on much more limited roles.

Others fear the idea that the UN might be a nascent world government. Those who put a premium on state sovereignty are concerned that a stronger UN might undermine local sovereignty and democracy. An even more anxious view sees the UN as a potentially totalitarian world government, eroding individual freedom everywhere. The *Left Behind* series of novels, immensely popular for a time in the United States, portrayed the anti-Christ as coming from the United Nations.

The Policy Connection

How to Reform the United Nations?

In recent years, there has been increasing dissatisfaction with certain aspects of UN organization and operation. Many countries are dissatisfied with the system of permanent seats on the Security Council, and various proposals have been made to revamp the Council to make it more representative. Many have also criticized the UN bureaucracy itself for being wasteful and sometimes corrupt, and have sought reform of the Secretariat.

In March 2005, UN Secretary General Kofi Annan announced a reform plan aimed at addressing many of the criticisms frequently aimed at the UN.[1] Annan minced no words about the need for reform: "This hall has heard enough high-sounding declarations to last us for some decades to come. We all know what the problems are and we all know what we have promised to achieve. What is needed now is not more declarations or promises, but action—action to fulfill the promises already made."[2] Annan proposed several goals:

- Restructure the Security Council. Annan outlined two proposals. In one alternative, the Security Council would be expanded by six permanent members and two rotating members (increasing the overall membership from fifteen to twenty-three and the number of vetos from five to eleven). The other alternative would add eight four-year members (a new category) and two two-year members. Overall membership would be twenty-five, with five states wielding vetos.
- "Revitalize" the General Assembly by adopting measures to streamline the agenda and ensure that the General Assembly tackles only the most pressing issues and conducts business more quickly.
- Reform the UN Secretariat (the permanent bureaucracy). Annan sought, among other things, to have the General Assembly review all mandates more than five years old to eliminate those that are no longer needed. He also sought authority to pursue a buyout of excess staff and to undertake a series of other reforms aimed at increasing transparency and efficiency.

- Transform the UN Human Rights Commission. Because its members are selected on a regional basis, some of the world's worst human rights violators, such as Cuba and Libya, have become members of the Commission, undermining the credibility of the commission and embarrassing the UN more broadly. Annan proposed electing members to the commission by a two-thirds vote of the General Assembly.
- Clarify the rules under which states could use preemptive military force. This proposal appeared to be a response to the U.S.-led attack on Iraq.
- Secure a commitment from developed states to contribute 0.7 percent of their GDP to development aid.

Annan's proposals did not get far. Even though there is widespread agreement on the problems, the solutions involve significant conflicts of interest. For example, increasing the number of permanent members of the Security Council creates conflict over who will get the additional seats, and dilutes the power of the existing five permanent members. Changing rules for selecting members for the Human Rights Commission will be opposed by those who know the goal is to keep them off.

Secretary General Ban Ki-moon, who succeeded Annan in 2007, adopted a more incremental strategy for reform. In 2009 he signed pacts with all senior managers to increase accountability and transparency, but in 2010, the head of the UN's internal watchdog agency accused Ban of neglecting the fight against corruption, saying, "I do not see any sign of reform in the organization."[3] The bigger problems, such as Security Council membership, continue to be intractable.

Critical Thinking Questions

1. What classic criticisms of the UN did Annan's plan attempt to address?
2. How would you reform the UN Security Council? What are the most difficult issues that need to be resolved?
3. Should countries dissatisfied with the progress of reform withhold their UN dues as a way of forcing change?

[1]"In Larger Freedom: Toward Development, Security, and Human Rights for All," UN General Assembly, March 21, 2005.
[2] BBC News, March 21, 2005, at http://news.bbc.co.uk/1/hi/world/americas/4367015.stm
[3]"UN Appoints New Director of Troubled Watchdog Group," *New York Times,* July 29, 2010, p. A18.

The UN as Irrelevant   In contrast to those who hope or fear that the UN will form a genuine world government, many see the UN as essentially irrelevant to international politics. The UN has little legal or military power to compel other actors. It does not even have enough financial resources to substantially influence most actors. In those rare cases when the great powers do agree, skeptics point out, they do not need the UN to help them coerce smaller states. Some of those who see the UN as irrelevant see this irrelevance as a good thing; others see it as unfortunate. U.S. billionaire Ted Turner, concerned that the UN was not as effective as it should be, committed to donate a billion dollars to the organization in 1997.

The UN as a Tool for States   According to liberal institutionalism, the UN is neither good nor bad in and of itself; nor does it have any commanding authority over states. Rather, the UN is a tool that states can use, when they want to, to achieve various goals. When states seek to collaborate, the UN provides an organization that facilitates such collaboration. When states disagree, as they often do, these disagreements can be voiced in the UN. In some cases, states may use the UN to help resolve disagreements and facilitate collaboration. In others, they may use the UN as an arena in which they can compete against their opponents.

The UN as a Source of Norms   From the perspective of constructivism, the United Nations and its related organizations have a powerful role, because much of their work focuses on defining internationally shared understandings of various problems. This view of the UN was advanced by Secretary General Ban Ki-moon in 2007: "Despite its universal outreach, the United Nations cannot be in all places, nor provide a solution to every challenge. But we can, and should, serve as a forum to set a global agenda and consensus."[7] By adopting one view on an issue, such as indigenous people's rights, ways of measuring poverty, or ideal standards for air quality, UN agencies legitimize that position. This is not power in a traditional realist sense, but it is power of the sort that constructivists find extremely important in international politics.

PROBLEMS AND PROSPECTS FOR THE UN

The UN engenders great hope and great fear around the world. Some lament its inability to solve pressing global issues; others fear that it will become too powerful relative to states. Both of these views are based on a perception of the UN as a single coherent actor. However, the UN is an international organization, with sovereign states as its members. It, therefore, reflects politics among states as much as it drives them. When state interests converge, the UN can be an important tool for pursuing them. When state interests diverge, the UN has limited power to change that and will be simply one more arena in which states pursue conflict. More important, however, is the role of the UN in shaping state interests. Its agenda-setting power and moral authority help create agreement on what issues states should focus on and how they should solve them.

The European Union

The UN is significant because it claims a broader mandate than any other IGO and claims to speak for the "community of states." The EU is significant for different reasons. It has pushed the bounds of international collaboration further than any other IGO, such that the boundary between international and domestic authority is now blurred. The EU appears to be achieving on a regional scale what some only dream of on the global scale: a supranational (above the states) level of government that, at least in some spheres, authoritatively governs relations between states. Defining attributes of the nation-state such as a joint military force and single foreign policy, have been elusive, despite much planning, but in many economic areas the EU functions like a single state.

Figure 12.2 European Union Expansion at a Glance

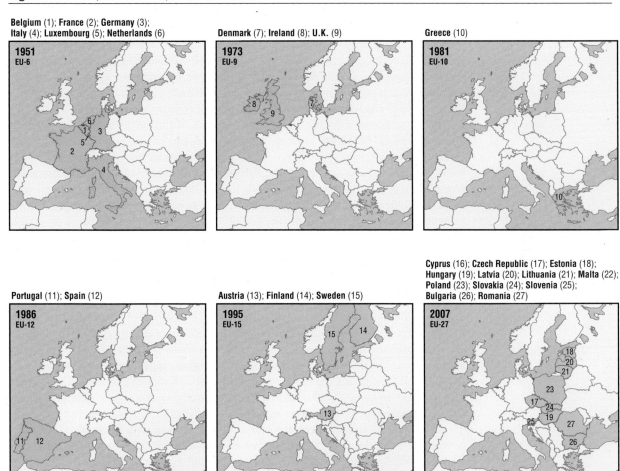

Belgium (1); **France** (2); **Germany** (3);
Italy (4); **Luxembourg** (5); **Netherlands** (6)

Denmark (7); **Ireland** (8); **U.K.** (9)

Greece (10)

Portugal (11); **Spain** (12)

Austria (13); **Finland** (14); **Sweden** (15)

Cyprus (16); **Czech Republic** (17); **Estonia** (18);
Hungary (19); **Latvia** (20); **Lithuania** (21); **Malta** (22);
Poland (23); **Slovakia** (24); **Slovenia** (25);
Bulgaria (26); **Romania** (27)

Source: Charles W. Kegley, *World Politics: Trend and Transformation,* 11th ed. (Boston: Wadsworth, 2007), p. 569.

HISTORICAL EVOLUTION OF THE EU

The ECSC and the Treaty of Rome   The EU originated in the European Coal and Steel Community (ECSC), which was formed in 1951 to coordinate the national markets for coal and steel in Europe in the aftermath of World War II. The economic purpose of the ECSC was to manage these key industries to promote industrial recovery from the war. The political purpose was to promote peace by binding the countries together in the economic sectors that were central to preparing for war. Those two motivations continue to be relevant today. European integration has provided substantial economic benefits as a result of decreased barriers to trade and a larger market and has helped bind together politically countries that had been almost constantly at war with each other in previous centuries.

Two of the early advocates of the EU, Robert Schumann of Germany and Jean Monnet of France, were instrumental in establishing a wide-ranging vision of European integration, declaring the goal of building an "ever-closer union." They recognized that this union could not be established in a single step. Instead, the strategy was to do as much as was politically feasible at any given time and to assume that each step would build an interest in collaboration and lead to demands for further steps, in a self-reinforcing process. This process, known as **spillover**, has indeed characterized the development of

spillover

A process by which small, incremental steps toward cooperation create the impetus for even further integration.

the EU since the 1950s. Even those who were skeptical about more idealistic notions of a "United States of Europe" were often willing to support small, incremental increases in integration for their concrete political and economic benefits.

Treaty of Rome

The 1957 treaty that established the European Economic Community, the predecessor of the European Union.

In 1957, the **Treaty of Rome**, widely regarded as the founding document of today's EU, was signed by six states: Belgium, France, West Germany, Italy, Luxembourg, and the Netherlands. To the ECSC were added Euratom, covering nuclear power, and the European Economic Community, which covered trade liberalization. The Treaty of Rome is widely regarded as the founding document of today's EU.

In the subsequent decades, European integration moved forward intermittently, both in terms of "widening" (adding new members) and "deepening" (extending cooperation between existing members). Widening occurred slowly until the 1990s. After being rejected by France in the 1960s, Britain became a member in 1972, adding a key economic and political power, along with Ireland and Denmark. When Greece joined in 1981 and then Spain and Portugal in 1986, the power of the EU in helping transform postauthoritarian societies was demonstrated. Austria, Sweden, and Finland, previously neutral, joined following the end of the Cold War, bringing total membership in 1995 to fifteen. Membership jumped to twenty-five in 2004 when ten of the former Communist countries joined, and then to twenty-seven when Bulgaria and Romania joined in 2007.

Over time, EU members cooperated on more and more issues, and as theorists of spillover predicted, each new level of cooperation required delegating more decision-making authority to EU institutions in Brussels. The most important component of the European Economic Community, as founded in 1957, was a customs union—a common external tariff toward all countries outside the community. At least in terms of tariffs, therefore, external producers faced the same conditions regardless of where they were trying to sell their goods. Moreover, tariffs inside the European Economic Community were reduced, so that countries were able to move even closer to a single integrated economic space, known as the Common Market.

As Table 12.2 shows, there are several stages of economic integration. As states pursued deeper economic integration, which provided for freer movement of goods, services, and labor, they had to agree to joint decision making in these areas.

By the 1980s, a great deal of integration had occurred, but two important barriers remained. First, the EU states continued to have separate currencies. Uncertainty about fluctuating exchange rates hindered trade. Second, conflicting regulations among the member states constituted a barrier to trade. For example, different environmental, health, and safety regulations meant that goods produced for one market might not be legal for another market. These conflicting regulations were, in effect, nontariff barriers to trade.

The 1986 Single European Act stated a commitment to forming a more genuine common market by 1992, by harmonizing domestic legislation across the members. This act also replaced the requirement of unanimous decision making (which enabled any state to veto any measure) with qualified majority voting, whereby some decisions could be made

Table 12.2 Stages of Economic Integration

	Free Trade Area	Customs Union	Common Market	Economic Union
Removal of tariffs among members	×	×	×	×
Common external tariff		×	×	×
Free movement of labor and capital			×	×
Harmonization of regulations				×

Source: Adapted from Theodore Cohn, *Global Political Economy: Theory and Practice*, 2nd ed. (New York: Pearson Longman, 2005).

by more than 50 percent (a simple majority) but not total unanimity. This major intrusion on state sovereignty was necessary to allow a larger, more diverse group of countries to make decisions on a widening array of issues.

The 1992 Maastricht Treaty set into motion the most important development in European structures since the Treaty of Rome. It officially changed the organization's name to the European Union and amended the Treaty of Rome. Most significantly, it added the creation of a common security and foreign policy to the agenda of the union and stated as a goal the establishment of a single currency. These two changes confirmed that the EU was now well beyond an economic union and were significant steps toward establishing a single political entity—since a distinct foreign policy and a separate currency and monetary policy are two central characteristics of a sovereign state. The Maastricht Treaty also established a common Justice and Home Affairs division, which further eroded differences among state policies.

Since 1992, the common foreign and security policy and the single currency have become much more of a reality than skeptics predicted, but perhaps less than optimists would have hoped. In the area of foreign and security policy, the EU now participates as a single entity in some significant international forums, such as the WTO and Middle East peace talks. This arrangement appears to give the states more influence together than they would have separately. Moreover, they have formed an EU rapid reaction force of 60,000 soldiers, for use in peacekeeping and related missions. This is the first European military force ever fielded.

However, deep divisions emerged over the U.S.-led invasion of Iraq in 2003. Several key states, including Britain, Italy, Spain, and Poland, supported the invasion and supplied troops. The majority, however, including France and Germany, were adamantly opposed. It was difficult to see how a common policy could emerge from such divergent positions. Similar divisions have emerged over other major foreign policy issues, including relations with Russia and policy toward the global financial crisis.

The Single Currency   In 1992, twelve of the fifteen EU members joined the single currency, and in 2002 euro coins and notes replaced traditional currencies such as the French franc, the Italian lira, and the German mark. A single currency reduces transaction costs and problems with instability, but it requires the states to agree on a single monetary policy and to live with it. Not all members of the EU have adopted the single currency: Britain, Denmark, and Sweden chose not to join, and many of the newer members have yet to meet the requirements for joining the single currency.

Monetary policy for the euro is now made by the European Central Bank, which is analogous to the U.S. Federal Reserve and is based in Frankfurt, Germany. The member states that adopted the euro have ceded their right to have an independent monetary policy. Initially, the single currency operated quite successfully, increasing its value relative to the dollar dramatically, and to some extent displacing the dollar as the standard currency for international transactions. But it was based on the optimistic assumption that the states could maintain a single monetary policy with divergent fiscal policies (and in divergent economic conditions), and in 2010, the euro zone was in crisis (see Chapter 10).

The European Constitution and the Lisbon Treaty   Once the EU had expanded to twenty-seven members of increasing diversity, it became apparent that its existing decision-making structures would have to be modified. The new states would have to be assigned voting weights, and this would naturally tend to dilute the influence of the existing states. Moreover, with more than twenty-five members, if the use of the single-state veto were not minimized, EU decision making, already considered cumbersome, might become completely immobile. To solve these problems, the members signed a new EU Constitution in 2004, to replace the Treaty of Rome. However, after France and Denmark failed to ratify the treaty, other states cancelled ratification votes and the Constitution

Figure 12.3 Evolution of the Structure of the European Union

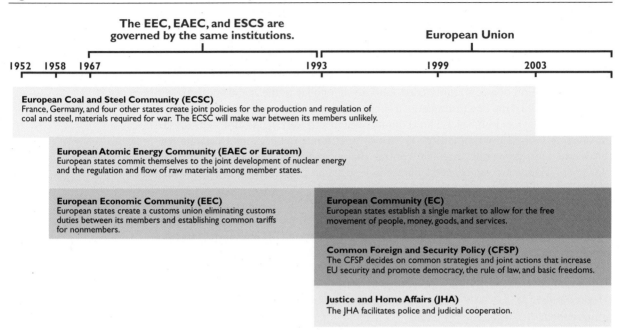

Source: Naomi Friedman

was scuttled. Instead, a modified version, the Treaty of Lisbon, entered force in 2009. Most importantly, the Lisbon Treaty created a genuine President of the EU Council, chosen by member states for a 2 ½ year term, rather than rotating the presidency from country to country every six months. It created a new High Representative for Foreign Affairs, to give the EU more weight in foreign affairs by combining the previously separate heads of External Affairs and Foreign and Security Affairs. In order to make it easier for the enlarged Union to make decisions, the voting system was modified the use of the veto was more narrowly circumscribed. Lastly, the weight of the European Parliament (representatives of voters) was increased relative to that of the European Council (representatives of governments).

ORGANIZATION OF THE EU

Like many nation-states, the EU has executive, legislative, and judicial branches. The organization of the EU engenders tensions between several competing goals, including efficiency of decision making, effectiveness of implementation, the sovereignty of the member states, and the rights of EU citizens.

European Commission

The body within the EU that carries out many executive branch functions.

The European Commission   The **European Commission** is analogous to the "cabinet" in a domestic government. Each commissioner heads a ministry (such as Justice, Freedom and Security, or Economic and Monetary Affairs). Although the commissioners come from the member states, their explicit mission is to govern for the benefit of the entire community, and they are not allowed to take instructions from their home governments. In this respect, the EU is a supranational organization (above the states), not merely an international organization of member-states. In addition to overseeing implementation of policy, the commission is also charged with drafting new legislation, either on its own initiative or at the request of the Parliament or Council. In most areas of policy, only the commission has the power to initiate legislation. In other words, a key part of the legislative process is in the commission's hands.

The Council   In contrast to the commission, the members of the **Council of the European Union** explicitly represent the governments of the member states. Once proposed by the commission, legislation is acted on by the Council and the Parliament. In a process known as "co-decision," both the council and the parliament must approve a bill in order for it to become law. Some issues require a unanimous vote in the council, but for many issues, a qualified majority is sufficient, meaning that the vote need not be unanimous but that more than 50 percent approval is required for passage. In the current formula, which will change in 2014 when the Treaty of Lisbon takes effect, a qualified majority is achieved if one of the following conditions is met:

■   The measure receives at least 255 of 345 votes (roughly 74 percent). (Larger states have more votes; see Table 12.3.)

■   A majority of member states approve the decision

■   Votes cast in favor represent at least 62 percent of the total EU population

Either a few large states or a large number of small ones can block legislation. The Treaty of Lisbon specifies the conditions under which a small number of large states can block a measure, changes the thresholds, and reduces the use of the veto.

> **Council of the European Union**
> The body within the EU that represents the governments of the member states and, along with the European Parliament, acts on legislation.

Table 12.3 Vote Quotas in the Council of the European Union

Country	Votes	Total Votes
Germany, France, Italy, United Kingdom	29 votes each	116
Spain, Poland	27 votes each	54
Romania		14
Netherlands		13
Belgium, Czech Republic, Greece, Hungary, Portugal	12 votes each	60
Austria, Bulgaria, Sweden	10 votes each	30
Denmark, Ireland, Lithuania, Slovakia, Finland	7 votes each	35
Cyprus, Estonia, Latvia, Luxembourg, Slovenia	4 votes each	20
Malta		3
TOTAL		345

The European Parliament   The European Parliament is the only EU institution whose members are elected directly by the citizens. It is also historically the weakest of the institutions. It has some power to amend legislation and to veto it on some issues, but in other areas it only has the right of consultation. Governments fear that, because members of the European Parliament are elected by citizens, they will cater to their constituents rather than to their home governments. Therefore, the member states have kept decision-making power concentrated in the arenas over which the member governments have most influence: the Council and the Commission. However, this arrangement has led to what some have called a "democratic deficit" in the EU: members of the institutions with the most power are not elected, and the one institution whose membership is elected has the least. Under the Treaty of Lisbon, the European Parliament is put on a par with the Council, so that they may be thought of a lower and upper house of a bicameral parliament.

The European Court of Justice   Almost all judicial functions in Europe continue to be handled by the courts of the member states. The European Court of Justice (ECJ) functions roughly analogously to the U.S. Supreme Court, handling disputes over the meaning of a particular law. It also hears charges that a member state is not fulfilling its obligations or that the European Commission has exceeded its authority. Thus, it is the arbiter of disputes among EU institutions.

PROBLEMS AND PROSPECTS FOR THE EU

The EU has undergone a remarkable transformation in the last two decades, from an organization with twelve members concerned primarily with implementing a customs union, to something approaching a European superstate, with twenty-seven members, 450

The Culture Connection

A European Identity?

Can Europe continue to move ever closer to a single state, rather than an organization of sovereign states? In the minds of many people, one fundamental barrier to the "United States of Europe" is people's strong sense of nationalism and national identity. Even as more decisions are made by European, rather than national, institutions, most individuals still identify themselves primarily with their traditional nation-states, rather than with Europe. There are Germans, Poles, and French people, but few who would call themselves primarily Europeans.

Is it possible that this can change? Can "European" supplant "German" the way that "German" supplanted "Frisian" and "Bavarian?" Europe's most popular sport, soccer, has a thorough Europeanization, both in the market for players and in the major competitions. Moreover, in at least one high-profile competition, golf's Ryder Cup, all of Europe is represented by a single team; previously, the competition pitted England against the United States. Passions, however, remain national, as the World Cup and European Championships demonstrate, or even local, as the violence sometime accompanying intracity rivalries shows.

Those who support movement toward a single European state have sought to promote this idea of European identity through the creation of European versions of nation-state symbols, including a flag and an anthem. The anthem chosen in 1985 is the "Ode to Joy" from Beethoven's Symphony No. 9 (without the words

from the Friederich Schiller poem on which Beethoven's piece was based).

One highly popular Europe-wide cultural event is the Eurovision song contest, sponsored by the European Broadcasting Union since 1956. The annual contest pits one musical group from each state against the others, with hundreds of millions of television viewers voting on the most popular The practice of having one group from each member state, however, shows that states and national identity are still considered essential. Moreover, traditional international politics are on display in the voting. There is a well-established pattern in which viewers tend to vote for performers from their neighbor countries or from countries with which they have ethnic or linguistic ties. For example, the 2007 winner from Serbia, gained five of its nine first-place votes from states that, like Serbia, had been part of Yugoslavia, whereas Albania, which is in conflict with Serbia over the territory of Kosovo, ranked Serbia last.[1] Thus, there have been bitter complaints that this cultural contest is driven by politics.

Critical Thinking Questions

1. What might the case of the United States reveal about efforts to create a single European identity?
2. Are identity differences such as those manifested in Eurovision voting driven by political differences, or do both political differences and voting behavior stem from something deeper?

[1] "Eurovision Song Contest 2007 Final," at http://www.eurovision.tv/addons/scoreboards/2007/final.html

million citizens, and economic power to rival that of the United States. The attractiveness of the EU is shown by the extraordinary efforts that the post-communist states have undertaken in order to join. Indeed, perhaps its greatest accomplishment in the past two decades has been its success in promoting and supporting democracy in the post-communist states.

Yet several challenges appear on the horizon. First, it remains uncertain how effective the twenty-seven-member union will be at decision making. The EU today is not only larger, but much more diverse than it was two decades ago. Moreover, widening and deepening was based on some optimistic assumptions about the common conditions and common interests. The economic crisis has caused major second thoughts about some of these steps. Second, the question of expansion continues to arise. The EU has successfully brought in much of post-communist Europe, but there is intense disagreement regarding further expansion, especially as it concerns Turkey. Third, agricultural subsidies continue to hinder the move to free markets in Europe. Throughout all the liberalization that has taken place in Europe in recent decades, agriculture has been sheltered and remains heavily subsidized. These subsidies, mandated by the Common Agriculture Policy, eat up nearly half of the EU budget. They are therefore a barrier to other spending priorities. Moreover, they substantially undermine the economic potential of agricultural producers in the developing world. Yet it is not clear that there is a politically acceptable strategy for dealing with this issue.

Despite the problems it faces, the process of European integration is almost universally regarded as a great success story. Countries that were once constantly preparing for war with each other now consider such conflict unimaginable. Economic integration has helped bring prosperity. The chance to join the EU has helped transform post-communist Europe. For these reasons, the EU has been seen as a model for other regions of the world.

Regional IGOs

The success of the European Union has helped increase enthusiasm around the world for similar regional groupings. Can the EU model be replicated? Most of these projects have focused on economic, rather than political, integration—but that is how the EU started as well. It is unclear whether the spillover that has pushed integration further in Europe will take place elsewhere or whether Europe will turn out to be a unique case.

Why do states form IGOs and why do they work through them? Different theoretical perspectives have different answers to this question. Neoliberal institutionalism provides

Table 12.4 Major Regional Economic Organizations, 2010

Name	Acronym	Year Founded	Number of Member Nations	Status
Association of Southeast Asian Nations	ASEAN	1967	10	Free trade area
North American Free Trade Agreement	NAFTA	1994	3	Free trade area
Economic Community of West African States	ECOWAS	1975	15	Various minor agreements
West African Economic and Monetary Union	UEMOA	1994	8	Monetary and Customs Union
Commonwealth of Independent States (Former Soviet Union)	CIS	1991	12	Negotiations toward single economic space stalled
Mercado Común del Sur (South America)	Mercosur	1991	4	Free trade area
Free Trade Area of the Americas (North/South America)	FTAA	Proposed	34	Negotiations stalled

the standard explanation: states form IGOs because it is in their interest to do so. Some problems can be solved more easily and less expensively through IGOs than without them. In particular, neoliberal institutionalism focuses on collective action problems (prisoners' dilemmas), such as the security dilemma, the temptation to enact competitive tariffs, and the difficulty in agreeing to protect the environment.

To address many of these problems, states need to coordinate their activities and monitor others to make sure they are living up to their commitments. For example, in the case of the security dilemma, states that seek to avoid nuclear proliferation needed to form the International Atomic Energy Agency to monitor the agreement and to help states complying with it to legally exploit nuclear energy. In the case of free trade, the WTO was formed to coordinate the negotiation of tariffs and to provide a mechanism for resolving disputes. In the case of the environment, the Intergovernmental Panel on Climate Change has been established to collect data and provide scientific analysis of climate change. Some of these tasks might be vastly more complicated and expensive to implement without the mechanism of IGOs. Others would be impossible. For example, without the reliable information on various countries' nuclear programs provided by the IAEA, the security dilemma, combined with uncertainty about other countries' programs, would likely compel far more countries to pursue nuclear weapons.

IGOs are sometimes created not to solve specific collective action problems, but to provide a forum for discussion. This is the primary function of the UN General Assembly. It has no predetermined agenda, but it provides a forum where states can discuss and debate issues that arise. The UN Security Council has a narrower agenda but is also primarily a forum. Similarly, one primary goal of the WTO is simply to organize meetings at which states negotiate to solve problems.

Transnational Actors

Transnational actors are changing the face of international politics today. Transnational (nongovernmental) actors are involved in almost every important issue in the world. Moreover, in terms of numbers, transnational organizations may be increasing their numbers even more rapidly than international organizations. As in the case of international organizations, the rise of transnational actors raises the question of whether the nature of international politics is fundamentally changing.

What Are Transnational Actors?

transnational actors
Actors whose activities cut across state boundaries.

Transnational actors are actors whose activities cut across state boundaries. This simple definition applies to an incredible number and variety of actors and organizations. Whereas there are roughly 200 states in the world and about 250 IGOs, there are roughly 60,000 transnational corporations and nearly 16,000 transnational nongovernmental organizations.[8] This section will focus on two major kinds of transnational actors. (Others include transnational terrorist groups, discussed in Chapter 8, and transnational criminal organizations, discussed in Chapter 14.)

■ Transnational (or multinational) corporations (TNCs or MNCs) are companies whose production and sales operations span more than a single country. In an era of globalization, the numbers are increasing rapidly, as even relatively small firms seek international suppliers and markets.

■ International nongovernmental organizations (INGOs) include a wide range of nongovernmental, nonbusiness organizations that operate across state boundaries.

They are distinguished from IGOs in that their members are individuals, not states. Included in this category are groups such as the International Olympic Committee and the International Committee of the Red Cross. An important subset of INGOs are transnational advocacy networks (TANs). These are groups that work on specific issues, which can range from helping to solve some world problem to spreading a particular belief system, to promoting the study of a particular subject. Examples are Human Rights Watch and Greenpeace.

A distinction should also be made between firms and organizations that are primarily national, with a small part of their operations abroad, and those that are fully transnational, with only a small part of their scope of operations in any one country. For example, the Labour and Conservative parties in the United Kingdom are both transnational actors in the sense that they collaborate with kindred parties in other states, but they are essentially British national organizations. By contrast, Human Rights Watch, although headquartered in the United States, has offices in seven other countries and conducts activities in many more.

What effect do transnational actors have on international politics? To some extent, this depends on how "international politics" is defined. The traditional "state-centric" view is that transnational actors need to be taken into account only to the extent that they influence states and the relations between states. A broader view holds that the activities of transnational actors are important in and of themselves and deserve to be studied as a major component of international affairs. Some transnational actors are powerful economically; others shape international norms, monitor governments, or provide humanitarian services.

Transnational Corporations

The transnational corporation is not a new invention: companies such as the British East Indies Company and the Hudson's Bay Company were formed in the seventeenth century to profit from economic opportunities opening up in regions newly discovered by Europeans. Until after World War II, however, there were few such companies, and they tended to be based in one country, going abroad only for sales or to purchase raw materials. After World War II, large corporations became increasingly international in their production operations.

Major corporations today pursue global strategies for production, sales, research, and investment. This behavior is perhaps most visible in the petroleum industry: firms such as Shell and Exxon/Mobil are present in nearly every country in the world, to pump oil, to refine it, or to sell the products made from it. It is increasingly true in parts of the retail sector as well: Coca-Cola, Unilever, and McDonalds are nearly everywhere. A single automobile may contain parts produced in several countries, and many information technology firms use programmers and engineers in multiple countries.

The role of transnational corporations in world politics has been a source of constant debate. This debate is often emotional as well as analytical. Claims have been made about the positive and negative effects of TNCs on the countries in which they operate. Also in question is their power vis-à-vis governments.

A central question for developing states has been whether TNCs tend to promote or to inhibit economic growth, a discussion closely tied to debates about globalization and development strategies. One view is that TNCs operating in developing countries seek only to extract raw materials and to take advantage of low labor costs, and therefore tend to contribute little to economic development. Opponents of TNCs further charge that TNCs use their economic influence to maintain low standards for labor and environmental protection (as in the sweatshop problem described in Chapter 11). The competing view is that the capital that TNCs invest helps boost productivity and that the local

Early Transnational Corporations: The British East India Company and the Hudson's Bay Company

The transnational corporation is considered a recent development, and in its modern form, it is. But today's TNC had predecessors in the joint-stock companies that were set up to finance shipping and trade between European states and their colonies in North America, India, and Southeast Asia during the age of exploration.

The British East India Company was founded in 1600 with 125 investors, £72,000, and, most important, a charter from the government granting it a monopoly on British trade with the East Indies (modern-day Indonesia). The company made its mark in India, and over the next few centuries became synonymous with the British colony there. By controlling the British trade with India and exploiting India's economic resources, the company was able to thrive. It was later central in establishing a British colonial presence in China that provoked the Opium Wars. By the mid-nineteenth century, the company effectively controlled most of India, Burma, Singapore, and Hong Kong.[1]

The British East India Company was much admired, and analogous companies were set up by the Dutch, whose firm displaced the British, as well as the Danish, French, and Swedish, in Indonesia. Not everyone was impressed with it, however. Adam Smith wrote, "The difference between the genius of the British constitution which protects and governs North America, and that of the mercantile company which oppresses and domineers in the East Indies, cannot perhaps be better illustrated than by the different state of those countries."[2]

The Hudson's Bay Company was formed in 1670, along a similar model, to exploit the growing demand for North American beaver pelts for the European hat industry. It too had the benefit of a state-granted monopoly over a massive territory, encompassing most of present-day Canada. As the fur trade died out, the Hudson's Bay Company was able to branch out into a wide variety of other ventures, since it owned most of western Canada. After Canadian independence in 1867, most of the company's land was ceded to the Canadian government, but it remained a force to be reckoned with. In World War I, it provided over 300 ships to the British war effort. The company still exists today, its trading post network having evolved into one of the largest department store chains in Canada.

Critical Thinking Questions

1. How has the political role of TNCs changed since the heyday of the British East India Company and the Hudson's Bay Company?

2. Do governments today have more or less power relative to TNCs than the British government had relative to the British East India Company and the Hudson's Bay Company? How has the power of governments changed in this regard?

[1]See Philip Lawson, *The East India Company: A History* (New York: Longman, 1993).
[2]Adam Smith, *The Wealth of Nations*, Book I, Chapter VIII (Chicago: University of Chicago Press, 1976).

PHOTO © ISTOCKPHOTO

workers and managers trained by TNCs add to the local skill pool, promoting further development. Moreover, supporters of TNCs point out that their presence expands the tax base in the host country. In recent years, the latter view has gained ground among governments, and more countries welcome the arrival of TNCs for the economic benefits they bring, even while being wary of their influence. Indeed, governments sometimes compete intensely, granting significant benefits in order to lure global firms. For example, the state of Alabama offered Mercedes Benz $250 million in aid to build a car factory near Tuscaloosa in 1993.

INFLUENCE OF TNCS ON GOVERNMENTS

To many, the competition for TNCs creates troubling implications. What effects do TNCs have on shaping local laws and local government decisions? Because some large firms are located in many countries, they can sometimes shift resources from one country to another to escape government policies they do not like, or to try to extract concessions from governments. This, it is argued, gives TNCs more leverage over governments. Some see this leverage as undesirable because it undermines the abilities of governments to promote higher social and environmental standards. Others see it as achieving some of the same benefits of the EU, by forcing states to adopt policies more compatible with the goals of TNCs.

However, not all economic assets are equally easy to move. "Portfolio investment" (investment in stocks) can be sold off and moved fairly easily, and cash can be moved quickly, but "bricks and mortar" investments, such as factories, cannot. Once a company invests significantly in immobile assets, power shifts from the company to the host government. In recent years, for example, after investing billions of dollars in development of energy infrastructure, foreign energy firms in countries as diverse as Bolivia, Russia, and Venezuela have been forced by the host governments to sell their investments for less than they were worth (a process known as *expropriation*).

A company with interests in two countries might lobby the government of one to pressure the government of the second on its behalf. This approach could open up a completely separate channel of corporate influence. It is precisely this concern that was raised through the post–World War II decades in Latin America, where U.S. government pressure on behalf of U.S. companies sometimes extended to the dispatching of troops to dispose of governments unfriendly to U.S. business. The lobbying of the U.S. firm ITT played an important role in causing the Nixon administration to have the CIA help bring the Chilean dictator Augusto Pinochet to power in 1973. Similarly, in recent years, both Russia and China have pressured other governments to enact policies that support the business interests of their companies.

TNCs also try to use governments as sales people. This is especially true of TNCs that are based in one country but sell around the world. In the aircraft business, for example, where Boeing is identified primarily with the United States and Airbus with the EU, governments frequently use foreign policy to help sell "their" companies' aircraft. In 1995, for example, U.S. President Bill Clinton was personally involved in forging a deal in which the government of Saudi Arabia bought six billion dollars' worth of U.S. aircraft.[9]

Overall, many believe that the various constraints placed on states by TNCs and the influence TNCs have on states are effectively eroding state sovereignty. One of the early works on TNCs was, therefore, called *Sovereignty at Bay*.[10] More recently, the increasing scope and power of TNCs is an important component in arguments that the sovereign state is rapidly losing its significance. In response to such concerns, states have worked through the United Nations to forge a "global compact" to promote agreed principles for TNC involvement. The compact includes principles such as that "businesses should... make sure they are not complicit in human rights abuses" and "businesses should work against corruption in all its forms, including extortion and bribery."[11]

Transnational Advocacy Networks

Among the many different INGOs, transnational advocacy networks have begun to play a role of growing importance in international politics and in particular countries. **Transnational advocacy networks (TANs)** are groups that organize across national boundaries to pursue some political, social, or cultural goal.[12] The range of groups, and the range of issues they cover, is so broad that it is difficult to devise a more precise definition. A few examples of well-known TANs serve to illustrate this point.

transnational advocacy networks (TANs)
Groups that organize across national boundaries to pursue some political, social, or cultural goal.

- Médicins Sans Frontières (Doctors Without Borders) organizes international teams of doctors to provide medical help in areas struck by disaster or war.

- Greenpeace organizes activists across the globe to lobby governments for stronger policies to protect the environment.

- Human Rights Watch monitors human rights abuses around the world and publicizes them in order to put pressure on governments.

These TANs have complex relations with governments. At times, they appear in adversarial roles, either opposing government policies or lobbying for change; at other times, they work closely with go vernments to achieve common goals that governments cannot achieve by themselves, in areas such as health care, human rights, and democratization.

LOBBYING GOVERNMENTS

Among the primary roles of TANs is lobbying governments across the world in favor of specific policies. In some cases, the goal can be to pressure a relatively small number of governments to cease certain practices. Some organizations perform a "watchdog" function, identifying and publicizing government shortcomings so that others can promote accountability. For example, Human Rights Watch and similar organizations seek to persuade states to adhere to certain standards of human rights. They have almost no means to compel governments. Instead, their main weapon is research and publication. Human Rights Watch, through its network of monitors, often gathers more reliable reporting on human rights practices than either governments or the private news media can provide. Therefore, both governments and the news media rely on Human Rights Watch reports. Although these reports do not stop human rights violations, they provide motivation to citizen groups and are often highly embarrassing, both to the governments in question and to their allies.

In other cases, the goal of a group can be to persuade all governments to adopt a new standard of behavior. The Campaign to Ban Landmines, for example, sought to persuade governments around the world to agree to a treaty banning the use of antipersonnel mines. Labor groups have established codes of workers' rights and have sought to convince transnational corporations to abide by these codes even in countries with lower standards.

There are perhaps two crucial differences between domestic and transnational lobbying. First, in transnational lobbying, resources raised in one country can be used in others. Therefore, especially in poorer countries, lobbying groups with transnational connections can be much more influential than they otherwise might be. This influence, of course, can spur a backlash from governments. Second, transnational lobbying can seek to move many countries at once toward a common policy position. When the goal in question is some kind of international agreement (as in the land mine treaty), moving policy in many states at once is crucial.

SETTING AGENDAS

TANs play a crucial role in setting international agendas, as emphasized particularly by constructivist international relations theory. It is very difficult, of course, for TANs to compel reluctant governments. But many times TANs raise an issue before it becomes one of importance to governments. On such issues, TANs can set the agenda by defining key goals, promoting norms, and setting standards. When an IGO or a group of states addresses this issue later, they may find that a set of standards and

Earthquake survivors queue for water at a makeshift housing compound in Port au Prince, Haiti, 2010.

Eddie Gerald/Alamy

expectations already exists. Although the IGO or the states are not forced to adopt these standards, often doing so is the easiest alternative. Thus, by raising the issues first and defining agendas, norms, and standards, TANs can influence the behavior of IGOs and states.

PROVIDING SERVICES

Many transnational advocacy networks do not merely advocate; they act. Organizations such as the International Committee of the Red Cross (ICRC), Doctors Without Borders, CARE, and thousands more provide many kinds of aid directly to people around the world. Especially in poor countries, where governments are incapable of providing for certain needs, these organizations play a role complementary to that of governments and help millions of people.

In the delivery of aid around the world, transnational aid organizations can often accomplish tasks that even the most powerful governments cannot. Because they are not affiliated with governments, they can often establish relationships and go places where official government representatives cannot. For example, the U.S. government cannot set up a permanent presence in villages around Uganda, but the ICRC, Doctors Without Borders, and related groups can. Similarly, the U.S. and Sudanese governments may be unwilling to collaborate with each other, but the NGOs and the Sudanese government are willing. Especially when needs arise rapidly, as in the case of natural disasters, governments often must rely on transnational aid organizations to deliver aid. The aid organizations have local knowledge and logistic networks that governments cannot easily set up quickly.

Similarly, in conflict-prone areas, where the presence of foreign government personnel might provoke violence, governments rely heavily on transnational aid organizations to deliver all sorts of aid. Aid organizations are often perceived as more neutral, and thus less threatening, than states or IGOs.

However, the relationship between transnational aid organizations and government is complicated and can sometimes create difficult ethical dilemmas. Even in the best of cases, there are often disputes about control. Governments, often concerned about sovereignty and about getting the political credit for providing aid, seek to control the distribution of aid. In some cases, they try to channel aid primarily to their supporters. Aid organizations, concerned that assistance be distributed according to certain principles and priorities and wishing to avoid theft and corruption, usually like to control the process as much as possible.

In cases where a country is experiencing internal conflict (often a primary cause of the problems that aid organizations help with), the government might seek to prevent aid organizations from delivering aid to those it sees as its adversaries. In the case of Sudan, one of the local agencies employed to distribute aid from the UN-led "Operation Lifeline Sudan" was, in fact, linked to one of the combatant groups. This agency distributed the aid in a way that it found politically useful, but in the process, it undermined the goals of minimizing death and suffering.[13] Fiona Terry shows how, in several cases, including the Rwandan genocide in 1994, the India-Pakistan war of 1971, and Palestinian refugees over many years, humanitarian groups provided food and shelter that unwittingly assisted "refugee-warriors" as they prepared to launch attacks, often on civilians.[14]

The End of the Westphalian State System?

The increasing importance of international organizations and transnational actors, combined with the broader processes of globalization, has led some analysts to argue that the Westphalian state system is essentially dead. There are three components to this argument. First, the increasingly free movement of goods, ideas, finance, and people across borders means that territorially bounded entities are inherently weaker than mobile ones. This chapter showed how transnational corporations can outmaneuver states, which, by definition, are territorially bounded. Second, supranational organizations (IGOs such as the WTO, the UN, and the EU) are being given more and more of the responsibilities that were formerly reserved for states. Third, TANs can coordinate lobbying activities across countries, and in many cases can accomplish tasks that states cannot.

These three processes are seen as reinforcing each other. International organizations tend to promote the harmonizing of laws and regulations that facilitate a rise in transnational activities. Transnational actors promote increasing the authority of international organizations, both directly through advocacy and indirectly through activities that give nation-states incentives to form common polices. For example, the tendency of TNCs to structure their transactions to minimize taxation gives states an incentive to coordinate tax policies. While the size of the state sphere has stayed constant or diminished, the size of the nonstate sphere has increased dramatically. Proportionally, then, the state has become much smaller. It has gone from being the only player on the international scene to being one of many.

For advocates of this view, the EU has been the ultimate example, even if recent difficulties have tarnished its image. Many of the traditional prerogatives of the sovereign state no longer exist in the twenty-seven separate European capitals, but rather are located in Brussels. But this is not simply a case of several sovereign states merging into a larger sovereign state, because the EU does not have many of the characteristics of a nation-state. Rather, Europe today seems to transcend the sovereign state framework entirely. It is ironic, perhaps, that the region that "invented" the sovereign state system in the sixteenth and seventeenth centuries is dismantling it in the twentieth and twenty-first centuries.

Those who are skeptical about the demise of the Westphalian system assert that the sovereign state is not only surviving, it is alive and well. Ultimately, they argue, sovereignty resides with the organization that, in Max Weber's terms, possesses a monopoly on the legitimate use of force. As nation-states combat organized crime and transnational terrorism, for example, they are recognized as the only actors that can legitimately use force—and thus still the source of sovereignty. The failure of international organizations—including the EU and the UN—to cope with the international security threats of recent years indicates that in the areas that matter most, states still dominate when they want to.

If transnational activities have increased, if international organizations have gained more authority, statists argue, it is because states have found it in their interest to allow this. For example, prominent realists as well as Marxists argue that the spread of TNCs in the last half-century occurred because it served the interests of the most powerful states in the system, and especially the United States, where many of these companies were based.

Similarly, some have viewed the EU not as an organization that curtails the power of states, but as one that increases states' power. Governments can get laws passed in Brussels that they could never get through their own legislatures. Thus, Europe's "democratic deficit" is seen as strengthening states over societies.

There is probably some truth in both views. It is true, as skeptics point out, that states have allowed globalization and the increase in transnational activities to occur and could probably reverse such changes if they made a concerted effort. However, there is little doubt that the costs of such a reversal, both in economic and political terms, are increasing. The state that retreated from the world economy would undergo substantial loss of income, and the government that tried to do this would likely meet powerful domestic opposition.

Perhaps it is a mistake, then, to view sovereign states as opposed to or in contradiction to international organizations. Clearly, international organizations and transnational actors are increasingly important in the world today. Much of the time, their interests and activities complement those of states, rather than contradict them. The question, therefore, is not which is more powerful, but rather how are international governmental organizations and transnational actors shaping state goals and the ways that states pursue solutions.

Reconsider the Case

Sudan: Who Can End the Genocide?

In July 2007, UN Security Council Resolution 1769 created the United Nations-African Union Mission in Darfur, a joint operation between the UN and the African Union. Headed by a diplomat from the Congo and reporting jointly to the AU and the UN, the mission had roughly 9000 troops deployed by the end of 2007. However, its effectiveness was severely undermined by a lack of helicopters, essential to moving troops around the region, which is the size of France but has few good roads. The peacekeepers were provided by African countries with few if any helicopters to spare for the mission.[15] Moreover, at the time of deployment, there was still no peace to keep; the peacekeepers would have a role that combined peace enforcement with delivery of humanitarian aid.

In 2010, the ICC indicted Bashir on genocide, a much more serious charge than war crimes, for which he had been indicted earlier. The indictment represented an official international recognition that what was happening in Darfur was indeed genocide. Advocates hoped that this step would increase international determination to use force to end the conflict and bring Bashir to justice, but by late 2010, this had not occurred.

Based on this chapter's discussion, several questions about Sudan can now be reexamined. First, consider the role of the United Nations. Why might the United Nations be expected to have difficulty ending the violence in Darfur? How would this situation have to be different for the UN to play a more effective role? How would the UN have to be different? Second, consider the roles of transnational actors in this case. Earlier chapters have discussed how state interests are formed. What determines the interests of transnational actors? How might different transnational actors approach Darfur or other humanitarian crises differently? Finally, consider the policies of those governments that hope to alleviate suffering in Darfur. Given limited resources, what should be the relative emphasis given to IGOs, INGOs/TANs, or their own state power in efforts to solve the problems there? Is there hope that new legal measures, such as indicting people and bringing them to trial, can better protect human rights in the future? These questions are taken up in the next chapter.

Critical Thinking Questions

1. What are the obstacles to effective UN action in Darfur?
2. How are the purposes of TANs and INGOs determined and who determines them?
3. How are the purposes of TANs different from those of states in this case? How do their means of effecting change differ?
4. What organization or combination of organizations do you think would be needed to stop the genocide in Darfur?

Summary

This chapter has considered how nonstate actors of various types are shaping international politics. Chapter 5 looked at nonstate actors within states, such as interest groups. Here, we looked at transnational actors, such as corporations and NGOs, that not only seek to influence states, but also go about their business in ways that sometimes ignore states, and sometimes create issues they have to deal with. We also considered IGOs. There are hundreds of these, and by examining two of the most prominent, the UN and the EU, we saw some of the potential as well as the potential limitations of IGOs.

Key Concepts

1. International organizations
2. Transnational actors
3. United Nations system
   a. General Assembly
   b. Security Council
   c. Specialized agencies
4. Peacekeeping
5. Spillover
6. Global governance
7. Transnational corporations (TNCs)
8. Transnational advocacy networks (TANs)

Study Questions

1. What is the difference between international organizations and transnational actors?
2. What are the competing understandings and evaluations of the UN?
3. What are the main issues involved in discussions on UN reform?
4. What are the key organs of the EU and what responsibilities do they have?
5. Why are other regions seeking to emulate the EU model and what barriers do they face?
6. How are transnational corporations influencing international politics?
7. How are transnational advocacy networks influencing international politics?
8. In what ways are international organizations and transnational actors undermining the Westphalian state system?

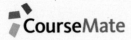 CourseMate

Endnotes

1. Eric Reeves, "The Case for NATO Intervention," *TNR Online,* at http://www.tnr.com/etc.mhtml?week=2005-07-17

2. For a more detailed definition, see Union of International Associations, ed., *The Yearbook of International Organizations 2008/2009 Volume I: Organization Descriptions and Cross-References* (Munich: Walter De Gruyter, 2008).

3. The author is grateful to Catherine Weaver for suggesting the inclusion of this table and for sharing a model.

4. UN Charter, Chapter IV, at http://www.un.org/en/documents/charter/chapter4.shtml

5. Global Policy Forum, "UN Budget: Tables and Charts," at http://www.globalpolicy.org/finance/tables/inxbuget.htm

6. The acronym UNICEF represents an earlier version of the organization's name, the United Nations International Children's Emergency Fund.

7. Ban Ki-moon, address at the Royal Institute of International Affairs, July 11, 2007, at http://www.un.org/apps/news/infocus/sgspeeches/statments_full.asp?statID=100

8. Peter Willetts, "Transnational Actors and International Organizations in Global Politics," in John Baylis and Steve Smith, eds., *The Globalization of World Politics* (Oxford: Oxford University Press, 2001), pp. 356–357.

9. "Clinton Helps Sell Saudis on Jet Deal Worth $6 Billion," *Los Angeles Times,* August 20, 1993, at http://articles.latimes.com/1993-08-20/news/mn-25730_1_u-s-aircraft-industry

10. Raymond Vernon, *Sovereignty at Bay: The Multinational Spread of U.S. Enterprises* (New York: Basic Books, 1971).

11. United Nations, "About the Global Compact," at http://www.unglobal compact.org/AboutTheGC/index.html

12. For a detailed discussion of transnational advocacy groups, see Margaret E. Keck and Kathryn Sikkink, *Activists Beyond Borders: Advocacy Networks in International Politics* (Ithaca, NY: Cornell University Press, 1998).

13. Fiona Terry, *Condemned to Repeat? The Paradox of Humanitarian Action* (Ithaca, NY: Cornell University Press, 2002), pp. 36–37.

14. Terry, *Condemned to Repeat?,* pp. 36–37.

15. "The Doves of War," *The Economist,* November 22, 2007.

13

International Law, Norms, and Human Rights

LEARNING OBJECTIVES

After completing this chapter, the student should be able to . . .

1. Define "international law."
2. Identify the sources of international law and rank their importance.
3. Analyze the problem of enforcing international law.
4. Articulate and defend an argument concerning the significance of international law.
5. Describe international law concerning human rights and its relationship with state sovereignty
6. Describe the structure and process of the International Criminal Court.
7. Define "international norms."
8. Explain the evolution of international norms and their influence on international politics.

◄ President Slobodan Milosevic on trial for war crimes at the UN tribunal in The Hague.
AP Photo/Pool

Consider the Case

The United States, the UN, and Iraq: 1990–1991 versus 2002–2003

After Iraq invaded Kuwait in August 1990, the United States and other nations resolved that, as U.S. President George H. W. Bush put it, "this will not stand." The United States and Kuwait immediately went to the UN Security Council, which approved a series of resolutions. The first, Security Council Resolution 660, passed within twenty-four hours of the invasion, condemned the Iraqi invasion and mandated a withdrawal of Iraqi forces from Kuwait.[1] Resolution 678, passed in November 1990, authorized UN member states to "use all necessary means to uphold and implement Resolution 660 and all subsequent relevant resolutions and to restore international peace and security."[2] The words "all necessary means," it was agreed, authorized the United States and others to attack Iraq to force it out of Kuwait. In January 1991, a force led by the United States but including contingents from thirty-three countries invaded Kuwait and forced Iraq to withdraw.

In 2002, the United States again prepared to invade Iraq and again sought authority from the UN Security Council. Resolution 1441, adopted on November 8, declared Iraq to be in violation of previous Security Council resolutions and stated that there would be "serious consequences" if Iraq did not comply.[3] Several members of the Security Council, including France, China, and Russia, stated that Resolution 1441 did not itself authorize war, since it did not contain clear authorization such as that in Resolution 678 from 1990.

The United States and Great Britain, understanding that a clear authorization of military attack would not be passed by the Security Council, asserted that Resolution 1441 and previous resolutions provided the legal basis to attack. Their case that the war was legal relied on two arguments: self-defense and the upholding of UN resolutions. First, they claimed that they were acting in self-defense, based on Article 51 of the UN charter, which states, in part, "Nothing in the present Charter shall impair the inherent right of individual or collective self-defense if an armed attack occurs." The Bush administration contended that the

right of self-defense included the right to preempt the use of weapons of mass destruction. More broadly, the **Bush doctrine** held that preventive war against potential nuclear proliferators was legal.

Second, they claimed that existing resolutions provided authorization for the use of force and that no new resolution was needed. U.S. Secretary of State Colin Powell, speaking before the Security Council in February 2003, stated, "Iraq has now placed itself in danger of the serious consequences called for in UN Resolution 1441. And this body places itself in danger of irrelevance if it allows Iraq to continue to defy its will without responding effectively and immediately."[4] They focused particularly on the words "serious consequences." Jack Straw, the British Foreign Minister, stated, "As far as the legal base is concerned, 1441 does not require a second resolution."[5] The governments also asserted the resolutions surrounding the first invasion of Iraq in 1991, including Resolution 678, were still in effect. The failure of Iraq to fully comply with the cease-fire reached in 1991, it was argued, meant that states were still authorized under Resolution 678 to resume hostilities.

Those who viewed the war as illegal were particularly critical of the argument that the attack was justified as self-defense under Article 51 of the UN Charter. Article 51 specifically allows self-defense " … if an armed attack occurs." Moreover, Article 51 allows states to use force without prior Security Council approval only "until the Security Council has taken measures necessary to maintain international peace and security." Because the Security Council had taken, through its various resolutions, the steps it believed were necessary, opponents argued, any attack was disallowed. Many observers disagreed with the position that Council Resolution 1441, authorized war with its threat of "serious consequences." Not only did the resolution not say anything about military force as a possible consequence, it did not authorize any actor to carry out those consequences.

In contrast to the 1991 invasion, there was widespread disagreement as to whether the 2003 invasion was legal and therefore legitimate. Global indignation was captured by UN Secretary General Kofi Annan, who stated in 2004, "From our point of view and the Charter point of view, it [the invasion] was illegal."[6] In subsequent years, U.S. prestige declined around the world, in part as a consequence of the perception that it should not have invaded Iraq (and in part because of the difficulties it encountered after the initial defeat of Iraq's army).

These two cases raise several questions. First, why did the United States and its allies even bother seeking UN approval for their actions? What were the perceived benefits of gaining UN authorization and the costs of not receiving it? Second, why did it matter to other states whether the United States and its allies did or did not have UN approval for their military plans? Third, was the invasion legal? Who decides legality in international affairs, and how does international law differ from domestic law? Fourth, in what ways did international law constrain the various actors in these cases? In what ways did it empower them? How would theorists from different schools of thought explain these cases?

International law is a very old idea that has attained renewed importance in recent decades. The more states interact with one another, the more they need to develop rules, formal and informal, to manage their relations. Yet the status of international law and the role that such rules can and should play are hotly debated. Since there is no recognized international government, who has the authority to make the laws and how can they be enforced? Some argue that without a reliable enforcement mechanism, international law is not really "law." Yet there is no doubt that international law, in the form of international treaties, courts, regimes, and norms, is expanding. Paradoxically, one of the oldest notions in international law, sovereignty, is now being questioned, as international intervention seems increasingly justified. How is the notion of law evolving to deal with this trend? This chapter explores these issues by examining both concrete cases and the concepts and arguments forwarded by realists, liberals, constructivists, and advocates of the other approaches to international relations.

Bush doctrine

A set of principles formed during the administration of U.S. President George W. Bush asserting the necessity of waging preventive war against potential aggressors possessing weapons of mass destruction.

What Is International Law?

International law can be defined as the set of rules and obligations that states recognize as binding on each other.[7] Three points are worth emphasizing. First, international law has traditionally been regarded as law among *states*. However, in recent decades, the increased importance of international organizations and transnational actors has led to pressure to give them an explicit role in international law. Second, only those rules that states *recognize* as binding are considered international law. Third, there is no presumption that all relations between states are regulated by international law. Only matters on which states recognize obligations are covered.

U.S. Secretary of State Colin Powell presents a vial that could contain anthrax as he tries to convince the UN Security Council that Iraq is developing weapons of mass destruction.

Ray Stubblebine/Reuters/Landov

international law

The set of rules and obligations that states recognize as binding on each other.

International law addresses a vast range of issues that arise between states. Treaty obligations between states, for example, deal with trade (the World Trade Organization), the environment (the Kyoto Protocol), and the conduct of war. The coverage of international law is very broad, but patchy. Some agreements cover one part of an issue but leave related matters unregulated. In other cases, some countries have signed treaties regulating conduct, while others, equally involved in the matter, have not.

The History of International Law

International law goes back as far as recorded history.[8] Early agreements dealt with relatively simple matters, such as territorial boundaries and rules for exchanging ambassadors. Even these simple agreements demonstrate why states need international law: It helps them regularize their conduct to avoid unwanted conflicts. States formed these laws and followed them not because they were compelled to do so, but because doing so was in their interest. This is a central theme in the study of international law.

The modern history of international law, like the nation-state system, has its roots in medieval Europe. The early European states still considered themselves part of a single political and religious space, the heir to the Roman Empire. Leaders and scholars believed that because all of the European states were explicitly Christian, their relations should be governed by rules rooted in church doctrine. Many of these rules concerned the laws of war. Because medieval European states were constantly at war with one another (or waging crusades in the Middle East), the appropriate reasons for going to war, and acceptable means of fighting war, were important issues.

In April 1139, representatives at the Second Lateran Council took two steps to try to limit the effects of the many wars between Europe's feudal states. First, they sought to regularize the "Truce of God," which prohibited fighting on holy days. Second, they banned the use of the crossbow, a newly developed and devastating weapon. This was probably the first arms control agreement. It should be noted that these prohibitions only applied to relations among Christians, and not to Muslims or other non-Christian enemies.

Grotius and the Theory of Just War

Efforts to forge a European international law based on the guidance of the Catholic Church persisted into the sixteenth century. However, the Protestant Reformation had destroyed the notion of a single Christian community, and increasingly violent religious conflict in Europe culminated in the Thirty Years War. In 1625, in the midst of that conflict, the Dutch lawyer Hugo Grotius published his work *The Law of War and Peace*.

just war theory

The theory of the circumstances in which it is ethical to go to war and the kinds of practices that are ethical in the prosecution of war.

Grotius sought to produce a systematic **just war theory**, and he defined the problem in ways that are still familiar to us today. He asked two basic questions. First, in what circumstances is it permissible to go to war? Second, what kinds of practices are acceptable in the prosecution of war? Looking only at U.S. involvement in Iraq since 2003, we can see that these questions remain salient today. Grotius based his answers on Christian theology, including the work of earlier theologians and political theorists such as St. Augustine and Thomas Aquinas. But he also revolutionized the study and practice of international law by advancing the concept of *natural law*—the idea that rational inquiry could reveal to people what behaviors should be legal.[9] He argued that war was just only if the reasons for going to war were just and the means used to prosecute the war were just.

Included in Grotius's approach are several familiar ideas:

- There must be just cause to go to war.
- War must be declared by legitimate authorities.

- The means used in war must not be inhumane.
- The means used in the war must be proportional to the ends obtained.

Although the succeeding centuries saw an increasing number of commercial and territorial treaties among states, the basic notions of international law did not change.

International Law in the Twentieth Century

It is not coincidental that the most violent century in history was also the century in which states and people renewed efforts to strengthen international law. A primary goal was to minimize or eliminate the use of war in resolving disagreements among states. That goal was not attained, but by the end of the century, international law was indeed becoming more prominent.

The horrors of World War I motivated the formation of the League of Nations. The goal of that body was to prevent war by getting states to join forces against aggression. Other treaties of the post-World War I period went further. The Kellogg-Briand Pact of 1928, signed by all of the major states, renounced war as an instrument of state policy. This treaty was quickly ignored and later mocked, but other treaties of the same era fared better, including the 1925 Geneva Protocol banning biological and chemical weapons.

The outbreak of World War II and the atrocities committed in that war convinced some that international law was pointless—and convinced others that it was more necessary than ever. Following the war, a convention against genocide and a Universal Declaration of Human Rights were adopted, both of which continue to be relevant today.

The new danger, however, was that of nuclear war between the United States and the Soviet Union. In the 1960s and 1970s, the two superpowers reached a series of bilateral treaties to limit the number of nuclear weapons produced. More important, perhaps, they collaborated in getting many other countries to sign the 1968 Nuclear Non-Proliferation Treaty.

Children at Auschwitz Concentration Camp in Poland, 1945. The atrocities of World War II spurred development of the Genocide Convention, which stated "Persons committing genocide . . . shall be punished, whether they are constitutionally responsible rulers, public officials, or private individuals."

AP Photo/CAF PAP

International law flourished in other areas. As the EU emerged and grew, it developed an increasingly large body of international law applying to its members. Similarly, the General Agreement on Tariffs and Trade, and then the WTO, developed a body of detailed agreements regulating the conduct of trade between states. In 1987, the first major international environmental agreement was signed: The Montreal Protocol banned the use of aerosol propellants that deplete the ozone layer. The twentieth century did not see sovereign states subjected to the rule of law from above—which would mean the end of the sovereign state system—but it did see the emergence of an increasingly thick web of agreements among states to govern their relations.

Sources of International Law

The origins of international law differ fundamentally from those of domestic law. Within nation-states, laws are made by sovereign governments. In international politics, there is no sovereign above the "subjects"—the states—and there is no international legislature. So where does international law come from? Who makes it?

Article 38 of the Charter of the International Court of Justice (ICJ)—the most authoritative international judicial body—lists three major sources of international law:

- International conventions [treaties], whether general or particular, establishing rules expressly recognized by the consenting states
- International custom, as evidence of a general practice accepted as law
- The general principles of law recognized by civilized nations

There are other sources of international law as well. Article 38 of the ICJ Charter states that as "subsidiary" sources of law, the court can consider other judiciary rulings and the opinions of experts. Moreover, states have delegated some legislative authority in specific areas to international organizations. A primary example is the EU's Council and Parliament.

It is worth noting as well what is *not* considered a source of international law: the United Nations. Any resolutions of the UN General Assembly intended to make the minority subject to the rule of the majority would violate state sovereignty. The role of the Security Council is slightly stronger: Its resolutions on matters brought before it are considered binding, but the Council has no authority to pass general laws that are binding on other states.

In one way or another, the source of all international law is states' agreement to accept certain obligations and be bound by them. Thus, the best domestic analogy is not the laws passed by legislatures, but the private agreements and contracts entered into by firms and individuals. At the international level, such agreements and contracts can be made formally, through treaties, or they can arise informally, as an outgrowth of international customs, general practices, or general principles of law. However, neither international custom nor general principles of "civilized nations" can come to exist without states' agreeing to them and recognizing them.

Over time, formal treaties have become increasingly important relative to other sources because it is so difficult to precisely interpret informal customs or principles. There has been a steady effort since World War II to codify essential aspects of custom and general principles into formal agreements. Codifying helps remove any ambiguity regarding what is meant and what is not. The International Law Commission of the UN was charged with this task.

Enforcement of International Law

Enforcement, in the view of many, is the central problem of international law. "Law" is only meaningful to the extent that the same rules apply to everyone. What happens when a state, an organization, or an individual violates the law? Domestic law relies on a process of determining guilt or innocence, assigning a penalty, and applying the penalty. Enforcement is a major issue in international law as well, but the process works quite differently. There are two potential mechanisms for enforcement of international law. One is enforcement by international organizations, such as the UN. The other is self-enforcement by states. Neither is perfectly reliable, and neither is fair.

Judgment

In order for enforcement to occur, there has to be some finding that international law has been violated. How does this occur in the international system? Essentially, there are two ways to make such a determination. The first is through the ruling of an international court or another international organization. The second is through a unilateral determination by a country. Both methods are problematic.

THE INTERNATIONAL COURT OF JUSTICE

The primary international court, empowered to determine when states have violated international law, is the **International Court of Justice (ICJ)**, also referred to unofficially as the "World Court," and based in The Hague in the Netherlands. It is the descendent of earlier courts, including the Permanent Court of International Justice that existed under the League of Nations. The ICJ is part of the UN system.

> **International Court of Justice (ICJ)**
>
> Also known as the "World Court," the body that adjudicates disputes that arise over treaty obligations.

The court consists of fifteen judges, including one each from the five permanent members of the UN Security Council. The ICJ adjudicates disputes between states on matters over which they have previously agreed that the court will have jurisdiction. Many international treaties include provisions that disputes over the treaty shall be resolved by the ICJ. Much more broadly, many states have signed agreements that they will submit their international conduct in general to the jurisdiction of the ICJ. In cases over which the court has jurisdiction, its rulings are considered final; there is no higher court to which the losing party can appeal. However, when states have not previously agreed to the court's jurisdiction, the court has none.

With those obvious limitations, the court is generally believed to function well. States do not like to be brought before the court and, in particular, to lose a case there, so states tend to avoid behavior that would likely lead to such an outcome. In that sense, the court may be influential even when cases are not brought to it.

Some examples of cases considered by the court in 2009-2010 illustrate its role.

- The ICJ found that the United States was in breach of its obligations by not following the court's ruling in an earlier case. In 2004, the court ruled that U.S. courts must reconsider the cases of fifty-one Mexican citizens awaiting death sentences in the United States, because the accused had not been granted all the rights required by an international consular treaty. The United States responded to the 2004 ruling by withdrawing its consent for ICJ jurisdiction on that treaty, but the ICJ asserted that it continued to have jurisdiction.

- The ICJ ruled on a case brought by Argentina against Uruguay in 2006, arguing that Uruguay had violated the 1975 Statute on the River Uruguay in building two pulp mills on the river. The

Figure 13.1 Primary Issue in Cases Brought Before the International Court of Justice (1981–2010). The ICJ has heard many different types of cases since its inception.

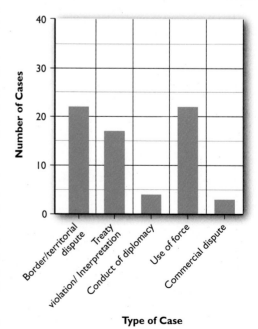

Source: International Court of Justice, "List of Cases referred to the Court since 1946 by date of introduction," at http://www.icj-cij.org/docket/index.php?p1=3&p2=2; Paul D'Anieri.

court ruled that Uruguay had violated the procedural requirements of the treaty, but not the substance. Argentina had asked the court to order Uruguay to dismantle the mills or pay compensation, and to order Uruguay to provide guarantees concerning future behavior under the treaty, but the court did neither.

■ At the request of the General Assembly, the ICJ issued an "advisory opinion" on the legality of Kosovo's 2008 declaration of independence. Various actors had asserted that the declaration of independence violated general principles of international law or UN Security Council Resolution 1244, which was adopted in 1999 to end fighting in Kosovo. In finding the declaration legal, the court found in particular that Resolution 1244 was not binding on the Kosovo Albanian authorities who declared independence.

■ The ICJ began considering a case in which Burkina Faso and Niger jointly submitted a border dispute for resolution. The two countries had agreed in a 2009 treaty to many of the details of their border, but agreement on one section remained contested, and they agreed to ask the ICJ to resolve the matter. In this instance, the court functioned in the role of arbitrator.

As these examples indicate, the ICJ seems to play a tangential role in the dominant issues of international politics. In two of the four cases previously described, the losing parties simply ignored the rulings, leaving the other parties with no further redress.

UNILATERAL DETERMINATION OF VIOLATIONS

A second means of judging violations of international law is for states simply to decide themselves when laws or treaties have been violated. Such findings obviously do not have the legitimacy of findings by the ICJ or another international body. They may, however, be a stronger deterrent to violations of agreements by other states. Because an aggrieved state may be more capable than an international organization of enforcing its judgment, states that contemplate violating agreements may be deterred. However, such enforcement is available only to relatively powerful states.

Enforcement

ENFORCEMENT BY UN ORGANS

In theory, enforcement of international law has been the responsibility of the UN system. The ICJ can issue judicial decisions on violations of international treaties in cases over which it has jurisdiction. However, the ICJ has never been central in resolving major instances of international conflict because it generally lacks jurisdiction in such cases. The most pressing threats to international security tend to be brought to the Security Council, as do cases in which rulings by the ICJ are ignored.

The limitations of the Security Council process were discussed in depth in Chapter 12. The Security Council can enforce international law only when the five permanent members either are on the same side of the issue in question or consider it to be of limited importance to them. Such cases have been relatively few. The most significant case in recent decades was the decision, in 1990, to authorize the use of force against Iraq after that country invaded Kuwait. That decision increased hopes that enforcement of international law would be strengthened by a newly unified Security Council, but the unity of that year did not last long.

ENFORCEMENT BY SPECIFIC TREATY ORGANIZATIONS

In recent decades, states have created judicial mechanisms within specific international treaties and organizations. Many treaties include provisions for rendering judgment on violations of those agreements. The WTO is a case in point. It has a dispute-resolution

The Culture Connection

Can Public Opinion Strengthen International Law?

International Law

Which of these two views is closer to yours?

Our nation should consistently follow int'l laws. It is wrong to violate int'l laws, just as it is wrong to violate laws within a country.		If our government thinks it is not in our nation's interest, it should not feel obliged to abide by int'l laws.

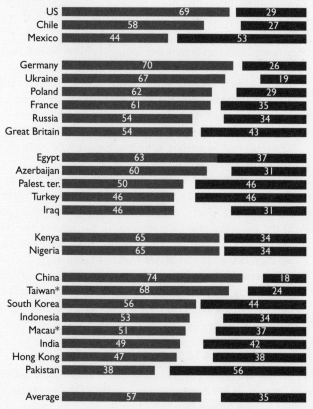

Country	Follow	Not obliged
US	69	29
Chile	58	27
Mexico	44	53
Germany	70	26
Ukraine	67	19
Poland	62	29
France	61	35
Russia	54	34
Great Britain	54	43
Egypt	63	37
Azerbaijan	60	31
Palest. ter.	50	46
Turkey	46	46
Iraq	46	31
Kenya	65	34
Nigeria	65	34
China	74	18
Taiwan*	68	24
South Korea	56	44
Indonesia	53	34
Macau*	51	37
India	49	42
Hong Kong	47	38
Pakistan	38	56
Average	57	35

* Excluded from average   WorldPublicOpinion.Org

The chart above shows public opinion about international law in a range of countries. In many of the countries, a majority of respondents supports their country abiding by international law. Skepticism about international law is evident in the many negative responses, but it is not as high as we might expect it to be. One might expect that this bodes well for the future of international law, but there are reasons for caution as well.

First, most of the relevant decisions on international law are not made according to public opinion polls, but by government negotiators. This raises the question of the influence of public opinion on foreign policy, discussed at length in Chapter 5. We could apply the general findings on public opinion on foreign policy to this question. One might wonder whether elite opinion in each of the countries surveyed is more or less favorable to international law than public opinion.

Second, we might expect the general idea of international law to be more popular than specific applications. Even those who support international law in principle might feel that their country should not be constrained by it in particular cases. Thus, the U.S. government consistently sought to carve out exceptions to account for the needs of the "war on terror." Even when Barack Obama replaced George W. Bush, the United States found it exceedingly difficult to change policies that many others saw as illegal.

In sum, the results of this poll show that in many countries, public opinion is not a major barrier to increased emphasis on international law. There is no sign, however, that public opinion is motivating any push to strengthen international law.

Critical Thinking Questions

1. What kind of additional data would we need to tell whether support for international law is increasing?
2. What might explain the variation in attitudes across countries?
3. What cases can you think of when international law became a focus of public discussion in your country?

mechanism that is empowered with judging whether a state has violated WTO rules. A central problem of the predecessor of the WTO, the General Agreement on Tariffs and Trade, was that states were left to their own devices to punish those they believed violated the agreements. This argument tended to lead to "tit-for-tat" disputes that spiraled out of control. It also allowed barriers to trade to increase more than many states desired.

In the WTO, enforcement mechanisms have been strengthened considerably. Member states of the WTO are required to accept the jurisdiction of the **WTO Dispute Settlement Body** (see the more detailed discussion of this body in Chapter 10). If a violation is found, the offending state can change its practice or can offer compensation. If it does not change its practice and does not make compensation agreeable to the plaintiff state, then the Dispute Settlement Body can allow the plaintiff to enact retaliatory tariffs against the offending state. The system is not without flaws. In particular, developing countries may not be able, even with authorized sanctions, to put much of a squeeze on powerful states that violate the agreement. However, in its mandatory jurisdiction and its fairly reliable system of obtaining compliance with its rulings, the WTO mechanism is perhaps the most robust piece of international law enforcement outside the EU. It may serve as a model for future enforcement mechanisms.

"BLENDED" ENFORCEMENT

The WTO mechanism might be described as an instance of **blended enforcement**. In this model, the authority for penalties comes from a recognized international organization

Reuters/Denis Balibouse

WTO Director-General Pascal Lamy opens an informal session of the Trade Negotiation Committee in Geneva.

and is clearly recognized by treaty, but the enforcement itself is carried out by the aggrieved state or by others acting on its behalf. The obvious advantage of such a mechanism is that it does not rely on an international force or international sanctions, which are extremely difficult to implement in practice.

The problem with this model is that it is still likely to lead to uneven enforcement. When enforcement is left to willing states, law is much more likely to be enforced only if the powerful want it enforced. In the case of the Iraqi invasion of Kuwait in 1990, Kuwait would have been out of luck if the United States had not taken such a strong interest in the case. Powerful states have been considerably less willing to invest resources in enforcing international law in places where they have less at stake, including much of Africa.

ENFORCEMENT BY INDIVIDUAL STATES

Most international law relies on **self-enforcement**, meaning that it is up to the individual states to enforce it. Unlike citizens in the domestic arena, states in the international arena continue to have the right to take justice into their own hands. The means open to them can include diplomatic pressure, economic sanctions, or even force. The consequence of self-enforcement of international law is that enforcement is very uneven, and hence the protection of the law is very uneven. Powerful states get the most protection from the law because others know that those states have the power to enforce the law themselves. Powerful states also can avoid being forced by weaker states to adhere to international law.

However, as supporters of international law point out, most international law is self-enforcing in a more basic way: Once states reach an agreement on an issue and are benefiting from their agreement, it is not in their interest to violate it. Although states that violate an agreement might get some short-term gain from doing so, they will suffer two

The Policy Connection

Is Humanitarian Intervention a Duty?

Traditionally, state sovereignty trumped international concerns about how other states treated their subjects. This bias toward nonintervention was deliberately built into the Westphalian system; the continuous wars that plagued early modern Europe could only be avoided by mutual agreement to respect the sovereign rights of other leaders, especially in religious matters. The principle of nonintervention did not mean that interventions did not occur, but that such interventions needed to be justified somehow as exceptions to that rule.

Following World War II, the Convention on Genocide altered the picture considerably, by explicitly allowing states to intervene in cases of genocide. The adoption of this convention meant that states faced two potentially conflicting rules, that of nonintervention and that of preventing massive human rights violations. However, the problem of unjustified intervention has turned out to be a relatively rare one. States' own self-interest often prevents them from inserting themselves into difficult situations in other countries. Although some interventions, such as the intervention of NATO troops in Kosovo in 1999, have been fairly controversial, others have been welcomed, such as Tanzania's intervention to oust the brutal Idi Amin from Uganda or the Vietnamese intervention in Cambodia to end the genocide there in 1978.

The bigger problem has been getting states to intervene in situations when intervention is clearly justified. The European Union, NATO, and the United States were all criticized for not intervening more quickly to prevent atrocities in the former Yugoslavia. The much more chilling case was that of Rwanda, where 800,000 people were killed, mostly with clubs and machetes, as the international community stood by and watched. The common refrain that arose after the Holocaust, "Never again," rang hollow.

The Rwanda genocide raised a difficult problem for international law and international ethics. It had been clearly established that states have a *right* to intervene in cases of genocide, but do they have a *duty* to do so? In terms of international law, they do not. In terms of public opinion or international norms, there may be a strong notion of duty in some cases, but it is a duty states may want to shirk. In the Rwanda case, senior officials in the U.S. government explicitly sought to avoid using the word *genocide* for fear that doing so would oblige the United States to intervene.[1]

If there is a duty to intervene, whose duty is it? Is it the duty of the UN, which has no forces? Of the United States, as the most powerful country in the world? Of regional leaders? These questions are fundamentally unresolved. Despite the perception of a moral obligation for someone to intervene in some cases, there is no international legal and organizational apparatus to fulfill such a duty.

Critical Thinking Questions

1. Is there a duty to intervene in cases of genocide? Exactly what is the duty and whose duty is it?
2. What hazards might arise from making the duty to intervene clear-cut?

PHOTO © ISTOCKPHOTO

[1]See Samantha Power, *"A Problem from Hell": America and the Age of Genocide* (New York: HarperCollins, 2002), especially Chapter 10, on Rwanda.

longer-term and broader costs. First, the agreement they violate will likely be shattered, so they will be deprived of any future benefits from it. Other states are unlikely to continue honoring their obligations to a state that has violated an agreement. The repeated version of the prisoner's dilemma, discussed in Chapter 3, shows that defecting in the short term can undermine cooperation that is beneficial in the long term. Second, once a state's reputation is damaged, it will become much more difficult for the state to reach future agreements on issues that may be of considerable importance. It is, therefore, costly to damage a reputation as a good partner.[10]

Is International Law Really Law?

The weakness and inconsistencies in enforcement of international law lead many to question whether international law should even be called "law." Is international law really law? Skeptics argue that international law is a contradiction in terms. States, they contend, obey international law only when it suits their interest. Others assert that international law is indeed law and that it has important effects on international behavior. These arguments over the status of international law arise from different theoretical approaches to international politics. Ultimately, both sides have a point. International law is different from domestic law in important ways, and enforcement is a particular issue. However, international law does have important effects on state behavior, and if it did not exist, it would probably need to be created.

The Case Against International Law

Realists and economic structuralists generally contend that international law is irrelevant. To the extent that it does matter, they say, international law is a tool used by the strong to control the weak. It does not, therefore, have a significant effect in constraining state behavior.

From this perspective, one central problem in international law is how agreements are made in the first place. Powerful states, it is argued, can use various threats to force weaker states to accept laws that favor the powerful. One fundamental example is the composition of the UN Security Council, where the great powers were able to set up a system that gives them more rights than others.

A second problem is enforcement. If international law is enforced by states, it will be enforced only when the powerful states benefit from it. This means that it can serve only the interests of the powerful. This, realists and economic structuralists contend, contradicts the very notion of the word "law" as something that applies equally to all actors without exception.

The Case for International Law

Those stressing the importance of international law argue that the skeptics have missed the point. This view tends to be held by those from the liberal and constructivist perspectives of international relations theory (feminist theorists might adopt either position on international law). Focusing entirely on coercive enforcement ignores the ways in which international law solves problems for states, and is therefore self-enforcing. The cost of destroying international treaties or ruining one's reputation is by itself often enough to ensure compliance. Enforcement, in this view, is not the key problem. As the scholar Louis Henkin famously wrote, "Almost all nations observe almost all ... of international law ... almost all of the time."[11]

International treaties and laws are established, according to this view, because states need them. If states could achieve common goals and avoid perils without international law, they would do so. International law is formed because the mutual assurances and common understandings it provides enable states to avoid dangerous situations.

Those who believe in the relevance of international law also point out that states that violate international law pay a price, sometimes a high one, for doing so. The U.S. invasion of Iraq in 2003 was widely perceived around the world to be a violation of international law because it was a preemptive attack not sanctioned by the UN Security Council. The opinion that it was illegal did not stop the United States from doing what it believed was necessary, but it did cost the United States considerably in terms of global opinion. This loss of prestige was not irrelevant, as the United States subsequently ran into considerable difficulties gaining collaboration on a variety of issues, such as tougher sanctions to stop Iran's nuclear program.

International and Domestic Law Compared

The similarities and differences between international and domestic law arise often in debates about international law. Skeptics tend to stress the differences between international and domestic law, whereas supporters either stress the similarities or argue that the comparison is not meaningful.

The central distinction between domestic and international law is the reliability of enforcement mechanisms. Clearly, for all the faults and inequities in domestic legal systems around the world, law enforcement is stronger even in poorly governed societies than in the international realm. The question, both at the domestic and at the international level, is how important is enforcement for compliance? Do people obey domestic laws primarily because of enforcement, or primarily because their normative beliefs or self-interest leads them to comply? To those who believe enforcement is crucial to compliance, international law looks very different from domestic law, and very weak. To those who believe that laws are adopted to serve actors' interests and values, most law is self-enforcing, and the distinction between international and domestic law is less significant.

The different approaches to international law can be illustrated through an analogy with domestic traffic rules. Skeptics liken international law to the speed limit on a highway. Speed limits are often meaningless without close enforcement. Supporters of international law compare it to the rule of driving on the correct side of the road. Without such a law, the highways would be chaotic and useless. Once that rule is established, and everyone drives on the same side, only a fool will violate the law.

Ultimately, both sides have a point. International law is different from domestic law in important ways, and enforcement is a particular issue. However, international law does have important effects on state behavior. States continue to create new international law, and nonstate actors advocate more (or different) international laws because international law is perceived to be at least somewhat effective.

International Regimes

Not all agreements among states achieve the status of international law. There is an important intermediate category of agreements that are not laws but are significant nonetheless in shaping state behavior. This category has been labeled *international regimes* by international relations scholars, and it has received much attention in recent decades. **International regimes** can be defined as shared understandings about how states will behave on a particular issue.[12]

In some cases, these shared understandings can be embodied in formal treaties and become international law. In other cases, they can become embodied in international organizations. Often, however, they remain unwritten and not represented by formal organizations. The fundamental point made by scholars of international regimes is that even when they are left informal, such regimes shape behavior.

international regimes
Shared understandings about how states will behave on a particular issue.

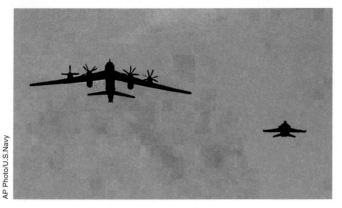

AP Photo/U.S.Navy

The United States and the Soviet Union, despite being involved in an intense political conflict, developed many informal rules of engagement to make sure that they kept the conflict within bounds. U.S. and Soviet aircraft frequently shadowed one another, but pilots developed "rules of the road" to avoid an incident.

A simple example is the nuclear nonproliferation regime. States have a shared interest in preventing the proliferation of nuclear weapons. This regime is institutionalized in several ways, including in the Nuclear Non-Proliferation Treaty (NPT), the International Atomic Energy Agency (an international organization), and the Nuclear Suppliers Group (a group of states that exports nuclear technology and has agreed to abide by guidelines for such exports). None of these agreements or organizations by themselves completely achieve the goals of the nonproliferation regime; the regime is a broader concept that helps explain what connects those formal institutions and why they exist.

International Norms

international norms

Shared ethical principles and expectations about how actors should and will behave in the international arena; and social identities, indicating which actors are considered legitimate.

Constructivists also point to the role played by **international norms** in contemporary affairs and to the ways in which changes in norms account for changes in behavior. These norms can take many forms:

- Ethical principles about how actors *should* behave
- Mutual expectations about how actors *will* behave in certain situations
- Social identities, indicating which actors are to be considered legitimate

Constructivist international relations theory focuses on how normative change leads states to redefine their interests and therefore to behave differently. It appears that there has been noticeable change in recent years, particularly in norms concerning human rights and state sovereignty.

In 1999, discussing NATO's decision to bomb Yugoslavia in response to its treatment of its Kosovar minority, former Czech President Vaclav Havel asserted that, "it seems that the enlightened endeavors of generations of democrats, the horrible experience of two World Wars, which contributed so substantially to the adoption of the Universal Declaration of Human Rights as well as the overall development of our civilization, are gradually bringing the human race to the realization that a human being is more important than a State . . . This change, among other things, should gradually antiquate the idea of noninterference, that is, the concept of saying that what happens in another state, or the measure of respect for human rights there, is none of our business."[13]

These issues remain controversial, but there has no doubt been a normative change—a change in general beliefs about what is right and wrong and about the priorities among different values. The point is not that norms *compel* states to behave in certain ways. Rather, they *motivate* states to behave in certain ways. Norms do not outweigh or compete with self-interest but often help redefine state interests.

HOW DO NORMS SPREAD?

There are a great number of advocates around the world promoting a wide variety of causes with great passion. In some cases, they may be promoting values that most everyone agrees on but that have not become a high priority. In other cases, groups and states may be advocating ideas that contradict established norms on a certain matter (for example, human rights versus state sovereignty). What determines which values gain the consensus necessary to motivate a large number of states to change policies? It is difficult

Figure 13.2 How International Norms Spread

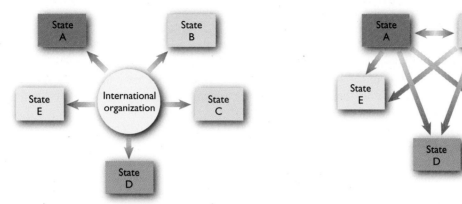

An international organization spreads a new norm.

New norms spread from one state to other states.

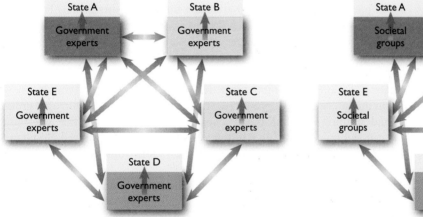

Government experts from different countries agree on norms and promote the norms within their governments.

Norms spread among societies, often through the efforts of transnational activists who attempt to persuade their governments to adopt the norms.

Source: Based on information found at http://papers.ssrn.com/sol3/papers.cfm?abstract_id=62934

to give a precise answer, but four channels can be identified through which norms are diffused across the international community.

First, norms can spread through international organizations. International organizations can establish standards on issues and, using their status, present those standards or norms as having international legitimacy. For example, the expertise of the World Bank helped spread the "Washington consensus" on development strategy. Transnational advocacy networks can also be powerful in stating and promoting new norms. Second, norms can spread from state to state. Success depends in part on the prestige and power of the governments spreading the norm. The prestige and economic power of the EU states has helped them spread many norms, including opposition to capital punishment, to the post-communist European states.

Third, transnational groups of government experts, all working on the same issues, often reach agreement among themselves first and then seek to promote the agreed-on norms with their respective societies and governments. This has been the case among scientists hoping to combat various environmental and health problems. Fourth, norms can spread across societies and then influence governments from the bottom up. Prior to 1994, the international norm against doing business with South Africa's apartheid government spread to the United States largely through the existing U.S. civil rights movement, which then worked to make it a national policy.[14] Transnational advocacy networks often seek to work from the bottom up, from societies to governments.

In sum, although international norms have always been a factor in international politics, people and governments around the world seem increasingly willing to explicitly take them into account in making policy. This does not mean that norms force compliance, but rather they often help change leaders' notions of what is desirable and what is acceptable.

NORMATIVE DISAGREEMENT

There is conflict as well as agreement over norms. Shared norms may motivate states to collaborate, but normative conflict can sometimes be intense and bitter. In recent years, the norm that UN Security Council approval is required for military intervention has been supported by many, rejected by a few, and accepted by others only within certain limits. This has led to intense resentment.

Moreover, even norms that are generally accepted do not always strengthen over time. A case in point is the norm against attacking noncombatants in war. For several centuries, this norm was generally followed throughout the world. In the first half of the twentieth century, however, it was completely abandoned, first in World War I, even more broadly in World War II, and then completely in U.S. and Soviet plans to annihilate each other's civilian populations.

Thus, there is no automatic mechanism requiring that normative consensus will increase within the international community. The rise of transnational terrorist groups indicates an undermining of a whole range of norms, including the norm that determines which actors can legitimately use force in the international system. Indeed, despite the development of international norms pointed to earlier, some would say we are living in a period of decreasing normative consensus.

Regardless of skepticism or idealism concerning the role of international law in international affairs, there is little doubt that states are creating more and more treaties that deal with increasingly far-reaching issues. States are also creating more sophisticated and potentially effective enforcement mechanisms.

Table 13.1 Major International Treaties Since 1990

Treaty	Year	Issue Covered	Scope
Maastricht Treaty (EU)	1992	Integration	12 (later 27) states; brings many traditionally domestic affairs into international treaty
WTO	1994	Trade	148 states; binding enforcement; trumps state legislation
Mine Ban Treaty	1997	Security	152 states; prohibits land mines
Kyoto Protocol	1997 (entered into force in 2005)	Environment	182 states; first major global environmental treaty; requires major domestic economic adjustments
International Criminal Court	1998	Crime/human rights	139 states; first permanent court to deal with "gravest international crimes"
Single European Currency (part of the Maastricht Treaty)	1999	Finance	12 states; national monetary policy surrendered to supranational authority

The scope of international legal commitments has broadened and deepened in the past two decades, and these commitments touch almost every aspect of international politics. Moreover, the treaties being reached are more detailed, contain more serious obligations, and interact much more deeply with states' domestic affairs than previously, as the examples in Table 13.1 illustrate.

As plenty of ongoing disagreements demonstrate, not every international challenge can be solved through international agreements and international laws. However, the examples in Table 13.1 show that on the most pressing issues facing the international community, new agreements and new organizations are being formed. Far from being viewed only as constraints on states, international agreements are seen as enabling states to deal with problems that cannot be solved individually.

human rights

An array of "inalienable" individual rights, including civil liberties and political rights. Some also include economic rights and cultural rights as well.

Human Rights

Human rights have become an increasingly salient area of international politics in recent years. Norms concerning human rights are changing, as are norms concerning the relative weight of human rights versus state sovereignty. Concerns about human rights have been at the center of many high-profile issues in recent years. Examples include military intervention in the former Yugoslavia; tension over the rights of China's Tibetan minority; economic aid; refugees, asylum-seekers, and migration; and questions about the treatment of suspected terrorists. In other words, nearly all the important issues considered in this book now have an important human rights dimension that influences how they are viewed and how policies are developed.

Chinese police apprehend a pro-Tibet protester in Beijing.

The scholar Charles Beitz divides human rights into five broad categories:

1. Personal rights, such as life, liberty, property, freedom of conscience, and religion.
2. Rights in law, such as equal protection, presumption of innocence, rights of the accused.
3. Political rights, such as freedom of speech, of the press, of assembly, and of association, as well as the right to choose one's government, and voting rights.
4. Economic and social rights, including the right to a job, a minimal standard of living, the right to join a union, and workplace rights.
5. Community rights, such as the rights of minority groups to self-determination, language choice, and cultural expression.[15]

The Universal Declaration of Human Rights, adopted in 1948 in the aftermath of World War II and the holocaust, is the central international statement enumerating and defining human rights. The declaration, which is aspirational, rather than binding law, lists an array of "inalienable" rights that every individual is presumed to possess. These include general rights to "life, liberty, and security of person" (Article 3), to fair trials and hearings (Articles 10 and 11), and to privacy (Article 12). The declaration also establishes more specific rights to freedom from torture (Article 5), to political asylum (Article 14), and to work (Article 23).[16]

Article 25 of the declaration states, "Everyone has the right to a standard of living adequate for the health and well-being of himself and of his family, including food, clothing, housing and medical care and necessary social services, and the right to security in

The Geography Connection

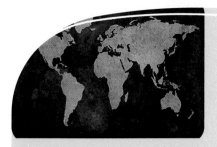

Freedom Around the World

The map above shows the level of political freedom in the world, as measured by the U.S.-based group Freedom House. Freedom House bases its rankings on factors such as freedom of expression and assembly, rights of the accused, and freedom of press.

2. What other kinds of factors might be used in assessing human rights?
3. Are there countries whose rankings you would disagree with? Or countries whose rankings would change if different criteria were used?

Critical Thinking Questions

1. What patterns or correlations can you see in the distribution of freedom around the world?

Freedom in the World 2007

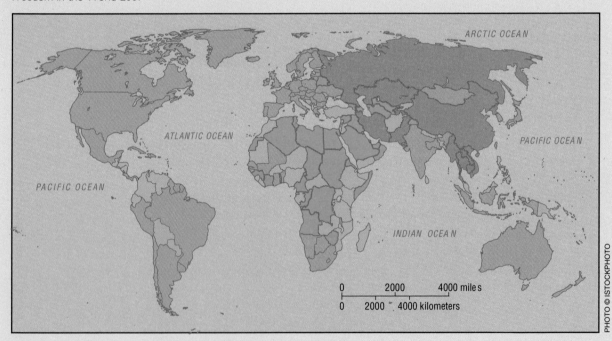

Source: Map based on Freedom House's survey, Freedom in the World 2007.

PHOTO © ISTOCKPHOTO

the event of unemployment, sickness, disability, widowhood, old age or other lack of livelihood in circumstances beyond his control." Thus, the deep poverty in which many people are mired can be seen not simply as an economic problem, but as a violation of human rights. This helps explain why so many people in the Third World believe that aid is an obligation.

Threats to human rights come from a variety of sources. In some cases, governments or other groups deliberately infringe them: China denies cultural rights to its Tibetan and Uighur minorities, and limits political rights of all its citizens. The Taliban in Afghanistan denies women a whole range of rights. The United States uses the death penalty, which many consider a human rights violation. Guerilla groups in Colombia target civilians. In many cases, however, human rights are violated unintentionally, as a result of other conflicts or problems. Around the world, people are forced from their homes and become refugees as a result of wars, famines, and natural disasters. Poverty causes the violation of many social and economic rights. In some places, governments are simply too ineffective to provide these rights—a competent government is a necessary condition for the provision of many basic human rights.

Many actors in international politics are concerned with improving protection of human rights. These include many of the transnational advocacy networks and international organizations discussed in the previous chapter, as well as domestic NGOs and even governments. A variety of means are employed, depending on the group and the specific right being pursued. Economic and social rights are often pursued through aid and development efforts. Political rights are often pursued through public pressure campaigns, sometimes linking transnational advocacy networks with domestic NGOs. Often these overlap with government efforts. In the case of Darfur, Western governments, pressure groups in Western countries, international NGOs, the UN, the African Union, and others, were all involved in trying to protect the rights of people in Darfur.

Although many human rights are not controversial by themselves, the question of how to protect them leads to some of the thorniest international political questions today. If states have made an *international* treaty commitment to protect these rights, and then fail to do so, does this make it a matter of concern to the international community? In recent years, more and more people—leaders as well as citizens—have answered this question affirmatively.

However, both the concept of human rights and the measures needed to protect them in the modern world clash with the Westphalian conception of sovereignty on which international law is based. The Westphalian system assumes that states control their own territory and citizens. Human rights assume that people have rights that states cannot deny and must protect. The Westphalian system assumes a territorial segmentation of authority. Human rights assume that rights, and the duty to protect them, are universal, spreading across territorial boundaries. Therefore, the recent focus on human rights promotion represents a fundamental revision of the Westphalian idea that governments have sovereignty over their internal affairs, including the right to rule as they see fit.[17] Practically, it raises the possibility that governments will intervene to protect the rights of individuals when those rights are being violated by their own governments. It could also lead to the possibility that outside governments will be legally obligated to intervene.

Intervention by one state in another—and military intervention in particular—is the most controversial aspect the human rights debate today. Intervention is often advocated, and not infrequently carried out, in the contemporary system. The case of Sudan (see Chapter 12) is one in which external intervention has been driven and legitimized by concerns over human rights. Similarly, intervention in the former Yugoslavia was motivated and justified not on grounds of international aggression, but of the violation of individuals' rights. When the government of Burma refused international offers of aid after a devastating cyclone in 2008, some argued that outside states should forcibly deliver aid to affected areas (this was not done). Even the U.S. invasion of Iraq was justified in part on the grounds that the government of Saddam Hussein consistently violated Iraqis' human rights. The cases are not infrequent, and are often highly controversial.

There remain powerful arguments against intervention, especially military intervention. First, many argue that such intervention is illegal under international law (that it

Table 13.2 Human Rights in International Treaties

	Universal Declaration of Human Rights	International Covenant on Civil and Political Rights	International Covenant on Economic, Social, and Cultural Rights
Life	×	×	
Liberty and security of person	×	×	
Protection against slavery	×	×	
Protection against torture and inhumane punishment	×	×	
Recognition as a person before the law	×	×	
Equal protection of the law	×	×	
Access to legal remedies for rights violations	×	×	
Protection against arbitrary arrest or detention	×	×	
Hearing before an independent and impartial judiciary	×	×	
Presumption of innocence	×	×	
Protection against ex post facto laws	×	×	
Protection of privacy, family, and home	×	×	
Freedom of movement and residence	×	×	
Freedom of thought, conscience, and religion	×	×	
Freedom of opinion, expression, and the press	×	×	
Freedom of assembly and association	×	×	
Political participation	×	×	
Freedom to own property	×		
Freedom to seek asylum from prosecution	×		
Recognition of nationality	×		
Protection against debtor's imprisonment		×	
Protection against arbitrary expulsion as an alien		×	
Protection against advocacy of racial or religious hatred		×	
Protection of minority culture		×	
Participation in free trade unions	×	×	×
Freedom to marry and found a family	×	×	×
Special protections for children	×	×	×
Self-determination		×	×
Social security	×		×
Work under favorable conditions	×		×
Rest and leisure	×		×
Food, clothing, and housing	×		×
Health care and social services	×		×
Education	×		×
Participation in cultural life	×		×

Source: Jack Donnelly, "State Sovereignty and International Intervention: The Case of Human Rights," in Gene M. Lyons and Michael Mastanduno, eds., *Beyond Westphalia? State Sovereignty and International Intervention* (Baltimore, MD: Johns Hopkins University Press, 1995).

violates state sovereignty). This argument is often made by states that might be the target of intervention. Second, many argue that intervention happens only when it serves the interest of the interveners, and therefore is illegitimate. Third, many argue that intervening states do not have the right to put their own citizen-soldiers at risk to solve somebody else's problem. Finally, it is sometimes argued that such intervention does not work; that the institutions that protect and advance human rights, such as democracy, rule of law, and a functioning economy cannot be established through external intervention. Supporters of intervention argue that human rights are as important an element of international law as sovereignty and that in many cases, only intervention can prevent massive suffering and genocide.[18]

THE CASE OF THE DEATH PENALTY

The global movement against the death penalty is a case that illustrates the spread of an international norm in the area of human rights. Until a few decades ago, international pressure to eliminate the death penalty would have been unimaginable for two reasons. First, very few countries had domestic norms against the death penalty. Second, almost no one believed that what one country did in this regard was any other country's business.

More recently, however, the countries of Europe have worked to persuade or compel other countries to abolish the death penalty. In 1983, a protocol prohibiting the death penalty was added to the European Convention for the Protection of Human Rights and Fundamental Freedoms. The EU has sought to spread this norm by making membership in key European institutions, such as the EU and the Council of Europe, dependent on abolition of the death penalty. Many of the post-Soviet states outlawed the death penalty in the 1990s as part of their efforts to be admitted to European institutions.

This norm is having an effect beyond Europe. In a very controversial ruling, the U.S. Supreme Court cited the international movement against the death penalty as one reason for banning the execution of those under age eighteen. In this case, a normative change has taken place over a relatively short period of time. In 1988, the court ruled that execution of those aged seventeen or eighteen was constitutional. In 2005, it reversed this ruling, citing "the evolving standards of decency that mark the progress of a maturing society." The majority opinion stated, "It is proper that we acknowledge the overwhelming weight of international opinion against the juvenile death penalty."[19] Legal briefs were submitted by the EU and the Council of Europe, among others. This position remained deeply controversial in the United States, however, with dissenting justices strongly criticizing both the overall decision and the notion that international opinion should be taken into account. Support for the death penalty in the United States remains high.

The International Criminal Court

An essential part of the effort to pursue human rights in the international realm is the effort to prosecute and punish those responsible for the most heinous violations. The recently formed **International Criminal Court (ICC)** and related efforts aim to create an international ability to prosecute war crimes and other crimes. The ICC seeks to offer some remedy for problems that the international community hoped were a thing of the past but that re-emerged in the 1990s: genocide and crimes against humanity on a massive scale. This development is of particular interest because states are seeking to establish international law in its narrow sense—law that leads to the apprehension, prosecution, and punishment of criminals. In that sense, the implications of the court for international law and for international politics more broadly are far-reaching.

International Criminal Court (ICC)

International court for the prosecution of war crimes and other heinous crimes.

war crimes

A set of transgressions established by the fourth Geneva Convention, including willful killing, torture or inhumane treatment, willfully causing great suffering or serious injury to body or health, unlawful deportation or transfer, or unlawful confinement of a protected person.

War crimes seized global attention as a result of the atrocities of World War II. The belief was that although many horrors of war are unavoidable, certain actions, such as the mass murder of Europe's Jews by Germany or the large-scale atrocities against civilian populations by Japan, went beyond what could be justified by the demands of war. Moreover, a central argument was that individuals could be held accountable for the actions of their countries and their armies. Twelve officials of Nazi Germany and seven officials of Imperial Japan were hanged as a result of the trials held in Nuremburg and Tokyo following World War II.

The fourth Geneva Convention, adopted in 1949, defines a range of behaviors as war crimes:

- Willful killing
- Torture or inhuman treatment, including biological experiments
- Willfully causing great suffering or serious injury to body or health
- Unlawful deportation or transfer or unlawful confinement of a protected person[20]

War crimes seemed more or less a historical matter until two events in the 1990s: the "ethnic cleansing" campaigns of the wars in former Yugoslavia and the Rwandan genocide of 1994, in which approximately 800,000 civilians were killed in the span of a few months. Efforts by the international community to stop the violence were slow in the case of Yugoslavia and nearly nonexistent in the case of Rwanda.

In both cases, there were calls for the initiators of mass murder to be punished for war crimes. In neither country, however, was there a functioning judicial apparatus that could bring them to justice. Therefore, the international community, through UN Security Council resolutions, established two separate tribunals, one for Yugoslavia and one for Rwanda. Most notable of the activities of these tribunals was the trial of former Yugoslav leader Slobodan Milosevic.

The role played by those two tribunals convinced many that a permanent version was needed. As one commentator lamented, "We have lived in a golden age of impunity, where a person stands a much better chance of being tried for taking a single life than for killing ten thousand or a million."[21] In 1998, by a vote of 120 to 7, with 21 abstentions, a conference in Rome approved an agreement forming the ICC.[22]

Perhaps the most innovative feature of the ICC is that individual criminals, not states, are its primary focus. Although the ICC was formed by an agreement among states, state governments are not represented at the court. In that sense, it has transcended the traditional notion of international law as "law among nations."

The ICC is charged with trying the most serious crimes: genocide, crimes against humanity, and war crimes.[23] It can begin proceedings against an individual either when the UN Security Council or a treaty signatory brings a case to its attention, or when the court's own prosecutor, based on his or her own investigations, believes an indictment is warranted. The court is based on the principle of "complementarity" with domestic courts, meaning that it only takes on cases in which domestic criminal courts are either unable or unwilling to get involved. Crucially, it is left to the ICC (not individual states) to determine when it should take on a case under these provisions. Opposition to this rule led the United States not to sign the agreement.

Until a case is actually brought to conclusion at the ICC, it remains to be seen how this organization will work in practice. Of the seven countries that chose not to sign the treaty, two—China and the United States—are expected to be among the most influential states in the world in coming decades. Their refusal to participate has spurred widespread criticism, but it is not difficult to understand.

The U.S. government feared that the ICC would be used as a political tool against the United States. Since the United States has more military missions around the world than any other country and is often looked to by other countries to get involved in

The History Connection

The Geneva Conventions

Much of contemporary international law on the conduct of war is codified in the Geneva Conventions. The first Geneva Convention was signed in 1864; the fourth was signed in 1949 and amended in 1977. The importance of these rules was demonstrated recently when the United States was accused of violating them at prisons in Iraq and Cuba.

Although limits on the conduct of war had been discussed for centuries, in the mid-nineteenth century, as the scale of warfare increased, there were few internationally agreed-on limits. In June 1859, a Swiss merchant named Henri Dunant witnessed the battle of Solferino, in what is today northern Italy. He was shocked to see that soldiers wounded on the battlefield died slow, agonizing deaths, sometimes succumbing to thirst because they could not be retrieved from the battlefield and treated.

Dunant returned to Geneva and began to campaign for arrangements that would allow for wounded soldiers to be treated. He called for a volunteer group of nurses and doctors to treat the wounded and for international recognition that these workers were neutrals and would not be harmed by warring armies. Soon an "International Committee for Relief to the Wounded" was established, which later became the International Committee of the Red Cross. This committee then lobbied for international recognition. In 1864, the Swiss government sponsored a diplomatic conference that established provisions for the care of the wounded and recognized the International Committee of the Red Cross.[1] The first Geneva Convention is known officially as "Convention for the Amelioration of the Condition of the Wounded in Armies in the Field, 1864." It protects medical workers, ambulances, and military hospitals, identified by the familiar red cross on a white background.

In 1906, the second Geneva Convention extended the provisions of the first convention to warfare at sea. The third convention, negotiated in 1925, introduced provisions for treatment of prisoners of war. Article 17 states, "No physical or mental torture, nor any other form of coercion, may be inflicted on prisoners of war to secure from them information of any kind whatever. Prisoners of war who refuse to answer may not be threatened, insulted, or exposed to unpleasant or disadvantageous treatment of any kind."

The third convention goes into considerable detail on the rights of prisoners and on definitions of who is a "lawful combatant" and thus covered by the convention. These definitional issues seemed fairly noncontroversial until the war in Afghanistan in 2001. There was considerable disagreement concerning which people captured by the United States and its allies were protected by the third convention and which were not.

The fourth Geneva Convention, adopted after World War II in 1949, dealt with protection of civilians during war. It attempted to deal with the fact that World War II had seen an unprecedented level of attacks on civilians, from the bombing of cities, practiced by all sides, to the Holocaust. This convention has been invoked in recent years to indict key leaders for war crimes in places such as Yugoslavia, Rwanda, and Sudan.

Critical Thinking Questions

1. How strong a limit do the Geneva Conventions create in practice? Do states obey the conventions only when it is convenient or do they act as though violating them carries a high cost?

2. How do you anticipate that the war on terror, with its debates about the utility of torture and the status of "enemy combatants," will affect the role of the Geneva Conventions?

PHOTO © ISTOCKPHOTO

[1]"International Humanitarian Law," at http://www.redcross.lv/en/conventions.htm.

conflict situations such as Yugoslavia and Rwanda, its soldiers and leaders are in many ambiguous situations, which some adversary might find useful in bringing charges before the ICC.

For example, given the view shared by many that the attack on Iraq in 2003 was illegal, might the U.S. president be accused of war crimes and made subject to international arrest? Presumably, if judges in The Hague found the war illegal, and the United States refused to prosecute its own president, the ICC could declare its jurisdiction over the case and issue an indictment. Hence, the U.S. government was unwilling to take the chance that the court would be used in this way. Similarly, one might fear that civilian casualties in Afghanistan or treatment of detainees might open U.S. soldiers or officials to charges of war crimes.

The U.S. concern was stated by Undersecretary of State John Bolton, "A fair reading of the treaty leaves one unable to answer with confidence whether the United States would now be accused of war crimes for legitimate but controversial uses of force to protect world peace. No U.S. presidents or their advisors could be assured that they would be unequivocally safe from politicized charges of criminal liability."[24] Others found Bolton's argument unconvincing, pointing out that since the United States has a fully functioning legal system, the ICC would never have jurisdiction over its actions. China, another nonsignatory, was apparently concerned about charges stemming from its treatment of Tibetan and Uighur minorities, and Israel was concerned about charges related to its control of the "occupied territories."

How strong a role the ICC will play in prosecuting and deterring the worst sorts of crimes remains to be seen. The process of indicting, capturing, and trying someone is sufficiently complex that it is hard to imagine this becoming a routine matter. As discussed in the previous chapter, the ICC has indicted Sudanese President Omar al-Bashir for war crimes and genocide, but it is unclear whether he will ever be brought before the court.

Defendants hear verdicts at the Nuremburg trials. These trials held at the end of World War II provided the prototype for tribunals addressing crimes committed in Yugoslavia, Cambodia, and Rwanda as well as for the International Criminal Court.

Reconsider the Case

The United States, the UN, and Iraq: 1990–1991 versus 2002–2003

At the outset of this chapter, we briefly considered the politics of UN Security Council resolutions concerning Iraq. In the middle of the chapter, we considered the legal arguments in more detail. We now return to the political questions. Why did the United States bother to seek legal authority to wage war? Why did others care if the United States went to war without it?

For the United States and Britain, gaining UN Security Council authorization to wage war had several potential advantages. Most important was the value of UN authorization in convincing skeptics at home and abroad to support the war In the 1990–1991 war, the U.S. Congress passed a resolution to authorize use of force only *after* UN Resolution 678 was passed, and even then by a closely divided vote (52-47 in the Senate; 250-183 in the House of Representatives).[25]

It also seems unlikely that thirty-two other states would have joined the coalition without UN authorization. In terms of the ability to fight and win the war, this may have made little difference, but clearly the United States believed that there were benefits to being perceived around the world as not only powerful, but also a force for good. The UN Security Council resolution, by expressing a common principle to motivate action, helped build the shared purpose that constructivists and liberals see as being essential to international collaboration.

Another factor focused on by constructivists, identity, was also shaped by UN authorization. Following the 1991 invasion, people around the world largely viewed the U.S. role as helping to build what President George H. W. Bush called "a new world order," in which power would be constrained

by law. In contrast, the decision to go to war in 2003, with authority that was widely questioned, recast the United States, in the eyes of many, as a country that would not allow its power to be constrained by law. Many states, even traditional allies of the United States, opposed this shift in principle even if they did not oppose the invasion. When supporting a U.S.-led invasion meant supporting the rule of law, most countries were willing to go along. When supporting a U.S.-led invasion meant undermining the rule of law, many more countries were unwilling to go along. For all except the most powerful, the prospect of power unconstrained by law is a sobering one.

Many countries continue to seek UN Security Council support for their efforts to pursue international security. For the United States and its allies, Security Council support is seen as essential to their efforts to prevent North Korea and Iran from building their nuclear arsenals. Many others have sought Security Council support in condemning Israel's policies regarding Palestinians. Many of these efforts result in frustration, but the value of Security Council support is high enough that states continue to seek it.

Critical Thinking Questions

1. What precedents were set by the decision to invade Iraq without a clear authorization in 2003?
2. Will the U.S. invasion embolden other states to claim international authority for their decisions to use force?
3. To what extent did the UN process actually constrain states in a meaningful way?

Summary

International law plays an important role in at least some areas of contemporary international politics. Especially in the European Union and in the WTO, international law is fairly clear, strict, and enforceable. In many other areas, states comply with international law because it would not be to their benefit to disrupt patterns of behavior that serve their interests. However, individuals and states are disappointed that international law cannot constrain powerful and determined states in many important areas.

The establishment of the ICC signals a fundamental reevaluation by most of the world's states about the relative importance of guarding the principle of national sovereignty versus pursuing international solutions to problems. By allowing the ICC to determine whether it has jurisdiction over actions committed by individuals, the signatories are making a substantial compromise of their sovereignty that would have been unimaginable in the past. Thus, the ICC is an important turning point in principle, even if it does not change much in practice.

The formation of the ICC is only one manifestation of this shift in views on the proper relationship between sovereignty and the rights of individuals. Since the end of the Cold War, much of the international community has striven to revise accepted notions concerning the boundary between domestic and international affairs. The case of Yugoslavia led to wider acceptance of the idea that the need to protect human rights "trumped" the traditional doctrine of noninterference in the internal affairs of sovereign states. Throughout Europe, there has been international pressure for states to reject the death penalty, and this has not been viewed as violating the international norm of sovereignty. However, consensus remains fragile at best; many powerful countries, including China, the United States, and Russia, continue to resist the notion that their domestic affairs can be the subject of international sanction.

The post–Cold War era has seen increasing focus on international law, but it remains unclear how much further recent developments will go. To what extent will states find it in their interest to have their behavior constrained, in return for having the behavior of others constrained? Will the most powerful states be more willing to enforce international law even on matters of little importance to them? Or will international law remain uneven in its formation and applications? The forces of globalization and new problems such as the deterioration of the environment give states more to gain from collaboration, but states have traditionally guarded their sovereignty jealously. So, the Westphalian system will likely evolve further, and it seems unlikely that it will be overthrown any time soon.

Key Concepts

1. Just war
2. International Court of Justice (ICJ)
3. International regimes
4. Enforcement

5. Self-enforcement
6. Human rights
7. International Criminal Court (ICC)
8. International norms

Study Questions

1. How is international law defined?
2. What are the major sources of international law?
3. What were the major tenets of Grotius's just war theory?

4. What are the major means of enforcing international law and what are the problems with them?
5. How is international law similar to and different from domestic law?

6. How should the imperatives of human rights and state sovereignty be weighed?

7. What are the sources and effects of changes in international norms?

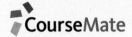
CourseMate

Endnotes

1. For the text of Security Council Resolution 660, see http://daccess-dds-ny.un.org/doc/RESOLUTION/GEN/NR0/575/10/IMG/NR057510.pdf?OpenElement

2. For the text of Resolution 678, see http://daccess-dds-ny.un.org/doc/RESOLUTION/GEN/NR0/575/28/IMG/NR057528.pdf?OpenElement

3. For the text of Resolution 1441, see http://daccess-dds-ny.un.org/doc/UNDOC/GEN/N02/682/26/PDF/N0268226.pdf?OpenElement

4. Rachel S. Taylor, "The United Nations, International Law, and the World in Iraq," *World Press Review Online*, at http://www.worldpress.org/specials/iraq/

5. Channel 4 News (UK), March 11, 2003, at http://www.channel4.com/news/2003/02/week_2/11_warlegal.html

6. "Annan Says Iraq War was 'Illegal'," *The New York Times*, September 16, 2004.

7. This definition is based on that in William R. Slomanson, *Fundamental Perspectives on International Law* (Minneapolis, MN: West, 1995), p. 3.

8. See Paul Christopher, *The Ethics of War and Peace*, 3rd ed. (Upper Saddle River, NJ: Pearson Prentice Hall, 2004), Chapter 1, pp. 8–16.

9. Christopher, *The Ethics of War and Peace*, Chapter 6, pp. 81–103.

10. A classic and readable rational choice approach to retaliation and reputation is Robert Axelrod, *The Evolution of Cooperation* (New York: Basic Books, 1984). On the importance of reputation, see John Mercer, *Reputation and International Politics* (Ithaca, NY: Cornell University Press, 1996).

11. Louis Henkin, *How Nations Behave*, 2nd ed. (New York: Columbia University Press, 1979).

12. The seminal work on international regimes is Stephen D. Krasner, ed., *International Regimes* (Ithaca, NY: Cornell University Press, 1982).

13. Address by President Vaclav Havel to the Senate and the House of Commons of the Parliament of Canada, 29 April 1999, at http://old.hrad.cz/president/Havel/speeches/1999/2904_uk.html

14. See Audie Klotz, "Norms Reconstituting Interests: Global Racial Equality and U.S. Sanctions Against South Africa," *International Organization*, Vol. 49, No. 3 (Summer 1995): 451–478.

15. Charles R. Beitz, "Human Rights as a Common Concern," *American Political Science Review* Vol. 95, No. 2 (June 2001): 247.

16. See the full declaration at http://www.ohchr.org/EN/UDHR/Pages/Language.aspx?LangID=eng for a complete list.

17. See Martha Finnemore, *The Purpose of Intervention: Changing Beliefs about the Use of Force*, (Ithaca, NY: Cornell University Press, 2003). p. 6.

18. Alex J. Bellamy and Nicholas J. Wheeler, "Humanitarian Intervention in World Politics," in John Baylis and Steve Smith, eds., *The Globalization of World Politics: An Introduction to International Relations* (New York: Oxford University Press, 2008), pp. 524 ff.

19. *Roper, Superintendent, Potosi Correctional Center v. Simmons*, 543 U.S. 551 (2005), p. 578.

20. The text of the fourth Geneva Convention can be viewed at http://www.icrc.org/ihl.nsf/FULL/380?OpenDocument

21. Michael P. Sharf, "Results of the Rome Conference for an International Criminal Court," *ASIL Insights* (August 1998), at http://www.asil.org/insights/insigh23.htm

22. The seven voting against were China, Iraq, Israel, Libya, Qatar, the United States, and Yemen.

23. International Criminal Court, "ICC at a Glance," at http://www.icc-cpi.int/menus/icc/about%20the%20court/icc%20at%20a%20glance/icc%20at%20a%20glance?lan=en-GB

24. John R. Bolton, "The United States and the International Criminal Court," remarks to the Federalist Society, Washington, D.C., November 14, 2002.

25. "Congress Acts to Authorize War in Gulf," *New York Times*, January 12, 1991, p. 1.

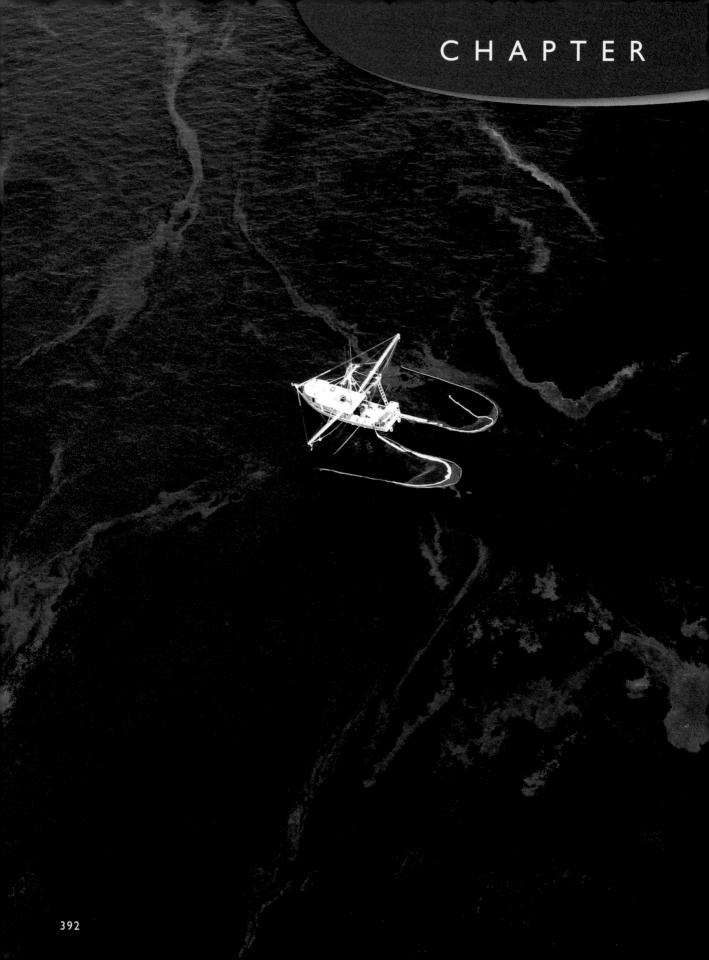

14

Emerging Grounds for Global Governance? Population, Crime, Health, and Environmental Problems

LEARNING OBJECTIVES

After completing this chapter, the student should be able to . . .

1. Define "transnational crime" and "human trafficking."
2. Identify the facets of globalization that contribute to the globalization of criminal, environmental, and health problems.
3. Evaluate the barriers to international collaboration on environmental problems.
4. Identify the main provisions of the Kyoto Protocol.
5. Identify the diseases that cause greatest international concern.
6. Assess the role of international governmental and nongovernmental organizations in dealing with global health problems.
7. Evaluate the likelihood of conflict and cooperation in the future on issues of transnational crime, health, and environmental problems.

◀ A shrimp boat is used to collect oil spilled by the BP Deepwater Horizon rig, May 2010.
AP Photo/Eric Gay

Consider the Case

Trafficking in Women

Trafficking in people has become an increasingly lucrative business in recent years. The transportation of people across borders for illegal purposes has its roots in poverty and in the huge differences in wage and income levels in different countries. The same breakdown in barriers to commerce that enables globalization also enables trafficking, which U.S. Secretary of State Condoleezza Rice described in 2007 as "a modern-day form of slavery, a new type of global slave trade."[1] Women and girls, because of their weaker economic, political, and social status in many countries, are especially vulnerable.

Women and girls are trafficked primarily for two purposes: sex and domestic servitude. In Europe, a particular problem is the trafficking of women from the former Soviet Union who are then forced into prostitution, essentially becoming sex slaves. In the Middle East, women are recruited from Asia as domestic servants. Recruiters prey on poor women in poor countries who are desperate for a better life and promise them good jobs in foreign countries. Typically, recruiters provide a passport and other necessary documents and smuggle the victims into another country. The women then find that promises about work and pay turn out to be untrue. In the case of domestic servants, women sometimes find themselves locked in their employers' homes, forced to work up to twenty hours per day, and paid next to nothing. In the case of sex slaves, they find themselves confined to brothels, serially raped, and beaten if they refuse to perform or try to escape.

Trafficking is a great business because once someone is smuggled successfully, she keeps earning profits for the criminal organization for years. The organizations that conduct trafficking are transnationally integrated enterprises. They have recruiters, shippers, forgers, and "government relations specialists" (who take care of bribing border officials and police). In many cases, because the criminals are transnationally integrated, they can compel a worker trafficked to one country through threats to her family back home.

Human trafficking creates a number of dilemmas for state governments. Who is more responsible for stopping the flow of trafficked people, the "exporting" countries or the "importing" countries? Is it possible to enforce immigration laws strictly without playing into the hands of traffickers? Once women are rescued from servitude, what kinds of programs can help them return to "normal" society, either in the country in which they find themselves or back home? How much priority should be given to combating trafficking relative to traditional concerns such as security and trade? Some of these questions are similar to those raised by the global drug trade and other forms of transnational crime.

The previous two chapters showed that states are creating more international organizations and an expanding web of international law to help manage the problems they face today. In this chapter, we see why. Many of today's most pressing problems do not stop at state borders. As a result, individual states are having increasing difficulty coping with them by themselves.

When it comes to crime and disease transmission, globalization becomes a threat rather than a benefit. Some environmental problems are global in scale, and there is no plausible way to deal with them on a state-by-state basis. Migration, which creates both opportunities and threats for states and individuals, is difficult for individual states to manage. Issues such as these create a demand for new international agreements and organizations and provide areas in which transnational actors seek to fill roles that states cannot.

These issues raise a much bigger question: Is it possible that the advent of ever-greater dangers that cannot be solved by individual states will lead actors to fundamentally revise the sovereign state basis of global politics? Or will conflict over these issues cause states to reassert their dominance?

U.S. Department of State

Sex workers in Hong Kong, many of whom were likely trafficked.

Population Growth and Demographic Change

In 2011, the world's population will surpass 7 billion, up from 3 billion in 1960, and headed, according to most estimates, toward 8 billion in another 12 to 14 years. Population growth is one of the major drivers of environmental problems, by placing increased demand on scarce resources, including land, housing, food, water, and energy, while creating increased pollution.

Population growth is very unevenly distributed. Although overall population is increasing, many wealthy states are experiencing stagnation. Moreover, **demographic change** is moving in very different directions around the world. In countries where population is growing, especially in developing countries, the ratio to young people to old people is increasing, while in advanced industrial states, the opposite is happening. Both situations create economic and social disruption. In societies with low population growth, the overall population is aging, such that there are ever fewer workers to pay for the pensions and health care needs of an increasing number of retirees. Throughout the developed world, pension systems will come under increasing strain in the coming decades. In countries with high population growth, there are an increasing number of workers for each retiree, potentially easing the pension burden. But that easing depends crucially on those young people being well educated and having economic opportunity. Lack of economic opportunity is one of the main sources of the urge to emigrate, while the need to bring more workers into the system is one of the main incentives for wealthy states to allow immigration.

Population is growing not because people are having more children (in many countries, they are having fewer), but because mortality has decreased dramatically. Increased agricultural productivity means that more people can live on the same land without succumbing to occasional famines. Prior the 1960s, many people in developing countries simply died of hunger, placing a check on population growth. The "green revolution," which focused on increased use of irrigation, fertilizer, pesticides, and high-yield crop breeds, as well as improved practices, dramatically increased yields in the developing world. At the same time, health care has improved dramatically. In much of the world,

demographic change

Change in the distribution of a population across categories such as age, gender, and wealth

diseases that routinely killed large numbers of people have been wiped out or brought under control. Smallpox, discussed later, used to kill millions, and has now been eradicated. Infant and maternal mortality has declined dramatically, although it is still higher in some countries than others.

In many societies, decreasing death rates have resulted, after some lag time, in decreased birthrates. Thus, in Japan, Russia, and much of Europe, birthrates have declined dramatically and are now lower than death rates, meaning that without immigration, population will decrease. For this reason, there is hope that the growth in global population will eventually slow down as more people move into the middle class and have fewer children. It is difficult to predict when that might happen.

Overpopulation and Environmental Problems

Since the eighteenth century, people have been predicting that at some point resource scarcity would lead to a massive population crash, and to political conflict. Historically, predictions of scarcity have often proven wrong: increases in economic productivity have more than kept up with population growth. The famines predicted by Thomas Malthus in 1795 did not take place because of increased agricultural production. Predictions of natural resource shortages in the 1970s also turned out to be wrong: As supplies decreased, prices rose. This gave consuming firms an incentive to use less of those materials. It also gave producers incentives to discover new supplies, and to extract more from existing supplies. Mines and mining techniques that were unprofitable at low commodity prices became profitable at higher prices, increasing the supply. The price of oil and other natural resources declined dramatically following the shortages of the 1970s. However, the notion that demand will lead to new supplies should not be overgeneralized. Resource shortages can lead to conflict as well as to innovation. Moreover, although materials shortages may automatically create the incentives to find solutions, that is probably not true for other environmental problems, such as pollution.

In the coming decades, population growth will not be the only driver of increased consumption and pollution. How much people consume is as important as how many of them are consuming. Growth in consumption in wealthy societies has as much environmental impact as population growth in poor societies. Geographer Jared Diamond estimates that if everyone in the developing world were to consume as much as the average American, it would have the same effect as increasing the global population to 72 billion people at current consumption levels.[2] Thus, the problems of increased consumption in the coming decades are much more dire than population growth alone implies. As 1.2 billion Chinese, a billion Indians, and many others move from poverty into the middle class, they will begin consuming like the middle class elsewhere, dramatically increasing demands on resources. The boom in the Chinese auto market, and the resulting increase in demand for oil and pollution in Chinese cities, is just one visible example. This is the environmental downside of the remarkable decline of poverty in some regions, and we deal with it at greater length in the section on the environment.

Migration

Populations are not just growing, they are moving, as they have since the dawn of time. Migration is an important part of globalization, and it is a powerful source of change and conflict in today's world. While the movement of goods and capital around the world has been dramatically liberalized in recent decades, states seek to retain close control over migration, and over immigration in particular.

Sources of Migration

What causes people to leave their homeland—perhaps with their family, perhaps without—to move to a strange country, with all the hardship and uncertainty that entails? A variety of hopes and fears may motivate the decision to emigrate.

- Security: Many people emigrate or become internally displaced unwillingly because of threats to their safety from war or famine. World War II, the Vietnam War, and Somali Civil War are all examples of conflict-driven migration.

- Economic opportunity: People go to places where there is economic opportunity. Historically, immigration from places such as Italy, Ireland, and Latin America has been driven by economic desperation. Although fewer in numbers, well-educated people also migrate to places where there is greater economic opportunity.

- Oppression: People flee authoritarian governments or religious persecution. Many fled the communist bloc during the Cold War. Today, people leave Cuba for both political and economic reasons.

- Family reunification: Once one member of a family migrates, for political or economic reasons, there is often an effort by others to follow. Immigration policy in many countries gives preference to such cases.

- Population growth and environmental degradation: Environmental constraints, particularly a lack of good land in agricultural societies, motivate people to migrate to places where land is more plentiful.

- Slavery: Historically, organized slave trading fed involuntary migration, leaving a profound legacy in Africa and in the western hemisphere. Today, trafficking for various purposes is less organized, but forcibly moves thousands each year.

After a hazardous crossing, African immigrants arrive in the Canary Islands, which belong to Spain, May 2006.

Refugees

Many people crossing borders do so involuntarily, prompted by oppression or conflict, and become **refugees** under international law. The 1951 Convention Relating to the Status of Refugees defines a refugee as any person who "owing to a well-founded fear of being persecuted for reasons of race, religion, nationality, membership of a particular social group, or political opinion, is outside the country of his nationality, and is unable to or, owing to such fear, is unwilling to avail himself of the protection of that country."[3] The UN High Commissioner for Refugees works with refugee populations around the world, and in 2009 was dealing with 10.5 million refugees.[4] The actual number is probably much higher, since not all refugees are protected by the UN High Commissioner for Refugees. Historically important examples include Jews who fled persecution in many countries, especially before and during World War II, huge populations moved in Europe as a result of World War II, and the "boat people" who left Vietnam after the communist victory in 1975. Today, the largest groups of refugees are in the Middle East and Southwest Asia, largely the result of the Iraq and Afghanistan wars, but also including large numbers of Palestinians.

The goal for many refugees, and for the states in which they become refugees, is that they will return to their homes. In practice, as the previous examples show, this is often impossible, and refugees are able to claim **asylum status**, which allows them to immigrate permanently to a new state. When refugees are not offered asylum status, or refuse

refugee

A person who leaves his or her country because of a well-founded fear of persecution or because of violent conflict.

asylum

Status granted to persons who cannot return to their home country without a well-founded fear of persecution.

to give up the hope of returning home, temporary refugee status can become somewhat permanent. Thus, the roughly 1 million Palestinians who left Israel as a result of the 1948 and 1967 Arab-Israeli wars continue to be refugees, as do their descendents, now numbering 4.6 million, according to the UN. Camps intended to be temporary become permanent, but are often unfit for permanent settlement.

Issues surrounding refugees and asylum seekers are closely connected with the human rights issues discussed in Chapter 13. Refugees and asylum seekers claim rights under international law, and under many states' domestic laws. But it is not clear which countries have an obligation to help refugees. Generally, the biggest burden falls on the immediate neighbors of the countries from which the refugees are fleeing. In addition to placing an economic burden on host governments, refugees can bring political instability and conflict as well. To the extent that they seek to migrate permanently, claims for asylum status may give them a better legal claim for permanent residence, but the same contentious issues about migration remain.

Dilemmas for Sending States

States whose citizens migrate elsewhere see both positive and negative effects, depending on the exact circumstances. In places where overcrowding and a lack of good jobs are creating unrest, economic emigration can help reduce tension and leave more resources and jobs for those who remain. More importantly, emigrants who leave family behind often send money back home, such that for some countries remittances from emigrants are a major contributor to GDP, as much as 25 percent for some countries. Globally, remittances from emigrants are roughly $300 billion per year, three times as large as all government foreign aid budgets combined.[5] The downside for these states is that they are often losing talented and ambitious citizens, a problem known as the "brain drain." This happens often when bright students from developing countries go to university in developed countries and then stay on to exercise their talent and creativity in their adopted countries. Even for less educated workers, however, it is likely that the most ambitious people are most likely to emigrate. In a world where human capital is perhaps the most valuable economic resource, the brain drain can be a problem.

However, the brain drain is mitigated by two factors. First, as previously mentioned, emigrants often send substantial resources back home. Second, emigrants themselves often return home to become entrepreneurs and investors, using the knowledge and money gained abroad to benefit their birth country. Thus, while many bright and ambitious Indian IT specialists have gone to Silicon Valley to work, some of these have returned to India to start the firms that have put India at the heart of the global information technology business.

Dilemmas for Receiving States

Developed states, because of their economic opportunity and strong commitment to human rights, are often migration targets for both economic and political migrants. Many of these developed states have low birth rates, and therefore a shortage of labor and a growing imbalance between workers and retirees. Migration potentially solves both problems: in places where labor is in short supply, migrants can provide it, often cheaply. In Germany, Turkish migrants were welcomed for decades because they provided unskilled labor that the domestic market could not supply. Similarly, agricultural interests in the United States argue that migrant workers are essential because U.S. workers will not do the same work at wages that are economical for the industry. Because migrants tend to be young, and tend to have more children than natives of developed countries, they help rebalance the demographic mix, and thus help keep pension systems solvent.

One reason why the United States does not face the same level of demographic problems as western Europe and Japan is that it has a much higher rate of immigration. Moreover, if sending countries suffer a brain drain, receiving countries experience a "brain gain." One study found that roughly 25 percent of U.S. technology firms started between 1995 and 2005 had a foreign-born chief executive officer or chief technology officer.[6]

Many perceive a downside to these benefits, which is why migration is such a volatile political topic in many countries. Economically, those who must compete for work with migrants see them as a threat to their livelihood, taking jobs away and driving wages down. To the extent that migrants are poor, and require social services, people also fear that they divert state resources from other missions. Cultural concerns are equally salient. Immigrants often bring their own languages, customs, traditions, and values, and when given the right to vote, they assert these values. Some natives of receiving countries resent having people around them speaking foreign languages. Others fear that immigrants will promote values contrary to their own.

All those concerns arise for legal immigrants. With illegal immigrants, the debate becomes even more divisive. Once an illegal immigrant is in a country, the options for the "host" state are not good. Finding illegal immigrants and sending them back home is expensive, disrupts the businesses and communities where they work, and often leads to bigger problems, such as children left in foster care when parents are deported. Moreover, many argue that deporting such people is immoral or that it violates their human rights. Finally, the treatment of illegal migrants can cause significant tension with the migrants' home governments, as has happened between the United States and Mexico. On the other hand, to the extent that a country does not treat illegal immigrants badly, it may encourage more to come, exacerbating the problem.

Transnational Crime

Transnational crime is a booming business, perhaps the biggest business in the world. The global drug trade alone generates roughly $300 billion per year, on par with the global oil trade. Only the trade in small arms is bigger. Crime helps support terrorists, undermines government stability, and contributes to misery for millions of victims. So far, only rudimentary international steps have been taken to combat it.

Transnational crime benefits from two characteristics of our increasingly globalized world. First, whereas criminal organizations are transnational and are able to move people, products, and finances across borders and around the world, law enforcement is not. Law enforcement is still organized country by country, and coordination of state-level law enforcement efforts is limited. It is comparatively easy, therefore, for transnational criminal organizations to outmaneuver their less mobile law enforcement counterparts.

Second, some regions of the globe have become safe havens for criminal enterprises. As noted throughout this book, the post–Cold War world is characterized by the breakdown and weakening of states in many regions. This weakening was demonstrated most dramatically in Afghanistan, which became a base for the Al-Qaeda terrorist organization (and has long been a base for heroin production). Somalia has become a base for pirates preying on shipping in the Indian Ocean. But state authority is also weakened in much of the post-communist world, including the former Yugoslavia, parts of Eastern Europe, and most of the former Soviet Union, a vast region stretching from the Mediterranean Sea to the Pacific Ocean.

This combination of safe havens and global mobility is ideal for transnational crime. Groups can set themselves up in places where they can be relatively free from harassment and still move more easily than ever before into the countries where they seek to do business.

Crime is essentially a business, although an illegal one; we can think of transnational criminal organizations as transnational actors, similar in their basic purpose to transnational corporations. The same aspects of globalization that have benefited legitimate transnational business are an asset to transnational criminal groups and have allowed them to increase their global mobility.

- The vastly increased amount of goods being shipped makes it easier to smuggle goods and people.

- Internet communications with modern encryption capabilities facilitate e-commerce but also make it easy for criminals to communicate with associates around the world with little fear of surveillance.

- Cheap cell phones, which can be replaced frequently, further facilitate communication and complicate surveillance.

- The same financial arrangements that fuel the flow of capital around the world also facilitate the movement and laundering of the profits from crime.

The Global Drug Trade

The global drug trade is among the largest industries in the world. In some regions, drug trafficking is by far the dominant economic activity. Mexico, for example, earns an estimated four times as much from drug exports to the United States as from oil, Mexico's leading legal export. In the "Golden Triangle" of Southeast Asia (Myanmar, Laos, and Thailand), where the overall economies are poorer, the role of drugs is even larger.

The United Nations Office on Drugs and Crime (UNODC) estimates that there are 185 million drug users in the world (3 percent of the population). Cannabis is the most widely used drug (150 million users), followed by amphetamines (30 million), opiates (15 million), cocaine (13 million), and Ecstasy (8 million).[7] The price of many drugs is actually going down, as globalization facilitates cheaper production and distribution.

The drug trade causes a variety of problems for national governments. Drugs, especially the more addictive ones, cause major health problems and are a significant source of other kinds of crime (especially property crime). Moreover, drugs that are injected (mainly heroin) are a primary vehicle for the transmission of human immunodeficiency virus (HIV)/AIDS and other illnesses. The drug trade has also become major source of funding for terrorist organizations.

Figure 14.1 This graph shows the street prices of opiates in Europe and the United States, 1990–2007, adjusted for inflation. How has globalization affected the price of these drugs?

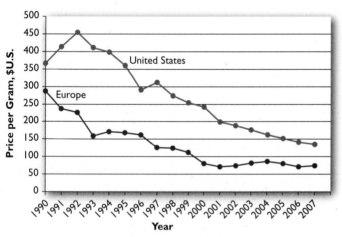

Source: ONDCP, The Price and Purity of Illicit Drugs: 1981–2007 (Reports prepared by the Institute for Defense Analysis for ONDCP. 1990–2000 (prices for 1 gram or less, at street purity), ONDCP, ONDCP, The Price & Purity of Illicit Drugs 1981–2003 (prices for < 2 grams) for 2001–03, Community Epidemiology Network–June 2005 (for 2004) and ONDCP (based on STRIDE) for 2005 to 2007.

Other Areas of Transnational Crime

Transnational crime is a significant problem in areas other than drugs, human trafficking, and money laundering:

- **The arms trade.** The legal arms trade is among the largest industries on the planet. The illegal arms trade is also massive. It has become much worse since the end of the Cold War, which left massive stockpiles of weaponry idle and poorly guarded throughout the former Soviet bloc. Illegally sold goods range from rifles and ammunition to submarines and air defense radars.

- **Cyber-crime.** Various kind of online crime, including identity theft and fraud, are carried out across borders, from countries in which enforcement is lax.

- **"Conflict diamonds."** Smuggled diamonds are used by government and rebel groups alike to finance some of the brutal wars that plague Africa. Despite international rules banning diamond sales from this region, a black market thrives.

- **Endangered species.** The Convention on International Trafficking in Endangered Species (CITES) bans trade in most endangered species, but a sophisticated network of organized crime has sprung up to circumvent it, pushing some species toward extinction.

- **Stolen automobiles.** Automobiles stolen in one state are often transported abroad and sold there. It is much easier to drive, and therefore to sell, a car outside the jurisdiction where it was stolen. Particularly problematic are the theft of cars in Western Europe for sale in the former Soviet Union and the theft of cars in the United States for sale in Mexico.

- **Piracy of copyrighted materials.** One of the fastest growing areas of transnational crime, piracy involves making copies of copyrighted goods, such as movies, CDs, and computer programs, and reselling them. This costs legal producers billions a year in lost revenues.

Transnational Crime and Terrorism

Transnational crime has become an important means of support for terrorist operations. Terrorists participate in criminal enterprises to finance their activities. **Money laundering** allows terrorists to hide their money from government authorities and to move the money to places where they seek to carry out operations. Human traffickers are experts at getting people across borders without official documentation or with false documentation, arms dealers can provide a wide range of illegal weaponry, and smugglers can be used to move weapons used in terrorist attacks. An increasing concern is that criminals could help terrorists procure more deadly weapons, ranging from shoulder-fired missiles to down aircraft to nuclear materials for radiological weapons.

money laundering
The process of making illegally gained money appear to have been earned legally.

International Enforcement

Compared with other types of international collaboration, very little is done in the area of law enforcement. **Interpol**, an international policing agency, helps the police agencies of member states pool information, but it has a staff of only a few hundred. Almost all law enforcement activities are carried out by states according to their own laws. Except within the EU, legal systems still remain state-level institutions, and there are important reasons for this. As noted in the previous chapter, there is great resistance to the idea of international agencies having lawmaking or law enforcement power over individual states. A basic conception of state sovereignty and democracy is that a political community makes its own laws and is not constrained by those of others.

Interpol
Informal name for the International Criminal Police Organization, an international agency that serves as an information clearinghouse for police agencies around the world.

International crime has not led to widespread calls for global law enforcement collaboration. Rather, it has led more to bilateral efforts in which one state or group of states tries to get another state to improve its domestic enforcement. Governments have not seen much need to actually adopt measures at the international level.

The Policy Connection

Interpol: Problems and Prospects

Interpol (whose official name is the International Criminal Police Organization) is an international law enforcement agency based in Lyon, France. It was founded in 1923. Despite the depictions that sometimes appear in the movies, Interpol does not have its own police officers or black-uniformed commandos. Instead, Interpol operates primarily as a clearinghouse for information for police agencies around the world. As of 2001, roughly 350 people worked for Interpol in Lyon.

Interpol provides three primary services to police agencies around the world:

■ A communication system to facilitate information exchange between police in different countries
■ Several databases on crime and criminals that help police agencies learn what is happening in other countries
■ Support for police operations in various countries

One important role of Interpol is its maintenance of an international "Wanted List." This is a list of individuals for whom individual states have issued arrest warrants and requested international attention. The list can include criminals ranging from terrorism suspects from Pakistan, to traffickers in women from Albania, to drug dealers from Colombia, to child molesters from California. How effective are these international warrants in bringing individuals to justice? In 2001, 1400 people were arrested as a result of Interpol "red notices."[1]

Another initiative, developed more recently, is a "Fusion Task Force" to monitor terrorism. The task force consists of specialists delegated to Interpol from state level law enforcement agencies. The task force, which is divided into groups that concentrate on different geographical regions, carries out two tasks. First, it seeks to disrupt movements of terrorists across international borders by focusing on the organized crime organizations that often provide the false documents and smuggling services needed. Second, it maintains a database of people who are known to have attended terrorist training camps and notifies the governments of the countries where they reside.[2]

Critical Thinking Questions

1. To what extent should the internationalization of crime lead to the internationalization of crime fighting? What sorts of measures would be effective?
2. What are the most important objections to greater international collaboration in criminal justice?

[1] "International Police Organization—Interpol," at http://en.wikipedia.org/wiki/Interpol
[2] "Fusion Task Force" at http://www.interpol.int/Public/FusionTaskForce/default.asp

COMBATING DRUG SMUGGLING

Most efforts to combat the drug trade occur at the national level. These include prosecuting suppliers and users of drugs, eradicating crops used to make drugs, and, in some countries, providing treatment for addicts.

International efforts are largely bilateral, usually involving a wealthy state that tends to consume a lot of drugs seeking to help (or compel) a supplying state to reduce the supply of drugs. There is often a significant amount of recrimination between poor supplier states and wealthy consumer states. Governments in importing states seek to get governments in exporting states to do more to reduce supplies. Governments in exporting states point out that if the governments in the importing states curbed drug use there, the demand would disappear.

One example of such a strategy is the U.S. **Plan Colombia**, which is aimed at reducing the supply of cocaine from Colombia. The plan includes substantial financial assistance, training, and equipment (including military aircraft) to assist the Colombian government in fighting the drug trade there. It also includes some funding to help farmers switch from coca to other crops. Although there have been some newsworthy successes on the ground in Colombia, there has been no noticeable effect on either the supply or price of cocaine in the United States.

COMBATING MONEY LAUNDERING

Law enforcement agencies have found that combating money laundering is often an effective way to attack international crime, especially the drug trade. The rise of transnational terrorism as a global concern has led to a substantial increase in concern about money laundering and has led governments around the world to take it much more seriously. In many states, tighter laws have been passed and more resources have been devoted to enforcement. There has been much more international cooperation in this area than in other aspects of law enforcement. The **Financial Action Task Force**, which has thirty-one members, establishes recommended policies for states to adopt to combat money laundering and monitors new trends in money laundering practices. It has been part of a campaign by the United States and the EU to put pressure on those states whose banking secrecy laws and absence of monitoring have made them havens for international criminal groups seeking to launder money. Switzerland, for example, was for decades the country of choice for illegally earned money because its banking system was both rock solid and highly secretive. Switzerland has now adopted international standards that allow law enforcement officials greater ability to investigate money laundering.

Plan Colombia

A U.S. program aimed at reducing the supply of cocaine from Colombia by providing substantial financial assistance, training, and equipment (including military aircraft) to assist the Colombian government in fighting the drug trade there.

Financial Action Task Force

An international task force that establishes recommended policies for states to adopt to combat money laundering and monitors new trends in money-laundering practices.

Transnational Crime as an Economic Problem

Some critics of standard "enforcement" approaches to drug and human trafficking argue that enforcement, by itself, is bound to fail. The market, they argue, is simply too powerful a force. As long as coca for cocaine and opium poppies for heroin are much more lucrative crops than grains and vegetables, impoverished farmers will grow them. In this view, economic desperation is the source of the drug supply, and economic development is the answer. In particular, advocates of a development approach point out that U.S. and European barriers to legal agricultural imports make it more difficult for poor country farmers to earn a living on legitimate crops.

Similarly, they argue, both human trafficking in particular and illegal immigration more broadly are driven by the desperation of poverty and will not abate as long as powerful economic incentives exist. The solution to both problems, in this view, is a global development strategy and a serious commitment of resources from wealthy countries to reduce the desperation that causes people to immigrate.

Raising Opium Poppies in Afghanistan. For many poor farmers around the world, producing crops that are converted into illegal drugs is a matter of feeding their families.

The Culture Connection

Global Film and Music Piracy

International crime seems like a concern far from the life of the average college student. In fact, however, as end consumers of the products of international crime, many college students are indeed involved. One avenue of involvement is, of course, drugs. Most of the drugs consumed on college campuses are trafficked by international criminal organizations. A second connection, growing in importance all the time, is the theft of intellectual property (unlawful copying of copyrighted or trademarked products).

Generally referred to as "piracy," the illegal copying and transfer of copyrighted material is an increasing economic problem for sellers and an increasing political problem for governments. Governments of countries where intellectual property is produced (such as the United States, which has large film and music industries as well as the software industry) seek to pressure countries that are less concerned about the issue. China and Russia, two countries that the U.S. government has watched closely, are less disturbed by the problem because their legitimate firms are losing little while their "entrepreneurs" (criminals) are gaining much.

The Motion Picture Association of American estimates that it is losing $3 to $4 billion per year on movie piracy.[1] (This is probably an overestimate, since it assumes that everyone who illegally copies a movie would otherwise have paid for it, rather than just doing without.) Organizations representing the entertainment and software industries have sought to convince consumers and governments that piracy is not a "victimless" crime. In 2004, the British Film Distributors' Association initiated a campaign to dampen the public's demand for pirated DVDs, stressing that those who sold them were not harmless entrepreneurs, but rather members of organized crime gangs and terrorists, who use profits from DVD sales to finance more brutal activities.[2]

In July 2004, two Americans were arrested in China for running a DVD piracy operation that sold pirated DVDs to customers in twenty countries for as little as $3 each. Their arrest was a result of collaboration between the U.S. Department of Homeland Security, which apparently discovered the sales in the United States, and Chinese law enforcement officials, who made the arrests in China, where the operation was based.[3] Overall, however this arrest remains the exception rather than the rule. Bootleg CDs, DVDs, and computer programs are widely available in China and are notoriously inexpensive. The *Financial Times* (London)

Global Environmental Problems

Threats to the environment are an increasing concern for states, societies, and the international community. Because many of these problems are transnational in nature, they are difficult to deal with at the state level. Yet most of the mechanisms for dealing with environmental matters lie within states. As with crime, the environment is an issue in which there is a mismatch between the scale of the problems and the tools available to deal with them. This mismatch has led to calls for greater international collaboration to combat environmental degradation. In some important cases, international agreements have been reached. On many others, most importantly global warming, agreement has been elusive.

The consequences of environmental problems will go well beyond narrowly "environmental" effects—polluted air, extinct species, damaged beaches. Resource shortages and climate change will likely have far-reaching economic, political, and security effects. For example, the spread of pests as the climate warms is already creating significant

reported that although the arrest of the two Americans and an antipiracy campaign were getting much publicity in China, it was "business as usual" in a district of Beijing known for the sale of pirated DVDs.[4] Despite this arrest, the United States continued to single out China as one of the most egregious violators of agreements on the protection of intellectual property.[5]

Pirated fashion items are also a huge business, as counterfeiters are able to produce fake Rolex watches, Louis Vuitton bags, and other fashion items that are nearly indistinguishable from the genuine versions. Such items are sold quite openly in the middle of New York City, but many buyers of "discount" merchandise on the Internet may also be purchasing counterfeits. Counterfeiters have increasingly gone down-market,

from faux-lex watches to fake sunglasses, basketball shoes, and designer t-shirts. U.S. firms lose roughly $200 billion a year to such crimes. The global economic downturn has fed the problem by idling factories, where managers are looking to make anything they can sell, and by making consumers more eager to save money in their quest for fashion.

Critical Thinking Questions

1. How high a priority should combating violations of intellectual property rights be? What are the arguments that this is a genuinely dangerous problem?
2. What advantages might governments see in not pursuing such violations too actively?

---

[1] BBC News World Edition, May 30, 2003, at http://news.bbc.co.uk/2/hi/entertainment/2949470.stm
[2] Film Distributors' Association, "Piracy Is a Crime—New Initiative 2004," at http://www.launchingfilms.com/piracy/index.html
[3] "2 Americans Held in China on Charges of Film Piracy," *New York Times*, July 31, 2004.
[4] "Business as Usual for DVD Piracy," *FT.com,* April 21, 2005, at http://news.ft.com/cms/s/d7bd428c-b1fa-11d9-8c61-00000e2511c8.html
[5] "Special 301 Report Finds Progress and Need for Significant Improvements; Results of China OCR Released, China Elevated to Priority Watch List," as quoted in "U.S.: China Has High Rate of Intellectual Property Infringement," U.S. Trade Representative Press Release, April 29, 2005, at http://www.america.gov/st/washfile-english/2005/April/20050429155355mbzemog0.5231745.html

---

economic damage. Increased intensity of storms will contribute to economic destruction and humanitarian disasters. Competition for natural resources, most importantly clean water, may lead to conflict. The United States Defense Department, in its major policy document, states: "Climate change and energy will play significant roles in the future security environment. . . . While climate change alone does not cause conflict, it may act as an accelerant of instability or conflict, placing a burden to respond on civilian institutions and militaries around the world. In addition, extreme weather events may lead to increased demands for defense support to civil authorities for humanitarian assistance or disaster response both within the United States and overseas."[8]

Types of Problems

Not all environmental problems are international problems. Some pollution and shortages are local and are entirely within the control of state governments. For example, the smog that pollutes Los Angeles and Beijing is produced locally and could be reduced through national or local regulations. The oil spilled into the Gulf of Mexico after the blowout of the British Petroleum's Deepwater Horizon well in 2010 polluted U.S. beaches and fisheries, and the responsibility for cleanup was taken by the U.S. government. Impurities in drinking water in many countries could be solved by improved sanitation at the local level. However, many environmental problems are shared across countries, and some are global.

Environmental problems that are transnational but not global include:

- Pollution of waterways that border more than one country
  - Danube River
  - Great Lakes
  - Gulf of Mexico
  - Mediterranean Sea
- Overconsumption of water from watersheds that supply more than one country
  - Jordan River (Jordan, Israel, Palestinian Authority)[9]
  - Ganges and Brahmaputra (India, Bangladesh, Nepal)
  - Tigris and Euphrates (Turkey, Iraq)
- Air pollution flowing across borders
  - United States and Canada
  - Europe
- Overfishing of shared bodies of water
  - Caspian Sea (overfishing of sturgeon for caviar)
  - Georges Bank (United States and Canada)

Environmental problems that are global include:

- Depletion of the ozone layer
- Global warming
- Loss of biodiversity
- Overpopulation
- Oil shortages

Barriers to Cooperation

Even at the domestic level, there are intense disagreements over how much environmental protection is appropriate and how it should be funded. Domestically, however, there are governments to resolve such disagreements. Such problems are much more difficult to resolve at the international level. International environmental problems are plagued by what scholars call "collective action problems" and other barriers to cooperation.

THE TRAGEDY OF THE COMMONS

collective action problem

A situation in which a group of actors has a common interest but cannot collaborate to achieve it.

A **collective action problem** is a situation in which a group of actors has a common interest but cannot collaborate to achieve it. One familiar way to explain it, with reference to environmental issues, is through a problem known as the "tragedy of the commons." The tragedy of the commons is analogous to the prisoner's dilemma discussed in previous chapters, although it can include many more than two actors.

Imagine a pasture that is shared by several farmers. How many head of cattle will each farmer graze in the pasture? What incentives do the farmers have? The pasture is shared, but the cattle belong to the individual farmers. When a farmer puts another cow on the pasture, the costs (in terms of decreasing the supply of grass) are shared by all the farmers. The benefits, however, accrue entirely to the owner of that cow. Therefore, each farmer has an incentive to put another cow on the pasture, and another, and another, until the pasture is depleted and none of them can graze their cattle there. The "tragedy" is that when each farmer acts according to his or her individual interest, the result is collective catastrophe. This example, known as the **tragedy of the commons**, is widely used as a model of what happens with shared resources.[10] Its logic is identical to the logic of the prisoner's dilemma, the security dilemma, and trade wars.

The same phenomenon occurs with a fishery shared by more than one actor (the actors could be individuals, corporations, or states). For every fish one actor takes out, the benefits accrue to that actor, and the costs are shared by all the others. Each actor has the incentive to take as much as possible before the others do. This explains the widespread depletion of unregulated fisheries around the world.

The same principle applies to air pollution: the costs of polluting are widely spread, while the benefits accrue to the polluting person or individual. In the international realm, states face the same incentives that individuals do in the domestic case. If one state refrains from producing carbon dioxide (CO_2) while others do not, the overall level of global warming may not change much, but that state will have taken on a significant cost. Because of this collective action problem, some have argued that strong international agreements will be needed to solve international environmental problems. There are four factors, however, that make international environmental collaboration especially difficult.

Conflict with Existing Agreements First, international environmental protection often complicates the issue of free trade. Environmental regulations are sometimes viewed as barriers to trade, and some important regulations have been struck down by the WTO for that reason.

Competing Priorities Second, the goal of environmental protection is a much greater priority for some countries than for others. For the poorest countries of the world, environmental protection is a luxury that appears unaffordable. The same thing is true for societies as a whole. For Third World governments with debts to pay, increasing exports to pay off those debts is likely to be a higher priority than protecting the environment, especially when they are under pressure from the World Bank or the IMF. However, it is not only poor countries that put economics ahead of the environment. The most prominent state refusing to sign the **Kyoto Protocol** on global warming (discussed in the next section) was the United States, which fears the economic consequences of reducing fossil fuel use.

For example, there has been immense focus in recent years on shifting from fossil fuels to biofuels such as ethanol. However, scientists posit a "trilemma" between reducing greenhouse emissions, shifting away from fossil fuels, and maintaining the food supply. As governments subsidize biofuels, farmers naturally try to produce more, either by bringing more land under cultivation or by diverting crops from food production to energy production. Bringing more land into production often means cutting down or burning rainforest, which puts more carbon into the atmosphere than is gained by switching to cleaner fuels. Diverting crops from food production drives up the price of food, which has drastic consequences for millions of people already on the edge. Scientists have therefore stressed that to be helpful, biofuel production must be carried out in very particular ways, such as by growing perennial grasses on abandoned fields.[11]

Equity Third, efforts to mitigate global environmental problems become tied up with the problems of inequality and underdevelopment. From the perspective of developing countries, it seems that the developed countries, having gotten rich by exploiting natural resources and despoiling the environment, are now trying to close the door before

tragedy of the commons
A version of the collective action problem in which a shared resource is overconsumed.

Kyoto Protocol
An international agreement that was signed in 1997 and went into effect in 2005 that aims to reduce greenhouse gas emissions in order to prevent global climate change.

Figure 14.2 Carbon Dioxide Emissions, 2007. How does carbon dioxide emission vary across the developed and developing world?

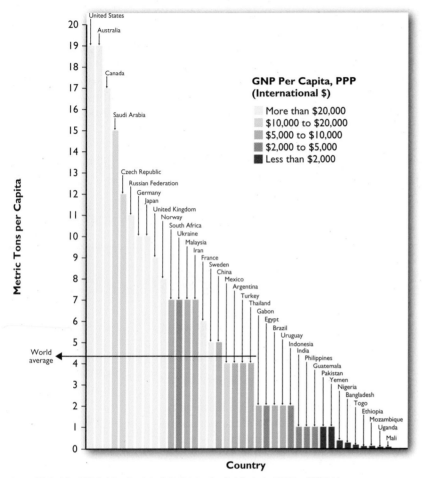

Source: IEA Statistics, "CO₂ Emissions/Population," *CO₂ Emissions from Fuel Combustion Highlights, 2009 Edition.*

the poorer countries can pursue the same strategies. In general, people in wealthier countries consume more resources and produce more pollution than those in poorer countries (see Figure 14.2).

It is difficult to imagine what would happen to the environment if a billion citizens of India raised their CO_2 output even to the German level, let alone the U.S. level. It is equally difficult to imagine Europeans and Americans undergoing enormous cuts in energy use. But poorer countries are understandably reluctant to accept the conclusion that they should forever consume less than the wealthy countries. This question of equity was the main cause of the failure of global climate talks at the Copenhagen summit in 2009.

Scientific Uncertainty   Finally, there is the problem of scientific uncertainty. It is difficult to undertake economic sacrifices when it is unclear how dangerous the threat is. Although most scientists now agree that the global climate is changing and that human activity is causing the change, there is a powerful dissenting current, especially in the United States. Organizations funded largely by energy companies have sown doubt by arguing that climate change science is inconclusive or politically biased. The development (or absence) of shared purpose is a key variable in international environmental collaboration. The role played by transnational actors and international organizations, and especially transnational groups of scientists, can be crucial in causing states to redefine their interests. The **Intergovernmental Panel on Climate Change (IPCC)** has been essential in marshalling scientific evidence to remove doubts about the seriousness of global warming. The importance of achieving scientific certainty and fostering shared purpose was expressed by the Norwegian Nobel Committee when it gave the 2007 Nobel Peace Prize to the IPCC and former U.S. Vice President Al Gore, but shared purpose on climate change has yet to fully emerge.

Intergovernmental Panel on Climate Change (IPCC)

An international body that assesses scientific research on climate change for decision makers.

International Environmental Agreements

THE KYOTO PROTOCOL AND COPENHAGEN SUMMIT

In December 1997, representatives of most of the world's states met in Kyoto, Japan, to finalize a treaty[12] limiting the emission of so-called **greenhouse gases**. Under the Protocol, thirty-nine "Annex I" countries, the largest producers of greenhouse gases, agreed to reduce their output of such gases to below their 1990 levels by 2012. Although the overall reduction would be 5.2 percent, the amount of reduction for each country would vary: The EU states are committed to reducing by 8 percent, the United States (which did not ratify the agreement) by 7 percent, and Japan by 5 percent.

All other countries (non-Annex I countries) are permitted to continue increasing their production of greenhouse gases, in recognition of the fact that they currently produce lower amounts and need to consume more fossil fuels to continue economic development. Essentially, the Annex I countries are the developed countries of the world and the post-Soviet states.

From Kyoto to Copengagen As with most domestic environmental measures, some believe the Kyoto Protocol is too restrictive, and others fear that it is too weak. Those who see it as too restrictive are concerned about the economic effects of cutting back on the use of fossil fuels in economies that are highly dependent on them. The economic cost of the agreement was a primary reason the U.S. government (under both President Clinton and the second President Bush) declined to seek Senate ratification.

Those who focus on the scope of global warming argued that the protocol was far too weak to deal with the problem. Even if emissions by Annex I countries were reduced to below 1990 levels, they contend, overall emissions would increase because developing countries are not covered and are rapidly increasing output (China surpassed the United States as the top emitter of greenhouse gases around 2005). Supporters of the Kyoto Protocol argued that although the agreement is imperfect, levels of greenhouse gases would rise much higher without the treaty. Most agreed further action was needed.

In December 2009, a summit was held in Copenhagen to devise a follow-up treaty to Kyoto, the provisions of which ran through 2012. Many hoped that a new binding agreement with stricter limits and coverage of more developing states would result. Before the summit even started, however, it was clear that a new treaty would not be agreed upon. The summit itself then broke down amidst intense recrimination about whether developed or developing states were to blame. The different positions of these two groups created a conflict of interest that simply could not be breached.

Most of the countries of Europe, and others such as Canada and Australia, had taken significant steps to limit greenhouse gas emissions since 1990. However, with the growth in the Chinese, Indian, and other developing economies between 1997 and 2009, it was clear that some limits on their production of greenhouse gases would eventually be needed. China had become the biggest single producer of greenhouse gases. The United States in particular resisted making any commitment if developing states did not do so.

However, the developing states steadfastly resisted limits on their own emissions, which in general were still lower on a per capita basis than were those in developed states. Moreover, led by China, they even resisted a treaty in which states chose their own limits, but took on a binding legal commitment to achieve them. Apparently, China and others found the idea of legally binding limits potentially dangerous to their future economic growth.

The breakdown at Copenhagen, and the bitterness that the process engendered, caused considerable pessimism about the likelihood that catastrophic global warming (generally defined as an increase of two degrees Celsius or more) will be averted. Those looking for a silver lining point out that many countries adopted significant voluntary limits before and after the summit and that these limits will help. Without serious commitments by the United States, China, and other developing states, however, it is difficult to see much potential to stabilize greenhouse gas emissions.

greenhouse gases
Gases in the atmosphere that trap heat in the earth's atmosphere. As they increase in concentration, the atmospheric temperature rises, causing climate change.

The Geography Connection

The Political Effects of Global Warming?

The map shows worldwide temperature increases from 2001 through 2005. These do not necessarily predict future trends, but the map might portray the differential effects around the world of climate change.

Critical Thinking Questions

1. Are there regions that might benefit economically from climate change? How might that occur?

2. How might climate change shape the global distribution of wealth and power?

3. Does the vulnerability of different states to climate change drive their policy on a global warming treaty?

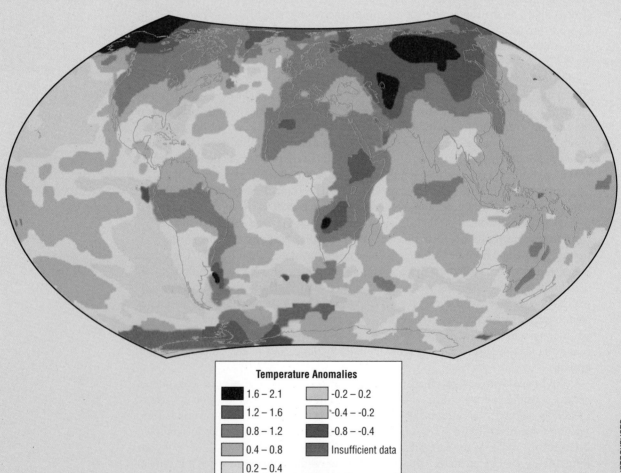

Temperature Anomalies

1.6 – 2.1		-0.2 – 0.2
1.2 – 1.6		-0.4 – -0.2
0.8 – 1.2		-0.8 – -0.4
0.4 – 0.8		Insufficient data
0.2 – 0.4		

Source: http://maps.grida.no/go/graphic/increases-in-temperature-2001-2005

OTHER INTERNATIONAL AGREEMENTS

In addition to the Kyoto Protocol, a variety of international environmental agreements— some regional, some global—address environmental problems. The **Montreal Protocol**, signed by twenty-four states plus the EU in 1987, now has over 180 signatories. It commits the signatories to reducing the production and use of gases that deplete the **ozone layer** in the atmosphere. The Montreal Protocol was significant because it was the first global environmental treaty and because its success convinced many skeptics that such cooperation was indeed possible. It was seen by many as a model for a treaty on greenhouse gases (the Kyoto Protocol). Cooperation to limit gases that deplete the ozone layer became possible in large part because scientific findings regarding the effect of certain chemicals on the ozone layer became indisputable. Similarly, there was wide consensus on the negative effects of increased ultraviolet radiation on human health.

The **Convention on Biological Diversity**, often called the "Biodiversity Treaty," was signed at the Rio Summit in 1992 and went into effect in 1993. It has since been signed by nearly 190 countries. The United States has signed the agreement, but it has not been ratified by the U.S. Senate. The treaty had three central goals: "the conservation of biological diversity, the sustainable use of its components and the fair and equitable sharing of the benefits arising out of the utilization of genetic resources."

The third goal has perhaps been most controversial because it addresses issues of economic equity. Developing countries, which often lack the cutting-edge technology and financial resources to discover the benefits of their biological resources and bring them to market, fear that the profits from exploitation of the resources will go primarily to corporations from developed countries. Thus, the treaty, rather vaguely, commits countries to a "fair and equitable sharing of benefits" from biological resources.

Critics claim that the treaty has done relatively little to protect biodiversity, while making the conduct of basic scientific research much more difficult. The treaty's provisions regarding the first goal are vague and have had little observable impact on the problem. At the same time, some scientists complain that the third goal has led to laws being passed in some countries that make conducting basic scientific research border on criminal activity.

Prospects for Cooperation

To many, the need for international cooperation on environmental problems is clear. However, there are serious obstacles to such agreements. International environmental collaboration runs into all the obstacles that domestic environmental measures encounter, plus the challenges of working with many governments rather than one. Of the agreements reached so far, only the Montreal Protocol on ozone-depleting chemicals is clearly a success. The goals of the others are sufficiently vague that it is difficult to know whether the treaties are really helping. The ongoing skepticism of key governments, most notably that of the United States but also that of China, about international environmental agreements also hampers their effectiveness. A key question for the future is whether governments will agree to more far-reaching limits on the production of greenhouse gases if the effects of global warming become more pronounced. Although some see environmental conflict as providing the incentive to shift to a much higher level of global governance, others see the opposite—a world of increased conflict driven by the effects of climate change population growth, coupled with battles for control of increasingly scarce resources such as oil and water.

International Health Issues

The speed with which the **SARS** (severe acute respiratory syndrome) virus spread around the globe in 2003, leaving medical and economic chaos in its wake, focused global attention on the increasing dangers of cross-border disease transmission in a globalizing world.

Montreal Protocol

An international agreement, signed in 1987, that commits the signatories to reducing the production and use of gases that deplete the ozone layer.

ozone layer

A layer of ozone in the upper atmosphere that reduces transmission of ultraviolet radiation. Ozone is a form of oxygen with three atoms per molecule (O_3) rather than the typical two (O_2). At ground level, ozone is a respiratory irritant.

Convention on Biological Diversity

An international agreement aimed at conserving biodiversity, signed in 1992.

SARS

Severe acute respiratory syndrome (SARS) is caused by a virus and spread by person-to-person contact. An outbreak in 2003 led to about 8000 infections and 774 deaths worldwide before it was contained.

The History Connection

The Flu of 1918

On March 11, 1918, soldiers at Fort Riley, Kansas, began falling ill. Within a week, Fort Riley had 500 cases of what its doctors recorded as pneumonia. By summer, forty-eight soldiers had died there.[1] Initially, the Fort Riley outbreak did not spread the disease to the rest of the United States. Instead, there was a lull. However, U.S. soldiers carried the flu overseas as they were deployed to Europe in the last months of World War I. As far as historians can tell, this was the beginning of the global flu pandemic of 1918, which killed between 20 million and 40 million people around the world. The number of victims is difficult to establish precisely because in poor areas such as India, where millions died, it is impossible to know the exact number.

This was not a flu that made people feel ill for a few days. It hit the young and strong and forced them into bed. Sometimes they were dead within a day, their lungs having filled with fluid. In the fall of 1918, the virus broke out in Europe, and it then became known as the "Spanish flu." It returned to the United States with returning soldiers, and in the fall of 1918, the flu ravaged the United States and other countries. In the United States, 600,000 people died within a few months—many of them young people in the prime of life. Scientists at the time struggled in vain to isolate the cause of the epidemic or to come up with treatments. Isolating those infected and keeping people apart in general were the only measures to combat the spread of the illness. In Philadelphia, public meetings were banned. It is difficult to imagine what sort of panic would occur today if such a number of people were to succumb to a new variant of the flu.

The 1918 flu continues to hold great interest for scientists and historians. Scientists are using modern genetic techniques on old tissue samples to try to figure out what made this particular strain of the virus so lethal. They are also trying to figure out whether it came to people from birds (where most flu viruses originate) or from pigs (which has been the predominant view of the 1918 flu).

These questions are not merely academic. Historically there has been a major flu outbreak about every thirty years, and the last one was in 1968. In Asia in recent years, there have been several scares. In Hong Kong in 1997, a particularly lethal flu virus began spreading from birds to people. Although the virus was deadly, it did not appear to spread from person to person, as is the case with epidemic flu viruses. By ordering the slaughter of every single bird in Hong Kong, the government was able to contain the virus. Since then, however, there have been many instances of a highly lethal flu virus spreading from birds to people. Most recently, the H1N1 "swine" flu virus created widespread disruption around the world in 2009–2010, even though it was not as lethal as initially feared. The great fear is that one of these viruses will mutate in such a way that it will become able to move from person to person. If this happens, we might have a new 1918 flu on our hands.

One key difference today is the speed with which people, and hence germs and viruses, can move about the world. A new outbreak today would potentially spread to every country within days or weeks. Another key difference today is the monitoring operations dedicated to identifying new flu viruses, developing vaccines, and administering those vaccines. In the event of a new outbreak, international collaboration in public health will race against the forces of globalization to try to get ahead of the flu.

Critical Thinking Questions

1. Who should make decisions regarding limitations on international travel—state governments or international organizations such as the WHO?
2. What different perspectives on the urgency of taking costly measures to combat a particular disease outbreak might poor and wealthy states have?

[1] PBS, "Influenza 1918," program transcript, at http://www.pbs.org/wgbh/amex/influenza/filmmore/transcript/transcript1.html

The H1N1 (swine) flu pandemic of 2009 had similar but larger effects. These cases are not unique, and the transnational spread of disease remains a significant threat. At the same time, transnational efforts to combat disease and improve health have become more significant. The past half century has seen several major efforts to combat diseases internationally, carried out by a mixture of national, international, and nongovernmental actors.

The Spread of Disease

The transnational spread of disease has a long history. The bubonic plague, or "Black Death," which wiped out a quarter of Europe's population in the late fourteenth century, came to Europe along the trade routes from central Asia, where the disease was more prevalent but less fatal. In 1918, just as World War I was winding down, a new strain of flu virus emerged and spread rapidly around the world, aided by the movement of infected soldiers. Within a year, the new flu had killed more people than four years of intense warfare.

The transnational spread of disease, therefore, follows our general discussion of globalization in an important respect. Although the phenomenon is not completely new, the speed with which disease can spread around the world has increased dramatically. However, there are also new solutions. Modern science and medical technology have made it possible to track the spread of disease much more effectively than in the past. In the 2008–2009 H1N1 flu pandemic, spread of the disease around the world was tracked and anticipated, and prompt development and distribution of vaccines limited the impact of the disease. Thus, there are clear incentives for countries to work together to combat the spread of disease and to eradicate existing disease.

The Politics of International Health

Compared with international environmental issues, there are fewer barriers to combating international health problems. Most importantly, there is no significant tension between protecting health and pursuing economic growth, as there appears to be with many environmental issues. However, protecting health, whether domestically or internationally, takes precious budgetary resources away from other goals, and so it is always subject to politics.

Although it is sometimes difficult to spend money on health care in the short term, doing so often saves money in the long term. This is a challenge to politicians from the local to the international level. The SARS outbreak in 2003, for example, was estimated to cost Hong Kong nearly 1 percent of its economic output for the year. The cost for Southeast Asia more broadly was estimated at 0.6 percent of GDP.[13] The German airline Lufthansa calculated its losses resulting from reduced travel to Asia at $62 million per week during the epidemic.[14]

Economic losses from health problems only begin with the direct costs of treating sick people. The days of work lost because of illness of workers or their family members create an additional expense to firms. Reduced travel to affected areas imposes losses on the travel industry, hotels, restaurants, and the governments that rely on tax revenues from such services. In countries where AIDS is killing a large number of people, it is also creating a large number of orphans, who are overwhelming social service networks. Societies will bear the costs of raising these children with no parents for decades to come. Despite those costs, it is often difficult for governments to fund health care provisions when they are under immense pressure to keep taxes at a minimal level.

In addition to global efforts at curbing the transnational spread of disease, international and transnational health programs aim at assisting health efforts within specific countries. These programs have much in common with development aid. In the case of development

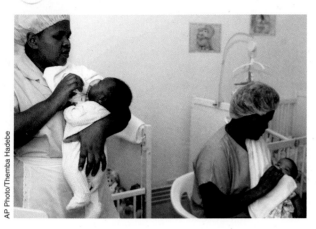

Midwives feed orphaned babies in Durban, South Africa. AIDS takes more than a human toll. The cost of treating the disease, and of managing the social consequences, such as orphaned children, is a serious economic problem in many countries.

aid, the "problem" exists in poorer countries, and wealthier countries (and transnational actors) try to help.

However, these two categories are increasingly being blurred as it becomes easier for individuals carrying infectious disease to move from one country to another. For example, for many years tuberculosis (TB) has been under control in much of the developed world, while still remaining a problem in developing countries. Today, however, there is fear that antibiotic-resistant strains of TB, which have emerged in developing countries and in Russia, will spread to Europe and North America, making a previously controlled disease much more difficult (and expensive) to deal with. In October 2006, the Red Cross and the World Health Organization warned that the EU was endangered by the potential spread of drug-resistant TB from the region to its east.[15] In May 2007, there was an international effort to find and quarantine an American man who had tested positive for extremely drug-resistant ("XDR") TB and to track down everyone who had come into contact with him.

EFFORTS TO FIGHT DISEASE

World Health Organization (WHO)

The UN's specialized agency that focuses on health issues.

The most important international organization working on health issues is the **World Health Organization (WHO)**, one of the UN's specialized agencies. The WHO has 192 member states and is based in Geneva, Switzerland. As well as managing ongoing programs to promote health and combat disease around the world, the WHO also coordinates the gathering of data on emerging crises and coordinates an international response. During the 2008–2009 H1N1 flu outbreak, for example, the WHO identified where the disease was present, encouraging people to avoid travel to those regions. The rapid enactment of such advisories was credited by many with containing the spread of the illness, although officials were less pleased in some places where a travel advisory had devastating economic effects.

Perhaps the most important historical success for the WHO was its role in coordinating the global eradication of smallpox. Smallpox outbreaks devastated populations around the world for centuries. The arrival of smallpox in North America with European settlers is viewed as the most significant cause of deaths for Native Americans. By the 1950s, even though a vaccine for smallpox was available, there were still 50 million cases worldwide, and smallpox still killed a quarter of its victims and left many others blind.

Beginning in 1967, the WHO began a program to completely eradicate the virus. If nearly everyone in the world were vaccinated, the virus would have no place left to live and would be wiped out. Achieving this goal required an extensive and well-coordinated program of vaccination in some of the most difficult working environments in the world. Over time, the disease was confined to Africa, and the last case of smallpox occurred in 1977 in Somalia. The WHO declared smallpox eradicated in 1980.[16] Except for research stocks of the virus and biological warfare agents, smallpox is now extinct, and although the fear remains that an accidental release of the virus or its deliberate use as a weapon will occur, one has no chance of acquiring the disease naturally.

Today, the WHO coordinates a variety of activities around the world. Its Global Outbreak Alert and Response Network coordinates the identification of and response to new disease outbreaks deemed to be of international significance. This group is called into action when there is an outbreak of a disease, such as SARS or the Ebola virus that threatens to spread transnationally. The WHO also responds to medical emergencies such as the tsunami that struck the Indian Ocean region in December 2004 and the earthquake in Haiti in 2010.

NGOs in International Health

In contrast to many other areas of international politics, NGOs take center stage in international health work. They are relied on by donor governments and recipient governments to do difficult jobs in difficult places because they have some key advantages over governmental actors.

- Health care workers from NGOs can operate in aid-receiving countries without raising the same concerns about sovereignty that would be raised if the work were being done by developed country officials.

- Health care workers from NGOs can operate in areas where government employees cannot. In places like Afghanistan, Sudan, and Iraq, NGOs could operate much more freely than British or American officials (although in each of these places there have been attacks on NGO workers).

- NGOs often have more expertise than government officials. A certain NGO may have years of experience with a particular issue or a particular country, whereas a government adopting a new program would have to start from scratch.

- NGOs can often react more quickly than governments can. In natural disasters and other emergencies, NGOs are often highly effective at moving people and materials into and within countries quickly, which can be difficult for massive government bureaucracies. The militaries of developed countries have significant capacity to move huge amounts of supplies to a stricken region but not to actually get those supplies distributed to the people who need them. Thus, an NGO, such as the International Committee of the Red Cross, is often at the center of relief efforts.

The nonstate character of NGOs makes them particularly effective in areas where health issues overlap with political disputes. Poverty and poor health care are often consequences of civil war and political instability.

There are thousands of international health-oriented NGOs providing assistance in various parts of the world. Some are funded primarily by private donations. Others receive all of their funding from a single government, essentially acting as private subcontractors for that government. It is worth looking at a few examples in detail to get an idea of the range of actors working in international health affairs.

A French Médecins Sans Frontières doctor quarantines a child with cholera.

The Agenda

There are, of course, thousands of diseases that cross national boundaries, but among these a small number have been identified as high priorities, either because they are causing immense suffering and economic disruption or because they threaten to do so.

HIV/AIDS

In much of the developed world, there is a perception that the HIV/AIDS epidemic has crested and is under control. On the global level, however, the epidemic is still growing and creating havoc. The number of infected individuals reached an estimated 39 million worldwide in 2004, with 4.9 million new cases that year. The hardest hit areas are in Africa and the Caribbean. In sub-Saharan Africa, 7.4 percent of the total population is affected,[17] and in the hardest-hit countries such as Zambia, 15 percent of the adult population is infected.[18] Infection rates at this level tear at the fabric of nearly every societal function. They overwhelm already stretched health care systems, hinder economic growth as key personnel fall ill (or must treat family members who do), and weaken societal cohesion by creating large numbers of orphans.

There is considerable concern about the potential "next generation" of HIV/AIDS epidemics. In several populous countries, including China, Russia, and India, HIV/AIDS appears to be at the "takeoff phase" of growth. In these countries, infection rates are currently low but are accelerating. The absence of adequate public information campaigns and other preventive measures leads researchers to believe that an explosion of cases is possible. The fear is that twenty years from now, these countries could have the level of infection present in sub-Saharan Africa today.

In places like Russia and China, intravenous drug users are the first community being affected. Because these individuals are often on the margin of society, monitoring of the disease among this community is poor, and sympathy for victims is low. However, from this group, the virus spreads to the general heterosexual population, and anyone with multiple partners is at risk. In India, 80 percent of new infections are a result of heterosexual sex.[19] Because HIV/AIDS victims in many countries are socially ostracized, losing their jobs or being expelled from school, people are very unwilling to be tested or to admit carrying the virus. This, of course, promotes further transmission. These countries' health systems will be badly overloaded if HIV/AIDS reaches anything like the anticipated levels.

In contrast, some developing countries have escaped the worst effects of HIV/AIDS by putting into place strong public health measures before the epidemic gets out of con-

Figure 14.3 Percentage of Adults in Need Who Have Access to Antiretroviral Drugs, 2004. Availability of the best HIV/AIDS treatments varies widely around the world, ensuring that the disease will continue to spread in many places

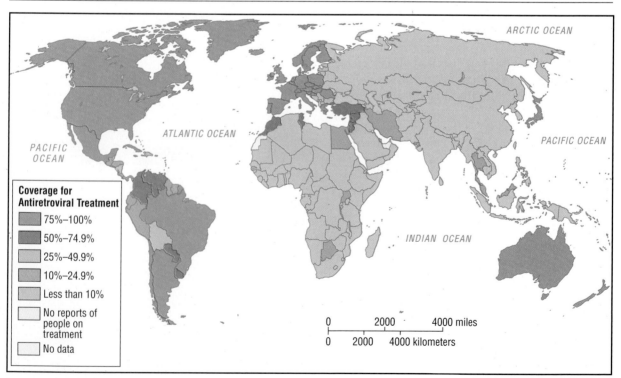

Coverage for Antiretroviral Treatment
- 75%–100%
- 50%–74.9%
- 25%–49.9%
- 10%–24.9%
- Less than 10%
- No reports of people on treatment
- No data

Source: http://www.who.int/3by5/en/coverage_march2004.jpg

trol. Senegal, Brazil, and Thailand are all considered countries where proactive measures have helped contain the spread of HIV/AIDS.

MALARIA

Malaria is perhaps the most widespread infectious disease problem, with some 2.3 billion people (roughly one-third of the earth's population) at risk of infection. Relatively little is heard about this disease in North America and Europe because it is a threat primarily in Africa and Asia (although global warming may change that). Malaria is caused by a parasite that is transmitted via the female *Anopheles* mosquito. Although efforts in the twentieth century to eradicate mosquitoes and treat people at risk helped with the problem in some regions, they did not help in the hardest-hit regions. In sub-Saharan Africa, the most heavily infected region, the problem has actually gotten worse in recent years.[20]

In technical terms, there is nothing difficult about combating malaria. Three strategies are used: killing mosquitoes, using mosquito netting to keep them away from people, and treating the infection. The problem has been finding sufficient resources to pay for these measures. In the case of eradicating mosquitoes, health promotion conflicts with environmental concerns because the pesticides used to kill mosquitoes can have far-reaching environmental effects. Because the hardest-hit countries are many of the poorest countries in the world, the victims and their governments are generally unable to bear the cost of prevention and treatment. For this reason, it has been essential for the international community to step in.

Efforts to combat malaria have been stepped up in recent years through programs such as "Roll Back Malaria" (organized by several UN agencies, including WHO) and the "Malaria Vaccines Initiative" (organized by the Bill and Melinda Gates Foundation). However, progress remains elusive, largely because the financial resources of those programs do not match the scope of the problem. Two leading experts wrote in 2004 that these approaches, unless given substantially more resources, "will get nowhere near eradicating the disease."[21] A particular challenge with malaria, as with other diseases, is the emergence of strains of the parasite that are resistant to the cheapest and most widely used treatment, chloroquine. Other treatments are much more expensive, and not widely available in quality medications.

Figure 14.4 Insecticide-treated nets are a proven way of combating malaria. Making them more widely available in Africa has been a key strategy for both governments and NGOs hoping to combat malaria

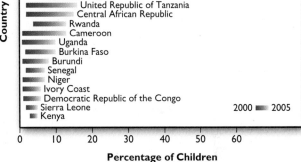

Source: http://www.who.int/whosis/whostat/EN_WHS08_Full.pdf, p. 19

TUBERCULOSIS

Tuberculosis, an infection of the lungs caused by a bacterium, was a significant cause of death throughout the nineteenth and early twentieth centuries. By the mid-twentieth century, however, antibiotics led to the near-elimination of TB in the developed world. Today, the disease continues to kill in the developing world and is making a comeback in Russia, where it was previously under control. Roughly one-third of the world's population carries the TB bacterium, although many carriers will not develop TB. Tuberculosis is particularly dangerous in combination with AIDS. Approximately one-third of AIDS deaths are caused by TB, and the vulnerability of AIDS victims to TB is helping TB to spread more rapidly.[22]

As with malaria, treatments for TB are well known. However, the tendency for antibiotics to be used improperly (for example, stopping a course of treatment before it is complete) has led to the development of drug-resistant strains of the bacterium. Effective second-generation treatments have been developed but are considerably more expensive. Moreover, new strains of the disease are resistant even to these second-generation drugs, leading to the possibility of a widespread increase in the incidence of the disease. The advent of drug-resistant TB has significantly increased the cost of dealing with the disease. There is hope of developing a vaccine for TB, but so far these efforts have not proven successful. Instead, the world now faces the spread of extremely drug-resistant TB.

PREVENTING A NEW FLU PANDEMIC

The flu (short for "influenza," a condition caused by a group of viruses that infect the respiratory system) is a fairly common illness in most of the world, with low fatality rates. However, the virus occasionally mutates, such that a new variant arises to which humans have little natural immunity. Moreover, in recent years there has been considerable concern about variants of influenza "jumping" from species of birds to humans. Not only the frail, but also the strong and healthy are at risk from these new variants. Three times during the twentieth century, new strains of the virus led to worldwide flu pandemics in which many people were killed. As noted in the History Connection feature, the worst of these outbreaks killed 20 million to 40 million people in 1918–1919. Outbreaks in 1957 and 1968 were less devastating but still considered major global pandemics.

The WHO coordinates the Global Influenza Surveillance Network, which relies on eighty-three national-level centers to identify new flu strains, determine which are most dangerous, and formulate a new vaccine every year based on such information.[23] The goal is to get ahead of a new virus outbreak by identifying it in its early stages and producing vaccines that can preempt the spread of the flu. The efforts at limiting the spread the H1N1 flu in 2008–2009 are widely considered to have been effective, but concerns remain about the ability to handle a more deadly or contagious strain of the virus.

Reconsider
the Case

Trafficking in Women

Trafficking in women, like the other issues considered in this chapter, is a problem that spans multiple states. As in the drug trade, some states (generally where poverty is high) tend to be "supplying" states; others (generally more wealthy states) tend to be "receiving" states. However, there is also a great deal of trafficking within states, especially in Asia, and some states, like China, are both importers and exporters of trafficked people.

Despite its transnational character, almost all action aimed at remedying the problem occurs at the state level. For example, the U.S. Congress passed the "Trafficking Victims Protection Act" in 2000, but it has little ability to influence prevention or enforcement efforts in other countries. And even the United States

has made this a fairly low priority, issuing reports but not spending a great deal of resources on the issue.

A powerful tactic used by traffickers to control victims is to confiscate their passports. Therefore, if the victims run away, they are illegal aliens, subject to arrest, extended detention, and deportation back to the place they originally sought to escape. Victims face these same consequences if they go to police. Ironically, the threat of law enforcement actually helps traffickers keep people under their control. The victims are punished, while the perpetrators often either vanish or bribe police.

One of the principal policy dilemmas for receiving states is what to do with victims once they are discovered. They have entered the country illegally and often have no documentation, and may be in need of costly social services. To allow them to stay might reward their initial decision to immigrate illegally and might encourage others to do the same. It might actually help traffickers in recruiting. However, imprisoning or deporting the trafficking victims gives the victims strong incentives to comply with their "owners." The only real solution is better prevention. As in the case of drug smuggling, the importing states sometimes have much greater interest in managing the problem than do the exporting states. Moreover, because trafficking tends to originate in countries where law enforcement is weak and susceptible to bribery, it is difficult to stop the supply "at the source," even when state leaders agree that doing so is a priority.

Clearly, part of the problem is that this is a low priority issue for governments in some countries. An internationally shared sense of purpose, a concept raised throughout this book, does not yet appear to exist. Why is trafficking in women a comparatively low priority? Is it because it is less of a threat than other forms of transnational crime, or as feminist scholarship would suggest, is it because problems that primarily afflict women are underemphasized in policy making that is still heavily masculine?

What conclusions can we reach about the measures that would most effectively and efficiently curb trafficking in women? Is enforcement against traffickers likely to be effective? Or will such efforts fail unless the official corruption on which traffickers rely is curbed? Or might we conclude that demand will always exist, and that the underlying cause of trafficking is the poverty that makes women desperate enough to put themselves at the mercy of traffickers in their search for better lives?

Critical Thinking Questions

1. What factors will influence whether there is deeper international collaboration to prevent trafficking in women?
2. To what extent might coercion be a useful tool to get more states to do more to combat trafficking?
3. If you wanted to solve this problem, would you accomplish more by pressing states to address the problem, or by supporting NGOs that work with women who are victims or potential victims?

Summary

Some theorists have speculated that new problems of transnational crime, human trafficking, environmental destruction, and disease, which cut across national boundaries, will force states to join together in new ways.[24] In this view, "international security" is becoming redefined: The new dangers to states and societies, it might be argued, come not from other states and societies, or from their armies, but from transnational criminal and terrorist groups, environmental degradation, and diseases, which threaten all states. Some see this development changing international politics in two ways. First, it makes all states "allies" against these common enemies. Especially in the case of health issues, this should make collaboration easier.

Second, some say, these problems simply cannot be solved by states working alone. Transnational criminal organizations will not be stopped by national-level law enforcement. Global warming will not be prevented without measures that have effects across all countries. Thus, some argue that these problems will *force* states to fundamentally revise the system of state sovereignty by giving real governmental authority to international organizations. In this view, states will not do so voluntarily, but through harsh necessity. Self-interest, in this view, will require surrendering state sovereignty, not defending it tenaciously.

Others view that perspective as hopelessly naïve.[25] From a more traditional realist perspective, there are two problems with the view that new shared dangers will increase cooperation. First, realists argue, such problems ignore the difficulty that states have always had overcoming individual interests in order to collaborate. They would cite the conflict over greenhouse gas emissions as evidence. Second, especially when viewing the environment, realists see sources of conflict, not cooperation. As resources become more scarce, states are more likely to fight over them. Oil and water appear to be the two strongest candidates that states may be willing to go to war over.

In that respect, some see international politics moving backward in time, not forward. Many see the U.S.-led wars in Iraq in 1991 and 2003 as the beginning of a new global conflict over oil. The rise of China as a huge oil consumer, and hence as a competitor for new global oil supplies, has many seeing oil as the key focus of resource conflict in the coming decades. Water, in some parts of the world, may also be a source of conflict, as states use force, rather than collaboration, to gain what they need.[26]

However, the two opposing scenarios just outlined are not mutually exclusive. Elements of both scenarios could play out at the same time. It is possible, for example, that there will be further collaboration on health issues and law enforcement and increased conflict over natural resources.

Key Concepts

1. Transnational crime
2. Human trafficking
3. Money laundering
4. Collective action problem
5. "Tragedy of the commons"
6. Kyoto Protocol
7. SARS
8. WHO

Study Questions

1. What characteristics of globalization have facilitated the growth of transnational crime?
2. How does transnational crime facilitate terrorism?
3. What environmental issues are global rather than national or regional in scope?
4. What are the major barriers to international collaboration on environmental problems?
5. In what way is international collaboration on environmental problems a collective action problem?
6. How does globalization affect the international transmission of diseases and efforts to combat it?
7. What kinds of political issues get embroiled in efforts to combat disease in developing countries?
8. Why do NGOs play such an important role in health care programs in developing countries?
9. What diseases present the biggest challenges today?
10. Will problems such as transnational crime, environmental degradation, and international health issues lead to more cooperation or more conflict among states?

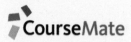
CourseMate

Endnotes

1. U.S. Department of State, "Trafficking in Persons Report, June 2007," at http://www.state.gov/documents/organization/82902.pdf

2. Jared Diamond, "What's Your Consumption Factor?" *The New York Times,* January 2, 2008, at http://www.nytimes.com/2008/01/02/opinion/02diamond.html

3. UNHCR, *Convention and Protocol Relating to the Status of Refugees*, at http://www.unhcr.org.au/pdfs/convention.pdf

4. UNHCR Fundraising Reports, 1 December 2009, at http://www.unhcr.org/4b04002b9.html

5. Jason DeParle, "Global Migration: A World Ever More on the Move," *New York Times*, June 25, 2010 (New York Edition):WK1.

6. Vivek Wadhwa, "Foreign Born Entrepreneurs: An Underestimated American Resource," Ewing Marion Kaufmann Foundation, at http://www.kauffman.org/entrepreneurship/foreign-born-entrepreneurs.aspx

7. UNODC, "World Drug Report 2004," p. 30.

8. U.S. Department of Defense, Quadrennial Defense Review Report, February 2010, pp. 7, 84, at http://www.defense.gov/qdr/images/QDR_as_of_12Feb10_1000.pdf

9. John K. Cooley, "The War over Water," *Foreign Policy* No. 54 (Spring 1984): 3–25.

10. Garrett Hardin, "The Tragedy of the Commons," *Science* No. 162 (1968): 1243–1248.

11. See David Tilman, Robert Socolow, Jonathan A. Foley, et al, "Beneficial Biofuels: The Food, Energy, and Environment Trilemma," *Science* (July 17, 2009): 270–271.

12. The treaty's official name is the "Kyoto Protocol to the United Nations Framework Convention on Climate Change." Technically, it is an amendment to the Framework Convention on Climate Change, which was negotiated at the Rio de Janeiro Earth Summit in 1992.

13. "Hong Kong Hit by SARS Costs," The *Guardian*, April 3, 2003, at http://www.guardian.co.uk/business/2003/apr/03/sars.medicineandhealth

14. "SARS Costs Lufthansa $62 million Weekly in Lost Revenues," at http://www.logisticsturku.fi/logistics/bulletin.nsf/0/5b2222e8914c6525c2256d2000230617?OpenDocument

15. "European Union 'faces TB crisis,' " BBC News, October 10, 2006, at http://news.bbc.co.uk/2/hi/europe/6036043.stm

16. "Smallpox," at http://www.who.int/mediacentre/factsheets/smallpox/en/index.html

17. GlobalHealthReporting.org, HIV/AIDS "Facts at a Glance," at http://www.globalhealthreporting.org/diseaseinfo.asp?id=23#global

18. U.S. Centers for Disease Control, at http://www.cdc.gov/globalaids/Global-HIV-AIDS-at-CDC/countries/Zambia/

19. *Hindustan Times*, December 5, 2003.

20. Richard Klausner and Pedro Alonso, "An Attack on All Fronts," *Nature* 430 (August 19, 2004): 930–931.

21. Klausner and Alonso, "An Attack on All Fronts," p. 930.

22. Bill and Melinda Gates Foundation, "Tuberculosis Backgrounder," at http://www.gatesfoundation.org/GlobalHealth/HIVAIDSTB/Tuberculosis/TuberculosisBackgrounder.htm

23. World Health Organization, "Influenza Fact Sheet," at http://www.who.int/mediacentre/factsheets/fs211/en/

24. Thomas F. Homer-Dixon labels those who believe that cooperation and ingenuity will ameliorate environmental problems "cornucopians" and those who believe that environmental issues will lead to conflict as "neo-Malthusians" (after the demographer and economist Thomas Malthus, whose 1798 *Essay on the Principle of Population* argued that population growth would inevitably lead to scarcity and conflict). See Thomas F. Homer-Dixon, "On the Threshold: Environmental Changes as the Cause of Acute Conflict," *International Security*, Vol. 16, No. 2 (1991): 76–116.

25. Robert Kaplan, "The Coming Anarchy," *The Atlantic Monthly*, 1994: 44–76.

26. For a sobering discussion of these issues, see Michael T. Klare, *Resource Wars: The New Landscape of Global Conflict* (New York: Metropolitan Books, 2001). See also Kenneth S. Deffyes, *Hubbert's Peak: The Impending World Oil Shortage* (Princeton, NJ: Princeton University Press, 2001).

Conclusion: Power and Purpose in a Changing World

LEARNING OBJECTIVES

After completing this chapter, the student should be able to . . .

1. Identify potential sources of change in international politics in coming decades.

2. Link claims about sources and effects of change to broader theoretical arguments.

3. Predict the effects of different potential developments in international politics.

◀ Commandos are in action near the Palace Hotel in Mumbai (Bombay), India, during the terrorist attack of November 26, 2008.

Bhaskar Paul/The India Today Group/Getty Images

Chapter 1 established three related goals for this book:

- To improve readers' understanding of international politics
- To prepare readers to make informed evaluations about important questions
- To enable readers to engage in intelligent, active debate on important public issues

With the hope that these goals have been achieved, this chapter now addresses questions that are perhaps even more difficult than those already considered. These are questions that will be asked with increasing frequency in coming years. They raise issues that will be the focus of public debate. They concern problems that will confront leaders and citizens with difficult choices. This conclusion looks to the future and asks what international politics might look like in the decades ahead. As Chapter 1 pointed out, our expectations about the future will determine the choices we make on important questions.

The contemporary era of international politics is defined by change. The collapse of communism in 1989–1991 brought the Cold War to an abrupt end. The terrorist attacks of 2001 ended the post–Cold War era. In the post-2001 era, new concerns such as terrorism, the environment, and globalization are shaping the international agenda. Economic and political power seems to be shifting from the United States and Europe to Asia. We do not yet know exactly what this era will look like or how it will evolve.

To reiterate the themes that have driven this book, power and purpose are both evolving. The distribution of power is changing, as resources, technology, and economic vitality change around the world. The sources of power are also changing, as terrorism empowers the weak and debt crisis redefines what it means to be strong. Purpose is evolving as well, as China contemplates global great power status, Europe rethinks the wisdom of integration, and people around the world contemplate the relative importance of sovereignty, international law, human rights, and economic well-being.

If "everything has changed" since September 2001, to what extent can the lessons of the past be applied to the future? Are the five major theoretical approaches to international politics still pertinent? In order to address these questions, we must assess the nature of the changes. Are the underlying patterns in the system changing, such that everything we have already learned is becoming irrelevant? Or does international politics continue to be defined by the same underlying patterns explored in this book? The answer, of course, is yes, to both questions. International politics today is defined by both continuity and change.

Assessing Continuity and Change

Previous chapters have often stressed the links between history and the present and the ways in which the present has diverged from the past. This chapter looks into the future while searching the past for insight. The early twenty-first century appears to be a revolutionary time. What sorts of precedents can be used for guidance? What new phenomena will require fundamentally new strategies that may not have been envisioned yet?

Robert Gilpin wrote in 1987 that modern realists know little today about international politics that Thucydides did not know when he was writing in the fifth century BCE.[1] Gilpin's point was that although much had changed in twenty-five centuries, the underlying nature of international politics had not. It was still a competition for security in a dangerous world in which power determined outcomes. Even if Gilpin was right in 1987, is that still true today? Is international politics changing in fundamental ways or is it changing in ways that retain the basic characteristics of the system?

An evaluation of potential changes in international politics demonstrates one important use of the conceptual tools that have been discussed in this book. We cannot predict what will happen in the future. But we can identify what might be the key signs that the situation is evolving in one direction or another. And we can also determine the likely consequences of different future scenarios.

The History Connection

The History of the Future

This chapter considers contemporary views of what the future will look like. Have past attempts to predict the future had any success? Looking back, examples can be found of both impressive prescience and errant forecasting.

Writing in 1795, Immanuel Kant predicted that eventually the horrors of war and the spread of liberal democracy would compel humankind to develop less violent ways of resolving their disputes. At the time he wrote, there were many wars and few democracies, and yet by the late twentieth century, many were claiming that Kant's perpetual peace had come into existence, at least among the advanced industrial democracies.

Norman Angell, a British journalist, published *Europe's Optical Illusion* (published in the United States as *The Great Illusion*) in 1909. Responding to the wave of economic integration and globalization then taking place, Angell argued that war among the powers of Europe would be so economically destructive that it was pointless, obsolete, and "a great illusion."[1] Only a few years later, World War I broke out. Looking back, many have seen Angell's book as demonstrating the folly of basing predictions on idealism, rather than on realism, although it could just as easily be argued that the economic disaster caused by World War I proved Angell's point. Angell won the Nobel Peace Prize in 1933.

In 1946, the world faced a genuine revolution: the advent of nuclear weapons. It was unclear how long the United States would retain its monopoly on the weapon and what implications nuclear weapons would have on diplomacy. In 1946, a year after the first nuclear weapons were used, a strategist at Yale named Bernard Brodie wrote *The Absolute Weapon: Atomic Power and World Order*. Brodie sought to deduce the effects of nuclear weapons on international politics, and he accurately predicted the shift of strategy from fighting to deterrence, writing, "Thus far the chief purpose of our military establishment has been to win wars. From now on its chief purpose must be to avert them. It can have almost no other useful purpose."[2] It took some time for leaders in the United States and the Soviet Union to accept this point of view, but by the 1960s, it was widely acknowledged to be so.

In recent years, which have seemed revolutionary to many people, there has been a new series of attempts to predict the future of international politics. Francis Fukuyama, in *The End of History and the Last Man*, asserted that ideological conflict had come to an end with the triumph of liberal democracy and capitalism.[3] Samuel Huntington, in *The Clash of Civilizations*, argued that conflicts between nation-states would be replaced with culturally driven conflicts between civilizations.[4] Thomas Friedman, in *The World Is Flat*, predicted a new world politics based on economic globalization.[5] Jared Diamond wrote *Collapse*, about the potential for ecological catastrophe to dominate the future.[6] They all make plausible arguments, but they cannot all be completely accurate at the same time.

Critical Thinking Questions

1. If successful as well as wildly erroneous predictions have been made in the past, how much confidence can we have that anyone can foresee the impact of the changes now taking place in world politics?
2. How might international relations theory help or hinder the pursuit of successful predictions?
3. Which is more useful, to predict accurately what will happen or to explore the implications of various potential scenarios?

[1] Norman Angell, *Europe's Optical Illusion* (London: Simpkin, Marshall, Hamilton, Kent, 1909).
[2] Bernard Brodie, *The Absolute Weapon: Atomic Power and World Order* (New York: Harcourt Brace & Company, 1946).
[3] Francis Fukuyama, *The End of History and the Last Man* (New York: The Free Press, 1992).
[4] Samuel P. Huntington, *The Clash of Civilizations and the Remaking of World Order* (New York: Simon and Schuster 1998).
[5] Thomas Friedman, *The World Is Flat: A Brief History of the Twenty-First Century* (New York: Farrar Straus and Giroux, 2005).
[6] Jared Diamond, *Collapse: How Societies Choose to Fail or Succeed* (New York: Viking, 2005).

Causes and Consequences of Potential Changes

Preceding chapters have identified several emerging sources of change in the international realm that might be viewed as revolutionary—as making the present (and future) fundamentally different from the recent past:

- The rise of transnational terrorism as a central problem in international politics
- The globalization of trade and finance
- The shift toward a system with only one military superpower
- The vast increase in global economic inequality
- The widespread acceptance of democracy as a form of government
- The erosion of the power of the sovereign state relative to societal, international, and transnational actors

The question is whether each of these developments is really fundamentally new, with no precedent, or whether it evolved from existing conditions. To the extent that developments are revolutionary, there will be relatively little experience to use in assessing them. On the other hand, to the extent that new developments are linked to phenomena already understood, there is some basis from which to generate expectations.

The prospect of fundamentally new developments in the workings of international politics can lead to both hope and fear about the future. For some, today's changes raise the hope that the traditional constraints on international politics will be weakened, allowing greater scope for collaboration, greater participation by disadvantaged actors, or greater opportunity to resolve conflicts without war. For example, the weakening of the sovereign state and growth of shared international norms about moral behavior provide, in some people's view, the prospect for greater international collaboration, strengthened global governance, and reduced conflict. For others, globalization seems likely to spread prosperity. Still others focus on the increased chances for global peace brought on by the spread of democracy.

From a different perspective, however, change seems to be a threat rather than a source of hope. As state governments have weakened in various parts of the world, terrorist organizations have found greater room to maneuver. A central aspect of the Westphalian system has been that only states could muster the military force to create serious security threats to the system. The potential emergence of nonstate actors wielding weapons of mass destruction has changed that basic assumption of traditional analyses. In this view, globalization is bringing threats along with hope: "The playing field is not being leveled only in ways that draw in and superempower a whole new group of innovators. It's being leveled in a way that draws in and superempowers a whole new group of angry, frustrated, and humiliated men and women."[2] In this view, the demise of the Westphalian system would be bad news. Of course, many do not accept the premise that the state is weakening.

If scholars, policy makers, and citizens are to deal adequately with the challenges of coming years, we must exercise judgment in assessing what is fundamentally new and what represents continuity with the past. By mistaking the old for something new, we overlook important lessons based on existing knowledge. By mistaking the new for something old, we become overconfident in thinking we understand a phenomenon that may have, in fact, substantially changed.

The six broad developments in international politics listed previously will shape the coming decades in essential ways. Each identifies an issue or debate already discussed in this book. This chapter aims the discussion squarely at the future and engages in a bit of speculation. The goal of this speculation is to explore the logical consequences of different assessments about how international politics works and how it is changing.

Terrorism: How Is It Changing International Politics?

As recently as the 1990s, international security was almost exclusively about the dangers states posed to other states. After September 2001, this narrow focus seems quaint. Terrorism has fundamentally changed the focus of most discussions of international politics. Today, when contemplating threats to international security, terrorist groups, rather than states, often come to mind first. Perhaps the most vexing question, at this point, is whether transnational terrorism is now a permanent part of international politics. Terrorism might be thought of not as a new kind of war, but as a new weapon. Just as the atomic bomb could not be "undiscovered," the tactics and techniques of terrorism are now widely known and can be used by any aggrieved group (or individual) with sufficient organizational skills.

What has changed less, perhaps, is how political actors deal with international security threats. Since 2001, military force has been at the center of efforts to combat terrorism. This has been especially true in the policy of the United States. The United States invaded Afghanistan and ousted the Taliban government in 2001 as a direct result of the September 11 events. Although the link between terrorism and the 2003 invasion of Iraq is more controversial, it is clear that the perceived threat from terrorism led to the widespread support for that attack among the American public.

Will terrorism empower a whole new group of actors, and if so, with what effects? By provoking the U.S. invasions of Afghanistan and Iraq, terrorism has had widespread economic, cultural, and political effects. But it remains unclear that it can be used to do more than disrupt. Thus, the power of terrorism—the ability to accomplish particular goals—remains in question. Although it may be very powerful at raising the costs of an occupying power, it is likely much less effective in pursuing other kinds of change.

Terrorism has blurred the lines between international and domestic security. The erosion of the distinction between international and domestic has long been recognized in economics, but until recently most analysts maintained the national/international distinction in security. That is now much harder to do. As a result, many countries have passed new antiterrorism laws that have altered long-held notions of civil liberties. Is it possible that the effort to combat terrorism will lead to a fundamental and long-term curtailment of civil liberties? Civil liberties have often been limited during wars in the past. But those wars were of finite duration. Even as democracy spreads, might it come to be defined differently than it traditionally has been?

Similarly, the **global war on terror** has led to the questioning of long-held notions about human rights and international law, questions of purpose. Governments widely admired for their commitment to human rights are now engaging in thinly veiled operations to torture suspected terrorists, and the vast majority of citizens are untroubled. What are the longer-term effects of democratic societies becoming comfortable with the idea of government-sponsored torture? We do not yet know. Similarly, as the war in Afghanistan has bogged down, the United States and its allies have relied increasingly on air attacks on suspected terrorist sites, often with civilian casualties. A heightened sense of insecurity can have far-reaching societal effects. The Cold War permeated every aspect of the societies involved, sometimes in ways that look incomprehensible in retrospect. The same could come to be true of the struggle against terrorism.

global war on terror
The George W. Bush administration's term for the U.S. response to the terrorists attacks of 9/11 on the World Trade Center.

POSSIBLE KEYS TO THE FUTURE

■ Do transnational terrorist groups obtain weapons of mass destruction? If so, terrorism will become much more important than it is even today. The sacrifices societies make to combat it would likely increase dramatically. The willingness of states to use military force to attack suspected supporters of terrorism would also likely increase. Torture may become more widely tolerated. On the other hand, if weapons of mass destruction,

AP Photo/U.S. Navy/Shane T. McCoy

Suspected Taliban and al-Qaida members are detained at Camp X-Ray, Guantanamo Bay, Cuba, January 2002.

and nuclear weapons in particular, come under more effective control, the level of anxiety may decrease.

■ Do scholars and politicians arrive at a more thorough understanding of the sources of terrorism? If so, do states have greater success in combating terrorism, limiting the number and scale of attacks? If it appears that terrorism is a "manageable" problem, then there could be a shift in focus to other problems.

Globalization

To many observers, the most important long-term change now underway is globalization. Globalization is undermining several of the fundamental assumptions of the international system. Enormous flows of trade and finance mean that more and more economic activity now occurs across, rather than within, states. The traditional state basis of economic policy making is thus undermined. The reduction in barriers to trade, and the ease with which goods, money, people, and information can now move, are making geographical distance less relevant than before.

In more and more economic sectors, the relevant market is global, rather than local, in scope. People with vastly different costs of living, wage expectations, and political rights are now competing economically. Moreover, as technology and education spread, societies that used to compete primarily through low wages are now competing by acquiring skill and knowledge. Rather than a "race to the bottom," some contend there is now a "race to the top," in which firms and workers in Asia compete with the traditional leaders in the most lucrative, knowledge-intensive parts of the economy, such as software development and biotechnology.

Is this really a revolution? The process of globalization is an old one. Disruption arising from changing trade and migration patterns has occurred for centuries. However, many argue that the world is not just experiencing more change, or more rapid change, but qualitatively new conditions, most notably a fundamental reduction in the ability of states to control economies.

If this is a revolution, is it inevitable? International trade began sharply expanding after World War II because the advanced industrial states, led by the United States, made free trade a high priority and sacrificed other goals to achieve it. If state policies led to an increase in trade, could state policies lead to a decrease? Historically, international trade has increased in some eras and decreased in others. Trade among the European states was very high before World War I but collapsed during that conflict. Similarly, global trade underwent a substantial reduction during the depression of the 1930s. It therefore seems possible that globalization could be slowed or even reversed. Antiglobalization activists hope to achieve just this, and free trade advocates argue that if trade is not expanded further, it may recede in the face of various challenges.

Others argue that states can no longer control globalization—that it has taken on a life of its own.[3] Because the global economy is so big relative to national economies, states now find it difficult, if not impossible, to control it. Moreover, some say, global competition will drive further globalization. Because free trade leads to greater efficiency and competitiveness, they argue, states that seek to "get ahead" of others will be pushed to accept free trade, even if they have reservations about its effects. Those that are less open to free trade will fall behind economically until they change course. Thus, economic competition is seen as driving globalization whether states like it or not.

Again, globalization has elements of both continuity and change: There is nothing new about increasing international trade, migration, and intercultural influence; these have been happening since the beginning of history. What is new is the difficulty that states are having in controlling this process and the influence it is having on domestic affairs. If it was once fairly easy to distinguish international from domestic economics, that is clearly no longer the case.

What are the likely consequences of these changes? How will states react if their control over international economic affairs continues to diminish? Might they try to regain control? What would be the consequences of such attempts? If state control of international economics continues to diminish, what might be the consequences for other state functions?

Most important, perhaps, if states do not govern the international economy, who will? What are the implications of tying national economies to a global economy that is essentially unregulated? In the economic crises of recent years, states have struggled to find joint solutions for shared problems. If government intervention is commonly used to avert crisis in domestic economies, how will crisis be avoided at the international level? In terms of effective governance, might the international economy be moving "back to the future?"[4]

Immigrants arriving at Ellis Island get their first glimpse of the Statue of Liberty, New York Harbor, early 20th century.

POSSIBLE KEYS TO THE FUTURE

- Will citizens rebel against globalization? Will citizen pressure force governments to reduce their free trade commitments?

- Will globalization alter the global distribution of wealth and power? If so, how will the losers respond? What will the winners do with their expanded power?

- Can an unregulated and unmanaged international economy avoid crisis? Will states be able to collaborate to prevent or at least manage crises? How bad can crises get if there is insufficient collaboration?

Unipolarity: Can It Persist? Does It Matter?

The mainstream media rarely use the term **polarity** in discussions of international politics, but the subject has, in fact, been a popular one in recent years. It has also absorbed a great deal of attention from government analysts and scholars. There is widespread agreement that with the collapse of the Soviet Union, the international system moved from bipolarity to unipolarity. The economic weakening of the United States and the rise of China now have many wondering whether the world is moving back to bipolarity or to multipolarity and what the consequences of such a shift might be.

polarity
The number of poles or centers of power within an international political system.

The distribution of power and the polarity of the international system were considered in Chapter 3. According to balance of power theory, unipolarity is highly unusual. Therefore, many have asked how this current unprecedented situation will change the dynamics of international politics. Hegemonic stability theory, in contrast, argues that having a single dominant power is beneficial for maintaining peace and prosperity in the international system.

According to hegemonic stability theory, it would only be natural for the United States to eventually lose its predominance, as hegemons have done throughout history. China's rise, both economically and militarily, seems inevitable.[5] From the perspective of realist hegemonic stability theory, the workings of the system do not depend on *who* the hegemon is. Does it matter, then, to anyone outside the United States or China, if China replaces the United States as hegemon?

One might fear such a development for two reasons. First, many are skeptical of the realist view that it does not matter who the hegemon is. Constructivists, feminists, and many liberals and economic structuralists argue that the *purpose* to which power is put is just as important as the distribution of power. From this perspective, Chinese hegemony might be very different—most assume much less benevolent— than U.S. hegemony. The fact that China is still an authoritarian country with a dismal record on human rights means that many people around the world would not welcome Chinese leadership. As much as they chafe under U.S. hegemony, Chinese hegemony might seem worse. Others might welcome a hegemon less inclined to intervene in other states' internal politics. This raises a question explored in Chapter 5: Does being a democracy or a nondemocracy substantially influence a state's foreign policy? More broadly, the prospect of Chinese hegemony raises the question of whether a state's foreign policy is more determined by internal or external factors. If China becomes a hegemon, will it simply behave as the previous states in the same position behaved?

hegemonic wars

Wars contested to determine who will be the dominant state in the system.

Second, and perhaps more disturbing, hegemonic stability theory finds that shifts in hegemony are often accompanied by **hegemonic wars**. This concept has been offered as the explanation for wars from the Peloponnesian War through World War I. According to this view, the United States would not give up its hegemony without a fight. Already, there are signs of tension. Prominent U.S. politicians and strategists have made maintaining U.S. preeminence a central political and military goal. China is viewed as the primary long-term threat to that preeminence. The 2006 "National Security Strategy of the United States of America" points to several areas of potential conflict between the two countries.[6] A Chinese general, speaking in July 2005, warned what would happen to the United States if it defended Taiwan in a war with China: "The Americans will have to be prepared that hundreds . . . of (their) cities will be destroyed by the Chinese."[7] Is a war between China and the United States imminent in coming decades? Not necessarily. But already both countries are viewing each other more seriously as military adversaries.

Russia's President Dmitri Medvedev, Brazil's President Luiz Inacio Lula da Silva, China's President Hu Jintao and India's Prime Minister Manmohan Singh, met at the BRIC summit in Brasilia, Brazil, April 2010.

Considerable uncertainty remains concerning these issues, however. One hegemon may not necessarily succumb to another. The current balance could remain unchanged. Or, one of two alternative possible realignments could emerge.

■ China rises, but the United States overcomes its recent problems and does not decline further. This might lead to bipolarity, such as that which characterized the period of the Cold War (1945–1989). Would bipolarity necessarily lead to the intense political conflict of that earlier period? Would China and the United States have the same level of ideological hostility as the Soviet Union and the United States? Could the mutual hostility be successfully managed without a great power war, as the Cold War was?

Figure 15.1 In GDP and military spending, China is closing the gap with the United States but is still well behind. Can we assume that present trends will continue?

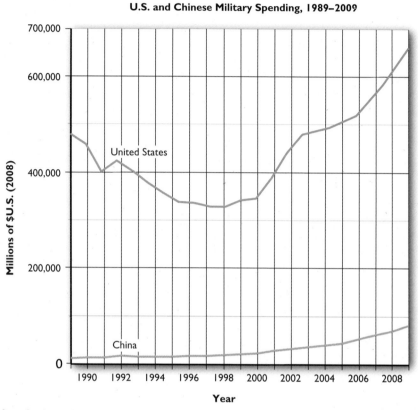

U.S. and Chinese Military Spending, 1989–2009

Source: Data from the Stockholm International Peace Research Institute (SIPRI), SIPRI Military Expenditure Database, http://milexdata.sipri.org. Used by permission.

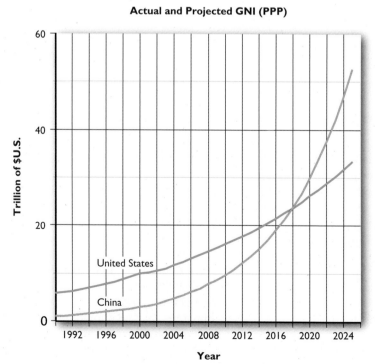

Actual and Projected GNI (PPP)

Source: World Bank for Actual. Projected figures based on average yearly growth from 1989–2006.

With only one modern case of bipolarity to learn from, it is difficult to predict what the consequences of bipolarity would be in the twenty-first century.

■ The United States continues to decline, but China does not rise far enough to dominate. Possible sources of U.S. decline are already visible: unsustainable trade and budget deficits, financial instability, military overcommitment, and a loss of support from other nations. Potential obstacles to China's rise are also visible: a weak banking system, potential political unrest, the aging of the population, and the need for further economic reforms. A U.S. decline that was not matched by a rise in Chinese influence would likely lead back toward multipolarity, which many states, such as France and Russia, have vocally promoted. Throughout history, the international system has had a great deal of historical experience with multipolarity. How would the substance of international politics change if the system shifted to multipolarity? Would collaboration become easier or harder? Would free trade be expanded or limited? Would the UN become more or less relevant?

The answers to these questions are not yet clear. What is clear is that, in terms of the polarity of the international system, we are in a time of transition and uncertainty. For realists, however, there is an underlying continuity: what happens in the international system will still be determined by the distribution of power among the largest states. Does that rule still hold? Did it ever? Those debates, covered in Chapters 3 and 4, remain salient.

POSSIBLE KEYS TO THE FUTURE

■ Can the United States solve the economic problems that threaten to undermine the basis of its global power? These problems include high budget deficits, low domestic savings, high trade deficits, the potential insolvency of the Social Security system, and heavy reliance on imported petroleum.

■ Can China continue to rise without further democratic reform? Can capitalist authoritarianism thrive or will further economic development require political liberalization?

■ Will the split of key allies such as France and Germany from the United States be temporary or permanent?

■ Will another country (India, Brazil, a united European Union, a resurgent Russia) rise to challenge the United States and/or China for top status?

Gaps in Wealth

There is nothing new about global poverty. However, the process of globalization means that people are now more than ever aware of the disparities in wealth. Moreover, the consequences of poverty, including immigration, disease, environmental degradation, and political instability, spread much further and more quickly today than in years past. Although there is certainly continuity in the existence of poverty and inequality, there is also significant change in recent years, in the emergence of shared purpose on global poverty. As the Millennium Development Goals indicate, many have come to view the alleviation of global poverty as a moral responsibility that cannot be ignored. Reduction of poverty has become a major priority for societies around the world. What will be the consequences if this goal is not achieved? What will be the consequences if it is?

Chapter 11 distinguished between two kinds of gaps in wealth: those between states and those within states. Disparities within states may be the more vexing problem in coming decades for two reasons. First, this problem afflicts wealthy states as well as poor ones. In the United States, for example, income inequality has been growing in recent

The Geography Connection

Projected Populations, 2050

The maps show countries according to their relative populations in 2000 and as projected for 2050.

Critical Thinking Questions

1. Which countries will have substantial changes?

2. How might changes in the relative populations of countries affect world politics?

3. What effects will overall population change have?

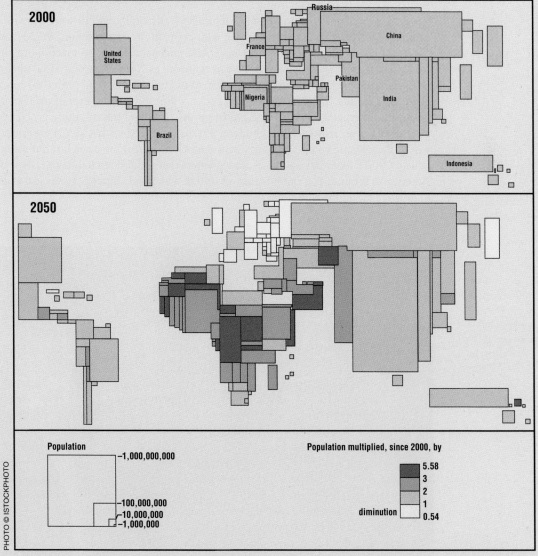

Source: These maps are published by the Institut de Recherche Pour le Développement (IRD) in a book entitled *Population et développement durable. Des cartes pour voir* (P. Peltre 2003, 32 p. + CD-ROM Mac/PC, 20 #). The data are taken from the UN population projections, 2000 edition. UN Population Division, *World Population Prospects: The 2000 Revision.*

decades for the first time in history. How well will democratic, market-based systems endure if ever-increasing inequality becomes a normal part of life? Because many social scientists find links between relative poverty and political instability, growing poverty might have a profound effect on other key goals, such as democratization.

What would be the consequences of a reduction in poverty? If workers in the poorest countries close the income gap, how will workers in the rich countries react? If creating jobs for the poorest people in the poorest countries means firing workers in a wealthier country, resentment is likely. To some extent, it may be that the poor in the poor countries will become more prosperous partly at the expense of the poor in the rich countries. Economic liberals, of course, strongly reject this view. Theory aside, it remains to be seen how globalization will affect gaps within countries.

Because money is linked to political power, it is worth asking how politics would change if the distribution of wealth and income changed significantly. At the state level, there are already some hints: poor countries tend to be weak internationally, whereas richer countries have more power. Not only do large markets create power, but wealth can be used to influence others or to buy weapons for that purpose. The increasing influence of China, as it moves from poverty to wealth, is an obvious example of the effect of reducing poverty on power politics.

What would international politics look like if per capita wealth were roughly even across the world? China and India, each with populations over a billion, would likely be the most powerful countries in the world. Asia in general would be much more powerful than it is now, and Africa would be as powerful as North America. How might this change politics? If gaps in wealth do shrink, would today's rich (and powerful) countries eventually see the trend as a threat? Experience has shown the sorts of problems that arise from international poverty. If global poverty is not addressed, those problems will get much worse. However, the modern international system has never experienced a world of economic equals. This may be too much of a dream to hope for. But economic equality would likely have political consequences that are difficult to imagine. How many Americans, for example, can imagine a world in which the United States is just a larger-than-average country and nothing more?

Hamas leader Ismail Haniyeh with security forces. Hamas, generally regarded in the West as a terrorist group, won democratic elections in an area controlled by the Palestinian Authority.

POSSIBLE KEYS TO THE FUTURE

- Does globalization help reduce disparities in wealth, as some predict, or increase them, as others predict? This question can address both inequality within countries, and inequality between countries. If the free market begins to reduce poverty, there may be less need for international aid. If globalization increases gaps in wealth, there may be a backlash on the part of the poor.

- Will strategies to assist the poor be politically sustainable in wealthy countries? So far, protection of agriculture in wealthy countries has been a higher priority than promoting development. Will this change? Will wealthy countries become willing to spend more on development aid? Or, with economic crisis dragging on and unemployment high, will wealthy states and their citizens focus more on their own problems?

The Spread of Democracy

The spread of democracy has been one of the major stories in international politics in the past two decades. Prior to 1989, democracy was still geographically limited, predominating only in western Europe and North America. With the collapse of communism in eastern Europe, the so-called **third wave of democratization** gained momentum. Democracy has become the norm in eastern Europe and in Latin America. It has made significant inroads as well in the former Soviet Union and in Africa, and in Asia. A significant change in the contemporary era is that there is no other model of government that is seriously viewed as a good alternative. In contrast to previous eras, there is no credible argument that authoritarian government is superior to democracy. In that sense, a key ideological battle has ended. In practice, of course, much authoritarianism remains, and democracy remains seriously flawed in many places.

> **third wave of democratization**
> The transitions of many autocratic states to democratic forms of government that began in 1974.

How will the spread of democracy affect international affairs? Chapter 5 examined in detail the argument that democracies are more peaceful than other states and found that the argument is only partly true. Democracies go to war as often as other states, but they rarely go to war with each other. As a result, a **zone of peace**, composed of states that will almost certainly not go to war with one another, appears to be expanding worldwide. On the surface, this would seem to be a momentous development, especially since the zone has expanded most rapidly in Europe, where history's most violent wars have been fought.

> **zone of peace**
> A group of states that tend not to war with each other because they are democratic.

Paradoxically, this trend may itself be a source of new conflicts. If democracies do not fight each other, much is at stake in promoting new democracies. It might be worthwhile to use force to overthrow an authoritarian government in order to establish a democracy that would safeguard peace in the future. This logic was used by the U.S. government to help justify its invasion of Iraq. Is it possible that the main source of international conflict in coming years will be a battle to spread democracy? Or will the U.S. experience in Afghanistan and Iraq deter states from pursuing such a strategy in the future?

There is also some uncertainty about whether the "democratic peace" that has existed until now will survive the spread of democracy into other states. Some research has indicated that new democracies are especially vulnerable to becoming aggressive.[8] Moreover, it appears that authoritarian leaders in several states are adopting much more moderate international policies than their populations would choose under democracy. In Pakistan, for example, it often appeared that its government was straining to resist a more combative policy toward India, which would have been popular. Many also fear that in places like Pakistan and Saudi Arabia, support for terrorism would be more likely to increase under democratic regimes than under authoritarianism.

The implications of democratization are especially interesting when considered together with the rise of China. The consequences of China's rise will likely be very

The Culture Connection

Islam and Modernization

Many of the most important questions about the future concern the role of Islam. Many non-Muslims see Islam as a potential danger, whether as an impediment to democracy, as a source of extremist political sentiments, or as a challenge to the rights of women. Many in the Islamic world see Islam, Muslims, and Muslim countries as constantly under attack by Western states. Some believe that Islam and its followers are likely to come into conflict with others; others see conflict as not necessarily inevitable. In 2006, the Pew Global Attitudes Project surveyed people in various countries about tensions between Islam and contemporary society, the results of which are shown in the graph.

Attitudes toward the compatibility between devotion to Islam and living in a modern society vary considerably. In France, Muslims and non-Muslims alike see little basis for conflict. In Germany, non-Muslims overwhelmingly see conflict, whereas Muslims do not. Overall, Muslims seem to see less conflict than do non-Muslims. As constructivists stress, predictions of conflict can sometimes be self-fulfilling. If people believe conflict will happen, they prepare for it, and in doing so, make it more likely.

Is there a conflict between being a devout Muslim and living in a modern society?

	No	Yes
United States	42	40
Germany	26	70
Spain	36	58
Russia	30	56
Great Britain	35	54
France	74	26
British Muslims	49	47
German Muslims	57	36
French Muslims	72	28
Spanish Muslims	71	25
Pakistan	17	47
Indonesia	52	43
Jordan	63	34
Turkey	60	29
Egypt	70	28
Nigerian Christians	34	41
Nigerian Muslims	64	33

Source: Pew Global Attitudes Project, "The Great Divide: How Westerners and Muslims View Each Other," June 22, 2006, at http://pewglobal.org/reports/display.php?ReportD=253. Reprinted by permission of The Pew Research Center.

Critical Thinking Questions

1. Why do non-Muslims in some countries see considerable tension between Islam and modernity, whereas Muslims see less?
2. What might explain the variation in attitudes within the Muslim world (for example, between Muslims in Pakistan and those in Egypt)?
3. Based on the data presented here, can you assess the likelihood of conflict between Islamic societies and others, or suggest how such conflict might be averted?

PHOTO © ISTOCKPHOTO

different depending on what kind of government evolves there. For realists, of course, this question is irrelevant: the rise of China will lead to rivalry with the United States regardless of what form of government China has. For advocates of the democratic peace theory, it does not matter how powerful China gets, as long as it becomes more democratic. We will simply have to wait and see which of these factors proves more influential.

An even more speculative topic is whether democracy will survive as the only legitimate form of government. In some parts of the world, extremists are gaining adherents to the argument that theocracy (rule by religious leaders) should be established. Other countries, including Russia and China, combine rigged elections, economic liberalism, and authoritarian control. To the extent that this "illiberal" democracy succeeds, will it come to challenge the liberal democratic model? And what will happen if efforts to build democracy in Afghanistan, Iraq, and other societies fail, as now seems to be certain? Will the world return to the notion—which was once considered conventional wisdom—that some societies simply are not yet ready for democracy and would be better off ruled by autocrats?

POSSIBLE KEYS TO THE FUTURE

- Will democracy spread in the Muslim world? If so, will the result be peace or instability? It is easy to imagine that a more democratic Pakistan, Egypt, or Saudi Arabia would take a more bellicose attitude toward neighbors than that held by their current authoritarian regimes.

- How will countries of the West view the tradeoff between maintaining democracy and combating terrorism? Where states with authoritarian rulers are viewed as allies in the struggle against terrorism, will Western states endanger the relationship by promoting democracy?

- Will peace between democracies survive the spread of democracy to less stable regions of the world?

The Demise of the Sovereign State?

Perhaps the most far-reaching changes in the field of international relations involve the most basic actor in the analysis: the sovereign state. Today many actors besides the state affect international politics. The state remains central but its role is clearly changing. The question for the future is whether the state will continue to play essentially the same role it has for the past 500 years, or whether some fundamental change is taking place. Many people have asserted that the state is losing its importance. Others find it as important as ever, even as its roles change.

Globalization means that many more of the problems states face extend beyond their geographical boundaries. Chapter 10 demonstrated that trade and finance now occur on a scale that cannot be governed by any single state government. State control is segmented territorially, but markets are not. Chapter 14 showed that migration, environmental problems, health problems, and crime are also beyond the control of any single state. Threats to states often come from actors besides states and from groups that easily cross state borders. To deal with these issues, states must work together in ways they have not before. This can mean collaborating more extensively with others or surrendering some decision-making power to international organizations. These problems can also prompt states to turn over some missions to nongovernmental organizations. These decisions convince many that states are losing their power to other actors.

Moreover, states seem to be losing power to actors from "below" as well. Domestic interest groups and nongovernmental organizations are becoming more and more involved in foreign policy issues. As business becomes more international, firms have a greater interest in foreign policy. Also, as more states become democratic, citizens may be gaining greater control over foreign policy. Finally, the adoption of market economics around the world means that a much greater share of economic activity is now out of the hands of states and is controlled instead by private entities.

However, some analysts see the state getting more powerful, not less. They point to the fact that states take advantage of advances in communications and information technology just as other actors do. Many key functions of state control, including surveillance, information storage and retrieval, and tax enforcement, are made easier by

The Policy Connection

The Use of Scenarios to Prepare for the Future

Governments, international governmental organizations, nongovernmental organizations, and firms all seek to prepare for the future by predicting what challenges they will need to respond to. However, because the future is uncertain, they are reluctant to base policies on a single prediction about the future that might turn out wrong. Instead, many planners generate a range of scenarios, each of which is based on different assumptions about how key variables will change. Generating scenarios still requires theory and predictions. Theory tells the scenario developers which variables to include in the scenarios, and predictions link different values for those variables to specific challenges. Several examples illustrate this approach.

The Intergovernmental Panel on Climate Change developed forty scenarios for future global warming based on assumptions suggested by different teams of scientists about what factors would most influence the process. The factors included levels of economic activity, technological advances, economic growth, and whether efforts to combat global warming occurred globally or locally. The panel grouped its scenarios into four general categories.[1] These were then used by other actors to generate more specific scenarios for specific regions. In the United States, for example, the Union of Concerned

Scientists (UCS) produced a Web site showing how far "south" states in the northeast United States would "move," in climatic terms, under different emissions scenarios. The UCS Web site shows that under a high-emissions scenario, New York City would have a climate similar to that of Charleston, South Carolina, by the end of this century, whereas with significant cuts in emissions, New York would "move" only as far "south" as Virginia Beach.[2]

The WHO created its scenarios for the future by looking at the recent past, at challenges that have arisen in recent years, focusing on three crises in particular. Looking at the anthrax scare in the United States in 2001, the WHO report pointed to the growing threat of biological attacks and the difficulty that existing public health systems have in facing them. The 2009 H1N1 virus spurred similar fears. The illicit dumping of toxic chemicals in Cote d'Ivoire in 2006 highlighted the health hazards of moving chemicals around the world for disposal. As thousands were sickened, the public health system was overwhelmed, and the country, already on the verge of civil war, was left with an environmental disaster it was unprepared to handle. The WHO expects these kinds of problems to define the coming years.[3]

technology. For example, immediately following the London Underground bombings in July 2005, British authorities circulated pictures of the bombers taken by closed-circuit television cameras posted throughout the system. Within days, several accomplices had been arrested. Similarly, although cell phones make it easy for criminals or terrorists to communicate, cell phone conversations are also easily intercepted by security agencies.

Analysts also point out that although states have surrendered decision-making authority over many issues in recent years, they can always take it back. Also, international collaboration should not always be seen as a weakening of states. In some cases, it appears to strengthen states at the expense of the society. For example, it has been argued that one effect of the EU is to empower European states to create new rules at

The U.S. government frequently uses scenario generation to combine different intelligence assessments without having to determine which is correct. The National Intelligence Council sponsored a major effort known as the "2020 Project" to assess what the international situation might look like in 2020. Based on what were considered "relative certainties" (globalization will continue, U.S. dominance will endure), the report then analyzed the perceived "key uncertainties" (whether gaps in wealth will narrow, whether other states will challenge U.S. dominance). The project takes for granted that China and India will become more important powers, but expresses uncertainty about how they will exercise that power. The report develops four fictional scenarios based on dominant trends: "Davos Man" (continued economic globalization), "Pax Americana" (continued U.S. dominance), "New Caliphate" (global challenge from Islam), and "Cycle of Fear" (concern about nuclear proliferation leading to reduction of civil liberties).[4]

The purpose of writing scenarios is not to predict the future accurately. Rather, it is to make perceived trends explicit and to consider their outcomes. Creating scenarios is perhaps more useful for highlighting the extent of uncertainty, and hence the range of possible future policy problems, than for providing targeted policy advice.

Critical Thinking Questions

1. What are the strengths and weakness of using scenarios to inform policy debates?
2. How might the creation of different scenarios complicate efforts to deal with emerging issues such as global warming?
3. In what areas is it most important to consider alternative scenarios?

[1] Intergovernmental Panel on Climate Change, *Special Report on Emissions Scenarios, 2000,* at http://www.ipcc.ch/ipccreports/sres/emission/index.htm
[2] Union of Concerned Scientists, "Impacts: Dramatically Changing Climates," at http://www.climatechoices.org/ne/impacts_ne/climates.html
[3] World Health Organization, *The World Health Report 2007—A Safer Future: Global Public Health Security in the 21st Century,* Chapter 3, "New Health Threats in the 21st Century," at http://www.who.int/whr/2007/07_chap3_en.pdf
[4] "Mapping the Global Future: Report of the National Intelligence Council's 2020 Project Base on Consultations with Experts Around the World," at http://www.dni.gov/nic/NIC_globaltrend2020.html#contents

the European level that they could never have gotten approved at the domestic level. Moreover, terrorism may strengthen the state by providing justification for surveillance and law enforcement measures that otherwise would not be tolerated.

What would be the consequences of a vastly weakened state? In places where the state has disintegrated, such as in Afghanistan and Somalia, the consequences are apparent: anarchy, violence, and sometimes starvation. Some fear that the weakening of states will shift the balance of power even further away from the poor and weak and toward powerful corporations. Others argue that the shift of economic control from states to unregulated markets was a major cause of the global financial crisis. As a result, support for state regulation of the economy has made a comeback. For those who believe that the state is already the tool of greedy corporations, its weakening is seen as opening up room for influence by citizen groups and nongovernmental organizations. Those who support a radical free market perspective also welcome the weakening of the state because they see it as an entity that creates regulations that needlessly interfere with freedom and productivity. Whatever evolution the state undergoes, it will most likely be slow, and it will vary across states. It may be that in some places, the state will weaken or collapse, whereas in others, it will strengthen. It might also be that even within individual states, some aspects of "stateness" might be augmented while others are eroded. For example, state surveillance of citizens might increase even as state involvement in certain parts of the economy decreases. These changes will undoubtedly influence who makes foreign policy and how states deal with the challenges they face.

However, one important element of continuity in the nature of the state should be stressed. The state, as a set of political institutions, has *never* been static. It has been constantly evolving since its emergence centuries ago. The idea that the state has some essential character that is now being shattered is based on a drastically oversimplified view of history. Therefore, the question to ask is which specific areas of state power are being augmented or eroded, and what happened in similar circumstances in the past.

POSSIBLE KEYS TO THE FUTURE

- Do states seek to "take back" the authority they have granted to international institutions? If so, do the states that do this suffer any disadvantages, or do others follow suit?

- Will the EU, the avatar of international integration, continue to broaden and deepen, or will one or both of those processes end (or even be reversed)? Will the EU model be adopted elsewhere?

- Will corporations and nongovernmental organizations continue to expand their influence, or can states insulate themselves from these actors? If the state weakens, will relatively more power accrue to citizens and nongovernmental organizations or to corporations?

- Can some other entity fulfill the functions of the Westphalian state? Or is it the case that if the state did not exist, it would have to be invented?

Summary

Will the world of 2050 look fundamentally different than the world of 2000? Undoubtedly—change has always been a normal part of international politics. By comparison, the changes in the first half of the twenty-first century may well be less revolutionary than those that characterized the first half of the twentieth century. At the beginning of the twentieth century, Britain dominated world politics, most of the world's population lived under colonial rule, and military technology had advanced as far as the horse and the machine gun. By 1950, the United States and the Soviet Union were engaged in a global standoff, colonialism was ending, and military technology consisted of missiles and long-range aircraft carrying nuclear weapons. Perhaps the difference between that era and this one is that the changes in place at the end of World War II were clearly visible to observers, and their implications seemed clear. As this chapter has indicated, the essential qualities of the twenty-first-century international system are subject to considerable uncertainty.

The sources of power in world politics are changing. In some respects, we will see the same roots of power that have existed for millennia—the military power to destroy, the economic power to create and to buy, and the cultural power to persuade. However, as more common problems emerge, another definition of power—the ability to collaborate—may become more salient. Moreover, if the sources of power are familiar, their distribution is not. Military power is spreading to nonstate actors such as terrorists and for-profit military contractors. Economic power is spreading away from states to billions of consumers and to global corporations. The power to collaborate is strongest, perhaps, in transnational advocacy networks, international organizations, and global corporations.

Similarly, purpose is evolving. Human rights as an important goal has moved from the periphery to the center of global debate. Disagreement about the role of the global community in individual states' human rights practices is a central issue in world politics today. How that dispute is resolved, and whether it is resolved, will be crucial. Environmental collaboration, especially in the area of climate change, is a relatively new issue on the agenda, and one that so far has not attained the high priority that many think it should. Whether states decide to collaborate on global warming will have an important effect on international politics in coming decades, both directly (in the degree of collaboration we see) and indirectly (in the widespread consequences of severe climate change).

This chapter has asked how international politics will evolve during the lifetimes of today's students. The answer is not predetermined. The evolution of the system will depend on the policies of states, organizations, and individuals. People, and the choices they make, will determine whether there will be more or less conflict, more or less poverty, more or less environmental degradation, and so on.

Throughout this book, nearly every question was found to have more than one good answer. Students, citizens, scholars, and leaders, therefore, have a task that is doubly difficult. They need not only to understand how the world works now but also to assess how much of what is true today is likely to be true tomorrow. It might seem like a hopeless task, but it is not. And it cannot be avoided. Policies can be based either on ignorance or on well-informed thinking—but they will have to be made one way or the other.

This book has aimed to inform the reader about some of the implications of different possible choices. Although it is not possible for any individual to shape the global situation as much as he or she might like, anybody—especially any citizen in a democratic society—can attempt to engage the problems discussed in this book. As citizens, volunteers, advocates, and leaders, we all can make choices to try to influence outcomes.

Endnotes

1. Robert Gilpin, "The Rich Tradition of Political Realism," in Robert O. Keohane, ed., *Neorealism and Its Critics* (New York: Columbia, 1987), pp. 308–309.

2. Thomas Friedman, *The World Is Flat: A Brief History of the Twenty-First Century* (New York: Farrar, Straus and Giroux, 2005), p. 8.

3. This argument has long been made by economic structuralists, beginning with Karl Marx. It is now made also by liberals, such as Thomas Friedman in *The World Is Flat*. The connection between Marx and the liberals on this matter is emphasized by John Gray; see "The World Is Round," *New York Review of Books*, August 11, 2005, p. 14.

4. Paul Krugman, *The Return of Depression Era Economics* (New York: W. W. Norton, 1999).

5. See Clyde Prestowitz, *Three Billion New Capitalists* (New York: Basic Books, 2005).

6. "The National Security Strategy of the United States of America," March 2006, at http://www.whitehouse.gov/nsc/nss/2006/nss2006.pdf, pp. 41–42.

7. "Sizing Up the Dragon," *The Economist*, July 23, 2005, p. 28.

8. Edward D. Mansfield and Jack Snyder, "Democratization and the Danger of War," *International Security*, Vol. 20, No. 1 (1995): 5–38.

Glossary

A

anarchy A condition in which there is no central ruler.

apartheid A system of official discrimination in South Africa in which the African majority was controlled by the white minority.

appeasement A strategy of avoiding war by acceding to the demands of rival powers.

asylum Status granted to persons who cannot return to their home country without a well-founded fear of persecution.

asymmetric conflict A conflict between actors with very different strengths, vulnerabilities, and tactics.

attribution The process whereby individuals attribute the behavior of others to one cause or another. Attribution can create unmotivated bias in decision makers.

audience costs The costs in loss of public support paid by leaders of democracies when they renege on a commitment.

B

balance of power A system in which no single actor is dominant; also, the distribution of power in such a system, which is not necessarily equal.

balance of trade Exports minus imports (measured in dollar value); a net accounting of how much in the way of goods and services is exported from a country compared to how much is imported.

Baltic states Refers collectively to Estonia, Latvia, and Lithuania, which lie on the Baltic Sea in northern Europe, just to the west of Russia.

basic human needs approach A development strategy focusing on the short-term alleviation of poverty as a prerequisite for further progress.

Berlin Wall Erected in 1961 to prevent citizens of communist East Germany from emigrating to West Germany, the Berlin Wall became a symbol both of the division of Europe and of the lack of freedom in the communist-controlled areas.

blended enforcement A model for implementing international law whereby the authority for penalties comes from a recognized international organization and is clearly recognized by treaty, but the enforcement itself is carried out by the aggrieved state or by others acting on its behalf.

bolstering The tendency of decision makers facing a difficult decision to increase their certainty once a decision is made.

bounded rationality A theory that decision makers try to be rational but face several inherent limits on their ability to do so.

bourgeoisie In Marxist jargon, the owners of capital.

Bretton Woods system The system that guided economic arrangements among the advanced industrial states in the post–World War II era. It included the GATT, the fixed exchange rate system, the IMF, and the World Bank. Bretton Woods was a resort in New Hampshire where the negotiations took place.

Bush doctrine A set of principles formed during the administration of U.S. President George W. Bush asserting the necessity of waging preventive war against potential aggressors possessing weapons of mass destruction.

C

capital Resources that can be used to produce further wealth.

city-state A state that centers on a single city, rather than a larger territory or a nation.

classes In economic structuralist theory, groups of people at different places in the economic hierarchy.

CNN effect The ability of the media to draw attention to an issue and force policy makers to address it.

coercion The use of a threat to change another actor's behavior.

cognitive dissonance theory A theory that holds that individuals tend to construct internally consistent views of the world and that psychological discomfort, or "cognitive dissonance," results when some new piece of information does not fit with an individual's existing beliefs.

Cold War A conflict between the United States and the Soviet Union during which no actual war broke out between the two superpowers. The Cold War dominated world politics from 1946 until 1991.

collective action problem A situation in which a group of actors has a common interest but cannot collaborate to achieve it.

collective security A doctrine nominally adopted by states after World War I that specified that when one state committed aggression, all other states would join together to attack it.

colonialism A type of imperialism in which the dominating state takes direct control of a territory.

competitive devaluation Competition between states to have the lowest-valued currency in order to boost domestic employment.

Concert of Europe An agreement reached at the Congress of Vienna in 1815 in which major European powers pledged to cooperate to maintain peace and stability.

conditionality The requirement that an aid recipient agree to a set of conditions that the donor believes will help promote development in the country.

Convention on Anti-Personnel Mines Also known as the Ottawa Convention. Agreement signed in 1997 and officially known as the "Convention on the Prohibition of the Use, Stockpiling, Production and Transfer of Anti-Personnel Mines and on Their Destruction."

Convention on Biological Diversity An international agreement aimed at conserving biodiversity, signed in 1992.

costs of adjustment Financial burdens that are imposed on a country as a result of changes in the international economic system.

Council of the European Union The body within the European Union that represents the governments of the member states and, along with the European Parliament, acts on legislation.

credibility The ability and will to carry out a threat.

crisis stability The likelihood that a crisis, once it begins, will have dynamics that tend to lead toward war.

Cuban missile crisis A crisis that arose in 1962 when the United States discovered Soviet missile bases in Cuba. The crisis nearly precipitated a nuclear war between the United States and the USSR.

D

debt crisis A crisis that occurs when a debtor country is no longer willing or able to make the scheduled payments on its debts.

declining terms of trade Conditions of international trade that force countries that primarily produce raw materials to export ever-increasing amounts of raw materials to earn the revenue needed to buy the manufactured goods they require.

decolonization The disbanding of nearly all colonial relationships between 1945 and 1975.

defenestration The ejection of someone from a window. The Second Defenestration of Prague in 1618 helped spark the Thirty Years War.

democracy The doctrine that the entire population of a nation, rather than a small elite or a single monarch, should control government.

demographic change Change in the distribution of a population across categories such as age, gender, and wealth.

depression and recession Decreases in overall economic output as measured by gross domestic product (GDP). The average recession lasts roughly a year and leads to an economic contraction of less than 10 percent of GDP. Longer, deeper slumps are called depressions. *See also* Great Depression.

deterrence A policy aimed at convincing a potential opponent not to attack by raising the costs of attack so that they are higher than the perceived benefits.

developmental state A state that takes an active role in economic development by fostering the accumulation of capital to invest in particular industries, and building the legal and bureaucratic infrastructure necessary for capitalism to thrive.

E

East and West Germany From the end of World War II in 1945 until 1990, there were two German states, the Federal Republic of Germany, or "West Germany," allied with the United States, and the German Democratic Republic, or "East Germany," allied with the Soviet Union. A year after the decision to bring down the Berlin Wall in 1989, Germany was reunited.

Economic and Social Council (ECOSOC) The UN council that oversees work on economic and social issues.

economic determinism The assumption that political behavior is driven by economic motivations and that political outcomes are determined by economic power.

economic imperialism Efforts by states to improve their economic situation through military expansion, usually to gain better control of resources and markets.

electromagnetic pulse weapons Weapons that use a powerful burst of energy to damage electronic circuits.

embedded liberalism The normative consensus that guided international economic arrangements after World War II. It combined a commitment to expansion of free trade with acceptance that states would have to intervene domestically to protect themselves from some of the effects of free trade.

European Commission The body within the European Union that carries out many executive branch functions.

exchange rate The price of one currency in terms of another.

expected utility theory A variant of the rational action model. The theory asserts that leaders evaluate policies by combining their estimation of the utility of potential outcomes with the likelihood that different outcomes will result from the policy in question.

export-led growth A development strategy that focuses on exporting to the global market.

F

fair trade A narrower approach to free trade that advocates retaliation against states that are perceived as "cheating" on free trade.

fascism A doctrine in which the rights or goals of individuals are subservient to those of the nation, which is viewed as a single organism.

feudal system A political system in which individuals within a society have obligations based on class (king, nobility, peasantry) and no single ruler has absolute authority over a given territory.

Financial Action Task Force An international task force that establishes recommended policies for states to adopt to combat money laundering and monitors new trends in money-laundering practices.

First-mover advantages Advantages enjoyed by firms or countries that first enter a new industry, including advantages gained from economies of scale, network effects, and access to investment funds.

fiscal policy The use of a government budget deficit or surplus to stimulate or slow economic growth. *See also* monetary policy.

fog of war A phrase coined by Prussian strategist Karl von Clausewitz to characterize the difficulties in controlling war once it starts.

force The use of violence or the threat of violence to achieve a political goal.

foreign policy analysis Analysis that attempts to understand states' behavior in terms of actors and processes at the domestic (state and sub-state) level.

foreign policy Policy (actions or statements intended to change behavior or outcomes) aimed at problems outside of the policy-making state's borders.

fundamental attribution bias The tendency to believe that if an adversary makes a concession, they were forced to, but if they make an unwelcome move, they did so freely due to bad intentions; and the tendency to have the opposite bias about ourselves.

G

G-8 Shorthand for the "Group of Eight" advanced industrial countries. It was originally formed as the "Group of Seven" in the 1970s. After the collapse of the Soviet Union, Russia was added, and the G-7 became the G-8.

Gates Foundation A private charity that has become a significant player in the field of international health.

gender A set of ideas that society has attached to the biological categories of male and female.

Gender Development Index A measure, published by the UN, of the economic equality of men and women.

gendered ideas Ideas that take "masculine" perspectives as "normal" and neglect "feminine" perspectives.

General Agreement on Tariffs and Trade (GATT) The main trade provision of the Bretton Woods system.

Gini coefficient A statistic developed by Italian statistician Corrado Gini to compare the incomes of the top and bottom fractions of a society.

global war on terror The George W. Bush administration's term for the U.S. response to the terrorists attacks of 9/11 on the World Trade Center.

globalization A process in which international trade increases relative to domestic trade; in which the time it takes for goods, people, information, and money to flow across borders and the cost of moving them are decreasing; and in which the world is increasingly defined by single markets rather than by many separate markets.

gold standard A system in which each currency represents a specific weight of gold. This facilitates stability but is highly inflexible.

good governance Governance that is transparent, controlled by the rule of law, accountable, and effective.

Great Depression The global depression that lasted from 1929 until World War II, during which the economies of the United States and Europe declined by as much as 25 percent. *See also* depression and recession.

great powers The UN Charter ascribed this status to Britain, China, France, the Soviet Union (Russia), and the United States.

greenhouse gases Gases in the atmosphere that trap heat in the earth's atmosphere. As they increase in concentration, the atmospheric temperature rises causing climate change.

gross domestic product (GDP) The total annual income of a country. Per capita GDP refers to the average annual income of the people in a country.

guerilla warfare Warfare in which tactics of harassment and ambush are favored over direct battle.

H

H1N1 A new strain of flu virus (also known as the "swine flu") that spread rapidly in 2009, causing many deaths and fear of a global flu pandemic such as that which killed millions in 1918.

hegemonic wars Wars contested to determine who will be the dominant state in the system.

Hezbollah A military and political force in Lebanon. It operates as a parliamentary party in Lebanese politics and is also a transnational terrorist movement, conducting attacks in Israel as well as in Lebanon.

hierarchy of goals A clear ranking of goals.

Human Development Index (HDI) A measure of poverty, produced by the United Nations Development Programme, that supplements per capita GDP (at purchasing power parity) with measures of life expectancy, literacy rates, and average years of schooling.

human rights An array of "inalienable" individual rights, including civil liberties and political rights. Some also include economic rights and cultural rights as well.

I

identity In constructivist theory, actors' and others' perceptions of who they are and what their roles are.

imperialism A situation in which one country controls another country or territory.

import substitution The strategy of producing domestically those goods that a country has been importing.

institutions Sets of agreed-upon norms, rules, and practices.

insurgency An effort to overthrow the political power in a territory through violence.

interests In constructivist theory, socially constructed goals that groups of people together define for society.

Intergovernmental Panel on Climate Change (IPCC) An international body that assesses scientific research on climate change for decision makers.

International Court of Justice Also known as the "World Court," the body that adjudicates disputes that arise over treaty obligations.

International Criminal Court (ICC) International court for the prosecution of war crimes and other heinous crimes.

international governmental organizations (IGOs) Organizations whose membership consists of three or more nation-states.

international law The set of rules and obligations that states recognize as binding on each other.

international norms Shared ethical principles and expectations about how actors should and will behave in the international arena; and social identities, indicating which actors are considered legitimate.

international organizations (IOs) Organizations formed by governments to help them pursue collaborative activity; a type of nonstate actor. More specifically know as international governmental organizations (IGOs).

international political economy The two-way relationship between international politics and international economics.

international regimes Shared understandings about how states will behave on a particular issue.

Interpol Informal name for the International Criminal Police Organization, an international agency that serves as an information clearinghouse for police agencies around the world.

isolationism The doctrine that U.S. interests were best served by playing as little a role as possible in world affairs.

J

just war theory The theory of the circumstances in which it is ethical to go to war and the kinds of practices that are ethical in the prosecution of war.

K

Kyoto Protocol An international agreement that was signed in 1997 and went into effect in 2005 that aims to reduce greenhouse gas emissions in order to prevent global climate change.

L

law of war A doctrine concerning when it is permissible to go to war and what means of conducting war are permissible (and not permissible).

League of Nations An international organization established after World War I that aimed to maintain world peace.

lender of last resort An actor that is committed to continuing to lend money to stressed economic actors when market institutions would refuse to do so.

lesson of Munich The lesson learned from British attempts to appease Hitler at the 1938 Munich peace conference, namely, that costly wars can be avoided by confronting hostile leaders promptly.

Levée en Masse A draft, initiated by Napoleon following the French Revolution, that allowed France to vastly expand its army.

level of analysis The unit (individual, state, or system) that a theory focuses on in its general explanation.

liberal approach Political approach focusing on the ability of actors to govern themselves without surrendering their liberty. International liberal theory focuses on the ability of states to cooperate to solve problems.

liberalization Reducing barriers to trade (increasing free trade).

M

mainstream effect The tendency for the public to follow political leaders and the media when those actors have consensus on an issue.

media The different means through which news and entertainment are conveyed.

mercantilism A trading doctrine that focused on state power in a conflictual world. It was based on the idea that the overall amount of wealth in the world was fixed by the amount of precious metals. Therefore, international trade was a zero-sum game, in which one state could gain only at the expense of another.

military industrial complex A term made popular by President Dwight D. Eisenhower that refers to a group consisting of a nation's armed forces, weapon suppliers and manufacturers, and elements within the civil service involved in defense efforts.

ministries The main institutions of the executive branch of government. In the United States, these institutions are called "departments."

mixed-motive game A situation in which actors have incentives that partially overlap with and partially contradict those of their partners. The prisoner's dilemma is one representation of a mixed-motive game.

monetary crisis A crisis that emerges when rapid sales of a particular currency cause its value to collapse.

monetary policy Raising or lowering central bank interest rates to stimulate or slow economic growth. *See also* fiscal policy.

money laundering The process of making illegally gained money appear to have been earned legally.

Montreal Protocol An international agreement, signed in 1987, that commits the signatories to reducing the production and use of gases that deplete the ozone layer.

motivated bias Bias that occurs as a result of some psychological need, such as the need for all of one's beliefs to be consistent with each other ("cognitive consistency") or the need to believe that a good solution to a problem is available.

multinational corporation A company with operations in more than one country; a type of nonstate actor; also called transnational corporation (TNC).

multiplier effect An economic effect whereby an increase in spending (for example, of funds provided to a country by a donor) produces an increase in national income and consumption greater than the initial amount spent. When aid flows out of a country, the benefit of aid may accrue to the donor rather than to the recipient.

Munich Crisis A crisis in 1938 precipitated by Germany's demand that it be allowed to occupy part of Czechoslovakia. War was averted when Britain and France agreed to Germany's demands.

mutual assured destruction (MAD) A situation in which each side in a conflict possesses enough armaments to destroy the other even after suffering a surprise attack.

N

national interest A foreign policy goal that is objectively valuable for the overall well-being of the state. The concept is important in realist theory and in foreign policy discussions, but some dispute that there is any single national interest.

national self-determination The doctrine that each state should consist of a single nation and each distinct nation should have its own state.

nationalism The doctrine that recognizes the nation as the primary unit of political allegiance.

natural selection The tendency for traits that increase the likelihood of individual survival to become more common in future generations of a species.

neomercantilism The belief that states should seek a trade surplus. This focus on the balance of trade makes trade a zero-sum game, as it was for traditional mercantilists.

nondiscrimination A principle guiding tariff policy that requires a country to apply equal tariffs on all of its trading partners; also referred to as the "most favored nation" principle.

nongovernmental organizations (NGOs) A broad category of diverse organizations, including groups similar to domestic interest groups but with transnational concerns and organizational structures, and groups that focus not on influencing governments, but on conducting activities in different countries.

nonstate actor A political actor that is not a state, such as an advocacy group, charity, corporation, or terrorist group.

normative theory A theory that aims to establish the proper goals of political action.

norms Shared ethical principles and expectations about how actors should and will behave in the international arena, and social identities, indicating which actors are to be considered legitimate.

O

Oil-for-food program Part of the pre-2003 UN sanctions against Iraq, whereby Iraq was allowed to sell oil to purchase humanitarian supplies.

one state, one vote A voting system in which each state has one vote, regardless of its size, population, or other characteristics. Used in the UN General Assembly and many other international organizations.

operationalizing Translating a theoretical concept into attributes that can be measured.

ozone layer A layer of ozone in the upper atmosphere that reduces transmission of ultraviolet radiation. Ozone is a form of oxygen with three atoms per molecule (O_3) rather than the typical two (O_2). At ground level, ozone is a respiratory irritant.

P

paradigm A theoretical approach that includes one or more theories that share similar philosophical assumptions.

peace enforcement The use of military force to compel an actor to cease or avoid some activity viewed as a threat to peace and security.

peacekeeping The introduction of foreign troops or observers into a region, in order to increase confidence that states will refrain from the use of force.

Peloponnesian War A war between Athens and Sparta from 431 BCE to 404 BCE. Thucydides's study of this war has been influential on later thinking about international relations.

Pentagon Papers A series of secret Defense Department reports on the origins of the Vietnam War that raised serious questions about U.S. involvement in the war.

per capita GDP The average income of the people in a country.

Plan Colombia A U.S. program aimed at reducing the supply of cocaine from Colombia by providing substantial financial assistance, training, and equipment (including military aircraft) to assist the Colombian government in fighting the drug trade there.

pluralism The presence of a number of competing actors or ideas.

polarity The number of poles or centers of power within an international political system.

politics of compromise The tendency among democracies to resolve disputes through bargaining.

portfolio investment Investments made by purchasing stocks rather than physical assets.

poverty The lack of sufficient income, which is often accompanied by insufficient nutrition, housing, and other necessities. Poverty can be defined in absolute terms as "income poverty" or in relative terms, with a focus on the range of choices open to individuals.

Powell Doctrine A set of criteria guiding military engagement, including establishing clear goals and using overwhelming force.

power The ability of an actor to achieve its goals. Exactly what constitutes power and how to measure it are vexing problems in international relations.

power transition theory A theory that postulates that war occurs when one state becomes powerful enough to challenge the dominant state and reorder the hierarchy of power within the international system.

precision-guided munitions Weapons with guidance systems and maneuvering capability that allow them to strike individual targets with a high degree of accuracy. Also known as "smart bombs."

prisoner's dilemma A game theory scenario in which noncooperation is the rational strategy, but leads to both players being worse off than if they had cooperated.

problem of late development The economic challenge faced by developing states because of economic competition from more advanced states.

proletariat In Marxist jargon, the working class.

prospect theory A theory that contends that how individuals weigh options is heavily influenced by whether a particular outcome is seen as a gain or a loss.

protectionism Measures taken by states to limit their imports.

proximate cause An event that immediately precedes an outcome and therefore provides the most direct explanation of it.

purchasing power parity (PPP) A measure used to calculate GDP that takes into account that goods cost different amounts in different countries.

purpose The goals that actors pursue, including the notion of "national interest." Whether actors see themselves as having shared or competing goals is a central concern.

Q

quota A numerical limit on the amount of a certain item that can be imported.

R

radiological weapons Weapons that use conventional explosives to distribute radioactive material, which has long-lasting poisonous effects. Also known as "dirty bombs."

rally around the flag effect The increase in popular support often gained by leaders of a country in times of war.

rational action model *See* rational choice theory.

rational choice theory A theory that bases explanations of decisions on the assumption that decision makers have clear goals, calculate the costs of various courses of action, and pick the policy that will best serve their goals.

reciprocity In international trading, an arrangement whereby two states agree to have the same tariffs on each other's goods. In game theory, the strategy of matching the other player's previous move.

recognition The acceptance by the international community of a state's sovereignty over its territory.

refugee A person who leaves his or her country because of a well-founded fear of persecution or because of violent conflict.

relative gains A problem with free trade arising from the fact that if one state can gain more wealth from a given transaction, it can potentially increase its military power vis-à-vis the other state.

reparations Payments that Germany was forced to make as a result of starting World War I. Reparations caused serious economic problems in Germany and were deeply resented by the German people.

S

SALT-I and SALT-II Agreements between the United States and the Soviet Union to limit the building of weapons.

SARS Severe acute respiratory syndrome (SARS) is caused by a virus and spread by person-to-person contact. An outbreak in 2003 led to about 8000 infections and 774 deaths worldwide before it was contained.

secretary general The head of the UN bureaucracy and the personification and public face of the UN.

Security Council The fifteen-member council within the UN in charge of dealing with threats to international security.

security dilemma The difficult choice faced by states in anarchy between arming, which risks provoking a response from others, and not arming, which risks remaining vulnerable.

self-enforcement Enforcement of law by individual states through diplomatic pressure, economic sanctions, or force.

sovereignty The principle that states have complete authority over their own territory.

spillover A process by which small, incremental steps toward cooperation create the impetus for even further integration.

standard operating procedures Procedures that bureaucracies adopt to deal efficiently with a large number of similar tasks.

state An entity defined by a specific territory within which a single government has authority; or the government and political system of a country.

state socialism A strategy for development in which the state rather than the market allocates resources.

state strength The degree to which a state is independent of societal influences.

state structure The form and function of state institutions.

status quo bias The tendency of leaders to take considerable risks to avoid a perceived loss.

structural adjustment A strategy adopted by the World Bank in the 1980s and 1990s aimed at strengthening the financial basis of a country's economy.

subsidies Direct payments to producers to help them remain profitable.

surplus value In economic structuralist theory, the difference between the value of raw materials and the value of the final product; presumably this is the value added by laborers.

T

tariff A tax on imports, used to protect domestic producers from foreign competition.

terrorism Use or threat of violence by nongovernmental actors to change government policies by creating fear of further violence.

theory A generalized explanation of a set of comparable phenomena.

theory of comparative advantage A theory developed by the English economist David Ricardo to show logically how and why trade is beneficial to both partners.

third wave of democratization The transitions of many autocratic states to democratic forms of government that begin in 1974.

Third World A term coined during the Cold War to describe those states that were neither in the group of advanced industrial states nor in the communist bloc; typically it refers to the many poor states in the southern hemisphere. The term is generally considered synonymous with "underdeveloped."

tied aid Aid that must be spent on goods or services from the donor country.

tragedy of the commons A version of the collective action problem in which a shared resource is overconsumed.

transgovernmental relations Direct interaction between bureaucracies in different countries without going through their heads of state.

transnational actors Actors whose activities cut across state boundaries.

transnational advocacy networks (TANs) Groups that organize across national boundaries to pursue some political, social, or cultural goal.

transnational corporation (TNC) A corporation with operations in more than one country; also called multinational corporation (MNC).

transnational relations Interaction between societal actors across nation-states.

Treaty of Rome The 1957 treaty that established the European Economic Community, the predecessor of the European Union.

Treaty of Versailles The agreement ending World War I that set up the League of Nations.

Treaty on the Non-Proliferation of Nuclear Weapons An agreement that states without nuclear weapons will refrain from getting them and that they will allow detailed inspections in order that other states can be certain that they are fulfilling their obligations.

Triple Alliance A pre–World War I agreement by Germany, Austria-Hungary, and Italy that if one state were attacked, the others would come to its aid.

Triple Entente   A pre–World War I agreement by Britain, France, and Russia that if one state were attacked, the others would come to its aid.

U

UN Millennium Development Goals   A set of goals and accompanying targets set by the UN aimed at addressing poverty and inequality.

unmotivated bias   Bias that occurs as a result of the simplifications inherent in the process of perceiving an ambiguous world.

U.S. Federal Reserve System   The central bank of the United States. The "Fed," as it is known, controls interest rates and the supply of currency to promote economic growth while preventing inflation.

W

war crimes   A set of transgressions established by the fourth Geneva Convention, including willful killing, torture or inhumane treatment, willfully causing great suffering or serious injury to body or health, unlawful deportation or transfer, or unlawful confinement of a protected person.

War Powers Resolution   A 1973 law that limits the U.S. president's ability to go to war without permission of Congress.

Washington consensus   A development strategy favored by leading donor countries and organizations that advocates open economies, free trade, and minimal interference by the state in the economy.

Westphalian system   The system of sovereign states that was recognized by the Treaty of Westphalia in 1648.

World Health Organization   The UN's specialized agency that focuses on health issues.

WTO Dispute Settlement Body   The enforcement body of the World Trade Organization, which can empower aggrieved states to impose retaliatory tariffs against countries that violate the organization's rules.

Z

zero-sum game   A situation in which any gains for one side are offset by losses for the other.

zone of peace   A group of states that tend not to go to war with each other because they are democratic.

References

Abbott, Kenneth, and Duncan Snidal. "Why States Act Through Formal International Organizations." *Journal of Conflict Resolution* 42, no. 1 (1998): 3–32.

Abdelal, Rawi. *National Purpose in the World Economy: Post-Soviet States in Comparative Perspective.* Ithaca, NY: Cornell University Press, 2001.

Adler, Emanuel, and Beverly Crawford, eds. *Progress in Post-War International Relations.* New York: Columbia University Press, 1991.

Aldrich, John, John L. Sullivan, and Eugene Borgida. "Foreign Affairs and Issue Voting: Do Presidential Candidates 'Waltz Before a Blind Audience'?" *American Political Science Review* 83 (1989): 123–142.

Allen, Tim. "Introduction: Why Don't HIV/AIDS Policies Work?" *Journal of International Development* 16, no. 8 (2004): 1123–1127.

Allison, Graham T. *Essence of Decision: Explaining the Cuban Missile Crisis.* Boston: Little Brown, 1971.

Anderson, Benjamin. *Imagined Communities: Reflections on the Origins and Spread of Nationalism*, rev. ed. London: Verso, 1991.

Arendt, Hannah. *On Violence.* New York: Harcourt Brace and World, 1969.

Aron, Raymond. "Biological and Psychological Roots." In *War*, edited by Lawrence Freedman. Oxford: Oxford University Press, 1994.

Axelrod, Robert. *The Evolution of Cooperation.* New York: Basic Books, 1984.

Ayoob, Mohammed. "Third World Perspectives on Humanitarian Intervention and International Administration." *Global Governance* 10, no. 1 (2004): 99–119.

Baglione, Lisa. *Writing a Research Paper in Political Science.* Belmont, CA: Wadsworth, 2006.

Barbieri, Katherine. *The Liberal Illusion: Does Trade Promote Peace?* Ann Arbor: University of Michigan Press, 2003.

Barkin, Samuel. "Realist Constructivism." *International Studies Review* 5 (September 2003): 328–342.

Barnett, Michael, and Martha Finnemore. *Rules for the World: International Organizations in World Politics.* Ithaca, NY: Cornell University Press, 2004.

Barnett, Michael, Hunjoon Kim, Madalene O'Donnell, and Laura Sitea. "Peacebuilding: What Is In a Name?" *Global Governance* 13, no. 1 (2007): 35–58.

Beasley, Ryan K., Juliet Kaarbo, Jeffrey S. Lantis, and Michael T. Snarr, eds. *Foreign Policy in Comparative Perspective.* Washington, DC: Congressional Quarterly, 2002.

Beitz, Charles R. "Human Rights as a Common Concern." *American Political Science Review* 95 (June 2001): 269–282.

Bell, David A. *The First Total War: Napoleon's Europe and the Birth of Warfare as We Know It.* New York: Houghton Mifflin, 2007.

Beneria, Lourdes. *Gender, Development, and Globalization: Economics as if All People Mattered.* New York: Routledge, 2003.

Bennett, Andrew, and Alexander George. *Case Studies and Theory Development in the Social Sciences.* Cambridge, MA: MIT Press, 2005.

Berejikian, Jeffrey D. "A Cognitive Theory of Deterrence." *Journal of Peace Research* 39 (2002): 165–183.

Best, Jacqueline. *The Limits of Transparency: Ambiguity and the History of International Finance.* Ithaca, NY: Cornell University Press, 2005.

Betts, Richard K. "Systems of Peace or Causes of War: Collective Security, Arms Control, and the New Europe." *International Security* 17, no. 1 (Summer 1992): 5–43.

Bhagwati, Jagdish. *In Defense of Globalization.* New York: Oxford University Press, 2004.

Blainey, Geoffrey. *The Causes of War*, 3rd ed. New York: The Free Press, 1988.

Blanton, Shannon Lindsey. "Foreign Policy in Transition? Human Rights, Democracy, and US Arms Exports." *International Studies Quarterly* 49 (December 2005): 647–667.

Blustein, Paul. *And the Money Kept Rolling In (and Out): Wall Street, the IMF, and the Bankrupting of Argentina.* New York: Public Affairs, 2005.

Boesen, Nils. *Enhancing State Capacity—What Works, What Doesn't, and Why?* Washington, DC: World Bank, 2004.

Bond, Michael. "The Making of a Suicide Bomber." *New Scientist*, May 15, 2004.

Bueno de Mesquita, Bruce. "Risk, Power Distributions, and the Likelihood of War." *International Studies Quarterly* 25, no. 4 (December 1981): 541–568.

Bueno de Mesquita, Bruce, James D. Morrow, Randolph M. Siverson, and Alastair Smith. "An Institutional Explanation of the Democratic Peace." *American Political Science Review* 93, no. 4 (December 1999): 791–807.

Bull, Hedley. *The Anarchical Society: A Study of Order in World Politics.* New York: Columbia University Press, 1977.

Calderisi, Robert. *The Trouble with Africa: Why Foreign Aid Isn't Working.* New York: Palgrave Macmillan, 2006.

Caporaso, James A., and Sidney Tarrow, "Polanyi in Brussels: Supranational Institutions and the Transnational Embedding of Markets," *International Organization* 63 (Fall 2009): 593–620.

Carlsnaes, Walter, Thomas Risse, and Beth Simmons, eds. *Handbook of International Relations.* London: Sage, 2002.

Carr, Edward Hallett. *The Twenty Years' Crisis, 1919–1939.* New York: Harper & Row, 1964 [1939].

Cashman, Greg, and Leonard C. Washington. *An Introduction to the Causes of War: Patterns of Interstate Conflict from World War I to Iraq.* Lanham, MD: Rowman and Littlefield, 2007.

Castaneda, Jorge G. "Latin America's Left Turn." *Foreign Affairs* 85, no. 3 (May–June 2006).

Chollett, Derek H., and James M. Goldgeier. "The Scholarship of Decision Making: Do We Know How We Decide?" In *Foreign Policy Decision-Making (Revisited)*, edited by Richard C. Snyder. New York: Palgrave MacMillan, 2002.

Christopher, Paul. *The Ethics of War and Peace*, 3rd ed. Upper Saddle River, NJ: Pearson Prentice Hall, 2004.

Clausewitz, Carl von. *On War.* Edited and translated by Michael Howard and Peter Paret. Princeton, NJ: Princeton University Press, 1984.

Cohen, Benjamin. *The Geography of Money.* Ithaca, NY: Cornell University Press, 1998.

Cohen, Eliot, Conrad Crane, Jan Horvath, and John Nagl. "Principles, Imperatives, and Paradoxes of Counterinsurgency." *Military Review* (March–April 2006): 49–53.

Cohn, Theodore. *Global Political Economy: Theory and Practice*, 2nd ed. New York: Longman, 2002.

Collier, Paul. *The Bottom Billion: Why the Poorest Countries Are Failing and What Can Be Done About It.* New York: Oxford University Press, 2007.

Collier, Paul, and David Dollar. *Development Effectiveness: What Have We Learnt?* Washington, DC: World Bank, 2001.

Collier, Paul, and Anke Hoeffler. "Resource Rents, Governance, and Conflict." *Journal of Conflict Resolution* 49, no. 4 (2005): 625–633.

Cooley, John K. "The War over Water." *Foreign Policy* 54 (Spring 1984): 3–25.

Craig, Gordon A., and Alexander L. George. *Force and Statecraft: Diplomatic Problems of Our Time*, 4th ed. Oxford: Oxford University Press, 1995.

Cronin, Audrey Kurth. "Behind the Curve: Globalization and International Terrorism." *International Security* 27, no. 3 (Winter 2002/2003): 32.

Das, Gurcharan. "The India Model." *Foreign Affairs* 85, no. 4 (July/August 2006).

de Beauvoir, Simone. *The Second Sex*. Translated and edited by H. M. Parshley. New York: Vintage, 1989 [1949].

Deffyes, Kenneth S. *Hubbert's Peak: The Impending World Oil Shortage*. Princeton, NJ: Princeton University Press, 2001.

Diamond, Jared. *Guns, Germs, and Steel: The Fates of Human Societies*. New York: W.W. Norton, 1999.

Diamond, Jared. "What's Your Consumption Factor?" *The New York Times*, January 2, 2008.

Dinan, Desmond. *Europe Recast: A History of European Union*. Boulder, CO: Lynne Rienner, 2004.

Donnelly, Jack. *Universal Human Rights in Theory and Practice*. Ithaca, NY: Cornell University Press, 2003.

Doyle, Michael W. *Empires*. Ithaca, NY: Cornell University Press, 1986.

Doyle, Michael W. "Kant, Liberal Legacies, and Foreign Affairs." *Philosophy and Public Affairs* 12, nos. 3 and 4 (Summer and Fall 1983): 205–235, 323–353.

Drezner, Daniel, ed. *Locating the Proper Authorities: The Interaction of Domestic and International Institutions*. Ann Arbor: University of Michigan Press, 2002.

Duffield, John. "What Are International Institutions?" *International Studies Review* 9 (2007): 1–22.

Easterly, William. "The Ideology of Development." *Foreign Policy* (July/August 2007): 31.

Easterly, William. *The White Man's Burden: Why the West's Efforts to Aid the Rest Have Done So Much Ill and So Little Good*. New York: Penguin, 2006.

Edelstein, David M. "Occupational Hazards: Why Military Occupations Succeed or Fail." *International Security* 29, no. 1 (Summer 2004): 49–91.

Eichengreen, Barry. *Globalizing Capital: A History of the International Monetary System*. Princeton, NJ: Princeton University Press, 1996.

Ellerman, David. *Helping People Help Themselves: From the World Bank to an Alternative Philosophy of Development Assistance*. Ann Arbor: University of Michigan Press, 2006.

Elshtain, Jean Bethke. "The Problem with Peace." *Millennium: Journal of International Studies* 17, no. 3 (1988): 441–449.

Elster, Jon. *Nuts and Bolts for the Social Sciences*. Cambridge: Cambridge University Press, 1990.

Enloe, Cynthia. *Bananas, Beaches and Bases: Making Feminist Sense of International Politics*. Berkeley: University of California Press, 1990.

Epstein, Helen. "God and the Fight Against AIDS." *New York Review of Books*, April 28, 2005.

Escobar, Arturo. *Encountering Development: The Making and Unmaking of the Third World*. Princeton, NJ: Princeton University Press, 1995.

Fabbro, David. "Peaceful Societies: An Introduction." *Journal of Peace Research* 15, no. 1 (1978): 67–83.

Falkenrath, Richard. "Analytical Models and Policy Prescriptions: Understanding Recent Innovation in U.S. Counterterrorism." *Studies in Conflict and Terrorism* 24, no. 3 (2001).

Fearon, James D. "Domestic Political Audiences and the Escalation of International Disputes." *American Political Science Review* 88, no. 3 (September 1994): 577–592.

Fearon, James D. "Rationalist Explanations of War." *International Organization* 49, no. 3 (Summer 1995): 379–414.

Festinger, Leon. *A Theory of Cognitive Dissonance*. Stanford: Stanford University Press, 1957.

Foyle, Douglas. "Foreign Policy Analysis and Globalization: Public Opinion, World Opinion, and the Individual." *International Studies Review* 5, no. 2 (June 2003): 165.

Freud, Sigmund. "Why War?" In *International War: An Anthology*, 2nd ed., edited by Melvin Small and J. David Singer. Chicago: The Dorsey Press, 1989.

Frieden, Jeffrey A. *Global Capitalism: Its Fall and Rise in the Twentieth Century.* New York: W.W. Norton, 2006.

Friedman, Thomas L. *The World Is Flat: A Brief History of the 21st Century.* New York: Farrar, Straus, and Giroux, 2005.

Gaddis, John Lewis. *The Cold War: A New History.* New York: Penguin, 2005.

Garrett, Geoffrey. "Global Markets and National Politics: Collision Course or Virtuous Circle?" *International Organization* 52, no. 4 (Autumn 1998): 787–824.

Geller, Daniel S. "The Stability of the Military Balance and War among Great Power Rivals." In *The Dynamics of Enduring Rivalries*, edited by Paul F. Diehl. Urbana: University of Illinois Press, 1998.

George, Alexander L. *Presidential Decisionmaking in Foreign Policy: The Effective Use of Information and Advice.* Boulder, CO: Westview Press, 1980.

Gerschenkron, Alexander. *Economic Backwardness in Historical Perspective.* Cambridge, MA: Belknap Press, 1962.

Gilbert, Martin. *The Second World War: A Complete History.* New York: Henry Holt, 1989.

Gilboa, Eytan. "Global Television News and Foreign Policy: Debating the CNN Effect." *International Studies Perspectives* (August 1995): 325–341.

Gilpin, Robert. *The Political Economy of International Relations.* Princeton, NJ: Princeton University Press, 1986.

Gilpin, Robert. *U.S. Power and the Multinational Corporation: The Political Economy of Direct Foreign Investment.* New York: Basic Books, 1975.

Glennon, Michael J. "Why the Security Council Failed," *Foreign Affairs* 82, no. 3 (2003): 16–34.

Goldstein, Judith L., Douglas Rivers, and Michael Tomz. "Institutions in International Relations: Understanding the Effects of GATT and the WTO on World Trade." *International Organization* 61 (2007): 37–67.

Grant, Rebecca, and Kathleen Newland, eds. *Gender and International Relations.* Bloomington: Indiana University Press, 1990.

Gray, John. "The World Is Round." *New York Review of Books,* August 11, 2005.

Grieco, Joseph. "Anarchy and the Limits of Cooperation: A Realist Critique of the Newest Liberal Institutionalism." *International Organization* 42 (Summer 1988): 485–508.

Gruber, Lloyd. *Ruling the World: Power Politics and the Rise of Supranational Institutions.* Princeton, NJ: Princeton University Press, 2000.

Hardin, Garrett. "The Tragedy of the Commons." *Science* 162 (1968): 1243–1248.

Harding, Sandra. *The Science Question in Feminism.* Ithaca, NY: Cornell University Press, 1986.

Hattori, Tomohisa. "Reconceptualizing Foreign Aid." *Review of International Political Economy* 8, no. 4 (2004): 633–660.

Hawkins, Darren, David Lake, Daniel Nielson, and Michael J. Tierney, eds. *Delegation and Agency in International Organizations.* Cambridge: Cambridge University Press, 2006.

Helleiner, Eric. "Economic Liberalism and Its Critics: The Past as Prologue?" *Review of International Political Economy* 10, no. 4 (2003): 685–696.

Henkin, Louis. *How Nations Behave*, 2nd ed. New York: Columbia University Press, 1979.

Hinsley, F. H. *Power and the Pursuit of Peace: Theory and Practice in the History of Relations between States.* Cambridge: Cambridge University Press, 1963.

Hirschman, Albert O. "Beyond Asymmetry: Critical Notes on Myself as a Young Man and on Some Other Old Friends." *International Organization* 32, no. 1 (Winter 1978).

Hobson, John. *Imperialism: A Study.* Ann Arbor: University of Michigan Press, 1965 [1902].

Hollis, Martin, and Steve Smith. *Explaining and Understanding International Politics*. Oxford: Clarendon, 1991.

Holsti, K. J. *Peace and War: Armed Conflicts and International Order, 1648–1989*. Cambridge: Cambridge University Press, 1991.

Holsti, Ole R. "Public Opinion and Foreign Policy: Challenges to the Almond-Lippman Consensus." *International Studies Quarterly* 36, no. 4 (December 1992): 439–466.

Homer-Dixon, Thomas F. "On the Threshold: Environmental Changes as the Cause of Acute Conflict." *International Security* 16, no. 2 (1991): 76–116.

Horowitz, Michael C. *The Diffusion of Military Power: Causes and Consequences for International Politics* (Princeton, NJ: Princeton University Press, 2010).

Howard, Michael, George Andreopoulos, and Mark R. Shulman, eds. *The Laws of War: Constraints on Warfare in the Western World*. New Haven, CT: Yale University Press, 1997.

Hudson, Rex A. *The Sociology and Psychology of Terrorism: Who Becomes a Terrorist and Why?* Washington, DC: Library of Congress, 1999.

Huntington, Samuel. *The Clash of Civilizations and the Remaking of World Order*. New York: Simon and Schuster, 1996.

Hurd, Ian. *After Anarchy: Legitimacy and Power in the United Nations Security Council*. Princeton, NJ: Princeton University Press, 2007.

Ignatieff, Michael. "Getting Iraq Wrong." *The New York Times Magazine*, August 5, 2007.

Iida, Keisuke. "Is WTO Dispute Settlement Effective?" *Global Governance* 10, no. 2 (2004): 207–236.

Janis, Irving L. *Groupthink: Psychological Studies of Policy Issues and Fiascoes*. Boston: Houghton Mifflin, 1982.

Janis, Irving L., and Leon Mann. *Decisionmaking: A Psychological Study of Conflict, Choice, and Commitment*. New York: The Free Press, 1977.

Jervis, Robert. *Perception and Misperception in International Politics*. Princeton, NJ: Princeton University Press, 1976.

Jervis, Robert. "The Political Effects of Nuclear Weapons: A Comment." *International Security* 13, no. 2 (Fall 1988): 80–90.

Johnson, Loch K., and James J. Wirtz. *Strategic Intelligence: Windows into a Secret World*. Los Angeles: Roxbury, 2004.

Johnston, Alistair Ian. "Is China a Status Quo Power?" *International Security* 27, no. 4 (Spring 2003): 5–56.

Joll, James. *The Origins of the First World War*, 2nd ed. Essex: Longman, 1992.

Jones, Kent. *Who's Afraid of the WTO?* New York: Oxford University Press, 2004.

Kaarbo, Juliet, and Ryan K. Beasley. "A Practical Guide to the Comparative Case Study Method in Political Psychology." *Political Psychology* 20 (June 1999): 369–391.

Kagan, Donald. *The Peloponnesian War*. New York: Penguin, 2003.

Kahneman, Daniel, and Amos Tversky. "Prospect Theory: An Analysis of Decision Under Risk." *Econometrica* 47 (1979): 263–291.

Kaplan, Robert. "The Coming Anarchy." *The Atlantic Monthly* (February 1994).

Kaplan, Robert. *Warrior Politics: Why Leadership Demands a Pagan Ethos*. New York: Random House, 2002.

Kara, Siddharth. *Sex Trafficking: Inside the Business of Modern Slavery* (New York: Columbia University Press, 2009).

Karns, Margaret P., and Karen A. Mingst. *International Organizations: The Politics and Processes of Global Governance*. Boulder, CO: Lynne Rienner, 2005.

Katzenstein, Peter J., ed. *Between Power and Plenty: Foreign Economic Policies of Advanced Industrial States*. Madison: University of Wisconsin Press, 1978.

Katzenstein, Peter J., ed. *The Culture of National Security: Norms and Identity in World Politics*. Ithaca, NY: Cornell University Press, 1996.

Katzenstein, Peter J. "Same War—Different Views: Germany, Japan, and Counterterrorism." *International Organization* 57 (Fall 2003): 734.

Katzenstein, Peter J. *A World of Regions: Asia and Europe in the American Imperium*. Ithaca, NY: Cornell University Press, 2005.

Katzenstein, Peter J., and Robert O. Keohane, eds. *Anti-Americanisms in World Politics*. Ithaca, NY: Cornell University Press, 2007.

Katzenstein, Peter J., Robert O. Keohane, and Stephen Krasner. "International Organization and the Study of World Politics." *International Organization* 52, no. 4 (1998): 645–685.

Kaufmann, Chaim. "See No Evil: Why America Doesn't Stop Genocide." *Foreign Affairs* 81, no. 4 (July–August 2002): 142–149.

Keck, Margaret E., and Kathryn Sikkink. *Activists Beyond Borders: Advocacy Networks in International Politics*. Ithaca, NY: Cornell University Press, 1998.

Kennedy, Paul. *The Parliament of Man: The Past, Present, and Future of the United Nations*. New York: Random House, 2006.

Kennedy, Paul. *The Rise and Decline of Great Powers*. New York: Random House, 1987.

Kennedy, Robert F. *Thirteen Days: A Memoir of the Cuban Missile Crisis*. New York: Norton, 1971.

Keohane, Robert O. *After Hegemony: Collaboration and Discord in the World Political Economy*. Princeton, NJ: Princeton University Press, 1984.

Keohane, Robert O. "International Relations Theory: Contributions of a Feminist Standpoint." *Millennium: Journal of International Studies* 18, no. 2 (1989): 245–253.

Keohane, Robert O., ed. *Neorealism and Its Critics*. New York: Columbia University Press, 1987.

Keohane, Robert O., and Joseph S. Nye. *Power and Interdependence*, 2nd ed. New York: HarperCollins, 1989.

Khagram, Sanjeev, Kathryn Sikkink, and James V. Riker, eds. *Restructuring World Politics: Transnational Social Movements, Networks, and Norms*. Minneapolis: University of Minnesota Press, 2002.

Khong, Yuen Foong. *Analogies at War: Korea, Munich, Dien Bien Phu, and the Vietnam Decisions of 1965*. Princeton, NJ: Princeton University Press, 1982.

Kindleberger, Charles. *The World in Depression 1929–1939*. Berkeley: University of California Press, 1973.

Kissinger, Henry. *A World Restored*. London: Wiedenfeld and Nicholson, 1957.

Klare, Michael T. *Resource Wars: The New Landscape of Global Conflict*. New York: Metropolitan Books, 2001.

Klotz, Audie. *Norms in International Relations: The Struggle against Apartheid*. Ithaca, NY: Cornell University Press, 1995.

Klotz, Audie, and Cecelia Lynch. *Strategies for Research in Constructivist International Relations*. Armonk, NY: ME Sharpe, 2007.

Krasner, Stephen D. "Are Democracies Important? (Or Allison Wonderland)." *Foreign Policy* 7 (Summer 1972): 159–172.

Krasner, Stephen D. "Global Communications and National Power: Life on the Pareto Frontier." *World Politics* 43, no. 3 (April 1991): 336–366.

Krasner, Stephen D., ed. *International Regimes*. Ithaca, NY: Cornell University Press, 1983.

Kristof, Nicholas. "Wretched of the Earth." *New York Review of Books*, May 31, 2007.

Krugman, Paul R. *The Return of Depression Era Economics*. New York: W.W. Norton, 1999.

Krugman, Paul R., and Maurice Obstfeld. *International Economics: Theory and Policy*, 3rd ed. New York: HarperCollins, 1994.

Lacher, Hannes. "Making Sense of the International System: The Promises and Pitfalls of Contemporary Marxist Theories of International Relations." In *Historical Materialism and Globalization*, edited by Mark Rupert and Hazel Smith. London: Routledge, 2002.

Lairson, Thomas D., and David Skidmore. *International Political Economy*, 3rd ed. Belmont, CA: Thomson Wadsworth, 2003.

Lake, David A. "Powerful Pacifists: Democratic States and War." *American Political Science Review* 86, no. 1 (March 1992): 24–37.

Laqueur, Walter. *No End to War: Terrorism in the Twenty-First Century*. New York: Continuum, 2004.

Larson, Deborah Welch. *Origins of Containment: A Psychological Approach*. Princeton, NJ: Princeton University Press, 1985.

Lebow, Richard Ned. *Between Peace and War: The Nature of International Crisis*. Baltimore, MD: Johns Hopkins University Press, 1981.

Lenin, V. I. *Imperialism: The Highest Stage of Capitalism*. New York: International Publishers, 1939 [1916].

Levy, Jack S. "The Causes of War: A Review of Theories and Evidence." In *Behavior, Society, and Nuclear War*, Vol. I, edited by Philip Tetlock, Jo L. Husbands, Robert Jervis, Paul C. Stern, and Charles Tilly. New York: Oxford University Press, 1989.

Levy, Jack S. "An Introduction to Prospect Theory." *Political Psychology* 13 (1992): 171–186.

Levy, Jack S. "Preventive War and Democratic Politics." *International Studies Quarterly* 52, no. 1 (March 2008): 1–24.

Levy, Jack S. "Prospect Theory, Rational Choice, and International Relations." *International Studies Quarterly* 41, no. 1 (March 1997): 87–112.

Lezhnev, Sasha. *Crafting Peace: Strategies to Deal with Warlords in Collapsing States*. Lexington, MA: Lexington Books, 2006.

Lipset, Seymour Martin. "The President, the Polls, and Vietnam." *Transactions* 3 (1966).

Lorenz, Konrad. *On Aggression*. New York: Harcourt Brace Jovanovich, 1966.

Lowenthal, Mark M. *Intelligence: From Secrets to Policy*. Washington, DC: CQ Press, 2006.

Magdoff, Harry. *The Age of Imperialism*. New York: Monthly Review Press, 1969.

Mansfield, Edward D., and Helen V. Milner. "The New Wave of Regionalism." *International Organization* 53 (1999): 589–627.

Mansfield, Edward D., Helen Milner, and B. Peter Rosendorf. "Why Democracies Cooperate More: Electoral Control and International Trade Agreements." *International Organization* 56, no. 3 (2002): 477–514.

Mansfield, Edward D., and Jon C. Pevehouse. "Democratization and International Organizations." *International Organization* 60 (2006): 137–167.

Mansfield, Edward D., and Jack Snyder. "Democratization and the Danger of War." *International Security* 20, no. 1 (Summer 1995): 302.

Maoz, Zeev, and Nasrin Abdolali. "Regime Types and International Conflict, 1816–1976." *Journal of Conflict Resolution* 33, no. 1 (March 1989): 3–35.

Maoz, Zeev, and Bruce Russett. "Normative and Structural Causes of Democratic Peace, 1946–1986." *American Political Science Review* 87, no. 3 (September 1993): 624–639.

Marx, Karl. *The Grundrisse*. In *The Marx-Engels Reader*, 2nd ed., edited and translated by Robert C. Tucker. New York: W.W. Norton, 1978.

Mearsheimer, John J. "The False Promise of International Institutions." *International Security*, 19, no. 3 (Winter 1994/1995): 5–49.

Mearsheimer, John. *The Tragedy of Great Power Politics*. New York: W.W. Norton, 2001.

Mercer, John. *Reputation and International Politics*. Ithaca, NY: Cornell University Press, 1996.

Migdal, Joel. *Strong Societies, Weak States: State-Society Relations and State Capabilities in the Third World*. Princeton, NJ: Princeton University Press, 1988.

Morgenthau, Hans J. *Power Among Nations: The Struggle for Power and Peace*, 5th ed. New York: Alfred A. Knopf, 1978.

Mousseau, Michael. "Market Civilization and Its Clash with Terror." *International Security* 27, no. 3 (Winter 2002/2003): 6.

Mueller, John E. "The Essential Irrelevance of Nuclear Weapons." *International Security* 13, no. 2 (Fall 1988): 55–79.

Mueller, John E. *War, Presidents, and Public Opinion*. New York: Wiley, 1973.

Munton, Don, and David A. Welch. *The Cuban Missile Crisis: A Concise History*. Oxford: Oxford University Press, 2006.

Nagl, John A. *Counterinsurgency Lessons from Malaya and Vietnam: Eating Soup with a Knife*. Westport, CT: Praeger, 2002.

Nisbett, Richard E., and Lee Ross. *Human Inference: Strategies and Shortcomings in Social Judgment*. Englewood Cliffs, NJ: Prentice Hall, 1980.

Nussbaum, Martha. *Women and Human Development: The Capabilities Approach*. Cambridge: Cambridge University Press, 2000.

Nye, Joseph S, Jr. *Soft Power: The Means to Success in World Politics*. New York: PublicAffairs Books, 2005.

Odell, John S. "Bounded Rationality and the World Political Economy." In *Governing the World's Money*, edited by David M. Andrews, C. Randall Henning, and Louis W. Pauly. Ithaca, NY: Cornell University Press, 2002.

Oren, Ido. "Can Political Science Emulate the Natural Sciences? The Problem of Self-Disconfirming Analysis." *Polity* 38, no. 1 (January 2006): 72–100.

Oren, Ido. "The Subjectivity of the 'Democratic' Peace." *International Security* 20, no. 2 (Fall 1995): 147–184.

Owen, John M. "How Liberalism Produces Democratic Peace." *International Security* 19, no. 2 (Fall 1994): 87–125.

Oye, Kenneth, ed. *Cooperation Under Anarchy*. Princeton, NJ: Princeton University Press, 1986.

Page, Benjamin I. *Who Deliberates? Mass Media in American Society*. Chicago: University of Chicago Press, 1996.

Pape, Robert. "The Strategic Logic of Suicide Terrorism." *American Political Science Review* 97 (2003): 343–361.

Parsons, Craig. "Showing Ideas as Causes: The Origins of the European Union." *International Organization* 56, no. 1 (Winter 2002): 47–84.

Pearce, Fred. *When the Rivers Run Dry: Water—the Defining Crisis of the Twenty-First Century*. Boston: Beacon Press, 2006.

Petraeus, David H. "Learning Counterinsurgency: Observations from Soldering in Iraq." *Military Review* (January–February 2006): 2–12.

Pevehouse, Jon, and Bruce Russett. "Democratic International Governmental Organizations Promote Peace." *International Organization* 60 (2006): 969–1000.

Philpott, Daniel. "The Challenge of September 11 to Secularism in International Relations." *World Politics* 55 (October 2002): 66–95.

Piazza, James A. "Incubators of Terror: Do Failed and Failing States Promote Transnational Terrorism?" *International Studies Quarterly* 52, no. 3 (September 2008): 469–488.

Porter, Andrew. *European Imperialism 1860–1914*. New York: Palgrave Macmillan, 1996.

Powlick, Philip J., and Andrew Katz. "Defining the American Public Opinion/Foreign Policy Nexus." *Mershon International Studies Review* 42 (1988): 29–61.

Prestowitz, Clyde. *Three Billion New Capitalists*. New York: Basic Books, 2005.

Price, Richard. "Transnational Civil Society and Advocacy in World Politics." *World Politics* 55, no. 4 (2003): 579–607.

Puchala, Donald J. "World Hegemony and the United Nations." *International Studies Review* 7 (2005): 571–584.

Putnam, Robert. "Diplomacy and Domestic Politics: The Logic of Two-Level Games." *International Organization* 42, no. 3 (1988): 427–460.

Rapley, John. *Understanding Development: Theory and Practice in the Third World.* Boulder, CO: Lynne Rienner, 2002.

Reimann, Kim D. "A View from the Top: International Politics, Norms and the Worldwide Growth of NGOs." *International Studies Quarterly* 50, no. 1 (2006): 4568.

Reiter, Dan, and Allan C. Stam III. "Democracy, War Initiation, and Victory." *American Political Science Review* 92, no. 2 (June 1998): 259–277.

Reuveny, Rafael, and William R. Thompson. "Uneven Economic Growth and the World Economy's North–South Stratification." *International Studies Quarterly* 52, no. 3 (September 2008): 579–605.

Risse-Kappen, Thomas. "Public Opinion, Domestic Structure, and Foreign Policy in Liberal Democracies." *World Politics* 43, no. 4 (July 1991): 479–512.

Rivoli, Pietra. *The Travels of a T-Shirt in a Global Economy: An Economist Examines the Markets, Power, and Politics of World Trade.* New York: Wiley, 2005.

Rosenau, James. "Pre-Theories and Theories of Foreign Policy." In *The Scientific Study of Foreign Policy,* edited by J. Rosenau. New York: The Free Press, 1971.

Rothgeb, John M., Jr. *Defining Power: Influence and Force in the Contemporary International System.* New York: St. Martin's Press, 1993.

Ruggie, John G. "International Regimes, Transaction, and Change: Embedded Liberalism in the Postwar Economic Order." *International Organization* 36, no. 2 (Spring 1983): 379–415.

Rupert, Mark. *Ideologies of Globalization: Contending Visions of a New World Order.* London: Routledge, 2000.

Rupert, Mark, and M. Scott Solomon. *Globalization and International Political Economy.* Lanham, MD: Rowman & Littlefield, 2006.

Russett, Bruce. *Grasping the Democratic Peace.* Princeton, NJ: Princeton University Press, 1993.

Sachs, Jeffrey D. *The End of Poverty: Economic Possibilities for Our Time.* New York: Penguin, 2005.

Salzinger, Leslie. *Genders in Production: Making Workers in Mexico's Global Factories.* Berkeley: University of California Press, 2003.

Schelling, Thomas. *Strategy of Conflict.* Cambridge, MA: Harvard University Press, 1960.

Schmidt, Brian C. *The Political Discourse of Anarchy: A Disciplinary History of International Relations.* Albany: State University of New York, 1998.

Schwartz, Herman. *States versus Markets: History, Geography, and the Development of the International Political Economy.* New York: St. Martin's, 1994.

Schweller, Randall. *Deadly Imbalances: Tripolarity and Hitler's Strategy of World Conquest.* New York: Columbia University Press, 1998.

Schweller, Randall. "Realism's Status Quo Bias: What Security Dilemma?" *Security Studies* 5, no. 3 (1995/1996): 90–121.

Sen, Amartya. *Development as Freedom.* New York: Anchor Books, 1999.

Sen, Amartya. *On Economic Inequality,* expanded ed. Oxford: Clarendon Press, 1997 [1973].

Shapiro, Robert, and Benjamin Page. "Foreign Policy and the Rational Public." *Journal of Conflict Resolution* 32, no. 2 (1988): 211–247.

Shue, Henry. *Basic Rights: Subsistence, Affluence, and Foreign Policy,* 2nd ed. Princeton, NJ: Princeton University Press, 1996.

Simmons, Beth. *Who Adjusts? Domestic Sources of Foreign Economic Policy During the Interwar Years.* Princeton, NJ: Princeton University Press, 1994.

Sjoberg, Laura. "Introduction to *Security Studies:* Feminist Contributions," *Security Studies,* 18 (2009): 182–213.

Slomanson, William R. *Fundamental Perspectives on International Law.* Minneapolis: West, 1995.

Smith, Alistair. "Diversionary Foreign Policy in Democratic Systems." *International Studies Quarterly* 40 (March 1996): 133–153.

Smith, James. "Inequality in International Trade? Developing Countries and Institutional Change in WTO Dispute Settlement." *Review of International Political Economy* 11, no. 3 (2004); 542–573.

Snyder, Jack. *Myths of Empire: Domestic Politics and International Ambition*. Ithaca, NY: Cornell University Press, 1991.

Spence, Jonathan D. *The Search for Modern China*. New York: W.W. Norton, 1999.

Springhall, John. *Decolonization Since 1945: The Collapse of European Overseas Empires*. New York: Palgrave Macmillan, 2001.

Spruyt, Hendrik. *The Sovereign State and Its Competitors: An Analysis of Systems Change*. Princeton, NJ: Princeton University Press, 1994.

Steans, Jill. *Gender and International Relations: An Introduction*. New Brunswick, NJ: Rutgers University Press, 2002.

Steele, Brent J. "Liberal-Idealism: A Constructivist Critique." *International Studies Review* 9, no. 1 (Spring 2007): 23–52.

Strange, Susan. *The Retreat of the State*. New York: Cambridge University Press, 1997.

Strayer, Joseph R. *On the Medieval Origins of the Modern State*. Princeton, NJ: Princeton University Press, 1970.

Sun Tzu. *The Art of War*. Translated by John Minford. New York: The Viking Press, 2002.

Sylvester, Christine. *Feminist Theory and International Relations in a Postmodern Era*. Cambridge: Cambridge University Press, 1994.

Tarp, Finn, ed. *Foreign Aid and Development: Lessons Learned and Directions for the Future*. London: Routledge, 2000.

Tarrow, Sidney. *The New Transnational Activism*. Cambridge: Cambridge University Press, 2005.

Terry, Fiona. *Condemned to Repeat? The Paradox of Humanitarian Action*. Ithaca, NY: Cornell University Press, 2002.

Thompson, Alex. "Coercion Through IOs: The Security Council and the Logic of Information Transmission." *International Organization* 60 (2006): 1–34.

Tickner, J. Ann. "Hans Morgenthau's Principles of Political Realism: A Feminist Reformulation." *Millennium: Journal of International Studies* 17, no. 3 (1998): 429–440.

Tilly, Charles. *Coercion, Capital, and European States, AD 990–1990*. Cambridge, MA: Blackwell, 1990.

Tilly, Charles, ed. *The Formation of National States in Western Europe*. Princeton, NJ: Princeton University Press, 1975.

United Nations Development Programme. *Human Development Report 2007/2008: Fighting Climate Change: Human Solidarity in a Divided World*. New York: UNDP, 2007.

United Nations Development Programme. *Millennium Development Goals: A Compact Among Nations to End Human Poverty*. New York: UNDP, 2003.

United Nations Millennium Project. *Taking Action: Achieving Gender Equality and Empowering Women*. London: Earthscan, 2005.

U.S. Department of the Army. *FM3-24: Counterinsurgency*. http://www.fas.org/irp/doddir/army/fm3-24.pdf.

Van Creveld, Martin L. *The Rise and Decline of the State*. New York: Cambridge University Press, 1999.

Van Evera, Stephen. "Offense, Defense, and the Causes of War." *International Security* 22, no. 4 (1988): 5–43.

Vasquez, John A. "The Realist Paradigm and Degenerative versus Progressive Research Programs: An Appraisal of Neotraditional Research on Waltz's Balancing Proposition." *The American Political Science Review* 91, no. 4 (December 1997): 899–912.

Vernon, Raymond. *Sovereignty at Bay: The Multinational Spread of U.S. Enterprises*. New York: Basic Books, 1971.

Vinci, Anthony. "Anarchy, Failed States, and Armed Groups: Reconsidering Conventional Analysis." *International Studies Quarterly* 52, no. 2 (June 2008): 295–314.

Voeten, Erik. "The Political Origins of the UN Security Council's Ability to Legitimize the Use of Force." *International Organization* 59 (2005): 527–557.

Wade, Robert. "Is Globalization Reducing Poverty and Inequality?" *World Development* 32, no. 4 (2004): 567–589.

Wade, Robert. "What Strategies Are Viable for Developing Countries Today? The World Trade Organization and the Shrinking of 'Development Space.'" *Review of International Political Economy* 10, no. 4 (2003): 621–644.

Waltz, Kenneth N. *Man, the State, and War: A Theoretical Analysis.* New York: Columbia University Press, 1959.

Waltz, Kenneth N. "The Origins of War in Neorealist Theory." *Journal of Interdisciplinary History* 83, no. 4 (Spring 1988): 620.

Waltz, Kenneth N. *Theory of International Politics.* New York: McGraw Hill, 1979.

Waltz, Kenneth N., and Scott D. Sagan. *The Spread of Nuclear Weapons: A Debate.* New York: W. W. Norton, 1995.

Walzer, Michael. *Just and Unjust Wars: A Moral Argument with Historical Illustrations*, 3rd ed. New York: Basic Books, 2000.

Watson, Adam. *The Evolution of International Society.* London: Routledge, 1992.

Weaver, Catherine. *Hypocrisy Trap: The World Bank and the Poverty of Reform.* Princeton, NJ: Princeton University Press, 2008.

Weaver, Catherine. "The World's Bank and the Bank's World." *Global Governance* (October 2007).

Weiss, Thomas G., and Sam Daws, eds. *The Oxford Handbook on the United Nations.* New York: Oxford University Press, 2007.

Weiss, Thomas G., David P. Forsythe, Roger A. Coate, and Kelly-Kate Pease. *The United Nations and Changing World Politics*, 4th ed. Boulder, CO: Westview Press, 2007.

Wendt, Alexander. "Anarchy Is What States Make of It: The Social Construction of Power Politics." *International Organization* 46, no. 2 (Spring 1992): 391–425.

Wetta, Frank Joseph, and Martin A. Novelli. "'Now a Major Motion Picture': War Films and Hollywood's New Patriotism." *Journal of Military History* 67 (2003): 861–882.

Wiener, Antje, and Thomas Diez, eds. *European Integration Theory.* New York: Oxford University Press, 2004.

Woo-Cummings, Meredith, ed. *The Developmental State.* Ithaca, NY: Cornell University Press, 1999.

Woods, Ngaire. *The Globalizers: The IMF, The World Bank, and Their Borrowers.* Ithaca, NY: Cornell University Press, 2006.

World Bank. *The East Asian Economic Miracle: Economic Growth and Public Policy.* New York: Oxford University Press, 1993.

Zaller, John. *The Nature and Origins of Mass Opinion.* Cambridge: Cambridge University Press, 1992.

Name Index

Subject Index

A

The Absolute Weapon: Atomic Power and World Order (Brodie), 425
Academics, foreign policy and, 60
Afghanistan
  human rights issues, 383
  issue of power, 67
  transnational crime, 399
Africa
  decolonization, 47–48
  HIV/AIDS, 415–416
  literacy rates, 104
  malaria, 417
  poverty in, 4
African National Congress (ANC), 132
African Union (AU), 5, 334
Aggression
  deterring and countering, 341–342
  and war, 18, 190–191
Aggressive states, 187
Agreement on the Peaceful Use of Nuclear Energy, 77
Agricultural protection
  Europe, 353
  Switzerland, 276
  World Trade Organization, 265
AIDS. *See* HIV/AIDS
Air pollution, 406, 407
Al-Askariya mosque, 24–25
Algeria, 128
Allied powers, 40
Al-Qaeda, 159, 225, 229, 230
Analysis, levels of, 18–20
Anarchy
  defined, 30, 62
  liberal institutionalism and, 76–77
ANC (African National Congress), 132
Apartheid, 96
APEC (Asian-Pacific Economic Cooperation) group, 280
Appeasement, 41, 69
Argentina
  diversionary theory of war, 190

ICJ rulings, 371–372
  resurgent socialism, 88
Armenians, massacre of, 52
Arms control
  Campaign to Ban Land Mines, 199
  Cold War, 197–198
  limits to, 199
  Nuclear Non-Proliferation Treaty, 198
  U.S. and Soviet Union/Russia, 78
Arms proliferation, 216
Arms trade, illegal, 400–401
Art of War (Sun Tzu), 209
Arusha Declaration, 110
ASEAN (Association of Southeast Asian Nations), 335, 353
Asia
  decolonization, 47–48
  literacy rates, 104
  malaria, 417
Asian Tigers
  export-led growth, 314–315
  state strength, 129
Asian-Pacific Economic Cooperation (APEC) group, 280
Association of Southeast Asian Nations (ASEAN), 335, 353
Asylum status, 397–398
Asymmetric conflict, 223
Attribution, 167
AU (African Union), 5, 334
Audience costs, 121
Auschwitz Concentration Camp, 369
Australia, 409
Austro-Hungarian Empire, 35, 38–39
Autarchic regimes, 184
Authoritarian regimes
  end of Cold War and, 50
  supporting, to promote democracy, 128
Automobiles, stolen, 401
Autonomous monetary policy, 283
"Axis of evil," 182
Axis powers, 40

B

Bailout, 270. *See also* Financial crisis
Balance of power theory, 29–30, 69
Balance of trade, 247–250, 251–253
Baltic states, 40
Basic human needs approach, 321
Basque terrorist group, 231
Battle of Agincourt, 20
Battle of Stalingrad, 193
Belgian Congo, 35
Berlin Wall, 50–51
Bilateral foreign aid, 326–329
Biological weapons, 218
Bipolarity, 70
Birthrates, 396
Black Death (bubonic plague), 413
Black Monday, 259
Blended enforcement, 374
Blistering agents, 218
Bolivia, resurgent socialism in, 88, 113
Bolstering, concept of, 174
Bombing
  coercion, 171
  Madrid, Spain, 224
  Oklahoma City, 229
  suicide, 6, 231
Bosnia-Herzegovina, 35, 38, 49, 97, 171
Bounded rationality, 167
Bourgeoisie, economic structuralism, 90
Brain drain, 398
Brazil
  independence of, 35
  political debate, 13
Brazilian-Argentine Agreement on the Peaceful Use of Nuclear Energy, 77
Bretton Woods system, 17, 45–46, 274, 287–288
Bricks and mortar assets, 290, 357
Britain
  lesson of Munich, 169
  MI6, 157
  Opium Wars, 310